ATLAS
OF THE
THIRD WORLD

ATLAS
OF THE
THIRD WORLD

by

George Kurian

Designed by
Andrew Elias and Eric Elias

FACTS ON FILE PUBLICATIONS
460 Park Avenue South
New York, New York 10016

ATLAS OF THE THIRD WORLD

by George Kurian

Published by Facts On File, Inc.
460 Park Avenue South, New York 10016

Library of Congress Cataloging in Publication Data

Kurian, George
  Atlas of the Third World.

  Includes index.
  1. Underdeveloped areas—Economic conditions—Maps.
2. Underdeveloped areas—National resources—Maps.
3. Underdeveloped areas—Social conditions—Maps.
I. Title.
G1046.G1K8   1983   912′.19724   82-675029
ISBN 0-87196-673-5

Printed in the United States of America

10 9 8 7 6 5 4 3 2 1

CONTENTS

INTRODUCTION...ix

PART I: THEMATIC PROFILES
PROLOGUE 1
GENERAL AND POLITICAL 5
POPULATION 10
ECONOMIC CONDITIONS.. 25
AID 40
DEFENSE 43
LABOR.. 50
FOOD AND AGRICULTURE 53
ENVIRONMENT... 68
EDUCATION 69
HEALTH... 74
ENERGY 86
TRADE 91
MEDIA & COMMUNICATIONS 97
LAW ENFORCEMENT 101

PART II: COUNTRY PROFILES
AFGHANISTAN 104
ALGERIA 108
ANGOLA 112
ARGENTINA... 114
BANGLADESH 118
BENIN 122
BOLIVIA.. 126
BRAZIL 128
BURMA 132
CAMBODIA 136
CAMEROON.. 138
CHAD 142
CHILE.. 146
COLOMBIA... 150
CONGO 154
COSTA RICA 156
CUBA 158
DOMINICAN REPUBLIC 162
ECUADOR 164
EGYPT 168
EL SALVADOR 172
ETHIOPIA 176
GABON 180

GHANA 184
GUATEMALA 188
GUINEA 192
GUYANA 194
HAITI 198
HONDURAS 200
INDIA 204
INDONESIA 208
IRAN 212
IRAQ 216
IVORY COAST 220
JAMAICA 224
JORDAN 228
KENYA 232
KOREA, NORTH 236
KOREA, SOUTH 238
LAOS 242
LEBANON 244
LIBERIA 246
LIBYA 250
MADAGASCAR 254
MALAWI 258
MALAYSIA 262
MAURITANIA 266
MAURITIUS 268
MEXICO 270
MOROCCO 274
MOZAMBIQUE 278
NEPAL 280
NICARAGUA 284
NIGER 288
NIGERIA 290
PAKISTAN 294
PANAMA 298
PERU 302
PHILIPPINES 304
SAUDI ARABIA 308
SENEGAL 312
SIERRA LEONE 316
SINGAPORE 320
SOMALIA 322
SRI LANKA 326
SUDAN 330
SYRIA 334
TANZANIA 338
THAILAND 342
TUNISIA 346
TURKEY 350
UGANDA 354

UPPER VOLTA 358
URUGUAY 360
VENEZUELA 362
YEMEN ARAB REPUBLIC 366
YEMEN, PEOPLE'S DEMOCRATIC REPUBLIC OF 368
ZAIRE 370
ZAMBIA 374
ZIMBABWE 376

INDEX 379

INTRODUCTION

THE ATLAS OF THE THIRD WORLD presents a comprehensive selection of maps and statistical information in graphic form organized under topical headings to depict important aspects of the current economic and social conditions in the Third World and their underlying historical dynamics. It is designed to be self-sufficient in scope but in many ways it supplements the ENCYCLO-PEDIA OF THE THIRD WORLD (three volumes, Facts On File and Mansell, 1982).

The ATLAS is divided into two parts: The 14 chapters of the First Part examine certain broad topics that have been identified as the critical issues affecting Third World development. Many indicators in this section are presented as a series of observations covering the past decade (in some cases, the past two decades) and allow the reader to gauge the direction of possible trends. In certain instances, by extrapolating available data, the statistician can function as a minor prophet and determine what conditions would develop if present trends were allowed to continue undisturbed. The Second Part presents charts and maps on 80 countries of the world with narrative introductions. Because of the complex interactions of factors affecting national life, it is interesting to read and compare country maps and charts, especially those relating to either neighboring countries, such as India and Pakistan, Ethiopia and Somalia, Bolivia and Peru, or to countries with different political systems, such as Mozambique and Zambia or North and South Korea.

Three broad types of indicators may be distinguished among those presented in the Second Part. The first describes the country's natural resources, including land area; the second the country's population—the key that determines all other indicators; and the third the country's social and economic performance as well as what is generally described as the quality of life. The first is the given in the equation of economic development, the second the fulcrum of growth and the third the engine of progress. If we think of development as a pyramid, the first indicator would form the base, the second the middle building block and the third the apex. No country in the developed or developing world possesses all three in their ideal shape or form, and developmental strategy consists in managing available resources to produce the most desirable quality of life. It should, however, be borne in mind that there are other elements in the equation which cannot be presented graphically because they are essentially nonquantifiable, such as the will to achieve growth or the ruling political ideology. Nevertheless, the charts and maps presented in each country chapter provide as complete a picture of the state of the country's economy as is possible using existing data.

The purpose of the ATLAS is to present a graphic report on the state of the Third World. To do so, we shall examine the picture under 11 headings.

1. DEVELOPMENT

The underlying theme in this ATLAS—the common thread that binds the more than 1,000 maps and charts—may be described as Development. (The word "development" has been chosen instead of "growth" because not all development is growth.) In the 1960s economists envisioned development as a linear process divided into stages, from "take-off" to "high mass consumption," with intermediate stages requiring such acrobatic feats as "breaking the vicious circle" and "catching up." All countries were seen as starting from the same point and facing the same obstacles as they proceeded over the same course. Some would simply move faster than others, the slower ones following at a distance and catching up later. The poorer countries could learn from the mistakes of others and benefit from the continued growth of the rich ones through spillover or trickle-down as well as generous economic aid.

Most of these assumptions have proved wrong. Indeed, the two so-called Development Decades have been described by K.K.S. Dadzie as "Decades of Disappointment." True, there has been growth in some areas in aggregate terms. As a whole, the Third World grew from 1950 through 1976 at an average rate of 5%, as against 4.2% for developed countries, and their aggregate manufactured exports increased at an impressive rate of 10%. Despite skyrocketing oil import bills, developing countries together managed to save and reinvest nearly a quarter of their national income. Agricultural production grew at a rate of 3.2% (2.8% for developed countries), manufacturing production 6.9% (4.0% for developed countries) and gross investment 8% (4.8% for developed countries). In terms of national well-being, their progress was equally striking. Life expectancy increased in the South in the past two decades by as much as it increased in the North in a century, and a number of diseases, such as malaria, were brought under control and others, such as smallpox, virtually eradicated. The Physical Quality of Life Index—a composite indicator of infant mortality, life expectancy and literacy—rose in the Third World from 39 in 1960 to 60 in the late 1982.

But what these accomplishments fail to reveal—and even, in some cases, mask—are the disparities that still persist. With a population growing by 2.2% annually, as against 0.7% for developed countries, much of the gains made in aggregate terms are lost in per capita terms. The North-South gap remains as substantial as ever. The South accounts for only 21% of the "gross global product" (GGP) of $8.8 trillion, 25% of the total world export earnings, 22% of the world military expenditures, 16% of the world's educational expenditures and 9% of the world's public health expenditures. Average life expectancy is still 16 years lower than in the North and infant mortality is five times as high. Some 800 million are living in absolute poverty and over 460 million (nearly half of them children) are malnourished. Only 52% of Third World residents can read and write, as compared with 99% in the developed world, and average educational expenditures are only $18 per capita, compared with $286 per capita in the developed world. About 850 million have no access to schools and rarely go beyond the primary grades. Less than half the people of the Third World have safe water supplies and only half of the urban households have minimally adequate housing. Most disastrous of all, development has been accompanied by a crushing burden of debt, which in 1983 amounted to $530 billion and is expected to triple in the next 10 years.

The past two decades have also introduced new inequalities and intensified the fissures between the developing countries themselves, making it necessary to introduce at least three new subcategories. The first subcategory comprises what are known as advanced developing countries (ADCs), or newly industrializing countries (NICs), and includes Brazil, Argentina and Mexico as well as the East Asian "Gang of Four": Singapore, Taiwan, Hong Kong and South Korea. Their economies enjoyed spectacular growth during the 1960s and 1970s. Their average annual per capital GNP growth rates from 1960 to 1977 were higher than that of the United States, even though their populations grew twice as fast. Their export performance was still more impressive, growing by 24%, as compared with 14% for the United States. The second subcategory consists of petroleum exporting countries (PECs), a disparate group with super-rich nations, such as Libya and Kuwait, at one end of the spectrum and lower-income nations, such as Nigeria and Indonesia, at the other. With a fifth of the Third World's population, PECs and ADCs account for 40% of its wealth. Another 40% is accounted for by the 45 middle-income countries (MICs), such as Thailand, Malaysia and the Philippines, with middling growth rates of 4 to 5% and 25% of the Third World's population. The remaining 35 countries, sometimes called the Fourth World, are the poorest in the world and their conditions have changed only for the worse during the past decade. Although they make up 35% of the developing world's population, they account for a mere 3% of the gross global product (GGP) and 5% of Third World exports. Their average per capita GNP was less than $230 in 1980.

Even in countries that have experienced relatively high growth rates, there have been no appreciable changes in the quality of life for the impoverished majority of their inhabitants. As economists have discovered, during transitional stages of development, wealth rarely trickles down but stays in puddles at the top. It requires active and deliberate government intervention to enable the benefits of development to reach lower-income groups. In fact, the divisions between the poor, the middle and the rich are sharper today in the developing world than they are in the developed world. The conclusion is that there is a Third World within every Third World country—a group that, in the words of the ILO, "has income insufficient to buy a basket of goods and services essential to a minimum level of welfare."

While economic development cannot be considered as an isolated phenomenon and is obviously related to numerous issues that do not yield to economic analysis, it may be simply stated that the heart of underdevelopment is overdependence. The institutions of the international economic system, particularly the key ones that control trade and credit, created during and in the immediate aftermath of World War II, are designed to function in such a way as to perpetuate the patron-client relationships of the colonial era. The developing countries have "milch cow economies"—*l'economie de trait,* as the French call it—producing for the needs of the North. In consequence, these economies are disarticulated and lack organic linkage between production and domestic demand. Tied to the coattails of richer economies, they are bereft of indigenous sources of dynamism. Despite all the power ascribed to producer cartels, the real economic decisions affecting the Third World are made in London, New York, Paris, Zurich and Tokyo.

During the past decade, Third World countries have pressed for reforms in international trade and monetary policies that they consider discriminatory. Their call for a New International Economic Order (NIEO) includes establishment of preferential treatment for their manufactured goods in the markets of industrialized countries, more stable and higher prices for their commodities, renegotiation of their external public debt, codes of conduct for the activities of multinational corporations, more transfer of technology to LDCs and a greater voice in the management of the world's monetary system. Simultaneously, developing countries have pursued the concept of "delinking," or loosening the historical connections between industrialized countries and former colonies and fostering greater economic cooperation among developing countries.

2. POLITICAL INSTABILITY

Next to poverty, the term most commonly associated with the Third World is political instability. Indeed, instability appears to be the concomitant of the process of modernization and part of the rites of passage as a developing country moves toward maturity. As a consequence of urbanization, industrialization, media and communications development and widespread rise in educational levels, the legitimacy that was once attached to traditional leadership erodes over a period of time. The spread of education creates significant changes in attitudes toward government and increasing demands for a share in its decision making and scrutiny of its performance. Modernization also produces new social structures and groupings and new leadership to articulate their aspirations. At first, these changes are rarely resisted openly by the powers that be. Even before independence, political elites in developing countries had come to accept the notion that they needed at least a facade of popular support to maintain their own edifices of power. They are also aware of the risk of violent revolution in postponing liberalization too long. Further, political structures in developing countries are often borrowed from developed nations or modeled on those of developed nations, and magic labels, such as "popular" and democratic," are sanctified by use in the media and indiscriminately appropriated by authoritarian regimes.

Paying only lip service to democratic ideals—with grandiloquent phrases embodied in their national constitutions—traditional power structures in developing countries managed to survive while circumventing the process of participatory democracy. One of the methods of survival used was to revert to a more primitive form, as in Iran, where the Pahlevi dictatorship gave way to the dictatorship of the mullahs under the guise of revolution. In some cases, the old leadership entrenched itself in a new network of patron-client groups, each dominating its political turf and excluding outsiders from the spoils of office. The patron—an important father figure in this stage of political evolution—acts as a mediator between the government on the one hand and his followers on the other. Another approach was for the old authority to cloak itself under some new but meaningless label, such as Marxism or Socialism, designed to mute any further demands for popular participation. If such devices failed, the army would step in and take over the state under the pretext of restoring law and order. The past two decades have thus witnessed a withering of democracy in the Third World. It is not surprising that three out of four Third World residents live under authoritarian regimes of one sort or another. As Samuel Huntington noted in *No Easy Choice,* the whiplash of illegitimate, authoritarian regimes is the price that many Third World countries have had to pay in their quest for quick modernization.

One contributory factor in this failure of democracy in the Third World is the prevalence of ethnic rivalries and conflicts. In fact, it is not possible to understand Third World politics without reference to its ethnic divisions and antagonisms. While many sociologists had expected such divisions to die out as a result of the cohesive and melting-pot pressures of modernization, the opposite has been the case. Particularly in Africa, ethnic loyalties override political loyalties and ethnic interests take precedence over national interests.

3. POPULATION

Rapid population growth continues to be the most formidable problem for developing countries as a whole. During the 1960s and 1970s, Third World population grew by 2.3% while the GNP increased by 4.5 to 5.0%. High fertility rates and reduced mortality rates thus combined to reduce the impact of what otherwise would have been a healthy growth rate for developing economies. Population explosion is a relatively recent phenomenon in the Third World. Until the 20th century, the real rate of population growth was held in check by a high mortality rate. With improved nutrition and medical services, death rates fell sharply without a corresponding reduction in birth rates and the problem became unmanageable and alarming. However, the birth rates peaked during the 1950s and then, to the amazement and relief of demographers, declined. This decline has been estimated at between 15 and 20% during the past 20 years and has been substantial in Asia, Latin America and the Pacific countries but less so in Africa. Even so, there is little room for optimism. It is important to recognize that the slowdown in population from 2.3 to 2.2% annually is not in itself large enough to have a significant impact on aggregate population figures. At the lower rate, the populations of developing countries will double every 30 years, rather than 31 years as before. If fertility rates continue to decline at the present rate, a global replacement level of reproduction (with the average of one surviving child for one parent) will be reached around 2020. Were this to happen, global population will eventually stabilize at about 11 billion.

This modest progress has been achieved as a result of the convergence of two factors: One is rapid urbanization, with urban couples generally having fewer children than their rural counterparts, and the other the improved availability of contraceptive devices. Between 1960 and 1975 more than 30 governments of developing countries adopted official policies and programs designed to encourage family planning and control.

4. FINANCE

1973 was a watershed year for the international monetary system; it marked not only the final collapse of the Bretton Woods system—which had been moribund for a number of years—but also the rise of OPEC as a kind of economic superpower, or more accurately, a monetary monster. It also added a new term to the vocabulary of international finance—petrodollar, a combination of two powerful words, petroleum and dollar. In fact, black gold became the de facto core of the monetary system.

Instability had been inherent in the international monetary system long before 1973. A few years earlier, the dollar had been displaced as the numeraire (the major currency for expressing the value of international transactions) and the principal intervention currency, and a floating system of exchange had been adopted. But the OPEC bombshell served to institutionalize this instability. The era immediately following the hike in oil prices was characterized by wild fluctuations in exchange rates, rapid swings in balances of payments and large accumulations of debt.

In the midst of these crises, the plight of the oil-importing developing countries (OIDC) went unnoticed. In just one year—1974 to 1975—their overall deficit went from $30 billion to $38 billion. They have also experienced average inflation rates of 25% or above since 1974. Unlike many developed countries that generated foreign reserves by receiving deposits from countries with surpluses or merely by printing money and receiving seigniorage rights, most developing countries had to earn their foreign reserves.

As a result, OIDCs have had to finance their debts through large-scale borrowing. The aggregate foreign debt of these countries exceeded $530 billion in 1983, $350 billion of it from private sources. Although statistics on short-term debt are not reliable, it is probably in the range of $170 billion. The bulk of this debt is managed by commercial banks, which provide almost two-thirds of the net external financial requirements of the OIDCs, as against only 3% supplied by the IMF. Commercial lending of recycled petrodollars increased by 11 times in real terms, swelling from one-fourteenth to one-fourth of the total flow of capital to developing countries. Developing countries preferred to deal with private lenders rather than the IMF, not only because the former had substantially larger assets—the eurocurrency market alone had 20 times the assets of the IMF—but because they considered the IMF's conditionality, or terms for standby lending, excessively stringent and an unwarranted interference in their domestic affairs. Moreover, most of the IMF credits are repayable in three to four years, a period economists generally consider too short a period for making the necessary economic adjustments.

The bulk of private-sector borrowing is concentrated in a small number of advanced developing countries (ADCs), which the commercial bankers consider as good risks because of their higher export potentials. By the end of the 1970s, four countries—Brazil, Mexico, Argentina and South Korea—accounted for 65% of all eurocurrency borrowings by developed countries. Other countries, especially the low-income ones, have had to rely on concessional assistance from multilateral aid agencies.

The financial plight of the OIDCs is likely to be even more serious in the 1980s than it was in the 1970s. Between 1980 and 1982, falling export income and rising debt service together had a negative impact of about $70 billion on the balance of payments of the developing countries. The proportion between payments on medium- and long-term debt and export income jumped from 18% in 1980 to 24% in 1982, and the ratio between debt outstanding and exports rose from 1:1 to 1:3. The record of the top 20 borrowers

—which are responsible for three-fourths of all Third World debt—was even worse. Their proportion between payments on medium- and long-term debt and export income reached 34%; the top four borrowers had debt service that exceeded 50% of their export income.

The sheer magnitude of this problem defies easy diagnosis. Obviously, its origins are in the worldwide recession of the late 1970s. The export sales of the developing countries were virtually stagnant in 1982, partially because of the protectionist measures adopted in developed countries. The terms of trade of the low-income countries have deteriorated by 30% between 1979 and 1982. In addition, about half the increase in Third World debt-service payments since 1980 has been due to higher interest rates. Real rates of interest averaged 2% in the 1960s, were negative in the mid-1970s and then jumped to 5% by 1981. A one-point increase in interest rates costs Mexico, Brazil and Argentina $1.2 billion a year.

Falling export sales and high interest rates have resulted in a rash of debt repayment problems. A number of countries—notably Zaire, Nicaragua, Turkey, Jamaica, Sudan and Mexico—have had to reschedule their outstanding debts, and four of the largest debtors—Mexico, Brazil, Argentina and Chile—have recently had to defer payments on the principals. Almost as many countries have had to reschedule loans in the past two years as in the previous 25 years. Eight of the 15 developing countries that rescheduled debt in 1981 and 1982 were low-income African countries, and seven of them had accumulated more debt than they could manage without disrupting their exports.

Commercial banks, especially the smaller ones, have understandably been sobered by these problems and have pulled back from lending to OIDCs. In the third quarter of 1982, the banks lent less to them than they took back in principal repayments. Nervousness about the capacity of borrowing countries to service existing debt has weakened the fabric of confidence on which all international economic transactions depend.

Nevertheless, there are at least three hopeful signs that indicate the current debt problem of the Third World can be brought under control. The first is that capital flows between developed and developing nations are not a recent phenomenon; they have been a normal feature of the international economy for over two centuries and have weathered wars, recessions, depressions, and near bankruptcies of nations. The second is that many developing countries have acquired, during the past two decades, a successful track record in managing economic stress and have demonstrated their ability to adjust to and survive adverse economic and political conditions. Essentially, their present problems are those of liquidity, not solvency. It is interesting to note that although many developing countries have defaulted on their debt, none has repudiated it, as the Soviet Union did not too many decades ago. The third is the resiliency and the robustness of the international banking system itself. The lending system is designed to absorb shocks when the going gets bumpy and has built-in corrective mechanisms.

Over the long haul, the financial surplus of OPEC coffers will continue to bring about a drastic shift in the patterns of resource transfers to and from the developing countries. Official development assistance will become much less important relative to private capital flows. Above all, the financial health of the developing countries will be a stabilizing element in the international monetary system.

5. TRADE

The one area where developing and developed countries clearly interact is that of trade. One-quarter of everything produced in the world is now traded across national borders, making it possible to speak of a global supply and a global demand. The South has learned to use trade as a developmental tool only within the past two decades. The basic strategy of Third World nations in the beginning was known as import substitution. It meant transfer of resources from agriculture to industry, and production for the internal market rather than for export. As a result, world primary exports grew very slowly, and the share of developing countries in this trade rapidly diminished. While their overall volume of exports grew in the 1950s and 1960s at a rate of 5%, their import purchasing power rose at a lower rate, 2%, because of deteriorating terms of trade.

During the 1970s, the demand for primary commodities increased more rapidly and the terms of trade stabilized. Many trade restrictions were phased out as liberalism came to be accepted as the standard official policy. International capital and technology transfers stimulated the expansion of trade. A few developing countries seized this opportunity to accelerate their exports and found a new niche in the South under the name advanced developing countries. The group included the so-called Gang of Four—Hong Kong, Singapore, Taiwan and South Korea—as well the South American giant, Brazil. These countries thus made trade itself an engine of growth. ADCs also found access to new sources of finance from international capital markets. At the same time, the expansion of trade created new fissures within the developing world as the low-income nations fell behind, their frail economies having little to contribute to the arena of trade. These economic basket cases became a Third World within the Third World.

A new factor entered into the picture with the 1973 oil embargo and the quantum jump in oil prices. While all OIDCs as a group have experienced consistent current account deficits since the first oil price shock, ADCs in particular have accumulated large deficits. Having to pay off their debts as well as their oil bills, these ADCs redoubled their efforts to export more goods despite less favorable opportunities for trade. For them exports became not merely an engine of growth but the very stuff of survival.

Thus the benefits of trade are heavily concentrated in a handful of Third World countries that can produce a diverse range of manufactured products at competitive prices. During the 1970s, they accounted for 98% of the gain in the export-derived purchasing power of the Third World. Seven countries are responsible for 75% of the manufactured exports of developing countries. However, by the end of the century, it is expected that the benefits of trade will become more widely diffused, enabling middle-income countries, such as Malaysia, Thailand, the Philippines, Colombia, Morocco and the Ivory Coast, to stake a presence in world markets. The poorer countries' share of world exports and their percentage of production exported will continue to fall in the remaining decades of this century because of uncertain and volatile market conditions in the industrialized world.

6. FOOD

The recent absence of food crises from the front pages of newspapers does not mean that food has ceased to be a critical issue for the

Third World. True, it is no longer the doomsday indicator that it once was and the crisis in the Sahel is now only a memory for those who do not live there. Since the early 1970s the world's food system has become more closely integrated than at any other time in human history. No longer a strictly national issue, food is now a global concern. Self-sufficiency in food is less urgent as a developmental imperative for the poorer nations when they have access to the overflowing silos of the richer countries. To rephrase the U.S. Presidential Commission on World Hunger, the war against famine in Africa is won on the farmlands of Kansas.

Yet surprisingly, the food beggars of the world are *not* the poorest nations but the relatively well-to-do, such as the Soviet Union, Japan, South Korea and Egypt. The typical customer in the global food market is not the destitute Djiboutian but the rotund Russian. The hungriest nations, in the starvation belt of Southeast Asia and the Sahel, have just barely increased their food imports over the past decade. India, for example, where half the world's undernourished people live, imported scarcely any grain between 1977 and 1981. Taiwan and South Korea, on the other hand, with a total population of 54 million, imported more grain (9.4 million tons in 1980) than all the low-income nations combined, with a total population 1.3 billion. An even greater irony is that the poorer nations use much of their scarce agricultural resources to produce coffee, cocoa, sugar, jute and bananas for the delectation of wealthy customers abroad. If land used to grow these products were given over to cereal production, then all Africa and Latin America would become truly self-sufficient in food.

Within a global context, food grain import costs still represent only a modest foreign exchange burden for most countries, averaging 20% of export earnings from agriculture and 5% of total export earnings. This share has remained fairly steady over the past 20 years.

Even though world food production has expanded steadily over the previous 30 years—by over 75% in developing countries—per capita production has only edged forward and in some cases declined. The problem lies not so much with the Third World farmer, who, as economist Theodore W. Schultz of the University of Chicago asserts, is "poor but efficient"; he responds to price incentives and has learned to maximize profits within available technology in much the same way as farmers in industrialized countries. The problem lies rather with official policies and external assistance programs that are targeted toward more visible and prestigious sectors, such as industry, to the exclusion of agriculture. The sector also suffers from price disincentives. Artificially low producer prices are, at least partially, the result of surplus disposal programs of richer countries. U.S. food aid, for example, has helped to depress agricultural prices in all countries to which it has been extended. National food policies also often distort market forces and frequently magnify the effect of short-term scarcities. In Egypt, official control over wheat, corn and rice led farmers to turn to fruits, vegetables and livestock (which were not price-controlled), with the result that Egypt now has to import six million tons of grain annually. Similarly, in India the production of rice lagged for years because it was relatively less profitable than wheat, which received government subsidies. It follows that official policies must reflect agricultural needs and allocate adequate resources to meet those needs.

7. EDUCATION

The 1948 U.N. *Universal Declaration of Human Rights* stated: "Everyone has the right to education. Education shall be free at least in the elementary and fundamental stages . . . Higher education shall be equally accessible to all on the basis of merit." Three decades later, this objective is far from reality. In the developing countries, less than 65% of children between the ages of 6 and 11 are enrolled in school and of them only about 50% reach the fourth grade. The enrollment rates of 12- to 17-year-olds and 18- to 23-year-olds are about 38% and 9% respectively. By 1985 UNESCO projects that the enrollment rates for these three age groups will be 68%, 42% and 12% respectively. The disparities in Africa and Asia will be even more striking. Twenty-eight of 46 African countries representing 77% of the continent's population and 14 of 27 Asian countries representing 88% of Asia's population will fall below the UNESCO projections. Youth not in school will increase by about 30 million. To maintain the current primary enrollment rate in the face of rapidly growing population, enrollment must increase by 30% over the next decade. Provision of basic education to the adult population is likewise inadequate. While the percentage of adult illiterates in developing countries declined by 12% between 1950 and 1975, it increased in absolute numbers to over 600 million by 1978 and is not expected to decrease before the year 2000.

In addition, there are unequal educational opportunities within countries based on sex, socioeconomic status, and differing rural, urban, regional and ethnic backgrounds. Of all these disparities, none is a greater hindrance to development than that based on sex. Aggregate data for developing countries as a whole show wide disparities between male and female enrollments, especially when compared with virtual parity in developed countries. In the primary age group the enrollment rate was 72% for boys and 56% for girls, in the secondary age group it was 44% for boys and 32% for girls and in the postsecondary age group it was 11% for boys and 6% for girls. The effect of other factors on enrollment is not always clearly distinguishable, but a few examples will illustrate conditions common throughout the developing world. The average enrollment rate for urban areas in Brazil is 92%, but the corresponding rate for the rural population is only 52%. The primary enrollment rate in the northern states of Nigeria is only 14%, compared with 76% in the southern states. In Indonesia, there is a gap of 15 percentage points between the enrollment rate for rural and urban children, increasing to about 40 percentage points by the last year of secondary school.

Educational programs in developing countries during the 1960s were aimed at expanding enrollment rather than changing the character of education. Although the newly independent countries replaced the foreign content in their school curricula with content related to national culture and traditions, these changes did not significantly alter other aspects of the educational system, such as the structure of cycles, the language of instruction, school calendars, or teaching and examination techniques. Nevertheless, a growing desire to assert national identity coupled with an urge to experiment with broader concepts of social development led to educational reforms, particularly in five areas: equality of educational opportunity, development of science teaching, improvement of the internal efficiencies of the school system, enhancement of the relevance of education to perceived national needs, and the indigenization of management and research. The new trends were most clearly defined in two areas: relevance and language. Relevance was identified as a function of education in the creation of an authentic national culture, especially one free of the vestiges of colonial rule. The quest for relevance also included efforts to establish, by official fiat, an indigenous national language as the medium of instruction. But the conflict proved to be not merely between the national and foreign languages but, even more so, between the national and local or ethnic languages. Linguistic chauvinism also served to sever the access that former colonies had hitherto enjoyed to the whole corpus of knowledge available only in Western languages as well as opportunities for higher education and training abroad. Confronted with such problems, few Third World countries have managed to evolve a clear and workable language policy. To nationalize the system of education, to make it relevant and to manage its growing complexities, many developing countries established units for planning and research. Unfortunately, these units have suffered from a lack of trained staff, sparseness of educational data, and a want of consensus regarding educational policies and programs.

Efforts to expand and equalize educational opportunities in developing countries face many constraints. The most obvious and frequent is the lack of resources—financial as well as human. Although during the past two decades developing countries have, on the average, steadily increased public expenditures for education as percentages of both their GNP and national budget, they are spending much less per student than developed countries and the gap is widening. Another major problem is that inefficiencies in the school system vitiate the quality of learning. Such inefficiencies are reflected in a high degree of waste—students dropping out and repeating, low student-teacher ratios and underused physical facilities. The relationship between education and work suffers from a shortage of training opportunities and work experiences, the discouraging prevalence of unemployment and the fact that even though education is considered primarily a passport to jobs, it is not always geared to employment opportunities in the economy. Finally, the development of national managerial and administrative as well as research capabilities lags behind the growth in size and complexity of the educational sector. Many school systems have poor management procedures, and decision-making responsibilities are distributed among numerous agencies without clear concomitant accountability.

8. HEALTH

Health problems in the South are very different from those in the North. In a typical developing country, more than 40% of the deaths are from infectious, parasitic and respiratory diseases (as against 10% in the North, where the major killers are cancer and heart and vascular diseases). One-half of the people, in middle-income countries and two-thirds of the residents of the world's poorest countries, drink contaminated water. The most widespread diseases in developing countries are diarrheal ones transmitted by human fecal contamination of soil, food and water. The parasitic diseases are usually more chronic and debilitating than acute, and they flourish in the poorest areas, such as slums. Diseases transmitted by insects, such as malaria, remain widespread in certain areas years after WHO believed they would be wiped out. Some 850 million people live in areas where malaria has been only partially controlled. Schistosomiasis, caused by a snail-borne parasite, is endemic in some countries with a population of 200 million. Ironically, development projects have increased the incidence of schistosomiasis and onchocerciasis (or river blindness) in many parts of Africa; drainage and irrigation canals provide habitat for the snails, and the spillways of dams for blackfly larvae.

Disease must be regarded as not merely a personal but a national waste, just as health must be considered a fundamental right, not merely a by-product of development. In no area is the North-South gap so dramatic as in that of health. The average life expectancy of a Northerner is 15 years greater than that of a Southerner, and 100 to 180 more live-born infants die per 1,000 in the Third World than in the developed world. In a typical developing country a third of all deaths are among children under five. The extent of sickness and disability is harder to document, but some studies suggest that a tenth of the life of an average Third World resident is seriously disrupted by illness.

Health is one of the least controversial developmental goals and receives considerable vocal support from Third World politicians. But when it comes to actual allocation of funds for health care, their performance has been disappointing. Most underdeveloped countries spend less than 1% of their GNP on health, compared with 6 to 12% in developed countries; in other words, only a few pennies per day per person is expended in the former compared with several dollars in the latter. Worse, even these exiguous amounts are spent on the urban and the rich, with the result that health services are practically nonexistent at the lowest levels. Such demographic and geographic discrimination is often aggravated by wrong choices in the forms and techniques of health delivery services. Western-type medical education prepares Third World doctors to look at medical episodes rather than at individuals holistically and to look at clinical conditions rather than at health problems. Increasingly complex and expensive medical technology is oriented toward hospital care rather than outpatient and home care. The quality of medical care in the Third World thus suffers on many levels: its availability, its orientation, its costs. Since health is the key element determining the national quality of life, the implications of an ill-guided and underfunded health-care system can be disastrous.

9. ENERGY

The future pace of energy consumption growth in developing countries will be dramatically different from that in developed countries. Consumption is expected to rise 200 to 250% in the former over the next 20 years, compared with only 50% in the latter. The proportion of commercial energy consumed in the Third World will grow from 18% in 1976 to 25% in 1990 and 30% in the year 2000.

Rapid escalation of energy demand is a correlate of development, because in the initial or transitional stages traditional sources of energy are replaced with more efficient ones, such as oil. The shift from traditional energy to oil could put significant additional pressure on the world's dwindling supplies of oil by the end of the century. The energy strategy of developing countries therefore needs to be directed toward three goals: producing more oil and gas, reducing dependence on oil and substituting renewable energy resources for it, and conserving energy.

Although 40% of the world's prospective oil-bearing terrain is located in OIDCs, including China, their share of proven oil reserves is only 11.5% of the world total. But much of this terrain remains underexplored. The intensity of drilling in the United States, for example, is 800 times as great as in Africa.

A second key element in the transition to the post-oil era is the exploitation and deployment of renewable energy resources, such as the sun, as well as more plentiful resources, such as coal and hydroelectric power. Developing countries account for 10% of the world's reserves of coal, most of it in India. Nevertheless, some 20 countries have considerable potential coal resources. Hydroelectric energy is more promising. About 70% of the world's potential large-scale hydroelectric resources is in developing countries, yet it accounts for only 20% of Third World energy production. While nuclear energy is not a viable alternative for many developing countries (because nuclear generating units currently generate electricity in amounts too large for these countries' delivery grids), solar power is an ideal energy resource for low-income nations. Not only do many of them have more sunlight than industrialized countries, but producing units can be adapted to small-scale rural development. In addition, their climatic conditions often permit faster growth of vegetation for firewood and biogasification.

Meanwhile, along with developed nations, Third World countries are learning to conserve energy and thereby cut back on imports, which already cost them $60 to $70 billion annually. But further cutbacks of oil imports could take a toll on development programs.

10. EMPLOYMENT

The most striking feature of the employment situation in the Third World is that nearly one-third of the working-age population is seriously *under*employed. The problem is the absence of productive jobs at fair wages for those who are technically considered employed. Unemployment, such as is found in the United States affecting 10% of the work force, is rarer in the Third World than it is in the industrialized world. The ILO reported in the mid-1970s that some 250 million people (or 35.7% of the Third World workforce) were underemployed. Not surprisingly, this is the same percentage of Third World residents who are reported to be living in absolute poverty.

The World Bank estimates that between now and the year 2000 the Third World labor force will increase to 1.25 billion, necessitating the creation of an additional 500 to 850 million jobs to absorb the new entrants into the labor force. In order to do so, the South will have to industrialize three to five times as rapidly as it did during the 1960s and 1970s as well as grow at an average annual rate of 20 to 25% over the next 17 years. Both these alternatives are impossible given the other constraints on growth already at work in the Third World. But it is not merely the length of the unemployment line that concerns Third World planners, it is also the generally poor productivity and the depressed quality of working life. Since agriculture is the least productive of all sectors, there is a need to encourage the shift of labor from agriculture to other sectors. Such a shift—one of the most reliable indicators of development—is already evident on the statistical charts but is too slow to make any impact on actual demographics. Between 1950 and 1970, it is estimated that the share of agricultural employment in low-income countries fell by only 3%.

One result of the difficult employment picture in the South is the vastly increased movement of workers from poor to rich countries, believed to be one of the largest such migrations in human history for economic and not political reasons. One widely cited source estimates the number of people involved at over 20 million. In recent years, these workers have tended to move principally to one of three areas: Western Europe, where there are now 5 to 6 million resident aliens from Southern Europe, Turkey and North Africa; the Arabian Peninsula, with 2 to 3 million workers from the not-so-rich Arab states and the Indian subcontinent; and the United States and Canada, with over 12 million (legal and illegal) aliens from Mexico, the Caribbean, Central America and northern South America.

The magnitude of transnational labor flows from the developing countries is not large enough to make a dent in their overall employment picture or afford them any significant relief. Migrants constitute less than 5% of their total out-of-work force. For the receiving countries, however, the influx may cause a significant imbalance in their ethnic makeup. For example, foreign workers constitute 75% of Kuwait's workforce and 25% of the workforces of Switzerland and Luxembourg. Outweighing this disadvantage is the fact that migrants contribute less expensive labor, which helps to hold down labor costs (and thus benefits employers) and prices (and thus benefits consumers).

There is considerable disagreement about the benefits of the brain drain and brawn drain for the developing countries themselves. The size of the annual remittances from migrant workers is at least one benefit. But more often than not, the people who migrate are professionals, skilled workers and entrepreneurs, whose talents are needed in their own societies. The prolonged absence of the predominantly male migrants may cause hardships, psychological and otherwise, to the mainly female dependents they leave behind. The remittances, therefore, are not always unmixed blessings for the sending nations.

11. INTERDEPENDENCE

Interdependence between developed and developing societies is not a new concept. But it has gained new urgency as a result of the events of the past two decades. It now defines not so much a passive state of awareness but an active resource energizing international transactions and helping to curb the excesses of short-sighted nationalism. It is also becoming an imperative in promoting a sustainable growth in world economy. The poor nations can no longer be dismissed as stragglers and basket cases; there is sound economic wisdom in any alliance between rich and poor nations because their ultimate interests coincide.

Increasingly, the developing countries are acting as engines of progress for the rest of the world. While the main transmission of economic activity is from the North to the South, the reverse effects are not negligible. Some estimates suggest that an extra percentage point in the growth rate of developing countries would add another 0.1 to 0.2% to the growth rate of developed nations. Another study calculatedthat by sustaining their imports during the mid-1970s while the rest of the world's slowed down, the middle-income countries had an impact on the industrialized countries equivalent to a signficant reflation of the economy of West Germany. They prevented the recession in the North from becoming even worse than it was.

The developing countries also play an increasingly important role in world trade. They will account for nearly 30% of the increase in world trade between 1980 and 1990. The OIDCs alone purhased 19% of EEC exports, 24% of U.S. exports and 32% of Japanese exports. In the trade in manufactured goods as a whole, industrial market economies enjoyed a surplus of $34.5 billion with the developing countries in 1978.

For Third World countries, the concept of interdependence has a particular significance because it is the most powerful argument they can advance for the greater involvement of the industrialized world in thier development. In one sense, all countries in the world are developing countries, just as all are dependent countries; it is this web of dependence and development that will sustain the continuing dialogue between North and South on the basis of equality and mutual respect.

A NOTE ON READING CHARTS

Charts presented in this book are based on basic data (frequency counts of persons, events etc.) or derived statistics (summary measures, such as averages, rates, ratios, proportions and percentage distributions). These data are often of uneven quality because data collection operations may not adhere to uniform standards. All data, however collected, are subject to some risk of inaccuracy or error. Even population figures, the most reliable of all, may vary by as much as 2%.

Two types of charts appear most often: bar charts, where the heights of vertical bars or the lengths of horizontal bars indicate magnitude, and line charts, whose connected points denote successive magnitudes or trends over time. The labels of the axes identify the variables and scales of measurement, which denote the values of the variables. At times, a break may appear on a bar denoting a single value that exceeds the limits of the chart scale. On many line charts time is represented on the x axis and the values of the variable are shown along the y axis. The line does not necessarily represent the values for periods between observations.

The ATLAS OF THE THIRD WORLD, like the ENCYCLOPEDIA OF THE THIRD WORLD and other projects before it, has been fortunate in that it had the steady skipper's hand of Edward W. Knappman, Executive Vice President of Facts On File, to guide it through the two years it was in gestation. I am completing this project with a large debt of gratitude for his patience and encouragement. The art department of Facts On File has done a magnificent job on the maps and charts within record time. My thanks are particularly due to Andrew Elias, the cartographer and graphic artist in chargeof the project. Andrew's comment that he had learned to understand the Third World more after working on the ATLAS is one that I hope every reader can make. This work can have no better purpose. My thanks are also due to my daughter, Sarah Claudine Kurian, who has helped me out on more occasions than I can count with her usual cheerfulness.

April 27, 1983   GEORGE THOMAS KURIAN

PART I:
THEMATIC PROFILES

PROLOGUE: THE NORTH-SOUTH GAP

FOOD PRODUCTION
(calories/person/day)

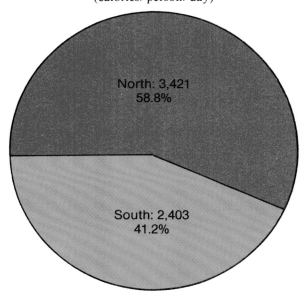

World Average: 2,590

POPULATION

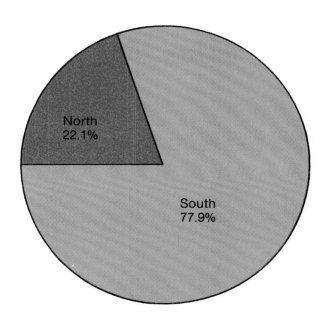

World (1979): 4,415,000,000
World (2000): 6,199,000,000

ENERGY PRODUCTION
(Quantities in thousand metric tons of oil equivalent)

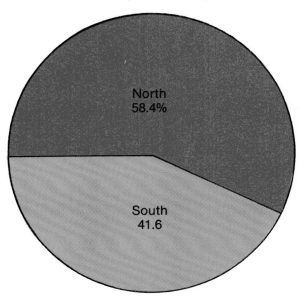

World (1979): 6,575,153

ENERGY CONSUMPTION
(Quantities in thousand metric tons of oil equivalent)

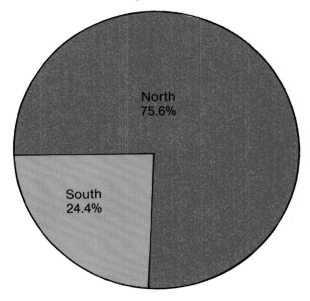

World (1979): 5,987,552

ADULT LITERACY RATE
(15 years and over)

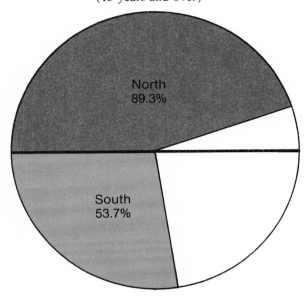

North
89.3%

South
53.7%

Data not available for China

CHILD DEATH RATE
(Age 1 to 4)

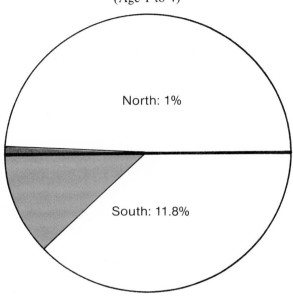

North: 1%

South: 11.8%

GNP

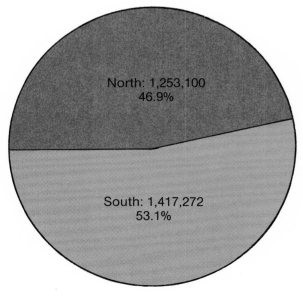

North
79%

South
21%

World (1980): $11.3 trillion

PRODUCTION OF PETROLEUM
(Thousand metric tons)

North: 1,253,100
46.9%

South: 1,417,272
53.1%

World (1979): 2,670,372

PUBLIC HEALTH EXPENDITURES

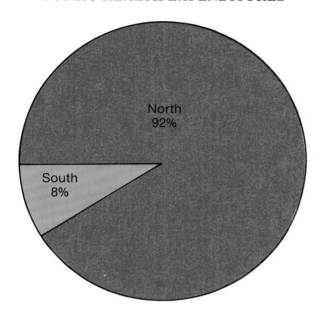

World (1978): $326.3 billion

MILITARY EXPENDITURES

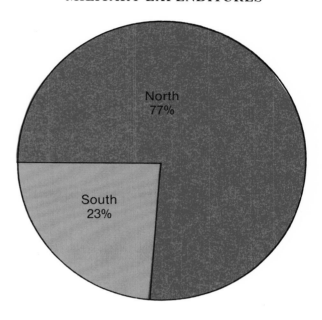

World (1978): $479.9 billion

PUBLIC EDUCATION EXPENDITURES

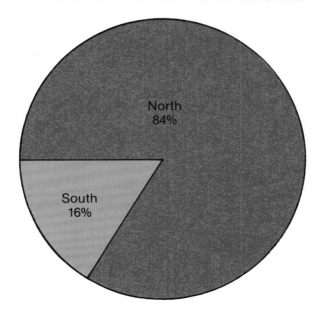

World (1978): $474.5 billion

NON-GOLD RESERVES
(billion SDRs)

December 1973
(Total, SDR 117.7 billion)

December 1981
(Total, SDR 342.4 billion)

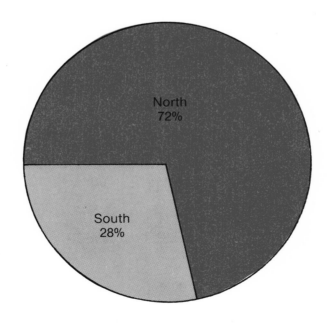

29.2

10.8

77.7

77.2

80.0

185.2

Industrial countries   Oil exporting countries   Non-oil developing countries

EXPORT EARNINGS

North
72%

South
28%

World (1979): $1,632.9 trillion

1: GENERAL AND POLITICAL

FIGURE 1-1
POLITICAL DIVISIONS

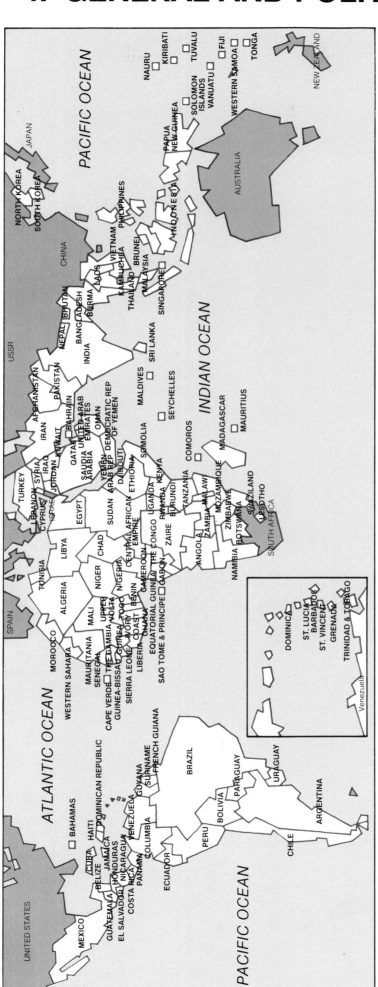

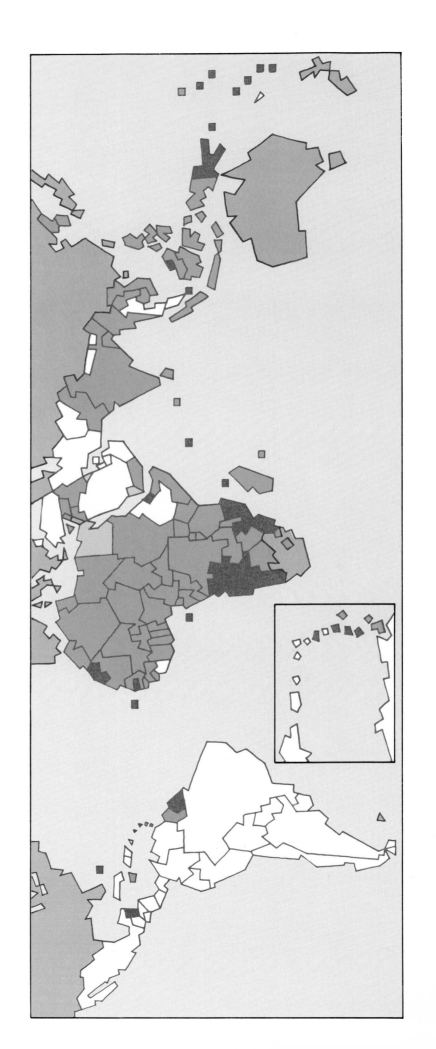

FIGURE 1-2
POLITICAL INDEPENDENCE

Gained independence
1900–1930

Gained independence
1931–1970

Gained independence
after 1970

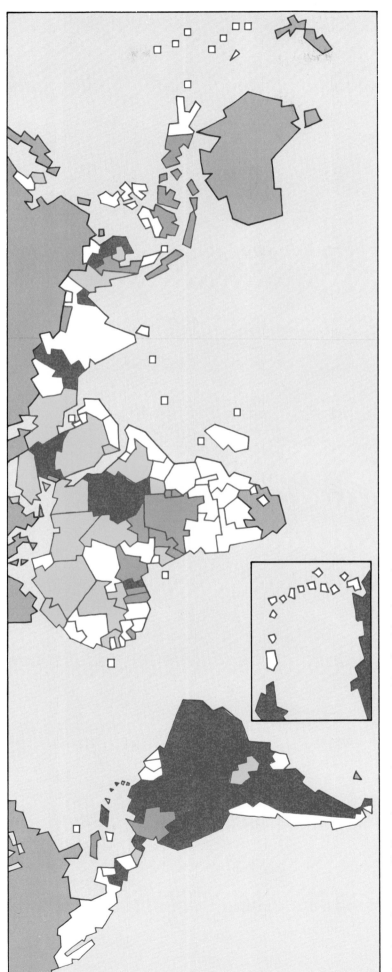

FIGURE 1-3
POLITICAL INSTABILITY
(1945-70)

Number of unconstitution changes in government leadership since 1945 (or year of independence if later)

One

Two

Three or more

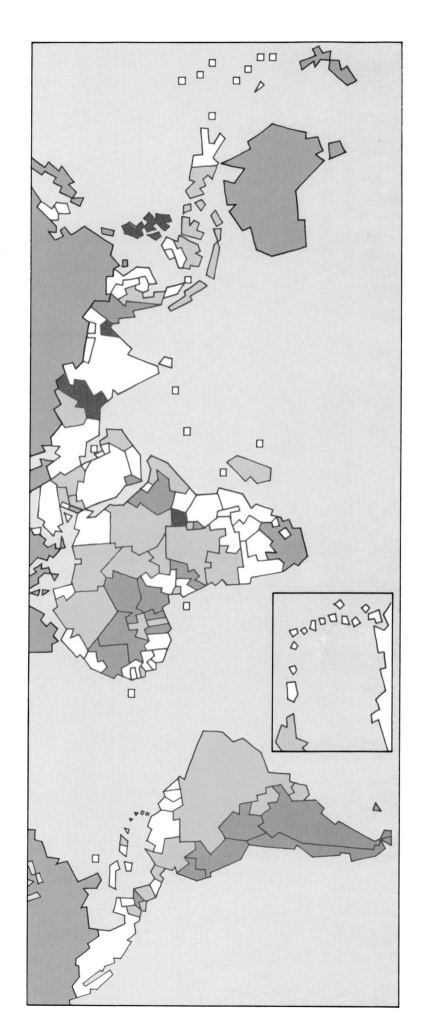

FIGURE 1-4
MILITARY GOVERNMENTS
(1978)

Governed by martial law

Military regimes

Substantial military
participation

FIGURE 1-5
THE MAP OF FREEDOM
(1981)

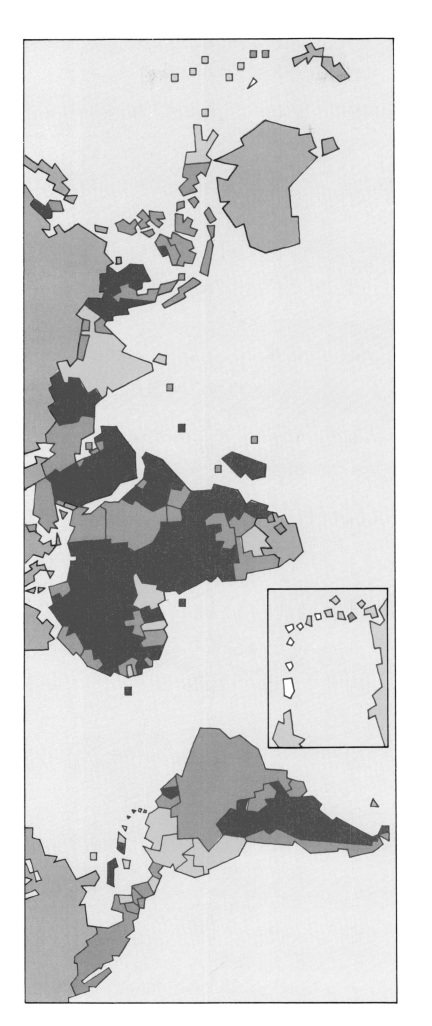

Free

Partly free

Not free

2: POPULATION

FIGURE 2-1
WORLD POPULATION

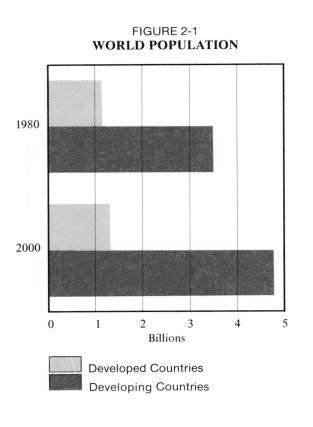

Billions

Developed Countries
Developing Countries

FIGURE 2-2
DISTRIBUTION OF WORLD POPULATION

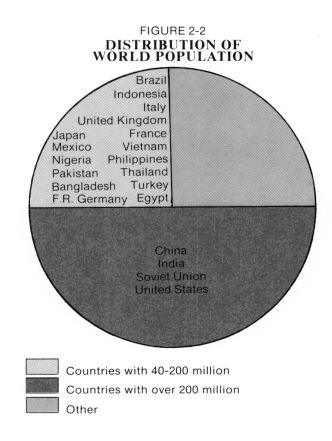

Brazil
Indonesia
Italy
United Kingdom
Japan   France
Mexico   Vietnam
Nigeria   Philippines
Pakistan   Thailand
Bangladesh   Turkey
F.R. Germany   Egypt

China
India
Soviet Union
United States

Countries with 40-200 million
Countries with over 200 million
Other

FIGURE 2-3

1975 POPULATION
(4,090 Million)

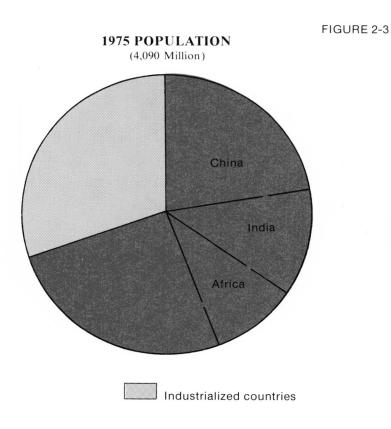

China

India

Africa

2000 POPULATION
(6,351 Million)

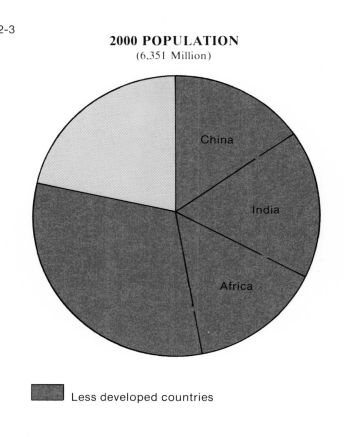

China

India

Africa

Industrialized countries   Less developed countries

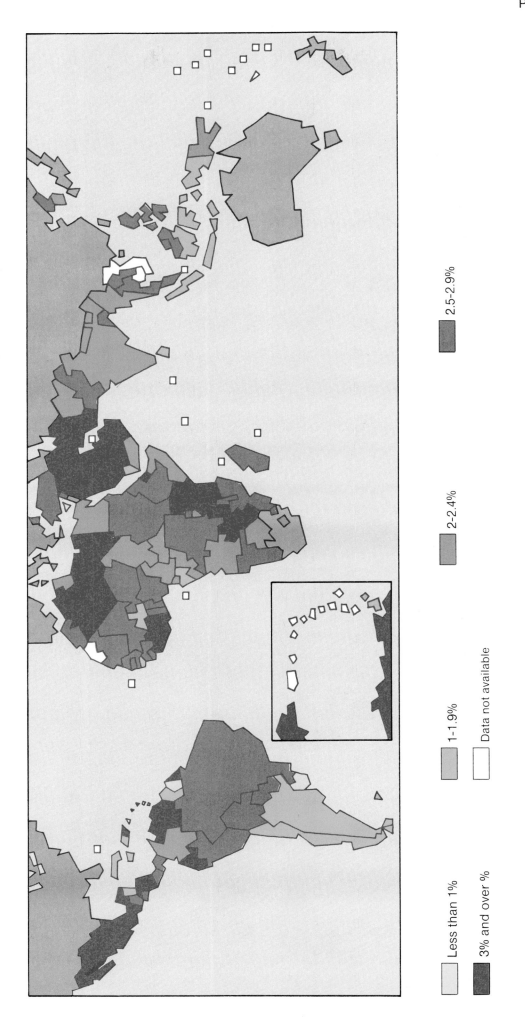

FIGURE 2-4
POPULATION GROWTH RATES
(1970-78)

Less than 1%

3% and over %

1-1.9%

Data not available

2-2.4%

2.5-2.9%

FIGURE 2-5a
NUMBER OF CHILDREN AGES 0-14
(1975)

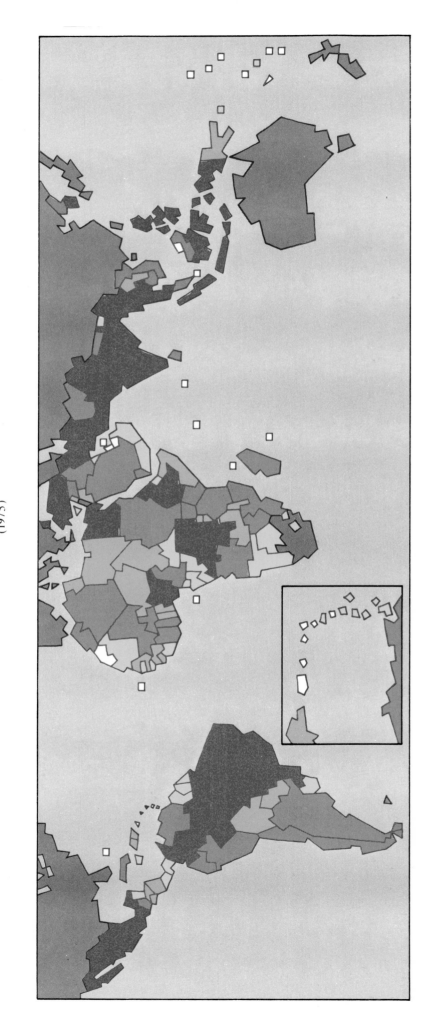

10,001,000 and over

2,501,000-10,000,000

1,001,000-2,500,000

0-1,000,000

Data not available

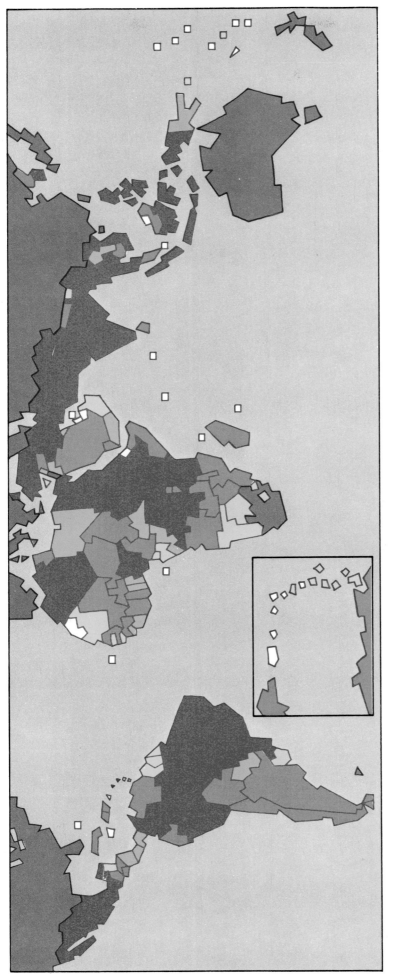

FIGURE 2-5b
NUMBER OF CHILDREN AGES 0-14
(2000)

0-1,000,000

1,001,000-2,500,000

2,501,000-10,000,000

10,001,000 and over

Data not available

FIGURE 2-6
BIRTH RATES AND DEATH RATES

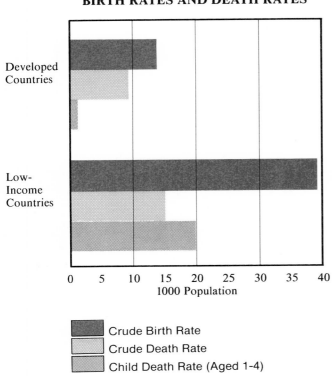

Developed
Countries

Low-
Income
Countries

0   5   10   15   20   25   30   35   40
1000 Population

Crude Birth Rate
Crude Death Rate
Child Death Rate (Aged 1-4)

FIGURE 2-7
POPULATION DENSITY BY REGION, 1977

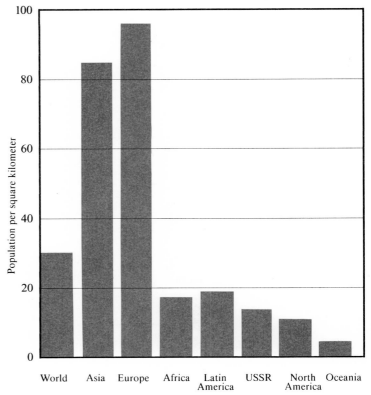

Population per square kilometer

World   Asia   Europe   Africa   Latin   USSR   North   Oceania
America   America

FIGURE 2-8
**POPULATION AND LAND AREA
BY REGION, 1977**

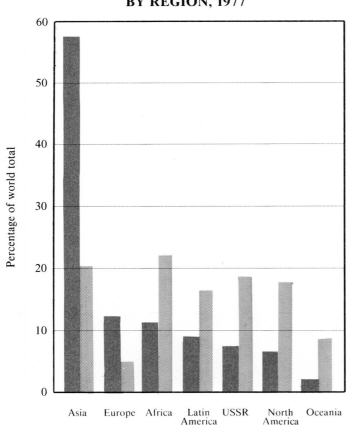

Percentage of world total

Asia   Europe   Africa   Latin   USSR   North   Oceania
America   America

Population   Land use

FIGURE 2-9
POPULATION OF THE WORLD

Billion

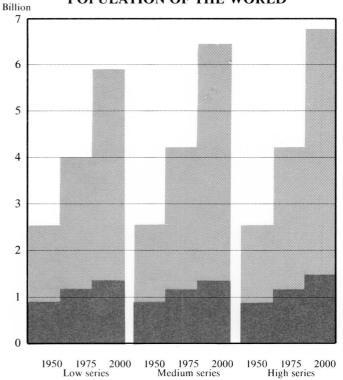

1950   1975   2000   1950   1975   2000   1950   1975   2000
Low series   Medium series   High series

Less developed regions

More developed regions

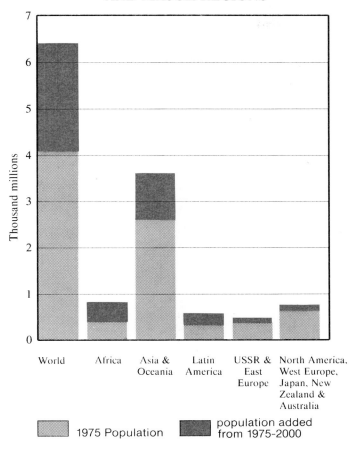

FIGURE 2-10
**TOTAL POPULATION OF THE WORLD
AND MAJOR REGIONS**

Legend:
- 1975 Population
- population added from 1975-2000

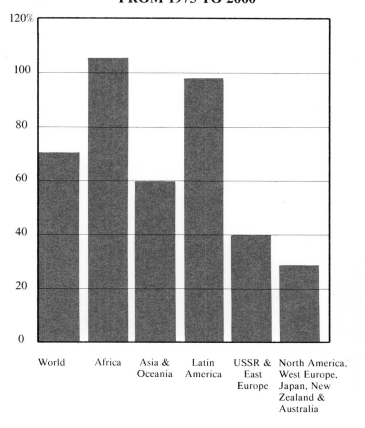

FIGURE 2-11
**NET GROWTH IN POPULATION
FROM 1975 TO 2000**

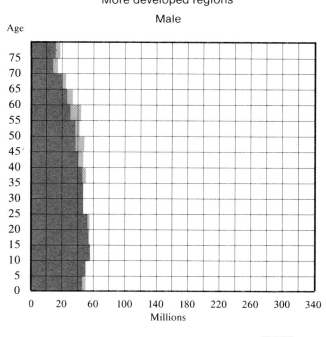

FIGURE 2-12a
AGE-SEX COMPOSITION

More developed regions

Male

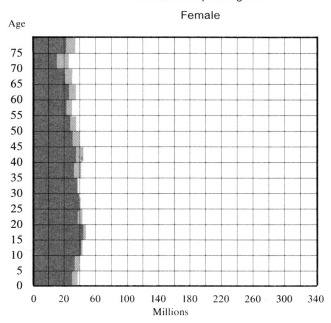

FIGURE 2-12b
AGE-SEX COMPOSITION

More developed regions

Female

Legend:
- 1975
- 2000

FIGURE 2-13a
AGE-SEX COMPOSITION
Less developed regions

Male

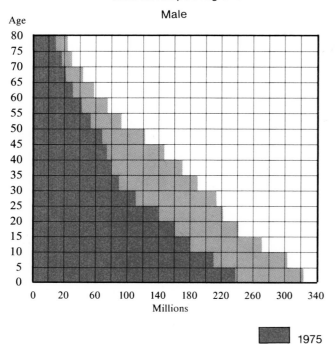

FIGURE 2-13b
AGE-SEX COMPOSITION
Less developed regions

Female

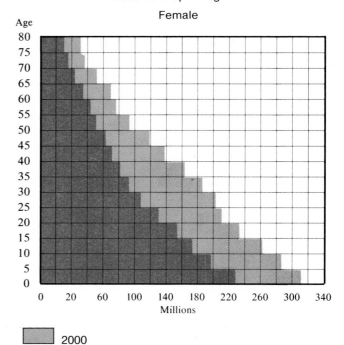

FIGURE 2-14
POPULATION OF THE WORLD
BY REGION: 1950-1979

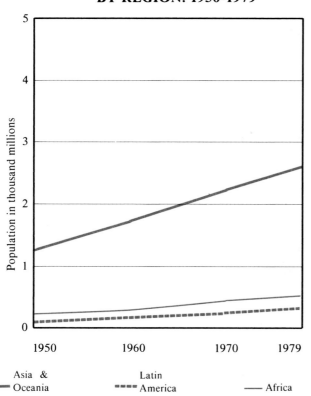

FIGURE 2-15
DISTRIBUTION OF WORLD POPULATION
BY REGION
(1979)

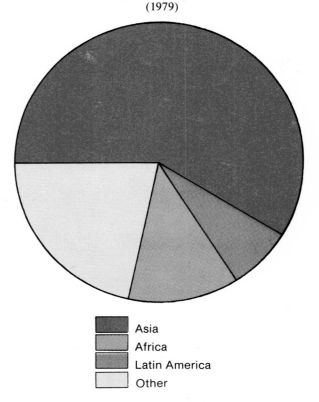

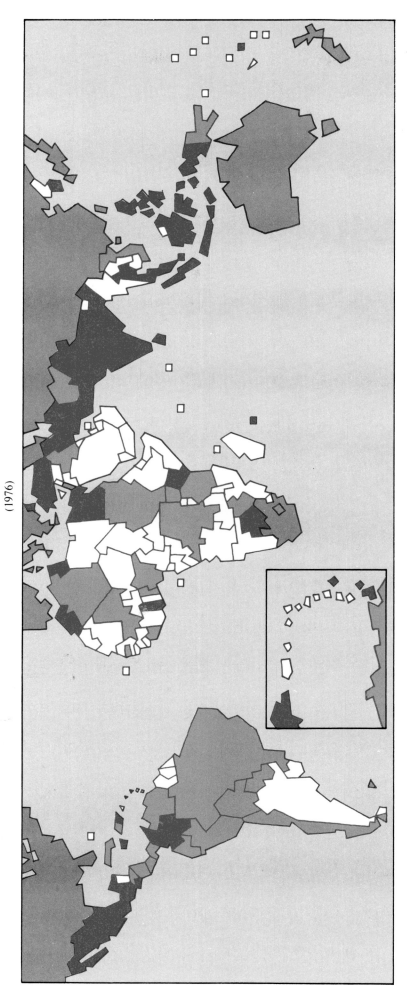

FIGURE 2-16
GOVERNMENT POSITIONS ON
POPULATION GROWTH AND FAMILY
PLANNING
(1976)

Official policy to reduce
growth rate

Official support of family
planning

Balance of developing
countries

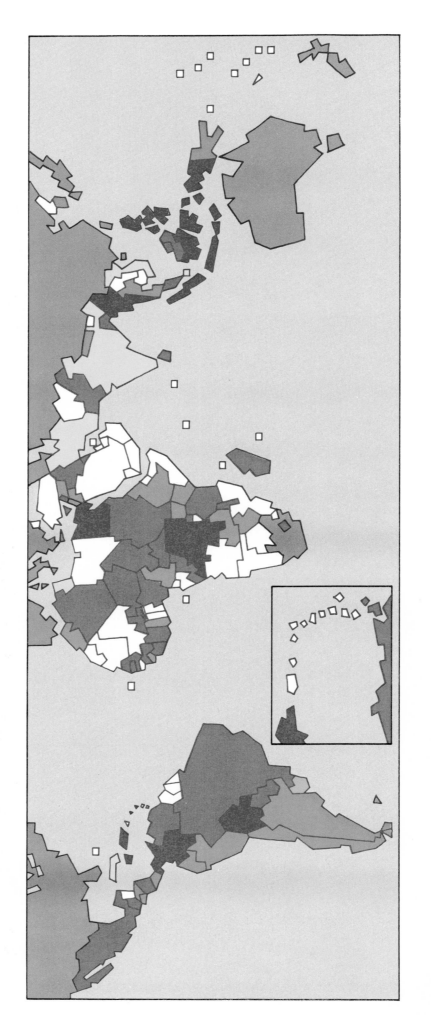

FIGURE 2-17
LEGAL STATUS OF ABORTION
(1979)

Legal on narrow medical
or juridicial grounds

Legal on medical,
juridical or eugenic
grounds

Legal on social/medical
grounds

Data not available

On demand

Illegal

FIGURE 2-18
BIRTH RATES, DEATH RATES AND AND RATES OF NATURAL INCREASE FOR THE WORLD: 1978

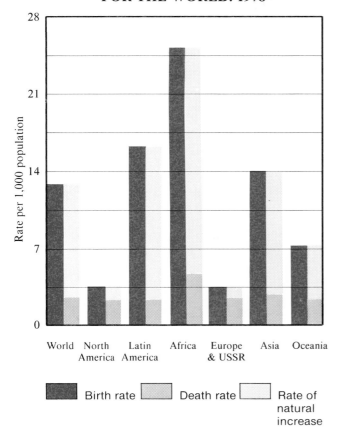

FIGURE 2-19
LIFE EXPECTANCY AT BIRTH FOR AFRICA

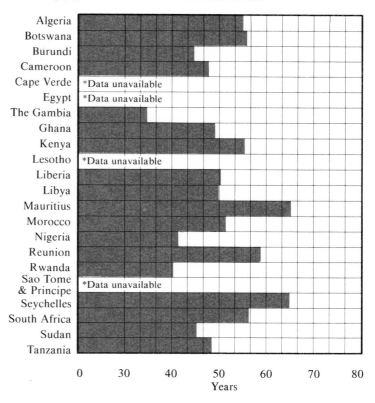

FIGURE 2-20
LIFE EXPECTANCY AT BIRTH FOR ASIA

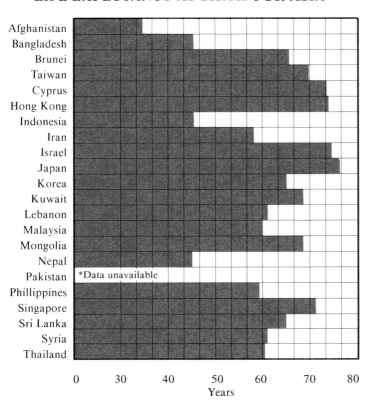

FIGURE 2-21
LIFE EXPECTANCY AT BIRTH FOR LATIN AMERICA

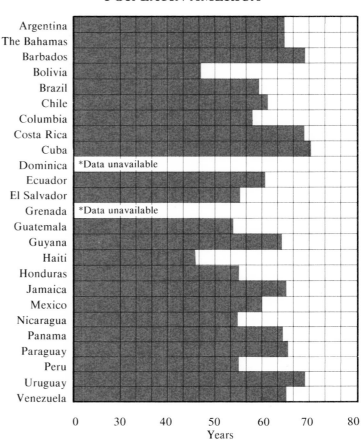

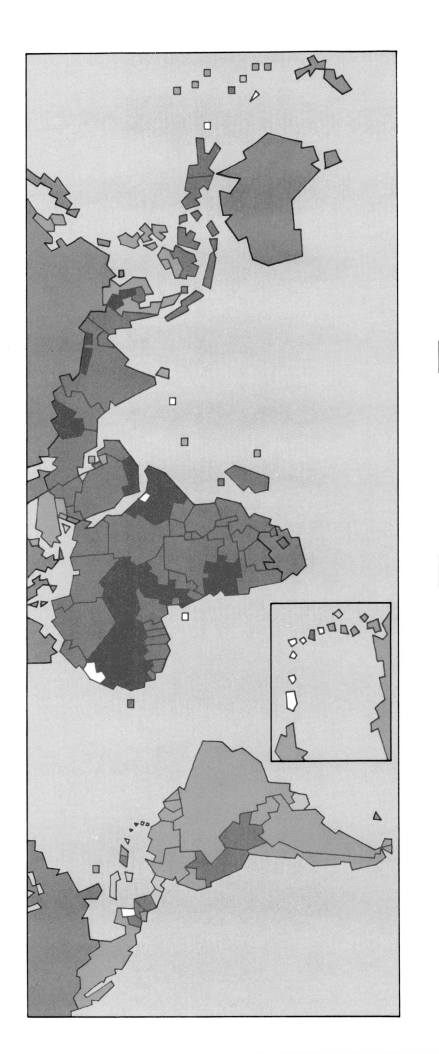

FIGURE 2-22
LIFE EXPECTANCY

70 and over   60-69   45-59   less than 45

Data not available

FIGURE 2-23
CONTRACEPTIVE USE

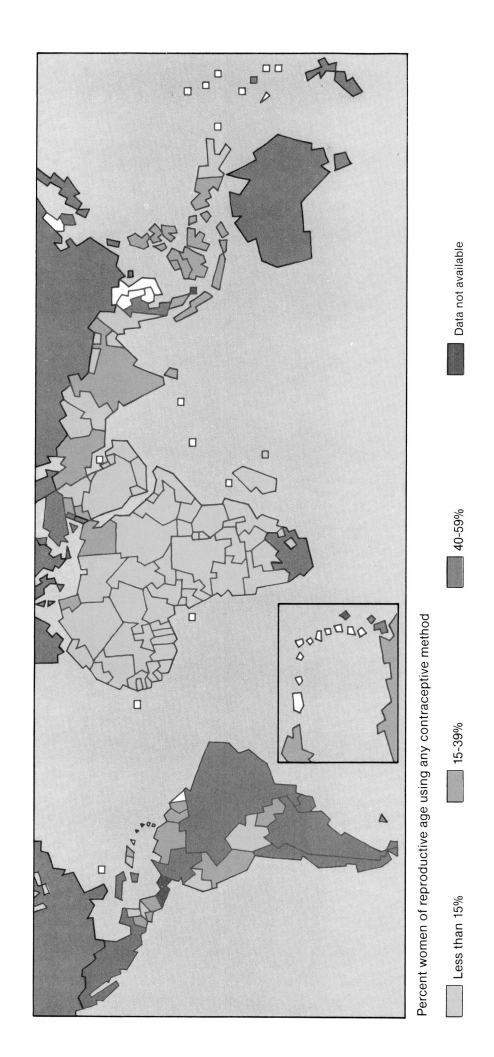

Percent women of reproductive age using any contraceptive method

Less than 15%   15–39%   40–59%   Data not available

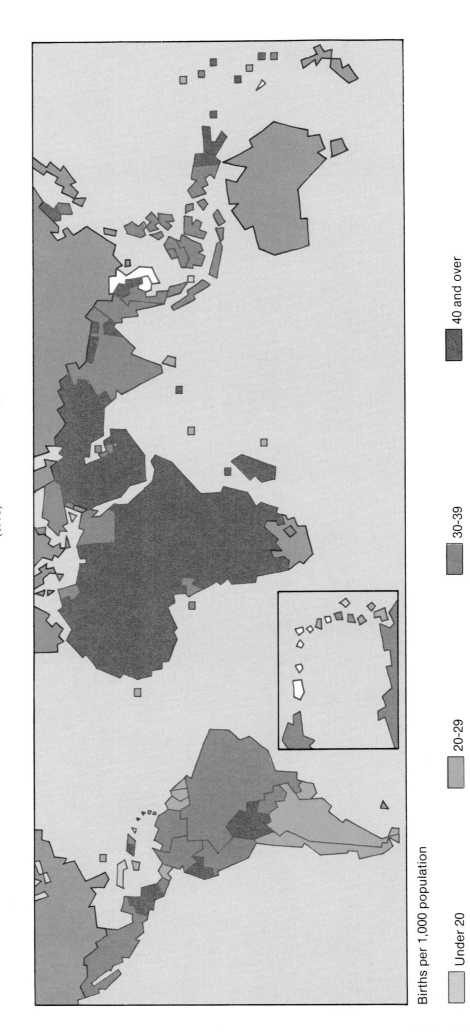

FIGURE 2-24
WORLD FERTILITY PATTERN
(1978)

Births per 1,000 population

Under 20

20-29

30-39

40 and over

Data not available

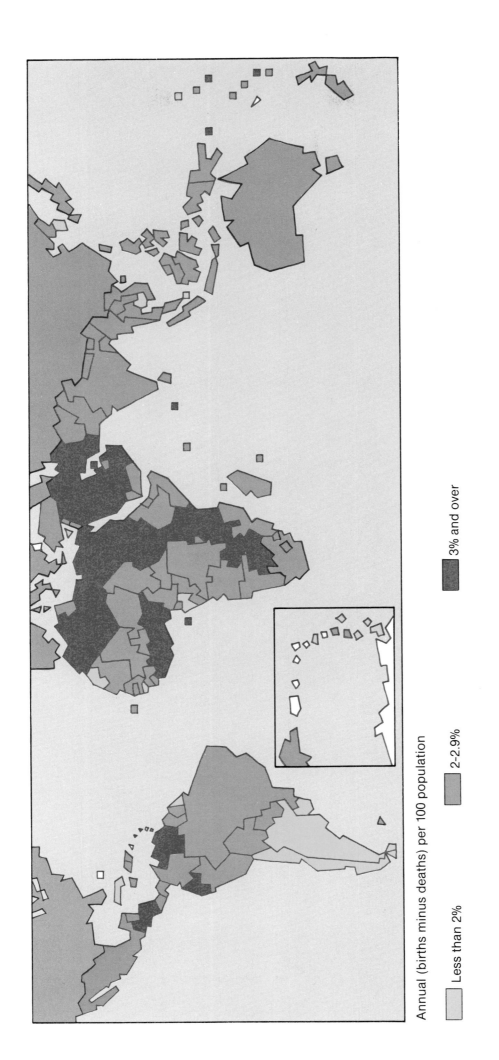

FIGURE 2-25
NATURAL INCREASE

Annual (births minus deaths) per 100 population

Less than 2%

2–2.9%

3% and over

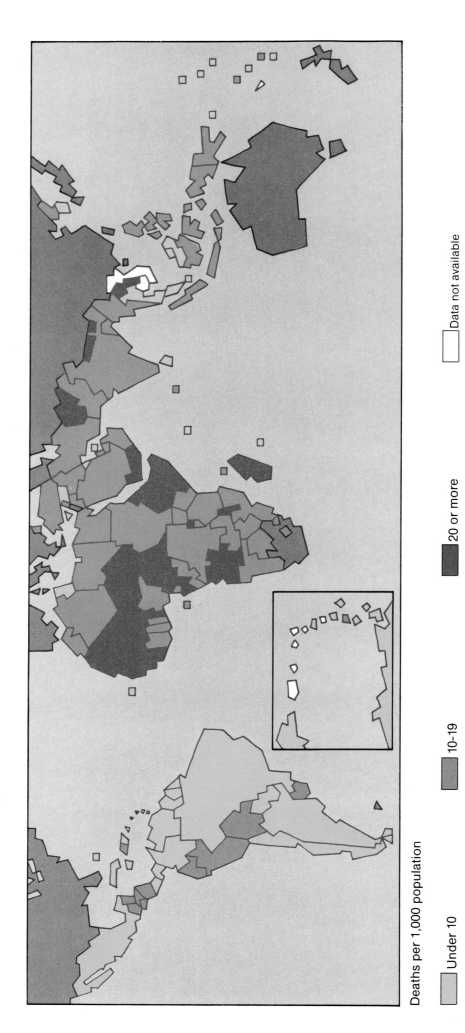

FIGURE 2-26
WORLD MORTALITY PATTERN
(1978)

Deaths per 1,000 population

☐ Under 10

■ 10-19

■ 20 or more

☐ Data not available

3: ECONOMIC CONDITIONS

FIGURE 3-1
THIRTY ONE YEARS OF WORLD CONSUMER PRICES
(per cent change over previous year)

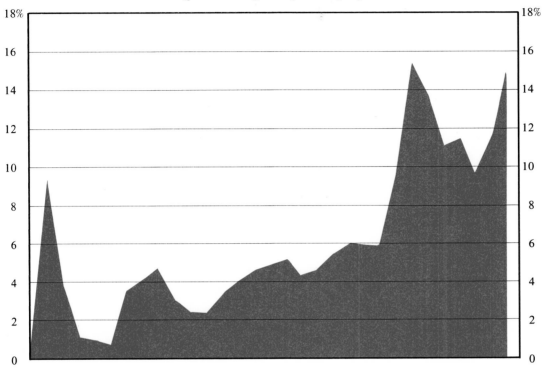

FIGURE 3-2
**DEVELOPING COUNTRIES:
TOTAL OUTPUT**
(per cent change from previous year)

FIGURE 3-3
CONSUMER PRICES
(per cent change over previous year)

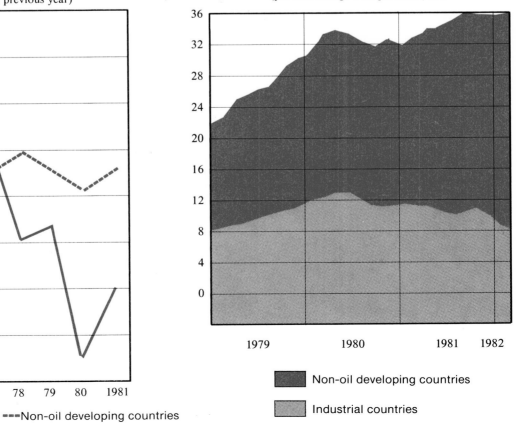

FIGURE 3-4
CENTRAL GOVERNMENT
DEFICITS AND SURPLUS
(as percentage of GDP)

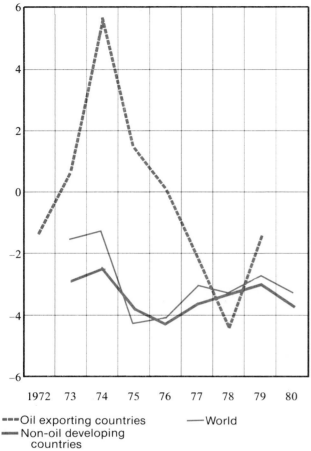

- - - - Oil exporting countries   ——— World
——— Non-oil developing
       countries

FIGURE 3-6
NON-OIL DEVELOPING CONTRIES
EXTERNAL DEBT SERVICE PAYMENTS

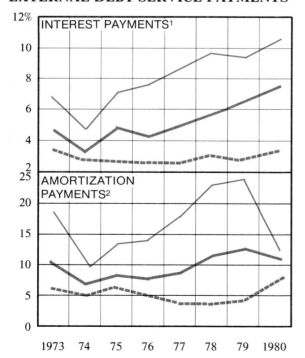

——— Net oil exporters   - - - - Low income countries
——— All non-oil developing countries

[1] As percentage of annual exports
[2] As percentage of annual exports

FIGURE 3-5
ECONOMIC TRENDS: 1960-79

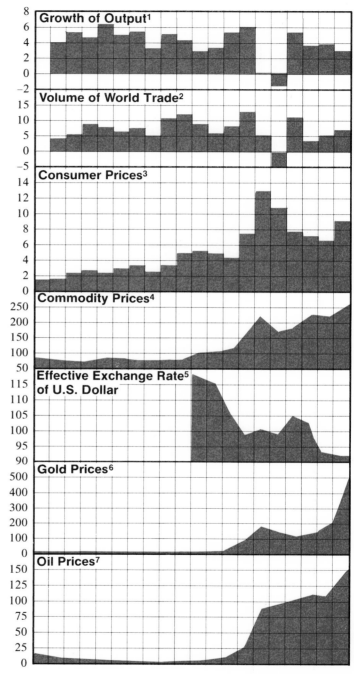

1960 61 62 63 64 65 66 67 68 69 70 71 72 73 74 75 76 77 78 1979

[1]GNP of industrial countries in real terms; percentage change from preceding year.
[2]Percentage change from preceding year, for Fund members and Switzerland.
[3]Index of industrial country prices; percentage change from preceding year.
[4]Index excluding oil and in terms of U.S. dollars; 1970 = 100.
[5]Based on IMF multilateral exchange rate model (MERM), 1975 = 100.
[6]London prices in U.S. dollars per fine ounce.
[7]Saudi Arabian light; index of wholesale prices, 1975 = 100.

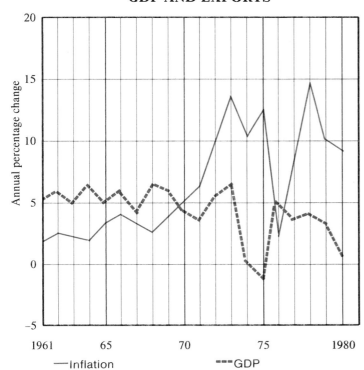

FIGURE 3-7
**INDUSTRIAL COUNTRIES'
GDP AND EXPORTS**

—Inflation   ╌╌GDP

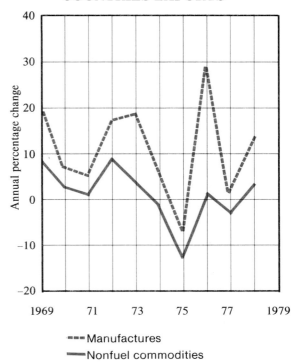

FIGURE 3-8a
**OIL-IMPORTING DEVELOPING
COUNTRIES EXPORTS**

╌╌Manufactures
▬Nonfuel commodities

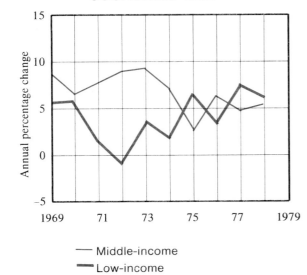

FIGURE 3-8b
**OIL-IMPORTING DEVELOPING
COUNTRIES' GDP**

—Middle-income
▬Low-income

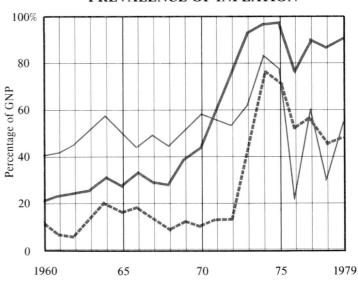

FIGURE 3-9
PREVALENCE OF INFLATION

Percent of countries with
— Rates greater than previous year
▬ 5% or more
╌╌ 10% or more

FIGURE 3-10
**NON-OIL DEVELOPING COUNTRIES:
REAL EXPORT EARNINGS**
(1972=100)

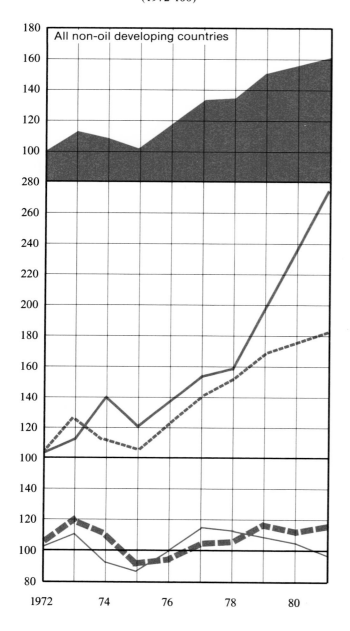

Oil exporters
Major exporters of manufactures
Other countries
Low-income countries

FIGURE 3-11
**NON-OIL DEVELOPING
COUNTRIES:
CURRENT ACCOUNT
DEFICITS**

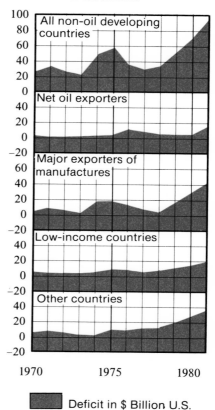

Deficit in $ Billion U.S.

FIGURE 3-12
**PRICES OF PRIMARY COMMODITIES,
EXCEPT OIL, EXPORTED BY
PRIMARY PRODUCING COUNTRIES**
(1975=$100)

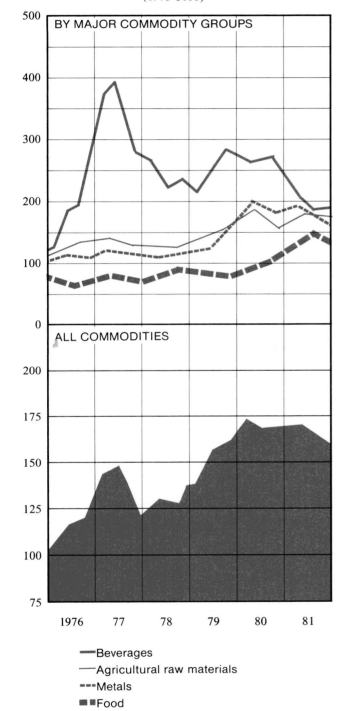

Beverages
Agricultural raw materials
Metals
Food

FIGURE 3-13
**NON-OIL DEVELOPING COUNTRIES:
RATIOS OF DEBT TO EXPORTS
AND DOMESTIC OUTPUT**

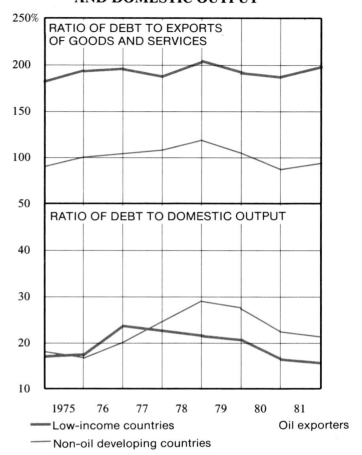

Low-income countries   Oil exporters
Non-oil developing countries

FIGURE 3-14
NUMBERS IN ABSOLUTE POVERTY

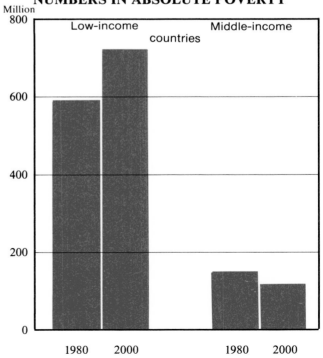

FIGURE 3-15
DEVELOPING COUNTRIES' GNP
(In 1980 dollars)

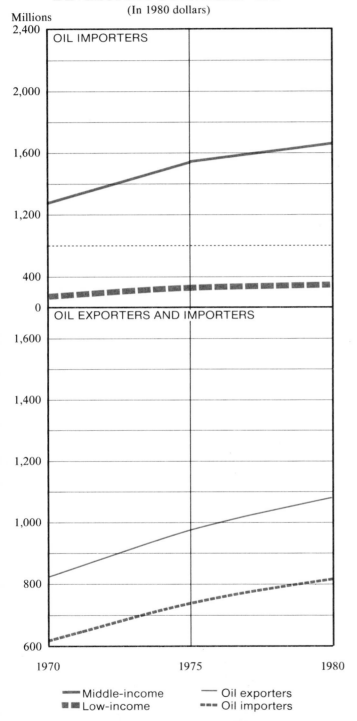

Middle-income   Oil exporters
Low-income   Oil importers

FIGURE 3-16
**DEVELOPING COUNTRIES'
OUTSTANDING DEBT**

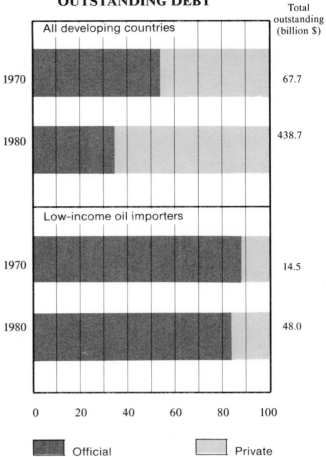

Official   Private

FIGURE 3-17
**DEVELOPING COUNTRIES' SAVINGS
AND INVESTMENT RATES**
(percentage of GDP)

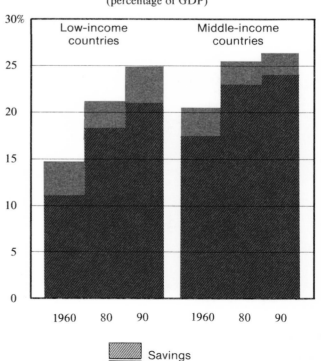

Savings
Investment

FIGURE 3-18
GNP PER PERSON
(In 1980 dollars)

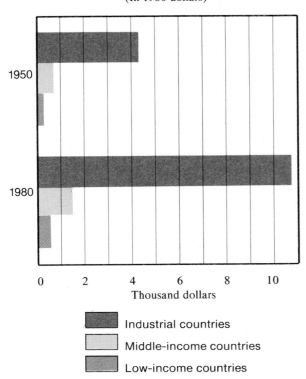

Thousand dollars

Industrial countries

Middle-income countries

Low-income countries

FIGURE 3-19
**OIL-IMPORTING
DEVELOPING COUNTRIES'
SOURCES AND USES OF
FINANCIAL FLOWS**
(Billions of 1978 dollars)

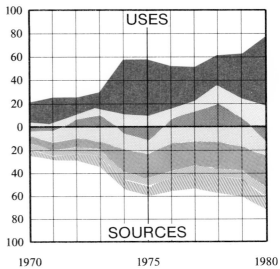

Resource transfer   Interest payments

Change in reserves and short term debt

Official Development Assistance

Medium and long-term commercial loans

Private direct investment

Workers' remittance

FIGURE 3-20
**OIL-IMPORTERS'
CURRENT ACCOUNT DEFICIT**
(Billions of 1978 dollars)

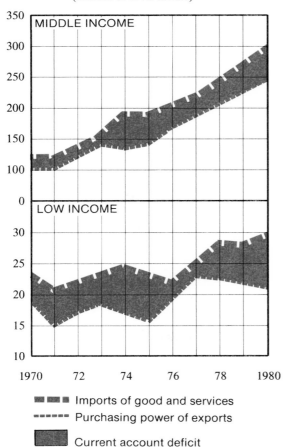

Imports of good and services

Purchasing power of exports

Current account deficit

FIGURE 3-21
**LONG-TERM PUBLIC DEBT OF NON-OIL
DEVELOPING COUNTRIES**

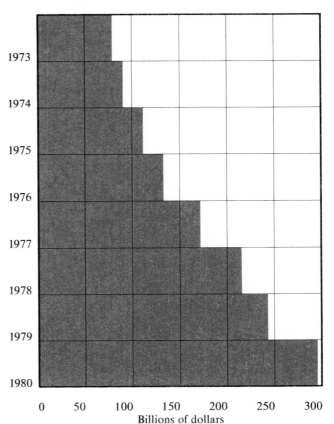

Billions of dollars

FIGURE 3-22
**THE EFFECT OF HIGHER OIL PRICES
ON NON-OPEC LDC'S**

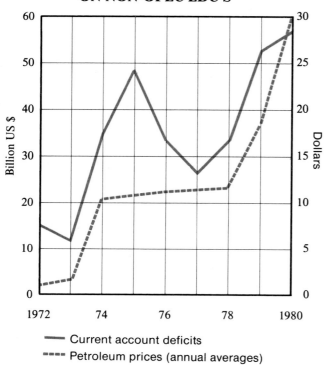

—— Current account deficits
- - - - Petroleum prices (annual averages)

FIGURE 3-23
**THE DROP IN LENDING TO
THE THIRD WORLD**
**New medium-term loans to developing
countries by international banks**
(In billions of dollars)

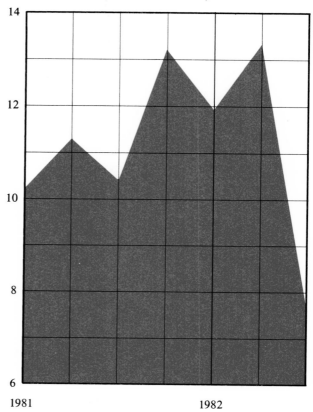

FIGURE 3-24
WEALTH AND POVERTY
Averages of income distribution

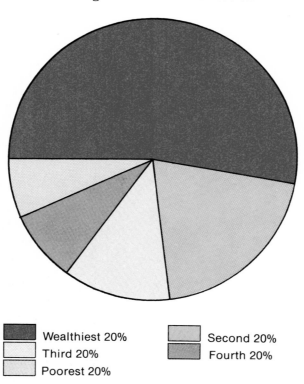

■ Wealthiest 20%   ▨ Second 20%
□ Third 20%   ▨ Fourth 20%
▨ Poorest 20%

FIGURE 2-25
PROJECTED GROWTH IN PER CAPITA INCOME

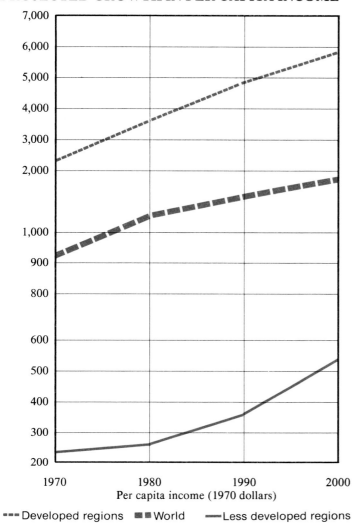

Per capita income (1970 dollars)

---Developed regions   ▪▪World   —Less developed regions

FIGURE 3-26
FOREIGN EXCHANGE RESERVES
(billion SDRs; end of period)

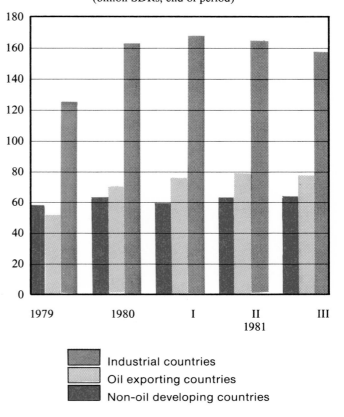

Industrial countries
Oil exporting countries
Non-oil developing countries

FIGURE 3-27
**COMPOSITION OF FOREIGN
EXCHANGE RESERVES**

Oil Exporting countries   Non-oil developing countries

Netherland guilder   French franc   Yen   U.S. dollar
Swiss franc   Pound sterling   Deutsche mark

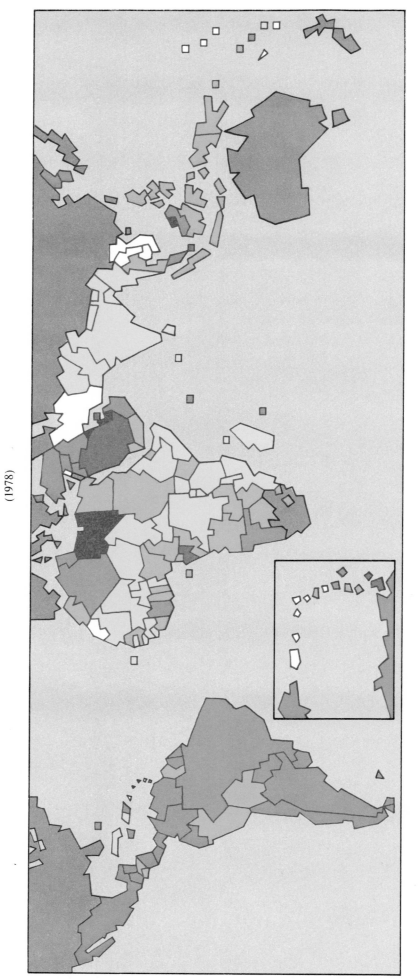

FIGURE 3-28
**GROSS NATIONAL PRODUCT PER
CAPITA**
(1978)

Less than $300

$7,000 and over

$300-$699

Data not available

$700-$2,999

$3000-$6,999

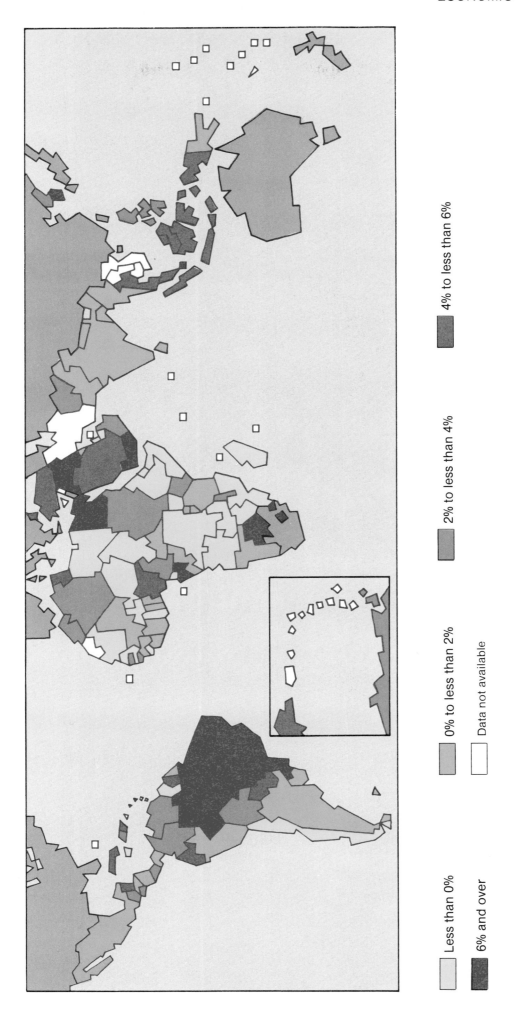

FIGURE 3-29
GNP PER CAPITA GROWTH RATE
(1970-78)

Less than 0%

6% and over

0% to less than 2%

Data not available

2% to less than 4%

4% to less than 6%

FIGURE 3-30
GNP PER CAPITA BY REGIONS
(1978)

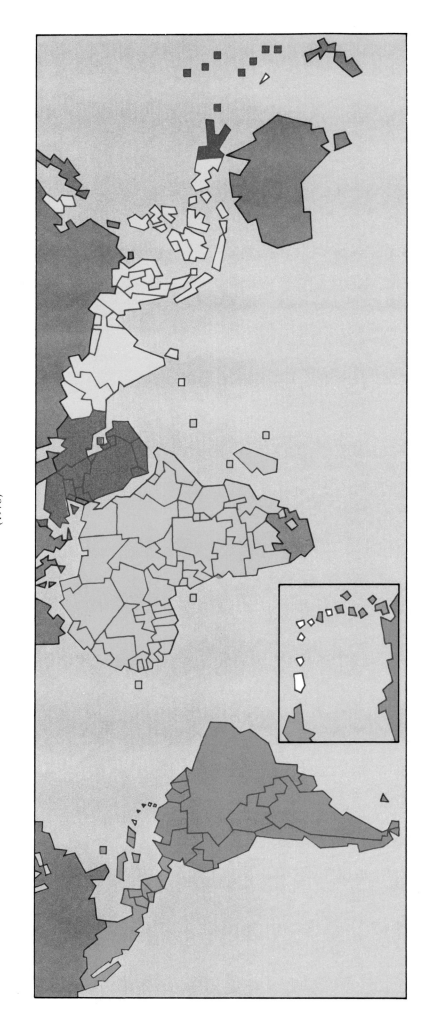

Oceania $6,230

Middle East $3,120

South America $1,470

Central America $1,260

Africa $560

Asia $280

FIGURE 3-31
THE BURDEN OF DEBT

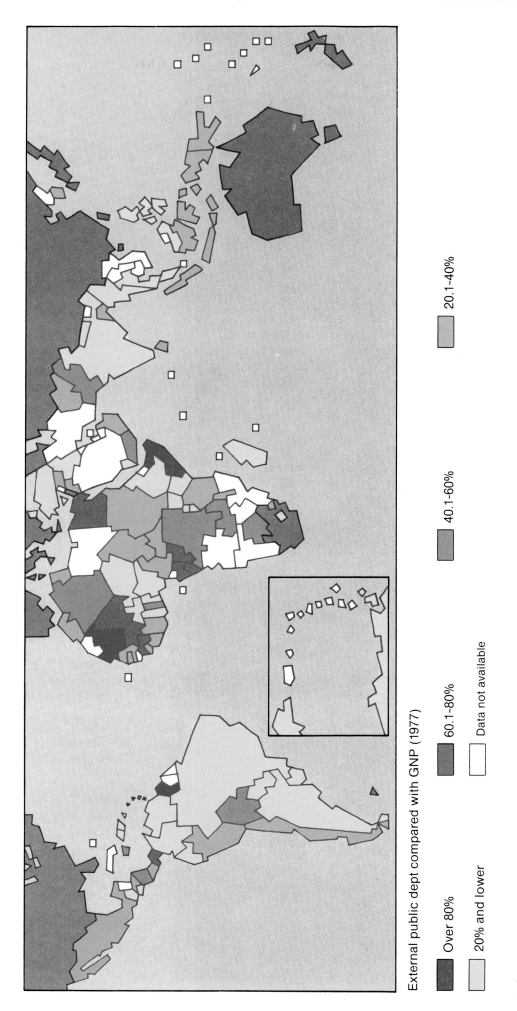

External public dept compared with GNP (1977)

Over 80%	60.1-80%
40.1-60%	20.1-40%
20% and lower	Data not available

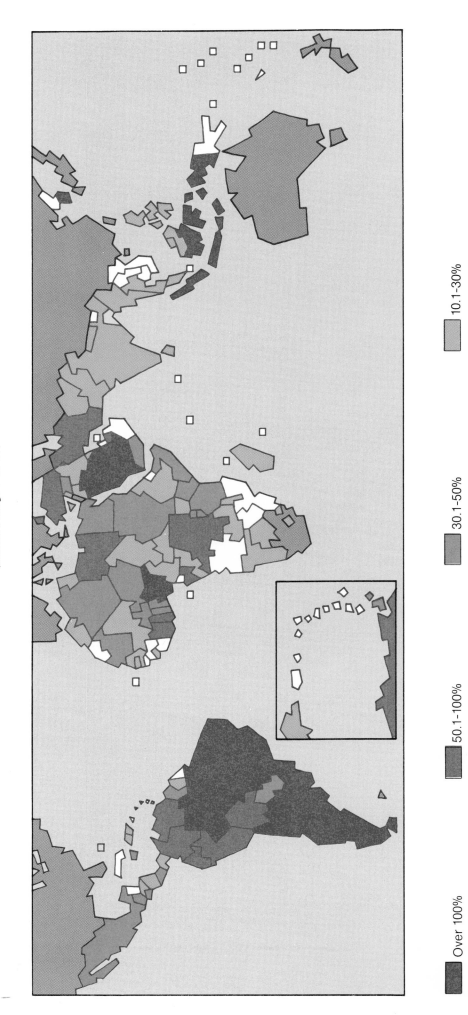

FIGURE 3-32
GROWTH IN MONEY SUPPLY
(Annual average 1968-77)

Over 100%

10% and below

50.1-100%

Data not available

30.1-50%

10.1-30%

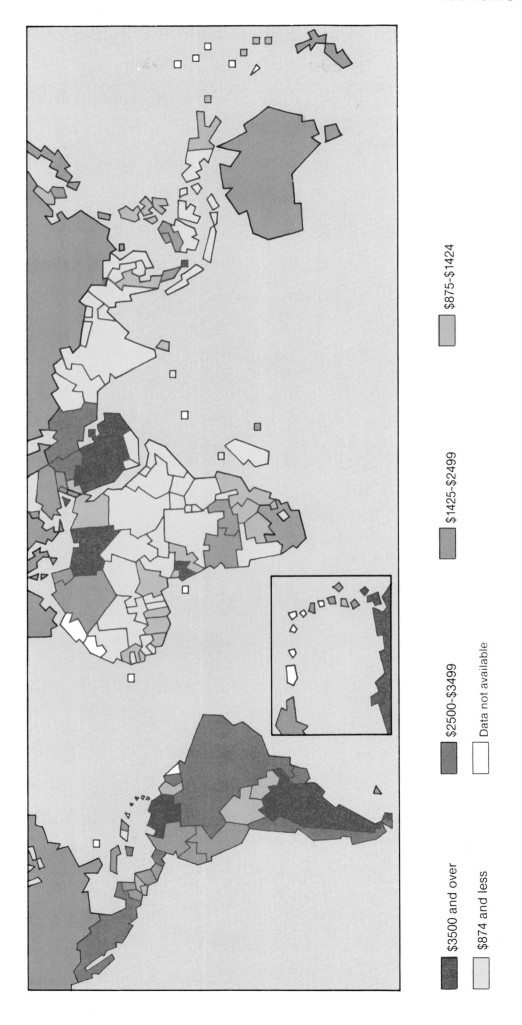

FIGURE 3-33
GROSS DOMESTIC PRODUCT
(Per capita)

$3500 and over

$2500-$3499

$1425-$2499

$875-$1424

$874 and less

Data not available

4: AID

FIGURE 4-1
OVERSEAS DEVELOPMENT ASSISTANCE
(In real terms)

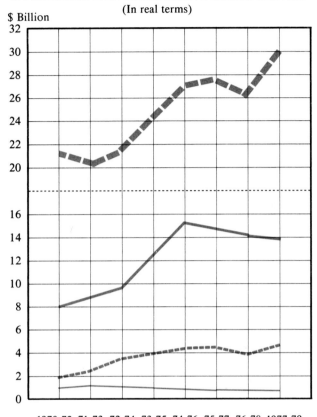

$ Billion

1970-72 71-73 72-74 73-75 74-76 75-77 76-78 1977-79

▪▪▪ All developing countries   — Least-developed countries
— Low-income countries   ■■■ Newly-industrialized countries

FIGURE 4-2
ODA IN REAL TERMS TO LOW-INCOME COUNTRIES

Billion

70-72 71-73 72-74 73-75 74-76 75-77 76-78 77-79

▪▪▪ Total   — From multilateral organizations
— From DAC countries   ■■■ From OPEC countries
(Development Assistance Committee)

FIGURE 4-3
EXTERNAL FINANCE TO DEVELOPING COUNTRIES

TRENDS

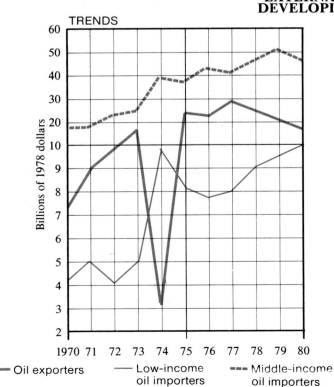

Billions of 1978 dollars

1970 71 72 73 74 75 76 77 78 79 80

— Oil exporters   — Low-income oil importers   ■■■ Middle-income oil importers

COMPOSITION

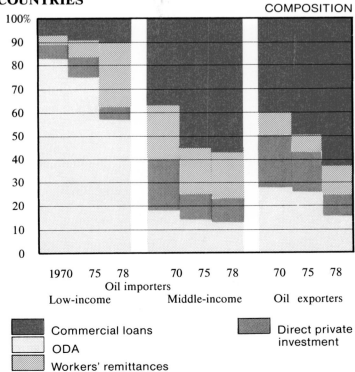

1970 75 78   70 75 78   70 75 78
Oil importers
Low-income   Middle-income   Oil exporters

■ Commercial loans   ▨ Direct private investment
□ ODA
▨ Workers' remittances

FIGURE 4-4
NET FLOWS OF CAPITAL TO
DEVELOPING COUNTRIES
Commercial terms

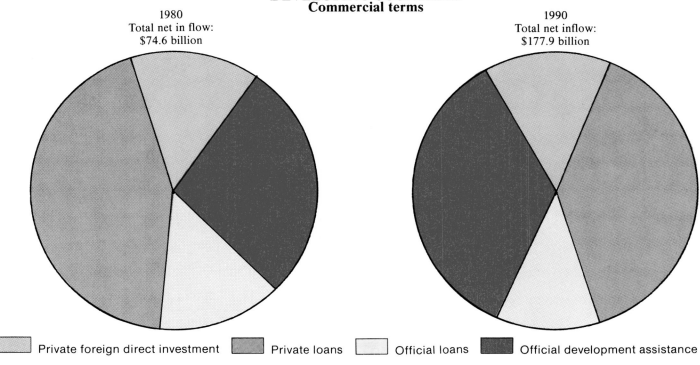

1980
Total net in flow:
$74.6 billion

1990
Total net inflow:
$177.9 billion

Private foreign direct investment   Private loans   Official loans   Official development assistance

FIGURE 4-5
TOTAL U.S. ECONOMIC AND MILITARY
ASSISTANCE TO THE THIRD WORLD
(1949-1979)

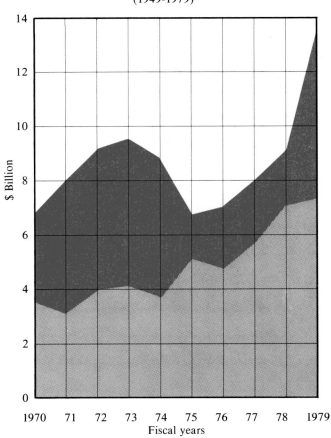

Military assistance   Economic assistance

FIGURE 4-6
ASSISTANCE FROM INTERNATIONAL
FINANCIAL INSTITUTIONS
(1968-1979)

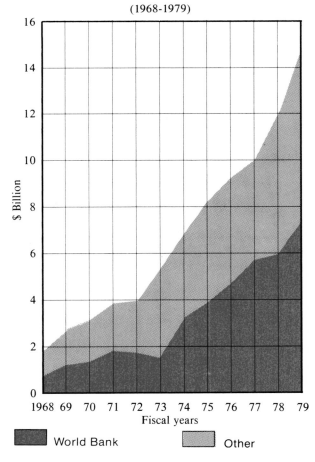

World Bank   Other

FIGURE 4-7
COMMUNIST MILITARY AID TO LESS
DEVELOPED COUNTRIES

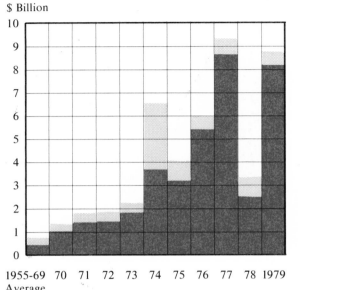

$ Billion

1955-69 70 71 72 73 74 75 76 77 78 1979
Average

Other
USSR

Total (1955-79): $53 Billion

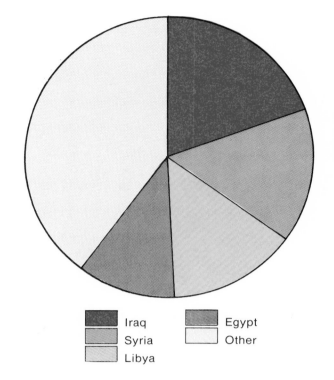

Iraq   Egypt
Syria   Other
Libya

FIGURE 4-8
COMMUNIST ECONOMIC AID TO LESS
DEVELOPED COUNTRIES

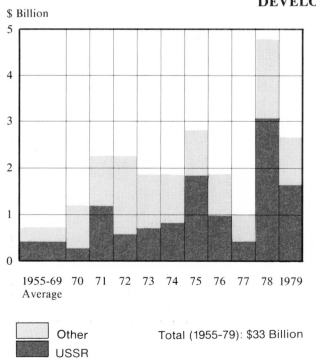

$ Billion

1955-69 70 71 72 73 74 75 76 77 78 1979
Average

Other
USSR

Total (1955-79): $33 Billion

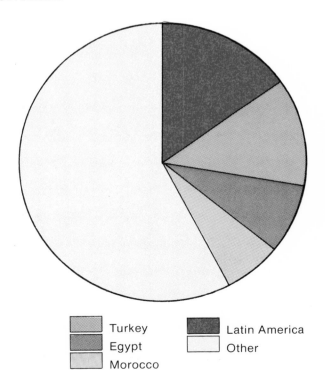

Turkey   Latin America
Egypt   Other
Morocco

5: DEFENSE

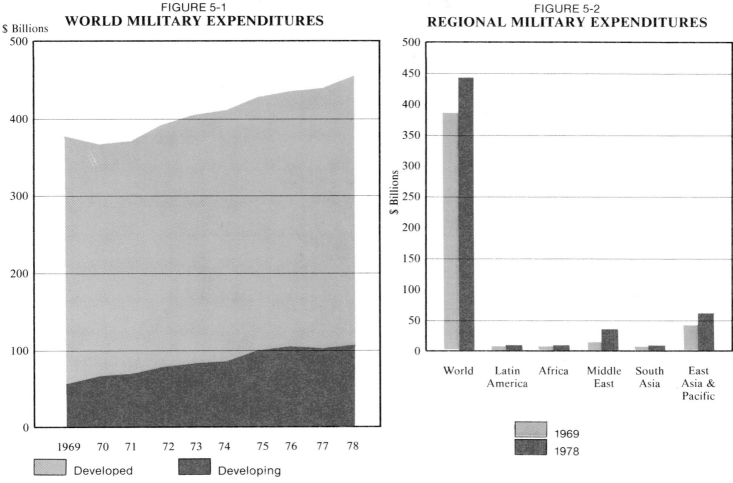

FIGURE 5-1
WORLD MILITARY EXPENDITURES

$ Billions

Developed
Developing

FIGURE 5-2
REGIONAL MILITARY EXPENDITURES

$ Billions

World · Latin America · Africa · Middle East · South Asia · East Asia & Pacific

1969
1978

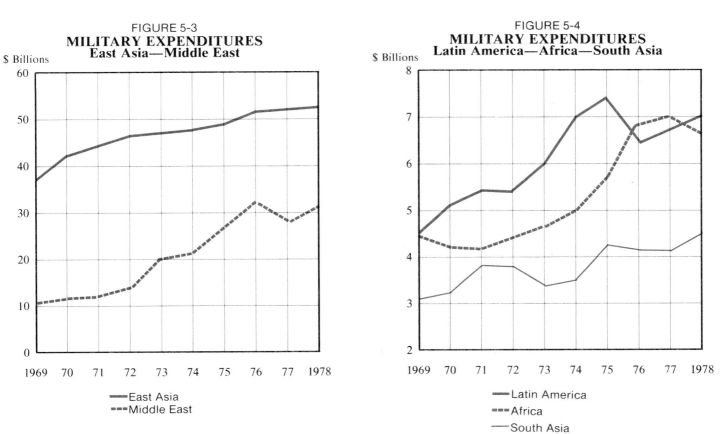

FIGURE 5-3
MILITARY EXPENDITURES
East Asia—Middle East

$ Billions

East Asia
Middle East

FIGURE 5-4
MILITARY EXPENDITURES
Latin America—Africa—South Asia

$ Billions

Latin America
Africa
South Asia

FIGURE 5-5
MILITARY EXPENDITURES

$ Billions

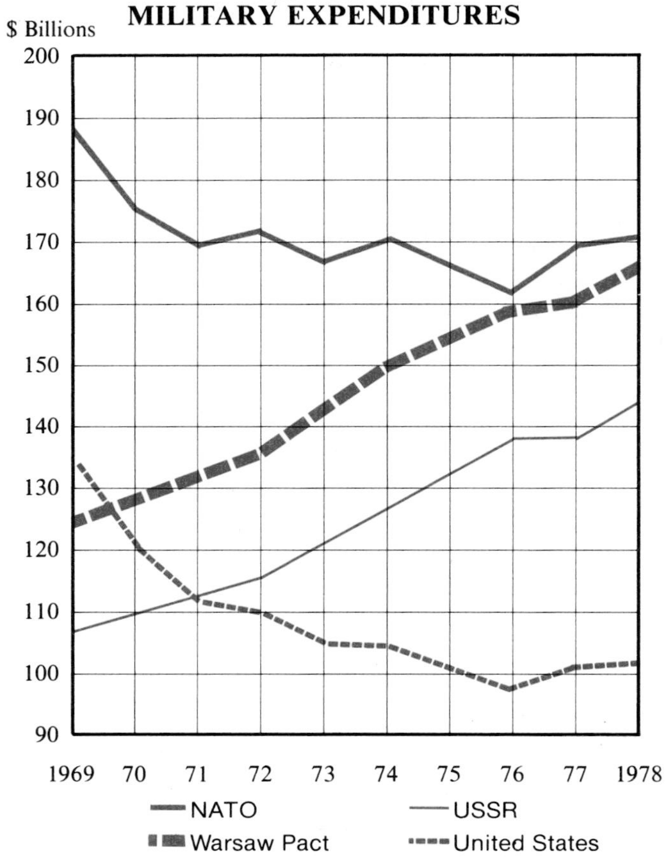

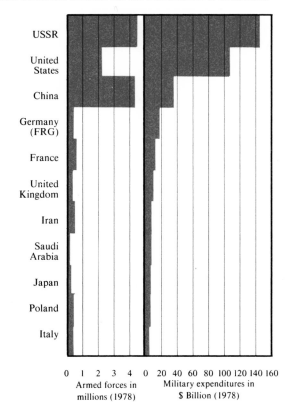

FIGURE 5-6
WORLD MILITARY EXPENDITURES

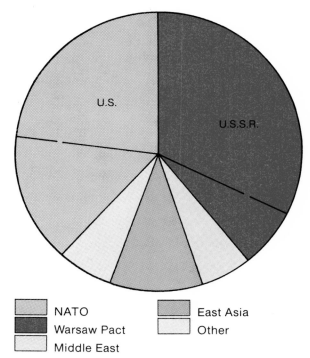

NATO   East Asia
Warsaw Pact   Other
Middle East

FIGURE 5-7
LEADING COUNTRIES IN MILITARY EXPENDITURES AND ARMED FORCES

FIGURE 5-8
MILITARY EXPENDITURES AS A PERCENTAGE OF COMBINED HEALTH AND EDUCATION EXPENDITURES

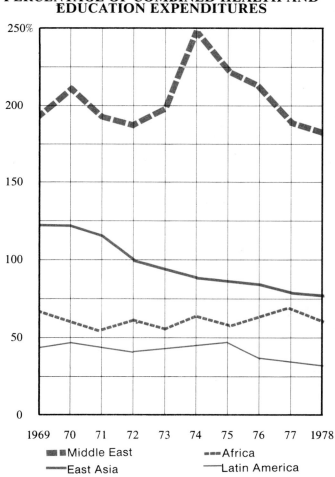

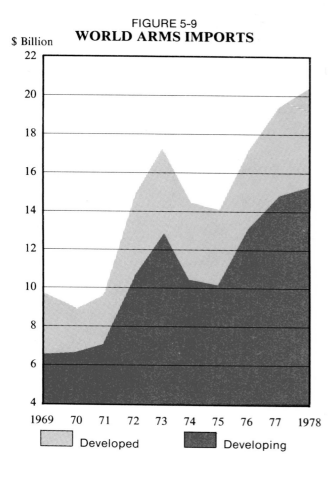

FIGURE 5-9
WORLD ARMS IMPORTS

$ Billion

Developed   Developing

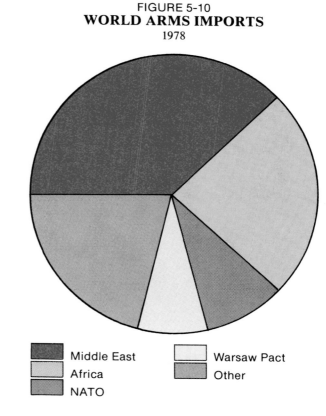

FIGURE 5-10
WORLD ARMS IMPORTS
1978

Middle East   Warsaw Pact
Africa   Other
NATO

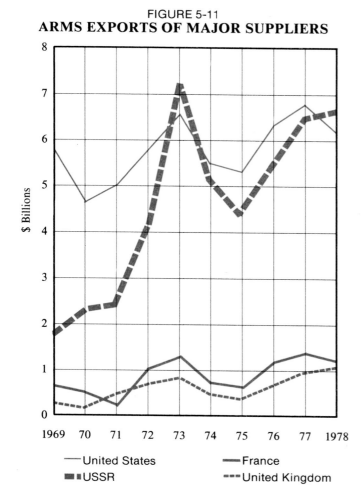

FIGURE 5-11
ARMS EXPORTS OF MAJOR SUPPLIERS

$ Billions

United States   France
USSR   United Kingdom

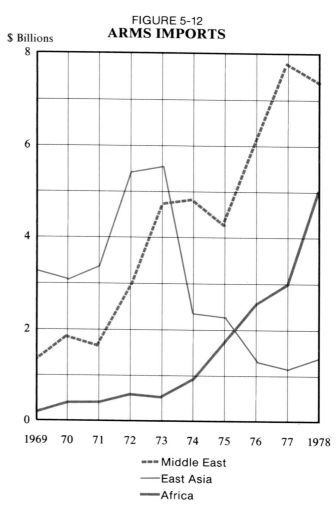

FIGURE 5-12
ARMS IMPORTS

$ Billions

Middle East
East Asia
Africa

FIGURE 5-13
WORLD ARMS EXPORTS
1978

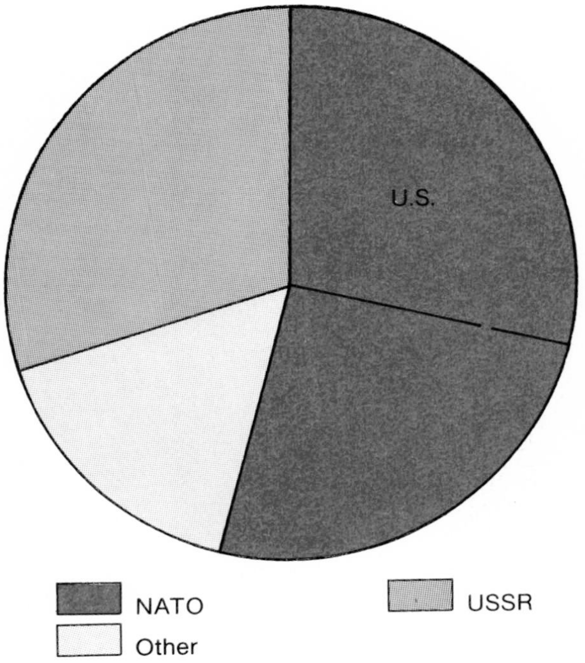

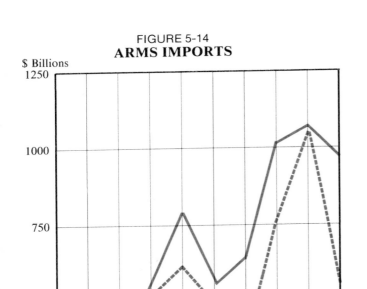

FIGURE 5-14
ARMS IMPORTS

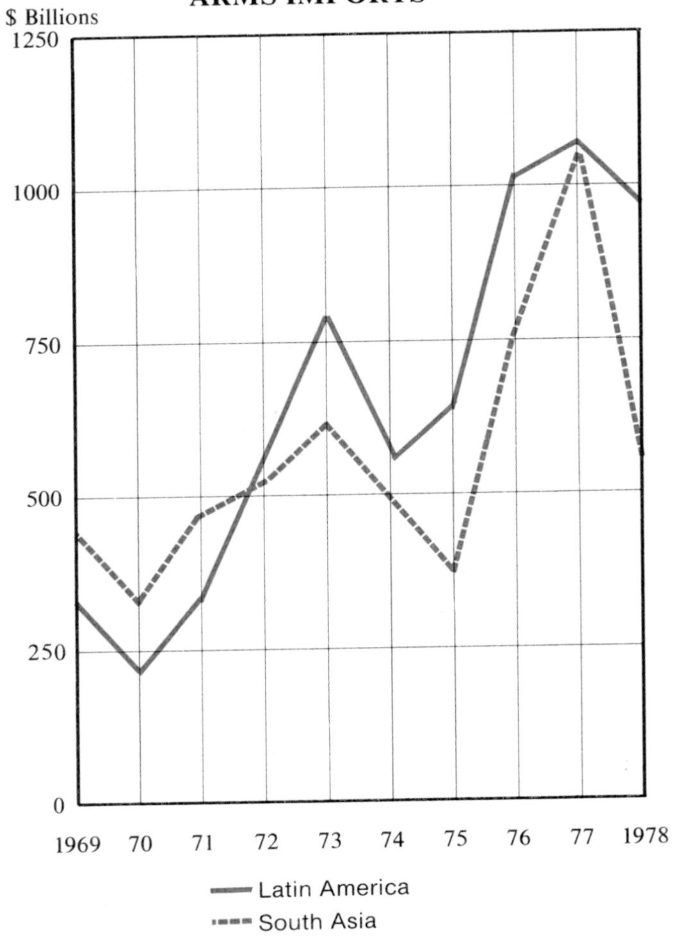

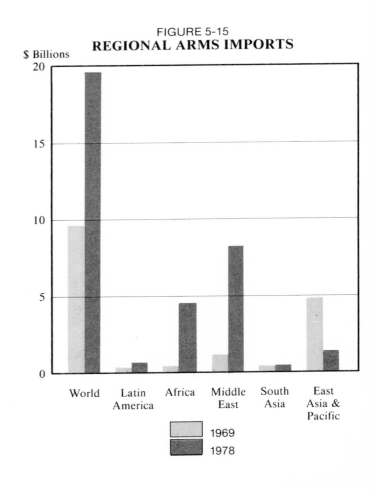

FIGURE 5-15
REGIONAL ARMS IMPORTS

FIGURE 5-16
LEADING COUNTRIES IN ARMS IMPORTS
1978

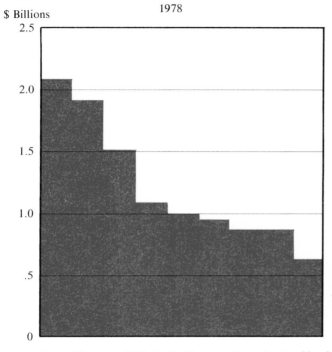

$ Billions

Iran Libya Iraq Ethiopia Saudi Israel Syria Soviet Algeria
                              Arabia   Union

FIGURE 5-17
TOTAL ARMS EXPORTS TO DEVELOPING STATES AND AID GRANTED 1974-1978

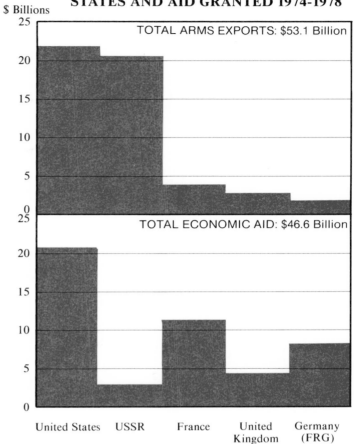

$ Billions

TOTAL ARMS EXPORTS: $53.1 Billion

TOTAL ECONOMIC AID: $46.6 Billion

United States USSR France United Germany
                                    Kingdom (FRG)

FIGURE 5-18
ARMED FORCES
(Developing countries)

FIGURE 5-19
ARMS IMPORTS
(Developing countries)

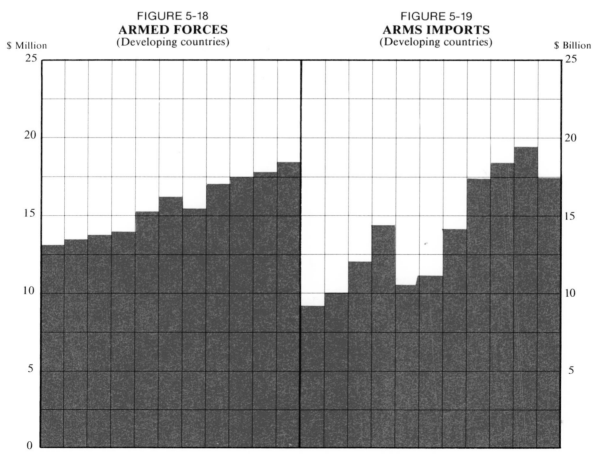

$ Million

$ Billion

1970 71 72 73 74 75 76 77 78 79 1980 1970 71 72 73 74 75 76 77 78 79 1980

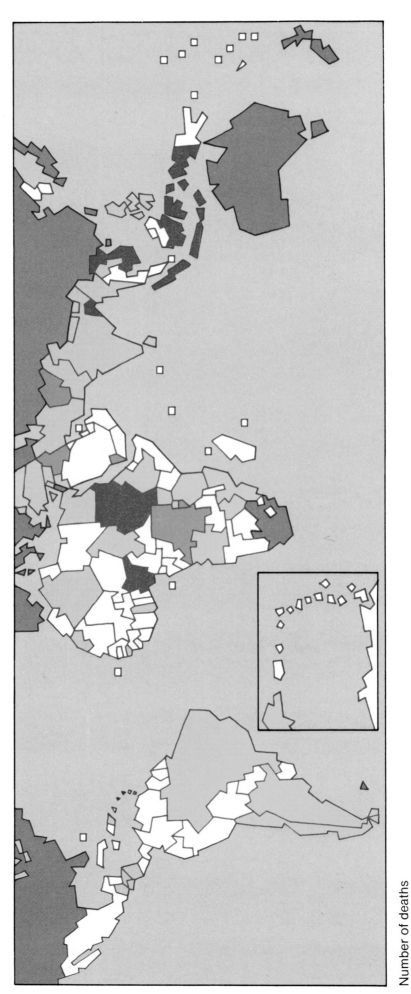

FIGURE 5-20
WAR AND DEATHS
(1960-82)

Number of deaths

█ 500,000 or more

▓ 100,000 to 499,999

░ 1,000-99,999

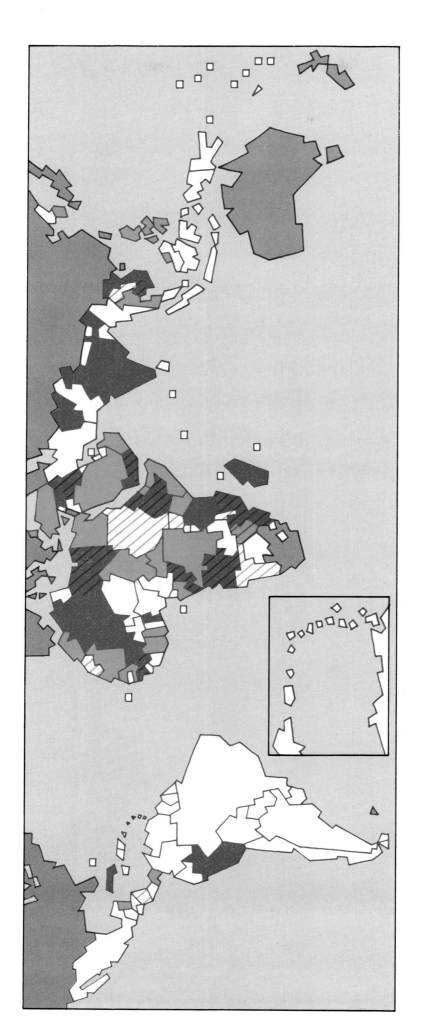

FIGURE 5-21
**MILITARY BASES AND PERSONNEL
ON FOREIGN TERRITORY**

NATO

Warsaw Pact

Other

6: LABOR

FIGURE 6-1
ESTIMATED WORLD LABOR FORCE
AT THE END OF 1987

Total: 2,045 million

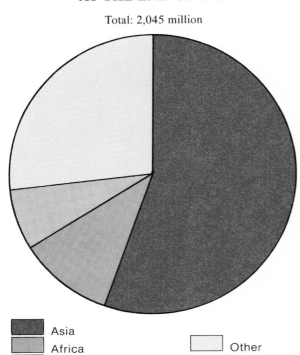

■ Asia
■ Africa
□ Other
▨ Latin America & the Caribbean

FIGURE 6-2
WORLD YOUTH POPULATION AT END
OF 1987

Total: 5,050 million

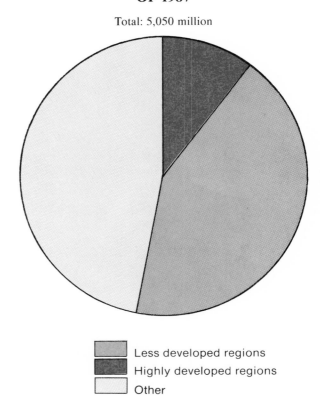

▨ Less developed regions
■ Highly developed regions
□ Other

FIGURE 6-3
WORLD DISTRIBUTION OF YOUNG
PEOPLE IN LESS DEVELOPED REGIONS

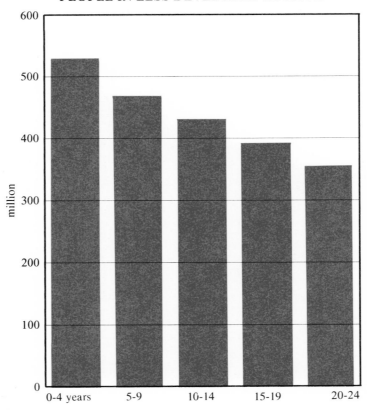

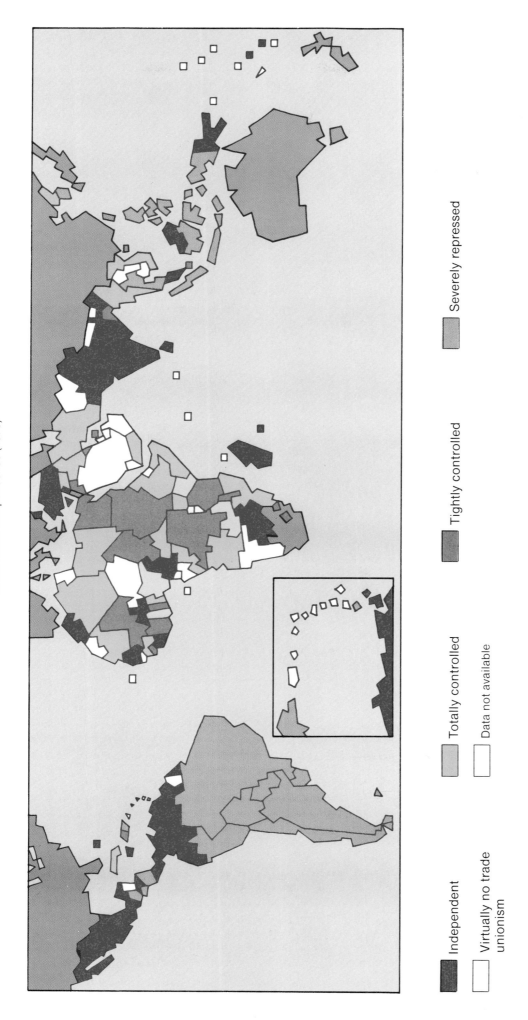

FIGURE 6-4
LABOR UNIONIZATION
Trade union independence (1978)

Severely repressed

Tightly controlled

Totally controlled

Data not available

Independent

Virtually no trade
unionism

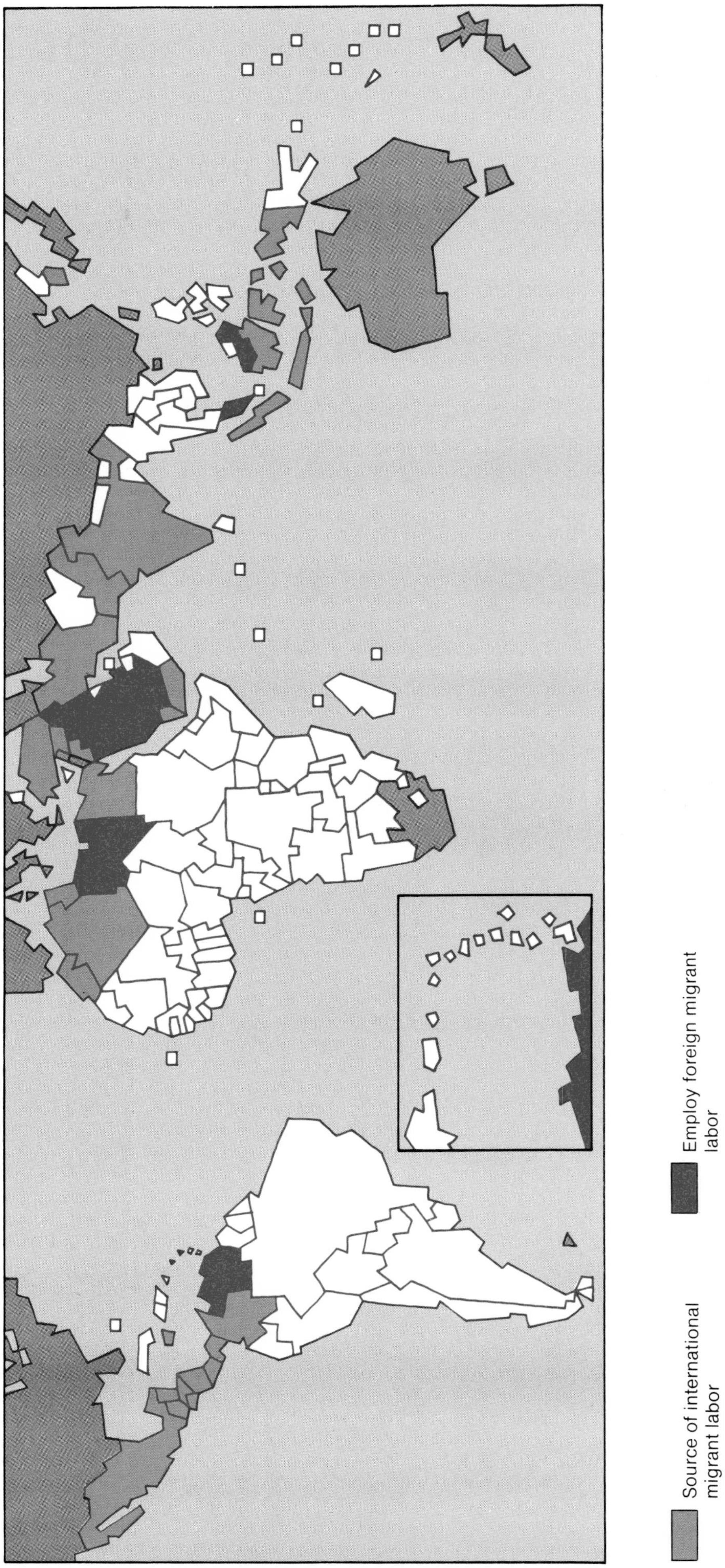

FIGURE 6-5
INTERNATIONAL LABOR MIGRATION

Source of international
migrant labor

Employ foreign migrant
labor

7: FOOD AND AGRICULTURE

FIGURE 7-1
FOOD PRODUCTION
(1950-1976)

HIGH-INCOME COUNTRIES

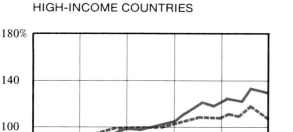

DEVELOPING COUNTRIES

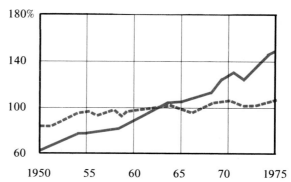

MIDDLE-INCOME COUNTRIES

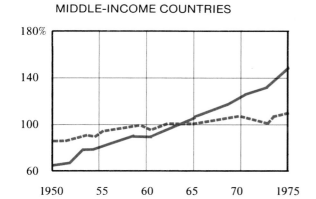

POOREST COUNTRIES

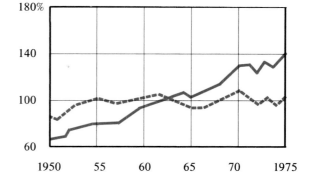

—— Total   ▪▪▪ Per capita

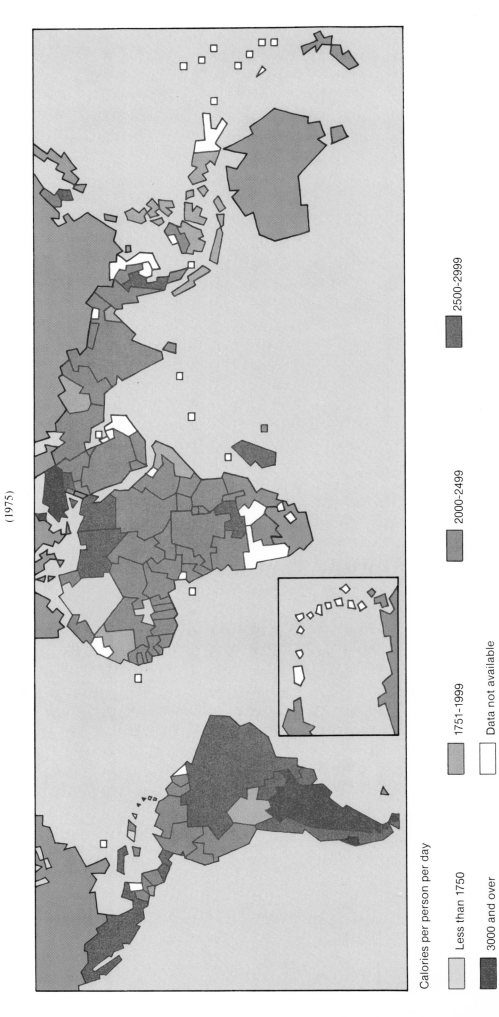

FIGURE 7-2
DIETARY ENERGY SUPPLY PER CAPITA
(1975)

Calories per person per day

Less than 1750

1751-1999

2000-2499

2500-2999

3000 and over

Data not available

FIGURE 7-3
LAND USE/VEGETATION
(1963-64)

OCEANIA

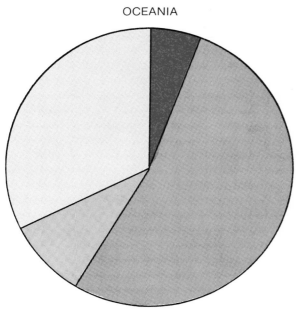

LATIN AMERICA

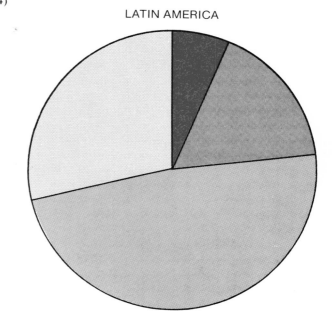

ASIA

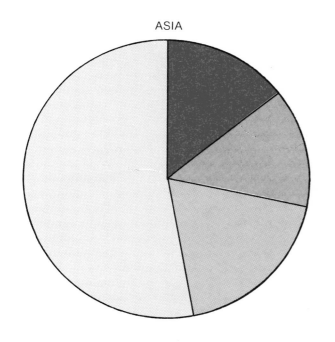

AFRICA

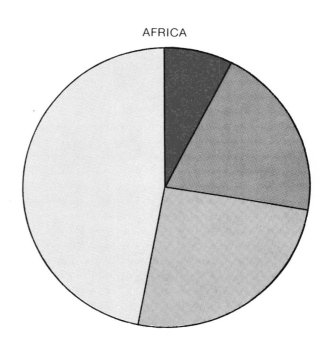

■ Available land

Meadow and pasture

Forested land

Built-on areas, wasteland, and other land

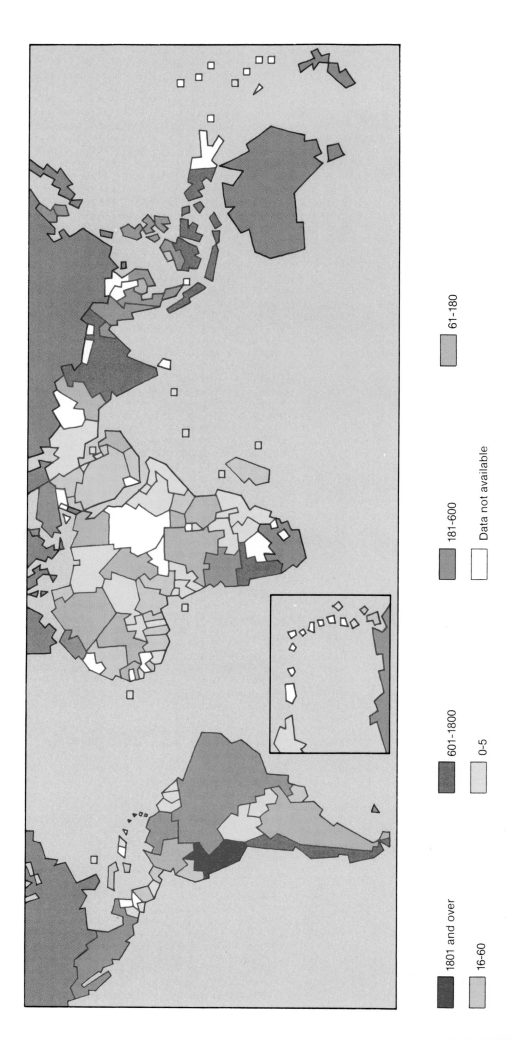

FIGURE 7-4
FISH LANDINGS
(1963-65 average)

1801 and over

601-1800

181-600

61-180

16-60

0-5

Data not available

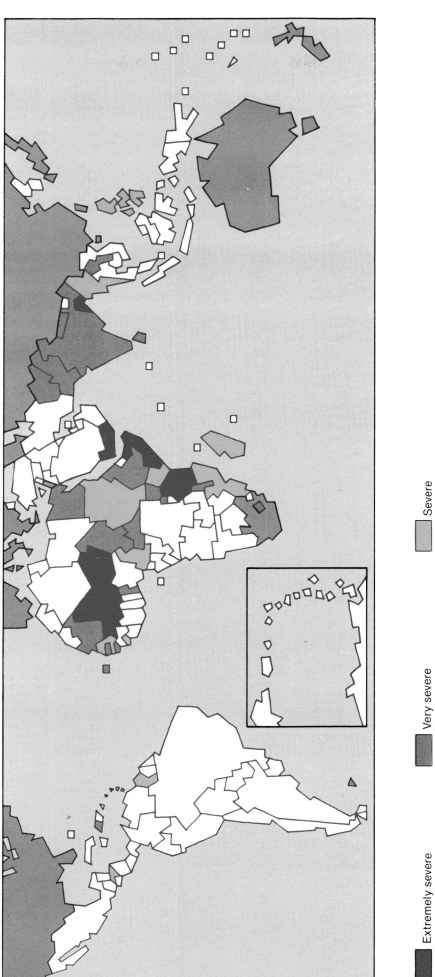

FIGURE 7-5
WORLD FOOD CRISIS

Extremely severe

Very severe

Severe

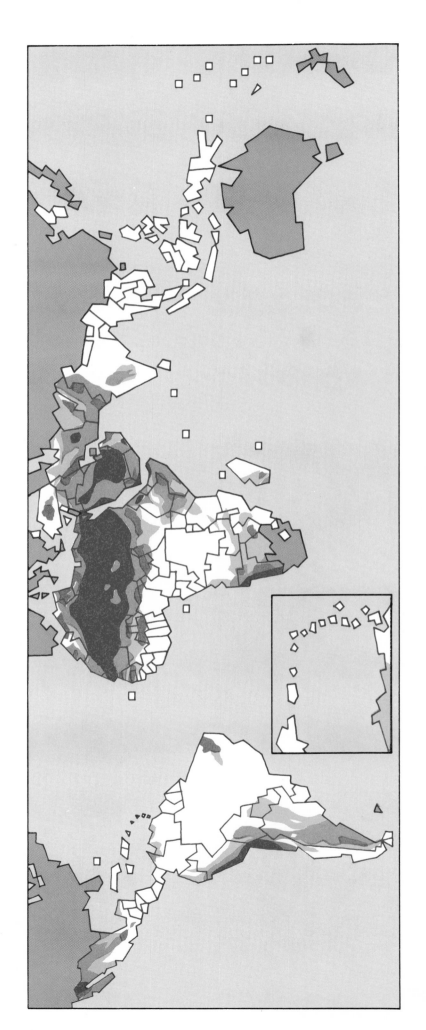

FIGURE 7-6
DESERTIFICATION

Existing deserts   Very high risk of desertification   High risk   Moderate risk

FIGURE 7-7
MEANS OF PRODUCTION—
IRRIGATED LAND
(1977)

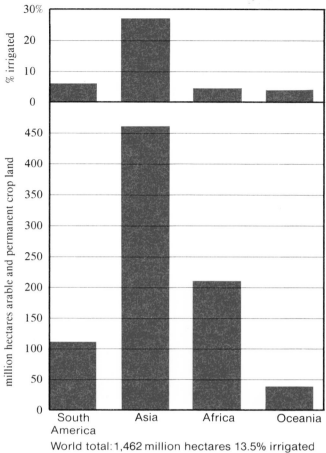

World total: 1,462 million hectares 13.5% irrigated

FIGURE 7-8
MEANS OF PRODUCTION—LABOR
(1978)

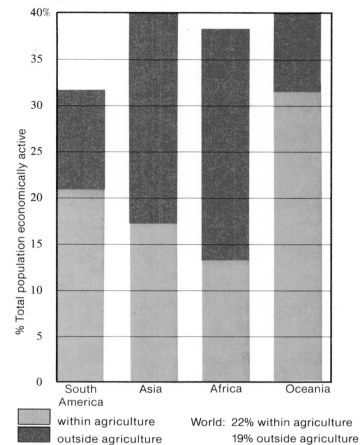

within agriculture   World: 22% within agriculture
outside agriculture   19% outside agriculture

FIGURE 7-9
WORLD FERTILIZER USAGE ON ARABLE AND
PERMANENT CROP LAND

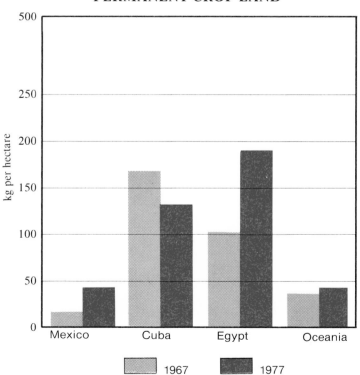

1967   1977

FIGURE 7-10
WORLD LAND USE
(1977)

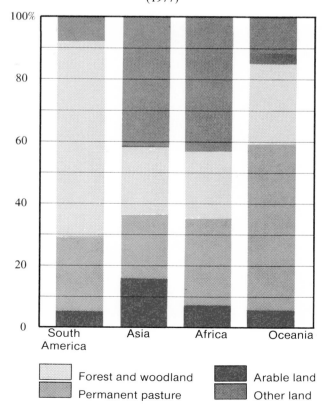

Forest and woodland   Arable land
Permanent pasture   Other land

FIGURE 7-11
AREAS OF ARABLE AND PERMANENT CROP LAND AND POPULATION
(1977)

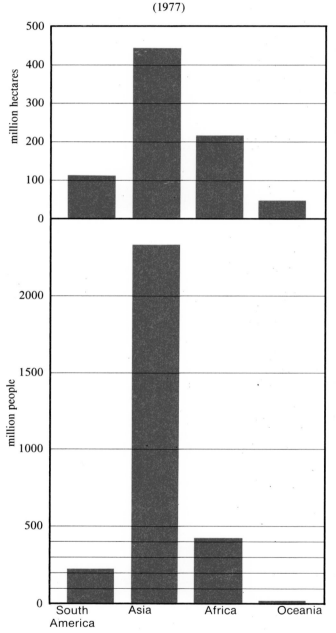

World: 4,104 million people
1,462 million hectares

FIGURE 7-12
WORLD FOOD SUPPLY—PROTEIN
(1975-77 average)

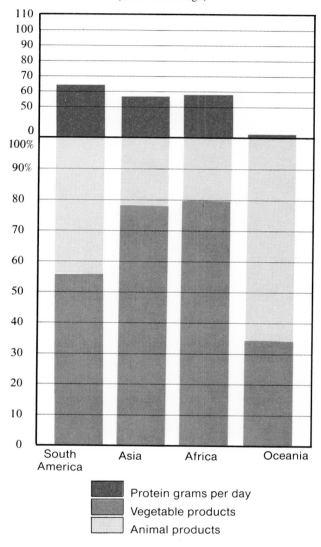

■ Protein grams per day
■ Vegetable products
□ Animal products

World average: 69.3 Protein grams per day
65% Vegetable products
35% Animal products

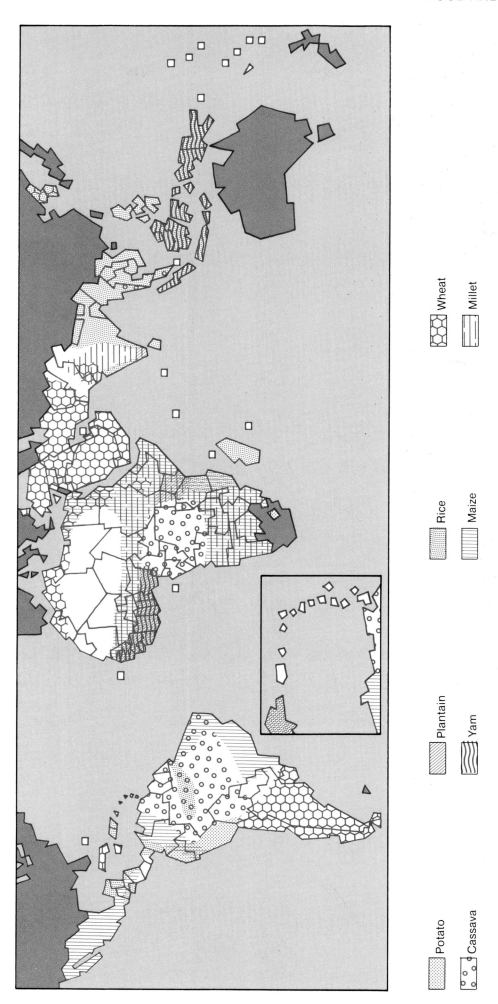

FIGURE 7-13
DOMINANT STAPLE CROPS OF THE WORLD

Potato

Cassava

Plantain

Yam

Rice

Maize

Wheat

Millet

FIGURE 7-14
WORLD FOOD SUPPLY—CALORIES
(1975-77 average)

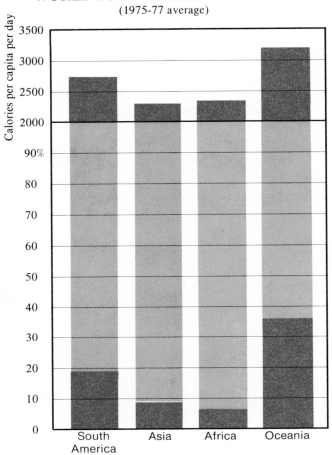

Vegetable products

Animal products

World average: 2590 Calories per capita per day
83% Vegetable products
17% Animal products

FIGURE 7-15
WORLD MEAT PRODUCTION
(1978)

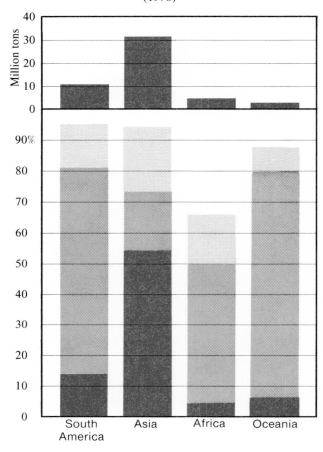

Pork

Beef

Poultry

World total: 133.4 million tons
37% Pork
35% Beef
19% Poultry

FIGURE 7-17
MEANS OF PRODUCTION—
AGRICULTURAL MACHINERY
(1977)

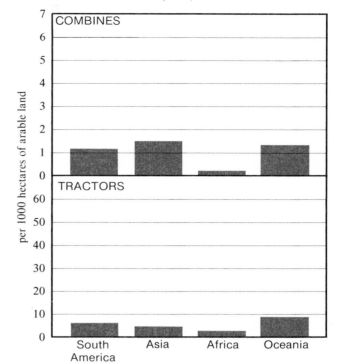

World average: 14 Tractors
2.3 Combines

FIGURE 7-16
WORLD CATTLE POPULATION, COW'S
MILK AND BEEF AND VEAL PRODUCTION
(1978)

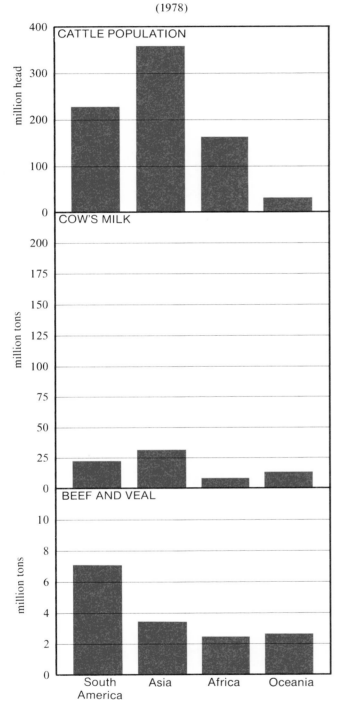

World total: 1213 million head
415 million tons milk
46.8 million tons beef and veal

FIGURE 7-18
WORLD FOOD SUPPLY—FAT
(1975-77 average)

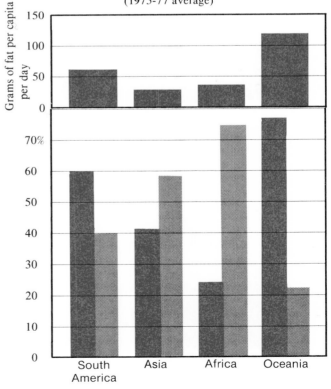

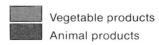
Vegetable products
Animal products

World average:
62.7 Grams
54% Animal
46% Vegetable

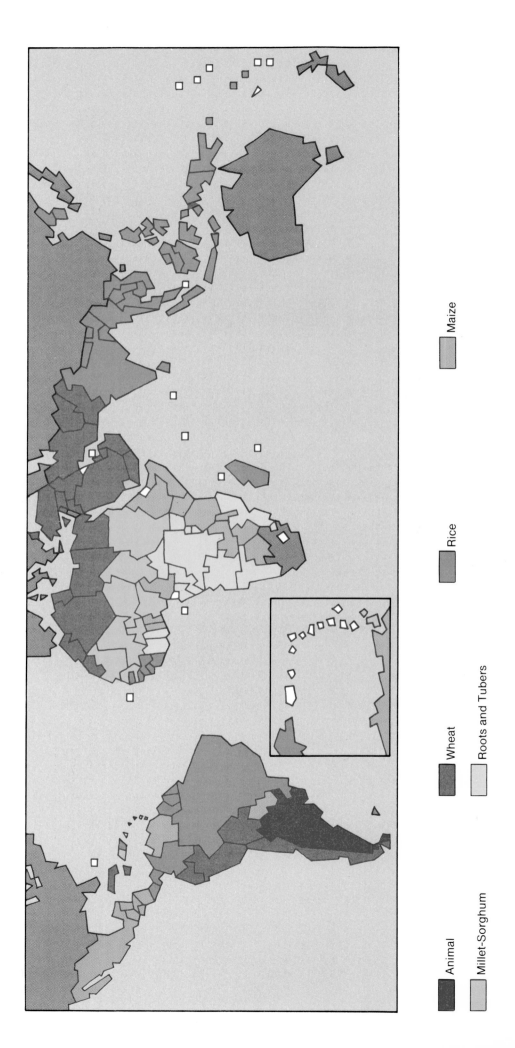

FIGURE 7-19
**WORLD FOOD RESOURCES AND
DIET PATTERNS**

Animal

Millet-Sorghum

Wheat

Roots and Tubers

Rice

Maize

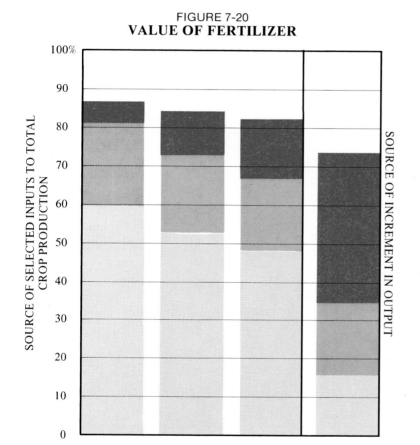

FIGURE 7-20
VALUE OF FERTILIZER

SOURCE OF SELECTED INPUTS TO TOTAL CROP PRODUCTION

SOURCE OF INCREMENT IN OUTPUT

1961-65   1969-71   1974-76   1961-65 to 74-76

■ Fertilizer
▨ Irrigation
☐ New cropped land

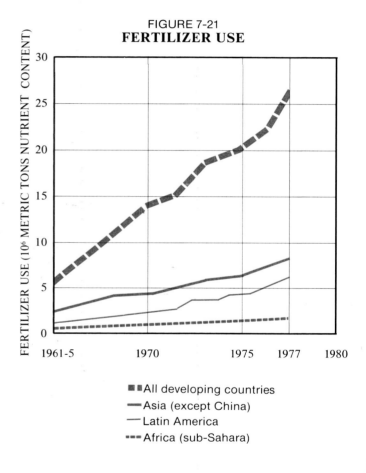

FIGURE 7-21
FERTILIZER USE

FERTILIZER USE (10^6 METRIC TONS NUTRIENT CONTENT)

1961-5   1970   1975   1977   1980

■■All developing countries
—Asia (except China)
—Latin America
===Africa (sub-Sahara)

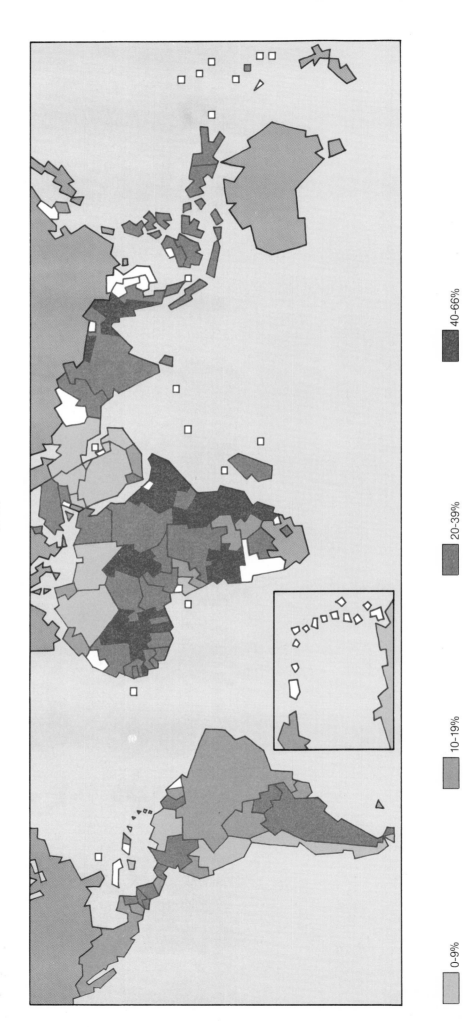

FIGURE 7-22
SHARE OF AGRICULTURE IN GDP
(1980)

0-9%

10-19%

20-39%

40-66%

Data not available

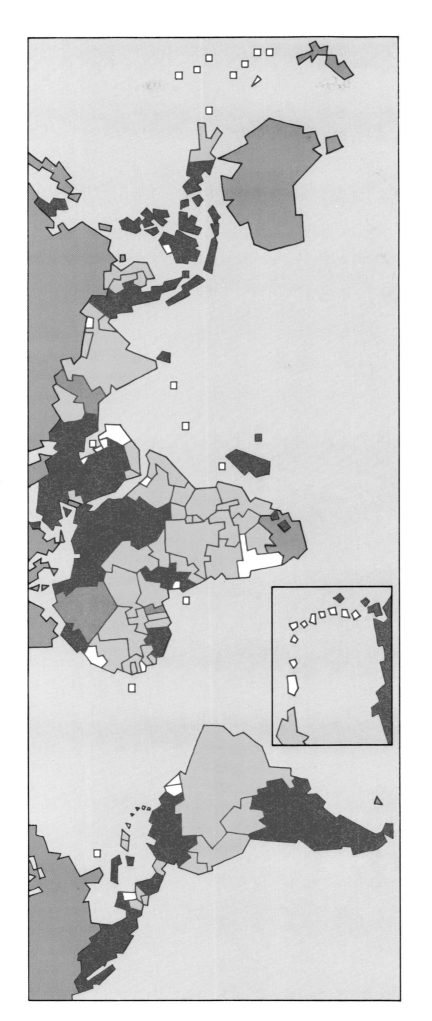

FIGURE 7-23
FOOD CONSUMPTION IN CALORIES
(National average)

Over 100% of requirement

100% of requirement

Under requirement

Data not available

8: ENVIRONMENT

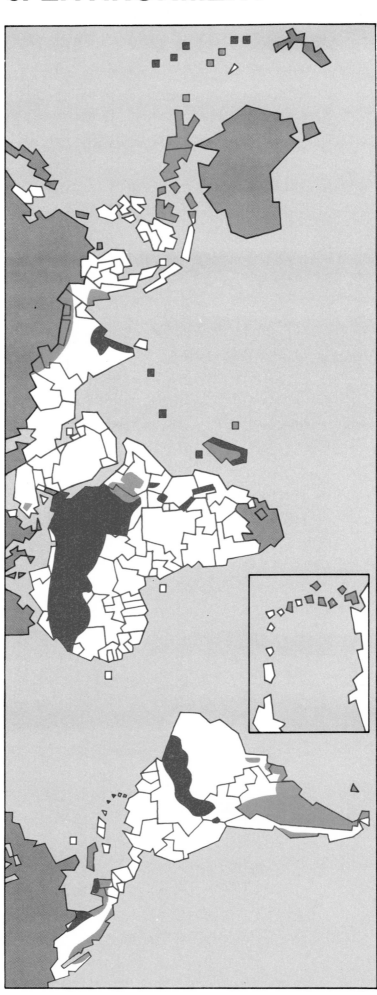

FIGURE 8-1
BIOGEOGRAPHICAL PROVINCES

No national parks or reserves

National parks or reserves less than 1000 km^2

9: EDUCATION

FIGURE 9-1
ADULT LITERACY IN MIDDLE AND LOW INCOME COUNTRIES

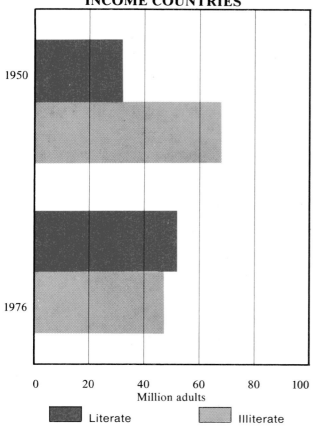

FIGURE 9-2
UNIT COSTS BY LEVEL OF EDUCATION
(1975)

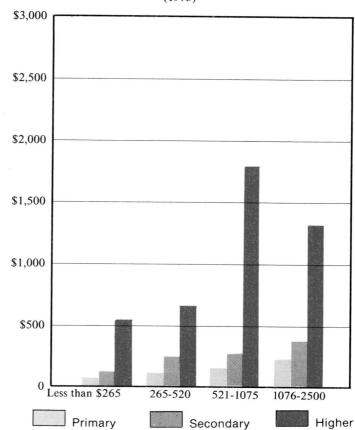

FIGURE 9-3
UNIT COSTS AS PERCENT OF GNP PER CAPITA
(1970-73)

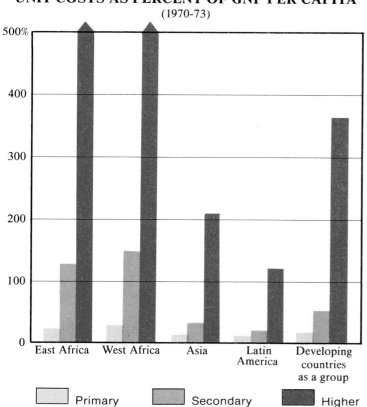

FIGURE 9-4
PUBLIC EXPENDITURES IN EDUCATION PER STUDENT
(1975)

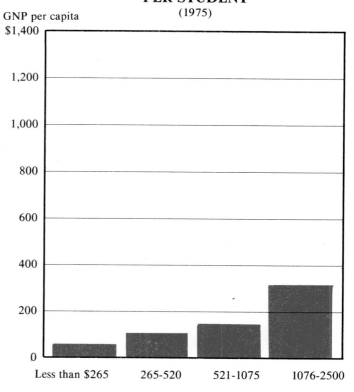

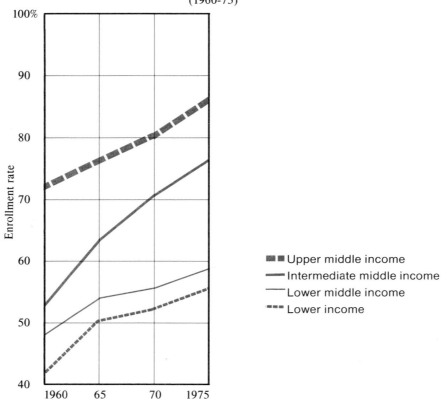

FIGURE 9-5
ENROLLMENT RATES OF CHILDREN AGED 6-11 YEARS
(1960-75)

- ▪▪ Upper middle income
- ── Intermediate middle income
- ── Lower middle income
- ▪▪▪ Lower income

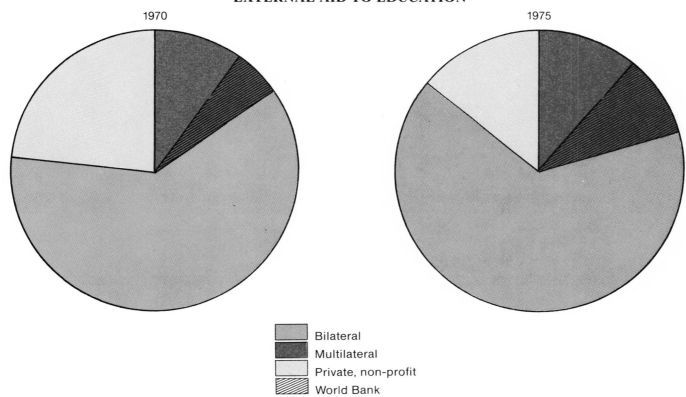

FIGURE 9-6
EXTERNAL AID TO EDUCATION

1970   1975

- Bilateral
- Multilateral
- Private, non-profit
- World Bank

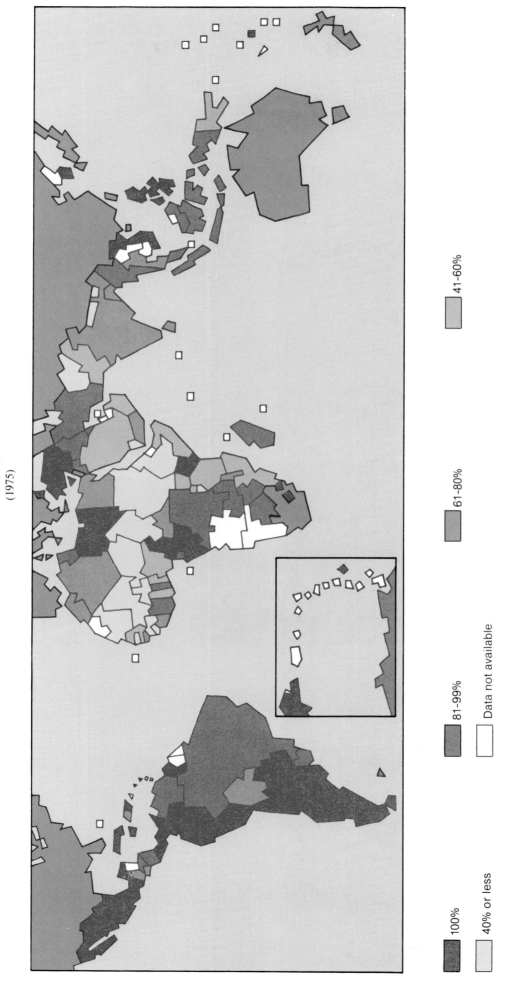

FIGURE 9-7
**PRIMARY EDUCATION ENROLLMENT
RATIOS**
(1975)

41-60%

61-80%

81-99%

Data not available

100%

40% or less

FIGURE 9-8
**SECONDARY EDUCATION
ENROLLMENT RATIOS**
(1975)

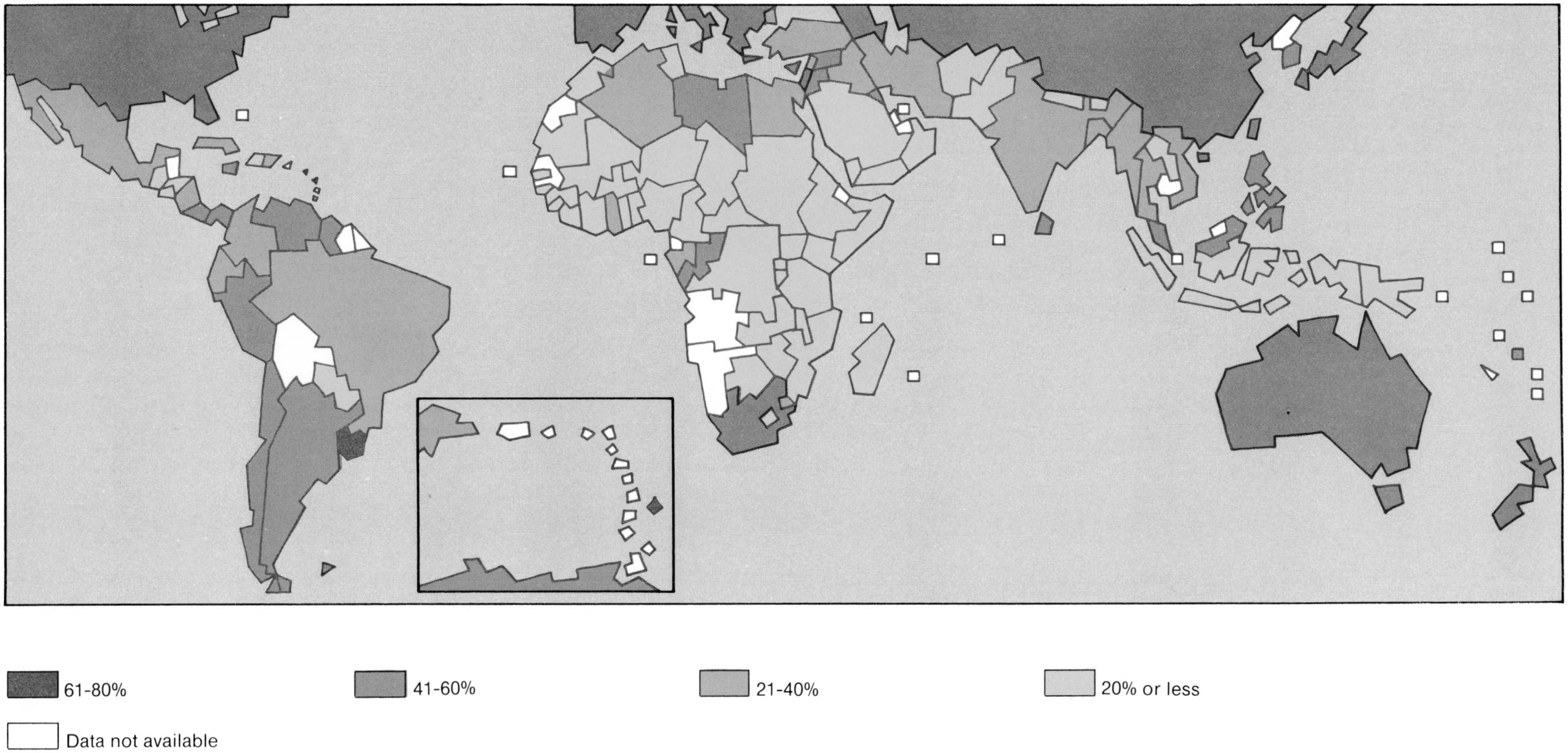

61–80%

Data not available

41–60%

21–40%

20% or less

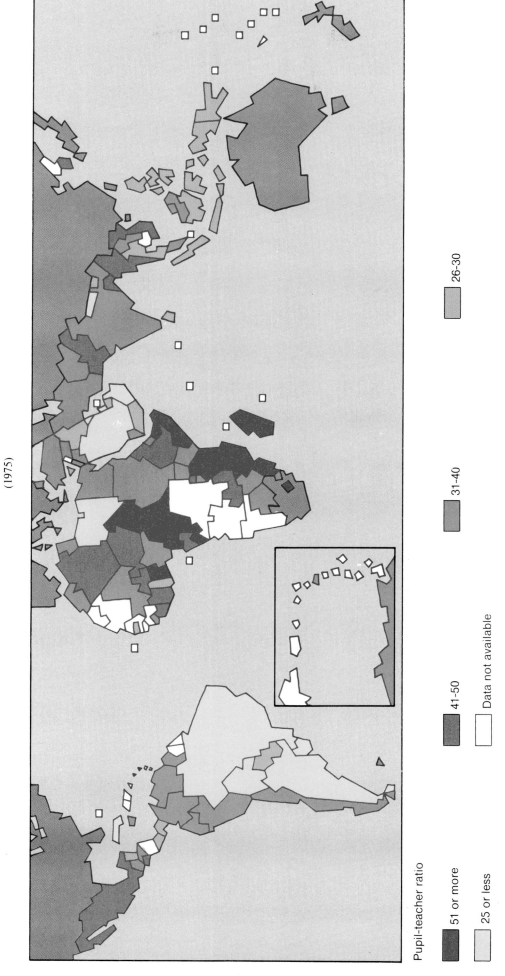

FIGURE 9-9
PUPIL-TEACHER RATIO IN PRIMARY EDUCATION
(1975)

Pupil-teacher ratio

51 or more

41-50

31-40

26-30

25 or less

Data not available

10: HEALTH

FIGURE 10-1
LIFE EXPECTANCY AT BIRTH

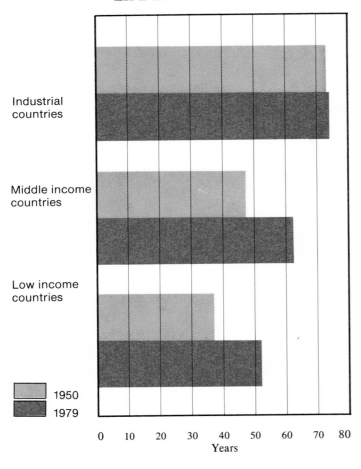

Industrial
countries

Middle income
countries

Low income
countries

■ 1950
■ 1979

0 10 20 30 40 50 60 70 80
Years

FIGURE 10-2
DRINKING WATER SUPPLY AND EXCRETA DISPOSAL SYSTEMS
(1975)

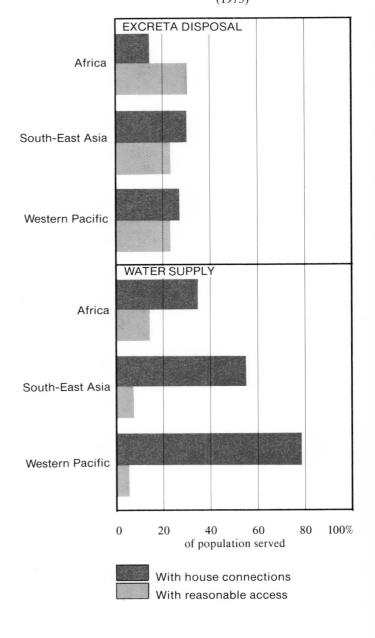

EXCRETA DISPOSAL

Africa

South-East Asia

Western Pacific

WATER SUPPLY

Africa

South-East Asia

Western Pacific

0 20 40 60 80 100%
of population served

■ With house connections
■ With reasonable access

FIGURE 10-3
ACCESS TO COMMUNITY WATER SUPPLY AND EXCRETA DISPOSAL SERVICES

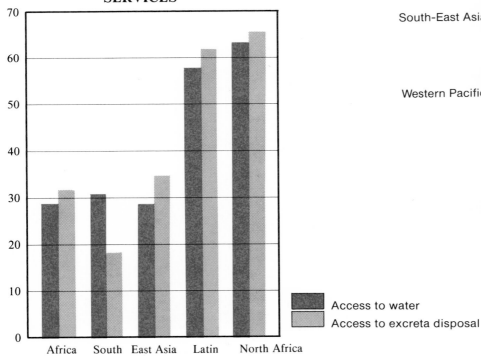

70

60

50

40

30

20

10

0

Africa
(South of
Sahara)

South
Asia

East Asia
& Pacific

Latin
America

North Africa
& Middle East

■ Access to water
■ Access to excreta disposal

FIGURE 10-4
DENSITY OF HEALTH OCCUPATIONS
(1975)

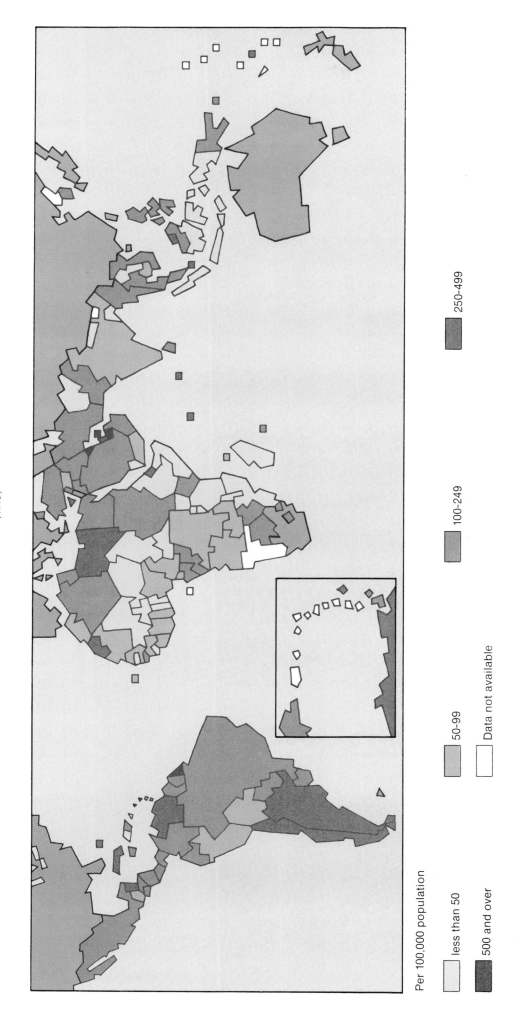

Per 100,000 population

less than 50

50-99

100-249

250-499

500 and over

Data not available

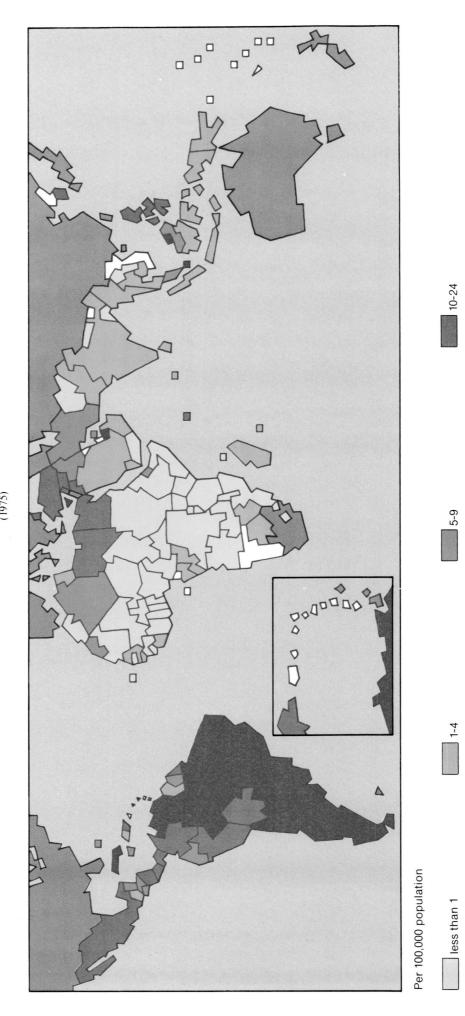

FIGURE 10-5
DENSITY OF DENTAL HEALTH
OCCUPATIONS
(1975)

Per 100,000 population

less than 1   1-4   5-9   10-24

25 and over   Data not available

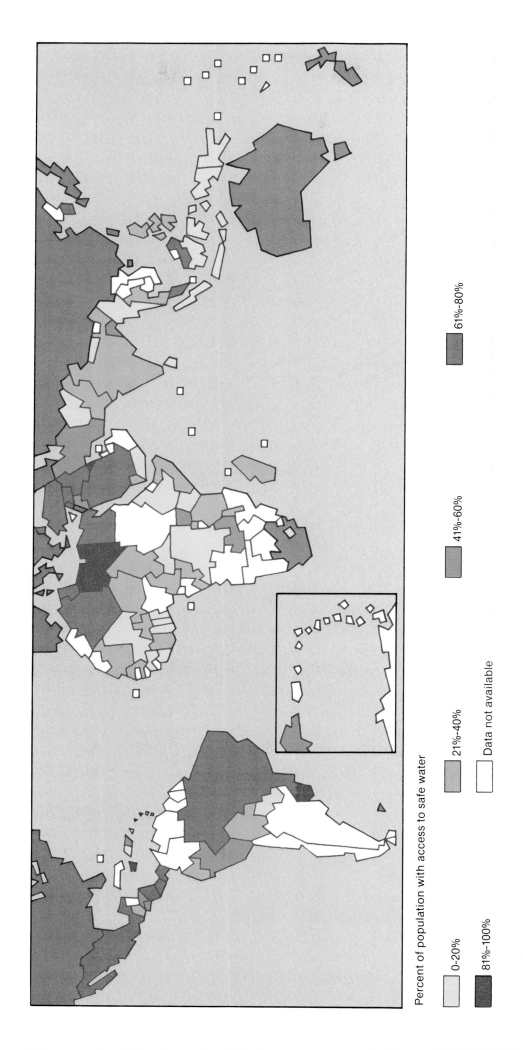

FIGURE 10-6
ACCESS TO POTABLE WATER

Percent of population with access to safe water

0-20%

81%-100%

21%-40%

Data not available

41%-60%

61%-80%

FIGURE 10-7
EFFECT OF MIGRATION ON
PHYSICIAN DENSITY

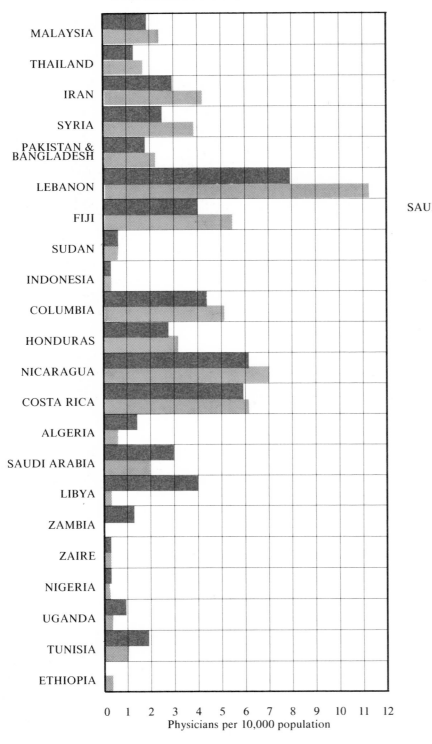

Physicians per 10,000 population

Actual coverage
Coverage without migration

FIGURE 10-8
EFFECT OF MIGRATION ON
PHYSICIAN DENSITY
(Recipient countries)

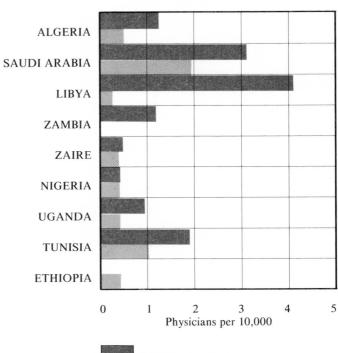

Physicians per 10,000

Actual coverage
Coverage without migration

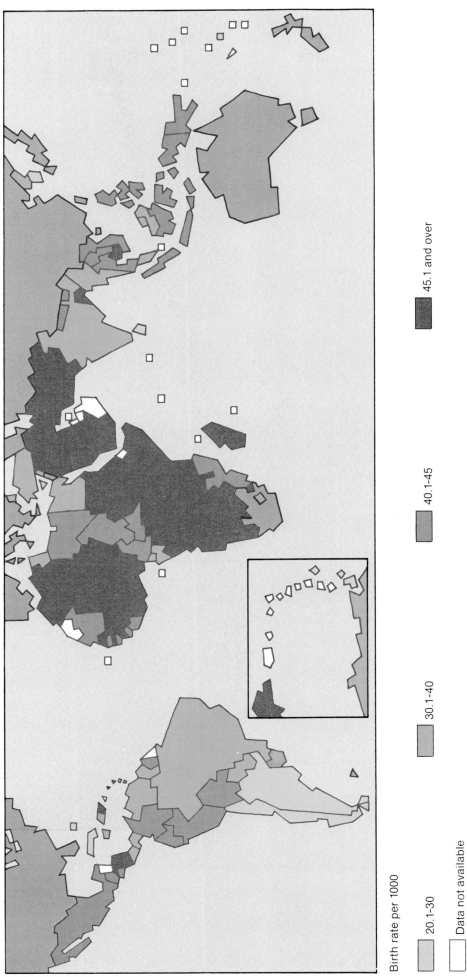

FIGURE 10-9
BIRTH RATES
(1975)

Birth rate per 1000

20.1-30

30.1-40

40.1-45

45.1 and over

Data not available

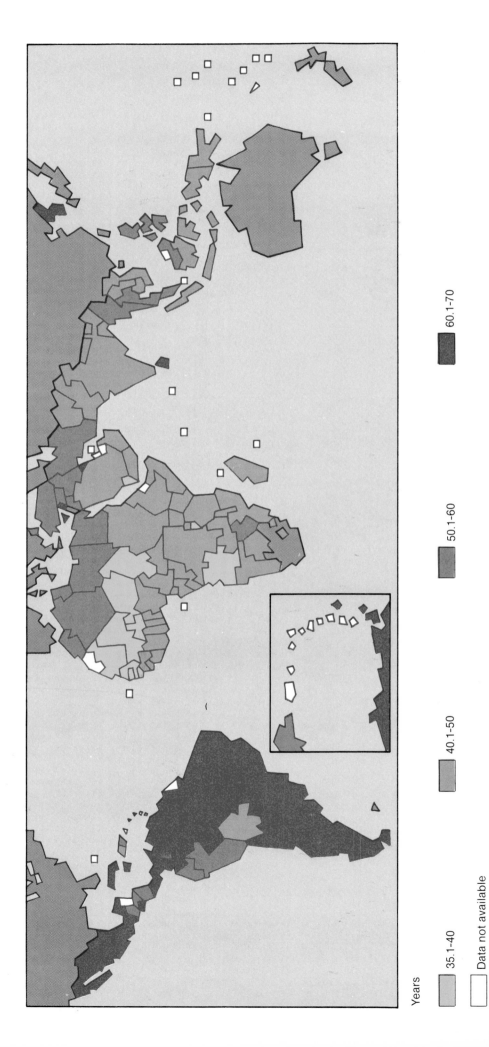

FIGURE 10-10
LIFE EXPECTANCY AT BIRTH
(1975)

Years

35.1-40

Data not available

40.1-50

50.1-60

60.1-70

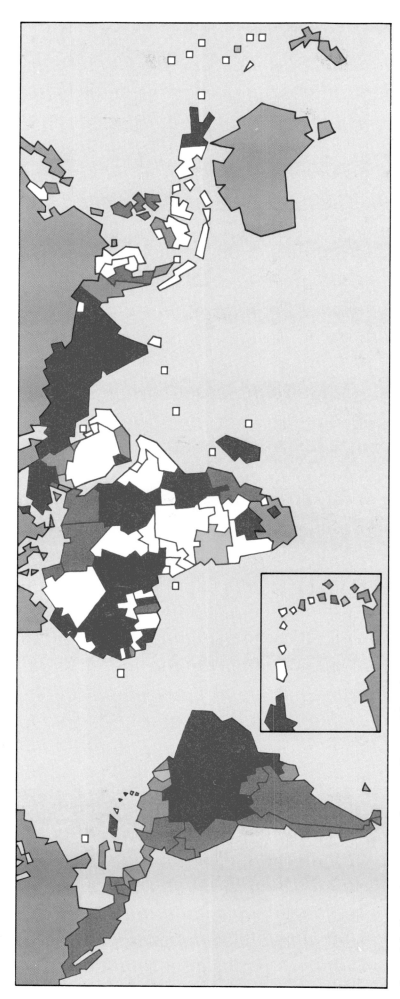

FIGURE 10-11
INFANT MORTALITY
(1970-75)

Annual deaths under one year of age per thousand live births

0-25

26-50

51-100

101 and over

Data not available

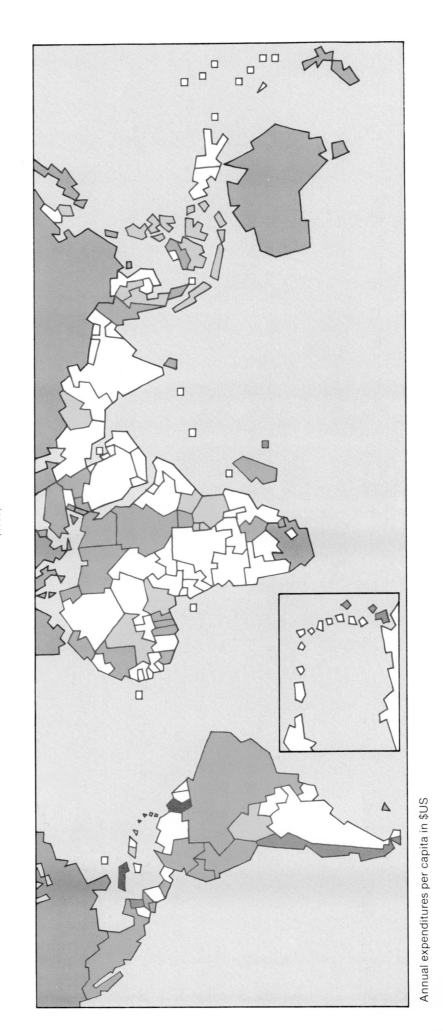

FIGURE 10-12
PUBLIC HEALTH EXPENDITURES
(1966)

Annual expenditures per capita in $US

10-20   5-10   1-5   0-1   Data not available

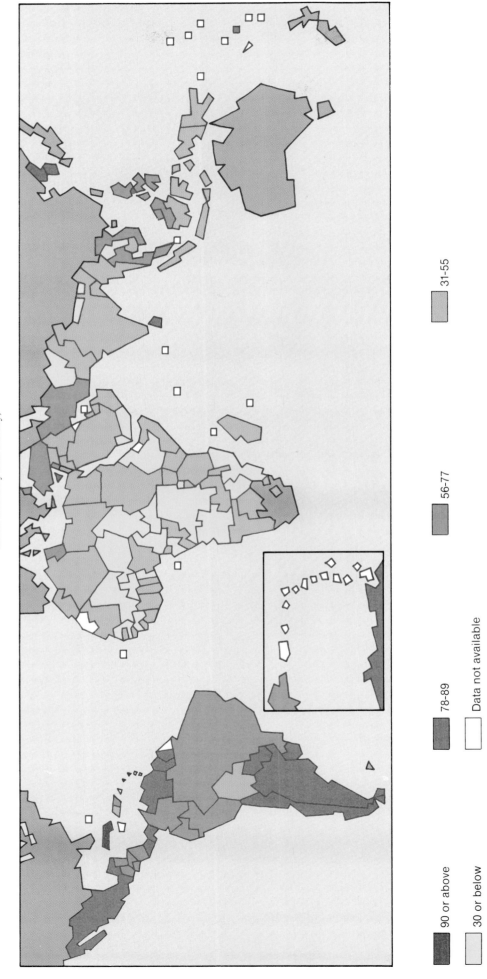

FIGURE 10-13
PHYSICAL QUALITY OF LIFE INDEX
(Average of life expectancy at age one,
infant mortality and literacy)

90 or above

78-89

56-77

31-55

30 or below

Data not available

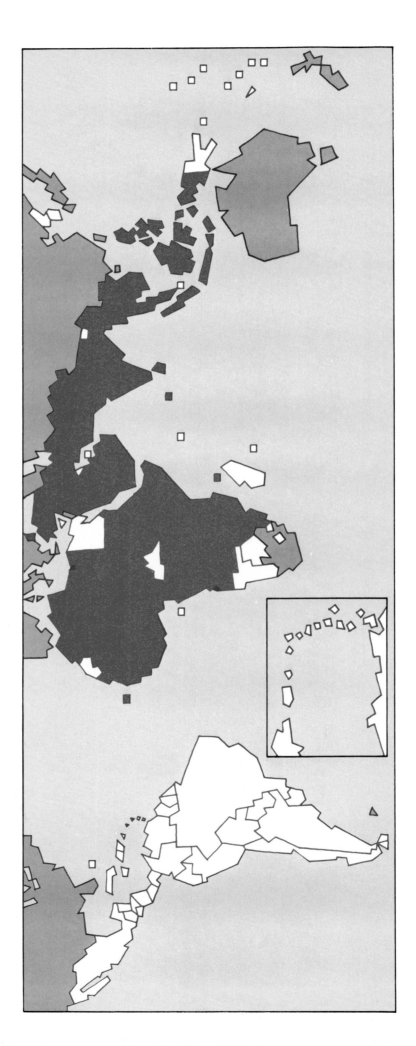

FIGURE 10-14
COUNTRIES REPORTING CHOLERA
(1961-80)

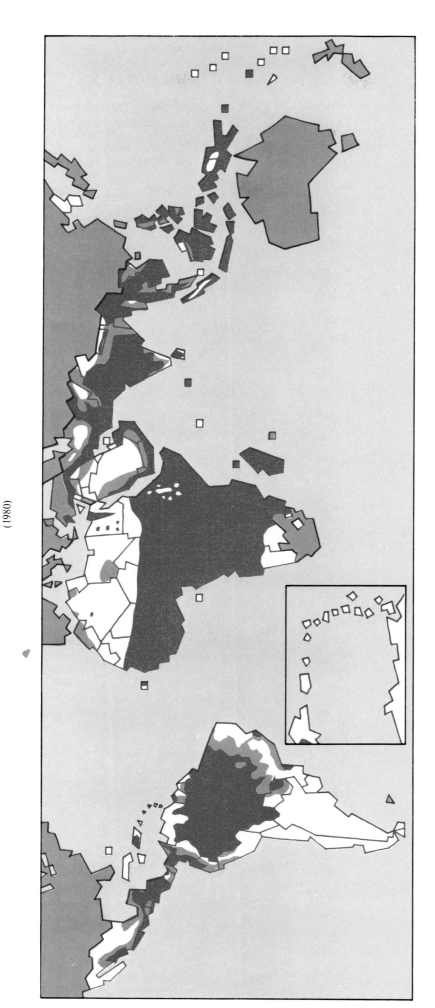

FIGURE 10-15
MALARIA
(1980)

Areas where malaria
transmission occurs

Areas with limited risk

11: ENERGY

FIGURE 11-1
**ENERGY PRODUCTION AND
CONSUMPTION GROWTH**
(1980-90)

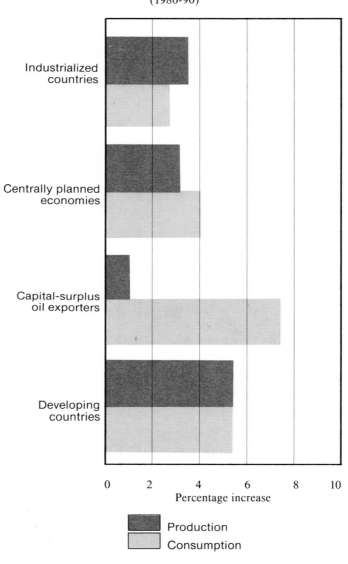

Percentage increase

Production
Consumption

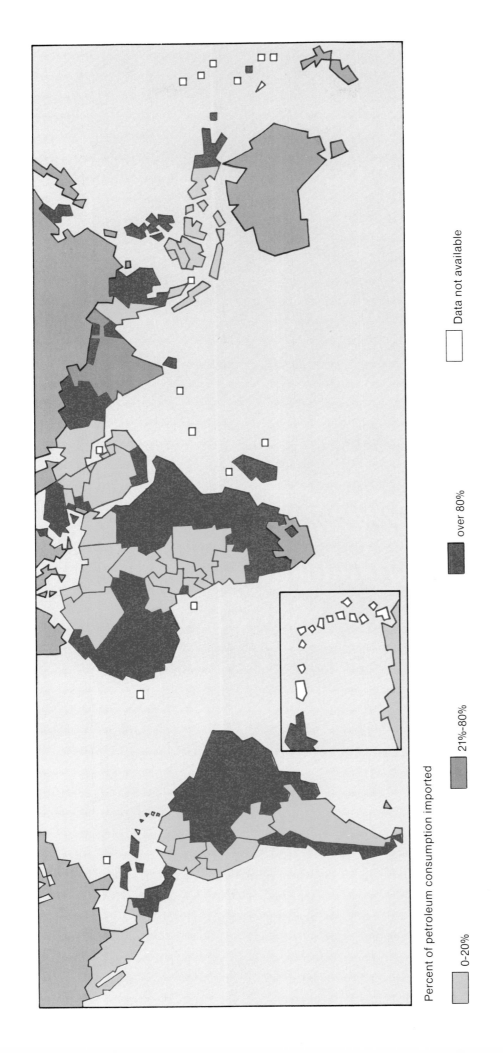

FIGURE 11-2
WORLD DEPENDENCE ON PETROLEUM

Percent of petroleum consumption imported

0-20%

21%-80%

over 80%

Data not available

FIGURE 11-3
ENERGY PRODUCTION
(1963-65 average)

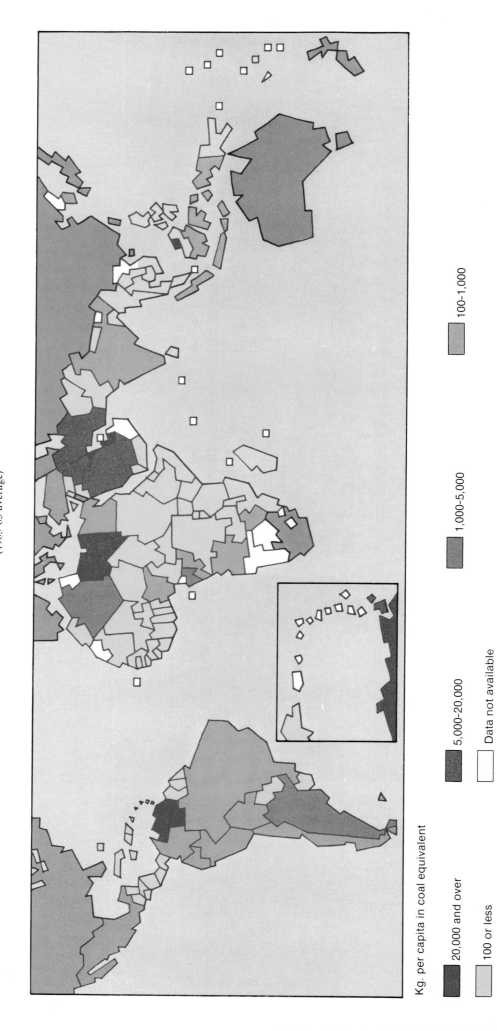

Kg. per capita in coal equivalent

20,000 and over

5,000-20,000

1,000-5,000

100-1,000

100 or less

Data not available

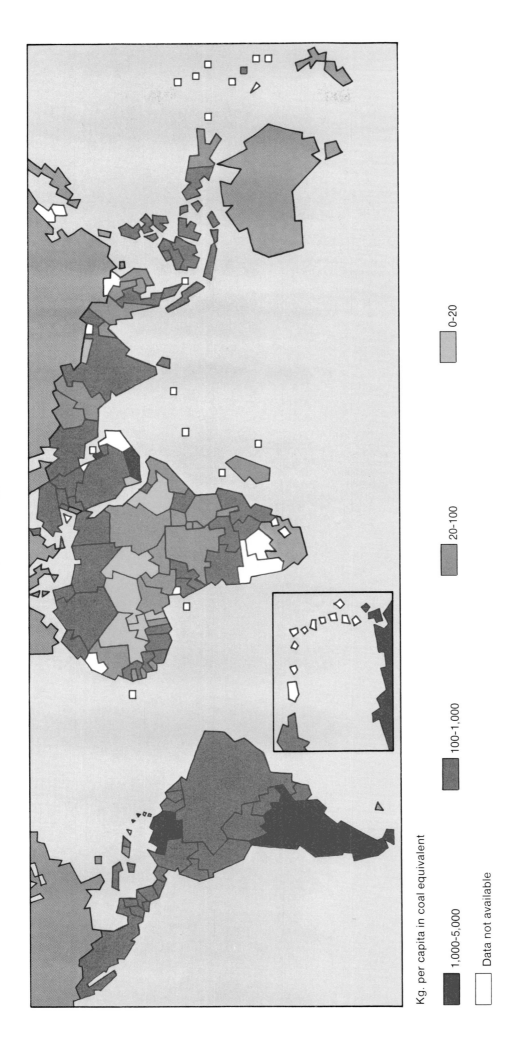

FIGURE 11-4
ENERGY CONSUMPTION
(1963-65 average)

Kg. per capita in coal equivalent

1,000-5,000

100-1,000

20-100

0-20

Data not available

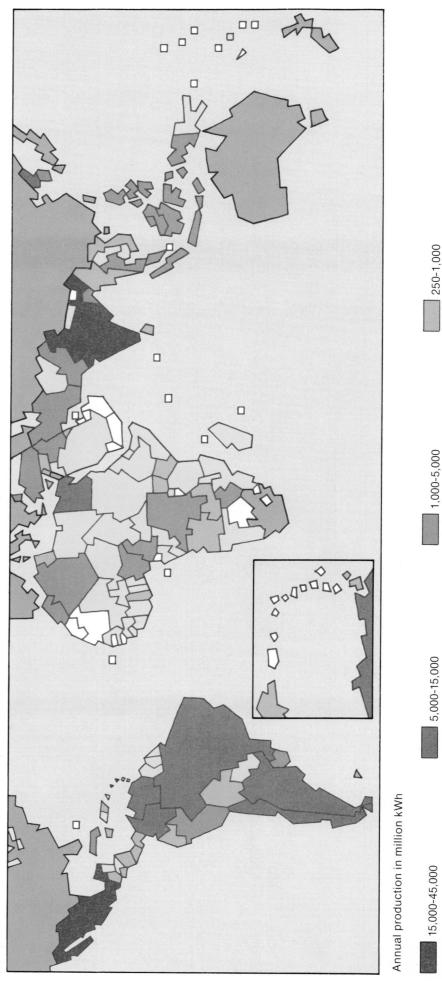

FIGURE 11-5
ELECTRICITY PRODUCTION
(1963-65 average)

Annual production in million kWh

15,000-45,000

250 or less

5,000-15,000

Data not available

1,000-5,000

250-1,000

12: TRADE

FIGURE 12-1
CHANGING DISTRIBUTION
OF WORLD TRADE

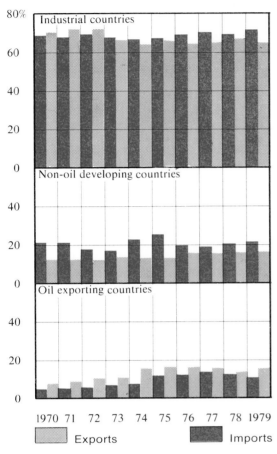

Exports   Imports

FIGURE 12-2
TRADE BALANCES

$ Billion

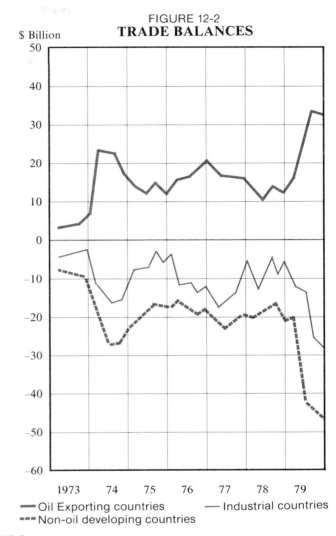

— Oil Exporting countries   — Industrial countries
■■■ Non-oil developing countries

FIGURE 12-3
COMMODITY COMPOSITION OF
WORLD TRADE
(Share of U.S. dollar totals)

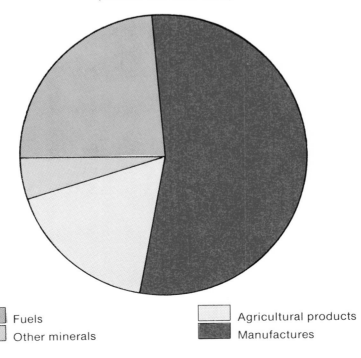

Fuels   Agricultural products
Other minerals   Manufactures

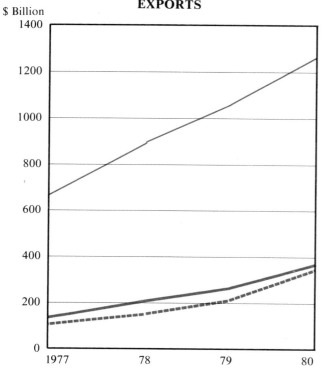

FIGURE 12-4
**INTERNATIONAL TRADE:
EXPORTS**

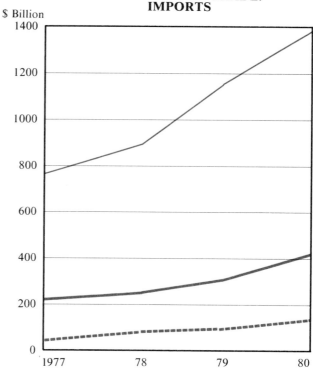

FIGURE 12-5
**INTERNATIONAL TRADE:
IMPORTS**

━━Non-oil developing countries
──Industrial countries
▬▬▬Oil exporting countries

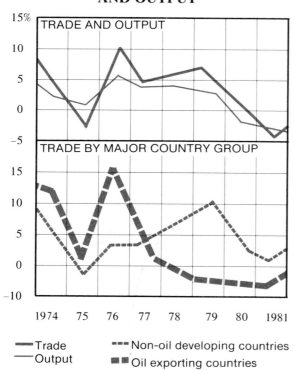

FIGURE 12-6
**GROWTH OF WORLD TRADE
AND OUTPUT**

TRADE AND OUTPUT

TRADE BY MAJOR COUNTRY GROUP

━━Trade   ▬▬▬Non-oil developing countries
──Output   ▬▬▬Oil exporting countries

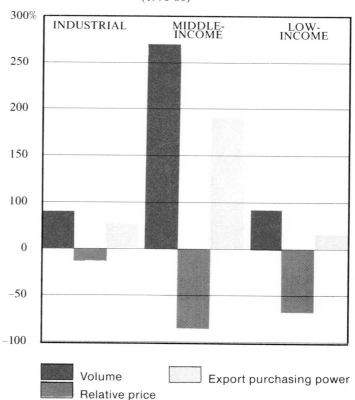

FIGURE 12-7
**INDUSTRIAL AND OIL-IMPORTING
DEVELOPING COUNTRIES'
MANUFACTURED EXPORTS**
(1970-80)

INDUSTRIAL   MIDDLE-   LOW-
                    INCOME   INCOME

▪ Volume   ▫ Export purchasing power
▪ Relative price

FIGURE 12-8
OIL-IMPORTING DEVELOPING COUNTRIES' PURCHASING POWER OF EXPORTS
(1965-80)

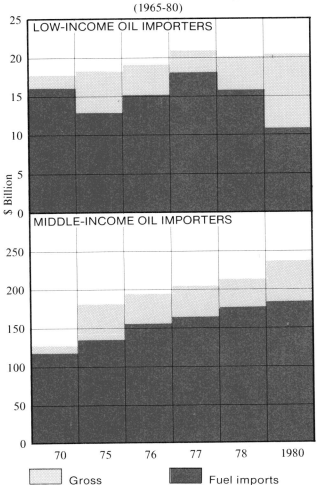

$ Billion

LOW-INCOME OIL IMPORTERS

MIDDLE-INCOME OIL IMPORTERS

70   75   76   77   78   1980

Gross   Fuel imports

FIGURE 12-9
DEVELOPING COUNTRIES' INCREASES IN EXPORT PURCHASING POWER
(1970-80)

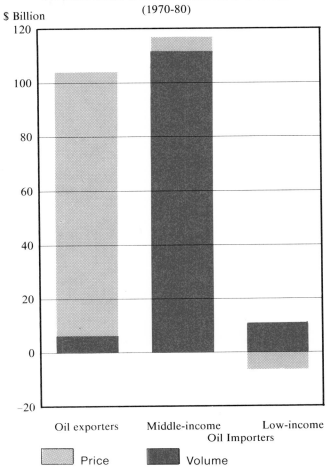

$ Billion

Oil exporters   Middle-income   Low-income
                        Oil Importers

Price   Volume

FIGURE 12-10
DEVELOPING COUNTRIES' EXPORTS TO INDUSTRIAL COUNTRIES
(1970=100)

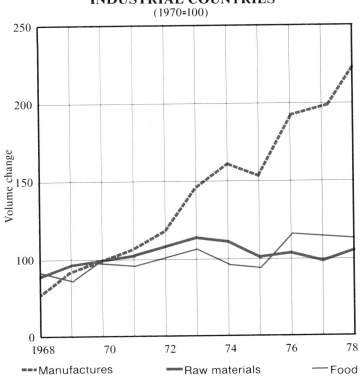

Volume change

1968   70   72   74   76   78

---Manufactures   —Raw materials   —Food

FIGURE 12-11
ANNUAL GROWTH IN U.S. EXPORTS TO DEVELOPING COUNTRIES

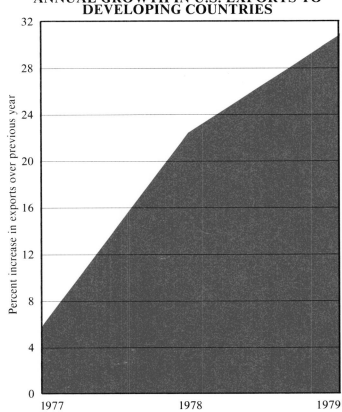

Percent increase in exports over previous year

1977   1978   1979

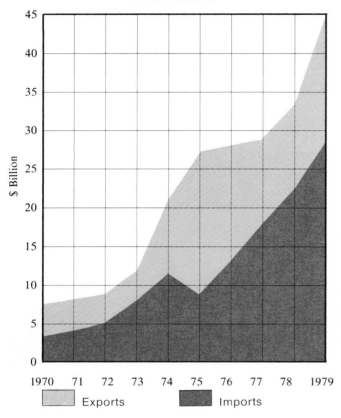

FIGURE 12-12
U.S. TRADE IN MANUFACTURED PRODUCTS WITH DEVELOPING COUNTRIES

Exports   Imports

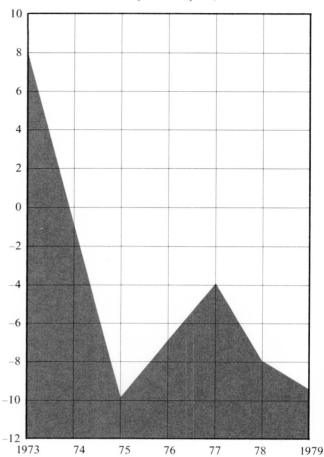

FIGURE 12-13
TERMS OF TRADE FOR NON-OIL DEVELOPING COUNTRIES
(The difference between the price of imports and the price of exports)

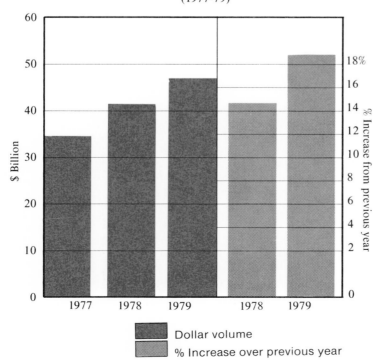

FIGURE 12-14
INCREASE IN U.S. DIRECT INVESTMENT POSITION IN DEVELOPING COUNTRIES
(1977-79)

Dollar volume

% Increase over previous year

FIGURE 12-15
U.S. EXPORTS TO DEVELOPING COUNTRIES
(1979)

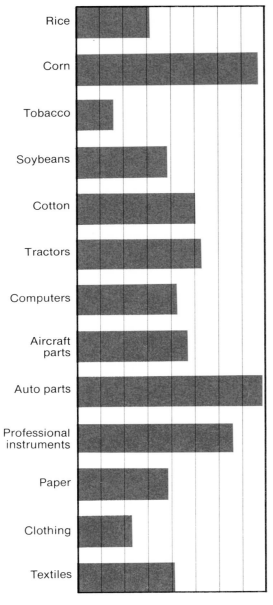

0   200 400 600 800 1000 1200 1400 1600
Millions of dollars

FIGURE 12-16
SHARES OF WORLD EXPORTS

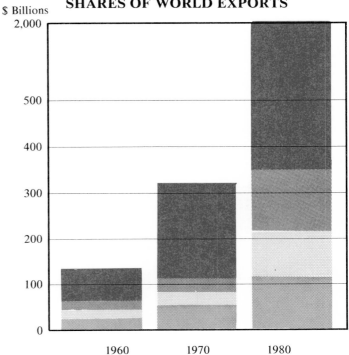

Developed Market Economies
Non-OPEC developing Market Economies
OPEC
Centrally Planned Economies

FIGURE 12-17
COMPOSITION OF WORLD EXPORTS

FIGURE 12-18
COMPOSITION OF WORLD IMPORTS

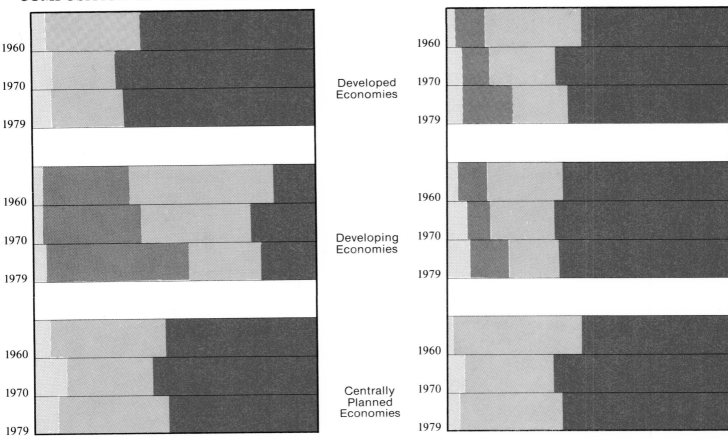

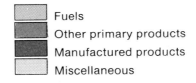

Fuels
Other primary products
Manufactured products
Miscellaneous

13: MEDIA & COMMUNICATIONS

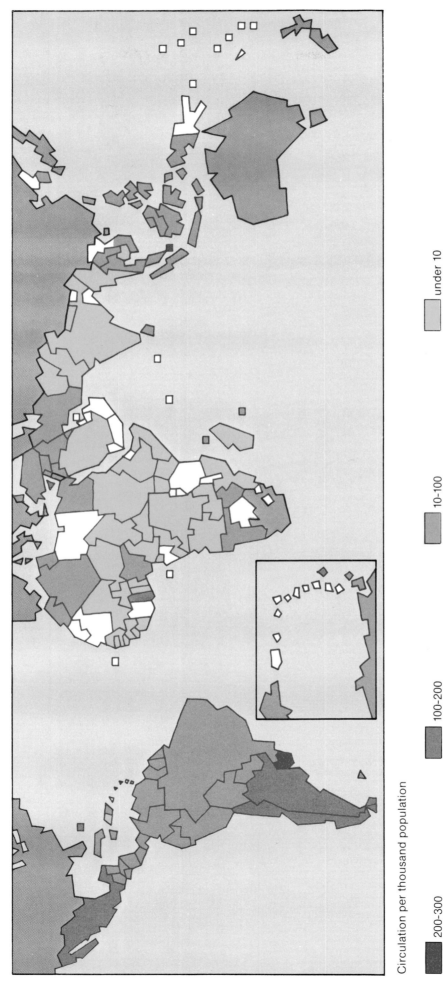

FIGURE 13-1
NEWSPAPER CIRCULATION
(1962–64 average)

Circulation per thousand population

200–300

100–200

10–100

under 10

Data not available

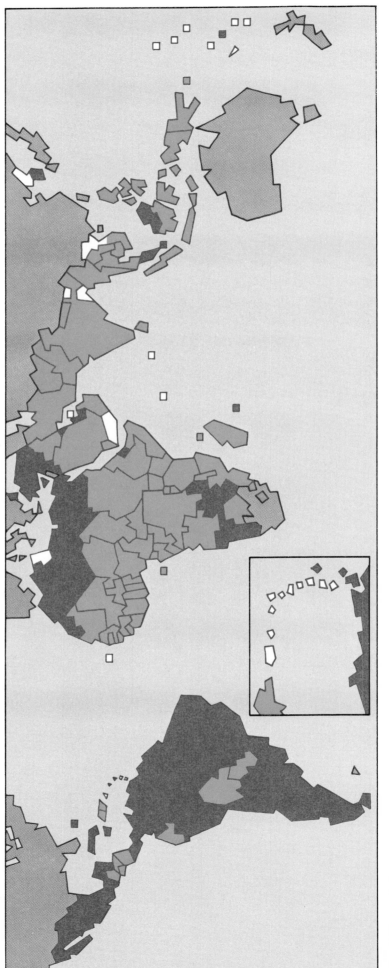

FIGURE 13-2
TELEPHONES IN USE
(1966)

Per 1000 population

10 and over

under 10

Data not available

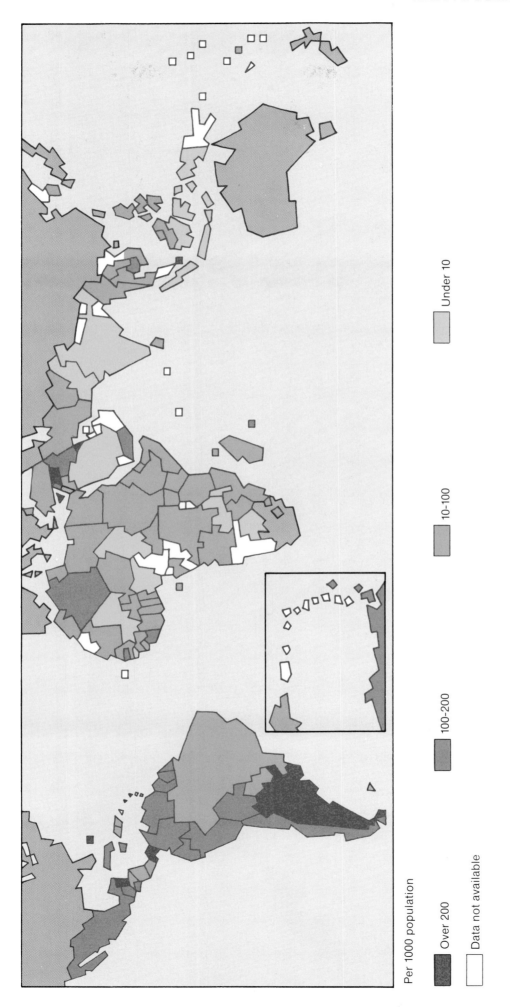

FIGURE 13-3
RADIOS IN USE
(1963-65 average)

Per 1000 population

Over 200

Data not available

100-200

10-100

Under 10

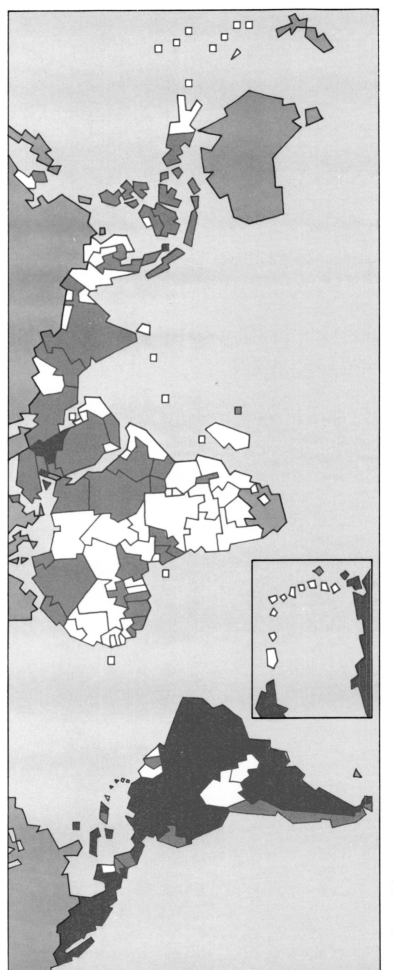

FIGURE 13-4
TELEVISIONS IN USE
(1963-65 average)

Per 1000 population

10 and over

Under 10

Data not available

14: LAW ENFORCEMENT

FIGURE 14-1
LAW ENFORCEMENT
(Early 1970s)

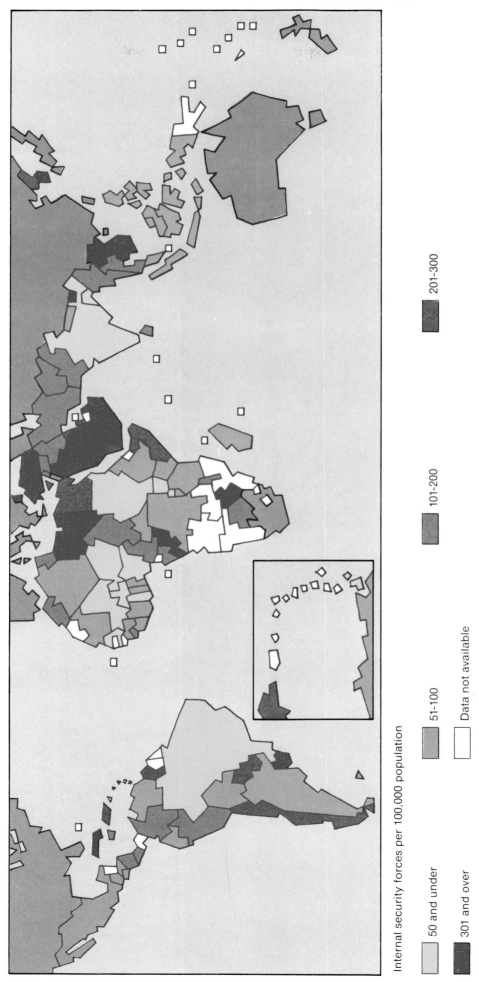

Internal security forces per 100,000 population

50 and under

51-100

101-200

201-300

301 and over

Data not available

PART II:
COUNTRY PROFILES

AFGHANISTAN

Afghanistan, a landlocked country in central Asia, ranks 34th in the world in land area and 38th in population. (Because a proper census has never been held, estimates of the country's population vary widely.) Although one of the least developed nations in the Third World, Afghanistan has substantial natural gas resources as well as reserves of high-quality iron ore in Bamiyam province and Hajigak. Gas exports contributed 21% of the national income in 1979. The country's seven-year economic development plan has been crippled by the Soviet occupation of 1979 and subsequent guerrilla warfare. By the summer of 1980 approximately 1 million Afghans had fled the country into neighboring Pakistan. As a Soviet satellite, Afghanistan receives massive loans and grants from the USSR, representing over 30% of government revenues. Economic and political relations with non-Communist countries have been downgraded or virtually abandoned.

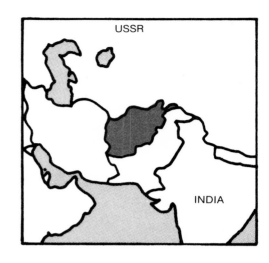

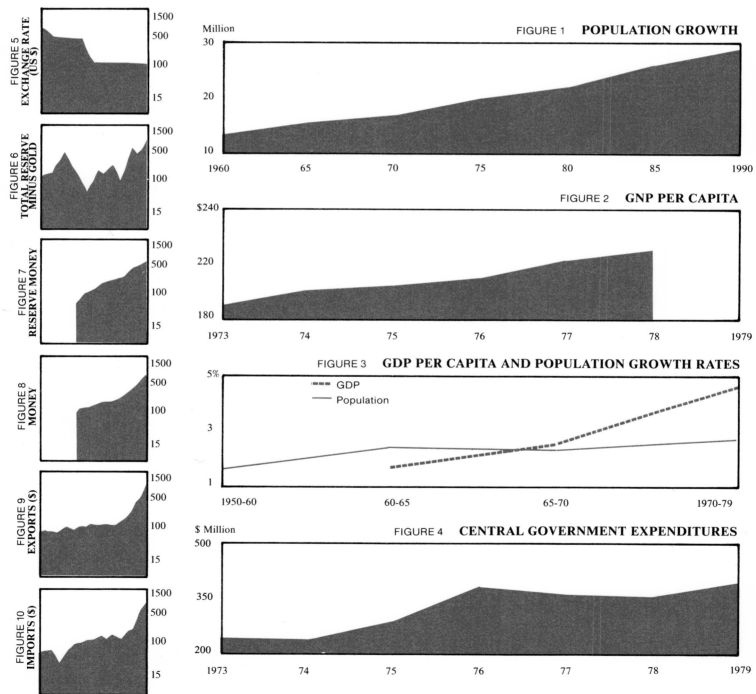

FIGURE 5 EXCHANGE RATE (US $)

FIGURE 6 TOTAL RESERVE MINUS GOLD

FIGURE 7 RESERVE MONEY

FIGURE 8 MONEY

FIGURE 9 EXPORTS ($)

FIGURE 10 IMPORTS ($)

FIGURE 1 **POPULATION GROWTH**

FIGURE 2 **GNP PER CAPITA**

FIGURE 3 **GDP PER CAPITA AND POPULATION GROWTH RATES**

FIGURE 4 **CENTRAL GOVERNMENT EXPENDITURES**

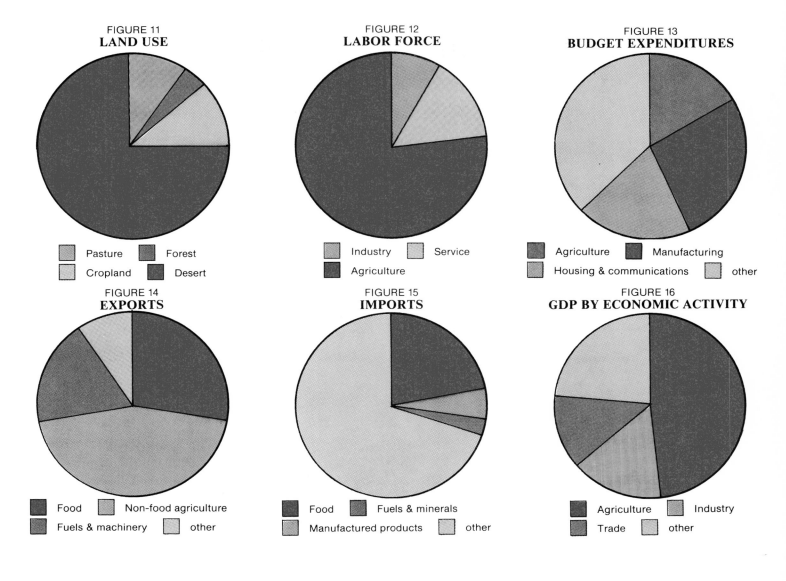

FIGURE 11
LAND USE

Pasture   Forest
Cropland   Desert

FIGURE 12
LABOR FORCE

Industry   Service
Agriculture

FIGURE 13
BUDGET EXPENDITURES

Agriculture   Manufacturing
Housing & communications   other

FIGURE 14
EXPORTS

Food   Non-food agriculture
Fuels & machinery   other

FIGURE 15
IMPORTS

Food   Fuels & minerals
Manufactured products   other

FIGURE 16
GDP BY ECONOMIC ACTIVITY

Agriculture   Industry
Trade   other

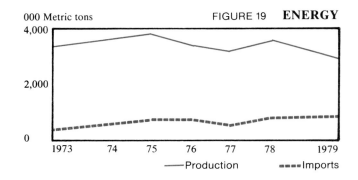

FIGURE 17   **EDUCATIONAL ENROLLMENT**

30

15

0

1960   65   70   73   75   1977

—— Primary   ==== Secondary

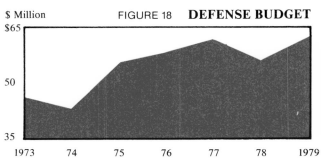

$ Million   FIGURE 18   **DEFENSE BUDGET**

$65

50

35

1973   74   75   76   77   78   1979

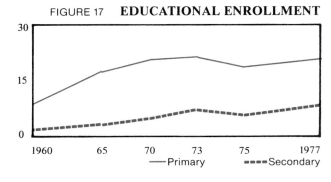

000 Metric tons   FIGURE 19   **ENERGY**

4,000

2,000

0

1973   74   75   76   77   78   1979

—— Production   ==== Imports

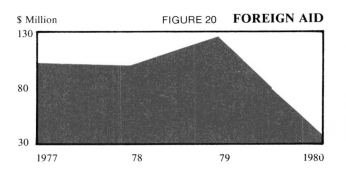

$ Million   FIGURE 20   **FOREIGN AID**

130

80

30

1977   78   79   1980

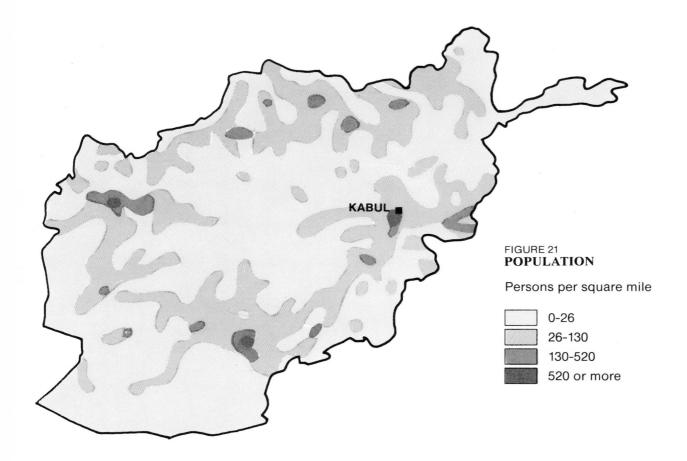

FIGURE 21
POPULATION

Persons per square mile

0-26
26-130
130-520
520 or more

FIGURE 23
ETHNOLINGUISTIC GROUPS

Pushtun
Hazara
Chahar Aimak
Tajik
Other

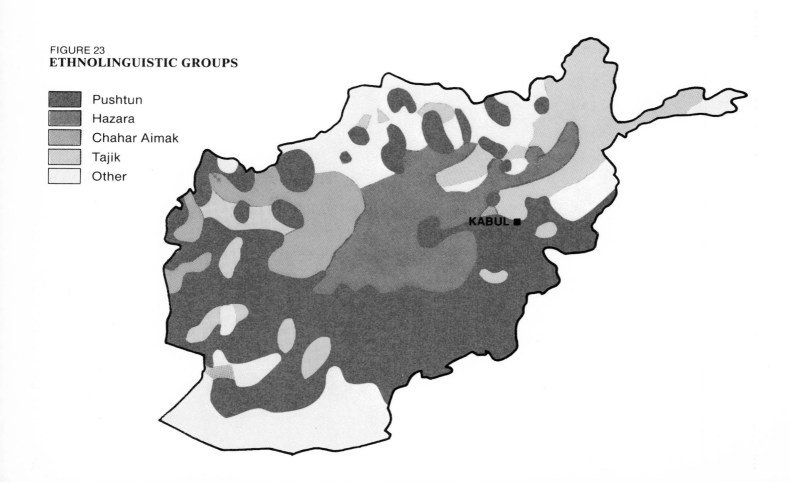

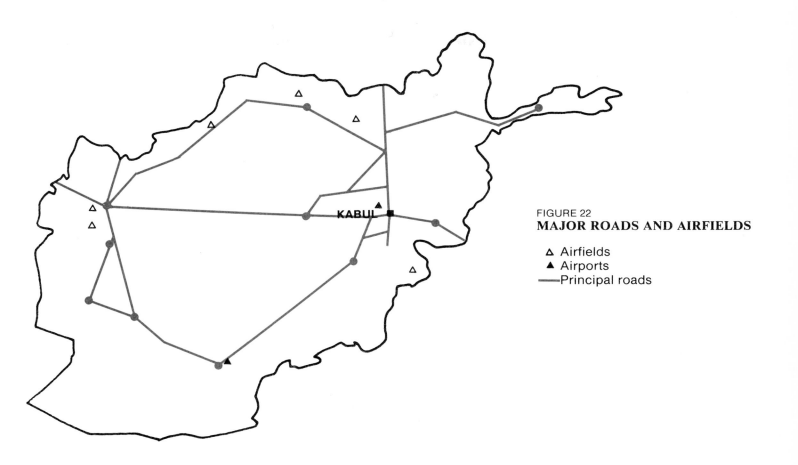

FIGURE 22
MAJOR ROADS AND AIRFIELDS

△ Airfields
▲ Airports
— Principal roads

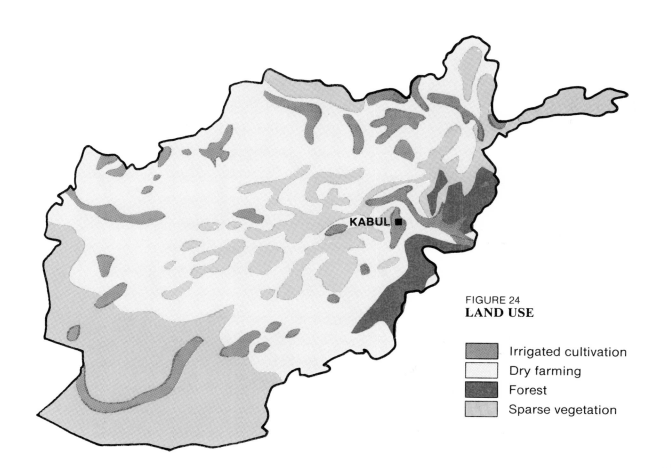

FIGURE 24
LAND USE

Irrigated cultivation
Dry farming
Forest
Sparse vegetation

ALGERIA

Located midway along the Maghrebian littoral, and extending southward into the heart of the Sahara, Algeria is the 10th largest country in the world but ranks only 37th in population. Despite its Islamic and Arabic orientation, Algeria is still part of the French cultural bloc. With a socialistic economy, the government dominates all sectors of national life. Its GNP is growing at a faster rate than its population. At the current rate of growth, Algeria has the potential to develop into a modern industrial state. Petroleum revenues have enabled Algeria to embark on a massive and ambitious program of industrialization. It ranks fifth in the world in annual industrial growth rate and seventh in industry's share of GDP. By the mid-1980s the country is expected to become the world's leading exporter of natural gas. Algeria's economic progress is matched by its political stability: it has not had a political crisis since the coup of 1965.

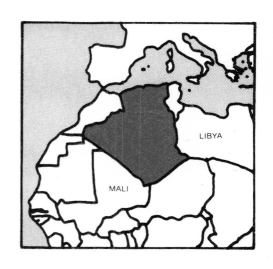

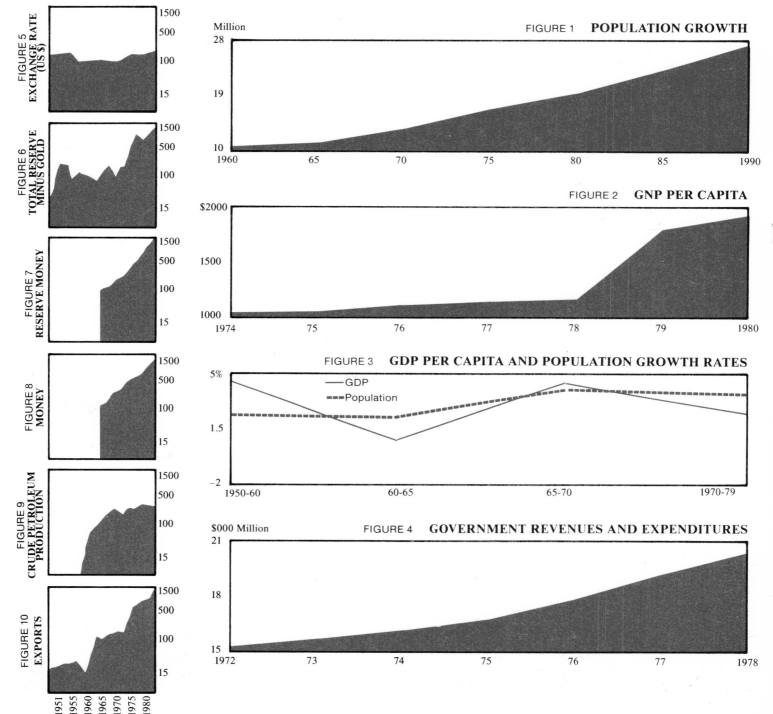

FIGURE 5 EXCHANGE RATE (US $)

FIGURE 6 TOTAL RESERVE MINUS GOLD

FIGURE 7 RESERVE MONEY

FIGURE 8 MONEY

FIGURE 9 CRUDE PETROLEUM PRODUCTION

FIGURE 10 EXPORTS

FIGURE 1 **POPULATION GROWTH**

FIGURE 2 **GNP PER CAPITA**

FIGURE 3 **GDP PER CAPITA AND POPULATION GROWTH RATES**

FIGURE 4 **GOVERNMENT REVENUES AND EXPENDITURES**

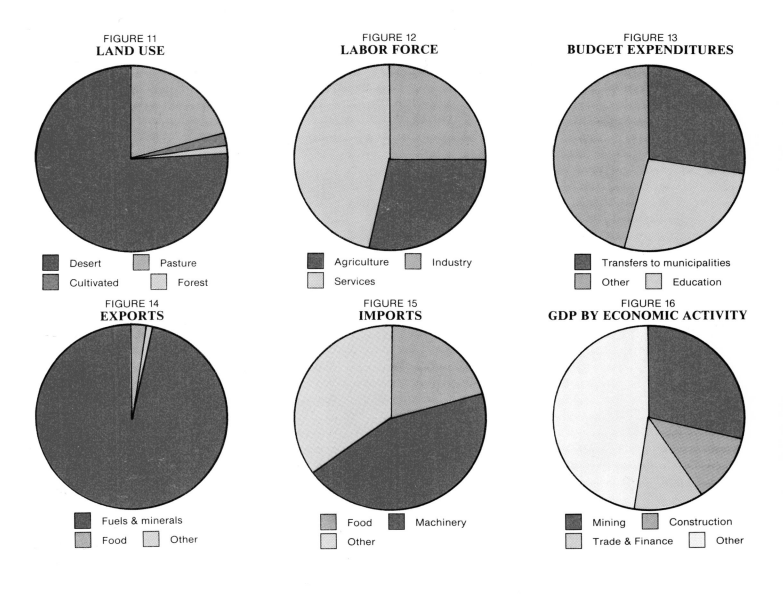

FIGURE 11
LAND USE

- Desert
- Pasture
- Cultivated
- Forest

FIGURE 12
LABOR FORCE

- Agriculture
- Industry
- Services

FIGURE 13
BUDGET EXPENDITURES

- Transfers to municipalities
- Other
- Education

FIGURE 14
EXPORTS

- Fuels & minerals
- Food
- Other

FIGURE 15
IMPORTS

- Food
- Machinery
- Other

FIGURE 16
GDP BY ECONOMIC ACTIVITY

- Mining
- Construction
- Trade & Finance
- Other

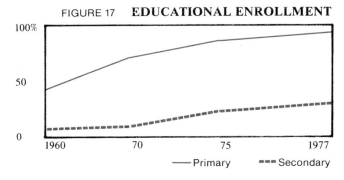

FIGURE 17 **EDUCATIONAL ENROLLMENT**

100%

50

0

1960　　70　　75　　1977

—— Primary　　▄▄▄ Secondary

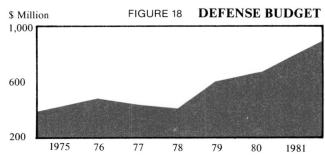

$ Million　　FIGURE 18 **DEFENSE BUDGET**

1,000

600

200

1975　76　77　78　79　80　1981

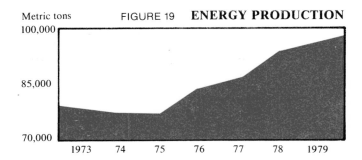

Metric tons　　FIGURE 19 **ENERGY PRODUCTION**

100,000

85,000

70,000

1973　74　75　76　77　78　1979

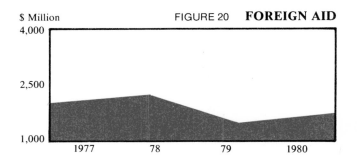

$ Million　　FIGURE 20 **FOREIGN AID**

4,000

2,500

1,000

1977　78　79　1980

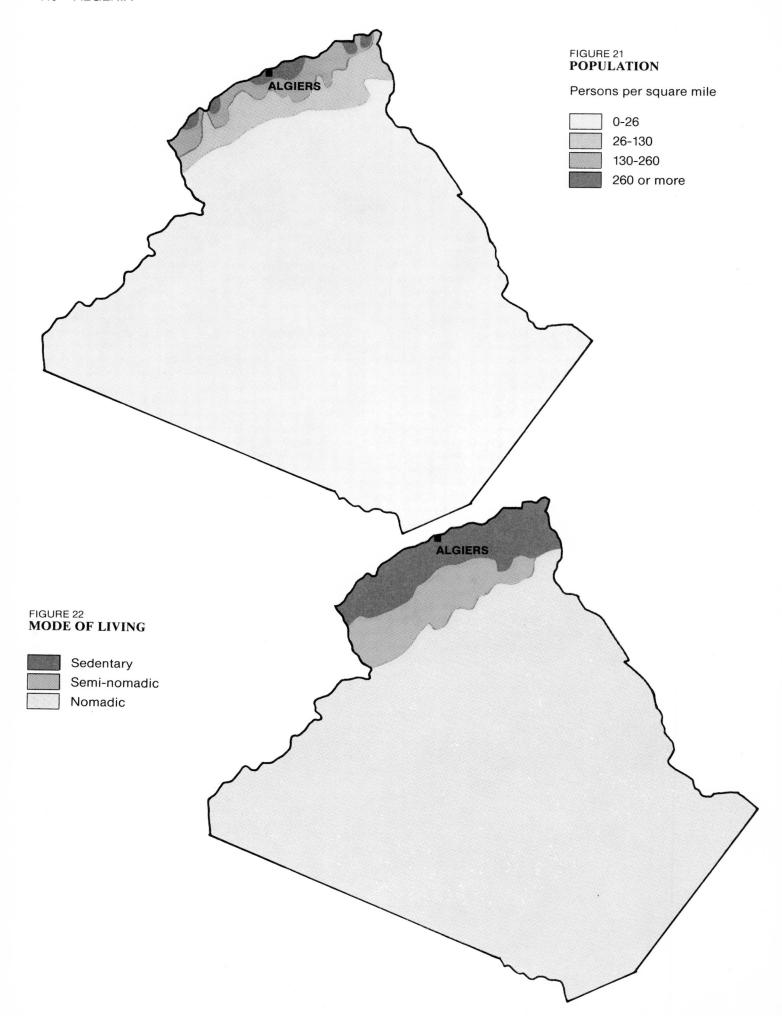

FIGURE 21
POPULATION

Persons per square mile

- 0-26
- 26-130
- 130-260
- 260 or more

ALGIERS

FIGURE 22
MODE OF LIVING

- Sedentary
- Semi-nomadic
- Nomadic

ALGIERS

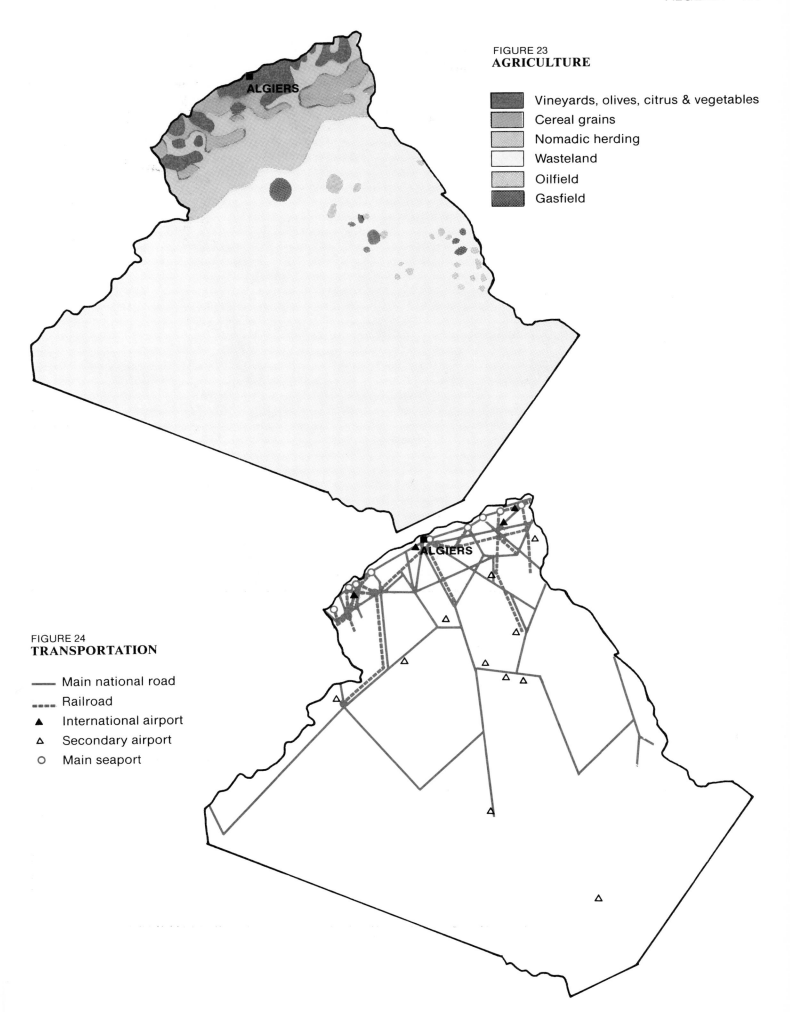

FIGURE 23
AGRICULTURE

Vineyards, olives, citrus & vegetables
Cereal grains
Nomadic herding
Wasteland
Oilfield
Gasfield

ALGIERS

FIGURE 24
TRANSPORTATION

—— Main national road
‑ ‑ ‑ ‑ Railroad
▲ International airport
△ Secondary airport
○ Main seaport

ALGIERS

ANGOLA

Located on the west coast of southern Africa, Angola ranks 20th in the world in land area and 71st in population. It is one of the richest countries on the continent in mineral resources, notably diamonds, iron ore and copper. Nevertheless, its erratic economic progress since the departure of the Portuguese has posed enormous barriers in achieving this potential. Although oil production has returned to near pre-war levels, other areas of the economy have experienced varying degrees of stagnation. Many of the stores and shops owned by the Portuguese before independence have not been reopened. In an effort to offset the gap in skilled workers, Cuba has sent 5,000 technicians and helped to train Angolan workers in Cuba. Under President Neto, Angola moved toward complete state control of the economy, including petroleum production and distribution. These policies have been continued by his successor, Jose Eduardo dos Santos.

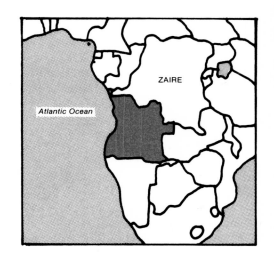

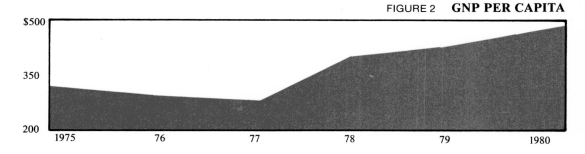

FIGURE 1 **POPULATION GROWTH**

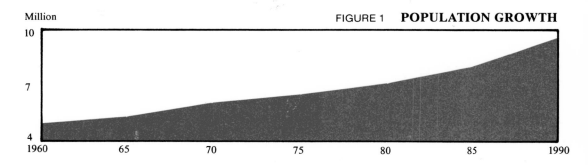

FIGURE 2 **GNP PER CAPITA**

I.M.F.
DATA
UNAVAILABLE

FIGURE 3 **GDP PER CAPITA AND POPULATION GROWTH RATES**

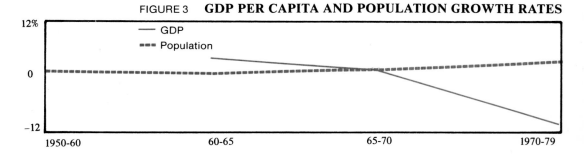

FIGURE 4 **URBANIZATION**

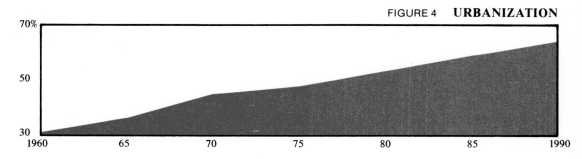

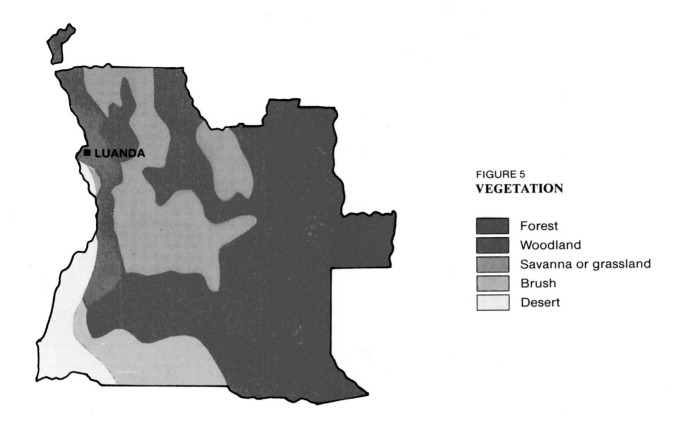

FIGURE 5
VEGETATION

Forest
Woodland
Savanna or grassland
Brush
Desert

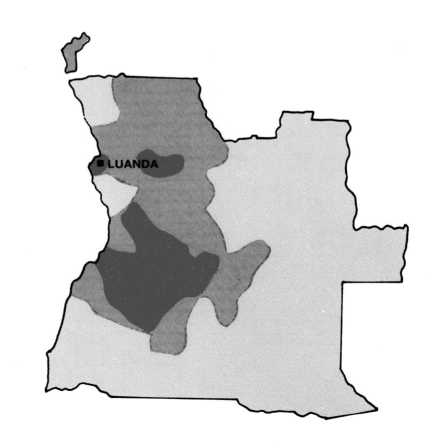

FIGURE 6
POPULATION

Persons per square mile

0-13
13-39
39 or more

ARGENTINA

The second largest country in Latin America and the eighth largest in the world, Argentina ranks only 30th in size of population because of low population density (less than 9 per sq km). Classified as an upper middle-income country, it has the third highest per capita income in Latin America and its GNP growth rate is more than double the population growth rate. Despite the third highest inflation rate in the world, the Argentines enjoy a better standard of living than most other Latin Americans. The bulwark of such economic well-being is the pampa, which, with its deep rich soil, is the granary of South America. The Argentine cattle herds are among the world's finest and the country is among the world's largest exporters of livestock products. Despite such immense resources, Argentina has never achieved its full potential because its economy is constantly muddied by labor and political unrest and violence, misguided military ambitions, lack of a coherent fiscal or industrial policy, high inflation, and a weak currency.

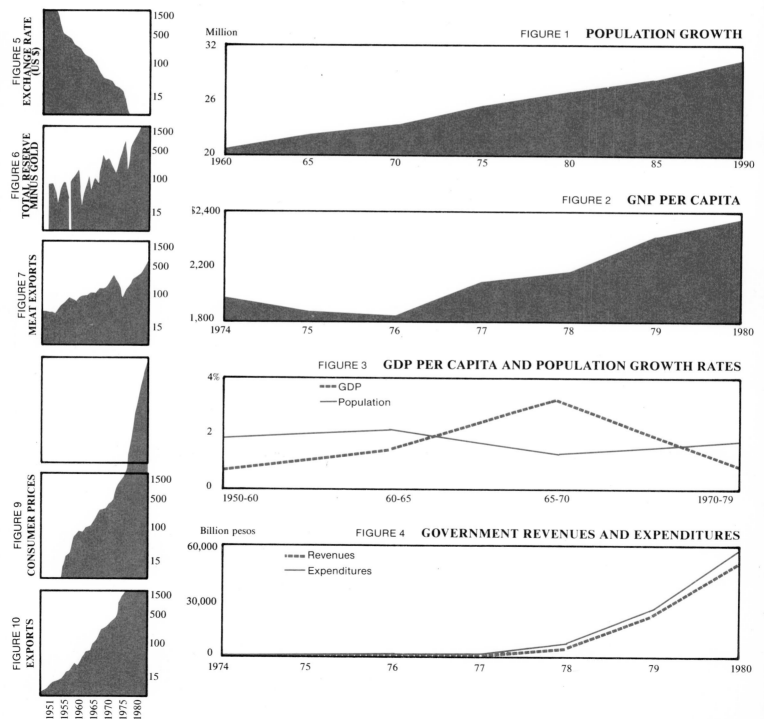

FIGURE 5 EXCHANGE RATE (US $)

FIGURE 6 TOTAL RESERVE MINUS GOLD

FIGURE 7 MEAT EXPORTS

FIGURE 9 CONSUMER PRICES

FIGURE 10 EXPORTS

FIGURE 1 **POPULATION GROWTH**

FIGURE 2 **GNP PER CAPITA**

FIGURE 3 **GDP PER CAPITA AND POPULATION GROWTH RATES**

FIGURE 4 **GOVERNMENT REVENUES AND EXPENDITURES**

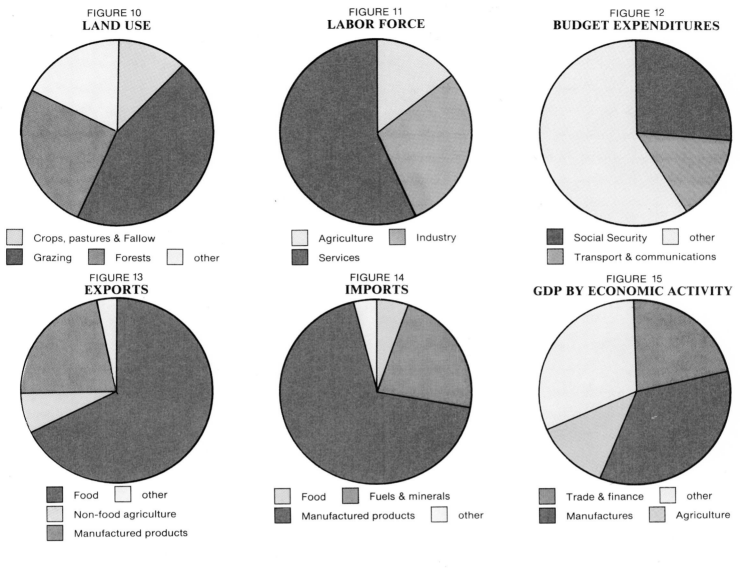

FIGURE 10
LAND USE

Crops, pastures & Fallow
Grazing
Forests
other

FIGURE 11
LABOR FORCE

Agriculture   Industry
Services

FIGURE 12
BUDGET EXPENDITURES

Social Security   other
Transport & communications

FIGURE 13
EXPORTS

Food   other
Non-food agriculture
Manufactured products

FIGURE 14
IMPORTS

Food   Fuels & minerals
Manufactured products   other

FIGURE 15
GDP BY ECONOMIC ACTIVITY

Trade & finance   other
Manufactures   Agriculture

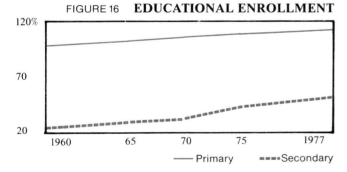

FIGURE 16   **EDUCATIONAL ENROLLMENT**

120%

70

20

1960   65   70   75   1977

—— Primary   ===Secondary

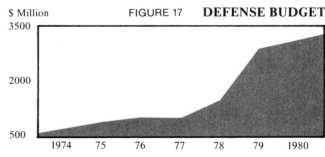

$ Million   FIGURE 17   **DEFENSE BUDGET**

3500

2000

500

1974   75   76   77   78   79   1980

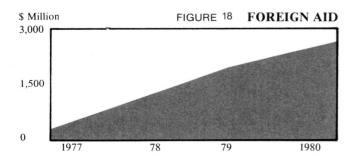

$ Million   FIGURE 18   **FOREIGN AID**

3,000

1,500

0

1977   78   79   1980

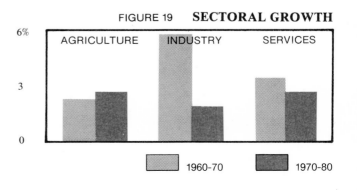

FIGURE 19   **SECTORAL GROWTH**

6%   AGRICULTURE   INDUSTRY   SERVICES

3

0

1960-70   1970-80

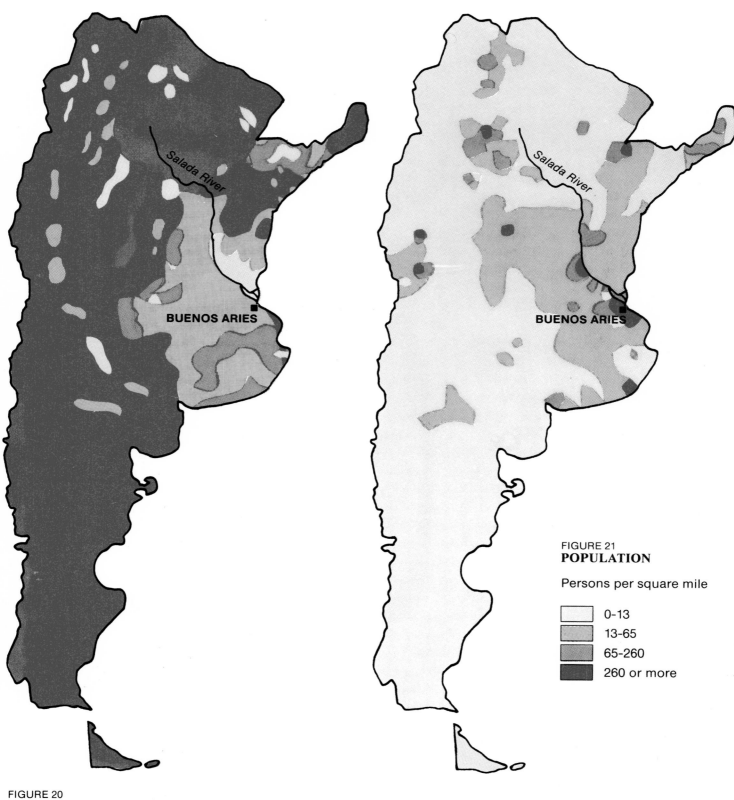

Salada River

BUENOS ARIES

Salada River

BUENOS ARIES

FIGURE 21
POPULATION

Persons per square mile

	0-13
	13-65
	65-260
	260 or more

FIGURE 20
VEGETATION

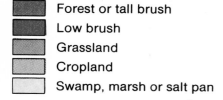

Forest or tall brush
Low brush
Grassland
Cropland
Swamp, marsh or salt pan

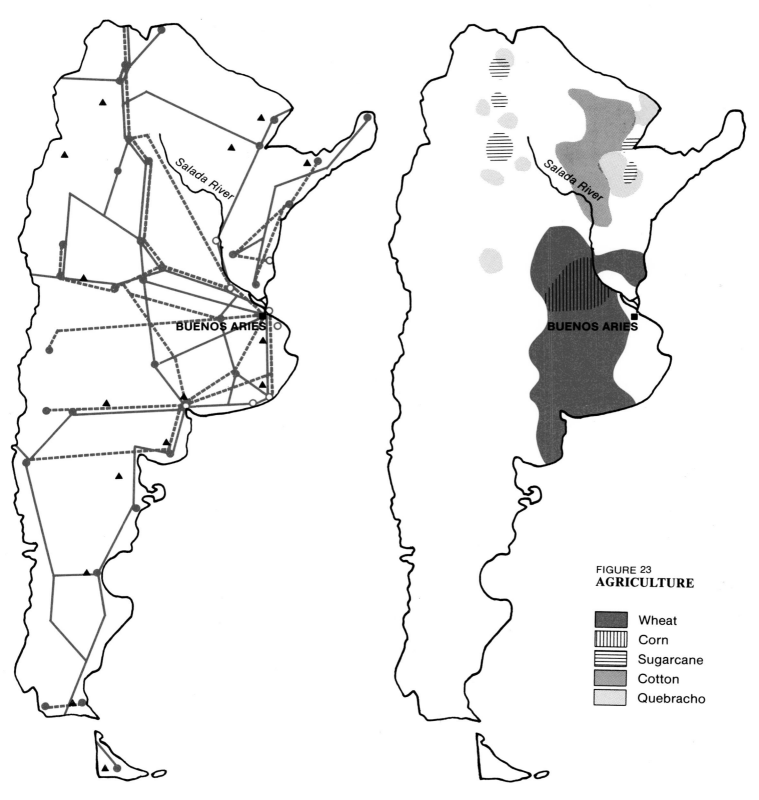

Salada River

BUENOS ARIES

FIGURE 23
AGRICULTURE

Wheat
Corn
Sugarcane
Cotton
Quebracho

Salada River

BUENOS ARIES

FIGURE 22
TRANSPORTATION

—— Roads
---- Railroads
▲ Airports
○ Ports

BANGLADESH

Located on the Indian subcontinent in the great combined delta of the Ganges, the Brahmaputra and the Meghna Rivers, Bangladesh ranks 87th in land area but eighth in size of population. The result is that Bangladesh has the highest density of population of any nation on earth other than small city states. It also has the 12th highest birth rate, sixth highest fertility rate and third highest death rate. An economic basket case, Bangladesh has learned to live on the brink of disaster, while surviving on its exiguous natural resources as well as handouts from the richer nations. Agriculture, on which 90% of Bangladeshis depend for their livelihood, remains the key to the continued survival of the country. However, it has few mineral resources, and its industrial sector is small and inefficient, making Bangladesh a classic textbook case of the underdevelopment-overpopulation-resourcelessness syndrome that afflicts most Third World nations.

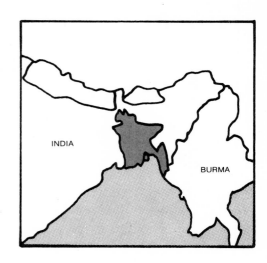

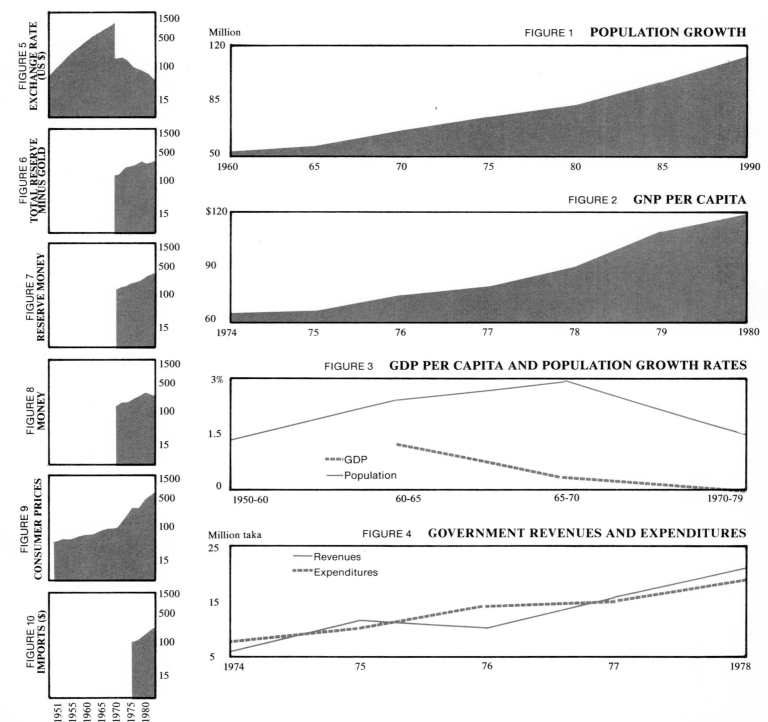

FIGURE 5 EXCHANGE RATE (US $)

FIGURE 6 TOTAL RESERVE MINUS GOLD

FIGURE 7 RESERVE MONEY

FIGURE 8 MONEY

FIGURE 9 CONSUMER PRICES

FIGURE 10 IMPORTS ($)

FIGURE 1 **POPULATION GROWTH**

FIGURE 2 **GNP PER CAPITA**

FIGURE 3 **GDP PER CAPITA AND POPULATION GROWTH RATES**

FIGURE 4 **GOVERNMENT REVENUES AND EXPENDITURES**

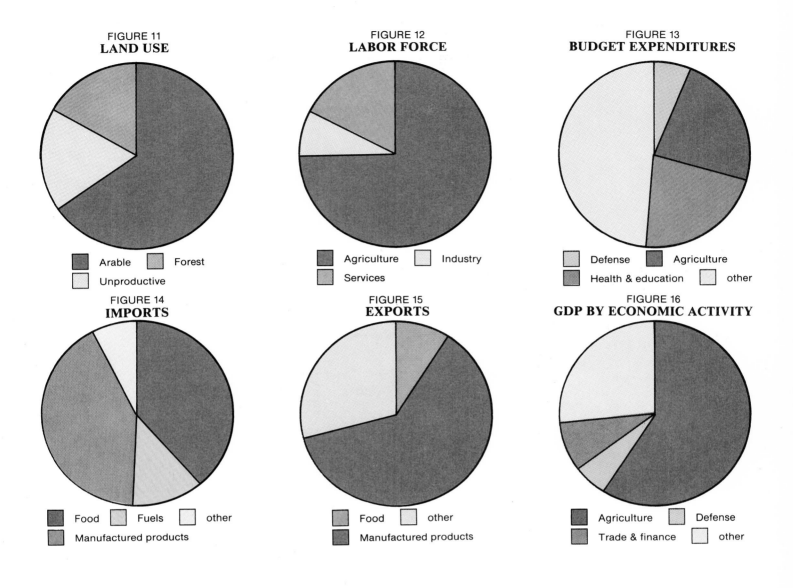

FIGURE 11
LAND USE

- Arable
- Forest
- Unproductive

FIGURE 12
LABOR FORCE

- Agriculture
- Industry
- Services

FIGURE 13
BUDGET EXPENDITURES

- Defense
- Agriculture
- Health & education
- other

FIGURE 14
IMPORTS

- Food
- Fuels
- other
- Manufactured products

FIGURE 15
EXPORTS

- Food
- other
- Manufactured products

FIGURE 16
GDP BY ECONOMIC ACTIVITY

- Agriculture
- Defense
- Trade & finance
- other

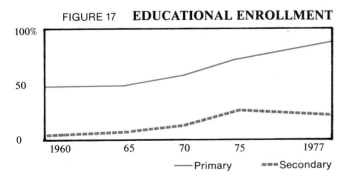

FIGURE 17   **EDUCATIONAL ENROLLMENT**

100%

50

0

1960   65   70   75   1977

—— Primary   ===Secondary

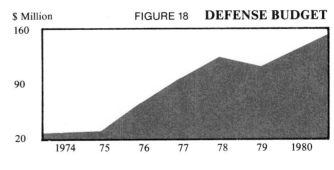

$ Million   FIGURE 18   **DEFENSE BUDGET**

160

90

20

1974   75   76   77   78   79   1980

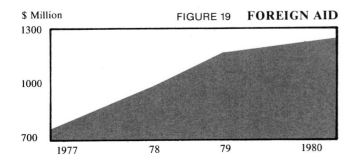

$ Million   FIGURE 19   **FOREIGN AID**

1300

1000

700

1977   78   79   1980

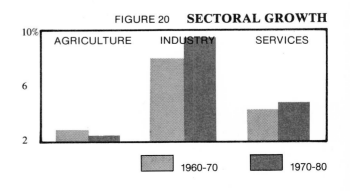

FIGURE 20   **SECTORAL GROWTH**

10%   AGRICULTURE   INDUSTRY   SERVICES

6

2

1960-70   1970-80

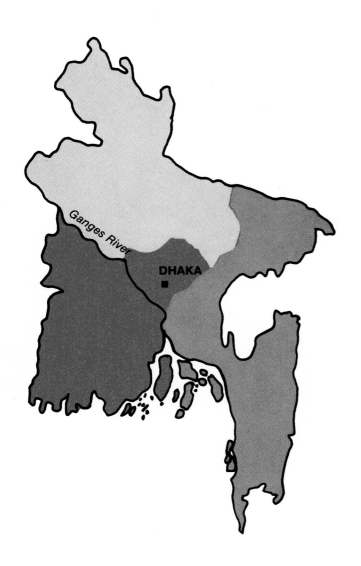

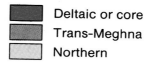

FIGURE 21
CULTURAL REGIONS

Deltaic or core
Trans-Meghna
Northern

FIGURE 22
PRINCIPAL REGIONS

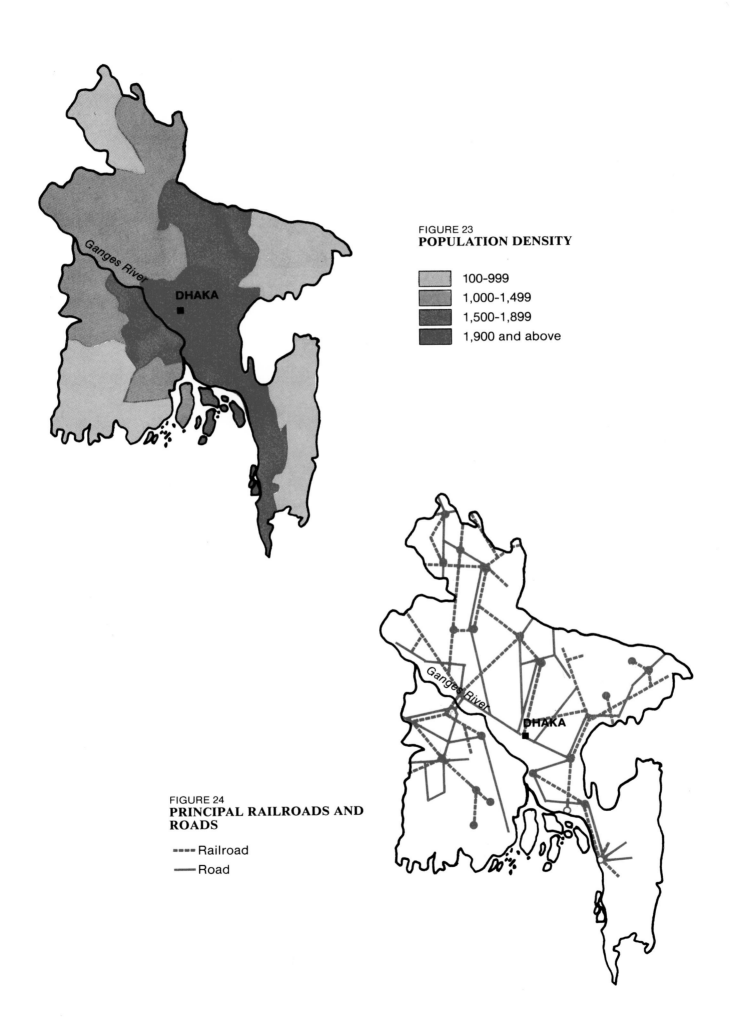

FIGURE 23
POPULATION DENSITY

100-999
1,000-1,499
1,500-1,899
1,900 and above

FIGURE 24
PRINCIPAL RAILROADS AND ROADS

---- Railroad
—— Road

BENIN

Sandwiched between Nigeria and Togo, on the western coast of Africa, Benin ranks 95th in land area and 103rd in population. It is one of the least developed countries in Africa with a per capita income in 1980 of $300. The economy is highly dependent on agriculture which provides 40% of the GDP and employs nearly 50% of the population. Government finances are sustained only through foreign aid, especially from France. In 1974 the government of President Mathieu Kerekou declared Benin as a Marxist-Lenninist state and launched a program of nationalization that virtually eliminated foreign investment from the economy. A series of three-year plans were launched in 1977 with only mixed results, and the country's agricultural exports, rather than increasing, have continued to decline. The most hopeful feature is the transportation sector which produces one-fourth of the nation's GDP and is rapidly growing because of Benin's key position as a transit point for Niger.

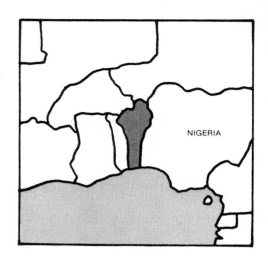

NIGERIA

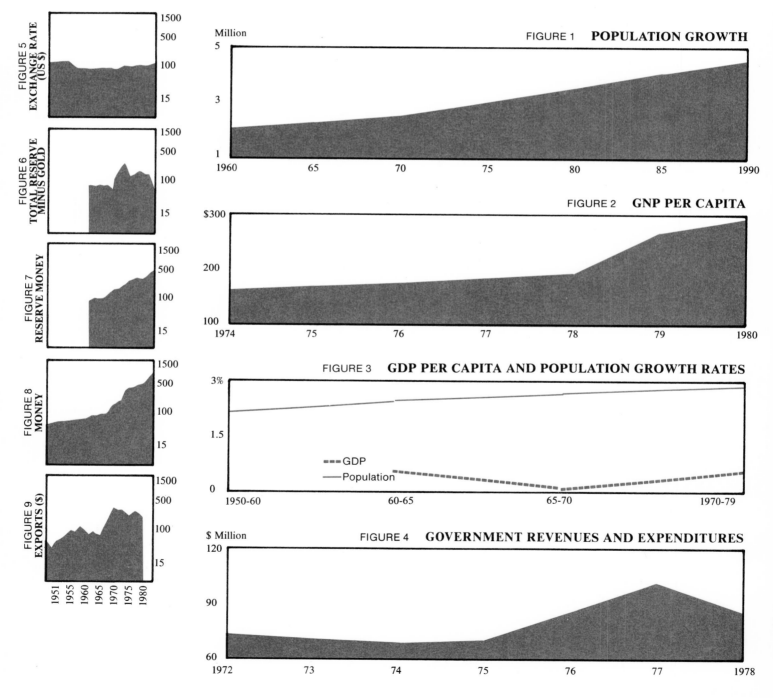

FIGURE 5 EXCHANGE RATE (US $)

FIGURE 6 TOTAL RESERVE MINUS GOLD

FIGURE 7 RESERVE MONEY

FIGURE 8 MONEY

FIGURE 9 EXPORTS ($)

FIGURE 1 **POPULATION GROWTH**

FIGURE 2 **GNP PER CAPITA**

FIGURE 3 **GDP PER CAPITA AND POPULATION GROWTH RATES**

GDP
Population

FIGURE 4 **GOVERNMENT REVENUES AND EXPENDITURES**

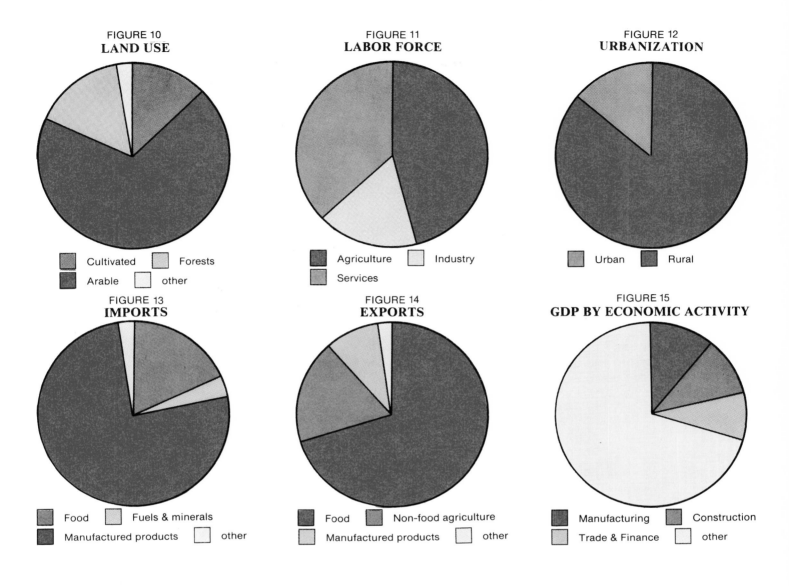

FIGURE 10
LAND USE

Cultivated   Forests
Arable   other

FIGURE 11
LABOR FORCE

Agriculture   Industry
Services

FIGURE 12
URBANIZATION

Urban   Rural

FIGURE 13
IMPORTS

Food   Fuels & minerals
Manufactured products   other

FIGURE 14
EXPORTS

Food   Non-food agriculture
Manufactured products   other

FIGURE 15
GDP BY ECONOMIC ACTIVITY

Manufacturing   Construction
Trade & Finance   other

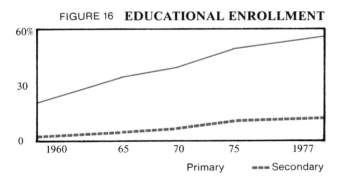

FIGURE 16   **EDUCATIONAL ENROLLMENT**

60%

30

0

1960   65   70   75   1977

Primary   Secondary

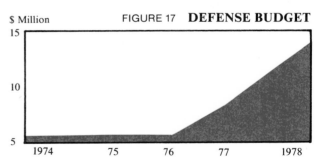

$ Million   FIGURE 17   **DEFENSE BUDGET**

15

10

5

1974   75   76   77   1978

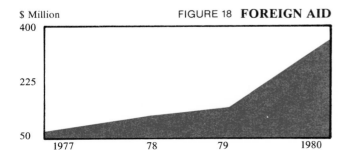

$ Million   FIGURE 18   **FOREIGN AID**

400

225

50

1977   78   79   1980

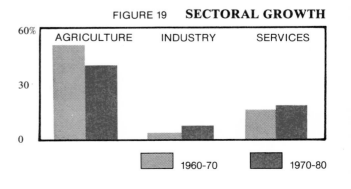

FIGURE 19   **SECTORAL GROWTH**

60%   AGRICULTURE   INDUSTRY   SERVICES

30

0

1960-70   1970-80

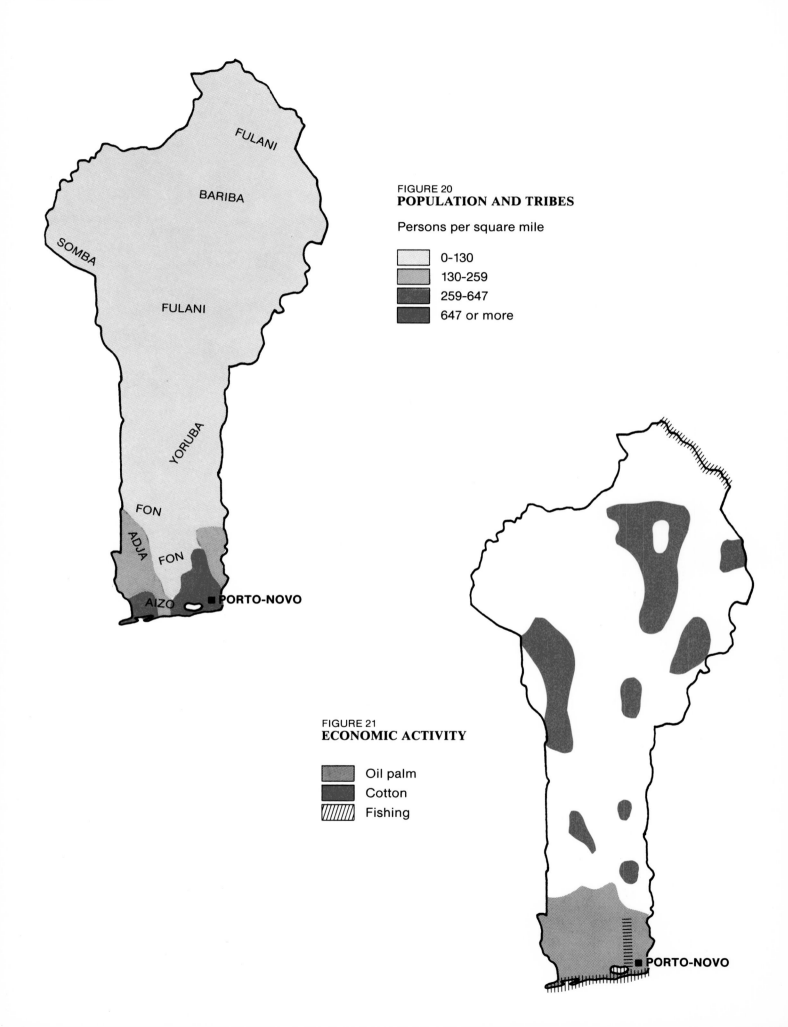

FIGURE 20
POPULATION AND TRIBES

Persons per square mile

- 0–130
- 130–259
- 259–647
- 647 or more

FIGURE 21
ECONOMIC ACTIVITY

- Oil palm
- Cotton
- Fishing

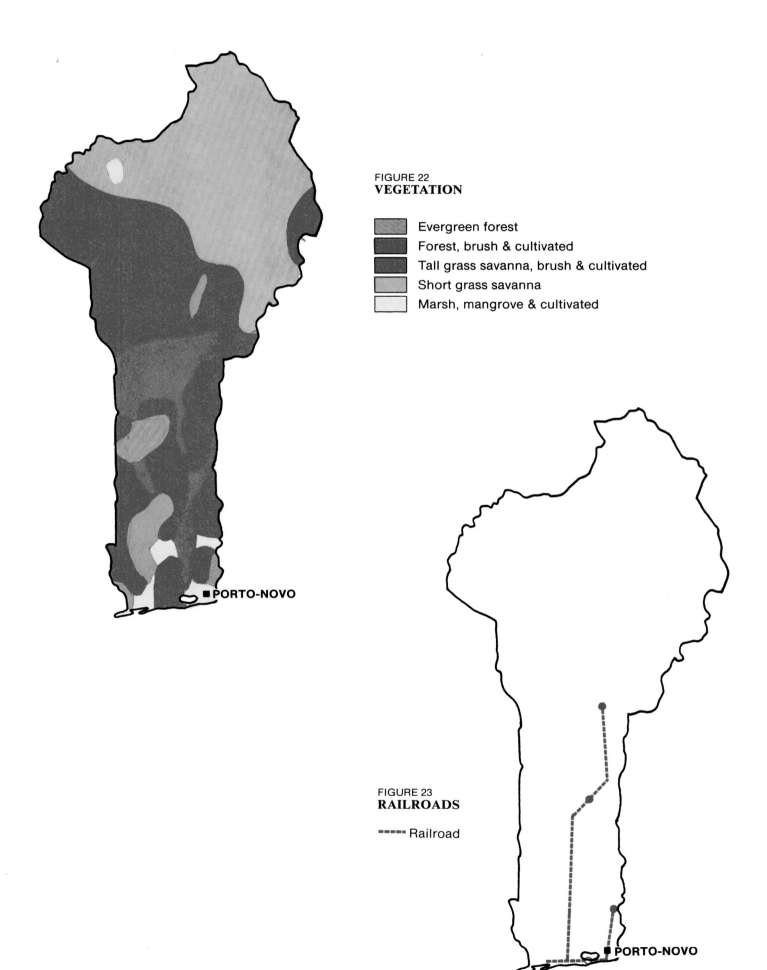

FIGURE 22
VEGETATION

Evergreen forest
Forest, brush & cultivated
Tall grass savanna, brush & cultivated
Short grass savanna
Marsh, mangrove & cultivated

■ PORTO-NOVO

FIGURE 23
RAILROADS

▪▪▪▪▪ Railroad

■ PORTO-NOVO

BOLIVIA

One of the two landlocked countries in South America, Bolivia ranks 25th in land area and 76th in population. It also has one of the highest concentrations of native Indians in Latin America, with Indians constituting 62% of the population. Bolivia is at once one of the richest as well as one of the poorest of Latin American countries. It is endowed with immense mineral resources, remarkable both for the size of the deposits and the variety of the ores. It is the largest tin producer in the Western Hemisphere and the second largest in the world. It is also the world's largest producer of bismuth and the second largest producer of antimony. At the same time, it is officially classified as a low-income country and the agricultural sector, which employs about two-thirds of the population, is mostly on the subsistence level. In 1952 Bolivia experienced a popular revolution which changed the social and political structure of the country. Since that time, the state has played an increasingly large role in the economy.

BRAZIL

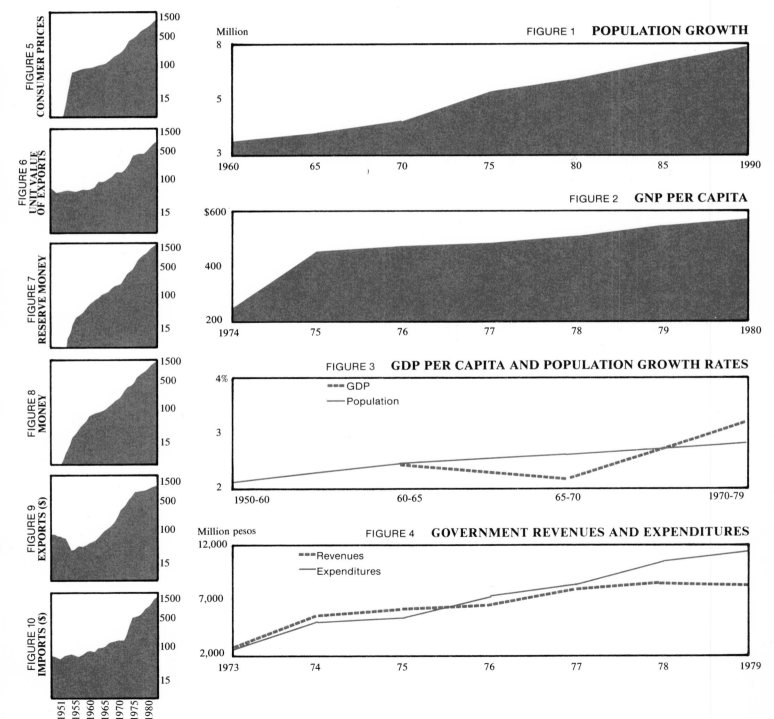

FIGURE 5 CONSUMER PRICES

FIGURE 6 UNIT VALUE OF EXPORTS

FIGURE 7 RESERVE MONEY

FIGURE 8 MONEY

FIGURE 9 EXPORTS ($)

FIGURE 10 IMPORTS ($)

FIGURE 1 **POPULATION GROWTH**

FIGURE 2 **GNP PER CAPITA**

FIGURE 3 **GDP PER CAPITA AND POPULATION GROWTH RATES**

FIGURE 4 **GOVERNMENT REVENUES AND EXPENDITURES**

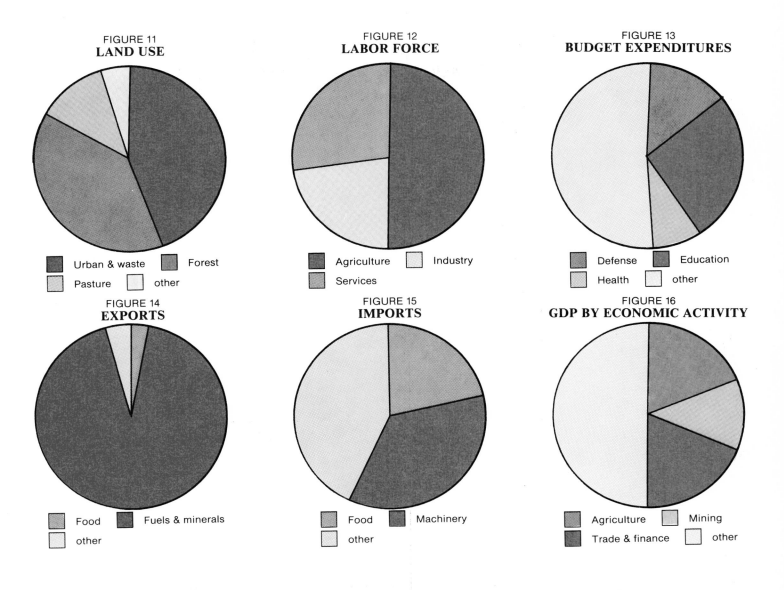

FIGURE 11
LAND USE

Urban & waste   Forest
Pasture   other

FIGURE 12
LABOR FORCE

Agriculture   Industry
Services

FIGURE 13
BUDGET EXPENDITURES

Defense   Education
Health   other

FIGURE 14
EXPORTS

Food   Fuels & minerals
other

FIGURE 15
IMPORTS

Food   Machinery
other

FIGURE 16
GDP BY ECONOMIC ACTIVITY

Agriculture   Mining
Trade & finance   other

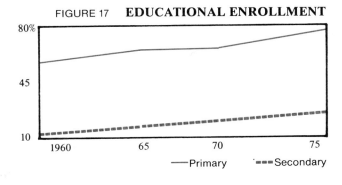

FIGURE 17   **EDUCATIONAL ENROLLMENT**

80%

45

10

1960   65   70   75

—— Primary   ---- Secondary

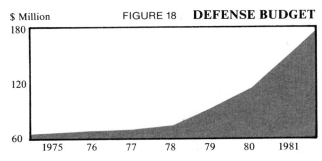

$ Million   FIGURE 18   **DEFENSE BUDGET**

180

120

60

1975   76   77   78   79   80   1981

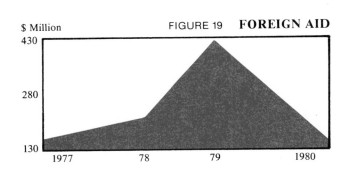

$ Million   FIGURE 19   **FOREIGN AID**

430

280

130

1977   78   79   1980

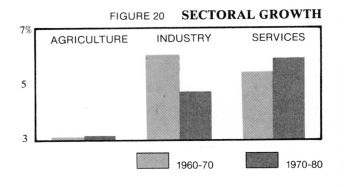

FIGURE 20   **SECTORAL GROWTH**

7%

AGRICULTURE   INDUSTRY   SERVICES

5

3

1960-70   1970-80

BRAZIL

The fifth largest country in the world, Brazil covers approximately one-half of the South American continent and also accounts for half of its population. Its international borders, the third longest in the world, touch every South American country except Ecuador and Chile. With a per capita income in 1980 of $2,050 Brazil is officially classified as an upper middle-income country. Brazil's GNP, the 10th highest in the world, has grown steadily since 1968, averaging about 10% annually. But its prosperity is being eroded by the seventh highest rate of inflation in the world, close to 26.1% from 1970 to 1976. The economy is in a transitional phase moving from an agricultural to an industrial base. The agricultural sector employs 45% of the population, accounts for 15% of the GNP and provides 60% of the exports. There is mounting evidence that Brazil's mineral resources may be among the world's richest. The public sector, led by Petroleo Brasileiro (Pterobas), has played a dominant role in the Brazilian miracle.

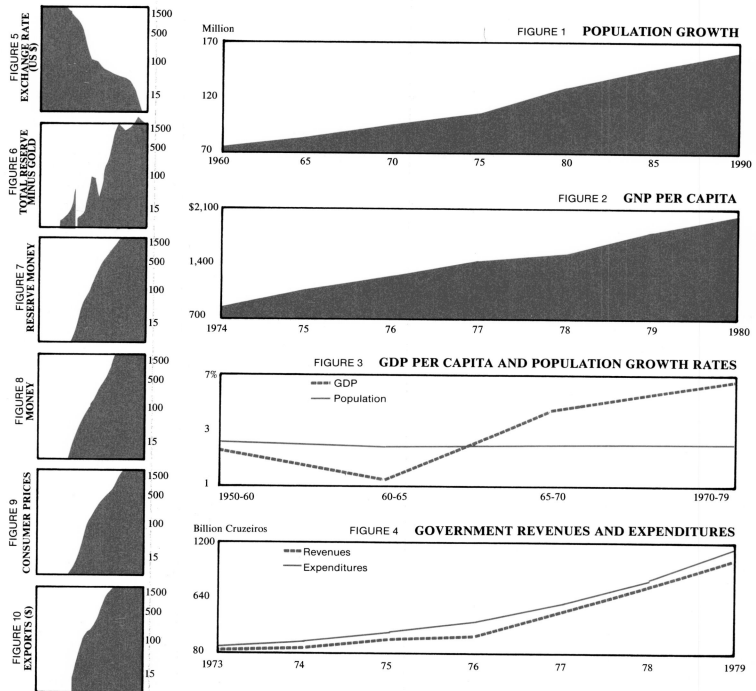

FIGURE 5 EXCHANGE RATE (US $)

FIGURE 6 TOTAL RESERVE MINUS GOLD

FIGURE 7 RESERVE MONEY

FIGURE 8 MONEY

FIGURE 9 CONSUMER PRICES

FIGURE 10 EXPORTS ($)

FIGURE 1 **POPULATION GROWTH**

FIGURE 2 **GNP PER CAPITA**

FIGURE 3 **GDP PER CAPITA AND POPULATION GROWTH RATES**

FIGURE 4 **GOVERNMENT REVENUES AND EXPENDITURES**

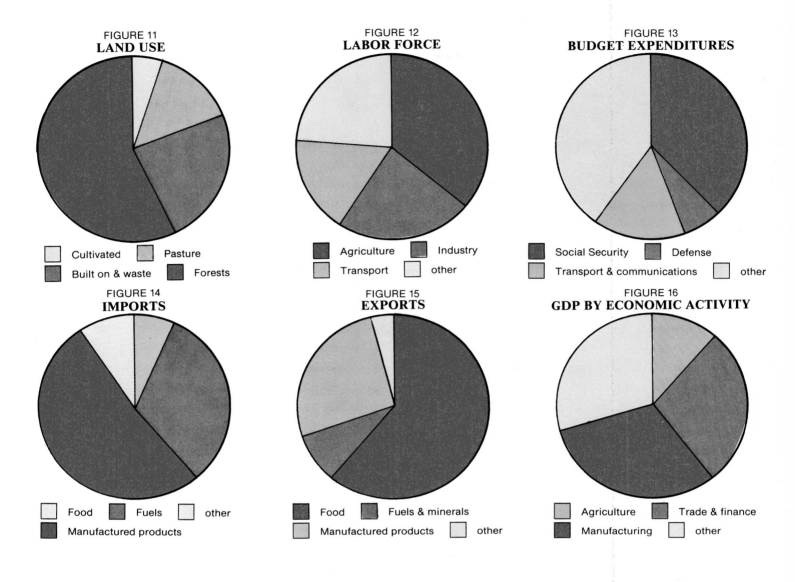

FIGURE 11
LAND USE

- Cultivated
- Pasture
- Built on & waste
- Forests

FIGURE 12
LABOR FORCE

- Agriculture
- Industry
- Transport
- other

FIGURE 13
BUDGET EXPENDITURES

- Social Security
- Defense
- Transport & communications
- other

FIGURE 14
IMPORTS

- Food
- Fuels
- other
- Manufactured products

FIGURE 15
EXPORTS

- Food
- Fuels & minerals
- Manufactured products
- other

FIGURE 16
GDP BY ECONOMIC ACTIVITY

- Agriculture
- Trade & finance
- Manufacturing
- other

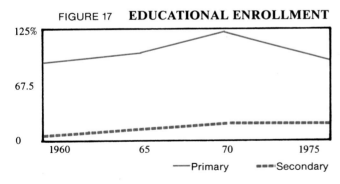

FIGURE 17   **EDUCATIONAL ENROLLMENT**

125%

67.5

0

1960   65   70   1975

—— Primary   ====Secondary

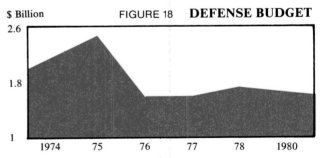

$ Billion   FIGURE 18   **DEFENSE BUDGET**

2.6

1.8

1

1974   75   76   77   78   1980

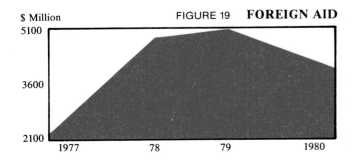

$ Million   FIGURE 19   **FOREIGN AID**

5100

3600

2100

1977   78   79   1980

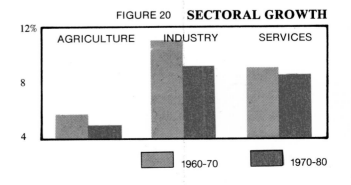

FIGURE 20   **SECTORAL GROWTH**

12%

AGRICULTURE   INDUSTRY   SERVICES

8

4

- 1960-70
- 1970-80

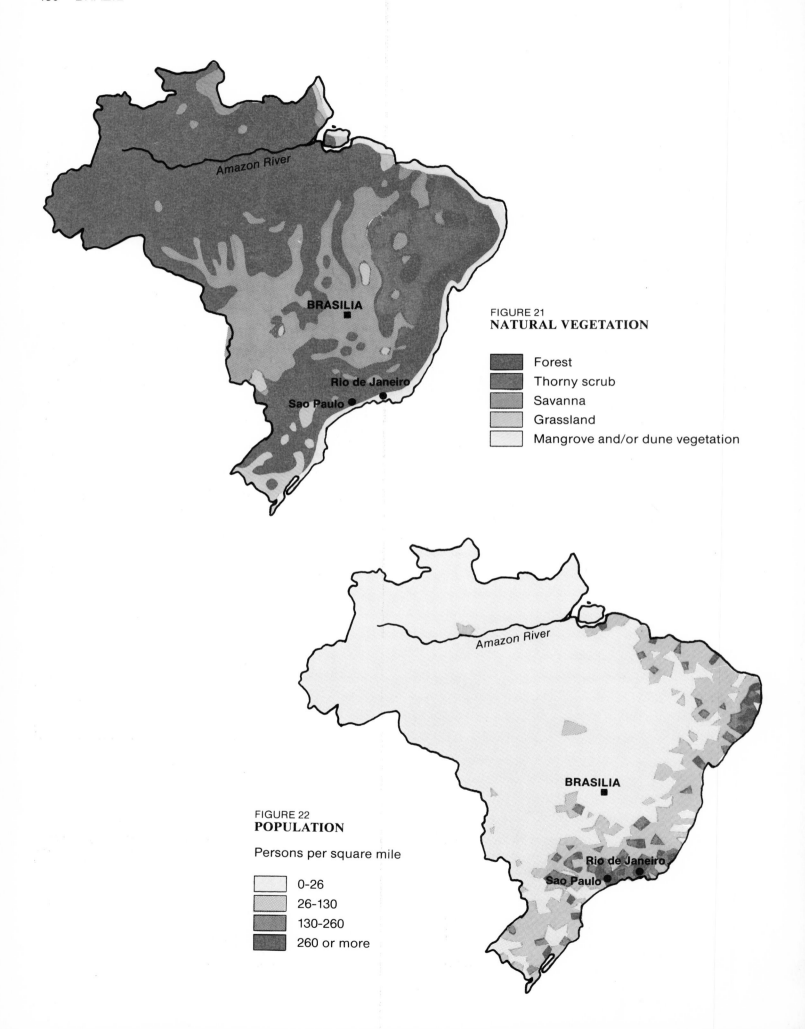

FIGURE 21
NATURAL VEGETATION

- Forest
- Thorny scrub
- Savanna
- Grassland
- Mangrove and/or dune vegetation

FIGURE 22
POPULATION

Persons per square mile

- 0-26
- 26-130
- 130-260
- 260 or more

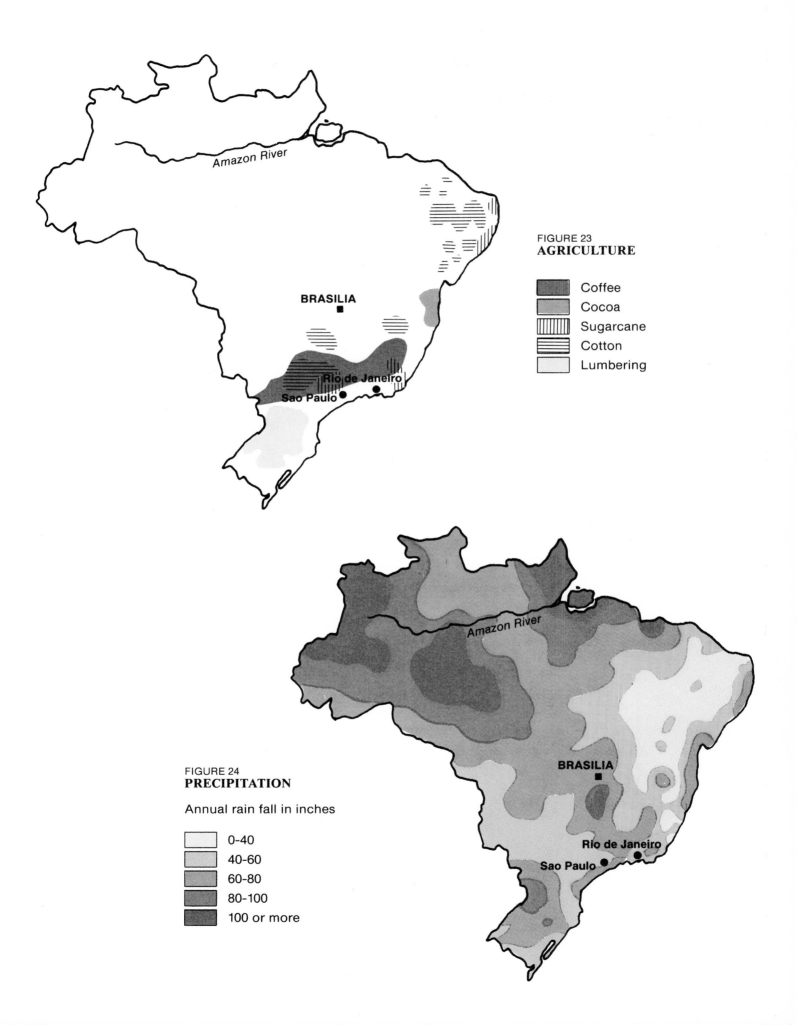

FIGURE 23
AGRICULTURE

Coffee
Cocoa
Sugarcane
Cotton
Lumbering

Amazon River

BRASILIA

Rio de Janeiro
Sao Paulo

FIGURE 24
PRECIPITATION

Annual rain fall in inches

0-40
40-60
60-80
80-100
100 or more

Amazon River

BRASILIA

Rio de Janeiro
Sao Paulo

BURMA

Burma, the largest country in mainland Southeast Asia, is the 37th largest country in the world and the 25th most populous. During the 1970s the population growth rate was curbed to 2.2% (down from 2.5% in the 1960s) while the GNP per capita growth rate rose to 2.0%, up from 0.9%. Much of this progress was achieved through three successive four-year plans which gave priority to agriculture, forestry and mining, rather than to industry. The economy is still primarily agricultural, and is dependent on rice cultivation, which accounts for 60% of the nation's export earnings. Another important component of the economy is the mineral and petroleum sector. Burma has also a substantial underground economy and a flourishing black market that supplies all foreign-made consumer goods at prices well above the official levels. Because of its ideological commitment to socialism, there has been no direct foreign investment in Burma since 1963 and even foreign borrowing was limited until the 1970s.

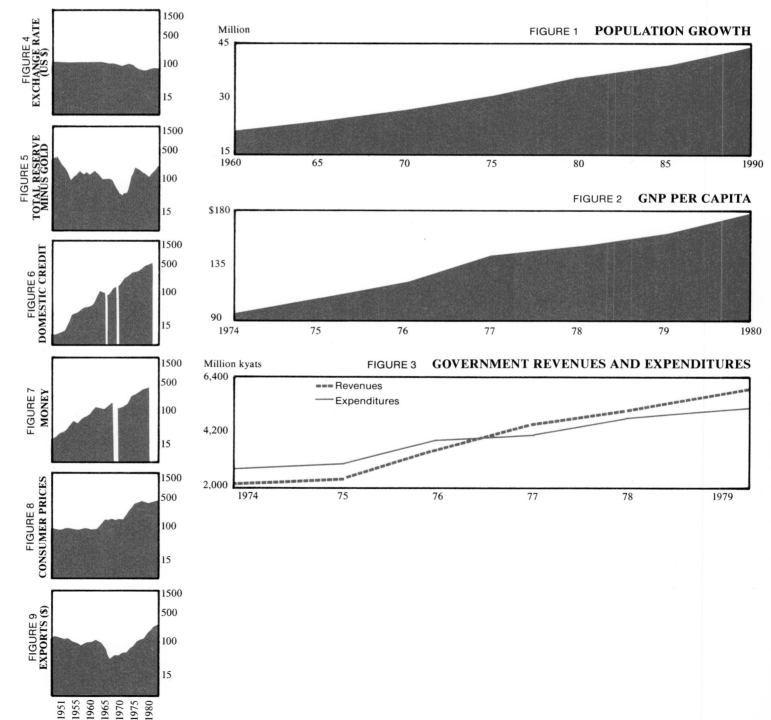

FIGURE 4 EXCHANGE RATE (US $)

FIGURE 5 TOTAL RESERVE MINUS GOLD

FIGURE 6 DOMESTIC CREDIT

FIGURE 7 MONEY

FIGURE 8 CONSUMER PRICES

FIGURE 9 EXPORTS ($)

FIGURE 1 **POPULATION GROWTH**

FIGURE 2 **GNP PER CAPITA**

FIGURE 3 **GOVERNMENT REVENUES AND EXPENDITURES**

Revenues
Expenditures

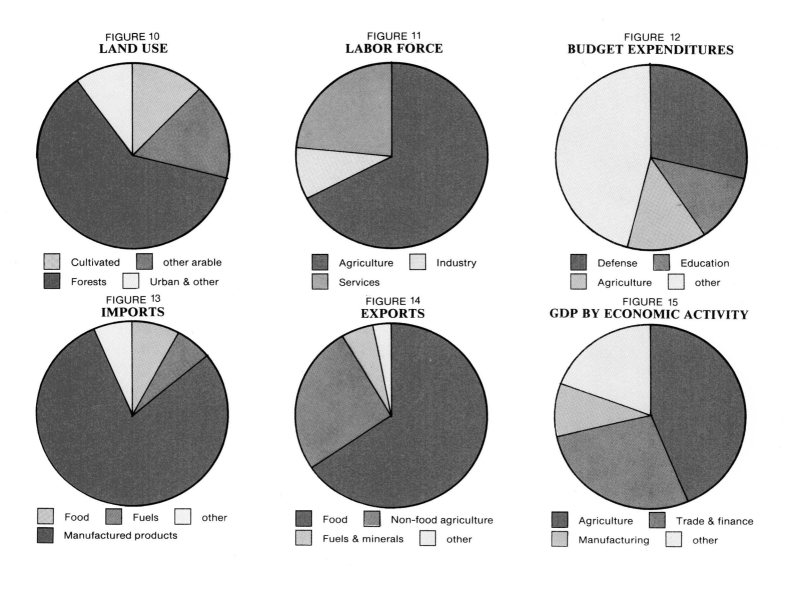

FIGURE 10
LAND USE

Cultivated   other arable
Forests   Urban & other

FIGURE 11
LABOR FORCE

Agriculture   Industry
Services

FIGURE 12
BUDGET EXPENDITURES

Defense   Education
Agriculture   other

FIGURE 13
IMPORTS

Food   Fuels   other
Manufactured products

FIGURE 14
EXPORTS

Food   Non-food agriculture
Fuels & minerals   other

FIGURE 15
GDP BY ECONOMIC ACTIVITY

Agriculture   Trade & finance
Manufacturing   other

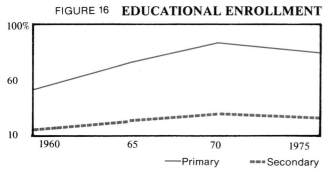

FIGURE 16   **EDUCATIONAL ENROLLMENT**

——Primary   ===Secondary

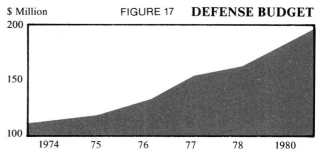

$ Million   FIGURE 17   **DEFENSE BUDGET**

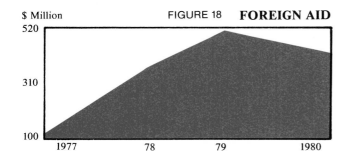

$ Million   FIGURE 18   **FOREIGN AID**

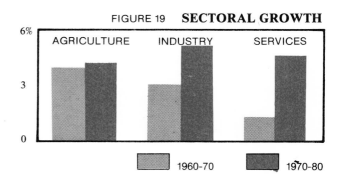

FIGURE 19   **SECTORAL GROWTH**

AGRICULTURE   INDUSTRY   SERVICES

1960-70   1970-80

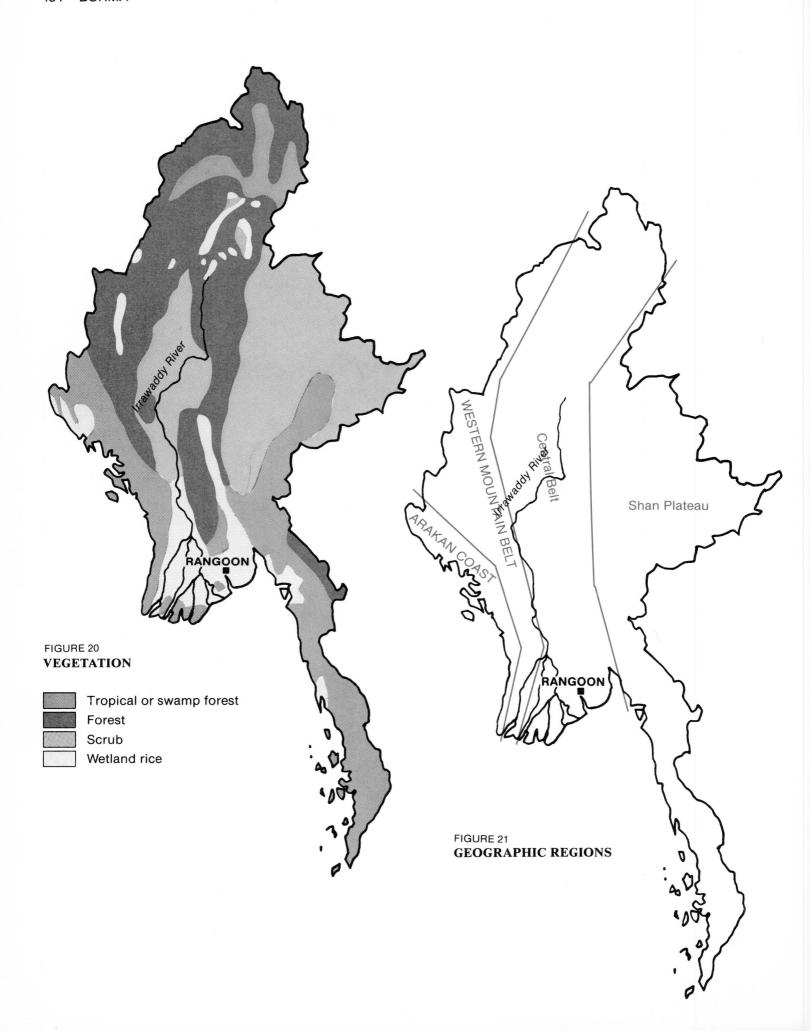

FIGURE 20
VEGETATION

- Tropical or swamp forest
- Forest
- Scrub
- Wetland rice

Irrawaddy River

RANGOON

FIGURE 21
GEOGRAPHIC REGIONS

ARAKAN COAST

WESTERN MOUNTAIN BELT

Irrawaddy River

Central Belt

Shan Plateau

RANGOON

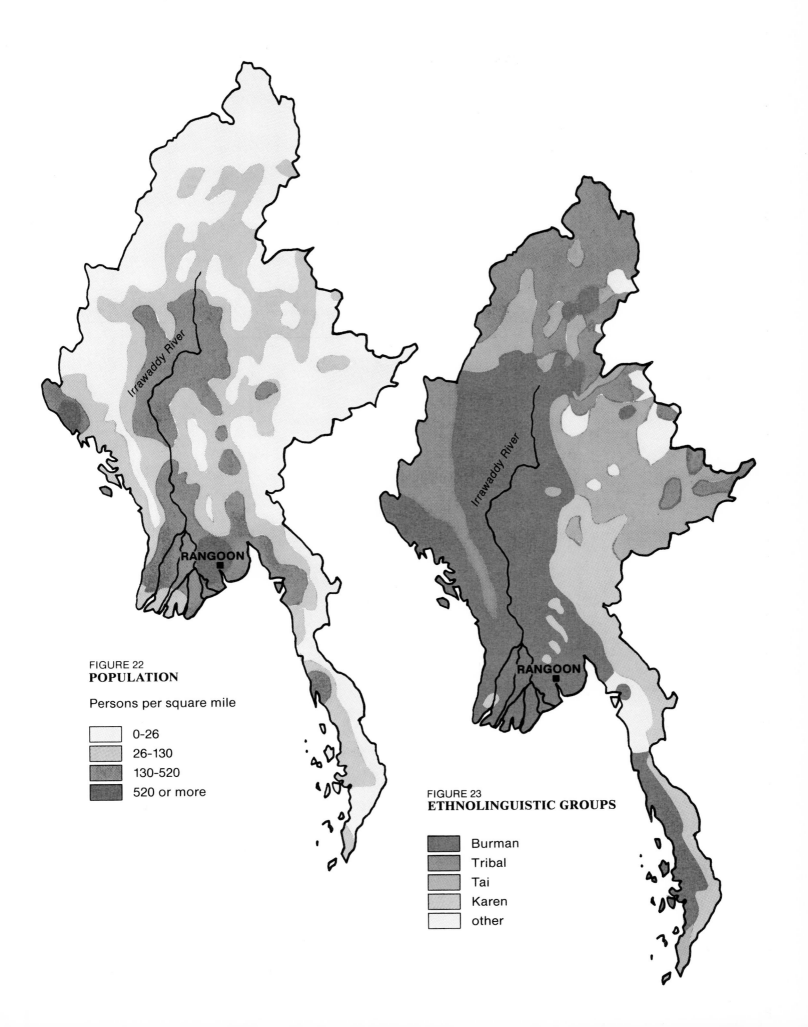

FIGURE 22
POPULATION

Persons per square mile

	0-26
	26-130
	130-520
	520 or more

FIGURE 23
ETHNOLINGUISTIC GROUPS

	Burman
	Tribal
	Tai
	Karen
	other

CAMBODIA

Cambodia, the smallest state in Southeast Asia, ranks 81st in land area and 64th in population. The severe disruptions following the Vietnamese takeover of the country have dried up even the small trickle of information that reached the West through unofficial channels. At present there is no means of determining the social condition or economic status of the country. Its annual population growth rate is modest compared to other countries of similar size in the developing world but this could be attributed to the decimation of the population through politically motivated massacres and forced relocation of urban populations and resulting starvation-deaths. A series of natural disasters (including flooding in the Mekong valley) and intensified internal insurgency combined to wipe out the economy. There is little prospect that Cambodia will again become what it once was—a productive land inhabited by a gentle and peaceful people.

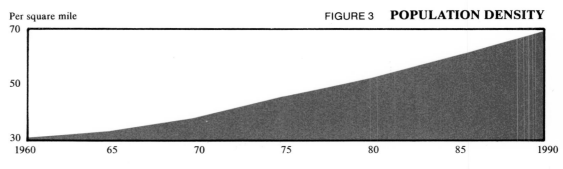

FIGURE 1 **POPULATION GROWTH**

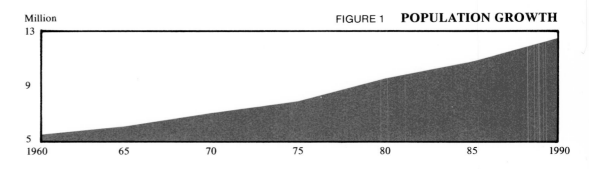

FIGURE 2 **URBANIZATION**

I.M.F.
DATA
UNAVAILABLE

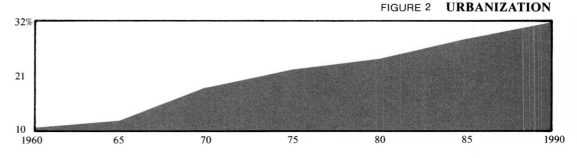

FIGURE 3 **POPULATION DENSITY**

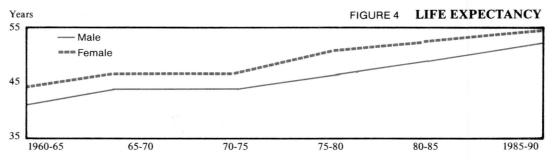

FIGURE 4 **LIFE EXPECTANCY**

Male
Female

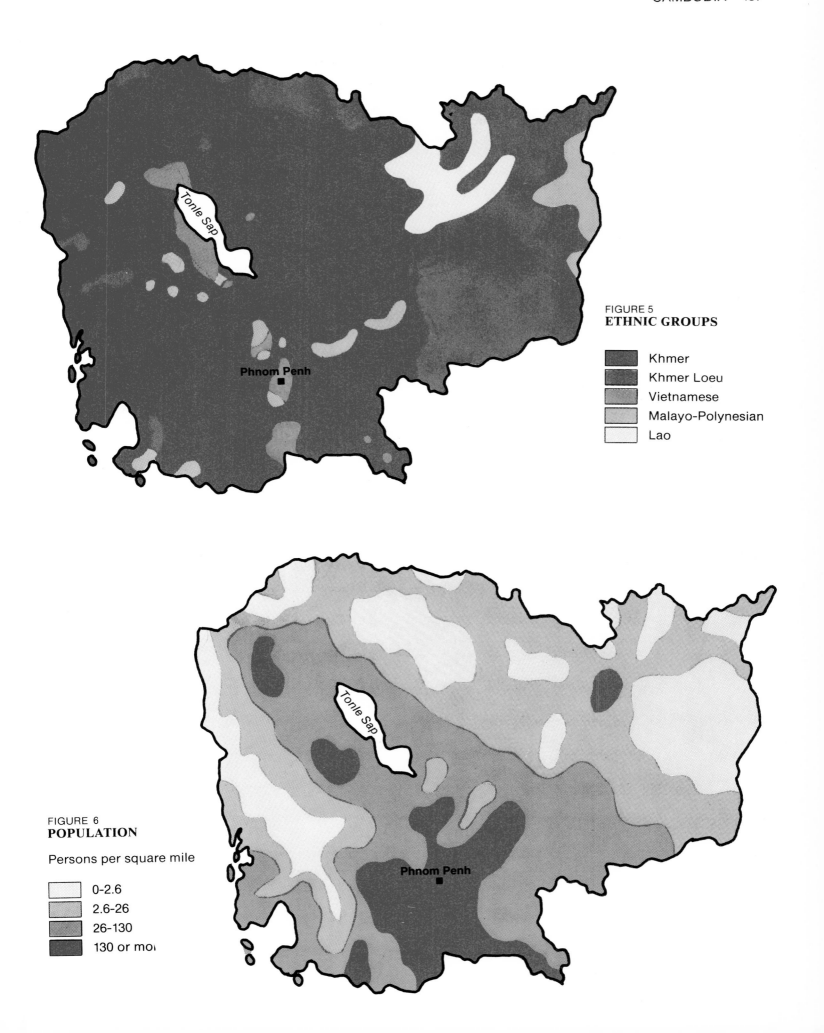

FIGURE 5
ETHNIC GROUPS

- Khmer
- Khmer Loeu
- Vietnamese
- Malayo-Polynesian
- Lao

Tonle Sap

Phnom Penh

FIGURE 6
POPULATION

Persons per square mile

- 0-2.6
- 2.6-26
- 26-130
- 130 or more

Tonle Sap

Phnom Penh

CAMEROON

Located on the western part of the waist of the African continent, Cameroon ranks 47th in land area and 73rd in population. The country's main distinctions are its political stability (since independence it has had only two presidents and its history is unmarred by coups or rebellions) and the fact that it is the only African country where both French and English are accorded official status. Cameroon has a very diverse ethnic configuration even by African standards, with over 200 tribes speaking 24 major African languages. The mainstay of the economy is agriculture, which employs 80% of the labor force and accounts for 70% of export earnings. The main cash crop is cocoa. Other major exports include coffee, timber, wool, aluminum ingots, cotton, rubber, peanuts, tobacco and tea. Offshore production of petroleum is expected to enable Cameroon to meet its domestic oil needs by the mid-1980s.

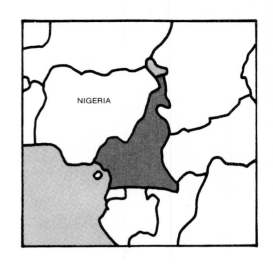

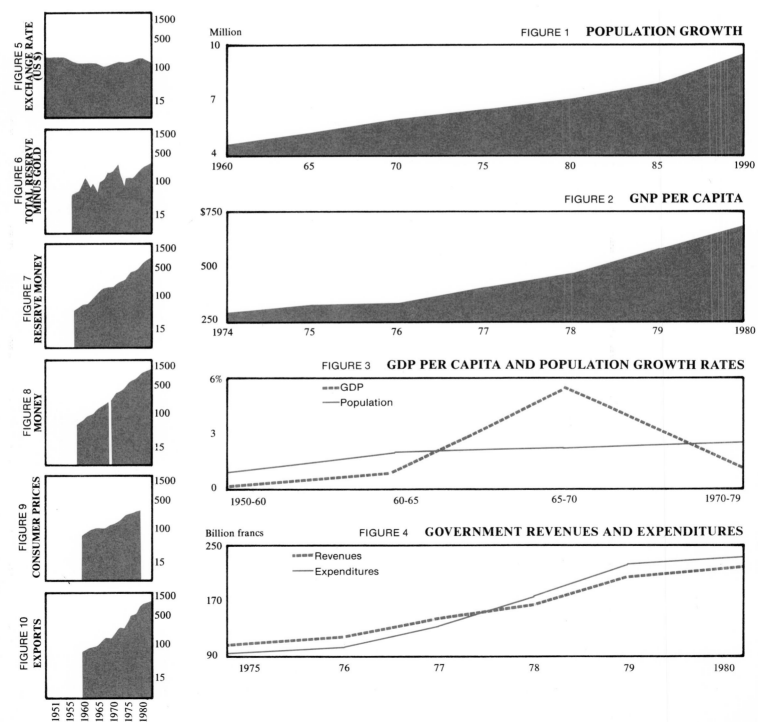

FIGURE 5 EXCHANGE RATE (US $)

FIGURE 6 TOTAL RESERVE MINUS GOLD

FIGURE 7 RESERVE MONEY

FIGURE 8 MONEY

FIGURE 9 CONSUMER PRICES

FIGURE 10 EXPORTS

FIGURE 1 **POPULATION GROWTH**

FIGURE 2 **GNP PER CAPITA**

FIGURE 3 **GDP PER CAPITA AND POPULATION GROWTH RATES**

FIGURE 4 **GOVERNMENT REVENUES AND EXPENDITURES**

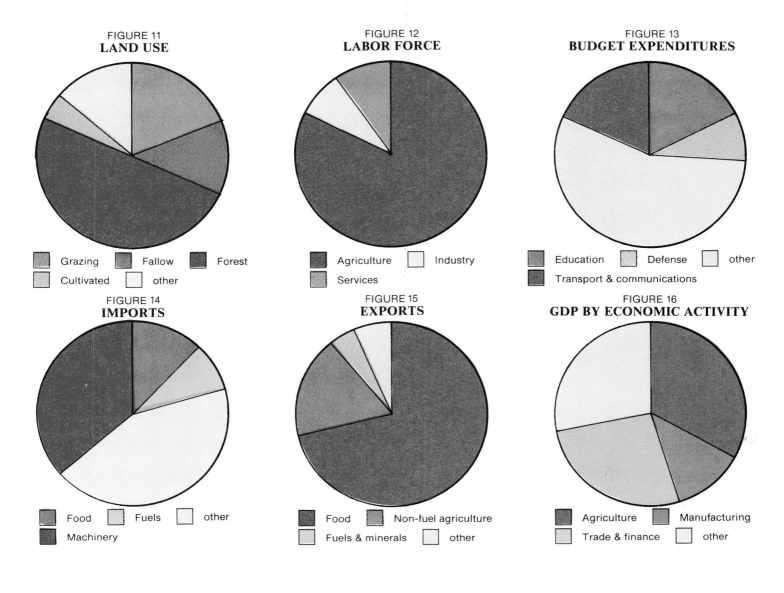

FIGURE 11
LAND USE

Grazing   Fallow   Forest
Cultivated   other

FIGURE 12
LABOR FORCE

Agriculture   Industry
Services

FIGURE 13
BUDGET EXPENDITURES

Education   Defense   other
Transport & communications

FIGURE 14
IMPORTS

Food   Fuels   other
Machinery

FIGURE 15
EXPORTS

Food   Non-fuel agriculture
Fuels & minerals   other

FIGURE 16
GDP BY ECONOMIC ACTIVITY

Agriculture   Manufacturing
Trade & finance   other

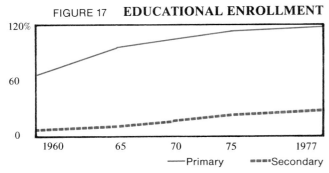

FIGURE 17   **EDUCATIONAL ENROLLMENT**

120%

60

0

1960   65   70   75   1977

——Primary   ■■■■Secondary

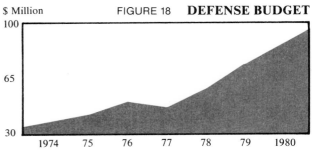

$ Million   FIGURE 18   **DEFENSE BUDGET**

100

65

30

1974   75   76   77   78   79   1980

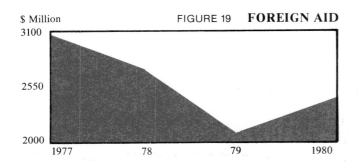

$ Million   FIGURE 19   **FOREIGN AID**

3100

2550

2000

1977   78   79   1980

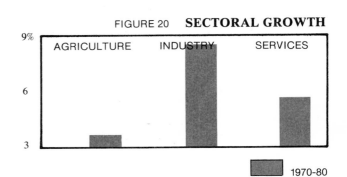

FIGURE 20   **SECTORAL GROWTH**

9%

AGRICULTURE   INDUSTRY   SERVICES

6

3

1970-80

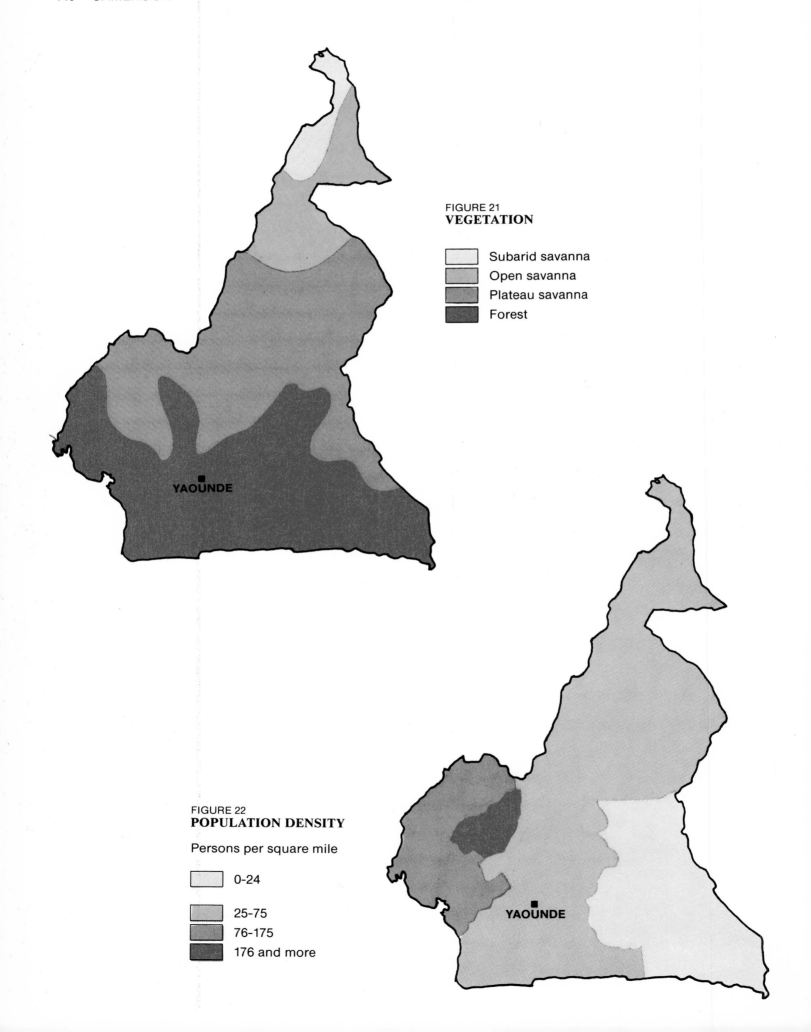

FIGURE 21
VEGETATION

Subarid savanna
Open savanna
Plateau savanna
Forest

FIGURE 22
POPULATION DENSITY

Persons per square mile

0-24

25-75
76-175
176 and more

YAOUNDE

YAOUNDE

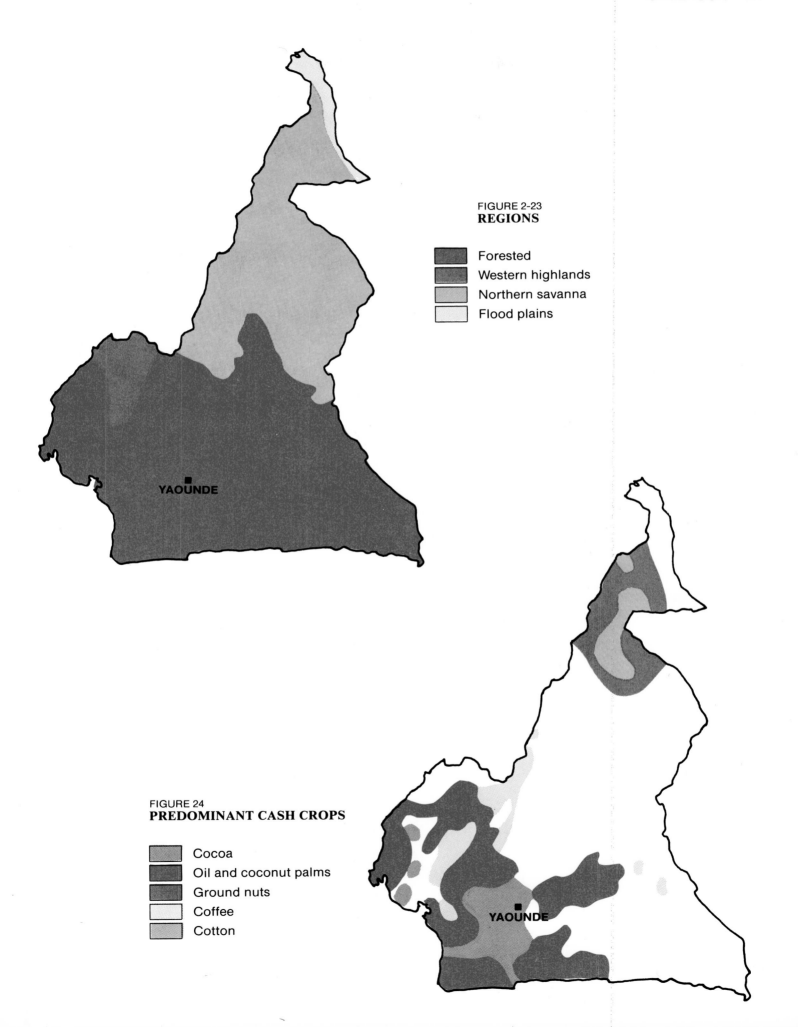

FIGURE 2-23
REGIONS

- Forested
- Western highlands
- Northern savanna
- Flood plains

YAOUNDE

FIGURE 24
PREDOMINANT CASH CROPS

- Cocoa
- Oil and coconut palms
- Ground nuts
- Coffee
- Cotton

YAOUNDE

CHAD

Chad, the largest among the countries of former French Equatorial Africa, ranks 18th in land area and 91st in population. The recent civil war and subsequent Libyan occupation of the country have retarded its economic and political growth to the point where conditions of anarchy and chaos prevail in many areas. Once the leading cotton producer in francophone Africa, its output has steadily dropped since 1975-76 when it produced a record high of 174,000 tons. The central government has only nominal control over the northern zone, an extension of the Sahara Desert, whose nomadic people consider themselves as having nothing in common with the southerners. In addition to political instability, Chad has substantial barriers to economic growth, not the least of which is its total lack of transportation facilities. It has no outlet to the sea, no railroads, little paved road mileage (what roads exist are nearly impassable in the rainy season) and little river shipping.

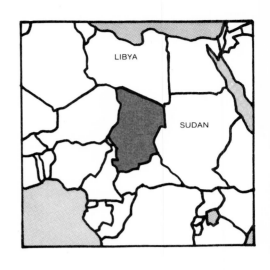

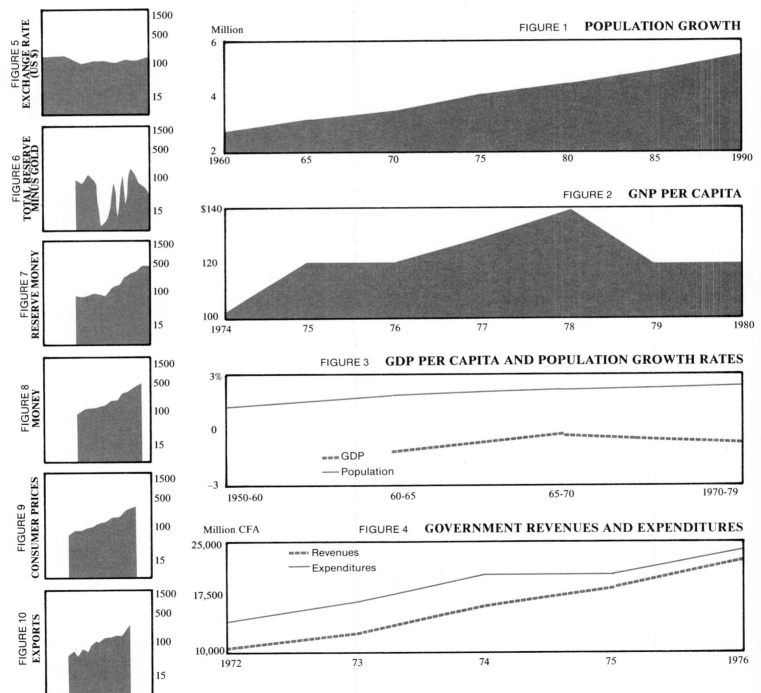

FIGURE 5 — EXCHANGE RATE (US $)

FIGURE 6 — TOTAL RESERVE MINUS GOLD

FIGURE 7 — RESERVE MONEY

FIGURE 8 — MONEY

FIGURE 9 — CONSUMER PRICES

FIGURE 10 — EXPORTS

FIGURE 1 — **POPULATION GROWTH**

FIGURE 2 — **GNP PER CAPITA**

FIGURE 3 — **GDP PER CAPITA AND POPULATION GROWTH RATES**

FIGURE 4 — **GOVERNMENT REVENUES AND EXPENDITURES**

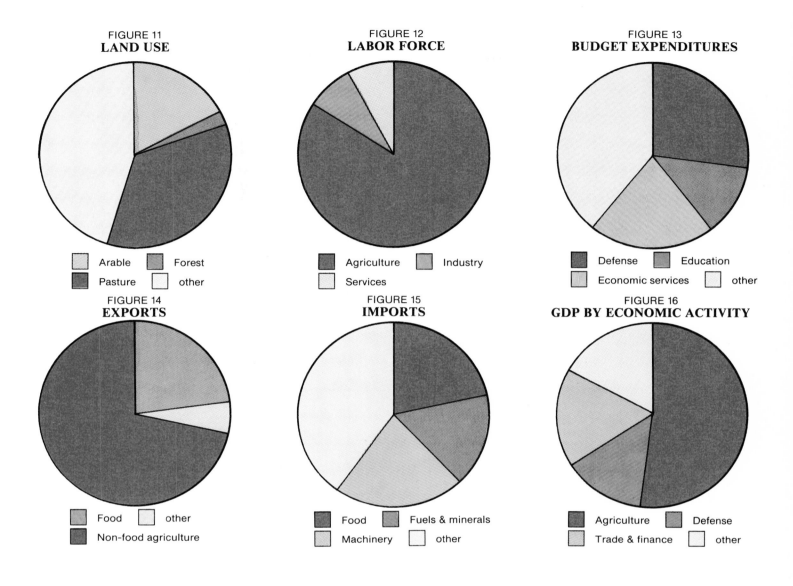

FIGURE 11
LAND USE

Arable
Pasture
Forest
other

FIGURE 12
LABOR FORCE

Agriculture
Services
Industry

FIGURE 13
BUDGET EXPENDITURES

Defense
Economic services
Education
other

FIGURE 14
EXPORTS

Food
Non-food agriculture
other

FIGURE 15
IMPORTS

Food
Machinery
Fuels & minerals
other

FIGURE 16
GDP BY ECONOMIC ACTIVITY

Agriculture
Trade & finance
Defense
other

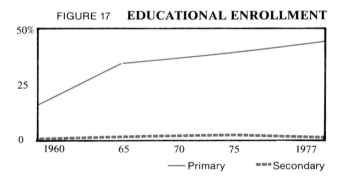

FIGURE 17 **EDUCATIONAL ENROLLMENT**

50%

25

0

1960   65   70   75   1977

—— Primary   ▬▬▬ Secondary

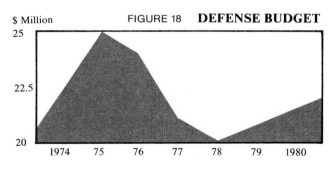

$ Million   FIGURE 18 **DEFENSE BUDGET**

25

22.5

20

1974   75   76   77   78   79   1980

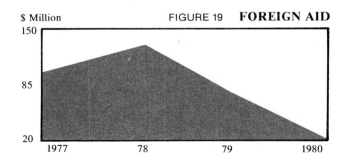

$ Million   FIGURE 19 **FOREIGN AID**

150

85

20

1977   78   79   1980

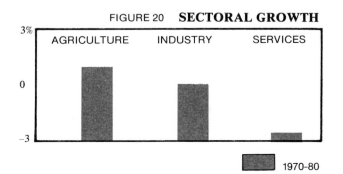

FIGURE 20 **SECTORAL GROWTH**

3%   AGRICULTURE   INDUSTRY   SERVICES

0

-3

1970-80

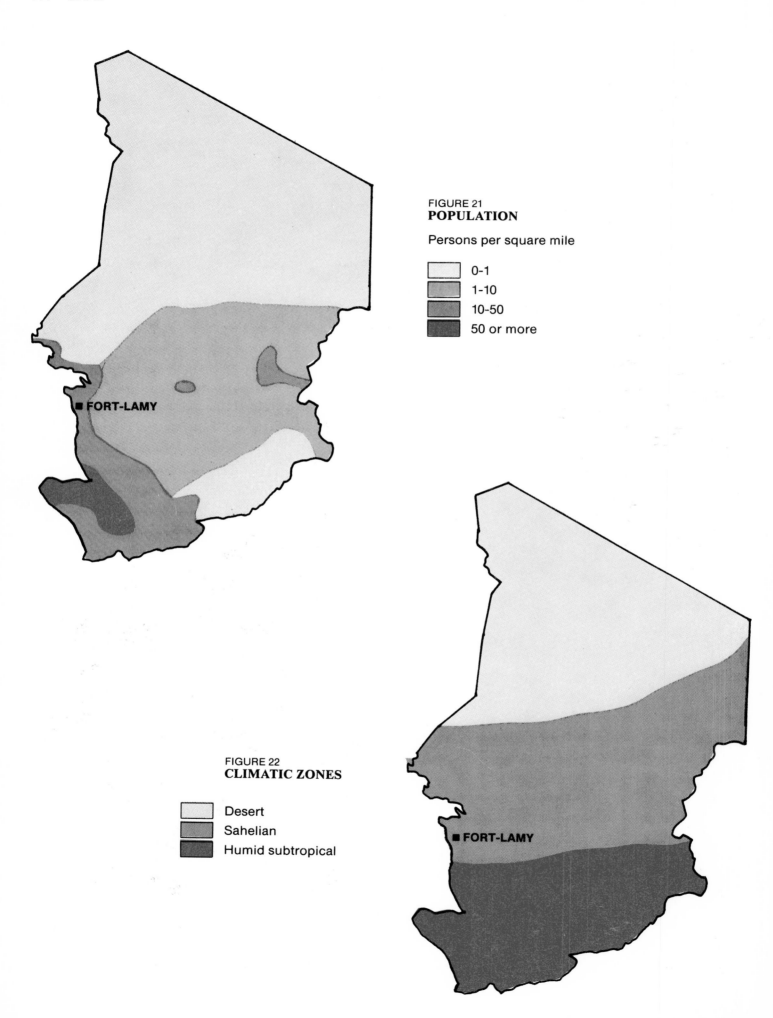

FIGURE 21
POPULATION

Persons per square mile

0-1
1-10
10-50
50 or more

FIGURE 22
CLIMATIC ZONES

Desert
Sahelian
Humid subtropical

FORT-LAMY

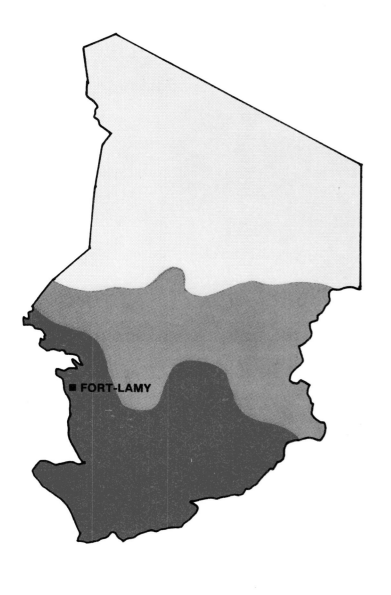

FIGURE 23
AGRICULTURE

- Subsistence crops (millet, sorghum, rice, peanuts
- Grazing
- Non-agricultural with some nomadic herding

■ **FORT-LAMY**

FIGURE 24
ETHNIC GROUPS AND TRIBES

- Muslim
- Animist-Christian

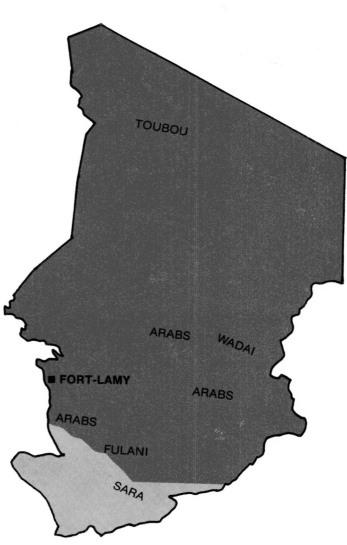

TOUBOU

ARABS   WADAI

■ **FORT-LAMY**

ARABS

ARABS

FULANI

SARA

CHILE

A country that is shaped like a narrow, pointed stake, extending 2,700 miles along the southwest coast of South America, Chile ranks 35th in land area and 54th in population. Over 70% of the population live in urban centers and more than one-third of the inhabitants are concentrated in and around Santiago and Valparaiso. Compared to other Latin American countries, Chile enjoys many significant advantages. Because of its geographical and cultural isolation, the population is extremely homogeneous. The country also has one of the highest literacy rates in Latin America at 85%. Despite these advantages the Chilean economy has been reeling for years under the highest inflation rate in the world. Based on 1970 = 100, the wholesale price index rose in the late 1970s to an astronomical 258,663. The reason for Chile's poor economic performance is partly the decline in agricultural output and partly the disastrous price controls and redistributive programs of the Salvador Allende regime.

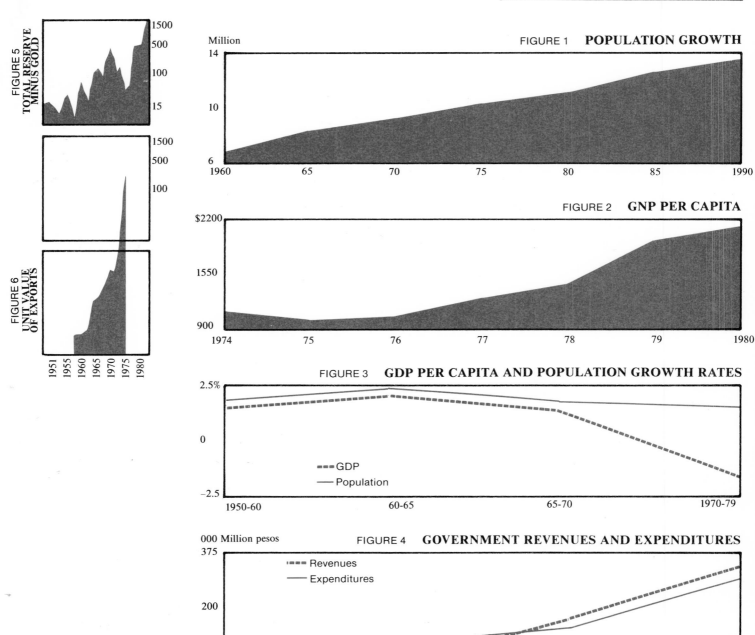

FIGURE 5 TOTAL RESERVE MINUS GOLD

FIGURE 6 UNIT VALUE OF EXPORTS

FIGURE 1 **POPULATION GROWTH**

FIGURE 2 **GNP PER CAPITA**

FIGURE 3 **GDP PER CAPITA AND POPULATION GROWTH RATES**

FIGURE 4 **GOVERNMENT REVENUES AND EXPENDITURES**

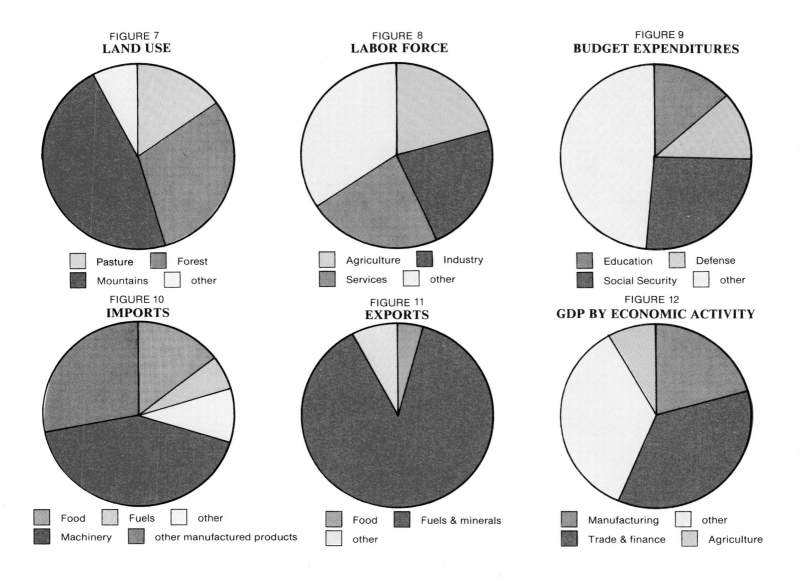

FIGURE 7
LAND USE

Pasture — Forest
Mountains — other

FIGURE 8
LABOR FORCE

Agriculture — Industry
Services — other

FIGURE 9
BUDGET EXPENDITURES

Education — Defense
Social Security — other

FIGURE 10
IMPORTS

Food — Fuels — other
Machinery — other manufactured products

FIGURE 11
EXPORTS

Food — Fuels & minerals
other

FIGURE 12
GDP BY ECONOMIC ACTIVITY

Manufacturing — other
Trade & finance — Agriculture

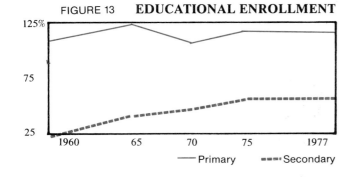

FIGURE 13   **EDUCATIONAL ENROLLMENT**

125%

75

25
1960   65   70   75   1977

—— Primary   ---- Secondary

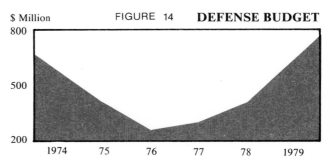

$ Million   FIGURE 14   **DEFENSE BUDGET**

800

500

200
1974   75   76   77   78   1979

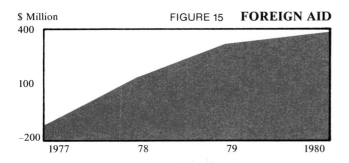

$ Million   FIGURE 15   **FOREIGN AID**

400

100

-200
1977   78   79   1980

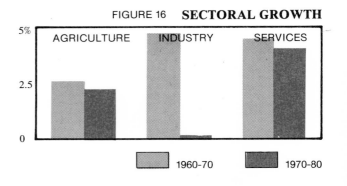

FIGURE 16   **SECTORAL GROWTH**

5%   AGRICULTURE   INDUSTRY   SERVICES

2.5

0

1960-70   1970-80

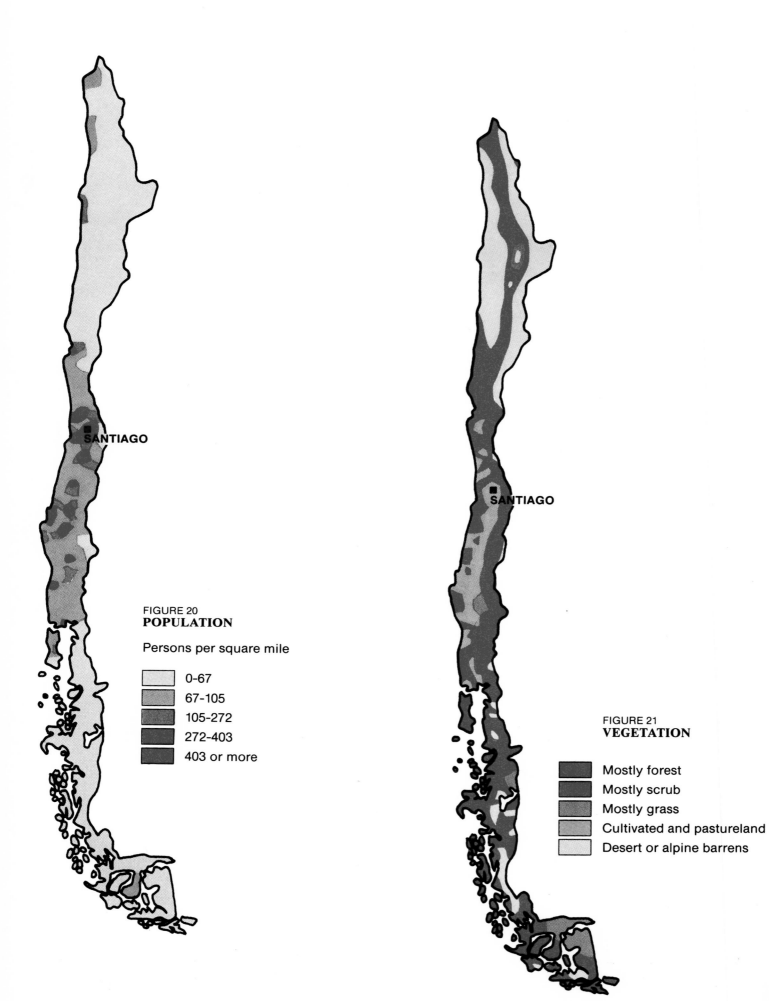

FIGURE 20
POPULATION

Persons per square mile

- 0-67
- 67-105
- 105-272
- 272-403
- 403 or more

SANTIAGO

FIGURE 21
VEGETATION

- Mostly forest
- Mostly scrub
- Mostly grass
- Cultivated and pastureland
- Desert or alpine barrens

SANTIAGO

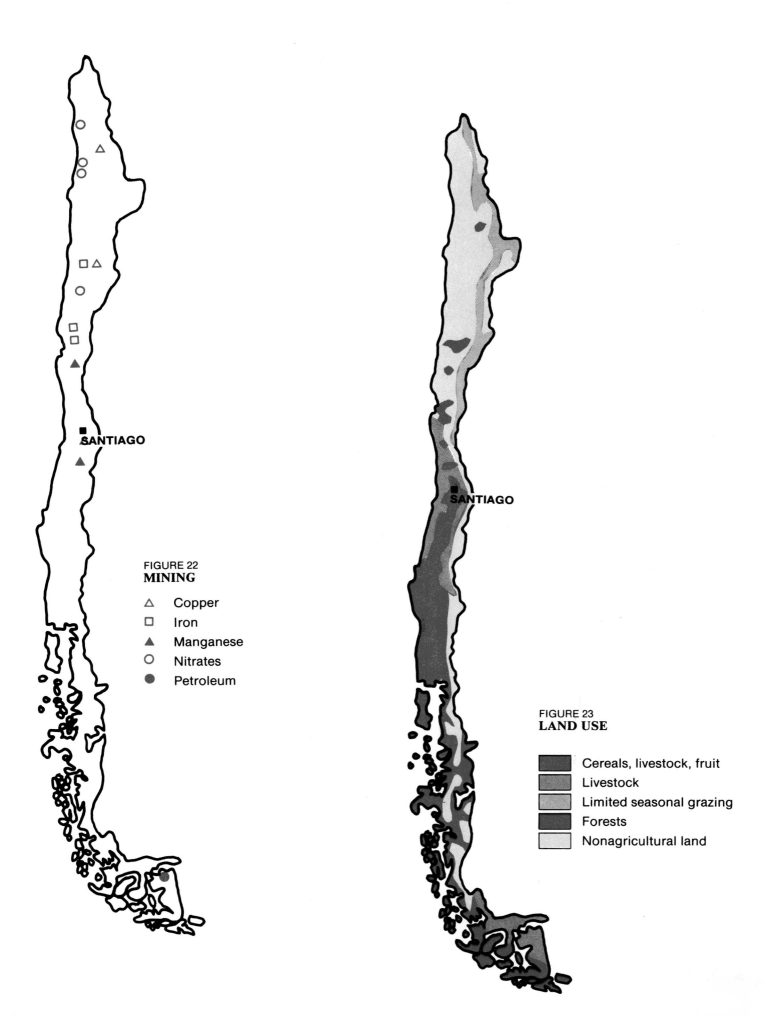

FIGURE 22
MINING

△ Copper
□ Iron
▲ Manganese
○ Nitrates
● Petroleum

SANTIAGO

SANTIAGO

FIGURE 23
LAND USE

Cereals, livestock, fruit
Livestock
Limited seasonal grazing
Forests
Nonagricultural land

COLOMBIA

The fourth most populous as well as the fourth largest country in South America, Colombia ranks 24th in land area and 27th in population in the world. As all coffee lovers know, Colombia is the world's second largest producer and exporter of coffee and coffee earnings constitute 30% of the GDP. The economy is predominantly agricultural; agriculture contributes over one-third of the GNP and employs one-half of the labor force. Colombia is also an important producer of cocoa. The country is rich in minerals and its 18 million tons of known coal reserves are the largest in Latin America. It is also the source of 90% of the world's emeralds. More recently, the country has gained some notoriety as the source of 70% of illegal drugs consumed in North America; drug-related income is estimated at $600 million annually. Despite a high rate of inflation and a 30% growth in money supply, the Colombian economy has maintained a steady rate of expansion.

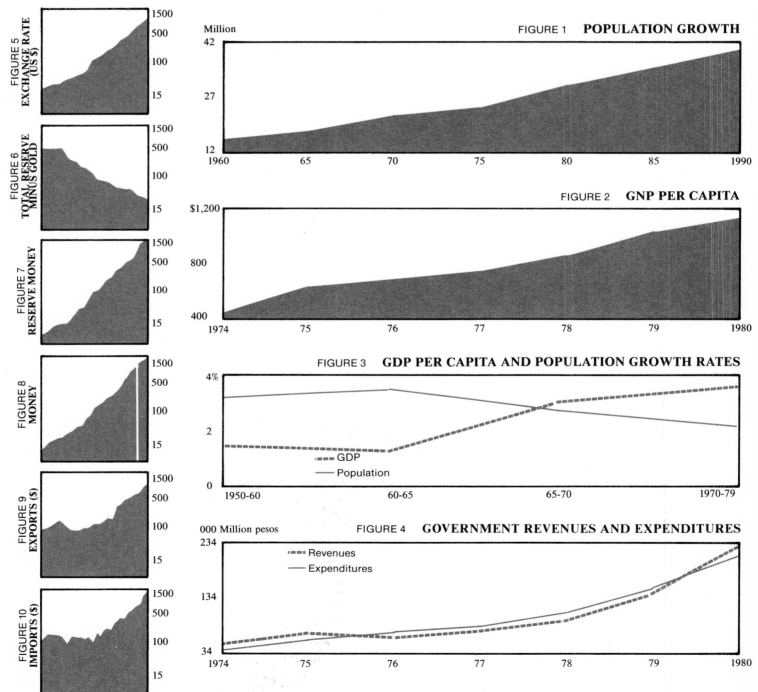

FIGURE 5 EXCHANGE RATE (US $)

FIGURE 6 TOTAL RESERVE MINUS GOLD

FIGURE 7 RESERVE MONEY

FIGURE 8 MONEY

FIGURE 9 EXPORTS ($)

FIGURE 10 IMPORTS ($)

FIGURE 1 **POPULATION GROWTH**

FIGURE 2 **GNP PER CAPITA**

FIGURE 3 **GDP PER CAPITA AND POPULATION GROWTH RATES**

GDP
Population

FIGURE 4 **GOVERNMENT REVENUES AND EXPENDITURES**

Revenues
Expenditures

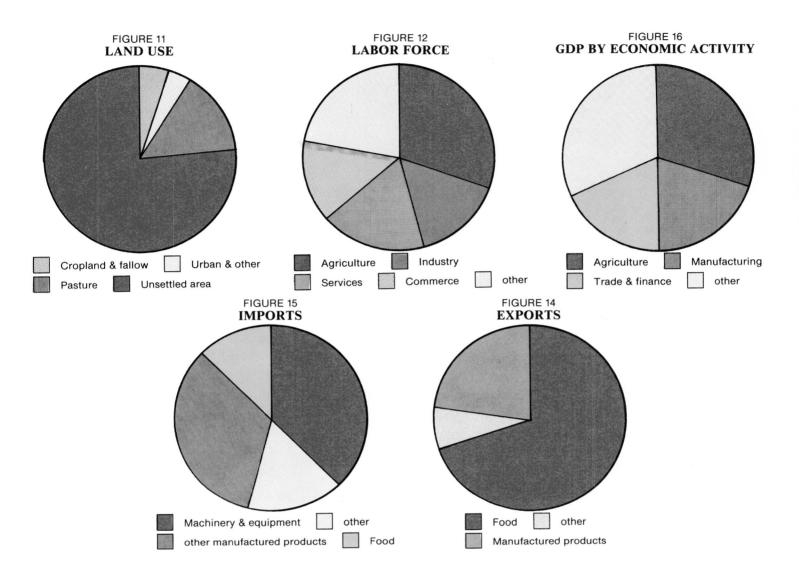

FIGURE 11
LAND USE

Cropland & fallow
Urban & other
Pasture
Unsettled area

FIGURE 12
LABOR FORCE

Agriculture
Industry
Services
Commerce
other

FIGURE 16
GDP BY ECONOMIC ACTIVITY

Agriculture
Manufacturing
Trade & finance
other

FIGURE 15
IMPORTS

Machinery & equipment
other
other manufactured products
Food

FIGURE 14
EXPORTS

Food
other
Manufactured products

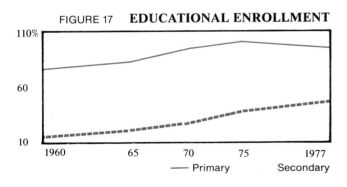

FIGURE 17   **EDUCATIONAL ENROLLMENT**

110%

60

10

1960   65   70   75   1977

— Primary   Secondary

$ Million   FIGURE 18   **DEFENSE BUDGET**

225

125

25

1974   75   76   77   78   79   1980

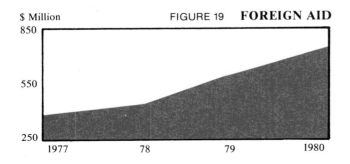

$ Million   FIGURE 19   **FOREIGN AID**

850

550

250

1977   78   79   1980

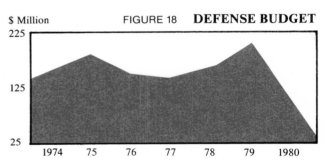

FIGURE 20   **SECTORAL GROWTH**

7%

AGRICULTURE   INDUSTRY   SERVICES

5

3

1960-70   1970-80

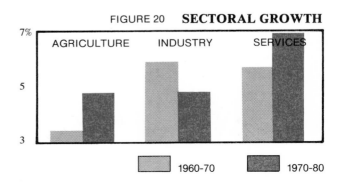

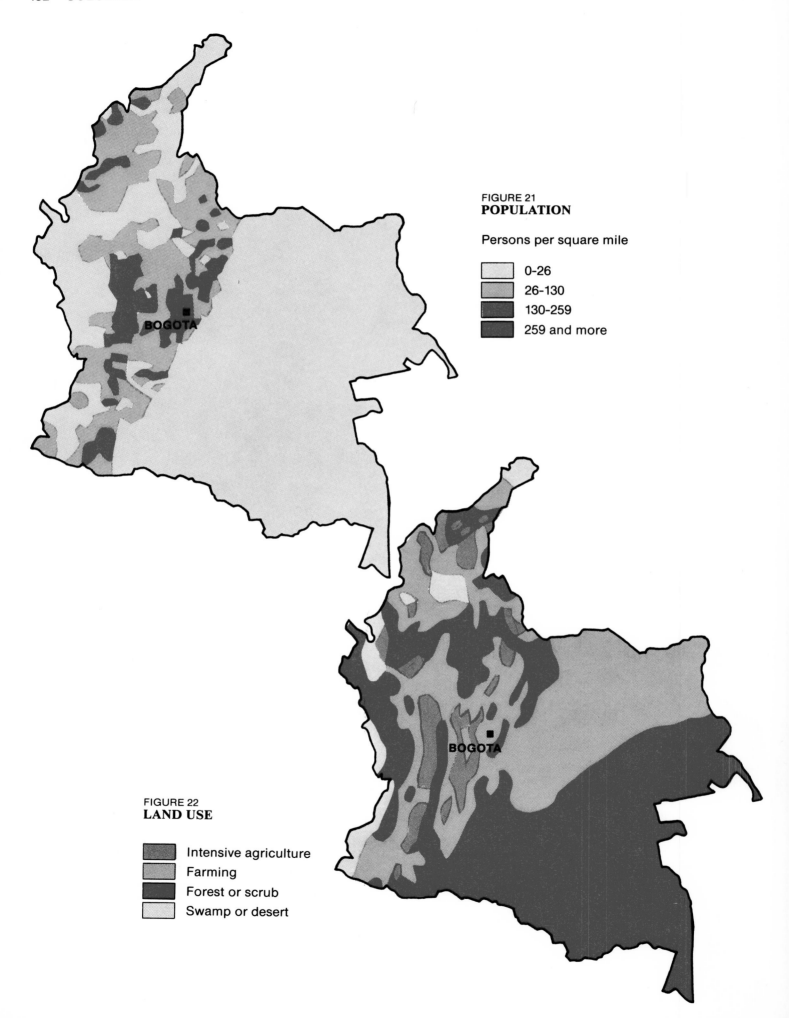

FIGURE 21
POPULATION

Persons per square mile

- 0-26
- 26-130
- 130-259
- 259 and more

BOGOTA

FIGURE 22
LAND USE

- Intensive agriculture
- Farming
- Forest or scrub
- Swamp or desert

BOGOTA

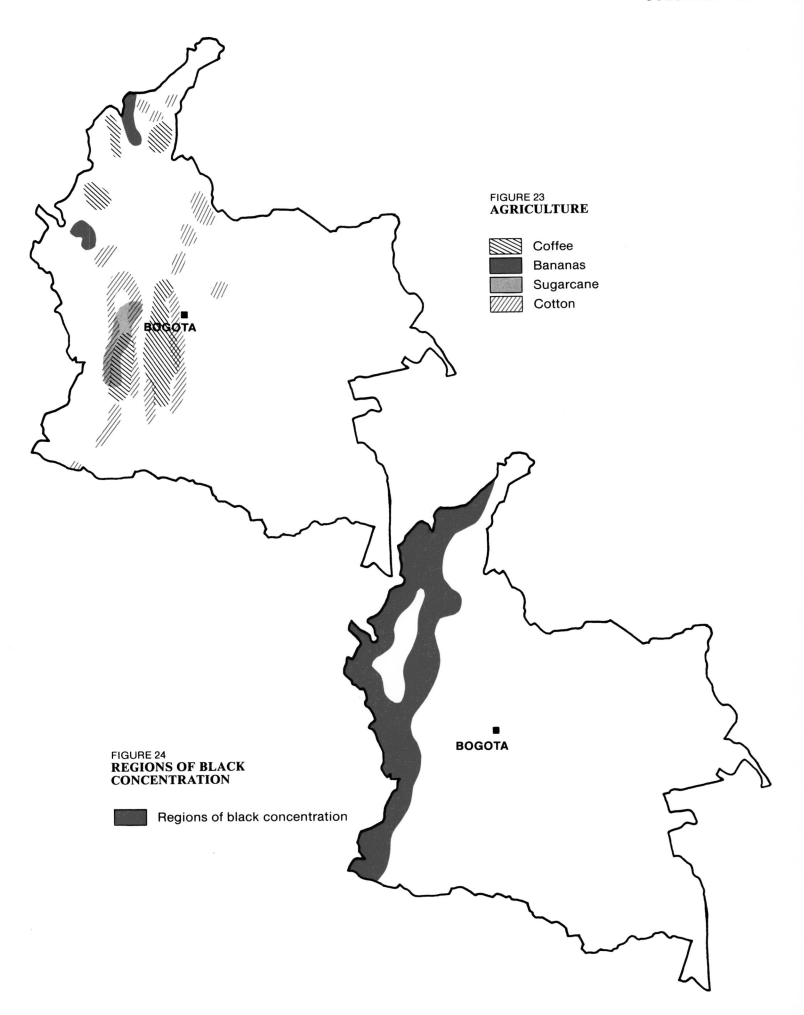

FIGURE 23
AGRICULTURE

Coffee
Bananas
Sugarcane
Cotton

BOGOTA

FIGURE 24
**REGIONS OF BLACK
CONCENTRATION**

Regions of black concentration

BOGOTA

CONGO

Located on the Equator in west-central Africa, Congo ranks 121st in land area and 126th in population. With a per capita income of $730, Congo is one of the few African countries that has managed to reach the lower middle-income level, perhaps because of its rich natural resources, low population density, high degree of urbanization, and high literacy. It is also the first Marxist African republic and in accordance with its official ideology state-owned enterprises play a major part in the economy. Congo is also a major transportation hub for western Africa with the Zaire and Ubangi rivers as key waterways serving the Brazzaville port. In addition, a railroad links the port of Point-Noire on the Atlantic with Brazzaville and Gabon. As a result of falling demand for oil and wood, the economy suffered severe reverses in the late 1970s, and its external public debt reached 50% of GNP. Recovery has been slow and erratic and many capital projects have been curtailed or abandoned as a result.

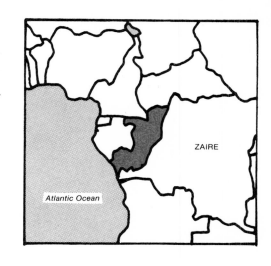

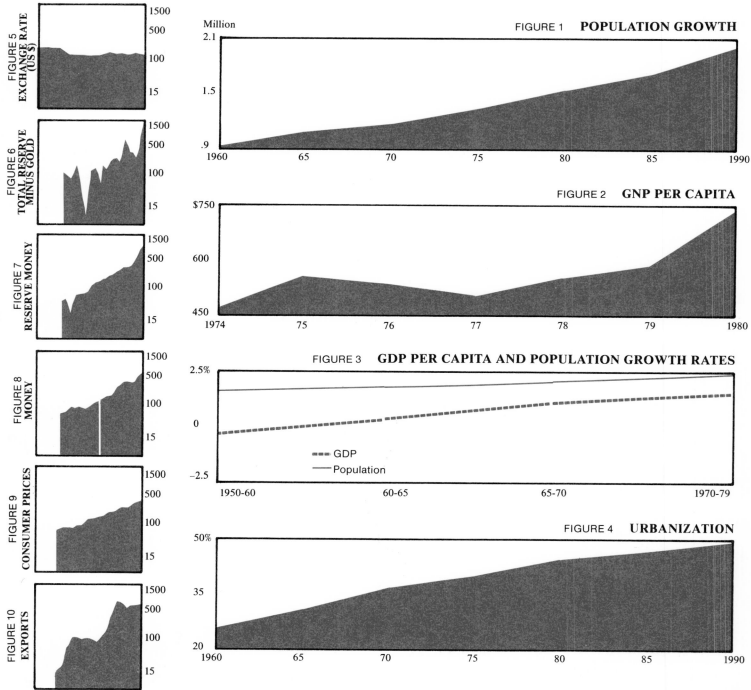

FIGURE 5 EXCHANGE RATE (US $)

FIGURE 6 TOTAL RESERVE MINUS GOLD

FIGURE 7 RESERVE MONEY

FIGURE 8 MONEY

FIGURE 9 CONSUMER PRICES

FIGURE 10 EXPORTS

FIGURE 1 **POPULATION GROWTH**

FIGURE 2 **GNP PER CAPITA**

FIGURE 3 **GDP PER CAPITA AND POPULATION GROWTH RATES**

FIGURE 4 **URBANIZATION**

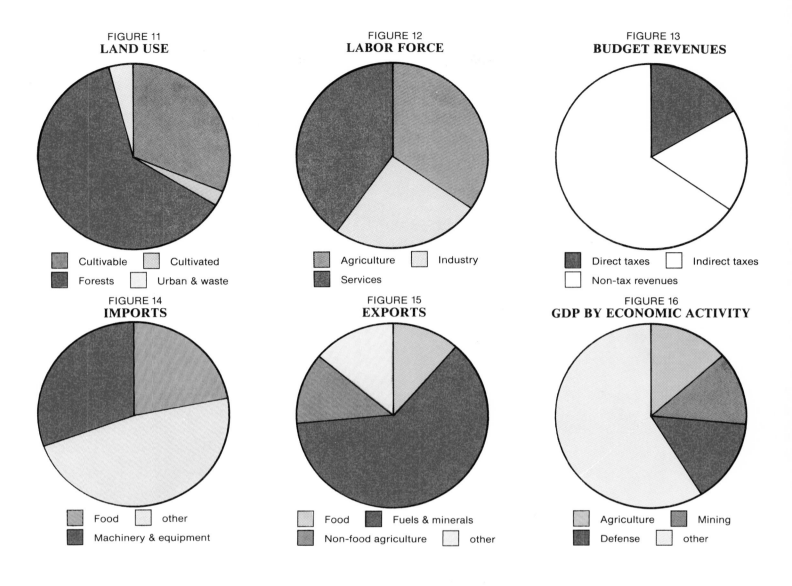

FIGURE 11
LAND USE

Cultivable
Cultivated
Forests
Urban & waste

FIGURE 12
LABOR FORCE

Agriculture
Industry
Services

FIGURE 13
BUDGET REVENUES

Direct taxes
Indirect taxes
Non-tax revenues

FIGURE 14
IMPORTS

Food
other
Machinery & equipment

FIGURE 15
EXPORTS

Food
Fuels & minerals
Non-food agriculture
other

FIGURE 16
GDP BY ECONOMIC ACTIVITY

Agriculture
Mining
Defense
other

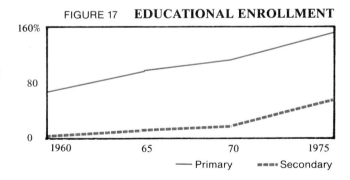

FIGURE 17   **EDUCATIONAL ENROLLMENT**

160%

80

0

1960   65   70   1975

—— Primary   ===== Secondary

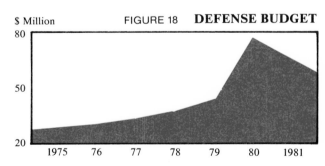

$ Million   FIGURE 18   **DEFENSE BUDGET**

80

50

20

1975   76   77   78   79   80   1981

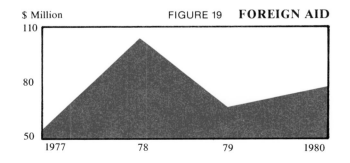

$ Million   FIGURE 19   **FOREIGN AID**

110

80

50

1977   78   79   1980

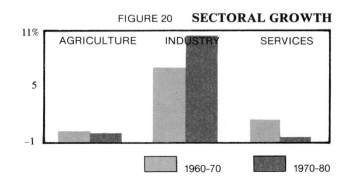

FIGURE 20   **SECTORAL GROWTH**

11%   AGRICULTURE   INDUSTRY   SERVICES

5

-1

1960-70   1970-80

COSTA RICA

The second smallest Central American republic, Costa Rica ranks 113th in land area and 117th in population. With a per capita income of $1,730 it is one of the 35 upper middle-income countries. Its main distinctions are that it is politically one of the most stable countries in Latin America, that it does not maintain a standing army and that it has a literacy rate of over 90%. Not only does Costa Rica have the highest per capita GNP in the region, but the national income is more evenly distributed than among its neighbors. This relatively equitable income distribution is one of the durable results of the Revolution of 1948 when the state became the dominant economic force. By the late 1970s industry and commerce had surpassed agriculture in their contribution to the GDP. At the same time, spiraling inflation and resulting demands for substantial wage increases by workers forced the government to adopt a broad stabilization program emphasizing monetary and fiscal restraint.

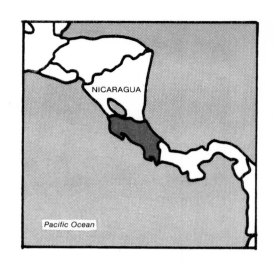

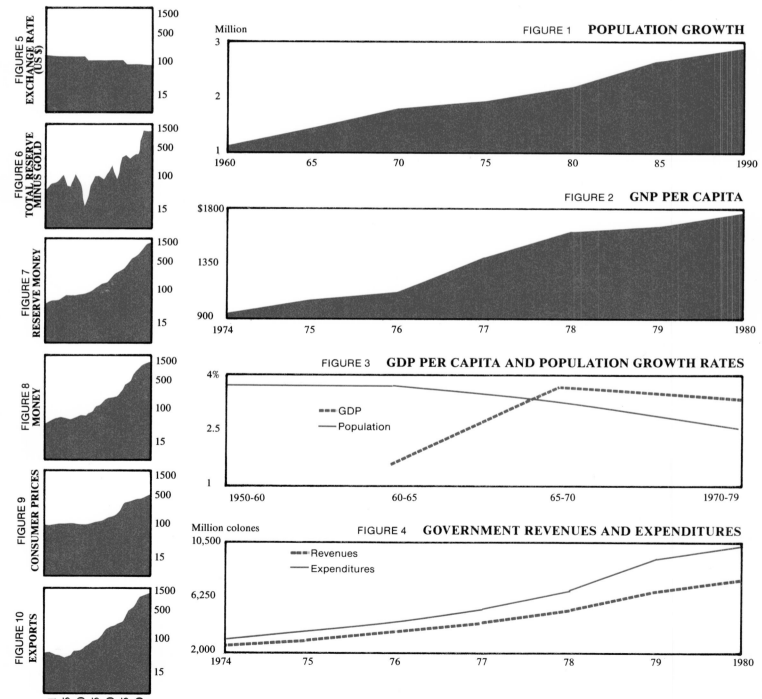

FIGURE 5 EXCHANGE RATE (US $)

FIGURE 6 TOTAL RESERVE MINUS GOLD

FIGURE 7 RESERVE MONEY

FIGURE 8 MONEY

FIGURE 9 CONSUMER PRICES

FIGURE 10 EXPORTS

FIGURE 1 **POPULATION GROWTH**

FIGURE 2 **GNP PER CAPITA**

FIGURE 3 **GDP PER CAPITA AND POPULATION GROWTH RATES**

FIGURE 4 **GOVERNMENT REVENUES AND EXPENDITURES**

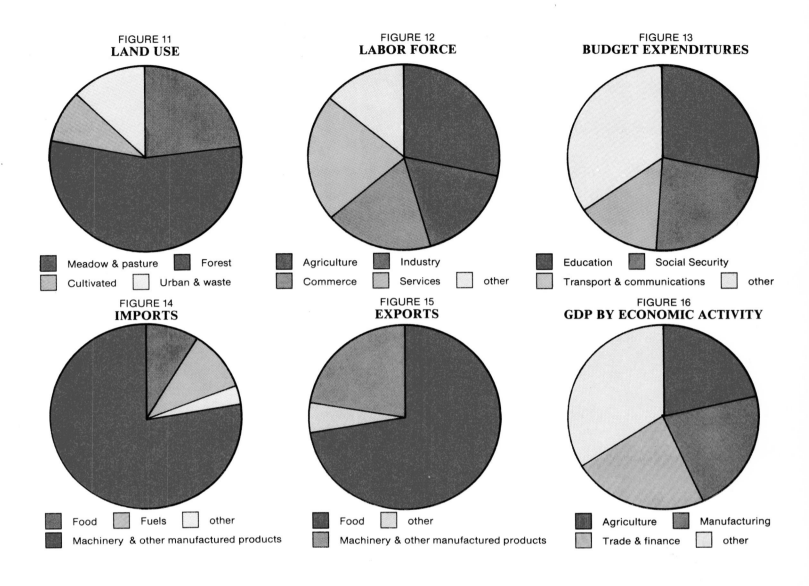

FIGURE 11
LAND USE

Meadow & pasture Forest
Cultivated Urban & waste

FIGURE 12
LABOR FORCE

Agriculture Industry
Commerce Services other

FIGURE 13
BUDGET EXPENDITURES

Education Social Security
Transport & communications other

FIGURE 14
IMPORTS

Food Fuels other
Machinery & other manufactured products

FIGURE 15
EXPORTS

Food other
Machinery & other manufactured products

FIGURE 16
GDP BY ECONOMIC ACTIVITY

Agriculture Manufacturing
Trade & finance other

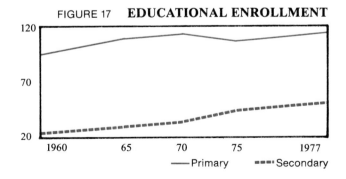

FIGURE 17 **EDUCATIONAL ENROLLMENT**

—— Primary ▪▪▪▪ Secondary

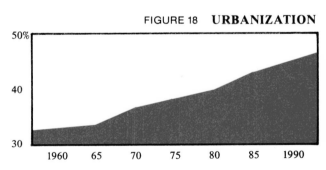

FIGURE 18 **URBANIZATION**

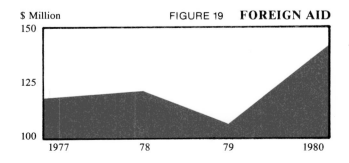

$ Million

FIGURE 19 **FOREIGN AID**

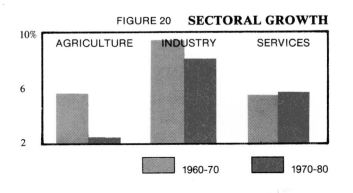

FIGURE 20 **SECTORAL GROWTH**

AGRICULTURE INDUSTRY SERVICES

1960-70 1970-80

CUBA

The largest and westernmost island in the West Indies, Cuba ranks 94th in land area and 56th in population. The Cuban economy is dominated by four factors: a heavy commodity concentration on the production and export of sugar; a loosely defined Communist ideology governing policy decisions; hostility toward the United States which reciprocates in kind; and a corresponding dependence on the Soviet bloc, especially the Soviet Union which has extended credits estimated at over $5 billion since 1959 in addition to nonrepayable trade subsidies, grants and technical assistance estimated at $10 billion. In 1972 Cuba bowed to Soviet pressure to join the Council for Mutual Economic Assistance (CMEA or Comecon) as a full member, receiving in return preferential trade terms and expanded technical assistance. Although Cuba's nickel deposits are among the largest in the world, extraction presents serious technical problems; however, production has increased substantially and nickel is now the country's second most valuable export item.

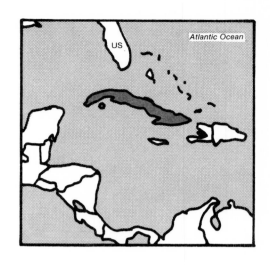

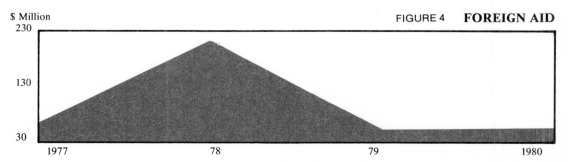

FIGURE 1 **POPULATION GROWTH**

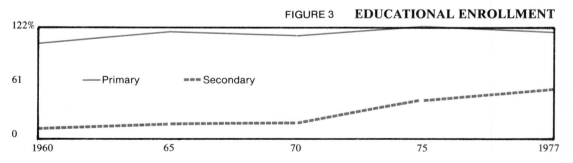

FIGURE 2 **GNP PER CAPITA**

I.M.F.
DATA
UNAVAILABLE

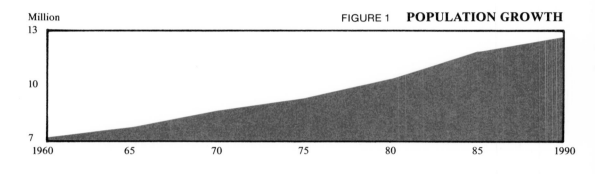

FIGURE 3 **EDUCATIONAL ENROLLMENT**

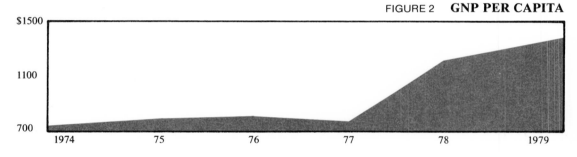

FIGURE 4 **FOREIGN AID**

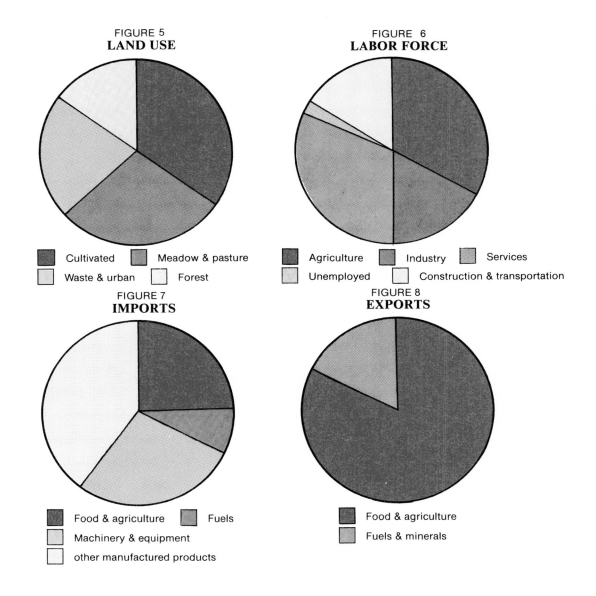

FIGURE 5
LAND USE

Cultivated　Meadow & pasture
Waste & urban　Forest

FIGURE 6
LABOR FORCE

Agriculture　Industry　Services
Unemployed　Construction & transportation

FIGURE 7
IMPORTS

Food & agriculture　Fuels
Machinery & equipment
other manufactured products

FIGURE 8
EXPORTS

Food & agriculture
Fuels & minerals

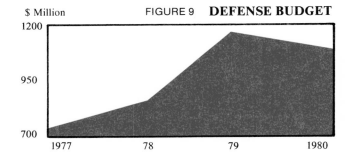

$ Million
FIGURE 9　**DEFENSE BUDGET**

1200

950

700

1977　78　79　1980

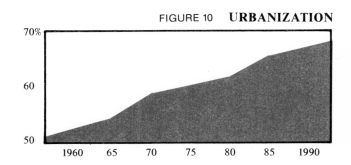

FIGURE 10　**URBANIZATION**

70%

60

50

1960　65　70　75　80　85　1990

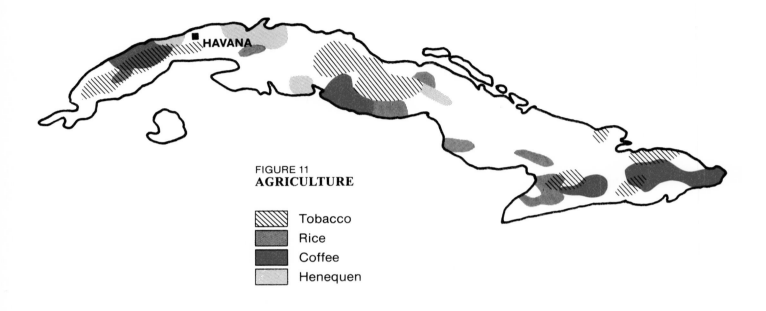

FIGURE 11
AGRICULTURE

Tobacco
Rice
Coffee
Henequen

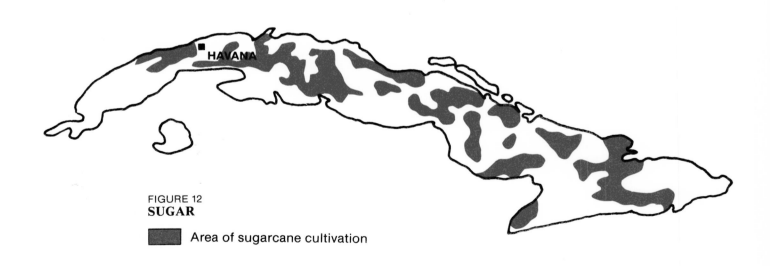

FIGURE 12
SUGAR

Area of sugarcane cultivation

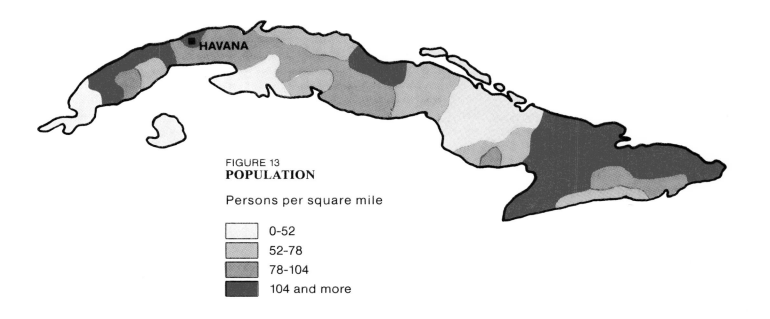

FIGURE 13
POPULATION

Persons per square mile

- 0-52
- 52-78
- 78-104
- 104 and more

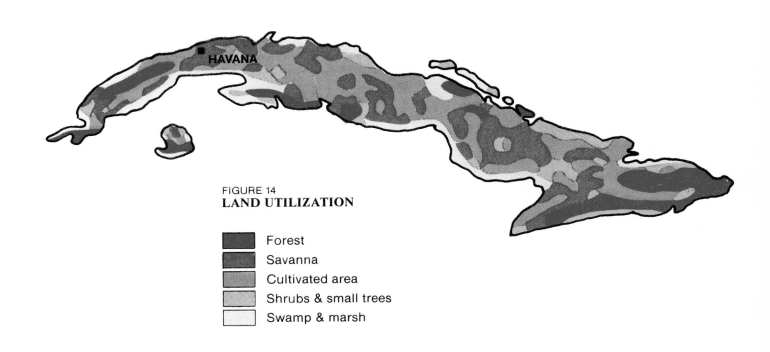

FIGURE 14
LAND UTILIZATION

- Forest
- Savanna
- Cultivated area
- Shrubs & small trees
- Swamp & marsh

DOMINICAN REPUBLIC

Occupying the eastern two-thirds of the island of Hispaniola in the Caribbean Sea, the Dominican Republic ranks 114th in land area and 79th in size of population. During the period 1968 to 1974 the country's GDP expanded at an annual rate of about 11%, one of the highest rates in the world. However, spiraling oil prices and the devastation caused by Hurricane David and the tropical storm Frederick reduced this growth rate by almost half by 1980. Agriculture accounts for well over half the country's foreign exchange earnings, although industry surpassed it some time ago in terms of contribution to the GDP. It has been estimated that, when properly developed, mineral resources alone could earn the Dominican Republic more than $1 billion in foreign exchange. Since the fall of Trujillo, the state has been an active participant in the economy, especially through the Corporacion Dominicana de Empresas Estatales (Corde), which administers some 26 enterprises.

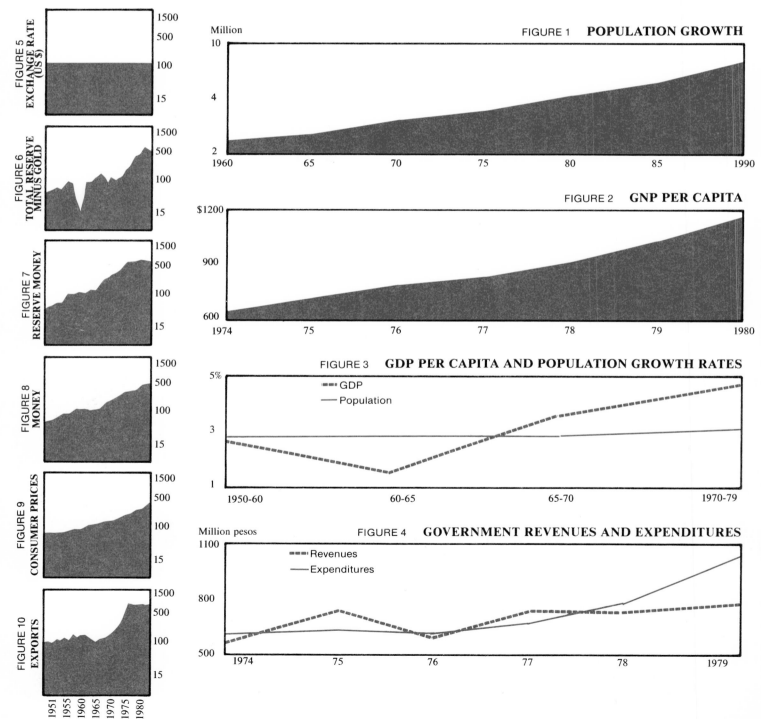

FIGURE 5 EXCHANGE RATE (US $)

FIGURE 6 TOTAL RESERVE MINUS GOLD

FIGURE 7 RESERVE MONEY

FIGURE 8 MONEY

FIGURE 9 CONSUMER PRICES

FIGURE 10 EXPORTS

FIGURE 1 **POPULATION GROWTH**

FIGURE 2 **GNP PER CAPITA**

FIGURE 3 **GDP PER CAPITA AND POPULATION GROWTH RATES**

FIGURE 4 **GOVERNMENT REVENUES AND EXPENDITURES**

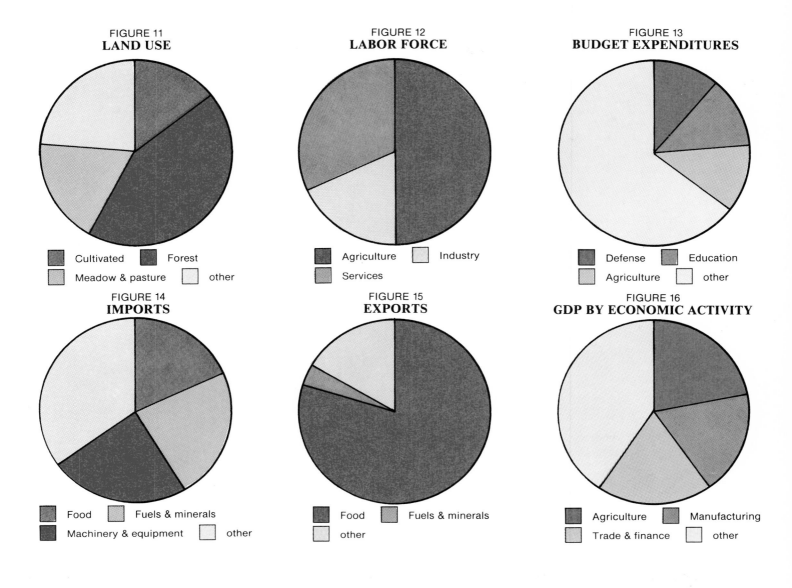

FIGURE 11
LAND USE

Cultivated ■   Forest ■
Meadow & pasture ■   other ■

FIGURE 12
LABOR FORCE

Agriculture ■   Industry ■
Services ■

FIGURE 13
BUDGET EXPENDITURES

Defense ■   Education ■
Agriculture ■   other ■

FIGURE 14
IMPORTS

Food ■   Fuels & minerals ■
Machinery & equipment ■   other ■

FIGURE 15
EXPORTS

Food ■   Fuels & minerals ■
other ■

FIGURE 16
GDP BY ECONOMIC ACTIVITY

Agriculture ■   Manufacturing ■
Trade & finance ■   other ■

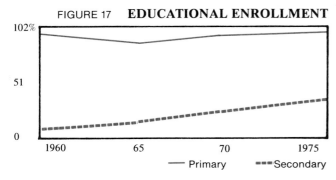

FIGURE 17   **EDUCATIONAL ENROLLMENT**

—— Primary   ===Secondary

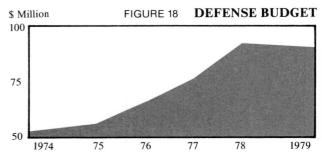

$ Million   FIGURE 18   **DEFENSE BUDGET**

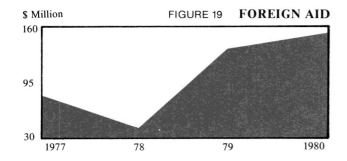

$ Million   FIGURE 19   **FOREIGN AID**

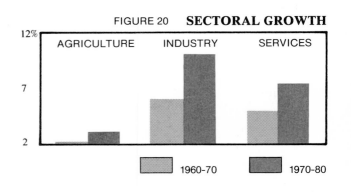

FIGURE 20   **SECTORAL GROWTH**

AGRICULTURE   INDUSTRY   SERVICES

■ 1960-70   ■ 1970-80

ECUADOR

Straddling the Equator on the Pacific coast of South America, Ecuador is the third smallest South American country, the world's 63rd largest and the 65th most populous. Recent growth in oil production has enabled the country to achieve a per capita annual GNP growth rate of 5.4% while the population growth rate has been pushed back to 3.3%. Currently, the petroleum industry accounts for over one-half of national export earnings and most of the foreign capital invested in the country. However, if significant new reserves are not found, Ecuador may cease to be a net exporter of petroleum by the late 1980s. Next to oil, agriculture is the mainstay of the economy, employing over one-half of the labor force and contributing over one-quarter of the GNP. Since the liberalization of the Andean Foreign Investment Code in 1976, Ecuador has gone further than other members of the Andean Common Market to open its doors to foreign investment. The United States accounts for two-thirds of total foreign investment.

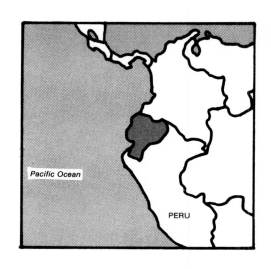

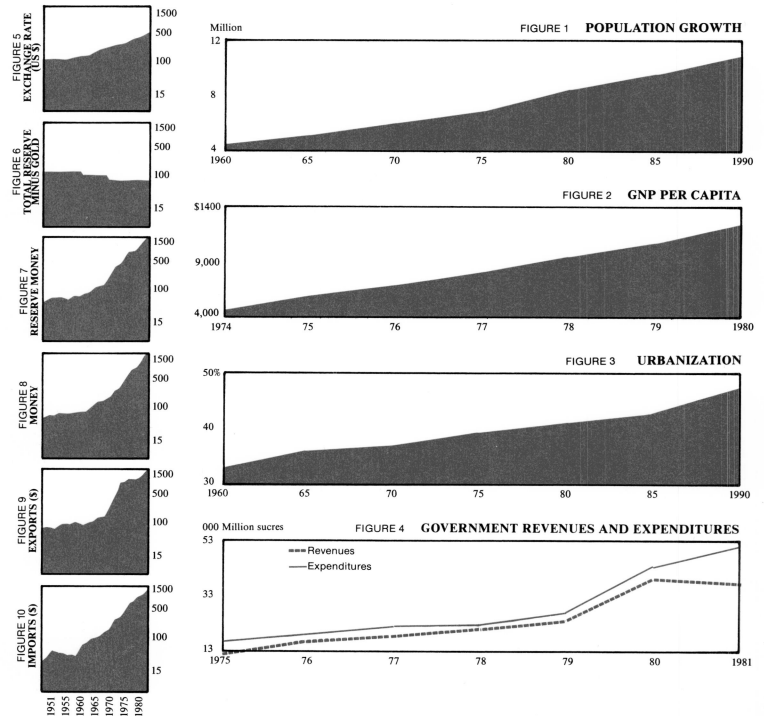

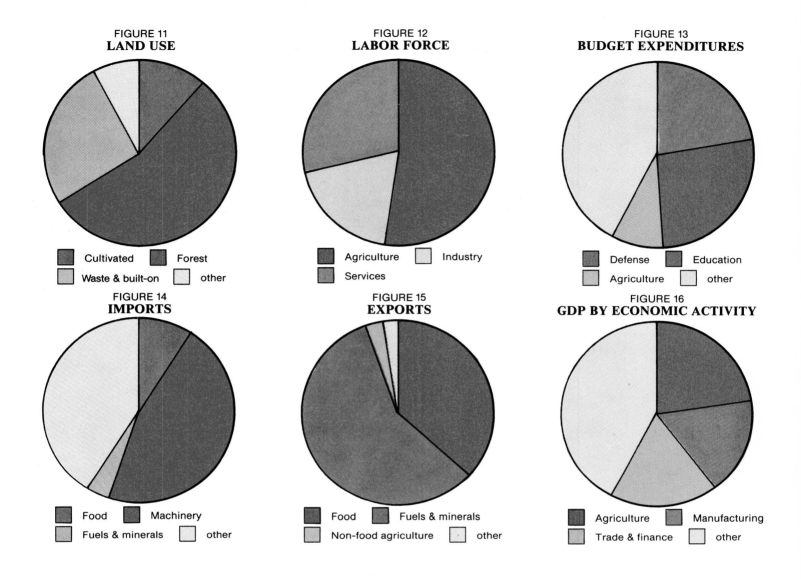

FIGURE 11
LAND USE

- Cultivated
- Forest
- Waste & built-on
- other

FIGURE 12
LABOR FORCE

- Agriculture
- Industry
- Services

FIGURE 13
BUDGET EXPENDITURES

- Defense
- Education
- Agriculture
- other

FIGURE 14
IMPORTS

- Food
- Machinery
- Fuels & minerals
- other

FIGURE 15
EXPORTS

- Food
- Fuels & minerals
- Non-food agriculture
- other

FIGURE 16
GDP BY ECONOMIC ACTIVITY

- Agriculture
- Manufacturing
- Trade & finance
- other

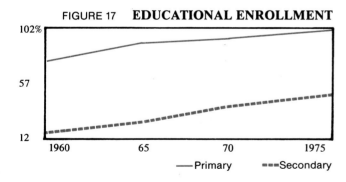

FIGURE 17   **EDUCATIONAL ENROLLMENT**

——Primary   ▪▪▪Secondary

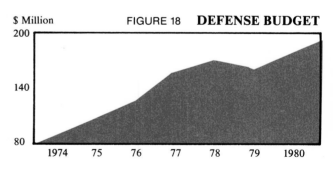

$ Million   FIGURE 18   **DEFENSE BUDGET**

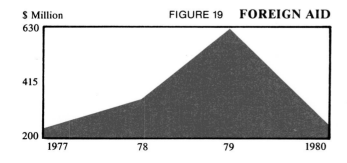

$ Million   FIGURE 19   **FOREIGN AID**

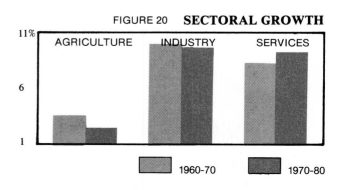

FIGURE 20   **SECTORAL GROWTH**

AGRICULTURE   INDUSTRY   SERVICES

- 1960-70
- 1970-80

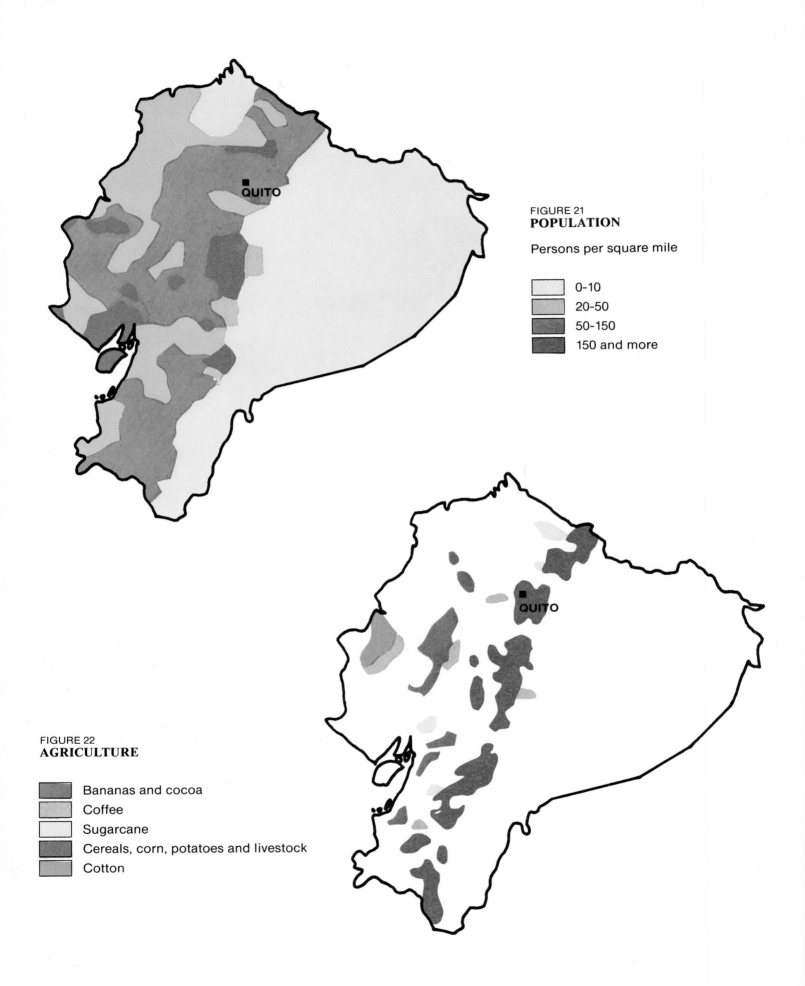

FIGURE 21
POPULATION

Persons per square mile

0-10
20-50
50-150
150 and more

FIGURE 22
AGRICULTURE

Bananas and cocoa
Coffee
Sugarcane
Cereals, corn, potatoes and livestock
Cotton

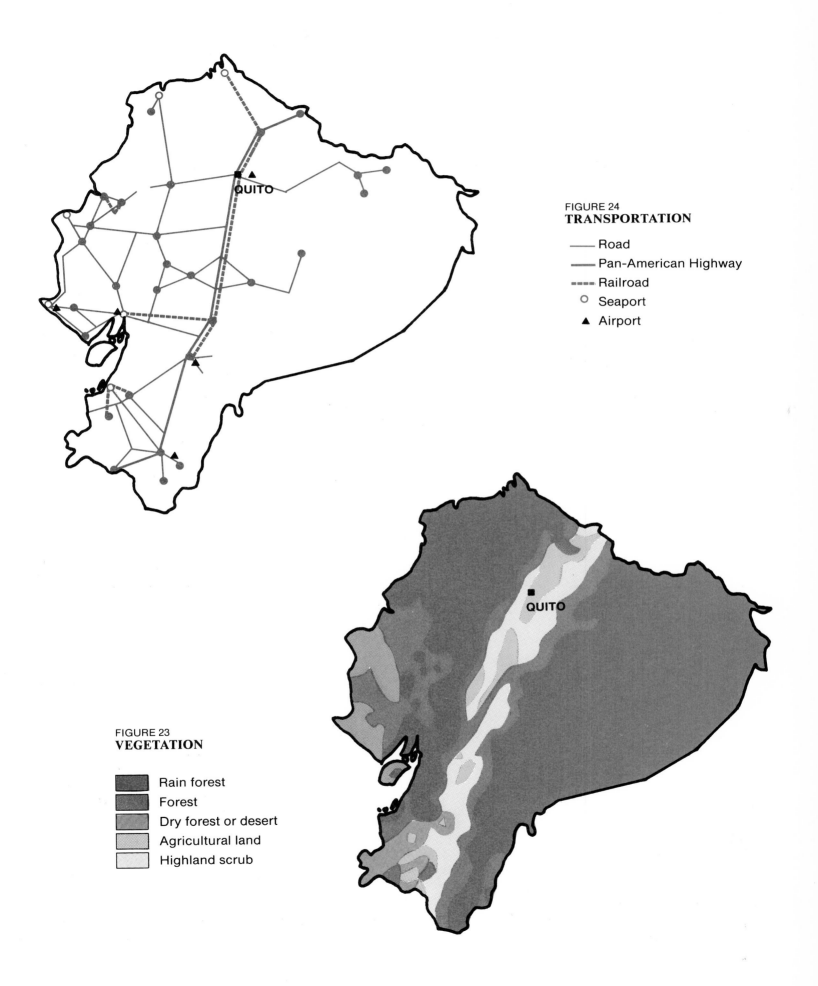

FIGURE 24
TRANSPORTATION

—— Road
—— Pan-American Highway
---- Railroad
○ Seaport
▲ Airport

QUITO

FIGURE 23
VEGETATION

Rain forest
Forest
Dry forest or desert
Agricultural land
Highland scrub

QUITO

EGYPT

Its territory straddling Africa and Asia, Egypt is the most populous Arab country, the second most populous in Africa and the 20th most populous in the world. Nearly 99% of its population is compressed into 3.5% of the land area, one of the most skewed population distributions in the world. In the valley of the Nile, the population density is the fifth highest in the world. The Egyptian economy is still predominantly agrarian, and the country's farmland is intensively cultivated, with two and sometimes three crops annually and extremely high per-hectare yields. Virtually 100% of the cultivated area is irrigated. Nevertheless, Egypt is not self-sufficient in food, because much of the arable area is devoted to cash crops, such as cotton, of which Egypt has long been one of the world's leading producers. Peace with Israel has been beneficial for Egypt because it has enabled it to divert funds to economic development and to receive more favorable trade terms and investment capital from the West.

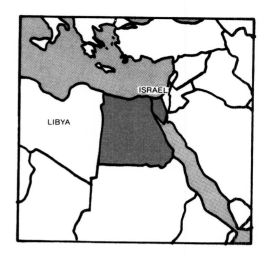

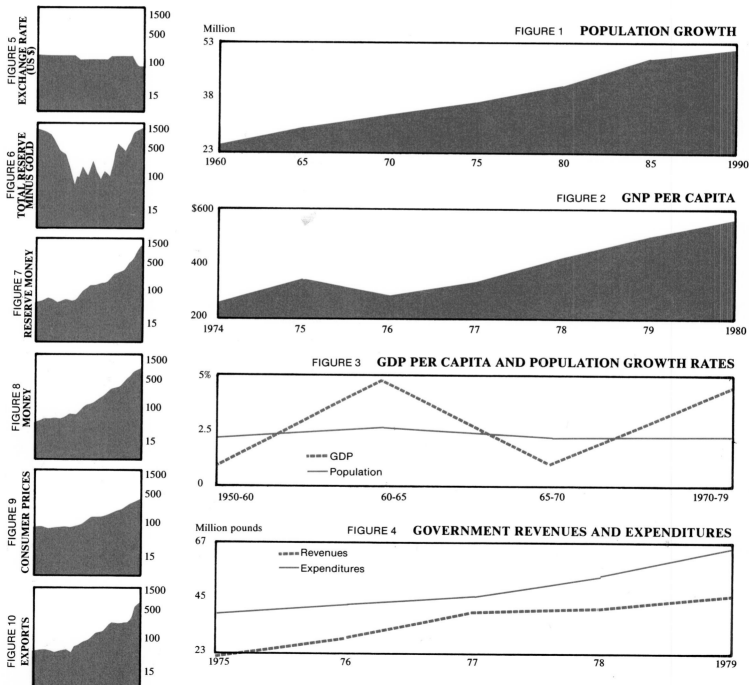

FIGURE 5 EXCHANGE RATE (US $)

FIGURE 6 TOTAL RESERVE MINUS GOLD

FIGURE 7 RESERVE MONEY

FIGURE 8 MONEY

FIGURE 9 CONSUMER PRICES

FIGURE 10 EXPORTS

FIGURE 1 **POPULATION GROWTH**

FIGURE 2 **GNP PER CAPITA**

FIGURE 3 **GDP PER CAPITA AND POPULATION GROWTH RATES**

FIGURE 4 **GOVERNMENT REVENUES AND EXPENDITURES**

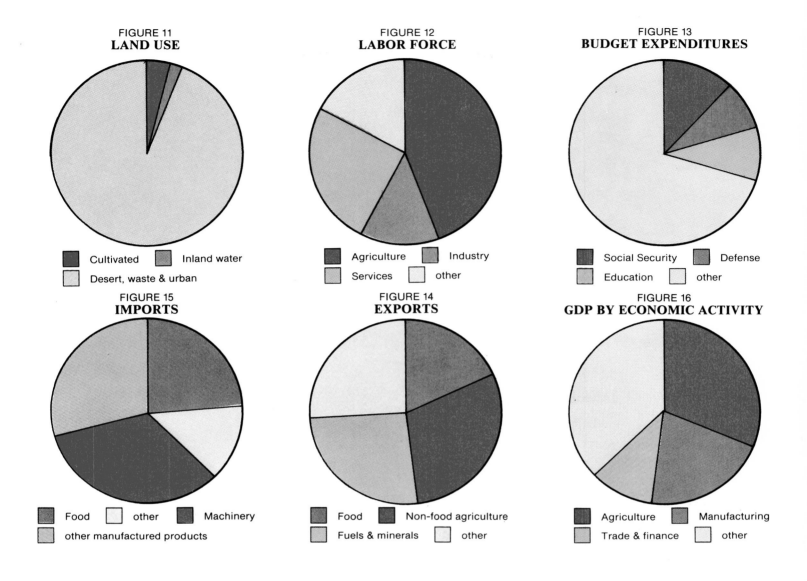

FIGURE 11
LAND USE

Cultivated Inland water
Desert, waste & urban

FIGURE 12
LABOR FORCE

Agriculture Industry
Services other

FIGURE 13
BUDGET EXPENDITURES

Social Security Defense
Education other

FIGURE 15
IMPORTS

Food other Machinery
other manufactured products

FIGURE 14
EXPORTS

Food Non-food agriculture
Fuels & minerals other

FIGURE 16
GDP BY ECONOMIC ACTIVITY

Agriculture Manufacturing
Trade & finance other

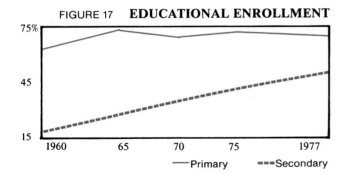

FIGURE 17 **EDUCATIONAL ENROLLMENT**

75%

45

15

1960   65   70   75   1977

——Primary ===Secondary

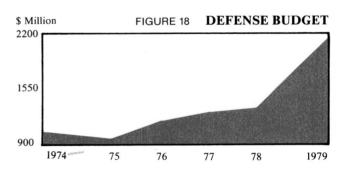

$ Million   FIGURE 18 **DEFENSE BUDGET**
2200

1550

900

1974   75   76   77   78   1979

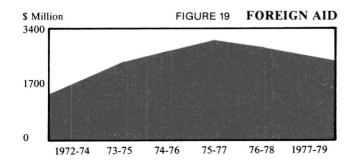

$ Million   FIGURE 19 **FOREIGN AID**
3400

1700

0

1972-74 73-75 74-76 75-77 76-78 1977-79

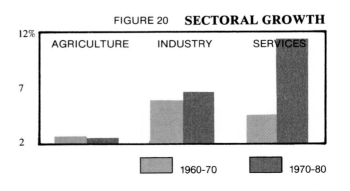

FIGURE 20 **SECTORAL GROWTH**

12% AGRICULTURE   INDUSTRY   SERVICES

7

2

1960-70   1970-80

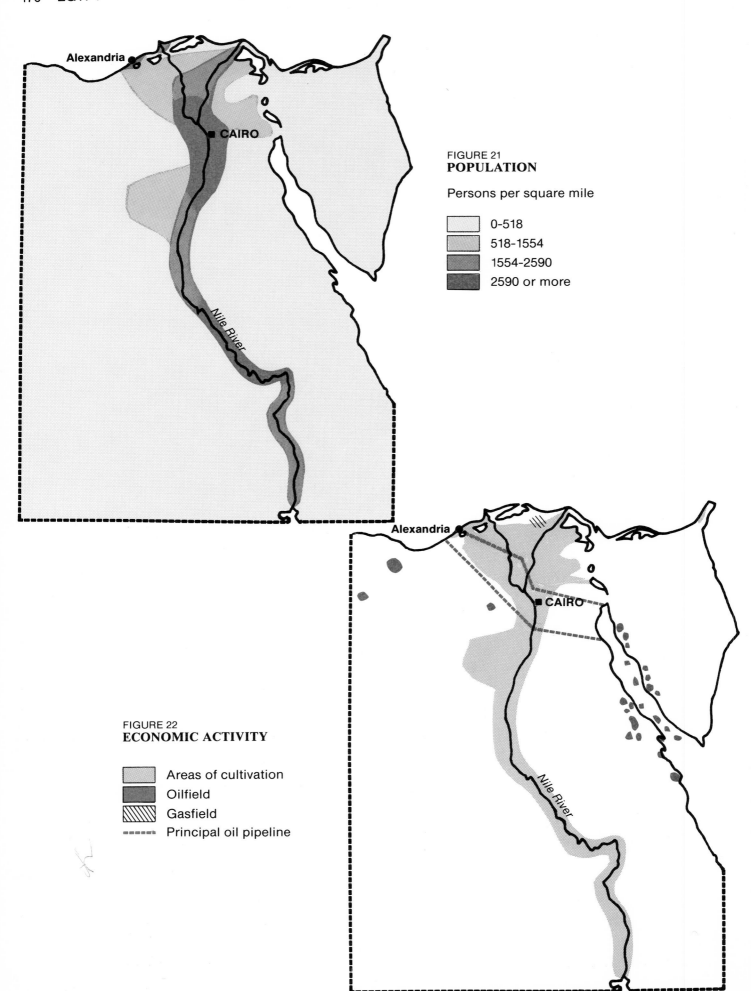

Alexandria

CAIRO

Nile River

FIGURE 21
POPULATION

Persons per square mile

	0-518
	518-1554
	1554-2590
	2590 or more

FIGURE 22
ECONOMIC ACTIVITY

	Areas of cultivation
	Oilfield
	Gasfield
- - - -	Principal oil pipeline

Alexandria

CAIRO

Nile River

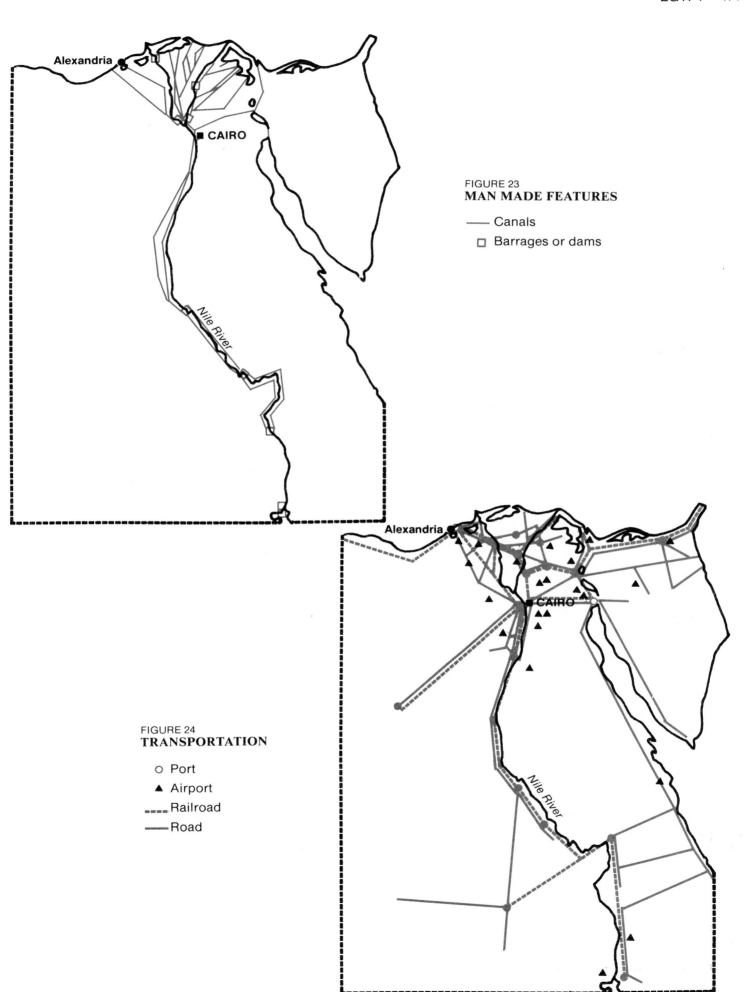

FIGURE 23
MAN MADE FEATURES

—— Canals
☐ Barrages or dams

Alexandria

CAIRO

Nile River

FIGURE 24
TRANSPORTATION

○ Port
▲ Airport
‑‑‑‑ Railroad
—— Road

Alexandria

CAIRO

Nile River

EL SALVADOR

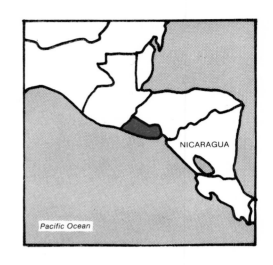

The smallest mainland American republic, El Salvador ranks 131st in land area and 89th in size of population. Its per capita GNP growth rate of 1.4% trails behind the annual population growth rate of 2.9%. The country's basic problems include heavy pressure on available land and a very uneven distribution of income. Although more industrialized than its neighbors, the Salvadoran economy is still agricultural but this sector has been dominated historically by the "14 families," a group of wealthy landowners and businessmen. Until 1980 when the ruling junta launched the country's first major land reforms, the richest 5% of Salvadorans controlled 40% of the national wealth while the poorest 20% received only 2%. The same 14 families also control the industrial sector. The current political turmoil has only served to intensify the country's economic problems and in 1980 the GNP declined by over 10% and nearly $1 billion in foreign investment is reported to have fled the country.

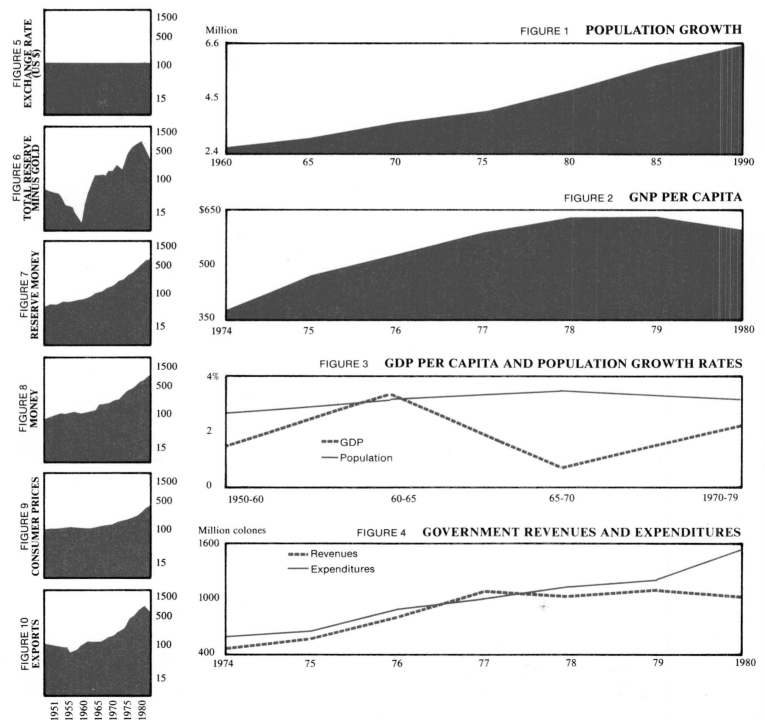

FIGURE 5 EXCHANGE RATE (US $)

FIGURE 6 TOTAL RESERVE MINUS GOLD

FIGURE 7 RESERVE MONEY

FIGURE 8 MONEY

FIGURE 9 CONSUMER PRICES

FIGURE 10 EXPORTS

FIGURE 1 **POPULATION GROWTH**

FIGURE 2 **GNP PER CAPITA**

FIGURE 3 **GDP PER CAPITA AND POPULATION GROWTH RATES**

FIGURE 4 **GOVERNMENT REVENUES AND EXPENDITURES**

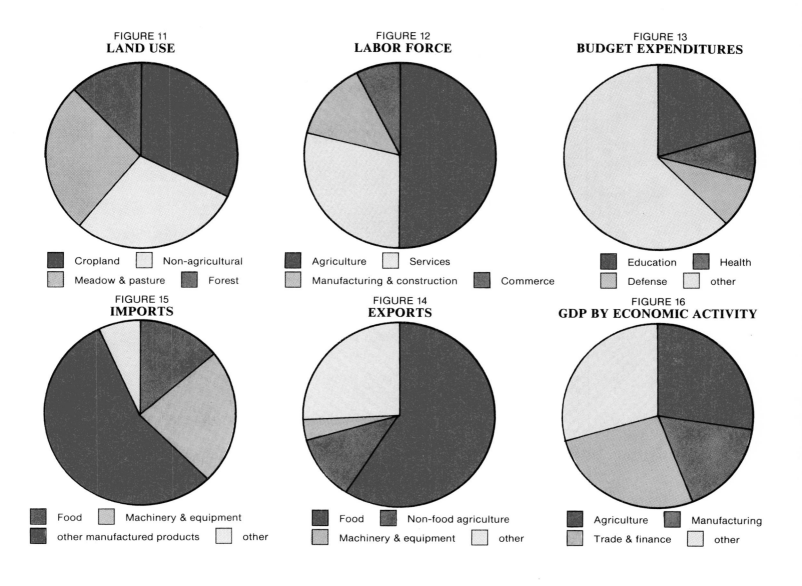

FIGURE 11
LAND USE

Cropland   Non-agricultural
Meadow & pasture   Forest

FIGURE 12
LABOR FORCE

Agriculture   Services
Manufacturing & construction   Commerce

FIGURE 13
BUDGET EXPENDITURES

Education   Health
Defense   other

FIGURE 15
IMPORTS

Food   Machinery & equipment
other manufactured products   other

FIGURE 14
EXPORTS

Food   Non-food agriculture
Machinery & equipment   other

FIGURE 16
GDP BY ECONOMIC ACTIVITY

Agriculture   Manufacturing
Trade & finance   other

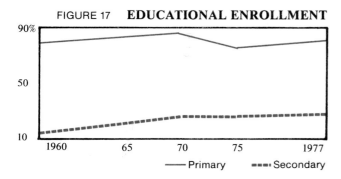

FIGURE 17   **EDUCATIONAL ENROLLMENT**

90%

50

10

1960   65   70   75   1977

——— Primary   ▬▬▪ Secondary

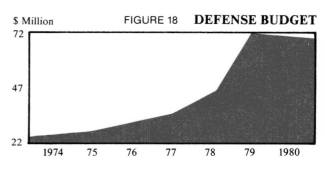

$ Million   FIGURE 18   **DEFENSE BUDGET**

72

47

22

1974   75   76   77   78   79   1980

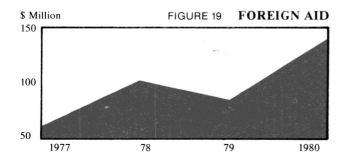

$ Million   FIGURE 19   **FOREIGN AID**

150

100

50

1977   78   79   1980

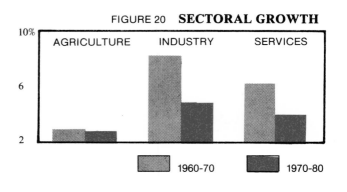

FIGURE 20   **SECTORAL GROWTH**

10%

AGRICULTURE   INDUSTRY   SERVICES

6

2

1960-70   1970-80

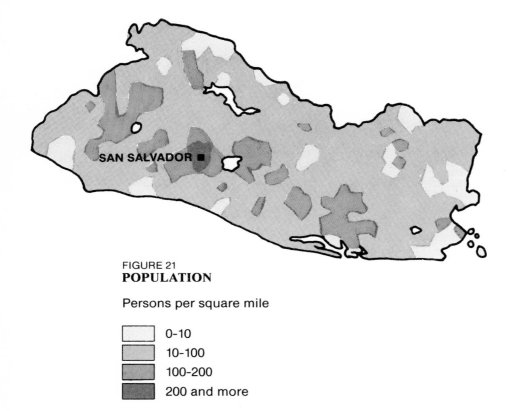

FIGURE 21
POPULATION

Persons per square mile

☐	0-10
☐	10-100
☐	100-200
☐	200 and more

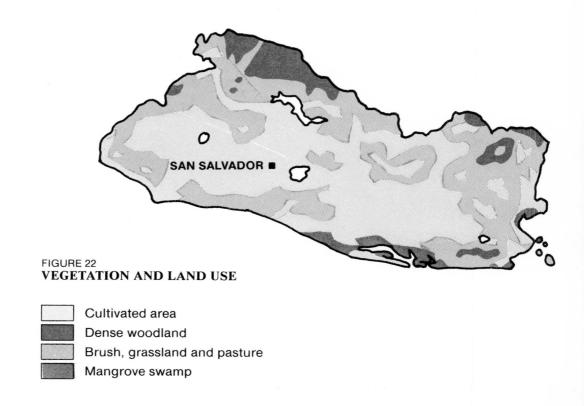

FIGURE 22
VEGETATION AND LAND USE

☐	Cultivated area
☐	Dense woodland
☐	Brush, grassland and pasture
☐	Mangrove swamp

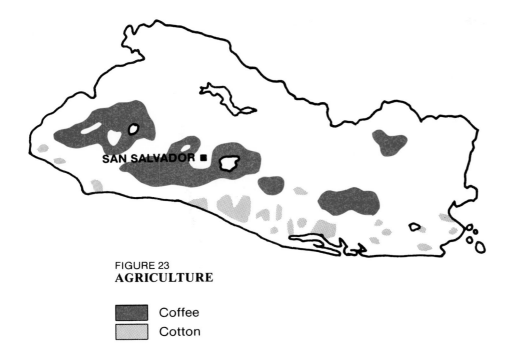

FIGURE 23
AGRICULTURE

■ Coffee
▨ Cotton

FIGURE 24
TRANSPORTATION

▪▪▪ Railroad
── Road

ETHIOPIA

One of the oldest nations of the world, the home of the now-forgotten Lion of Judah, Ethiopia ranks 22nd in land area and 26th in population. With a per capita GNP of $140 and a GNP growth rate of 0.3% annually (both among the lowest in the world), Ethiopia is acknowledged to be among the poorest even among the poor nations of the world. More than 75% of its population subsist in absolute poverty. Despite such destitution, Ethiopia in recent years has undergone a political transformation and consolidation that has made it a power to be reckoned with in the Horn of Africa. Many of the vestiges of former feudalism have been wiped out, the Eritrean secessionists and Somali irredentism have been dealt severe blows, and the country has been placed firmly within the Soviet bloc. However, it is too soon to tell whether these gains are permanent or whether the Dergue, as the Ethiopian ruling junta is known, will self-destruct before the establishment of a socialist economy.

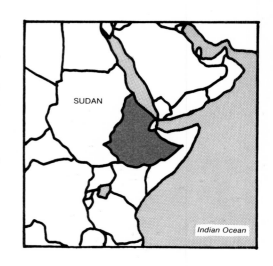

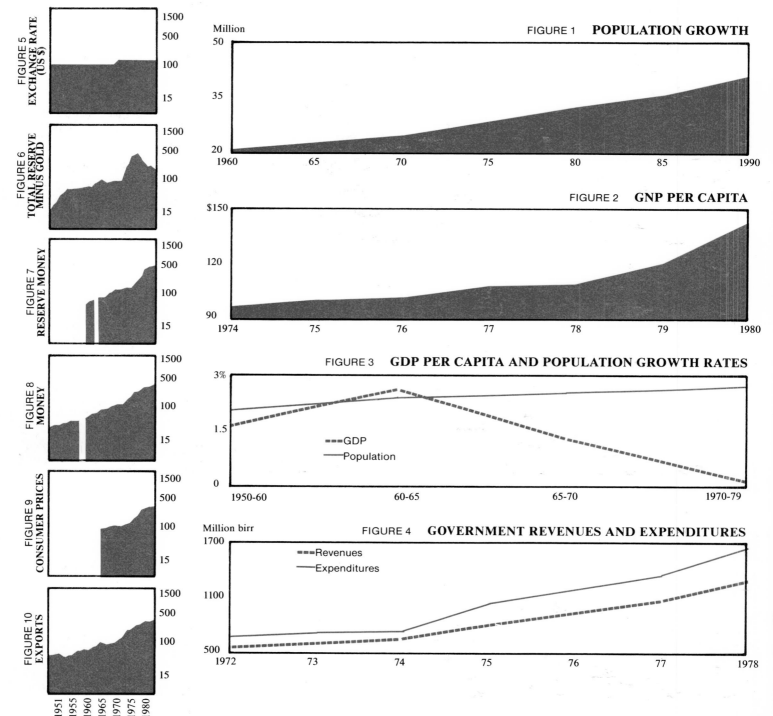

FIGURE 5 EXCHANGE RATE (US $)

FIGURE 6 TOTAL RESERVE MINUS GOLD

FIGURE 7 RESERVE MONEY

FIGURE 8 MONEY

FIGURE 9 CONSUMER PRICES

FIGURE 10 EXPORTS

FIGURE 1 **POPULATION GROWTH**

FIGURE 2 **GNP PER CAPITA**

FIGURE 3 **GDP PER CAPITA AND POPULATION GROWTH RATES**

GDP
Population

FIGURE 4 **GOVERNMENT REVENUES AND EXPENDITURES**

Revenues
Expenditures

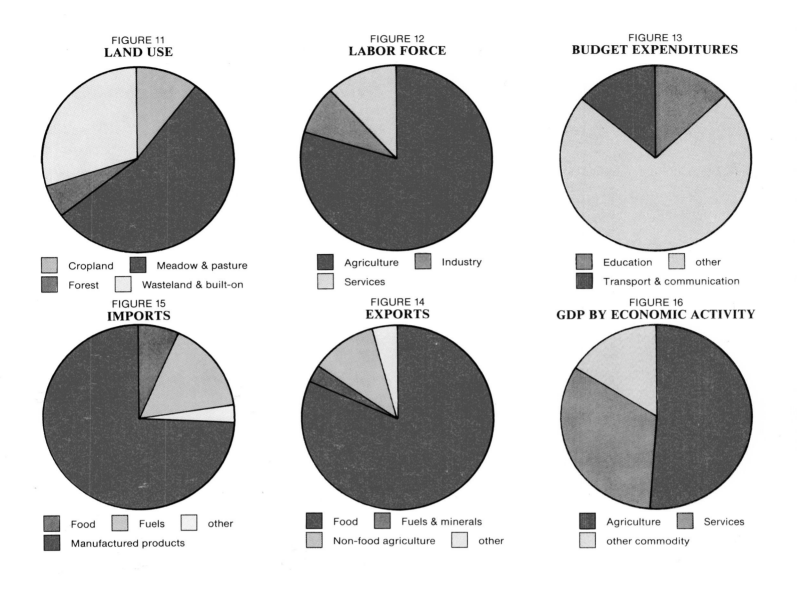

FIGURE 11
LAND USE

Cropland
Forest
Meadow & pasture
Wasteland & built-on

FIGURE 12
LABOR FORCE

Agriculture
Services
Industry

FIGURE 13
BUDGET EXPENDITURES

Education
Transport & communication
other

FIGURE 15
IMPORTS

Food
Manufactured products
Fuels
other

FIGURE 14
EXPORTS

Food
Non-food agriculture
Fuels & minerals
other

FIGURE 16
GDP BY ECONOMIC ACTIVITY

Agriculture
other commodity
Services

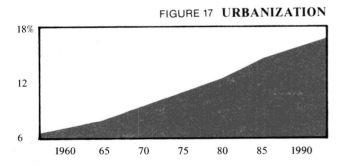

FIGURE 17 **URBANIZATION**

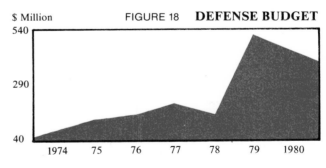

$ Million   FIGURE 18   **DEFENSE BUDGET**

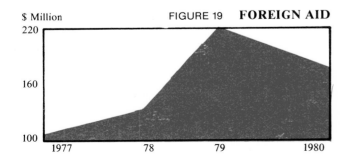

$ Million   FIGURE 19   **FOREIGN AID**

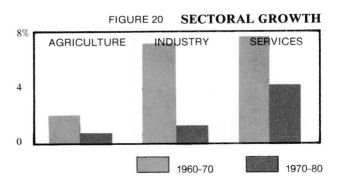

FIGURE 20   **SECTORAL GROWTH**

AGRICULTURE   INDUSTRY   SERVICES

1960-70   1970-80

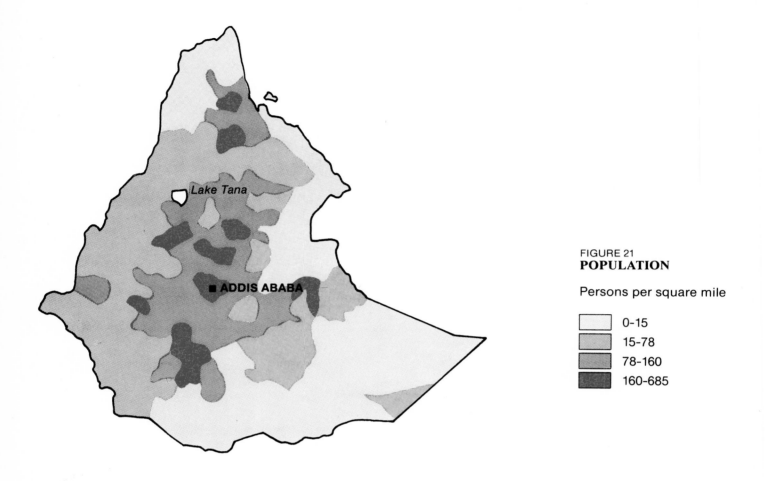

FIGURE 21
POPULATION

Persons per square mile

0-15
15-78
78-160
160-685

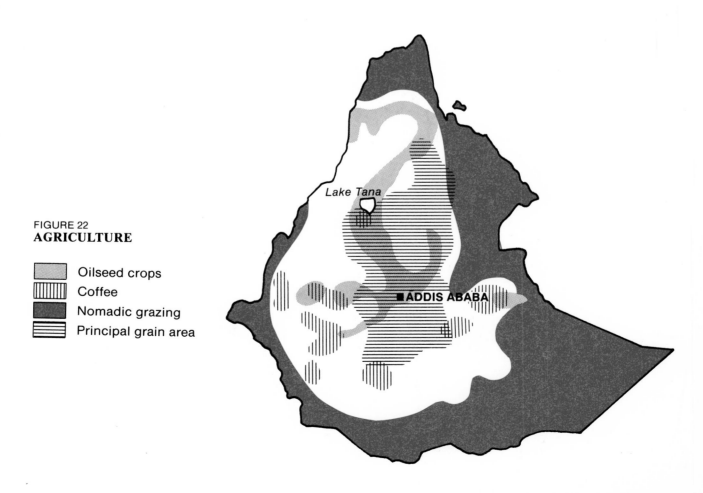

FIGURE 22
AGRICULTURE

Oilseed crops
Coffee
Nomadic grazing
Principal grain area

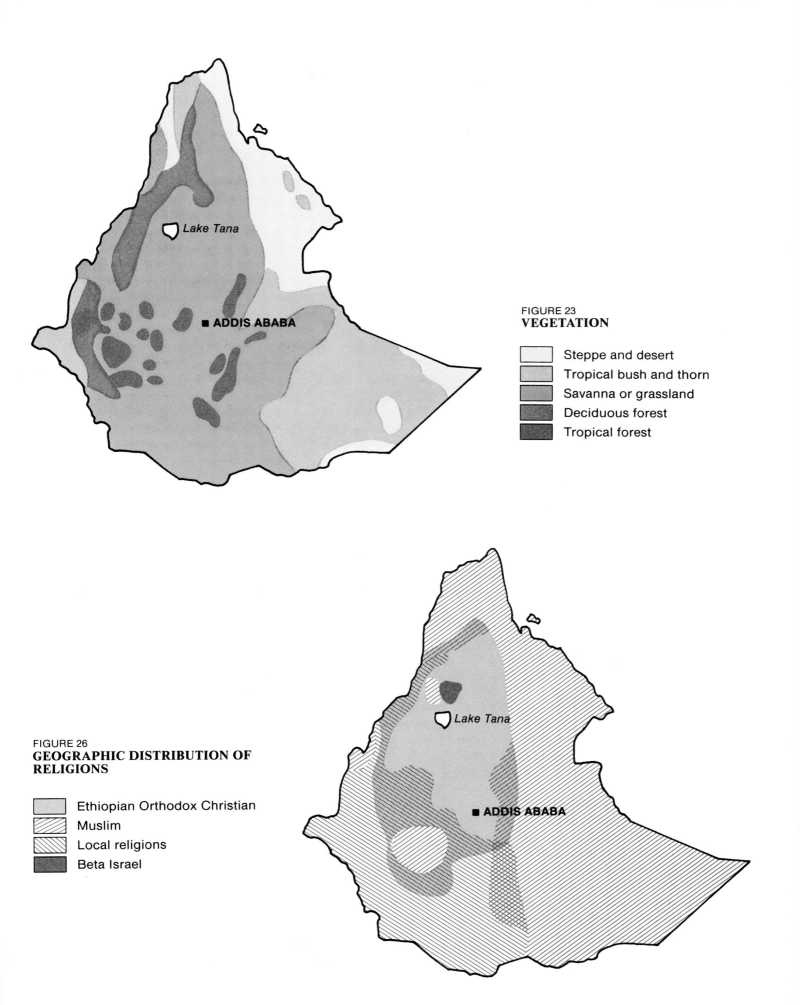

FIGURE 23
VEGETATION

Steppe and desert
Tropical bush and thorn
Savanna or grassland
Deciduous forest
Tropical forest

Lake Tana

■ ADDIS ABABA

FIGURE 26
GEOGRAPHIC DISTRIBUTION OF RELIGIONS

Ethiopian Orthodox Christian
Muslim
Local religions
Beta Israel

Lake Tana

■ ADDIS ABABA

GABON

Spanning the Equator on the west coast of Africa, Gabon ranks 48th in land area and 141st in population. A small population and enormous mineral resources have combined to make Gabon one of the wealthiest nations in black Africa, one of the four African nations in the upper middle-income group. Despite this apparent prosperity, the benefits of national wealth have not trickled down to the lower classes. Although agriculture employs more than half the labor force, less than 1% of the land is cultivated and agricultural contribution to the GDP is negligible. Manufacturing is also a relatively small sector. On the other hand, petroleum, the country's most valuable export, accounts for more than one-half the government revenues. The output of the offshore wells may be exhausted by 1985 and vigorous efforts are being made to find new sources. If oil does run out, Gabon has other mineral resouces to bank on, including 1 billion tons of iron ore and 20,000 tons of uranium.

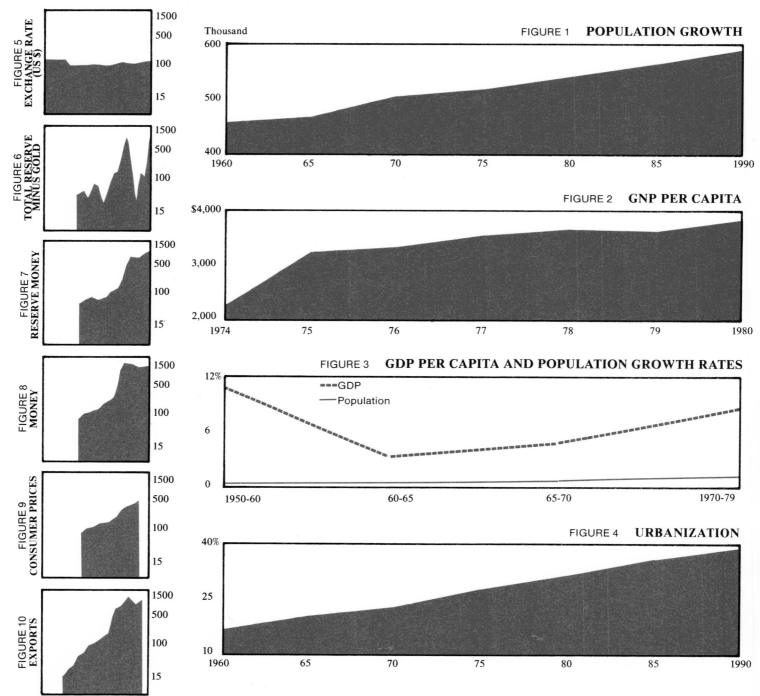

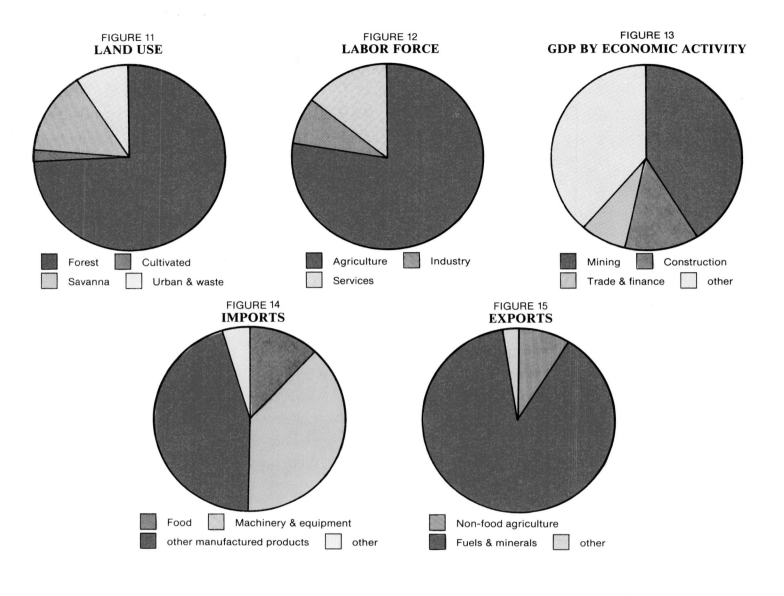

FIGURE 11
LAND USE

Forest   Cultivated
Savanna   Urban & waste

FIGURE 12
LABOR FORCE

Agriculture   Industry
Services

FIGURE 13
GDP BY ECONOMIC ACTIVITY

Mining   Construction
Trade & finance   other

FIGURE 14
IMPORTS

Food   Machinery & equipment
other manufactured products   other

FIGURE 15
EXPORTS

Non-food agriculture
Fuels & minerals   other

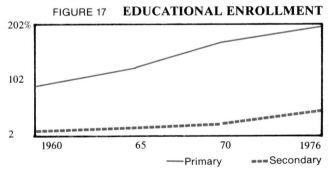

FIGURE 17   **EDUCATIONAL ENROLLMENT**

202%

102

2

1960   65   70   1976

—— Primary   ===Secondary

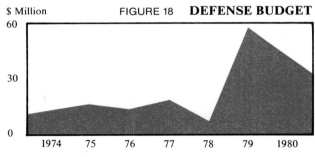

$ Million   FIGURE 18   **DEFENSE BUDGET**

60

30

0

1974   75   76   77   78   79   1980

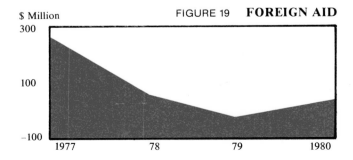

$ Million   FIGURE 19   **FOREIGN AID**

300

100

-100

1977   78   79   1980

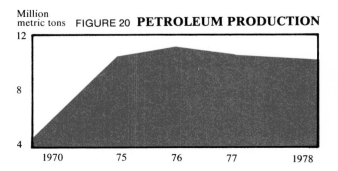

Million
metric tons   FIGURE 20   **PETROLEUM PRODUCTION**

12

8

4

1970   75   76   77   1978

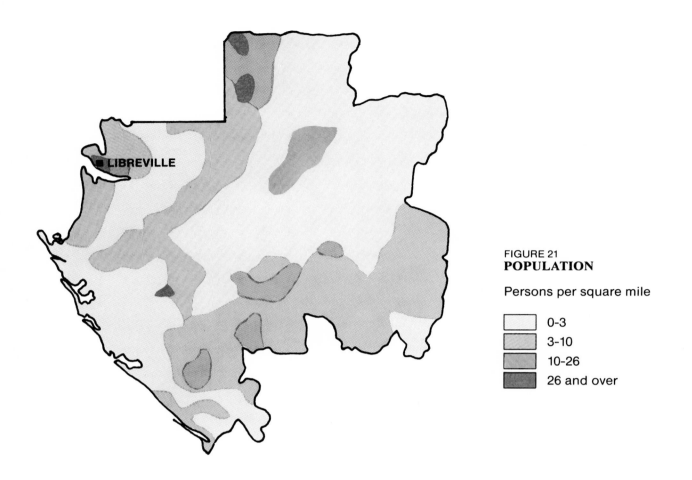

FIGURE 21
POPULATION

Persons per square mile

0-3
3-10
10-26
26 and over

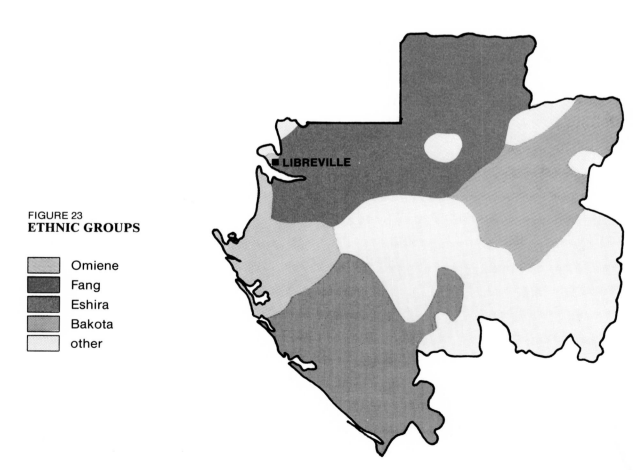

FIGURE 23
ETHNIC GROUPS

Omiene
Fang
Eshira
Bakota
other

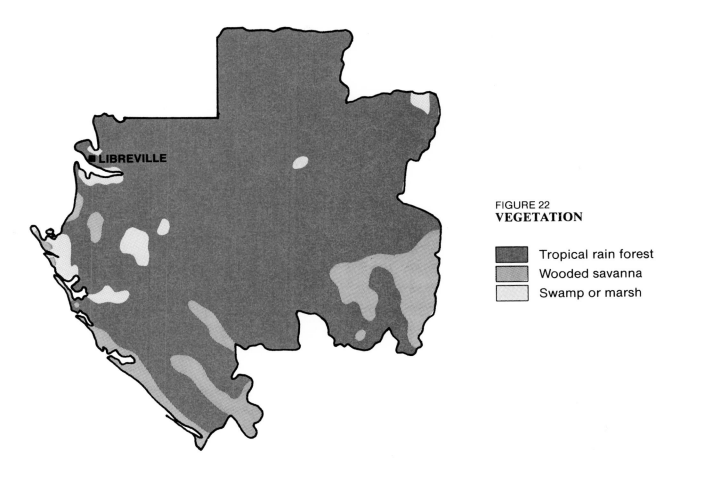

FIGURE 22
VEGETATION

Tropical rain forest
Wooded savanna
Swamp or marsh

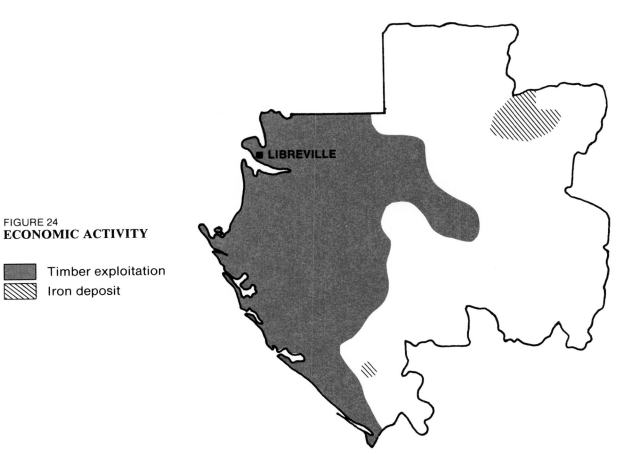

FIGURE 24
ECONOMIC ACTIVITY

Timber exploitation
Iron deposit

GHANA

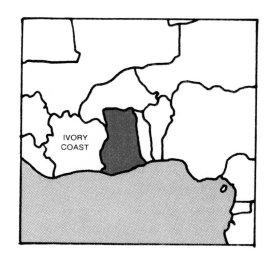

Located on the west coast of Africa and known as the Gold Coast before independence, Ghana ranks 71st in land area and 53rd in population. Once a prosperous country and the world's leading cocoa producer, Ghana was one of the first Anglophone countries to gain independence and for a while served as a model and mentor for its neighbors. But Kwame Nkrumah's disastrous political and economic experiments set the country on a bumpy road leading to what the *Economist* once described as an "abysmal chaos," characterized by chronic instability, inefficiency, corruption, mismanagement and shortages of almost everything. Succeeding governments have tried to remedy the situation but ended up making it worse. The inflation rate stood at 100% in 1980, industry was operating at 30% of capacity because of shortages of raw materials and the GDP declined by 5%. The return of Lt. Jerry Rawlings to power has brought some positive signs for the immediate future but economic recovery is still not in sight.

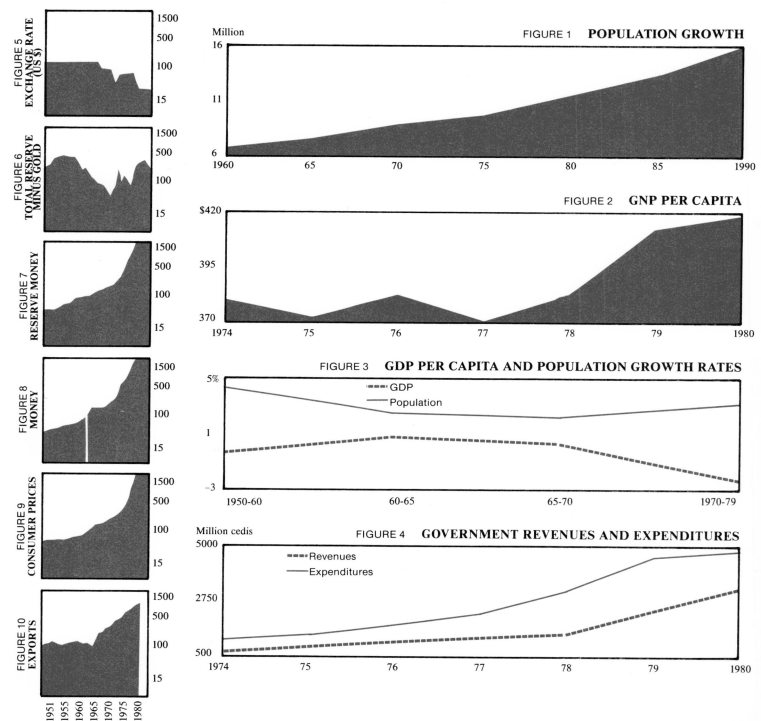

FIGURE 5 EXCHANGE RATE (US $)

FIGURE 6 TOTAL RESERVE MINUS GOLD

FIGURE 7 RESERVE MONEY

FIGURE 8 MONEY

FIGURE 9 CONSUMER PRICES

FIGURE 10 EXPORTS

FIGURE 1 **POPULATION GROWTH**

FIGURE 2 **GNP PER CAPITA**

FIGURE 3 **GDP PER CAPITA AND POPULATION GROWTH RATES**

FIGURE 4 **GOVERNMENT REVENUES AND EXPENDITURES**

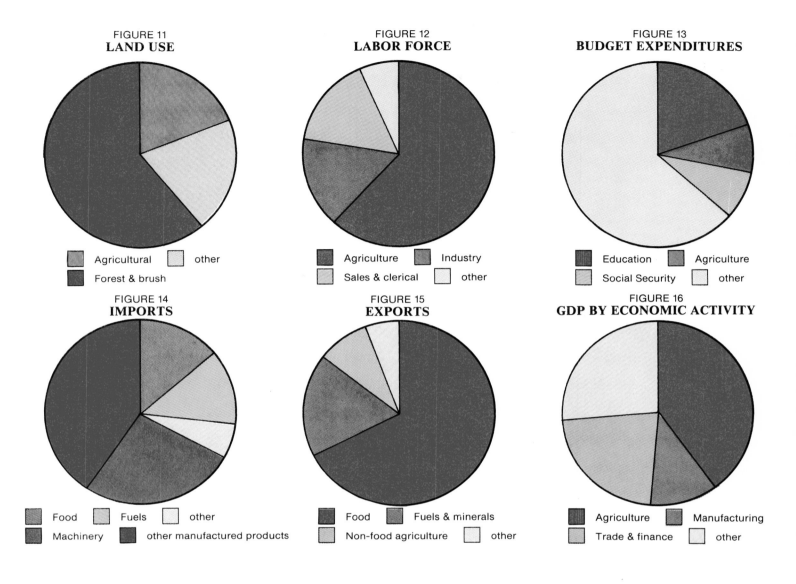

FIGURE 11
LAND USE

Agricultural | other
Forest & brush

FIGURE 12
LABOR FORCE

Agriculture | Industry
Sales & clerical | other

FIGURE 13
BUDGET EXPENDITURES

Education | Agriculture
Social Security | other

FIGURE 14
IMPORTS

Food | Fuels | other
Machinery | other manufactured products

FIGURE 15
EXPORTS

Food | Fuels & minerals
Non-food agriculture | other

FIGURE 16
GDP BY ECONOMIC ACTIVITY

Agriculture | Manufacturing
Trade & finance | other

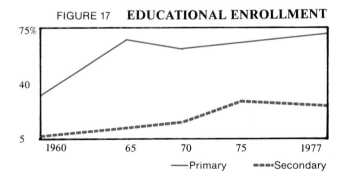

FIGURE 17   **EDUCATIONAL ENROLLMENT**

75%

40

5

1960   65   70   75   1977

——Primary   ▪▪▪▪Secondary

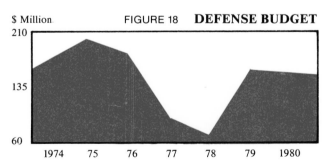

$ Million   FIGURE 18   **DEFENSE BUDGET**

210

135

60

1974   75   76   77   78   79   1980

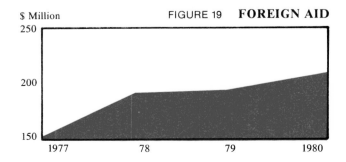

$ Million   FIGURE 19   **FOREIGN AID**

250

200

150

1977   78   79   1980

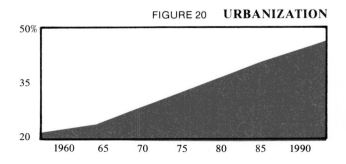

FIGURE 20   **URBANIZATION**

50%

35

20

1960   65   70   75   80   85   1990

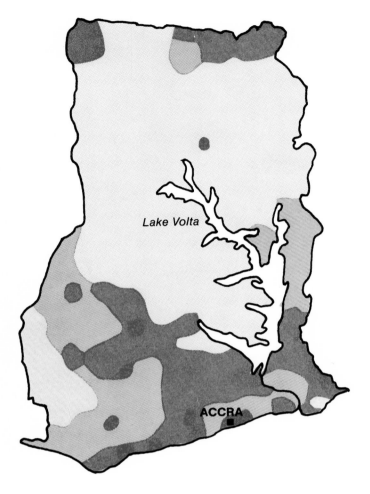

FIGURE 21
POPULATION

Persons per square mile

0-50

50-100

100-400

400 and over

FIGURE 22
ETHNIC GROUPS

Akan

Ewe

Guan

Gur subfamily

Ga-Adangbe

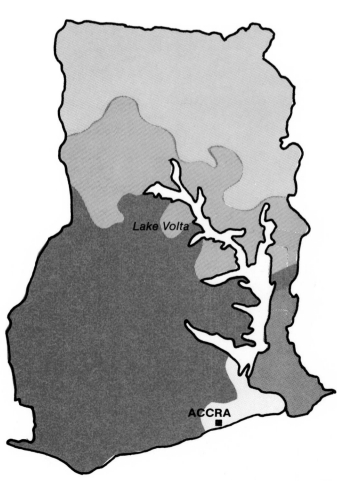

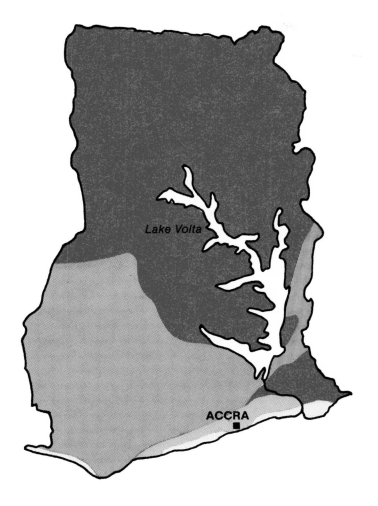

FIGURE 23
VEGETATION

▓	Savanna
▒	Broadleaf forest
░	Coastal grassland
□	Coastal swamp or marsh

FIGURE 24
ECONOMIC ACTIVITY

 Cocoa (area of maximum production—
Northern limit of cocoa growing
 Diamonds

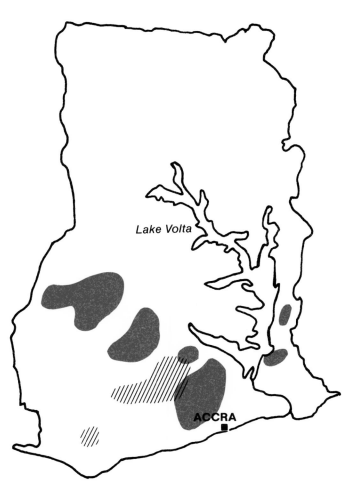

GUATEMALA

The northernmost and the most populous of the Central American republics, Guatemala ranks 99th in land area and 72nd in population. As in other countries of the region, the economy is characterized by extreme disparities in the distribution of income and this has produced social tensions spilling over into the political sphere in the form of sporadic insurgencies. The agricultural sector accounts for over one-quarter of the GDP and two-thirds of export earnings, the principal products being coffee, sugar and bananas. The country's agricultural wealth is concentrated in the hands of a small group of ladinos and foreigners (although the legendary United Fruit—later United Brands—has sold out its interests in Guatemala, U.S. interests are still substantial) who also control the larger manufacturing industries as well as trade and finance. The richest 2% are believed to control between 50% and 80% of the cultivable land, and the government's halfhearted land reform efforts have proved ineffective.

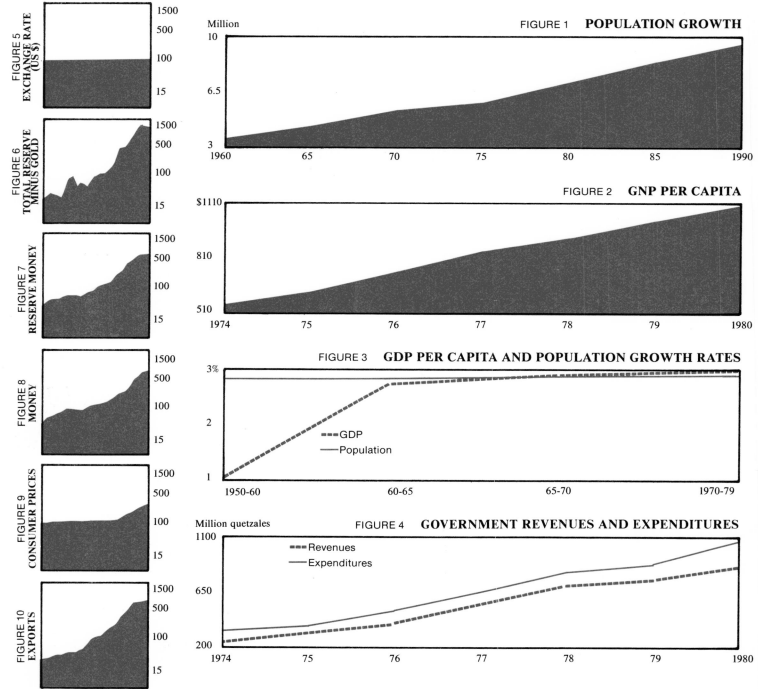

FIGURE 5 EXCHANGE RATE (US $)

FIGURE 6 TOTAL RESERVE MINUS GOLD

FIGURE 7 RESERVE MONEY

FIGURE 8 MONEY

FIGURE 9 CONSUMER PRICES

FIGURE 10 EXPORTS

FIGURE 1 **POPULATION GROWTH**

FIGURE 2 **GNP PER CAPITA**

FIGURE 3 **GDP PER CAPITA AND POPULATION GROWTH RATES**

FIGURE 4 **GOVERNMENT REVENUES AND EXPENDITURES**

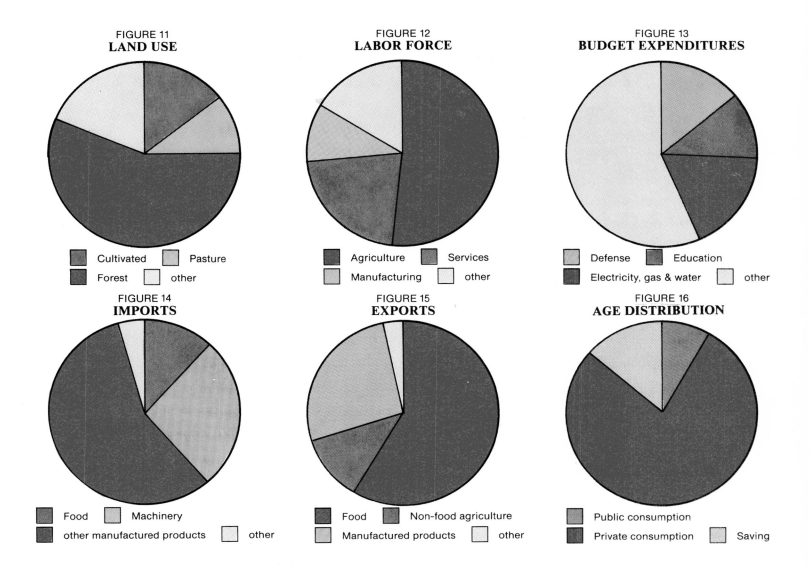

FIGURE 11
LAND USE

Cultivated Pasture
Forest other

FIGURE 12
LABOR FORCE

Agriculture Services
Manufacturing other

FIGURE 13
BUDGET EXPENDITURES

Defense Education
Electricity, gas & water other

FIGURE 14
IMPORTS

Food Machinery
other manufactured products other

FIGURE 15
EXPORTS

Food Non-food agriculture
Manufactured products other

FIGURE 16
AGE DISTRIBUTION

Public consumption
Private consumption Saving

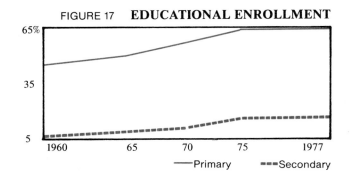

FIGURE 17 **EDUCATIONAL ENROLLMENT**

65%

35

5

1960   65   70   75   1977

——Primary ===Secondary

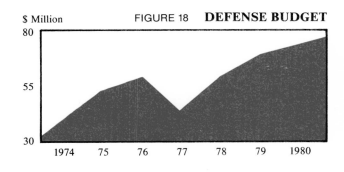

$ Million   FIGURE 18 **DEFENSE BUDGET**

80

55

30

1974   75   76   77   78   79   1980

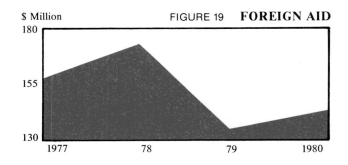

$ Million   FIGURE 19 **FOREIGN AID**

180

155

130

1977   78   79   1980

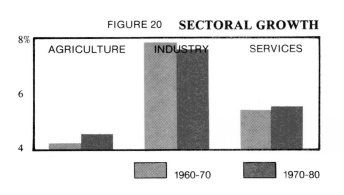

FIGURE 20 **SECTORAL GROWTH**

8%   AGRICULTURE   INDUSTRY   SERVICES

6

4

1960-70   1970-80

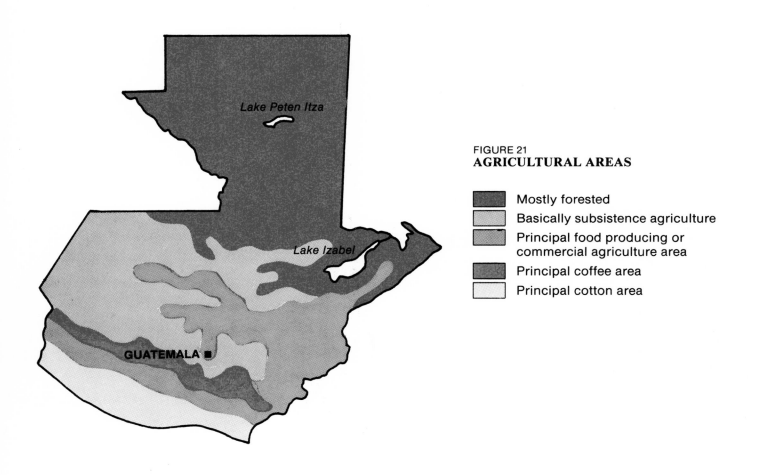

FIGURE 21
AGRICULTURAL AREAS

- Mostly forested
- Basically subsistence agriculture
- Principal food producing or commercial agriculture area
- Principal coffee area
- Principal cotton area

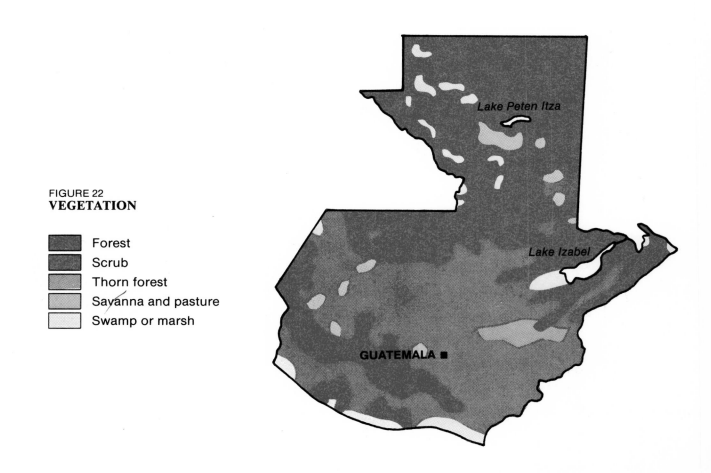

FIGURE 22
VEGETATION

- Forest
- Scrub
- Thorn forest
- Savanna and pasture
- Swamp or marsh

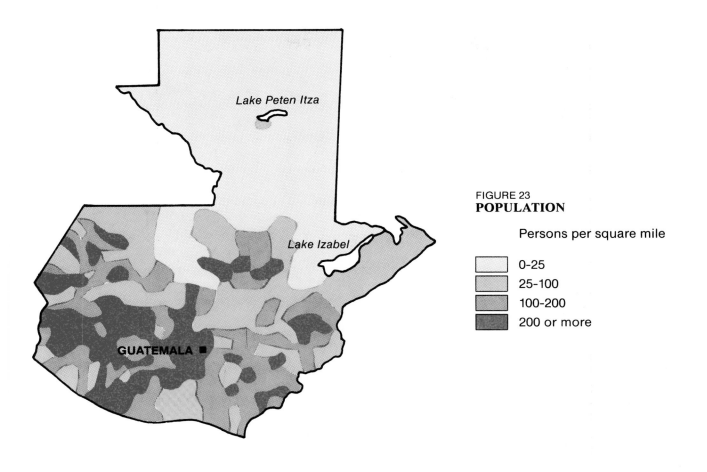

FIGURE 23
POPULATION

Persons per square mile

0-25

25-100

100-200

200 or more

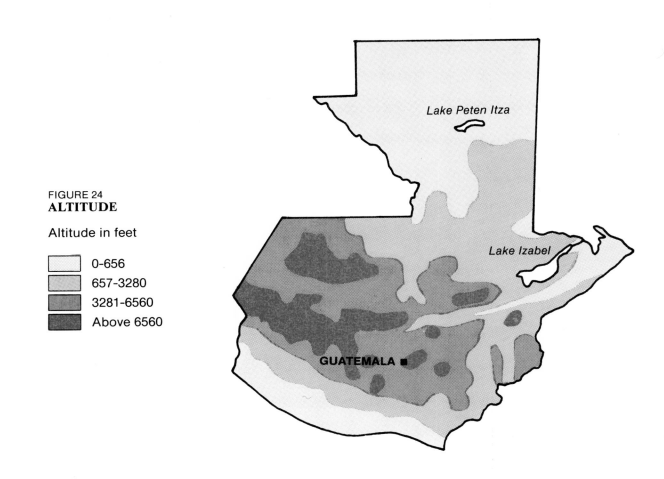

FIGURE 24
ALTITUDE

Altitude in feet

0-656

657-3280

3281-6560

Above 6560

GUINEA

Located on the bulge of West Africa, and one of the most politically stable countries in Africa, Guinea ranks 69th in land area and 81st in population. Despite enormous mineral resources—its bauxite resources are reputed to be the third largest in the world—the Guinean economy has never really taken off and by all standard indicators it remains one of the poorest countries in the world, where 75% of the population subsists in absolute poverty. Many of the country's intractable problems could be traced to President Toure's unbending dedication to his concept of a centrally planned economy, especially as applied to agriculture, which employs 85% of the work force and contributes 30% of the GDP. After 25 years of independence, the collectivized economy has been a dismal failure resulting in the loss of the country's former self-sufficiency in food. More recently, however, the government has been restoring elements of private enterprise to all sectors and stepping up the exploitation of mineral resources to generate investment capital.

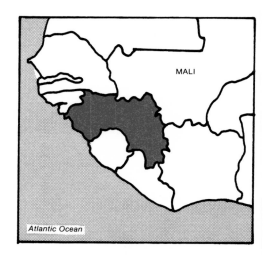

I.M.F.
DATA
UNAVAILABLE

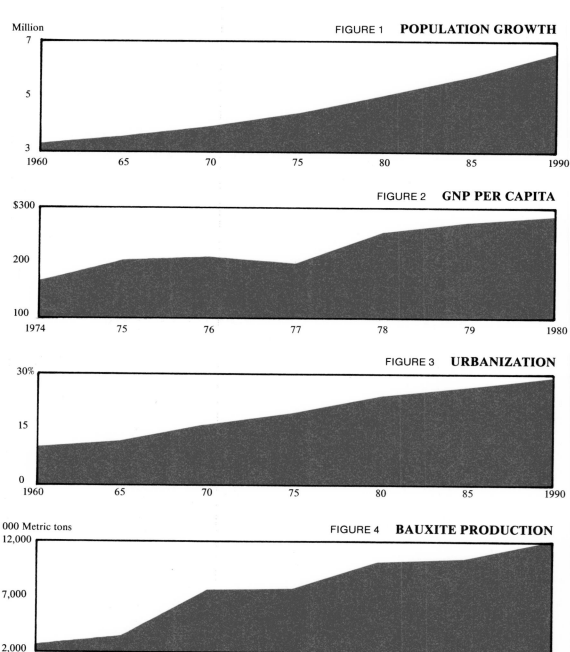

FIGURE 1 **POPULATION GROWTH**

FIGURE 2 **GNP PER CAPITA**

FIGURE 3 **URBANIZATION**

FIGURE 4 **BAUXITE PRODUCTION**

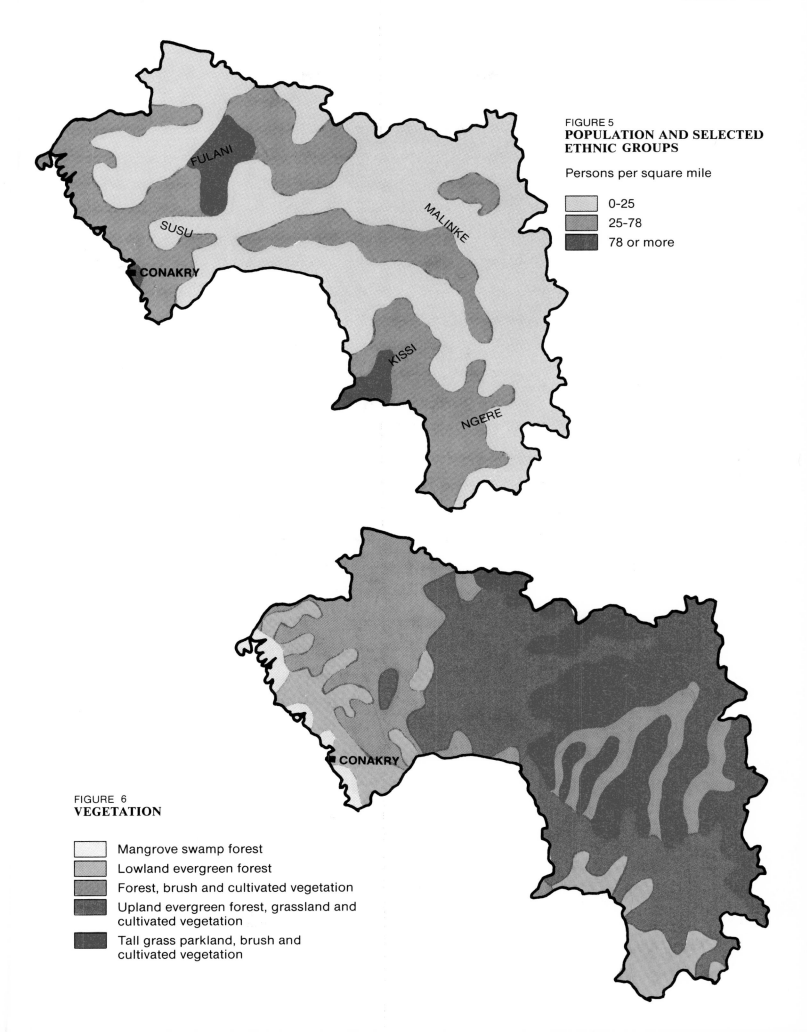

FIGURE 5
POPULATION AND SELECTED ETHNIC GROUPS

Persons per square mile

0-25

25-78

78 or more

FULANI

SUSU

CONAKRY

MALINKE

KISSI

NGERE

FIGURE 6
VEGETATION

Mangrove swamp forest

Lowland evergreen forest

Forest, brush and cultivated vegetation

Upland evergreen forest, grassland and cultivated vegetation

Tall grass parkland, brush and cultivated vegetation

CONAKRY

GUYANA

Located on the northern Atlantic coast of South America, Guyana ranks 75th in land area and 133rd in population. A former British enclave, Guyana shares very little, culturally or politically, with its Luso-Hispanic neighbors. It has an ethnic and religious variety quite unknown in the larger countries of the South American continent and, in fact, has more in common with the former British West Indian territories. In 1980, it adopted a socialist constitution, the first state in South America to do so. In accordance with its socialist goals, the government has carried out a nationalization program affecting all large enterprises in agriculture, industry and mining. Three commodities—bauxite, sugar and rice—account for over 80% of the country's foreign exchange earnings, bauxite alone accounting for half that figure.

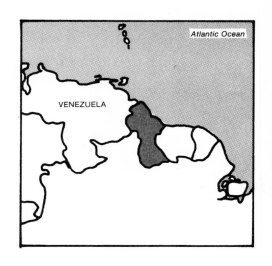

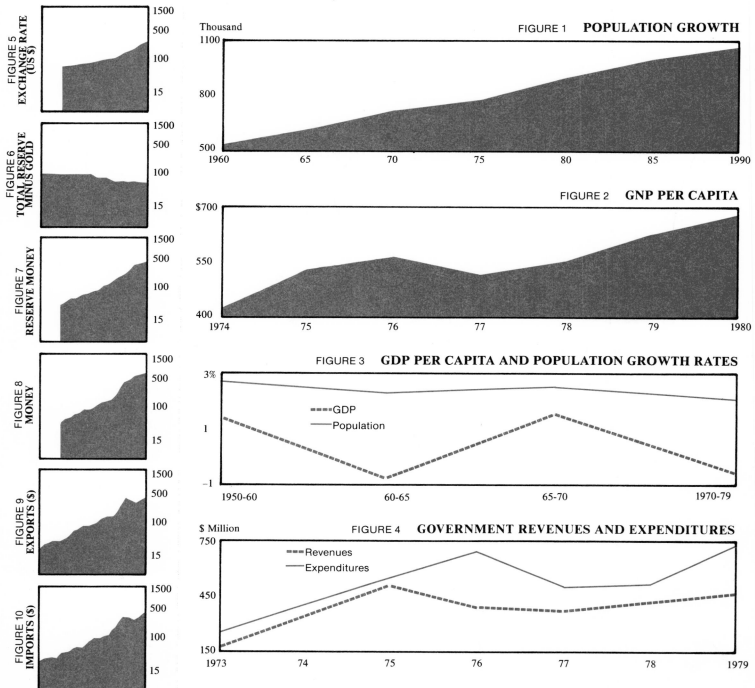

FIGURE 5 EXCHANGE RATE (US $)

FIGURE 6 TOTAL RESERVE MINUS GOLD

FIGURE 7 RESERVE MONEY

FIGURE 8 MONEY

FIGURE 9 EXPORTS ($)

FIGURE 10 IMPORTS ($)

FIGURE 1 **POPULATION GROWTH**

FIGURE 2 **GNP PER CAPITA**

FIGURE 3 **GDP PER CAPITA AND POPULATION GROWTH RATES**

FIGURE 4 **GOVERNMENT REVENUES AND EXPENDITURES**

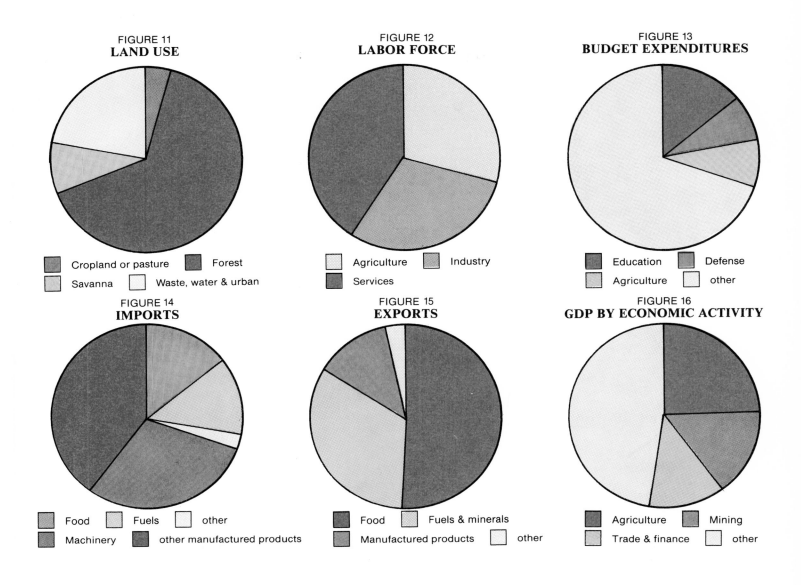

FIGURE 11
LAND USE

Cropland or pasture   Forest
Savanna   Waste, water & urban

FIGURE 12
LABOR FORCE

Agriculture   Industry
Services

FIGURE 13
BUDGET EXPENDITURES

Education   Defense
Agriculture   other

FIGURE 14
IMPORTS

Food   Fuels   other
Machinery   other manufactured products

FIGURE 15
EXPORTS

Food   Fuels & minerals
Manufactured products   other

FIGURE 16
GDP BY ECONOMIC ACTIVITY

Agriculture   Mining
Trade & finance   other

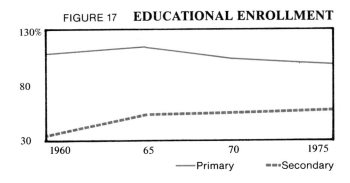

FIGURE 17   **EDUCATIONAL ENROLLMENT**

130%

80

30

1960   65   70   1975

——Primary   ■■■Secondary

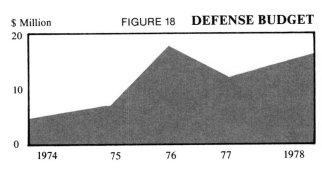

$ Million   FIGURE 18   **DEFENSE BUDGET**

20

10

0

1974   75   76   77   1978

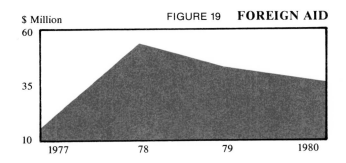

$ Million   FIGURE 19   **FOREIGN AID**

60

35

10

1977   78   79   1980

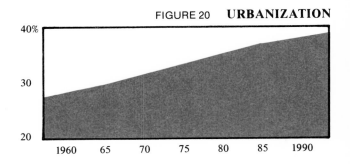

FIGURE 20   **URBANIZATION**

40%

30

20

1960   65   70   75   80   85   1990

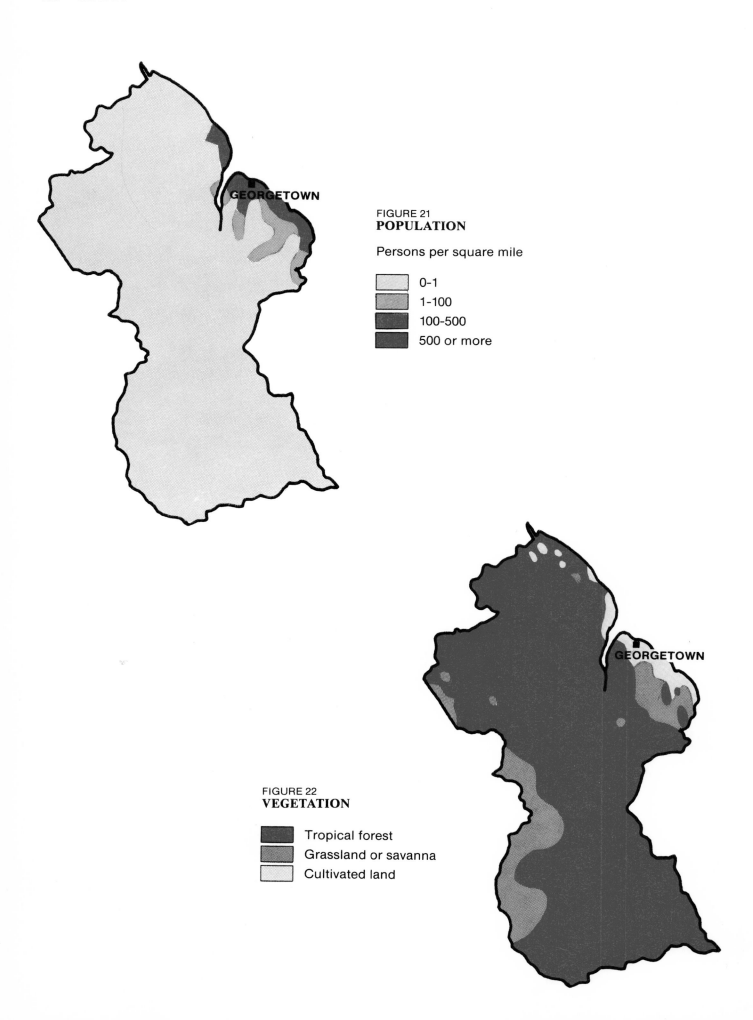

FIGURE 21
POPULATION

Persons per square mile

0-1
1-100
100-500
500 or more

GEORGETOWN

FIGURE 22
VEGETATION

Tropical forest
Grassland or savanna
Cultivated land

GEORGETOWN

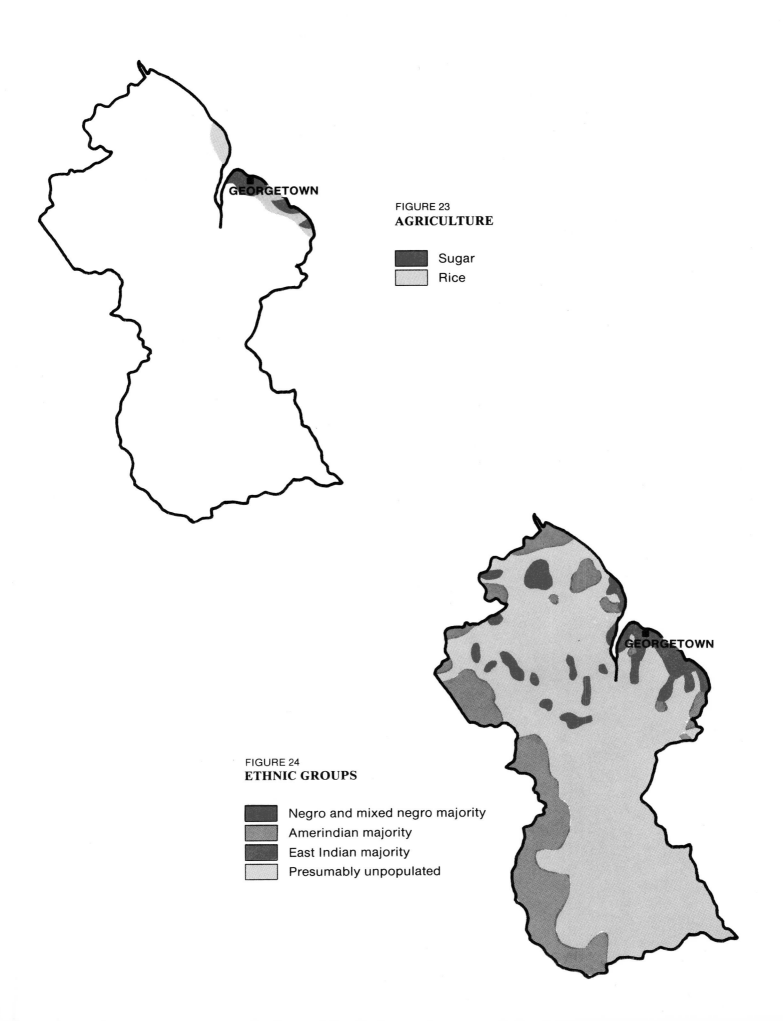

FIGURE 23
AGRICULTURE

Sugar
Rice

FIGURE 24
ETHNIC GROUPS

Negro and mixed negro majority
Amerindian majority
East Indian majority
Presumably unpopulated

HAITI

Haiti occupies the western third of the island of Hispaniola in the Caribbean and ranks 128th in land area and 87th in population. The sixth most densely populated country in the Western Hemisphere, Haiti is also one of the poorest with a per capita income of $270. Apart from its poverty and its voodoo practices, Haiti is best known as the only republic in the Western Hemisphere where French is the sole official language. Haiti ranks poorly in all physical quality of life indicators. Health conditions are substandard except in the capital, illiteracy approaches 80%, and nearly 25% are unemployed and 50% underemployed. While 90% of the population lives in absolute poverty, the richest 5% account for over half the national income. Agriculture employs 80% of the work force and contributes two-fifths of the GNP. Economic progress is also impeded by a lack of infrastructure. Apart from Port-au-Prince, the country is largely without electric power, telephone service, safe water supplies, paved roads and rail transportation.

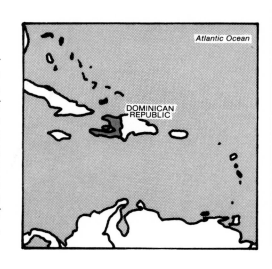

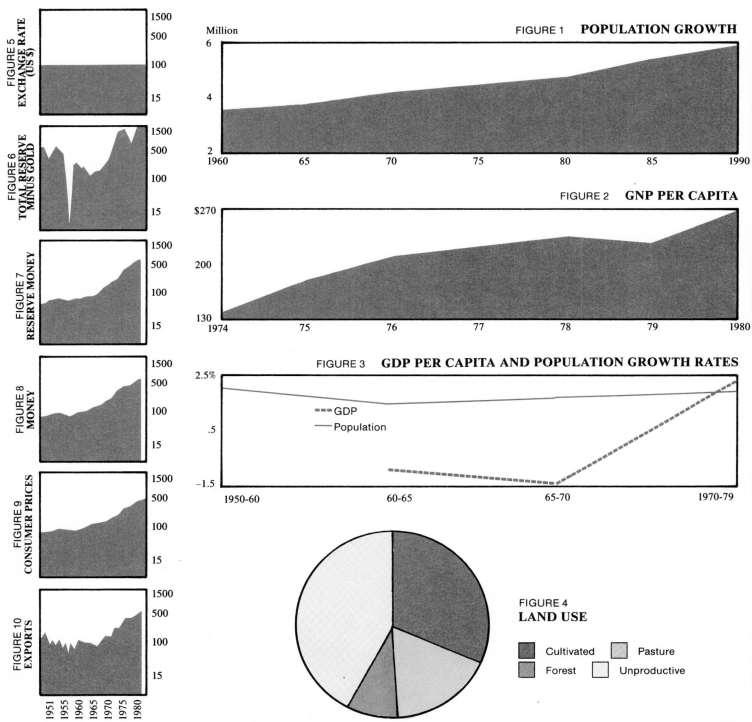

FIGURE 5 EXCHANGE RATE (US $)

FIGURE 6 TOTAL RESERVE MINUS GOLD

FIGURE 7 RESERVE MONEY

FIGURE 8 MONEY

FIGURE 9 CONSUMER PRICES

FIGURE 10 EXPORTS

FIGURE 1 **POPULATION GROWTH**

FIGURE 2 **GNP PER CAPITA**

FIGURE 3 **GDP PER CAPITA AND POPULATION GROWTH RATES**

- - - GDP
—— Population

FIGURE 4
LAND USE

Cultivated   Pasture
Forest   Unproductive

FIGURE 5
POLITICAL DIVISIONS

FIGURE 6
TOPOGRAPHIC FEATURES

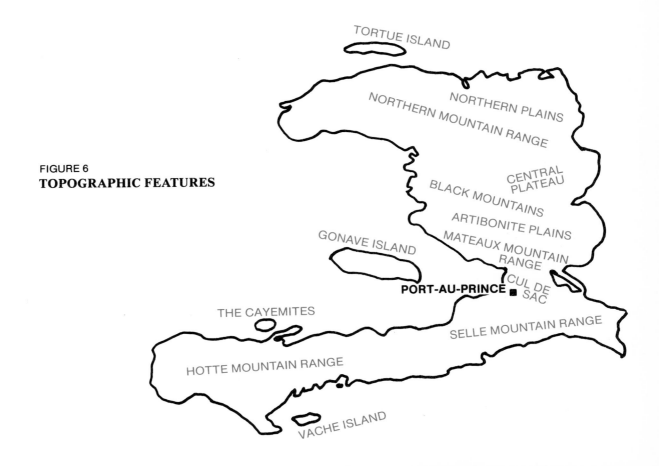

HONDURAS

One of the banana republics of Central America, Honduras ranks 96th in land area and 109th in population. Although less adversely affected by the political unrest that has plagued its neighbors, Honduras still suffers from a population growth rate that is seven times higher than its GNP growth rate (3.4% as against 0.5%). Nevertheless, the economic prognosis is better for Honduras than other Central American republics, and all sectors, particularly agriculture, industry, commerce and tourism, have been expanding at impressive rates. Until 1976, bananas constituted the leading export crop but coffee has become the major foreign-exchange earner since then. Honduras has the most attractive investment climate in Central America, particularly because it has no restriction on the repatriation of dividends, interest or capital. Investors can also import basic materials and equipment duty free. Four of the five largest foreign corporate ventures are U.S.-owned, reflecting substantial U.S. involvement in the economy.

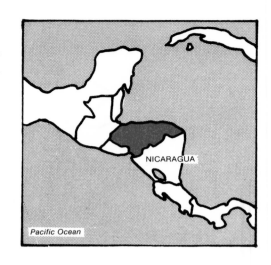

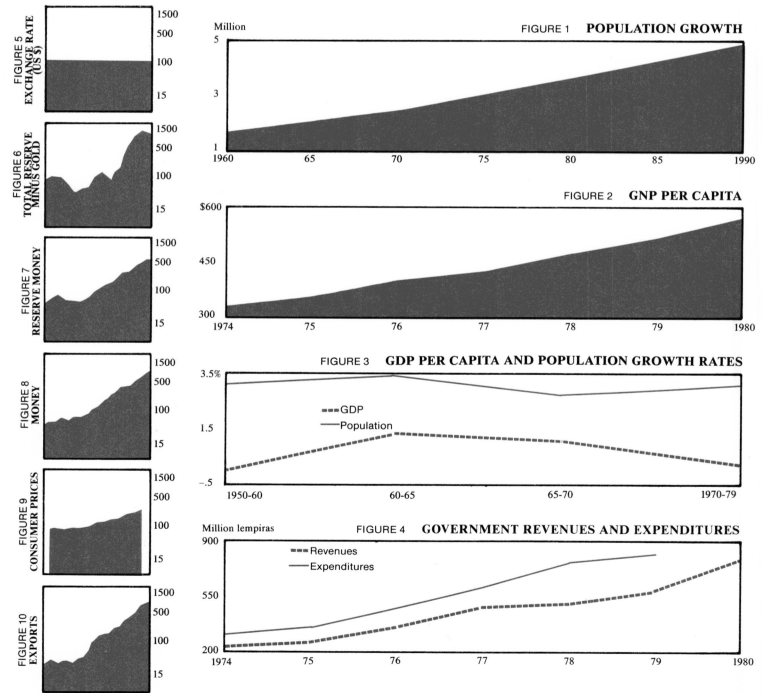

FIGURE 5 EXCHANGE RATE (US $)

FIGURE 6 TOTAL RESERVE MINUS GOLD

FIGURE 7 RESERVE MONEY

FIGURE 8 MONEY

FIGURE 9 CONSUMER PRICES

FIGURE 10 EXPORTS

FIGURE 1 **POPULATION GROWTH**

FIGURE 2 **GNP PER CAPITA**

FIGURE 3 **GDP PER CAPITA AND POPULATION GROWTH RATES**

- - - GDP
—— Population

FIGURE 4 **GOVERNMENT REVENUES AND EXPENDITURES**

- - - Revenues
—— Expenditures

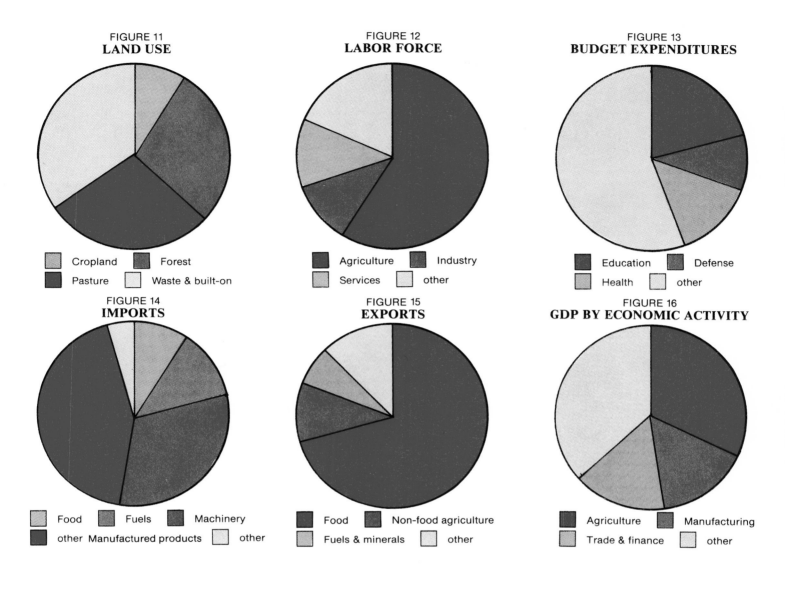

FIGURE 11
LAND USE

☐ Cropland   ☐ Forest
☐ Pasture   ☐ Waste & built-on

FIGURE 12
LABOR FORCE

☐ Agriculture   ☐ Industry
☐ Services   ☐ other

FIGURE 13
BUDGET EXPENDITURES

☐ Education   ☐ Defense
☐ Health   ☐ other

FIGURE 14
IMPORTS

☐ Food   ☐ Fuels   ☐ Machinery
☐ other   Manufactured products   ☐ other

FIGURE 15
EXPORTS

☐ Food   ☐ Non-food agriculture
☐ Fuels & minerals   ☐ other

FIGURE 16
GDP BY ECONOMIC ACTIVITY

☐ Agriculture   ☐ Manufacturing
☐ Trade & finance   ☐ other

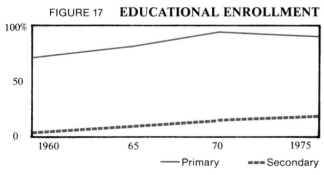

FIGURE 17   **EDUCATIONAL ENROLLMENT**

100%

50

0

1960   65   70   1975

—— Primary   ═══ Secondary

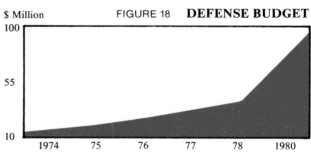

$ Million   FIGURE 18   **DEFENSE BUDGET**

100

55

10

1974   75   76   77   78   1980

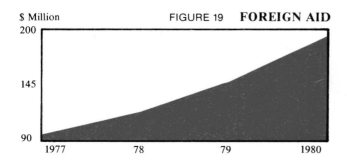

$ Million   FIGURE 19   **FOREIGN AID**

200

145

90

1977   78   79   1980

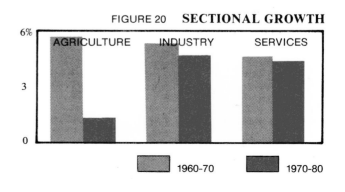

FIGURE 20   **SECTIONAL GROWTH**

6%   AGRICULTURE   INDUSTRY   SERVICES

3

0

☐ 1960-70   ☐ 1970-80

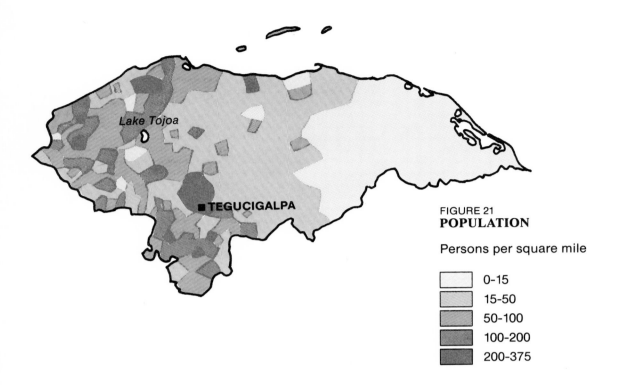

FIGURE 21
POPULATION

Persons per square mile

	0-15
	15-50
	50-100
	100-200
	200-375

FIGURE 22
LAND UTILIZATION

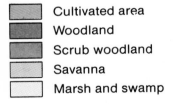

Cultivated area
Woodland
Scrub woodland
Savanna
Marsh and swamp

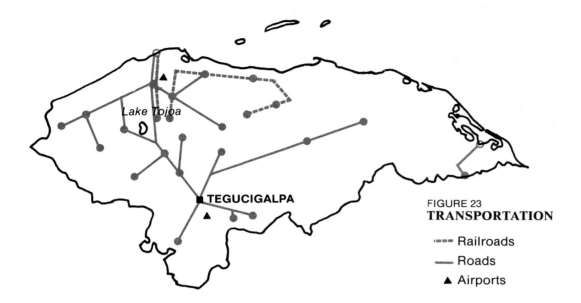

FIGURE 23
TRANSPORTATION

==== Railroads
—— Roads
▲ Airports

FIGURE 24
ALTITUDE

Altitude in feet

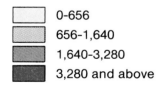

0-656
656-1,640
1,640-3,280
3,280 and above

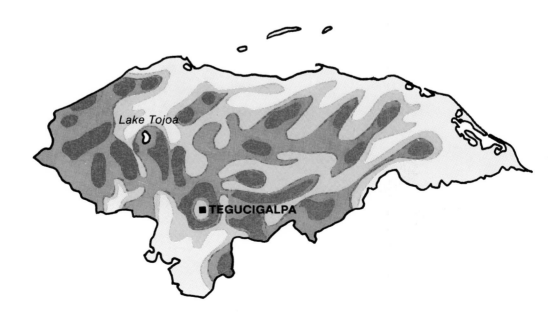

INDIA

The largest country on the Indian subcontinent, India is the second most populous country in the world and the seventh largest. Although it occupies only 2.09% of the world's land surface, it supports 14% of the world's population and the latter percentage is growing at an alarming rate. More languages are spoken and more religions professed in India than in any other country in the world. Only 12 countries exceed India in aggregate GNP but, because of its high population, it ranks among the poorest in per capita income. Despite the socialist commitment of the Nehru and Gandhi governments, extremes of wealth and poverty remain. A sizable public sector exists cheek by jowl with a vigorous but shrinking private sector. Agriculture is the mainstay of the economy and one bad harvest usually sends shock waves through every sector. India's economy remains vulnerable and subject to many constraints; it has yet to reach the 5 to 6% aggregate growth rate necessary for a low-income country to escape the poverty cycle.

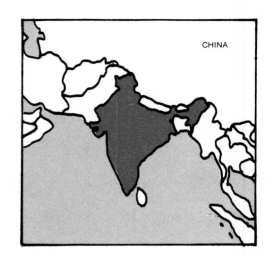

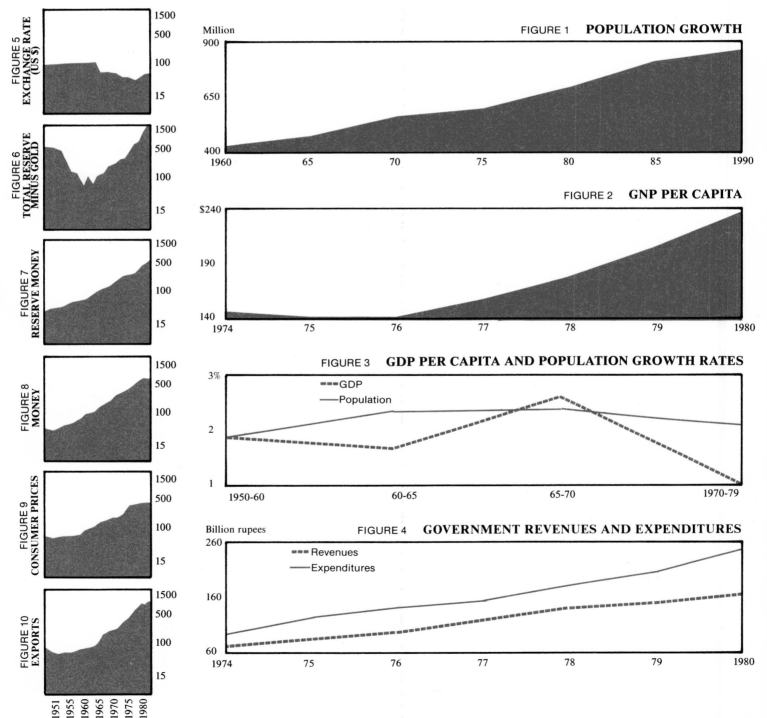

FIGURE 5 EXCHANGE RATE (US $)

FIGURE 6 TOTAL RESERVE MINUS GOLD

FIGURE 7 RESERVE MONEY

FIGURE 8 MONEY

FIGURE 9 CONSUMER PRICES

FIGURE 10 EXPORTS

FIGURE 1 **POPULATION GROWTH**

FIGURE 2 **GNP PER CAPITA**

FIGURE 3 **GDP PER CAPITA AND POPULATION GROWTH RATES**

FIGURE 4 **GOVERNMENT REVENUES AND EXPENDITURES**

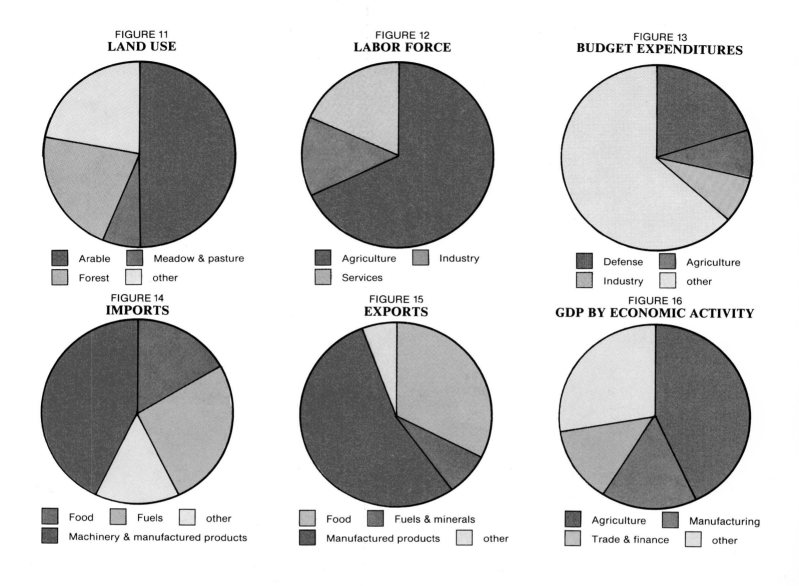

FIGURE 11
LAND USE

- Arable
- Meadow & pasture
- Forest
- other

FIGURE 12
LABOR FORCE

- Agriculture
- Industry
- Services

FIGURE 13
BUDGET EXPENDITURES

- Defense
- Agriculture
- Industry
- other

FIGURE 14
IMPORTS

- Food
- Fuels
- other
- Machinery & manufactured products

FIGURE 15
EXPORTS

- Food
- Fuels & minerals
- Manufactured products
- other

FIGURE 16
GDP BY ECONOMIC ACTIVITY

- Agriculture
- Manufacturing
- Trade & finance
- other

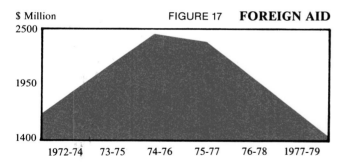

$ Million   FIGURE 17   **FOREIGN AID**

2500

1950

1400

1972-74   73-75   74-76   75-77   76-78   1977-79

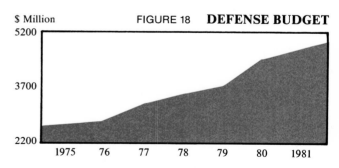

$ Million   FIGURE 18   **DEFENSE BUDGET**

5200

3700

2200

1975   76   77   78   79   80   1981

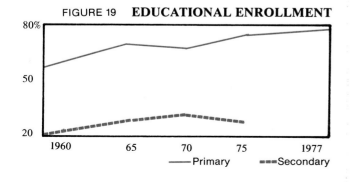

FIGURE 19   **EDUCATIONAL ENROLLMENT**

80%

50

20

1960   65   70   75   1977

——— Primary   ===Secondary

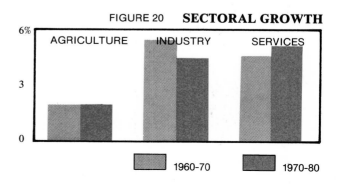

FIGURE 20   **SECTORAL GROWTH**

6%

AGRICULTURE   INDUSTRY   SERVICES

3

0

- 1960-70
- 1970-80

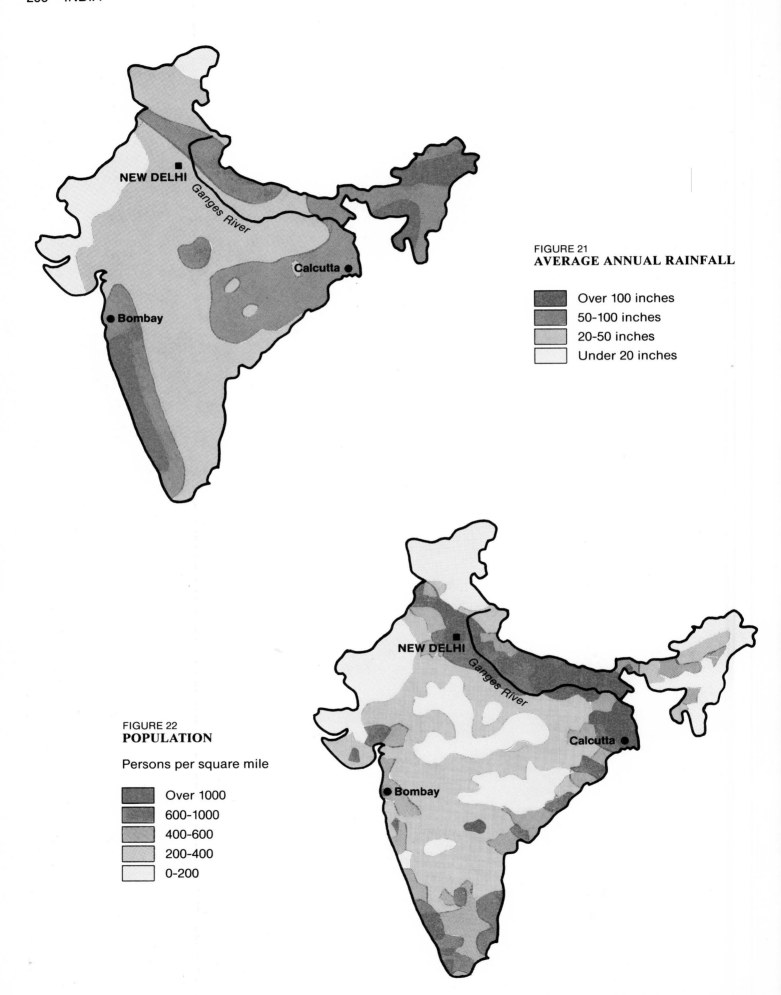

FIGURE 21
AVERAGE ANNUAL RAINFALL

Over 100 inches
50-100 inches
20-50 inches
Under 20 inches

FIGURE 22
POPULATION

Persons per square mile

Over 1000
600-1000
400-600
200-400
0-200

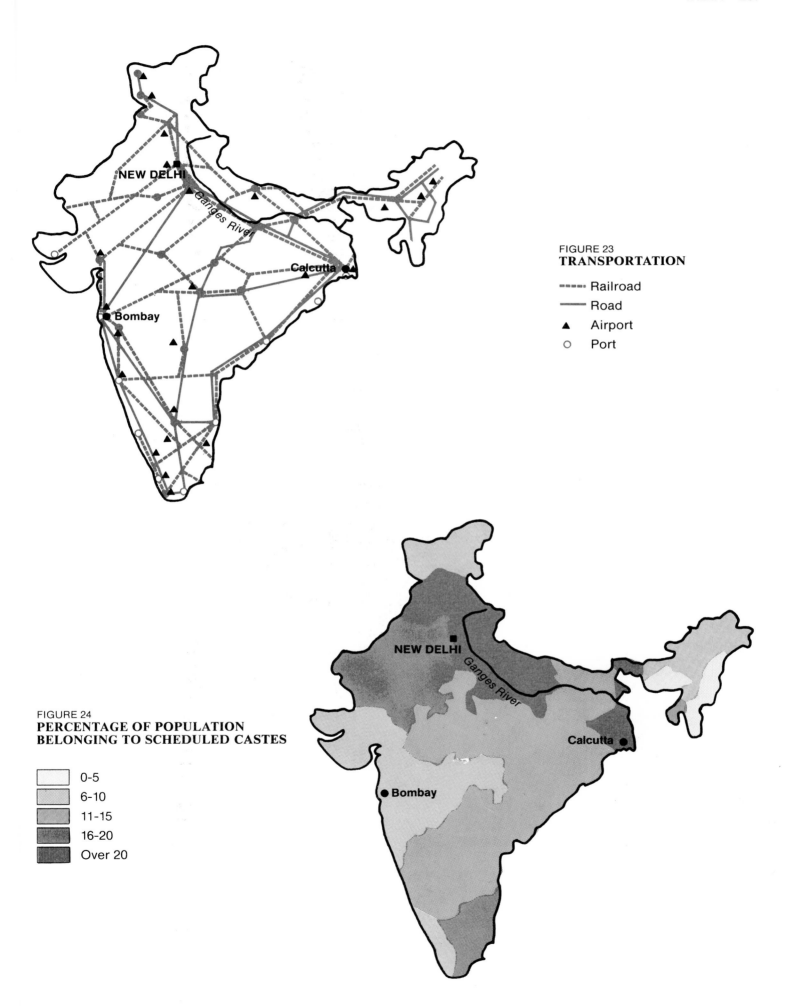

FIGURE 23
TRANSPORTATION

------- Railroad
——— Road
▲ Airport
○ Port

FIGURE 24
**PERCENTAGE OF POPULATION
BELONGING TO SCHEDULED CASTES**

0-5
6-10
11-15
16-20
Over 20

INDONESIA

An archipelago of some 13,500 islands extending along the Equator for over 3,000 miles, Indonesia is the fifth most populous nation in the world and the 16th largest in land size. Although overall density is moderate, Java is one of the most densely populated areas of the world with over 75 million inhabitants compressed into an area no larger than New York state. Despite its rich natural resources, Indonesia is classified as a low-income country and it is the only oil producer in this category. The economy is loosely divided between public and private sectors, the former dominated by the government and the latter by the Chinese. Agriculture employs over 60% of the work force but contributes only one-third of the GDP. Although soil and climate favor multiple cropping and high yields, the country is not self-sufficient in rice. The three five-year development plans—known as Repelitas—have resulted in increasing the contribution of industry to GDP from one-seventh in 1960 to one-third in 1980.

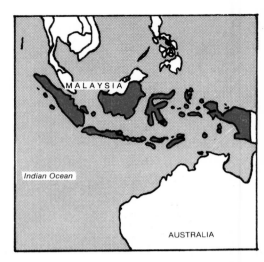

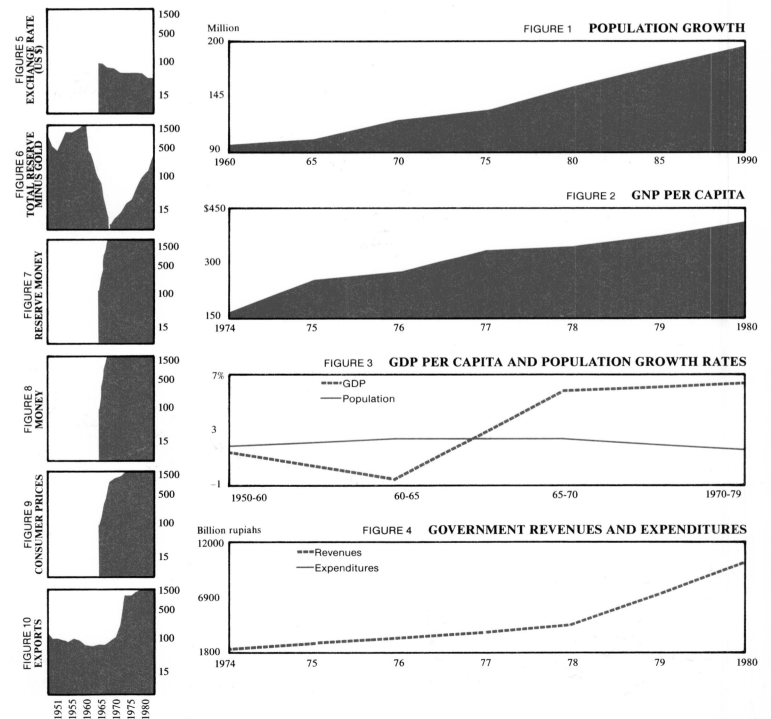

FIGURE 5 EXCHANGE RATE (US $)

FIGURE 6 TOTAL RESERVE MINUS GOLD

FIGURE 7 RESERVE MONEY

FIGURE 8 MONEY

FIGURE 9 CONSUMER PRICES

FIGURE 10 EXPORTS

FIGURE 1 **POPULATION GROWTH**

FIGURE 2 **GNP PER CAPITA**

FIGURE 3 **GDP PER CAPITA AND POPULATION GROWTH RATES**

FIGURE 4 **GOVERNMENT REVENUES AND EXPENDITURES**

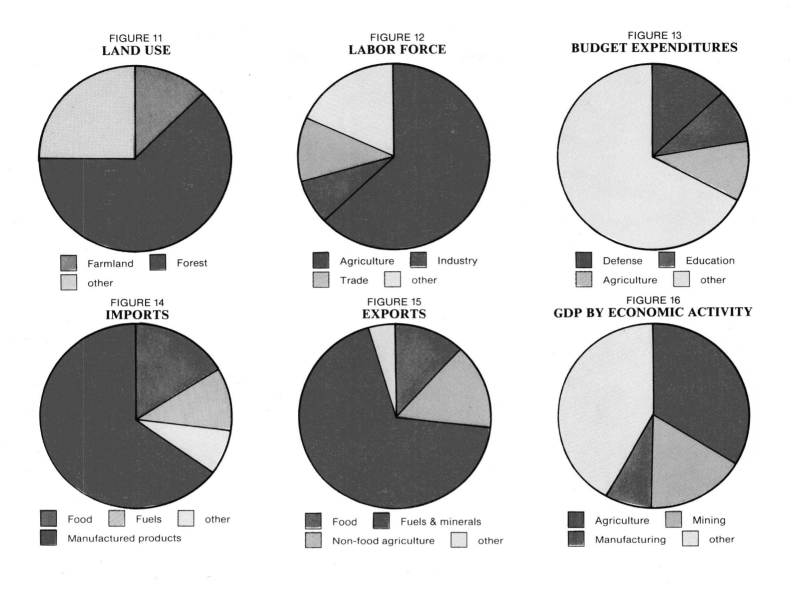

FIGURE 11
LAND USE

Farmland Forest other

FIGURE 12
LABOR FORCE

Agriculture Industry Trade other

FIGURE 13
BUDGET EXPENDITURES

Defense Education Agriculture other

FIGURE 14
IMPORTS

Food Fuels other Manufactured products

FIGURE 15
EXPORTS

Food Fuels & minerals Non-food agriculture other

FIGURE 16
GDP BY ECONOMIC ACTIVITY

Agriculture Mining Manufacturing other

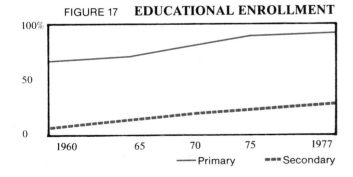

FIGURE 17   **EDUCATIONAL ENROLLMENT**

100%

50

0

1960   65   70   75   1977

Primary   Secondary

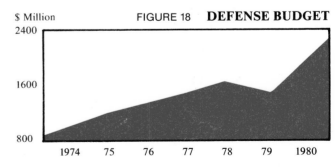

$ Million   FIGURE 18   **DEFENSE BUDGET**

2400

1600

800

1974   75   76   77   78   79   1980

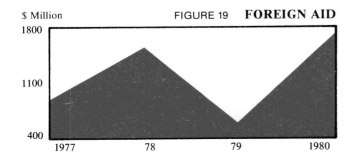

$ Million   FIGURE 19   **FOREIGN AID**

1800

1100

400

1977   78   79   1980

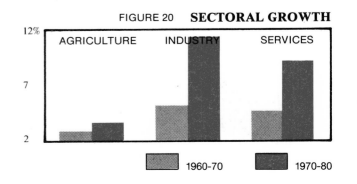

FIGURE 20   **SECTORAL GROWTH**

12%

AGRICULTURE   INDUSTRY   SERVICES

7

2

1960-70   1970-80

FIGURE 21
ETHNOLIGUISTIC DISTRIBUTION

Javanese
Coastal Malays
Balinese-Sasak
Papuan
Minangkabau

FIGURE 22
POPULATION

Persons per square mile

0-26
26-130
130-260
260 or more

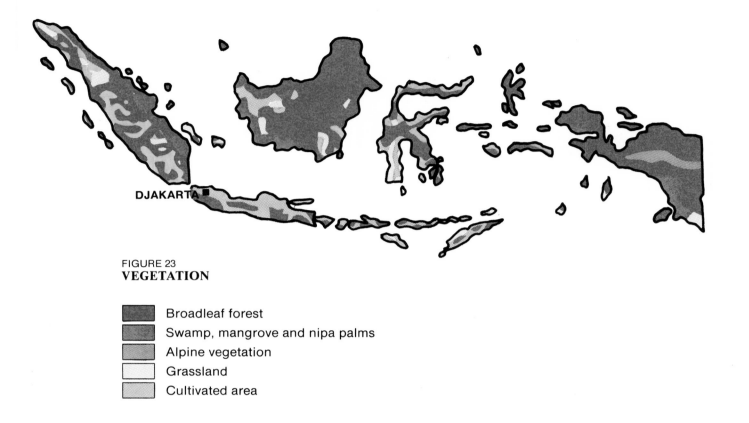

FIGURE 23
VEGETATION

- Broadleaf forest
- Swamp, mangrove and nipa palms
- Alpine vegetation
- Grassland
- Cultivated area

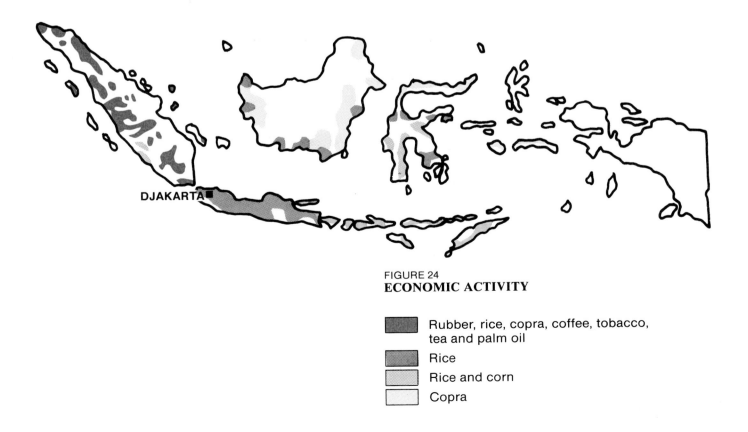

FIGURE 24
ECONOMIC ACTIVITY

- Rubber, rice, copra, coffee, tobacco, tea and palm oil
- Rice
- Rice and corn
- Copra

IRAN

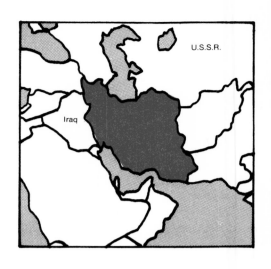

Located in southwestern Asia and larger than all countries of the EEC, Iran ranks 14th in land area and 21st in population. The only country in the world ruled by mullahs, Iran's theocratic government and civil turmoil have not seriously affected its economic structure, which continues to thrive on gushing oil revenues and coffers full of petrodollars. Only Saudi Arabia among OPEC countries produces or exports more oil than Iran. Oil revenues have enabled Iran not only to survive the political crises that followed the ouster of the shah and the seizure and occupation of the U.S. embassy in Tehran, but also to repel the Iraqis in one of the longest wars in the Middle East. However, only time will tell whether these have been Pyrrhic victories, reducing Iran's long-term potential to become a first-rank industrial power. Conflicting reports from Tehran on the state of the economy make it even more difficult to assess the situation. Nevertheless, it is well known that the oil industry has performed poorly since the revolution.

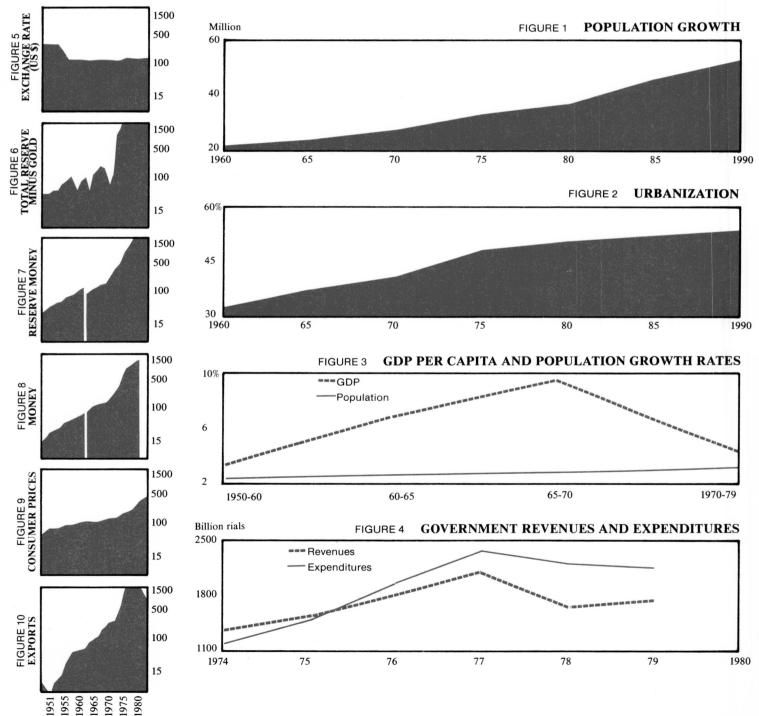

FIGURE 5 EXCHANGE RATE (US $)

FIGURE 6 TOTAL RESERVE MINUS GOLD

FIGURE 7 RESERVE MONEY

FIGURE 8 MONEY

FIGURE 9 CONSUMER PRICES

FIGURE 10 EXPORTS

FIGURE 1 **POPULATION GROWTH**

FIGURE 2 **URBANIZATION**

FIGURE 3 **GDP PER CAPITA AND POPULATION GROWTH RATES**

FIGURE 4 **GOVERNMENT REVENUES AND EXPENDITURES**

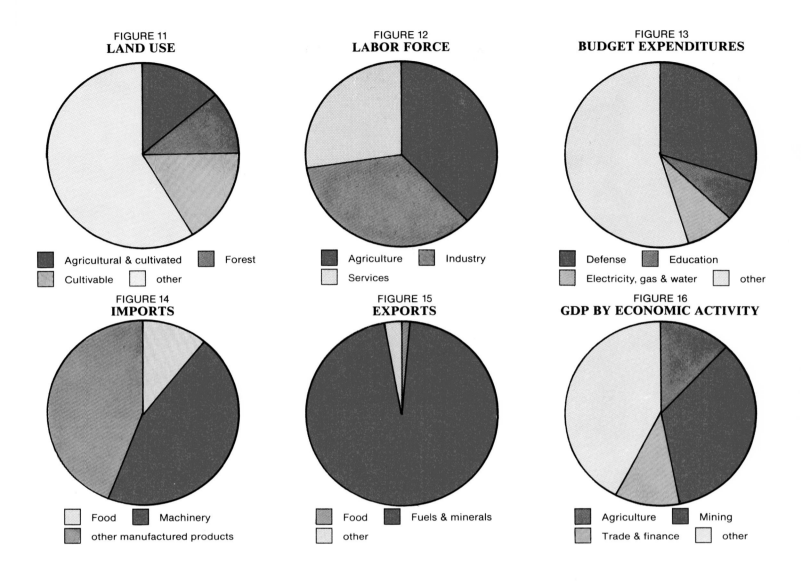

FIGURE 11
LAND USE

■ Agricultural & cultivated   ■ Forest
■ Cultivable   □ other

FIGURE 12
LABOR FORCE

■ Agriculture   ■ Industry
□ Services

FIGURE 13
BUDGET EXPENDITURES

■ Defense   ■ Education
■ Electricity, gas & water   □ other

FIGURE 14
IMPORTS

□ Food   ■ Machinery
■ other manufactured products

FIGURE 15
EXPORTS

■ Food   ■ Fuels & minerals
□ other

FIGURE 16
GDP BY ECONOMIC ACTIVITY

■ Agriculture   ■ Mining
■ Trade & finance   □ other

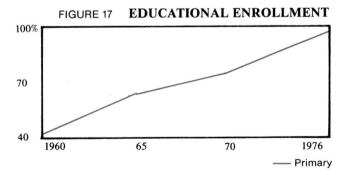

FIGURE 17   **EDUCATIONAL ENROLLMENT**

—— Primary

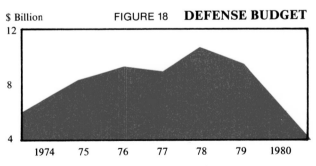

$ Billion   FIGURE 18   **DEFENSE BUDGET**

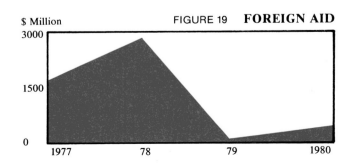

$ Million   FIGURE 19   **FOREIGN AID**

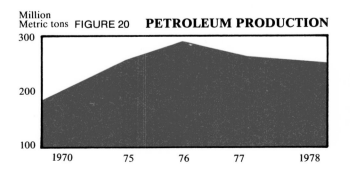

Million
Metric tons   FIGURE 20   **PETROLEUM PRODUCTION**

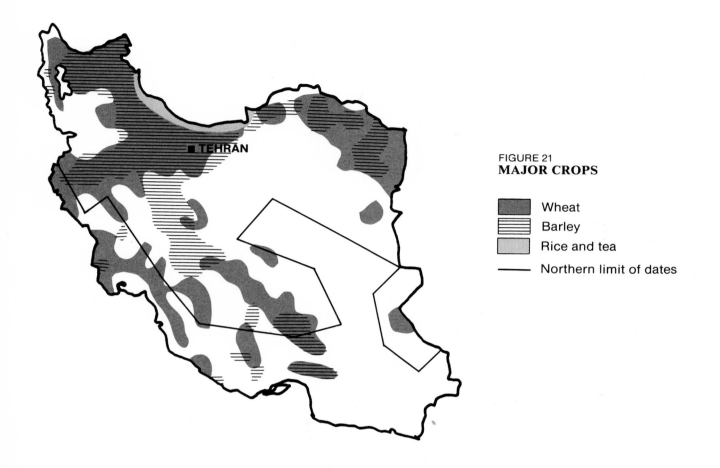

FIGURE 21
MAJOR CROPS

Wheat
Barley
Rice and tea
Northern limit of dates

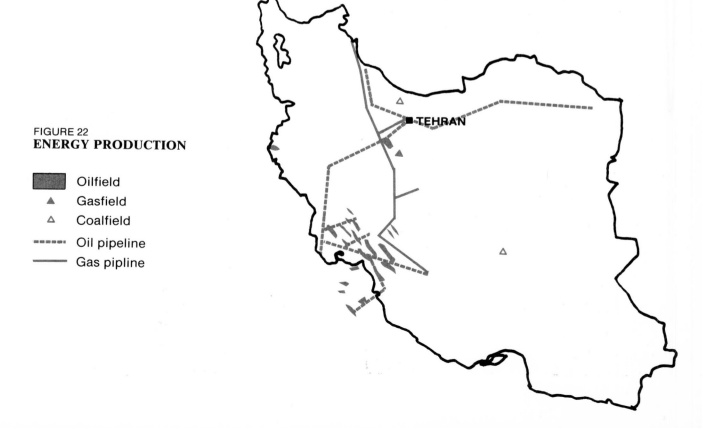

FIGURE 22
ENERGY PRODUCTION

Oilfield
Gasfield
Coalfield
Oil pipeline
Gas pipline

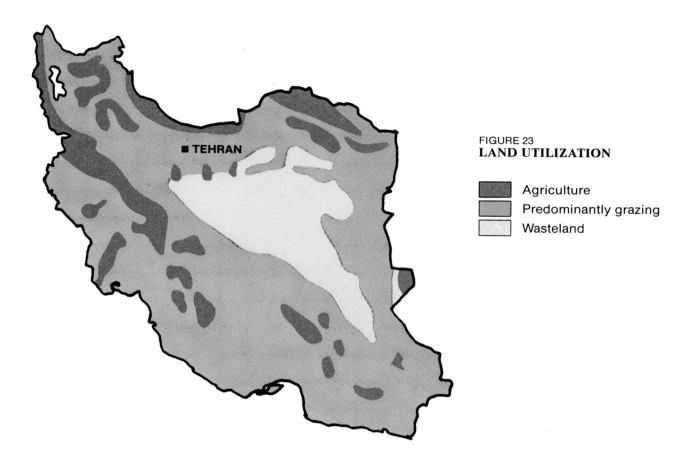

FIGURE 23
LAND UTILIZATION

Agriculture
Predominantly grazing
Wasteland

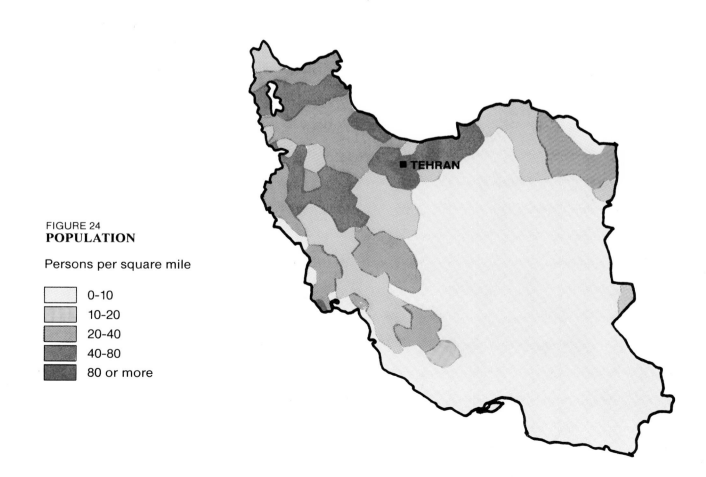

FIGURE 24
POPULATION

Persons per square mile

0-10
10-20
20-40
40-80
80 or more

IRAQ

Known as Mesopotamia, or the land between the rivers (i.e., the Tigris and the Euphrates), Iraq ranks 51st in land area and 52nd in population. Except for a short coastal strip on the Persian Gulf, Iraq is virtually a landlocked country and one of its longheld ambitions is to expand its coastline at the expense of Iran. Iraq is the sixth largest oil producer in the world and the fourth largest in the Middle East and its potential reserves are considered second only to Saudi Arabia's. The oil industry was completely nationalized by 1977 as part of a program that brought under total state control the manufacturing and mining sectors. Burgeoning oil revenues have enabled the Baath governments to launch a carefully planned modernization and industrialization program as well as a multi-billion dollar building program for new schools, houses and hospitals. More recently, Iraq has been forced to make substantial purchases of military equipment for its war against Iran; the economic effects of this war are, as yet, unclear.

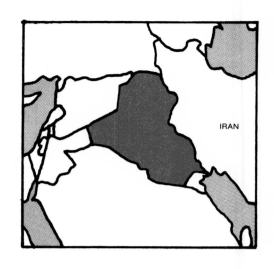

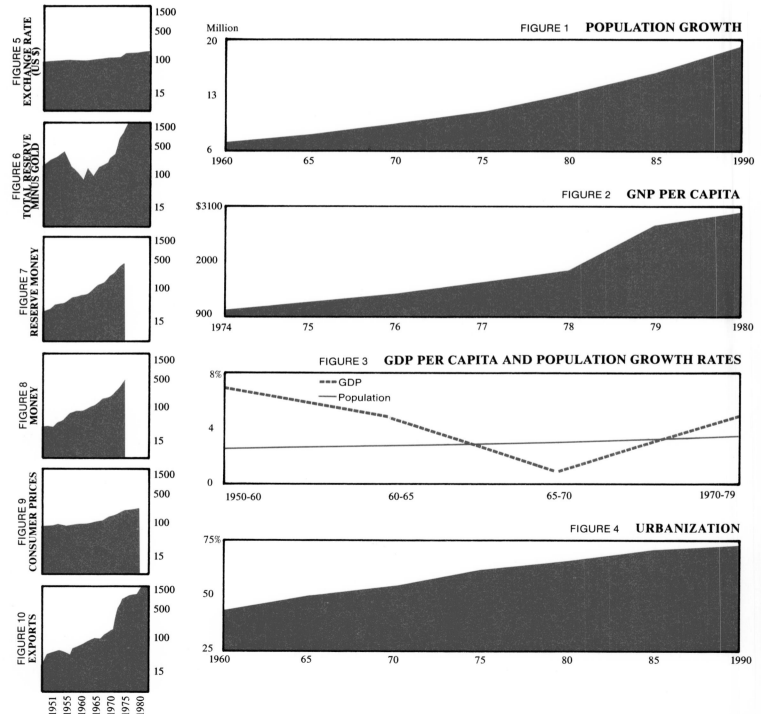

FIGURE 5 EXCHANGE RATE (US $)

FIGURE 6 TOTAL RESERVE MINUS GOLD

FIGURE 7 RESERVE MONEY

FIGURE 8 MONEY

FIGURE 9 CONSUMER PRICES

FIGURE 10 EXPORTS

FIGURE 1 **POPULATION GROWTH**

FIGURE 2 **GNP PER CAPITA**

FIGURE 3 **GDP PER CAPITA AND POPULATION GROWTH RATES**

FIGURE 4 **URBANIZATION**

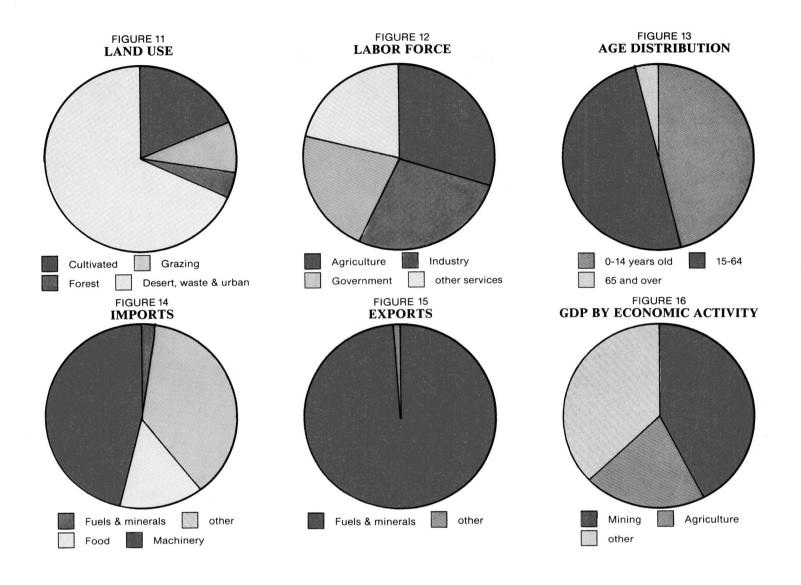

FIGURE 11
LAND USE

Cultivated ◼
Grazing ▨
Forest ◼
Desert, waste & urban ▤

FIGURE 12
LABOR FORCE

Agriculture ◼
Industry ◼
Government ▨
other services ▤

FIGURE 13
AGE DISTRIBUTION

0-14 years old ▨
15-64 ◼
65 and over ▤

FIGURE 14
IMPORTS

Fuels & minerals ◼
other ▨
Food ▤
Machinery ◼

FIGURE 15
EXPORTS

Fuels & minerals ◼
other ▨

FIGURE 16
GDP BY ECONOMIC ACTIVITY

Mining ◼
Agriculture ▨
other ▤

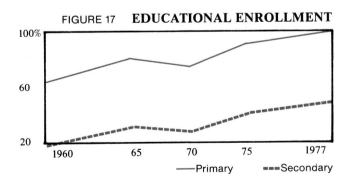

FIGURE 17   **EDUCATIONAL ENROLLMENT**

100%
60
20

1960   65   70   75   1977

——Primary   ===Secondary

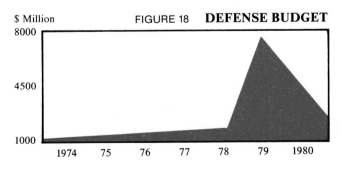

$ Million   FIGURE 18   **DEFENSE BUDGET**

8000
4500
1000

1974   75   76   77   78   79   1980

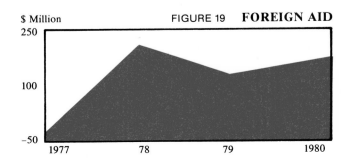

$ Million   FIGURE 19   **FOREIGN AID**

250
100
-50

1977   78   79   1980

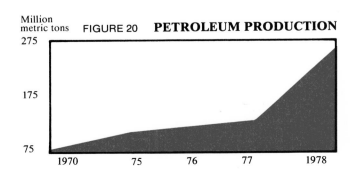

Million metric tons   FIGURE 20   **PETROLEUM PRODUCTION**

275
175
75

1970   75   76   77   1978

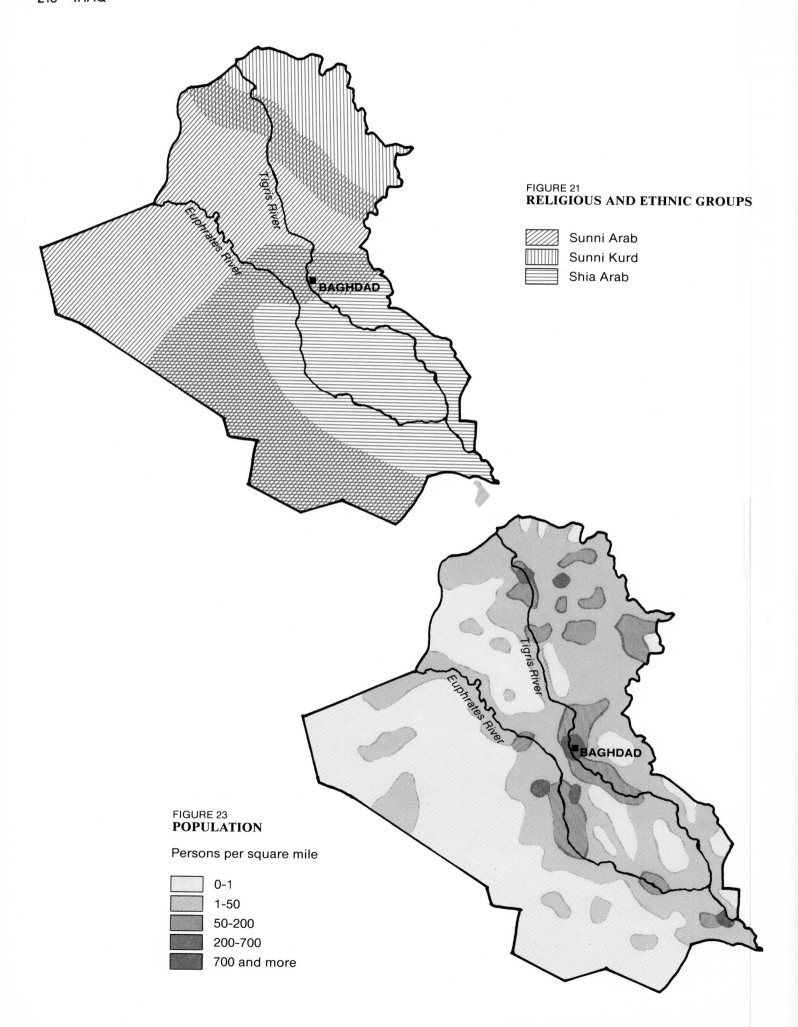

FIGURE 21
RELIGIOUS AND ETHNIC GROUPS

Sunni Arab
Sunni Kurd
Shia Arab

FIGURE 23
POPULATION

Persons per square mile

0-1
1-50
50-200
200-700
700 and more

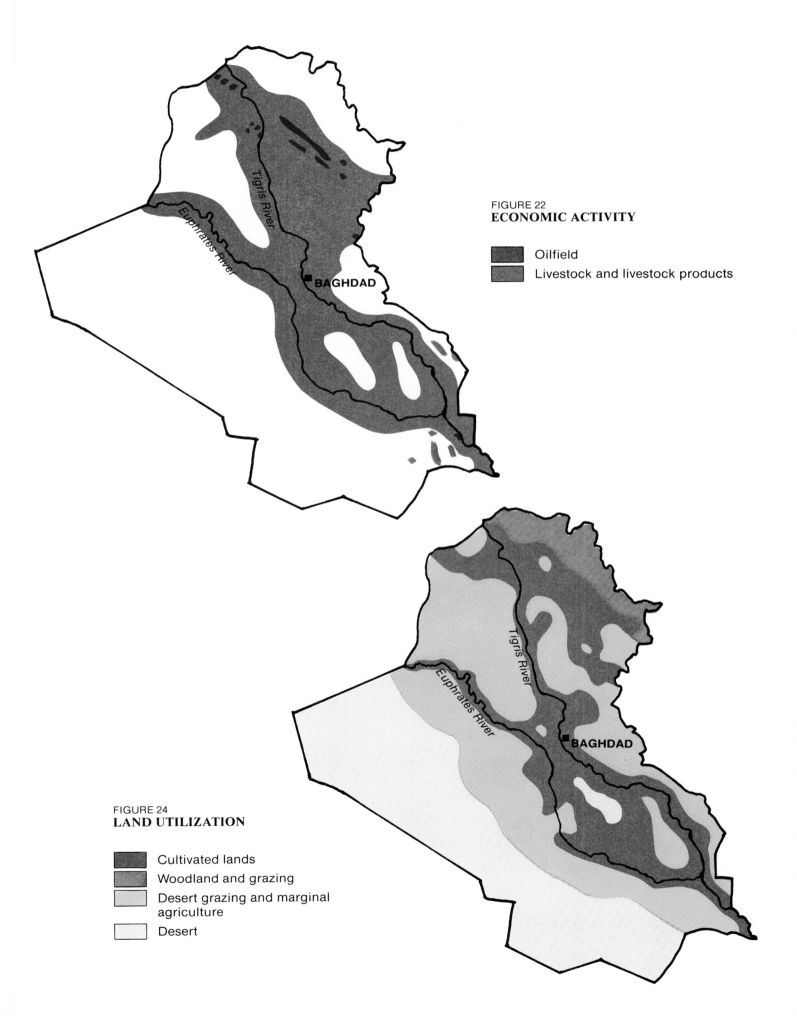

FIGURE 22
ECONOMIC ACTIVITY

- ▨ Oilfield
- ▨ Livestock and livestock products

FIGURE 24
LAND UTILIZATION

- ▨ Cultivated lands
- ▨ Woodland and grazing
- ▨ Desert grazing and marginal agriculture
- ▨ Desert

IVORY COAST

One of the richest and most self-sufficient of African states, Ivory Coast ranks 58th in land area and 83rd in population. In the 23 years since independence, it has gained a reputation for political stability and moderation and economic vitality. Such an extended period of growth was made possible by export earnings from the country's two principal commodities: coffee and cocoa. It ranks as Africa's major producer of both crops as well as the leading exporter of logs and lumber. The Houphouet-Boigny government has created the necessary climate for economic growth through liberal investment policies designed to encourage the inflow of foreign capital, technology and management expertise. Although the government remains committed to Ivorianization, it has welcomed expatriate administrative and technical skills, with the result that the country has one of the largest non-national white populations in sub-Saharan Africa, including 60,000 French and over 100,000 Lebanese, the latter engaged mostly in commerce.

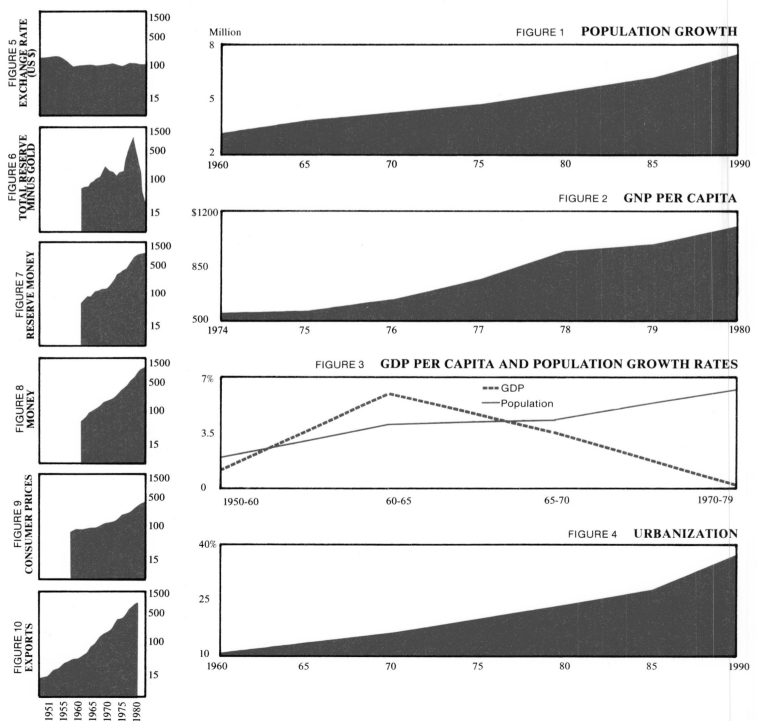

FIGURE 5 EXCHANGE RATE (US $)

FIGURE 6 TOTAL RESERVE MINUS GOLD

FIGURE 7 RESERVE MONEY

FIGURE 8 MONEY

FIGURE 9 CONSUMER PRICES

FIGURE 10 EXPORTS

FIGURE 1 **POPULATION GROWTH**

FIGURE 2 **GNP PER CAPITA**

FIGURE 3 **GDP PER CAPITA AND POPULATION GROWTH RATES**

FIGURE 4 **URBANIZATION**

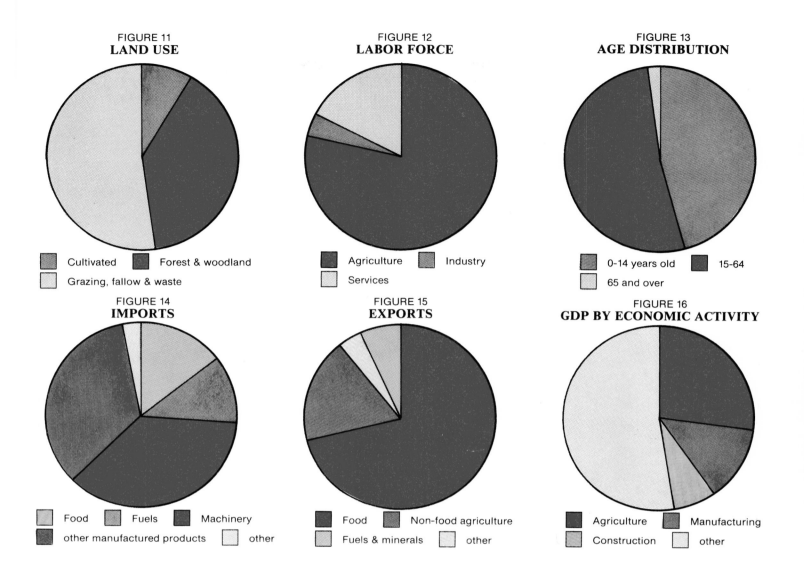

FIGURE 11
LAND USE

Cultivated
Forest & woodland
Grazing, fallow & waste

FIGURE 12
LABOR FORCE

Agriculture
Industry
Services

FIGURE 13
AGE DISTRIBUTION

0-14 years old
15-64
65 and over

FIGURE 14
IMPORTS

Food
Fuels
Machinery
other manufactured products
other

FIGURE 15
EXPORTS

Food
Non-food agriculture
Fuels & minerals
other

FIGURE 16
GDP BY ECONOMIC ACTIVITY

Agriculture
Manufacturing
Construction
other

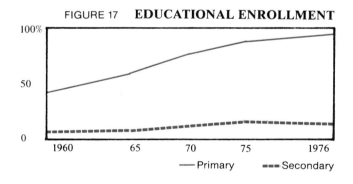

FIGURE 17   **EDUCATIONAL ENROLLMENT**

100%
50
0
1960   65   70   75   1976

— Primary   ■■■ Secondary

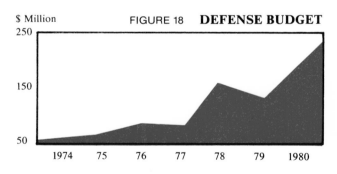

$ Million   FIGURE 18   **DEFENSE BUDGET**

250
150
50
1974   75   76   77   78   79   1980

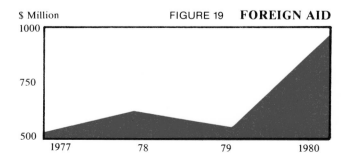

$ Million   FIGURE 19   **FOREIGN AID**

1000
750
500
1977   78   79   1980

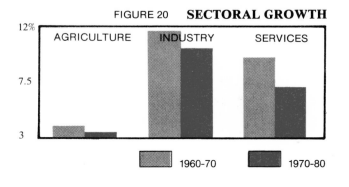

FIGURE 20   **SECTORAL GROWTH**

12%
7.5
3
AGRICULTURE   INDUSTRY   SERVICES

1960-70   1970-80

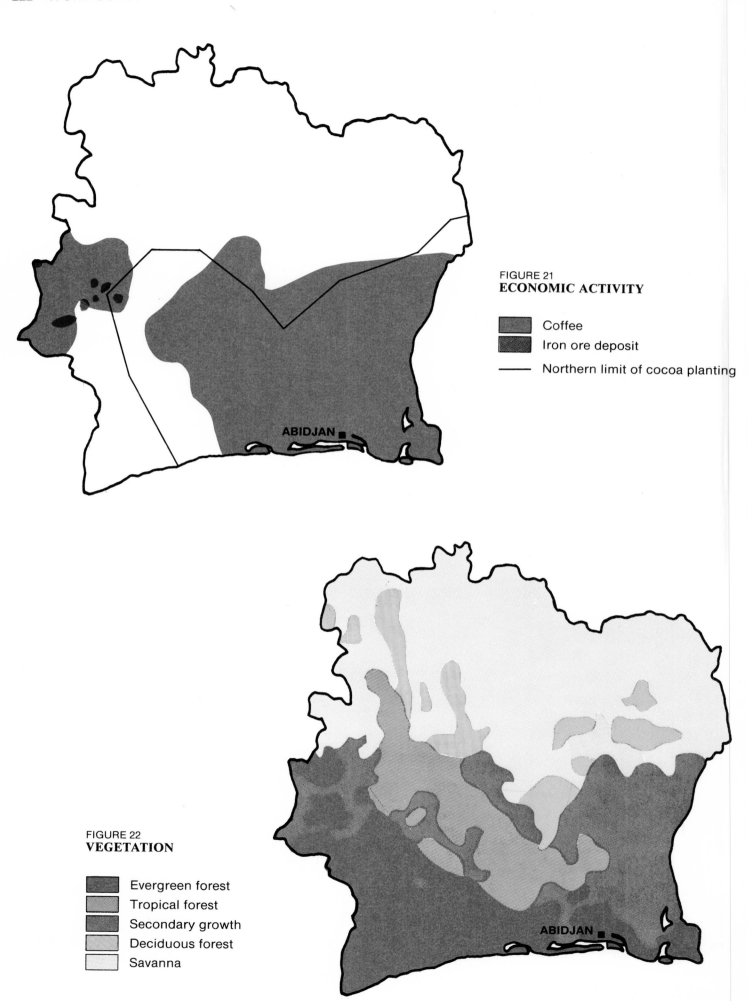

FIGURE 21
ECONOMIC ACTIVITY

■ Coffee
■ Iron ore deposit
— Northern limit of cocoa planting

ABIDJAN ■

FIGURE 22
VEGETATION

■ Evergreen forest
■ Tropical forest
■ Secondary growth
■ Deciduous forest
□ Savanna

ABIDJAN ■

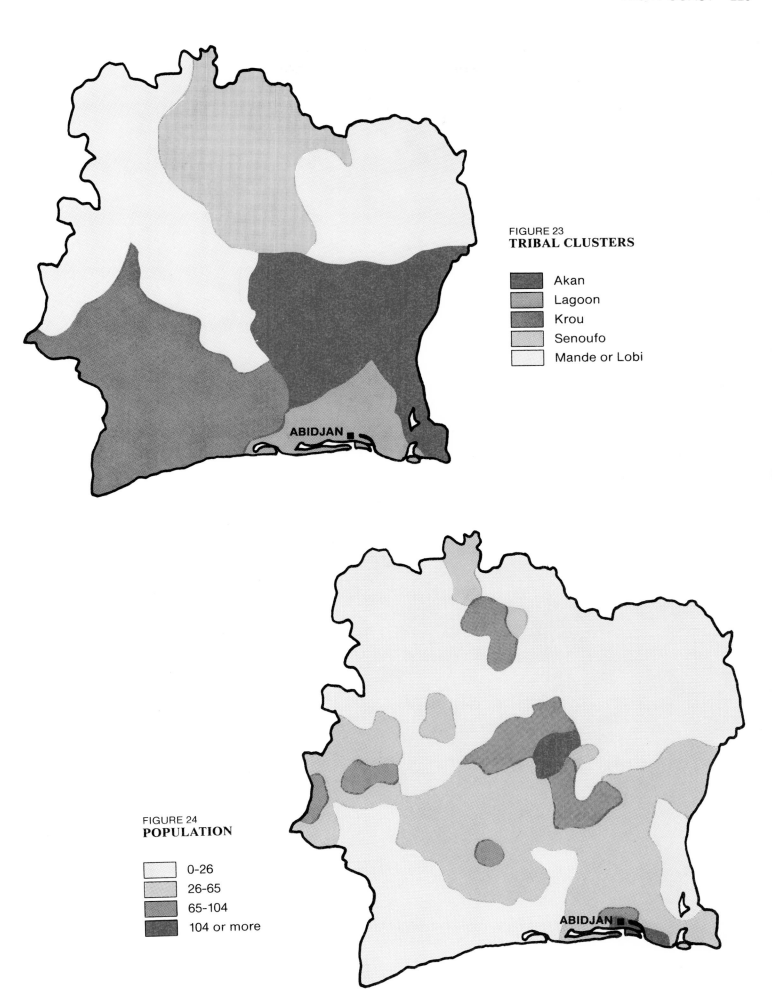

FIGURE 23
TRIBAL CLUSTERS

Akan
Lagoon
Krou
Senoufo
Mande or Lobi

ABIDJAN ■

FIGURE 24
POPULATION

0-26
26-65
65-104
104 or more

ABIDJAN ■

JAMAICA

The third largest island in the Caribbean, Jamaica ranks 140th in size and 119th in population. Until the mid-1970s, it had a prosperous economy based partly on agricultural exports and partly on bauxite, of which it was the world's second largest producer. However, in the mid-1970s a number of circumstances combined to precipitate a downward spiral that has brought the country to the brink of bankruptcy. The principal factor in this crisis was the Manley government's imposition of a levy on aluminum ingots, which led to a decline in their output from 15 million tons in 1974 to 10 million tons in 1976. Reduced production of bauxite combined with drastically increased energy costs caused a gap in the balance of payments that continued to widen through the early 1980s. Tourism, Jamaica's second largest foreign exchange earner, has also faltered in recent years. Despite IMF credits totaling approximately $350 million, Jamaica has had negative economic growth for nearly every year during the past decade.

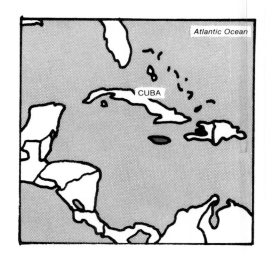

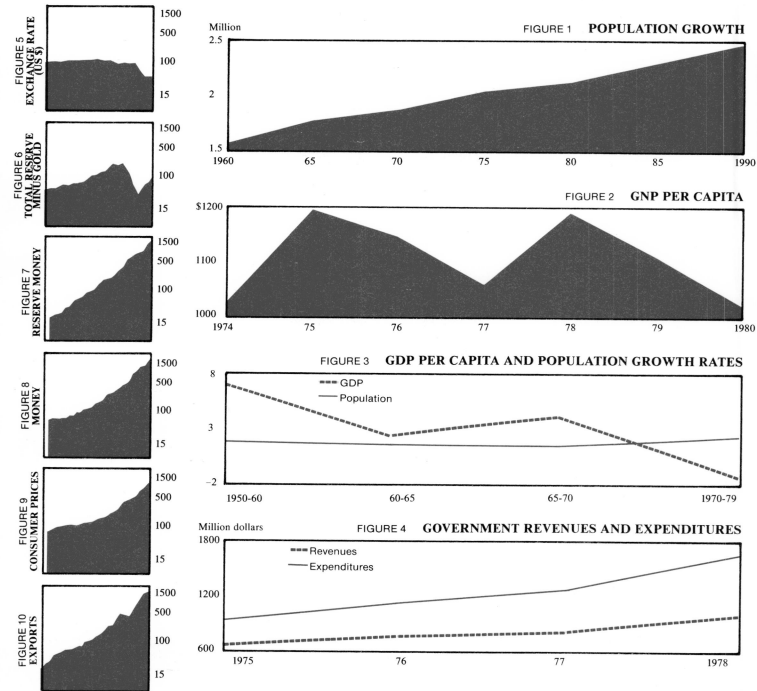

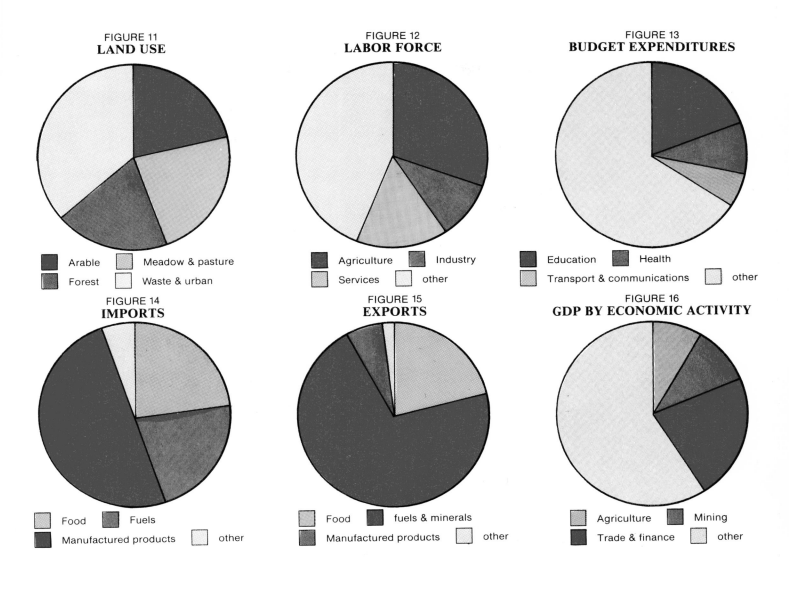

FIGURE 11
LAND USE

Arable Meadow & pasture
Forest Waste & urban

FIGURE 12
LABOR FORCE

Agriculture Industry
Services other

FIGURE 13
BUDGET EXPENDITURES

Education Health
Transport & communications other

FIGURE 14
IMPORTS

Food Fuels
Manufactured products other

FIGURE 15
EXPORTS

Food fuels & minerals
Manufactured products other

FIGURE 16
GDP BY ECONOMIC ACTIVITY

Agriculture Mining
Trade & finance other

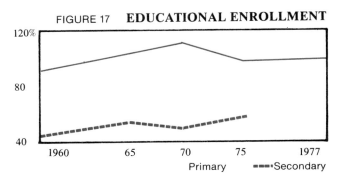

FIGURE 17 **EDUCATIONAL ENROLLMENT**

120%

80

40

1960   65   70   75   1977

Primary   ━━━Secondary

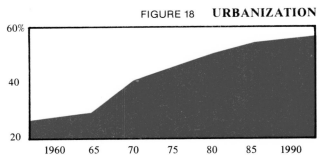

FIGURE 18 **URBANIZATION**

60%

40

20

1960   65   70   75   80   85   1990

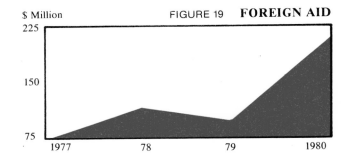

$ Million
225

FIGURE 19 **FOREIGN AID**

150

75

1977   78   79   1980

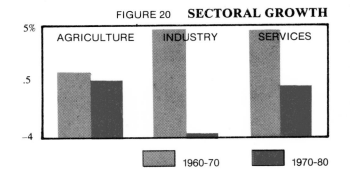

FIGURE 20 **SECTORAL GROWTH**

5%

AGRICULTURE   INDUSTRY   SERVICES

.5

-4

1960-70   1970-80

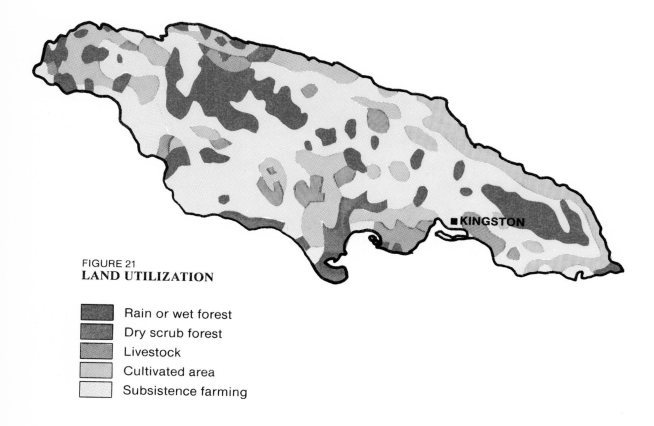

FIGURE 21
LAND UTILIZATION

Rain or wet forest
Dry scrub forest
Livestock
Cultivated area
Subsistence farming

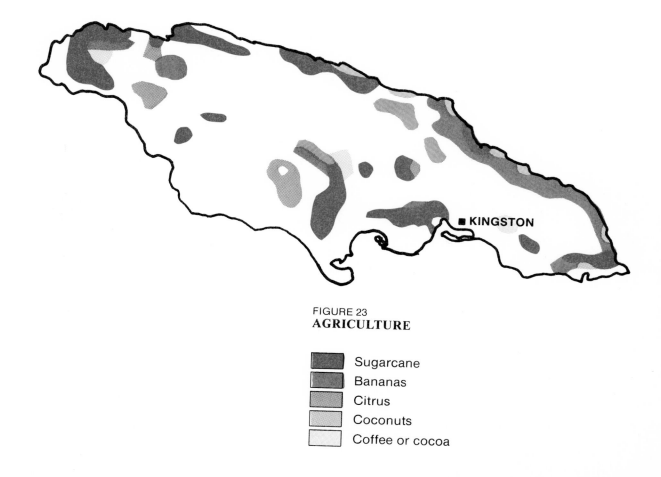

FIGURE 23
AGRICULTURE

Sugarcane
Bananas
Citrus
Coconuts
Coffee or cocoa

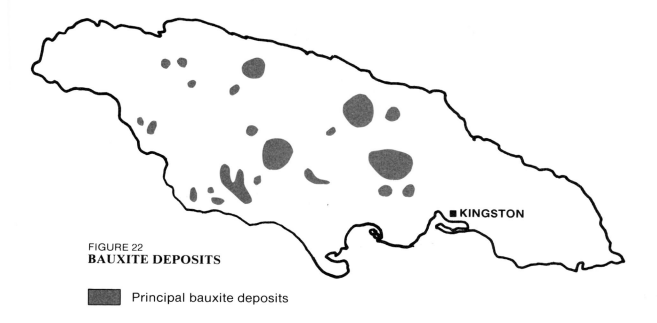

FIGURE 22
BAUXITE DEPOSITS

Principal bauxite deposits

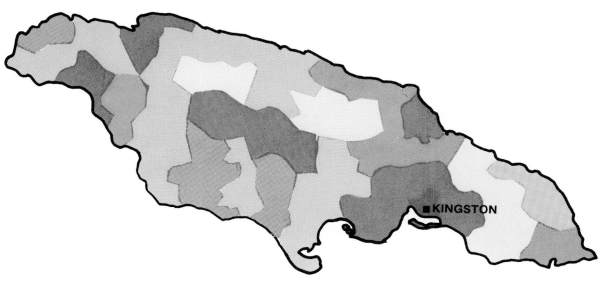

FIGURE 24
POPULATION

Persons per square mile

125-200
200-300
300-400
400-650
5,000-40,000

JORDAN

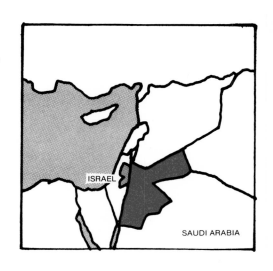

ISRAEL

SAUDI ARABIA

A nearly landlocked nation in the heart of the Arab world, Jordan ranks 103rd in land area and 108th in population. While classified as a lower middle-income country, Jordan has many advantages over other Middle Eastern countries: overall political and economic stability, dependable allies in the Arab world as well as in the West, and a liberal investment code. Barriers to growth are almost as numerous: a limited domestic market, lack of mineral resources other than phosphate, and a shortage of skilled labor aggravated by the flight of skilled labor to oil-rich Arab countries. The burden of hostilities with Israel (of which Jordan bore the brunt in the 1960s and 1970s) has been reduced following the no-war, no-peace stalemate of recent years while generous aid has been forthcoming from both the United States and Saudi Arabia. The economy has adjusted itself to the severe setbacks it sustained following the 1967 war, especially the loss of the agriculturally rich West Bank.

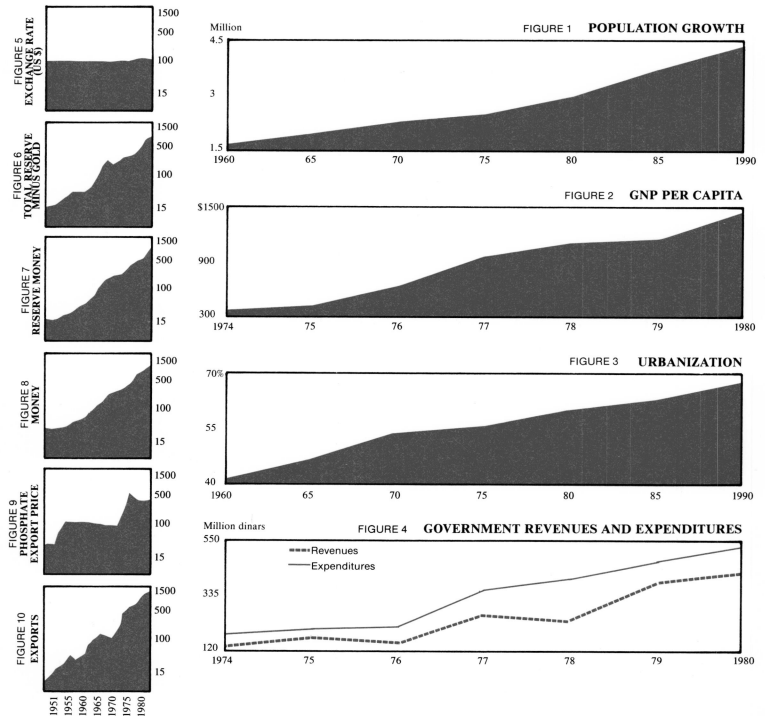

FIGURE 5 EXCHANGE RATE (US $)

FIGURE 6 TOTAL RESERVE MINUS GOLD

FIGURE 7 RESERVE MONEY

FIGURE 8 MONEY

FIGURE 9 PHOSPHATE EXPORT PRICE

FIGURE 10 EXPORTS

FIGURE 1 **POPULATION GROWTH**

FIGURE 2 **GNP PER CAPITA**

FIGURE 3 **URBANIZATION**

FIGURE 4 **GOVERNMENT REVENUES AND EXPENDITURES**

Million dinars

- - - Revenues
—— Expenditures

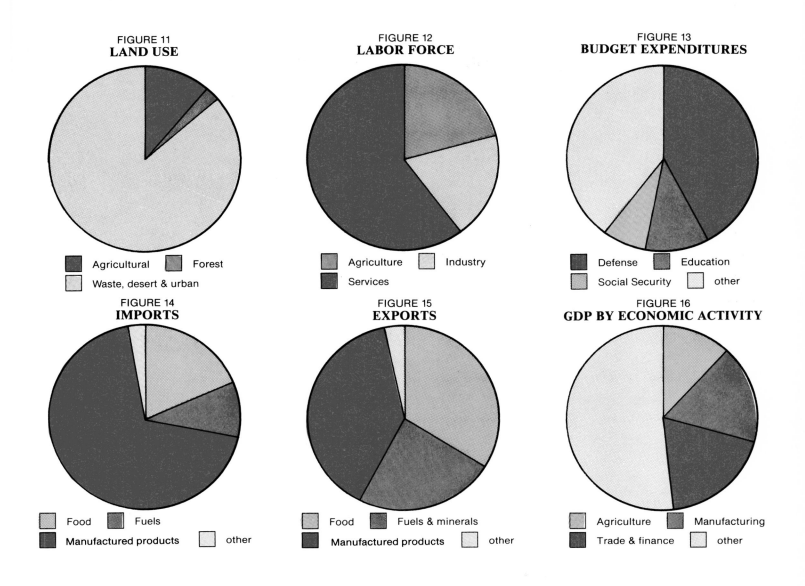

FIGURE 11
LAND USE

Agricultural   Forest
Waste, desert & urban

FIGURE 12
LABOR FORCE

Agriculture   Industry
Services

FIGURE 13
BUDGET EXPENDITURES

Defense   Education
Social Security   other

FIGURE 14
IMPORTS

Food   Fuels
Manufactured products   other

FIGURE 15
EXPORTS

Food   Fuels & minerals
Manufactured products   other

FIGURE 16
GDP BY ECONOMIC ACTIVITY

Agriculture   Manufacturing
Trade & finance   other

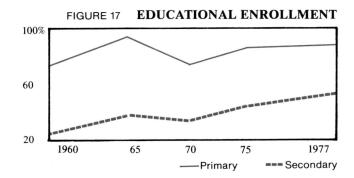

FIGURE 17   **EDUCATIONAL ENROLLMENT**

——Primary   ===Secondary

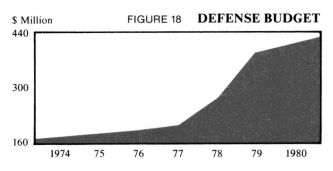

$ Million   FIGURE 18   **DEFENSE BUDGET**

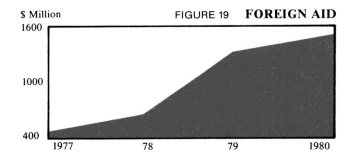

$ Million   FIGURE 19   **FOREIGN AID**

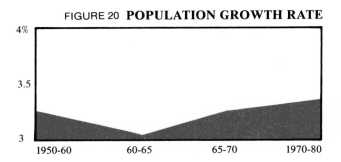

FIGURE 20   **POPULATION GROWTH RATE**

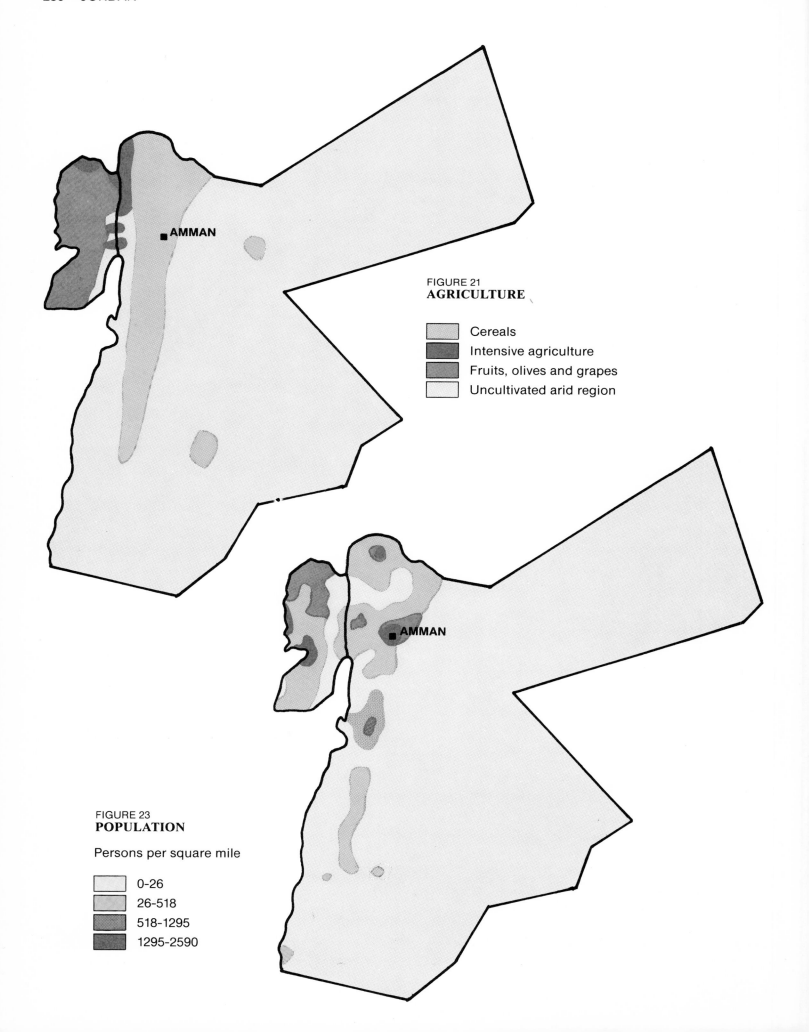

FIGURE 21
AGRICULTURE

Cereals

Intensive agriculture

Fruits, olives and grapes

Uncultivated arid region

FIGURE 23
POPULATION

Persons per square mile

0-26

26-518

518-1295

1295-2590

AMMAN

AMMAN

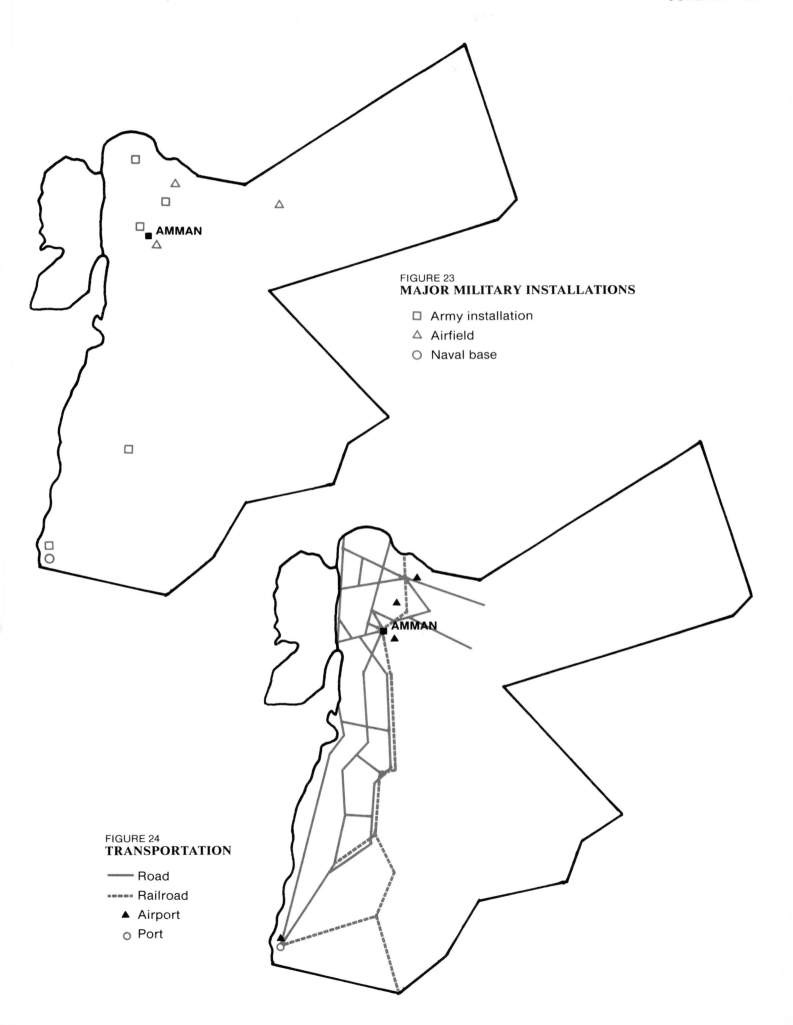

FIGURE 23
MAJOR MILITARY INSTALLATIONS

□ Army installation
△ Airfield
○ Naval base

AMMAN

FIGURE 24
TRANSPORTATION

── Road
----- Railroad
▲ Airport
○ Port

AMMAN

KENYA

A country of striking topographical and climatic variety located on the Equator, Kenya ranks 43rd in both land area and population. It inherited from the British a strong agricultural and industrial base and was for long considered the bellwether of the East African economy. Independence has not borne out this potential but, by the same token, it has been spared much of the political instability and economic disruptions suffered by some of its neighbors. Since independence some 20 years ago, Kenya has launched four development plans, all calling for a mixed economy. Despite impressive progress in certain areas, nearly a fifth of the GDP still originates outside the monetary economy and more than half the agricultural output consists of subsistence farming. President Daniel Arap Moi has acknowledged corruption and smuggling as major problems facing the economy. Most observers believe that Kenya will weather its present problems and be back on track in the 1980s.

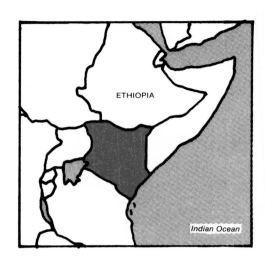

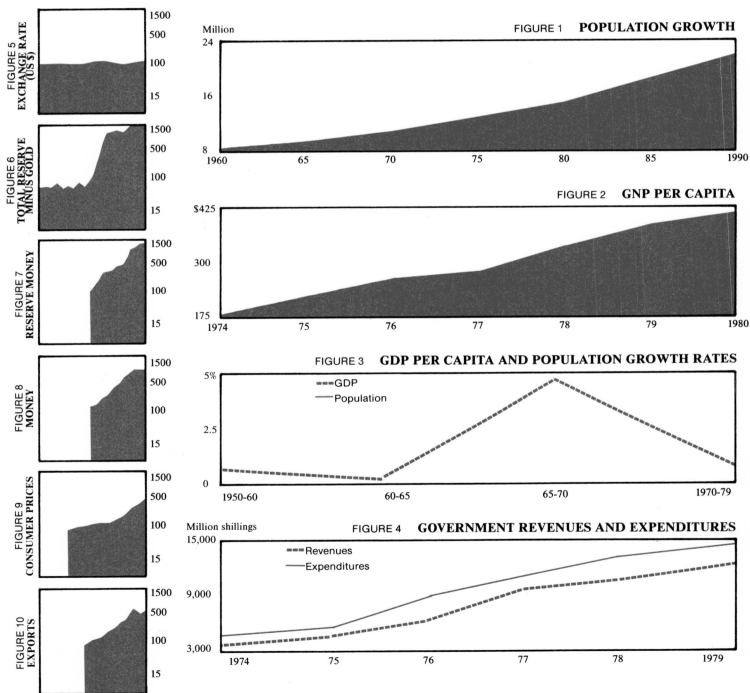

FIGURE 5 EXCHANGE RATE (US $)

FIGURE 6 TOTAL RESERVE MINUS GOLD

FIGURE 7 RESERVE MONEY

FIGURE 8 MONEY

FIGURE 9 CONSUMER PRICES

FIGURE 10 EXPORTS

FIGURE 1 **POPULATION GROWTH**

FIGURE 2 **GNP PER CAPITA**

FIGURE 3 **GDP PER CAPITA AND POPULATION GROWTH RATES**

- - - GDP
—— Population

FIGURE 4 **GOVERNMENT REVENUES AND EXPENDITURES**

- - - Revenues
—— Expenditures

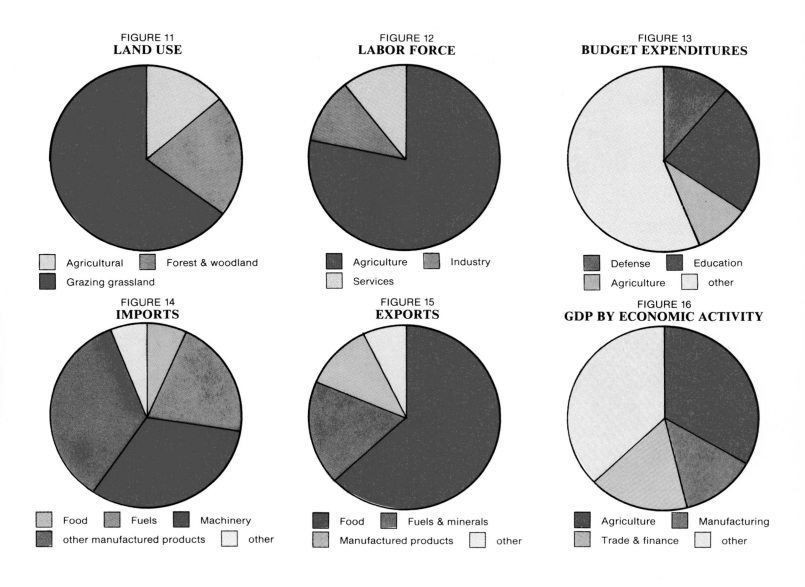

FIGURE 11
LAND USE

☐ Agricultural ☐ Forest & woodland
☐ Grazing grassland

FIGURE 12
LABOR FORCE

☐ Agriculture ☐ Industry
☐ Services

FIGURE 13
BUDGET EXPENDITURES

☐ Defense ☐ Education
☐ Agriculture ☐ other

FIGURE 14
IMPORTS

☐ Food ☐ Fuels ☐ Machinery
☐ other manufactured products ☐ other

FIGURE 15
EXPORTS

☐ Food ☐ Fuels & minerals
☐ Manufactured products ☐ other

FIGURE 16
GDP BY ECONOMIC ACTIVITY

☐ Agriculture ☐ Manufacturing
☐ Trade & finance ☐ other

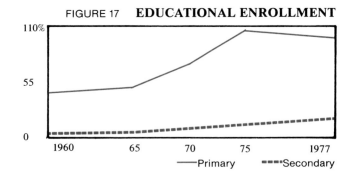

FIGURE 17 **EDUCATIONAL ENROLLMENT**

110%

55

0

1960 65 70 75 1977

—— Primary ===== Secondary

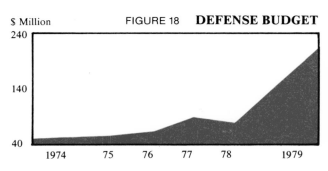

$ Million FIGURE 18 **DEFENSE BUDGET**

240

140

40

1974 75 76 77 78 1979

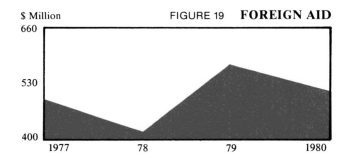

$ Million FIGURE 19 **FOREIGN AID**

660

530

400

1977 78 79 1980

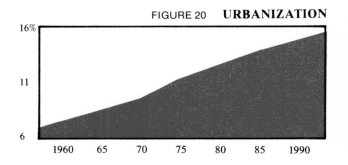

FIGURE 20 **URBANIZATION**

16%

11

6

1960 65 70 75 80 85 1990

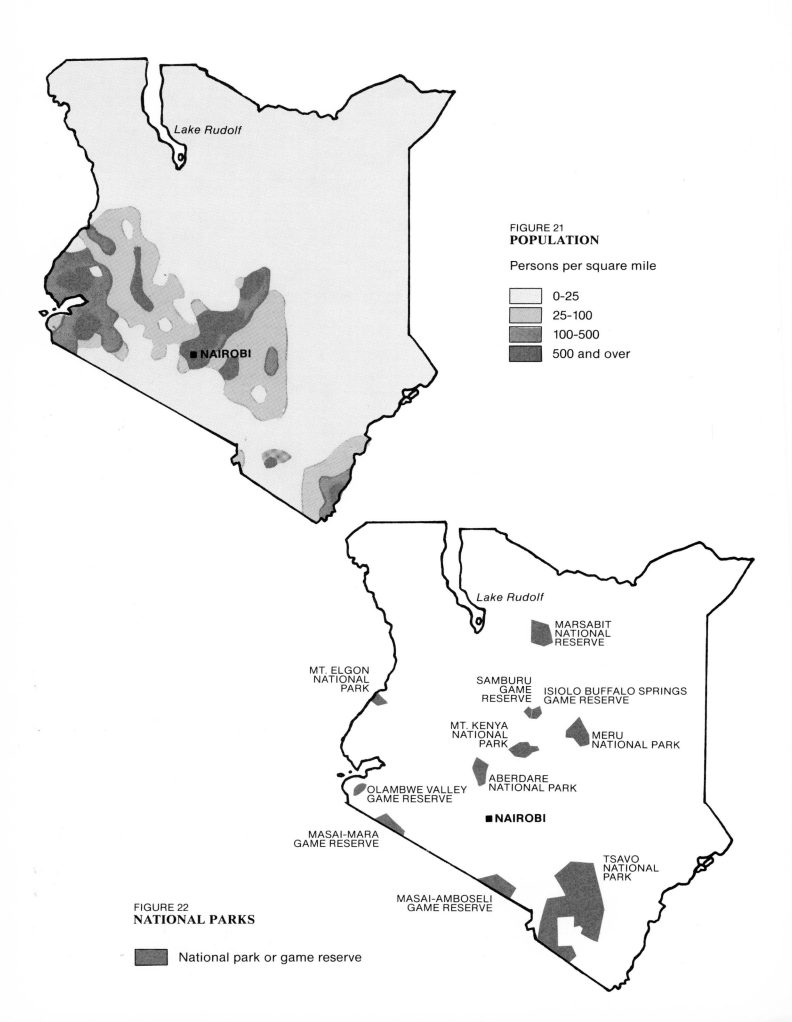

FIGURE 21
POPULATION

Persons per square mile

0-25

25-100

100-500

500 and over

Lake Rudolf

■ NAIROBI

Lake Rudolf

MARSABIT NATIONAL RESERVE

MT. ELGON NATIONAL PARK

SAMBURU GAME RESERVE

ISIOLO BUFFALO SPRINGS GAME RESERVE

MT. KENYA NATIONAL PARK

MERU NATIONAL PARK

ABERDARE NATIONAL PARK

OLAMBWE VALLEY GAME RESERVE

■ NAIROBI

MASAI-MARA GAME RESERVE

TSAVO NATIONAL PARK

MASAI-AMBOSELI GAME RESERVE

FIGURE 22
NATIONAL PARKS

National park or game reserve

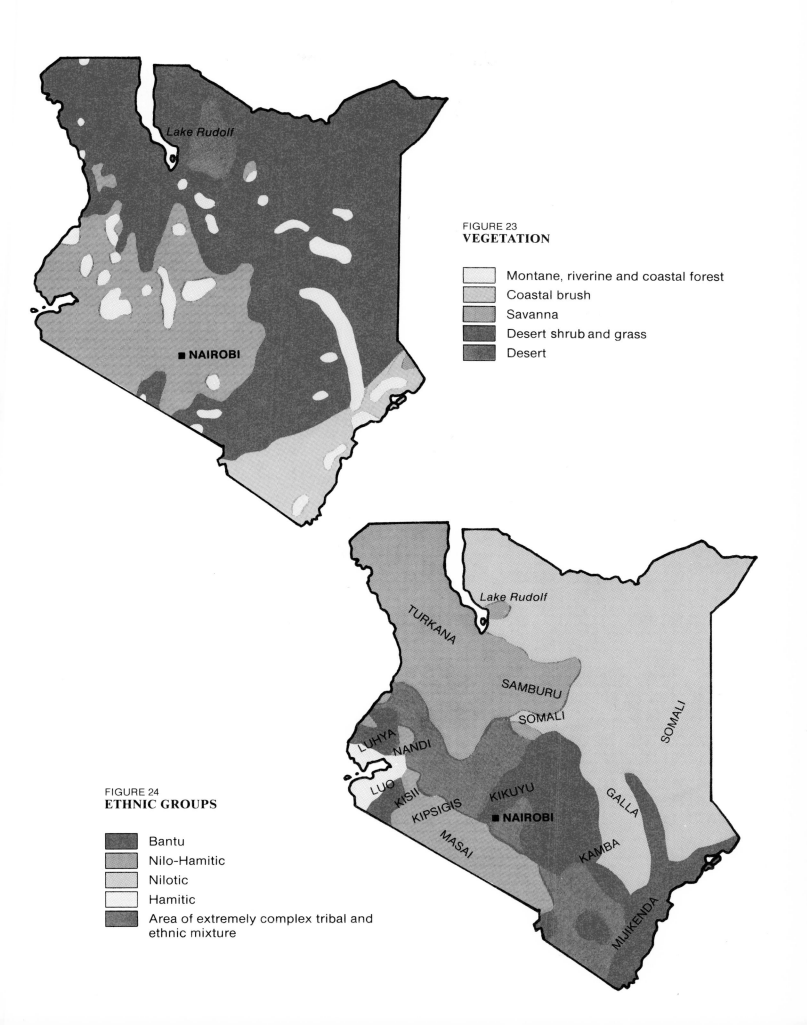

FIGURE 23
VEGETATION

- Montane, riverine and coastal forest
- Coastal brush
- Savanna
- Desert shrub and grass
- Desert

FIGURE 24
ETHNIC GROUPS

- Bantu
- Nilo-Hamitic
- Nilotic
- Hamitic
- Area of extremely complex tribal and ethnic mixture

NORTH KOREA

Located on the northern half of the Korean Peninsula, North Korea (or the Democratic People's Republic of Korea) ranks 92nd in land area and 39th in population. On most indicators, it ranks poorly compared with South Korea. As a socialist, centrally planned, "command" economy, it has no market sector. Even agriculture is fully collectivized. Although heavy dependence on foreign aid (from the USSR as well as China) marked the early years of the republic, official emphasis is on *chuch'e sasang*, or self-reliance, elevated to the status of an ideology by Kim Il Sung, the only president the country has known since the end of World War II. The sparseness of official statistics makes it difficult to assess the current condition of the economy. However, travelers report that, while many consumer goods are not available, the standard of living is not much lower than that of South Korea, because most citizens receive free medical care, subsidized housing and adequate food supplies.

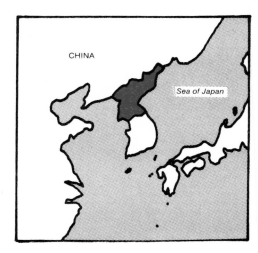

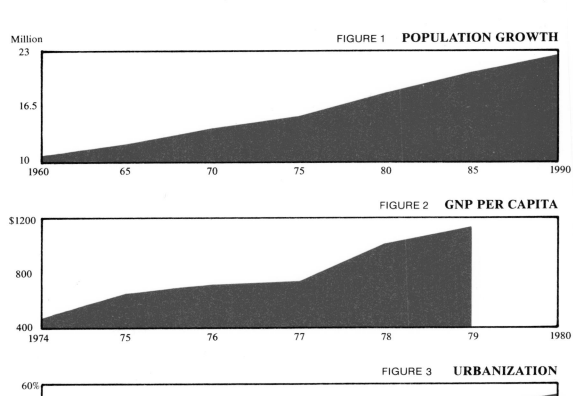

FIGURE 1 **POPULATION GROWTH**

FIGURE 2 **GNP PER CAPITA**

I.M.F.
DATA
UNAVAILABLE

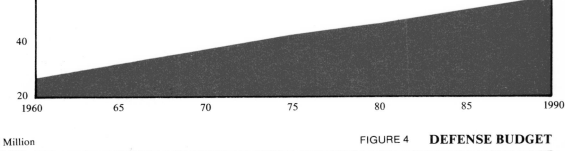

FIGURE 3 **URBANIZATION**

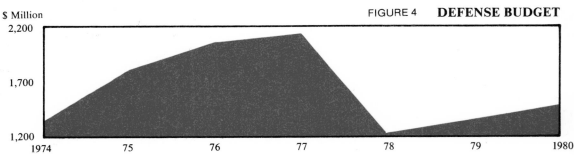

FIGURE 4 **DEFENSE BUDGET**

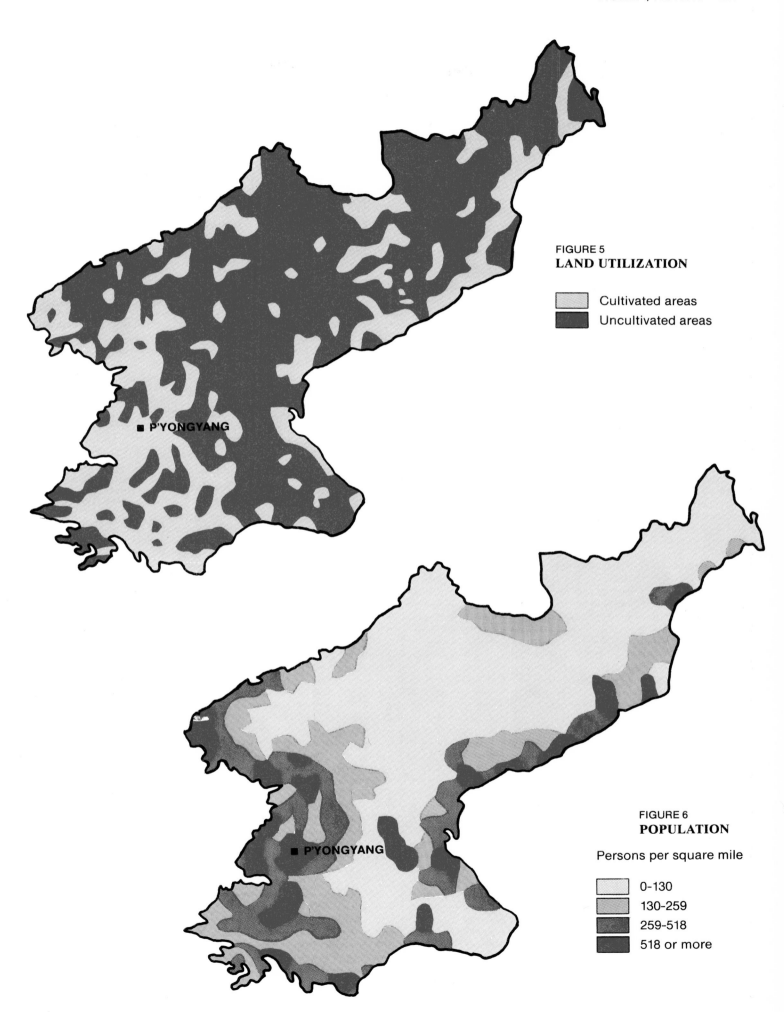

FIGURE 5
LAND UTILIZATION

Cultivated areas
Uncultivated areas

P'YONGYANG

FIGURE 6
POPULATION

Persons per square mile

0–130
130–259
259–518
518 or more

P'YONGYANG

SOUTH KOREA

Located on the southern half of the Korean Peninsula, South Korea ranks 102nd in land area and 22nd in population. Although it has less natural resources than its neighbor to the north, it outstrips North Korea on virtually all indicators. Its extraordinary economic growth during the 1960s and 1970s has enabled it to join the ranks of the so-called ADCs (advanced developed countries) along with many others, such as Brazil, and to become one of the "Gang of Four," with Taiwan, Hong Kong and Singapore. South Korea's economic miracle has been attributed to many factors, the most significant being strong central government intervention in the economy, incentives to private enterprise, constraints on unionization and wage pauses. The entire industrial sector was geared for export rather than import-substitution. In the mid-1970s, South Korea began to diversify, moving into heavy capital goods, chemicals and construction of industrial plants abroad. By 1990 it is expected to become a developed country.

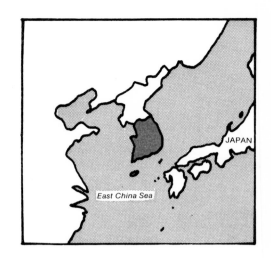

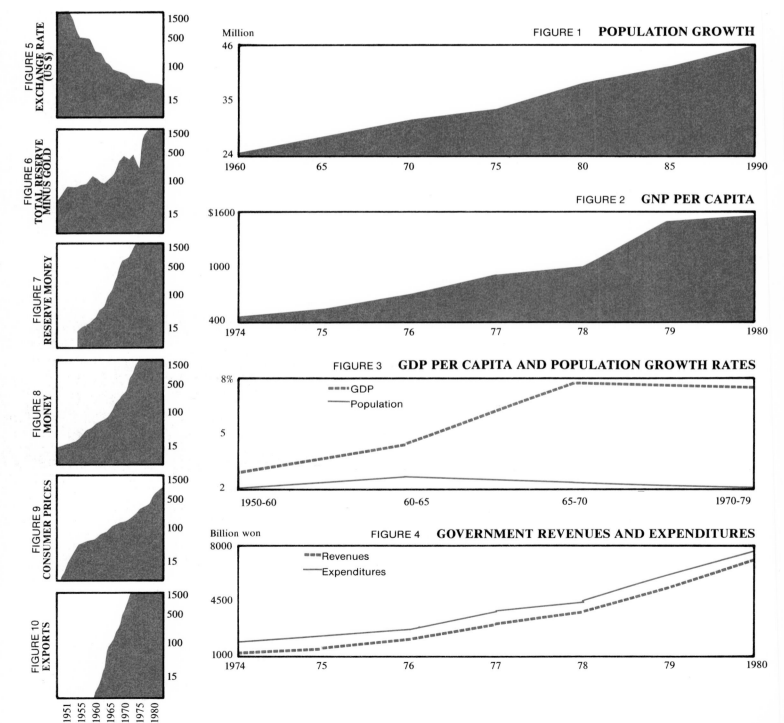

FIGURE 5 EXCHANGE RATE (US $)

FIGURE 6 TOTAL RESERVE MINUS GOLD

FIGURE 7 RESERVE MONEY

FIGURE 8 MONEY

FIGURE 9 CONSUMER PRICES

FIGURE 10 EXPORTS

FIGURE 1 **POPULATION GROWTH**

FIGURE 2 **GNP PER CAPITA**

FIGURE 3 **GDP PER CAPITA AND POPULATION GROWTH RATES**

FIGURE 4 **GOVERNMENT REVENUES AND EXPENDITURES**

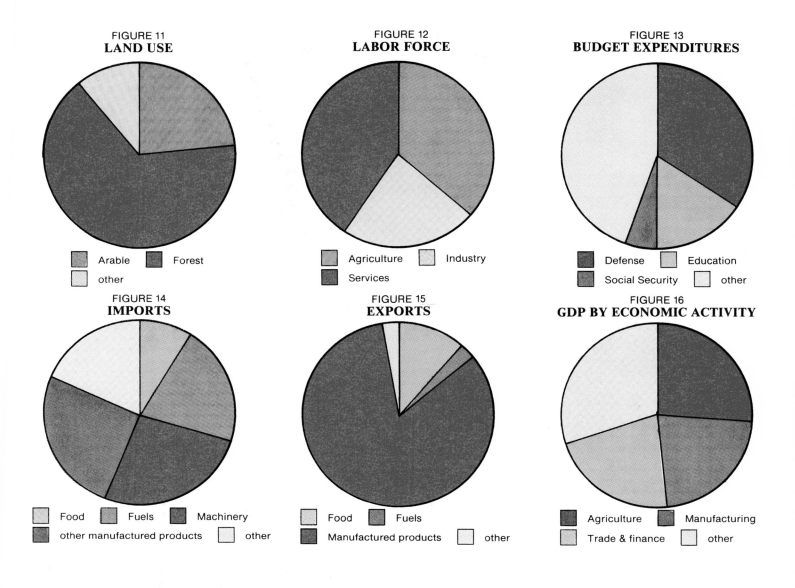

FIGURE 11
LAND USE

Arable Forest
other

FIGURE 12
LABOR FORCE

Agriculture Industry
Services

FIGURE 13
BUDGET EXPENDITURES

Defense Education
Social Security other

FIGURE 14
IMPORTS

Food Fuels Machinery
other manufactured products other

FIGURE 15
EXPORTS

Food Fuels
Manufactured products other

FIGURE 16
GDP BY ECONOMIC ACTIVITY

Agriculture Manufacturing
Trade & finance other

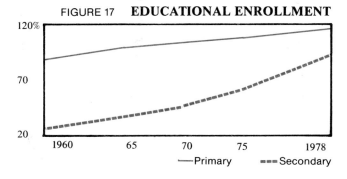

FIGURE 17 **EDUCATIONAL ENROLLMENT**

120%

70

20

1960   65   70   75   1978
——Primary ===Secondary

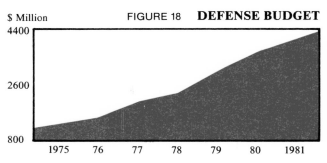

$ Million   FIGURE 18 **DEFENSE BUDGET**

4400

2600

800
1975   76   77   78   79   80   1981

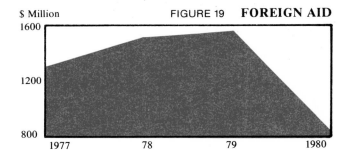

$ Million   FIGURE 19 **FOREIGN AID**

1600

1200

800
1977   78   79   1980

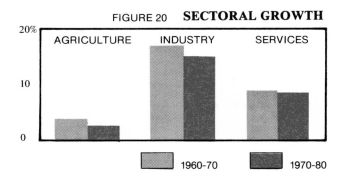

FIGURE 20 **SECTORAL GROWTH**

20%

AGRICULTURE   INDUSTRY   SERVICES

10

0

1960-70   1970-80

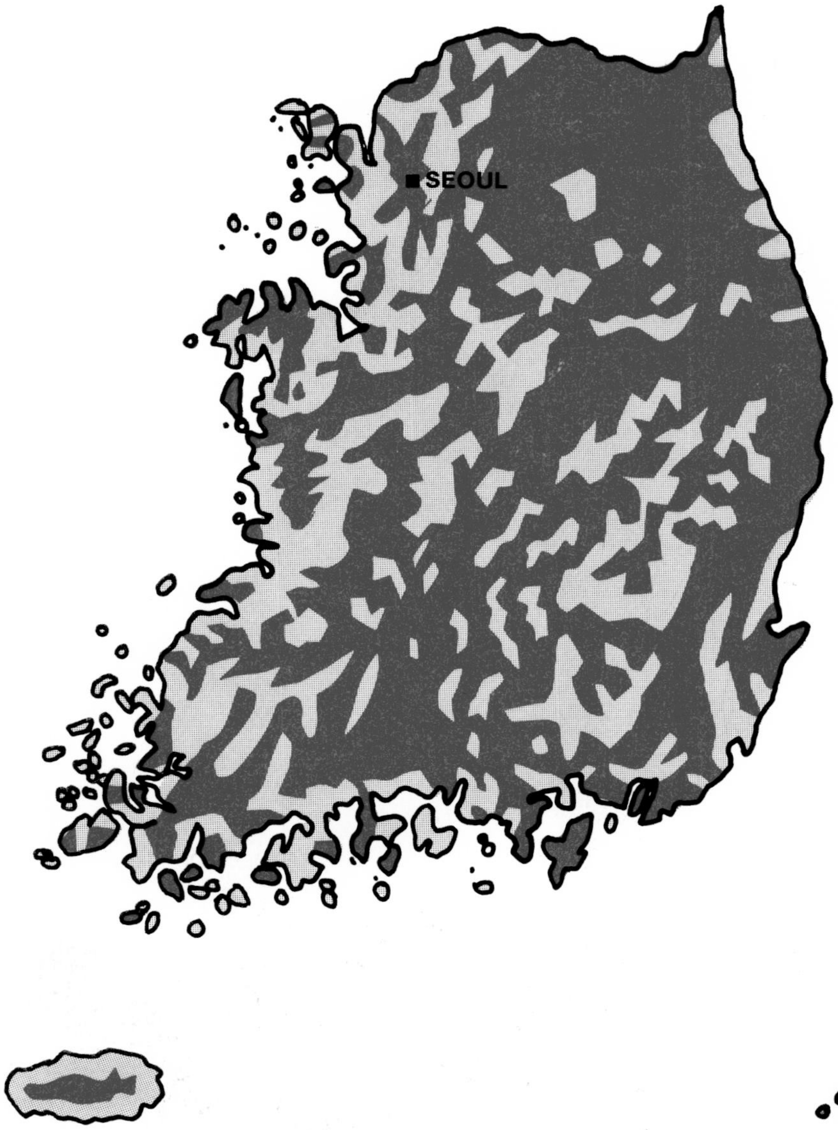

FIGURE 21
LAND UTILIZATION

Cultivated areas
Uncultivated areas

■SEOUL

FIGURE 22

Persons per square mile

0–130
130–259
259–518
518 and more

■SEOUL

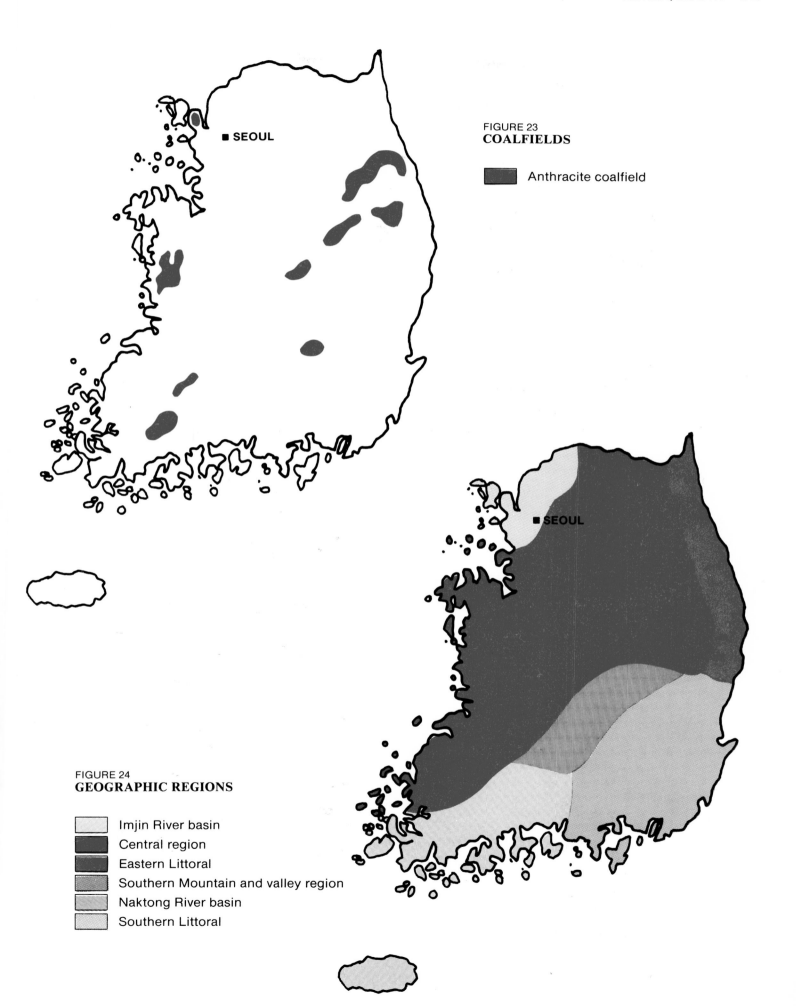

FIGURE 23
COALFIELDS

Anthracite coalfield

SEOUL

FIGURE 24
GEOGRAPHIC REGIONS

Imjin River basin
Central region
Eastern Littoral
Southern Mountain and valley region
Naktong River basin
Southern Littoral

SEOUL

LAOS

One of the five landlocked countries in Asia, Laos ranks 73rd in land area and 101st in population. Even after the end of the civil war that lasted nearly 20 years, Laos remains among the least developed nations of the world. The current Marxist government's policies, such as collectivized farming and stringent barriers affecting internal trade, met with more resistance in the countryside than Vientiane had anticipated and more recent reports indicate a relaxation of these policies and a shift in national priorities. The Laotian monetary unit, the kip, once the weakest currency in the world, was replaced with the liberation kip, in an effort to reduce the money supply. The food prices paid to farmers were raised in order to inhibit smuggling and induce higher production. Extra pay was offered to civil servants to reduce the exodus of trained employees. The tax system was reformed and private traders were permitted to import without limit from Thailand. These reforms have helped to restore some vital signs to what once appeared to be a dying economy.

FIGURE 1　**POPULATION GROWTH**

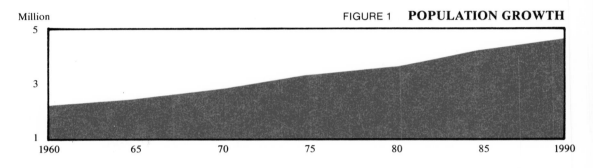

FIGURE 2　**GNP PER CAPITA**

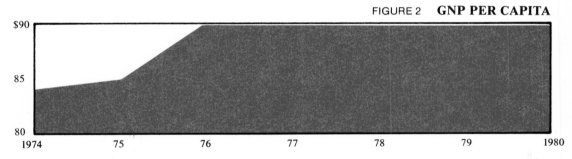

I.M.F.
DATA
UNAVAILABLE

FIGURE 3　**URBANIZATION**

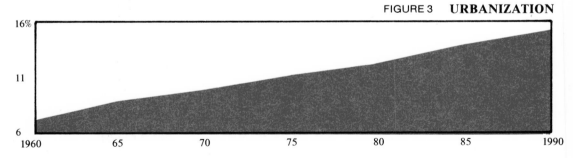

FIGURE 4　**FOREIGN AID**

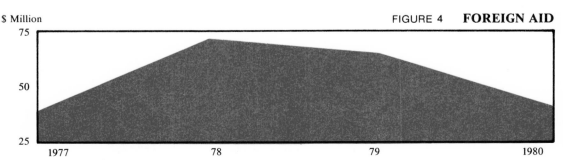

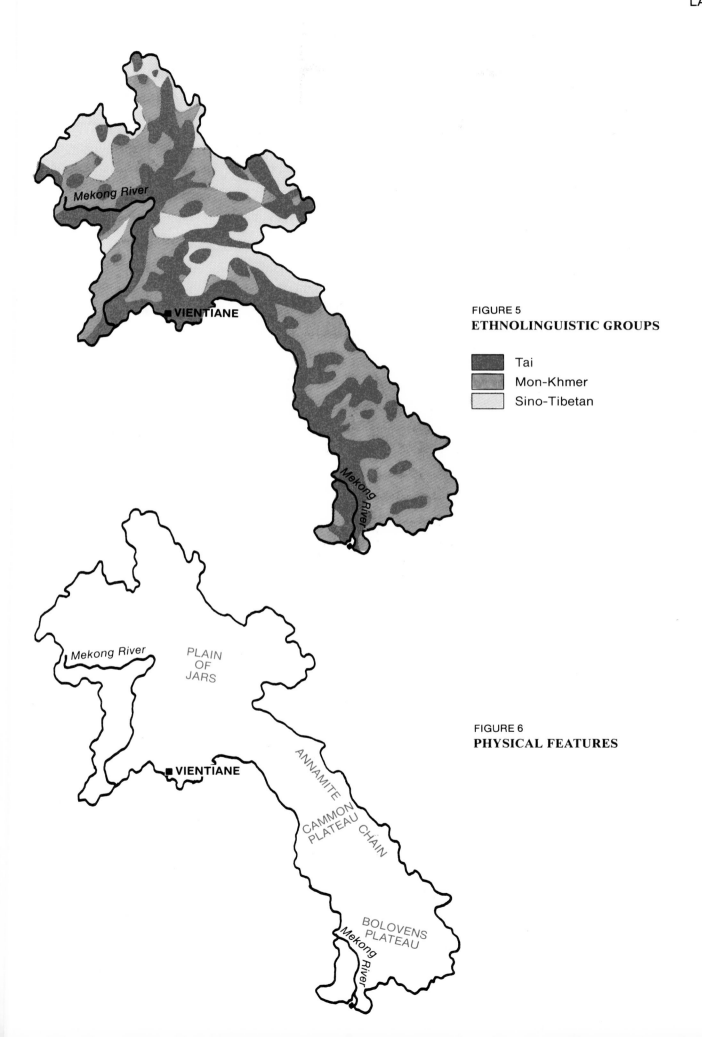

FIGURE 5
ETHNOLINGUISTIC GROUPS

Tai
Mon-Khmer
Sino-Tibetan

FIGURE 6
PHYSICAL FEATURES

LEBANON

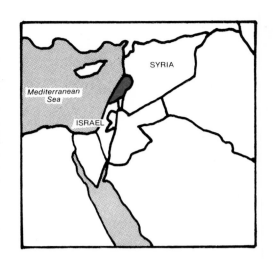

Once known as the "Switzerland of Asia," strife-torn Lebanon ranks 141st in land area and 114th in population. Until the civil war, Beirut was the focal point of trading activity in the Middle East, especially in such service areas as banking, insurance, tourism and shipping. Lebanese universities attracted students from all over the Arab world. The civil war changed all this within the closing years of the seventies, and until the expulsion of the Palestinian guerrillas by the Israelis in 1982, the state of Lebanon was more a fiction than a fact. As all statistical activities have been suspended (except perhaps for the counting of casualties), no significant economic information has been collected or published for nearly a decade. Nearly half the nation's GNP is believed to have been lost between 1975 and 1977 and 700,000 skilled workers emigrated to other countries during this period. Nevertheless, the economy has proved remarkably resilient—owing much to the entrepreneurial ability of the populace—and could make a strong recovery once peace is restored.

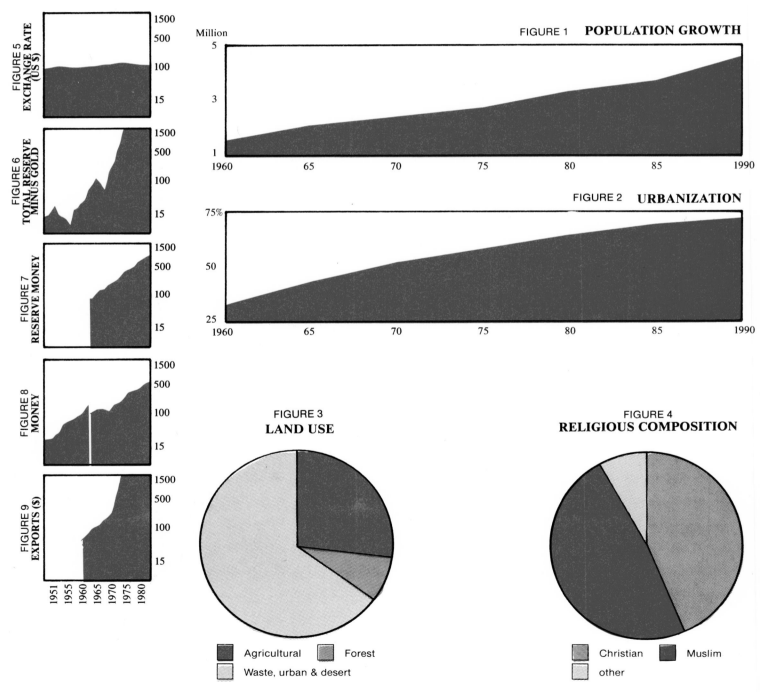

FIGURE 5 EXCHANGE RATE (US $)

FIGURE 6 TOTAL RESERVE MINUS GOLD

FIGURE 7 RESERVE MONEY

FIGURE 8 MONEY

FIGURE 9 EXPORTS ($)

FIGURE 1 **POPULATION GROWTH**

FIGURE 2 **URBANIZATION**

FIGURE 3 **LAND USE**

Agricultural   Forest
Waste, urban & desert

FIGURE 4 **RELIGIOUS COMPOSITION**

Christian   Muslim
other

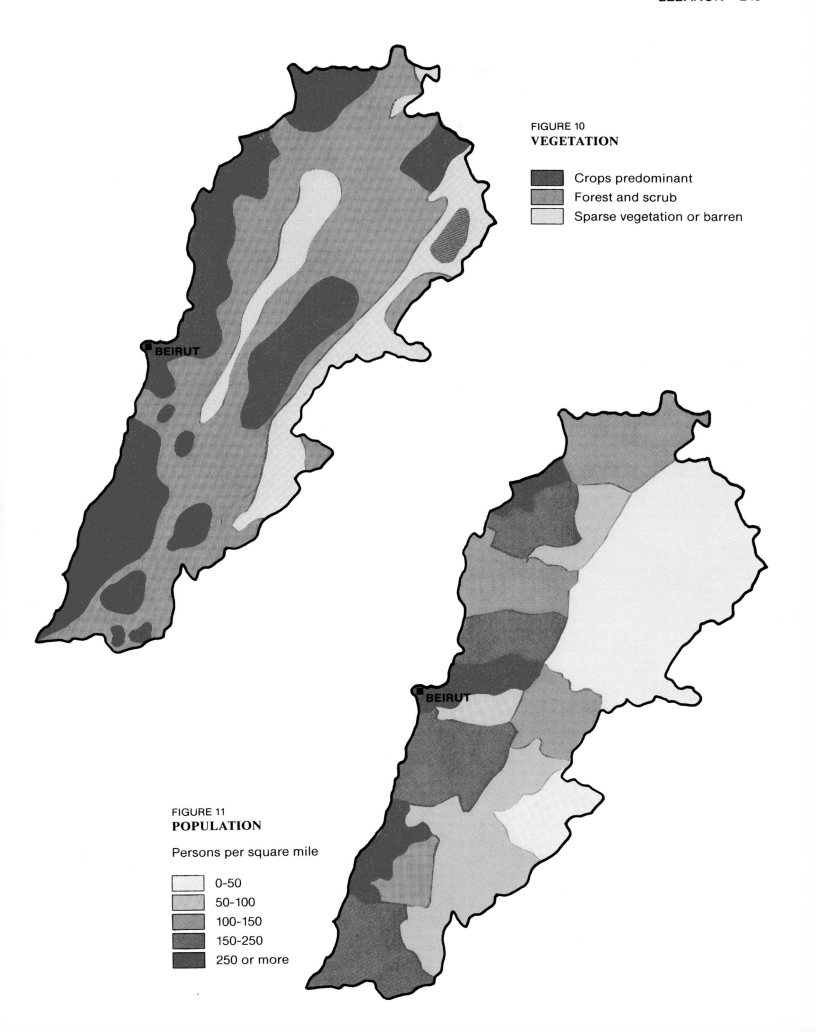

FIGURE 10
VEGETATION

■ Crops predominant
■ Forest and scrub
□ Sparse vegetation or barren

BEIRUT

FIGURE 11
POPULATION

Persons per square mile

□ 0-50
□ 50-100
■ 100-150
■ 150-250
■ 250 or more

BEIRUT

LIBERIA

The oldest black republic in Africa, Liberia ranks 97th in land area and 121st in population. Liberia is most closely identified with two things: ships and rubber. In terms of gross registered tonnage, the Liberian merchant marine is the world's largest because the Liberian flag is the most popular flag of convenience. Rubber plantations initiated by the U.S. rubber manufacturer Firestone have made Liberia the world's sixth ranking rubber producer. More recently, rubber has been superseded by iron ore, which now accounts for approximately 75% of Liberian exports. In the three years prior to the coup that brought Samuel Kenyon Doe to power and ended the dominance of the Americo-Liberians, the Liberian economy was in the doldrums. In 1977, the country registered its first trade deficit since 1963. On assuming power Doe outlined a series of economic goals, including more jobs, better pay scales for military and civil servants, better health care and education and an end to administrative corruption. Only slow progress has been made in achieving these goals.

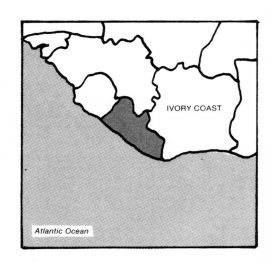

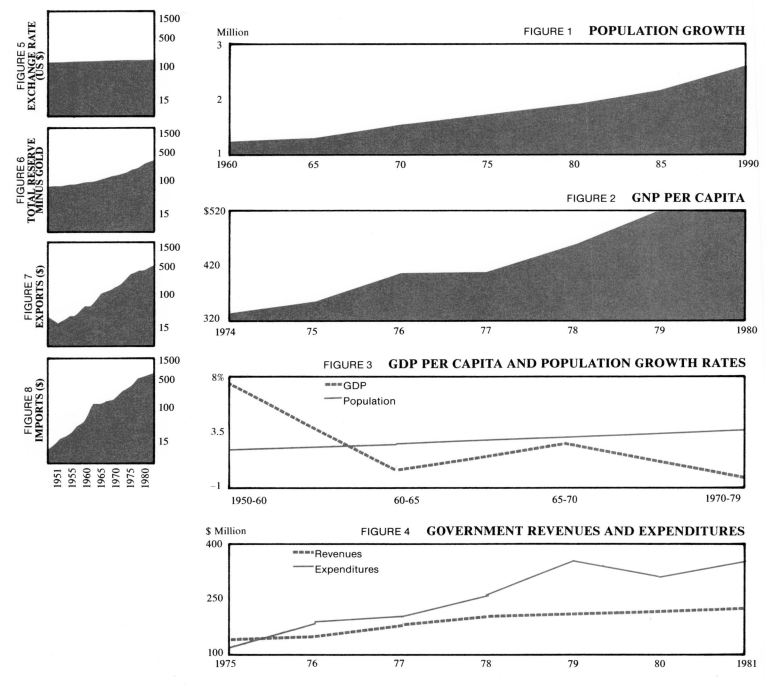

FIGURE 5 EXCHANGE RATE (US $)

FIGURE 6 TOTAL RESERVE MINUS GOLD

FIGURE 7 EXPORTS ($)

FIGURE 8 IMPORTS ($)

FIGURE 1 **POPULATION GROWTH**

FIGURE 2 **GNP PER CAPITA**

FIGURE 3 **GDP PER CAPITA AND POPULATION GROWTH RATES**

FIGURE 4 **GOVERNMENT REVENUES AND EXPENDITURES**

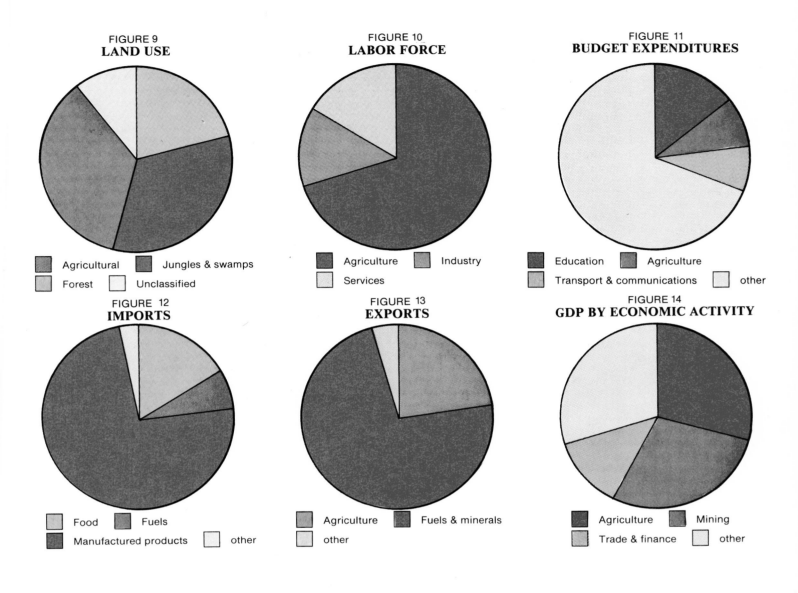

FIGURE 9
LAND USE

- Agricultural
- Jungles & swamps
- Forest
- Unclassified

FIGURE 10
LABOR FORCE

- Agriculture
- Industry
- Services

FIGURE 11
BUDGET EXPENDITURES

- Education
- Agriculture
- Transport & communications
- other

FIGURE 12
IMPORTS

- Food
- Fuels
- Manufactured products
- other

FIGURE 13
EXPORTS

- Agriculture
- Fuels & minerals
- other

FIGURE 14
GDP BY ECONOMIC ACTIVITY

- Agriculture
- Mining
- Trade & finance
- other

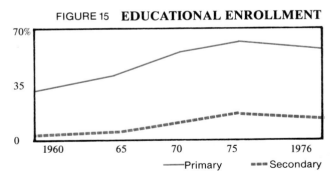

FIGURE 15 **EDUCATIONAL ENROLLMENT**

—— Primary   ▪▪▪ Secondary

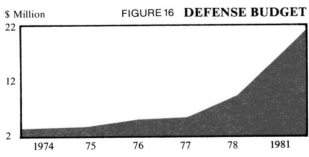

$ Million   FIGURE 16 **DEFENSE BUDGET**

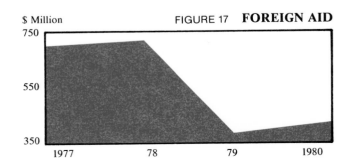

$ Million   FIGURE 17 **FOREIGN AID**

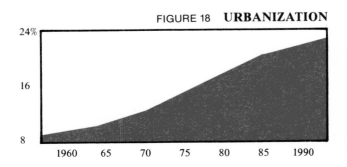

FIGURE 18 **URBANIZATION**

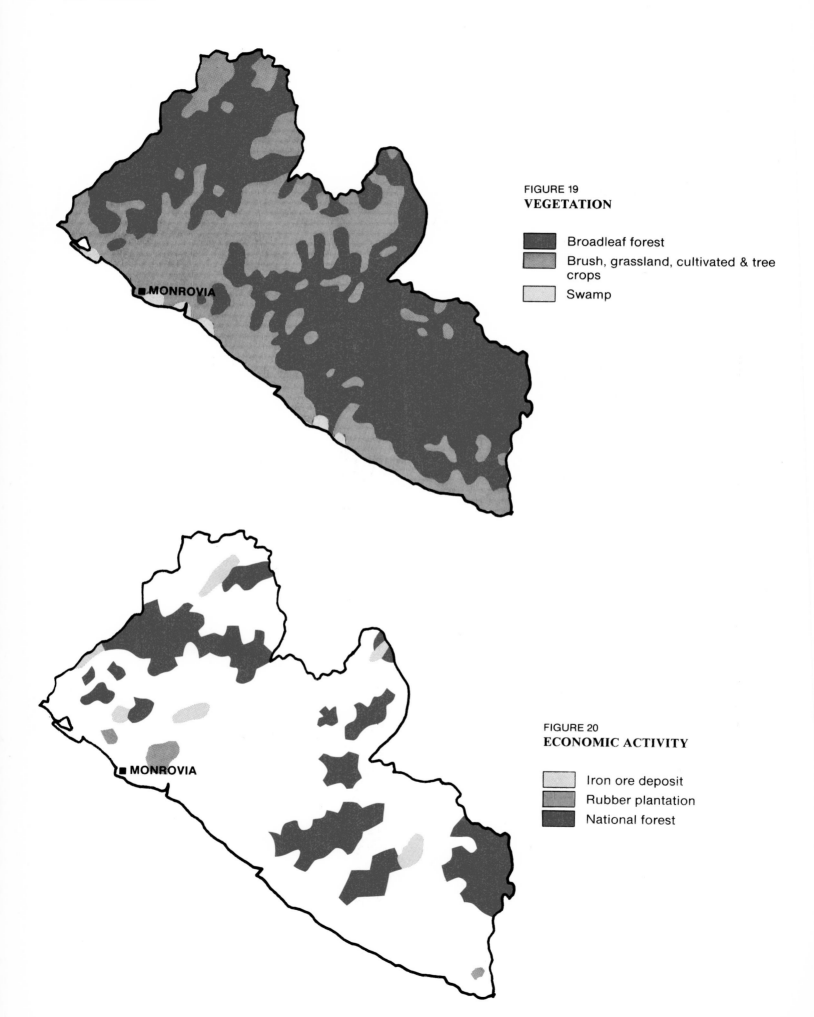

FIGURE 19
VEGETATION

Broadleaf forest

Brush, grassland, cultivated & tree crops

Swamp

FIGURE 20
ECONOMIC ACTIVITY

Iron ore deposit

Rubber plantation

National forest

MONROVIA

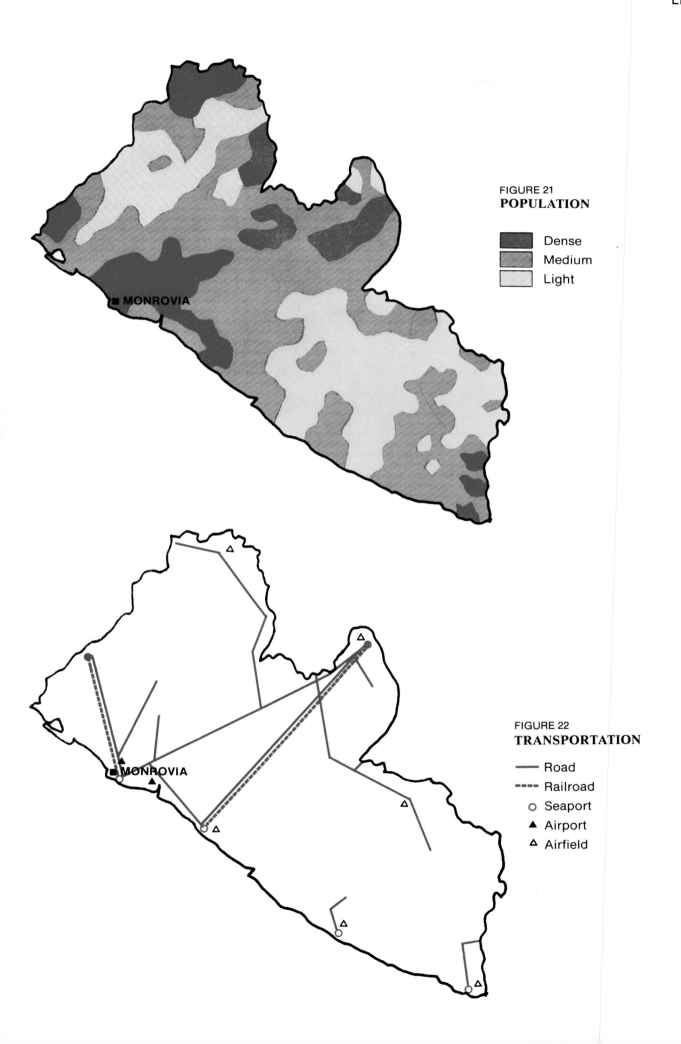

FIGURE 21
POPULATION

Dense
Medium
Light

MONROVIA

FIGURE 22
TRANSPORTATION

Road
Railroad
Seaport
Airport
Airfield

MONROVIA

LIBYA

The enfant terrible of the Arab world, Libya ranks 13th in land area but only 113th in population. Whereas the country had been classified in 1954 by the World Bank as one of the world's poorest countries, its per capita income in the early 1980s was the highest in Africa. During the same period the country has witnessed a political transformation as well, moving from a conservative monarchy to an Islamic-Marxist *jamahariya* (roughly translated as state of the masses) whose ideology is nothing more than the sum total of the idiosyncracies of its founder, Muammar Quadhafi. With the eighth largest petroleum reserves in the world, Libya ranks 10th in crude oil production and its crude commands the highest price in the spot markets. The petroleum industry, which employs only 10% of the labor force, contributes over one-half the country's GDP (down from over 60% in 1970) and more than 99% of its export earnings. Libya is also one of the most militant members of OPEC and was one of the first to nationalize foreign oil companies.

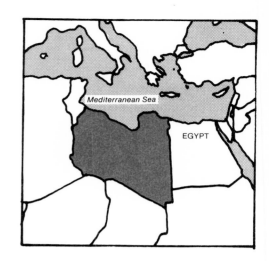

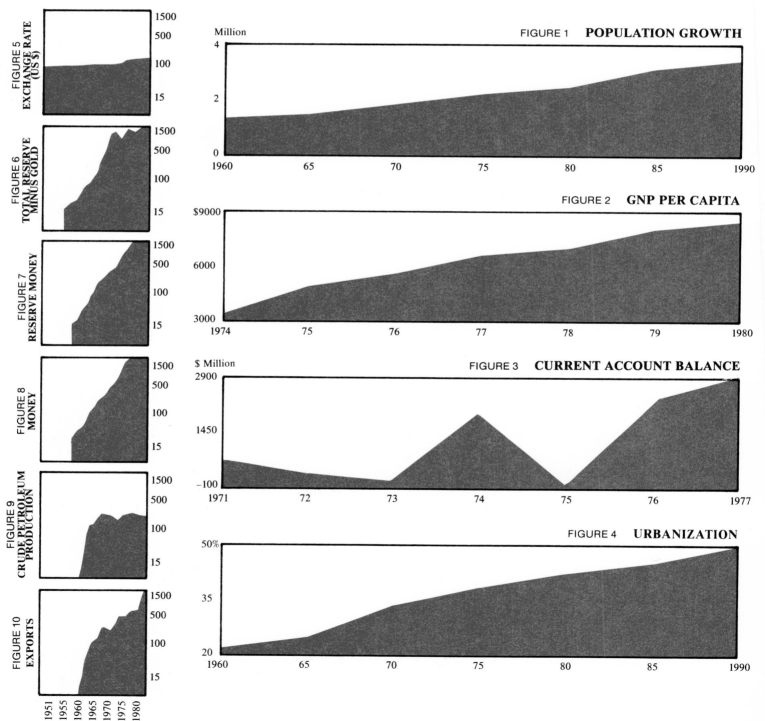

FIGURE 5 — EXCHANGE RATE (US $)

FIGURE 6 — TOTAL RESERVE MINUS GOLD

FIGURE 7 — RESERVE MONEY

FIGURE 8 — MONEY

FIGURE 9 — CRUDE PETROLEUM PRODUCTION

FIGURE 10 — EXPORTS

FIGURE 1 — **POPULATION GROWTH**

FIGURE 2 — **GNP PER CAPITA**

FIGURE 3 — **CURRENT ACCOUNT BALANCE**

FIGURE 4 — **URBANIZATION**

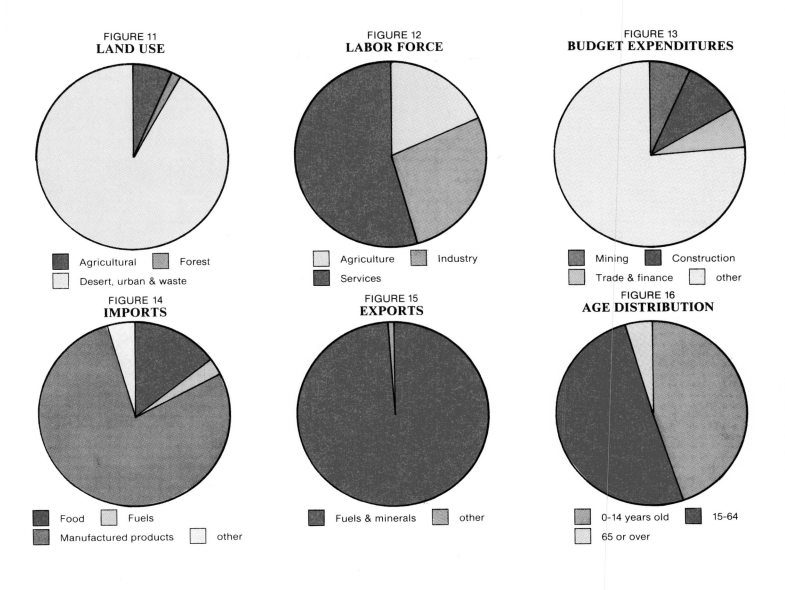

FIGURE 11
LAND USE

Agricultural   Forest

Desert, urban & waste

FIGURE 12
LABOR FORCE

Agriculture   Industry

Services

FIGURE 13
BUDGET EXPENDITURES

Mining   Construction

Trade & finance   other

FIGURE 14
IMPORTS

Food   Fuels

Manufactured products   other

FIGURE 15
EXPORTS

Fuels & minerals   other

FIGURE 16
AGE DISTRIBUTION

0-14 years old   15-64

65 or over

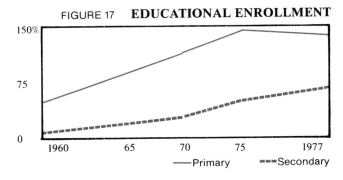

FIGURE 17   **EDUCATIONAL ENROLLMENT**

——Primary   ===Secondary

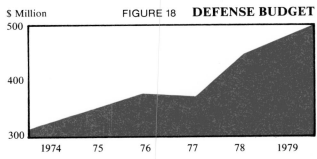

$ Million   FIGURE 18   **DEFENSE BUDGET**

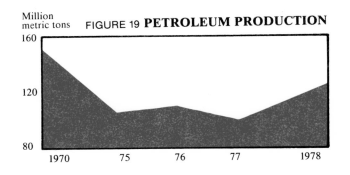

Million
metric tons   FIGURE 19 **PETROLEUM PRODUCTION**

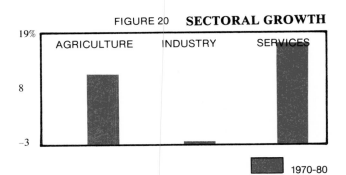

FIGURE 20   **SECTORAL GROWTH**

AGRICULTURE   INDUSTRY   SERVICES

1970-80

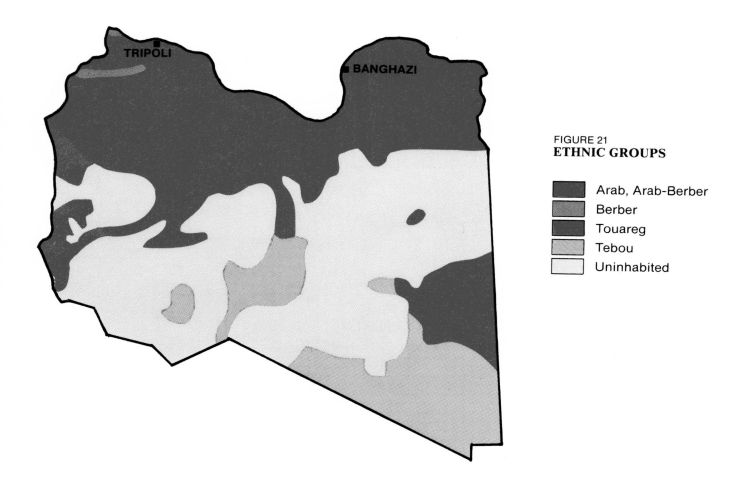

FIGURE 21
ETHNIC GROUPS

- Arab, Arab-Berber
- Berber
- Touareg
- Tebou
- Uninhabited

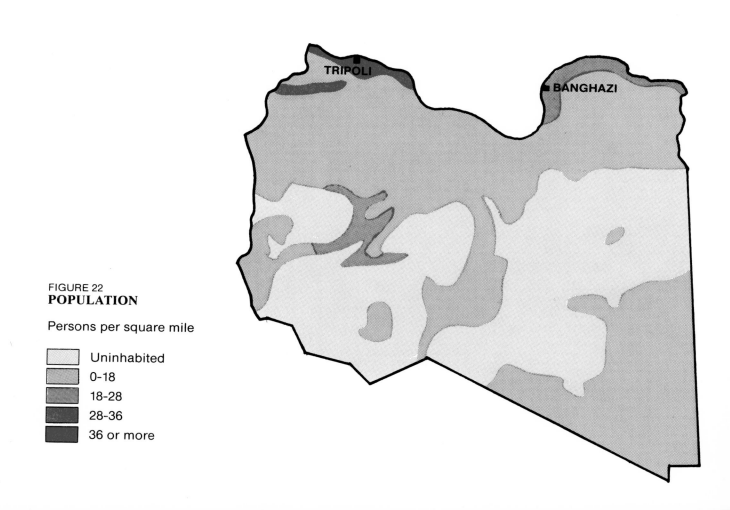

FIGURE 22
POPULATION

Persons per square mile

- Uninhabited
- 0-18
- 18-28
- 28-36
- 36 or more

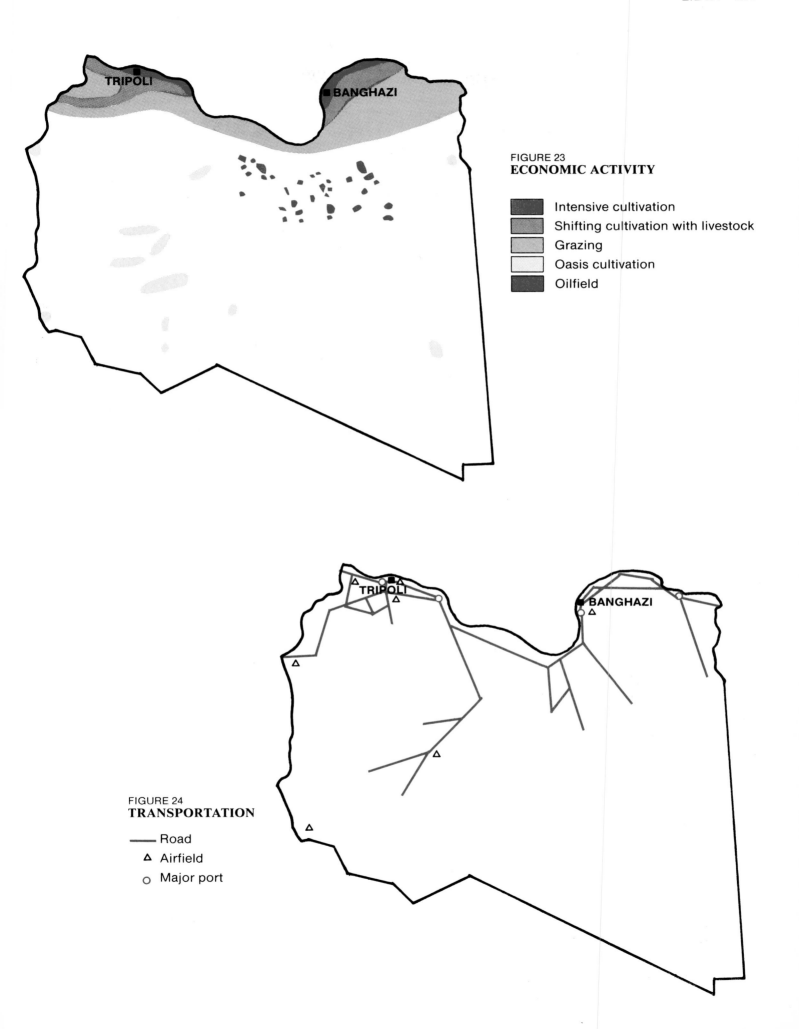

FIGURE 23
ECONOMIC ACTIVITY

Intensive cultivation
Shifting cultivation with livestock
Grazing
Oasis cultivation
Oilfield

TRIPOLI

BANGHAZI

FIGURE 24
TRANSPORTATION

—— Road
△ Airfield
○ Major port

TRIPOLI

BANGHAZI

MADAGASCAR

The world's fourth largest island, Madagascar ranks 42nd in land area and 59th in population. The turning point in Malagasy economic history was the socialist orientation introduced by President Didier Ratsiraka in the mid-1970s. Under his leadership, Madagascar has successfully nationalized all major industrial sectors, including plantations established under the French rule. Whereas the government owned or controlled only 13% of the economy's productive base in 1975, the proportion had risen to 70% by 1980. Nevertheless, agriculture remains the mainstay of the economy, contributing nearly two-fifths of the GDP and employing nearly 80% of the economically active population. The principal crops are coffee (which accounts for nearly half the total export earnings), vanilla and cloves; Madagascar is the world's leading producer of these last two. Until the 1970s foreign investors controlled approximately 85% of the industrial sector; currently direct foreign investment is limited to minority participation.

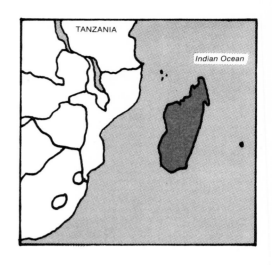

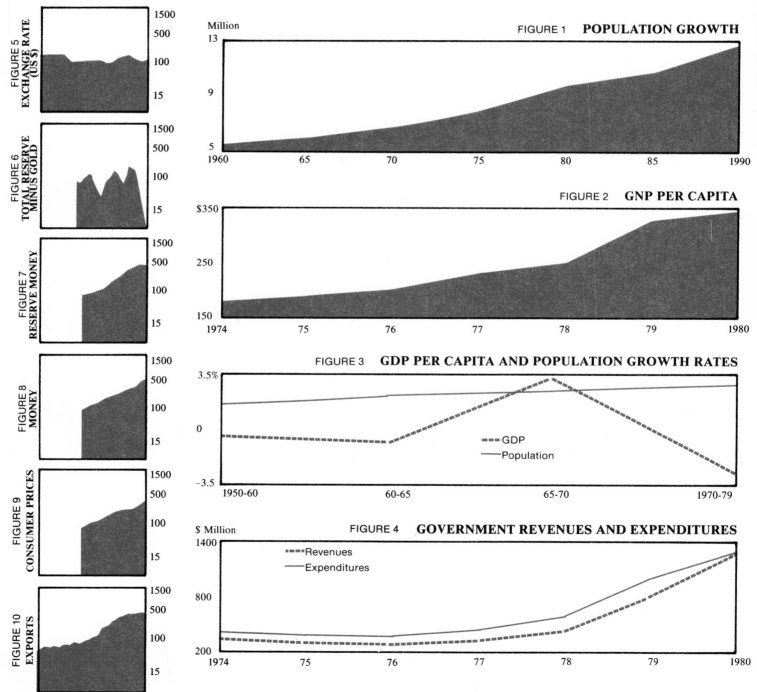

FIGURE 5 EXCHANGE RATE (US $)

FIGURE 6 TOTAL RESERVE MINUS GOLD

FIGURE 7 RESERVE MONEY

FIGURE 8 MONEY

FIGURE 9 CONSUMER PRICES

FIGURE 10 EXPORTS

FIGURE 1 **POPULATION GROWTH**

FIGURE 2 **GNP PER CAPITA**

FIGURE 3 **GDP PER CAPITA AND POPULATION GROWTH RATES**

FIGURE 4 **GOVERNMENT REVENUES AND EXPENDITURES**

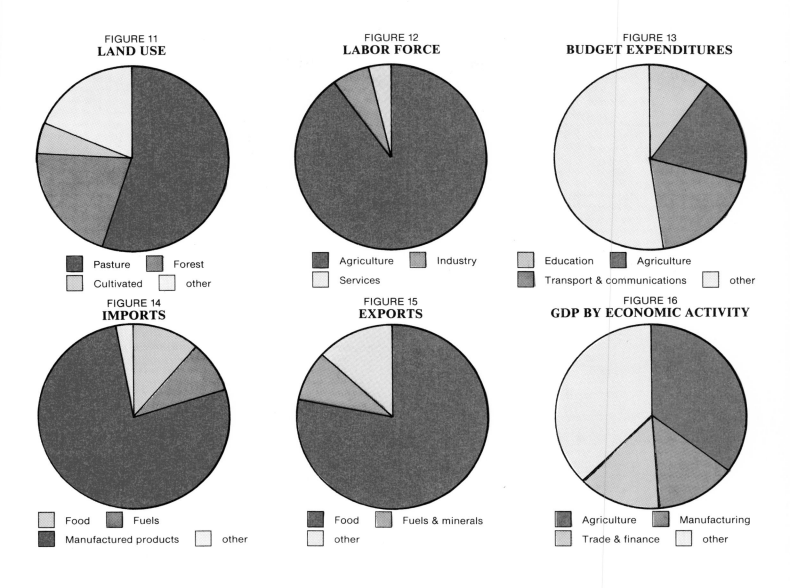

FIGURE 11
LAND USE

Pasture   Forest
Cultivated   other

FIGURE 12
LABOR FORCE

Agriculture   Industry
Services

FIGURE 13
BUDGET EXPENDITURES

Education   Agriculture
Transport & communications   other

FIGURE 14
IMPORTS

Food   Fuels
Manufactured products   other

FIGURE 15
EXPORTS

Food   Fuels & minerals
other

FIGURE 16
GDP BY ECONOMIC ACTIVITY

Agriculture   Manufacturing
Trade & finance   other

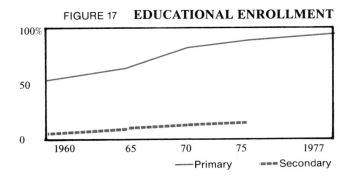

FIGURE 17   **EDUCATIONAL ENROLLMENT**

100%

50

0

1960   65   70   75   1977

——Primary   ===Secondary

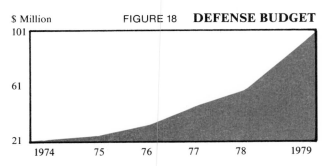

$ Million   FIGURE 18   **DEFENSE BUDGET**

101

61

21

1974   75   76   77   78   1979

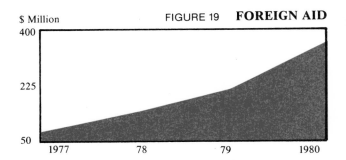

$ Million   FIGURE 19   **FOREIGN AID**

400

225

50

1977   78   79   1980

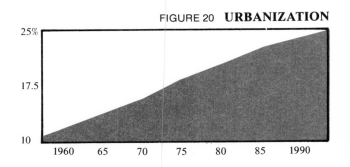

FIGURE 20   **URBANIZATION**

25%

17.5

10

1960   65   70   75   80   85   1990

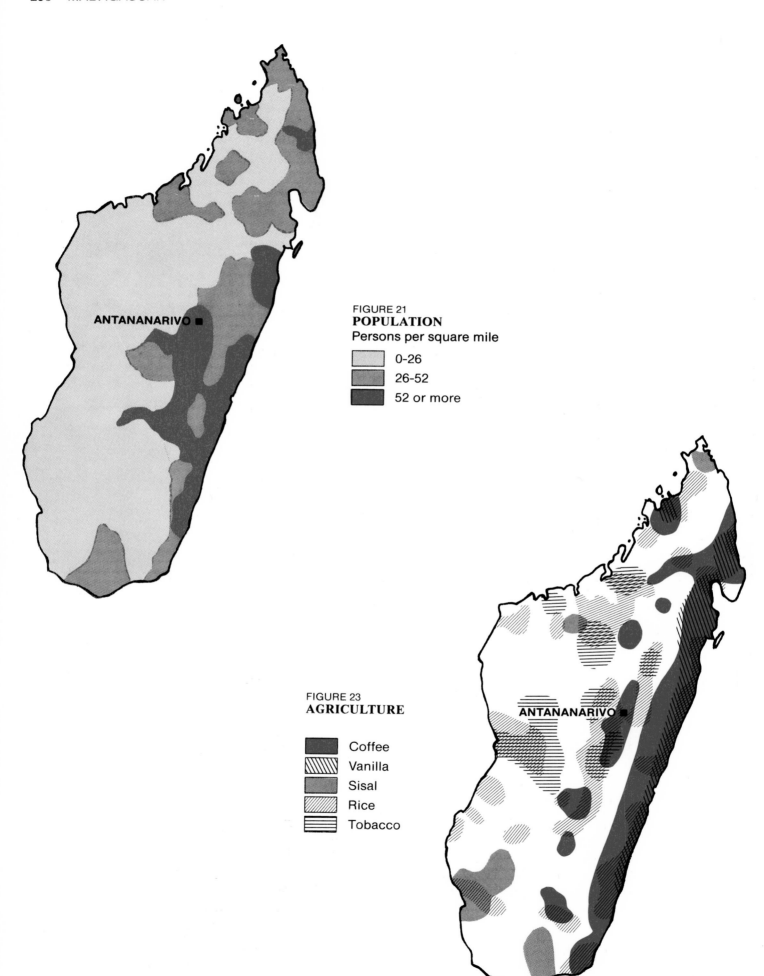

FIGURE 21
POPULATION
Persons per square mile

- 0-26
- 26-52
- 52 or more

FIGURE 23
AGRICULTURE

- Coffee
- Vanilla
- Sisal
- Rice
- Tobacco

ANTANANARIVO ■

ANTANANARIVO ■

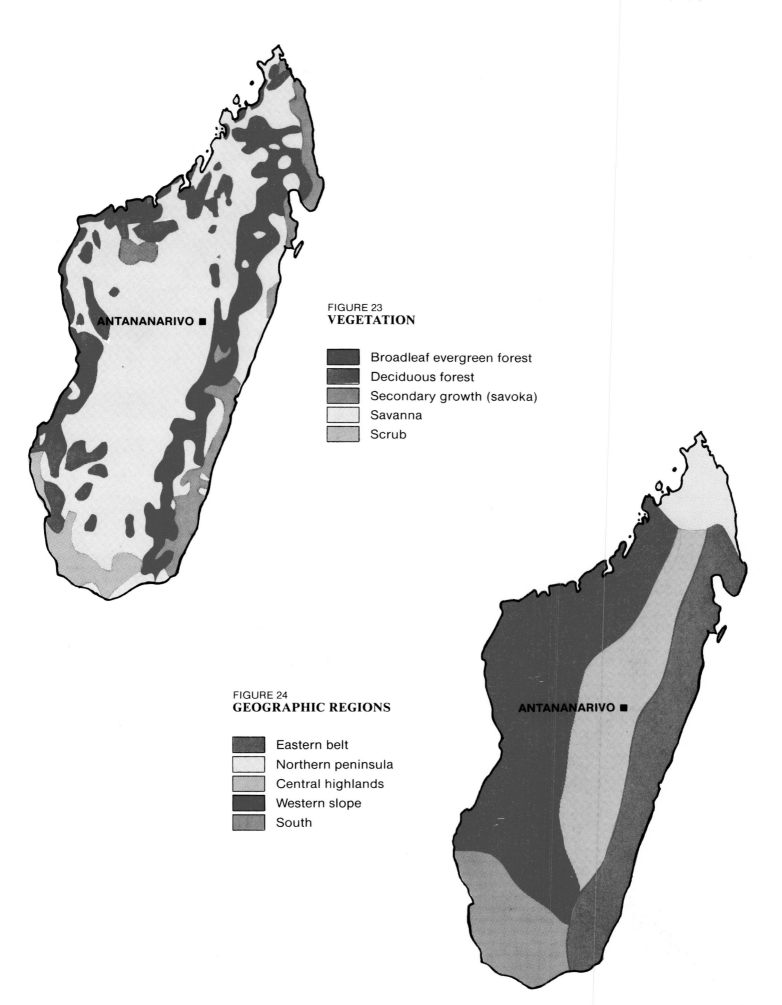

FIGURE 23
VEGETATION

- Broadleaf evergreen forest
- Deciduous forest
- Secondary growth (savoka)
- Savanna
- Scrub

FIGURE 24
GEOGRAPHIC REGIONS

- Eastern belt
- Northern peninsula
- Central highlands
- Western slope
- South

MALAWI

A landlocked nation on the western side of the lake that bears the same name, Malawi ranks 93rd in land area and 82nd in population. While the population growth rate is not much higher than the African average, the country has experienced a steady growth in per capita GNP throughout most of the 1970s. Much of the growth was accounted for by the agricultural sector, particularly the smallholdings. Malawi is among the few African countries totally self-sufficient in basic foodstuffs. Another reason for Malawi's remarkable growth record is its ability to attract the right type of foreign donors and investors. Several of the nation's largest agricultural estates and manufacturers are foreign owned, including the Imperial Group, Lonrho and Portland Cement. As a pragmatist, President Banda has maintained close ties with Pretoria, even at the expense of alienating his black neighbors, but the same pragmatism may dictate a closer relationship with the latter in the future, particularly in the areas of transportation, communication and energy.

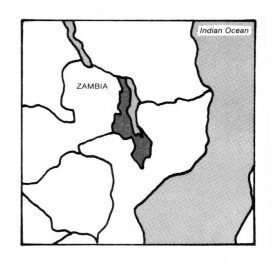

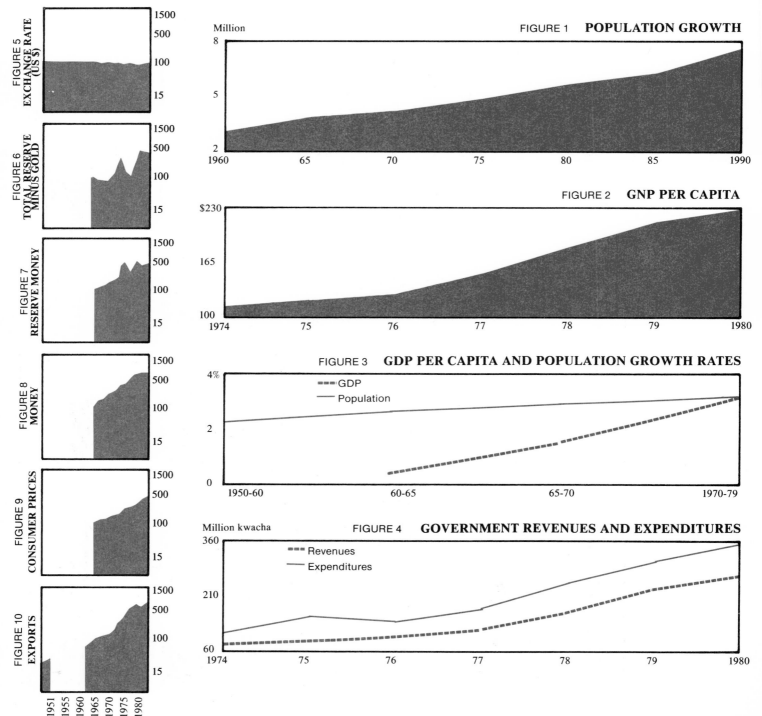

FIGURE 5 EXCHANGE RATE (US $)

FIGURE 6 TOTAL RESERVE MINUS GOLD

FIGURE 7 RESERVE MONEY

FIGURE 8 MONEY

FIGURE 9 CONSUMER PRICES

FIGURE 10 EXPORTS

FIGURE 1 **POPULATION GROWTH**

FIGURE 2 **GNP PER CAPITA**

FIGURE 3 **GDP PER CAPITA AND POPULATION GROWTH RATES**

FIGURE 4 **GOVERNMENT REVENUES AND EXPENDITURES**

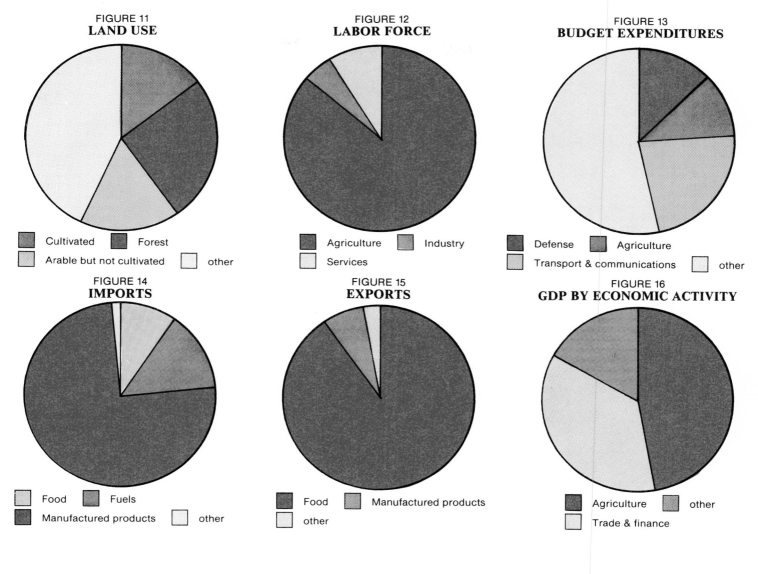

FIGURE 11
LAND USE

Cultivated — Forest — Arable but not cultivated — other

FIGURE 12
LABOR FORCE

Agriculture — Industry — Services

FIGURE 13
BUDGET EXPENDITURES

Defense — Agriculture — Transport & communications — other

FIGURE 14
IMPORTS

Food — Fuels — Manufactured products — other

FIGURE 15
EXPORTS

Food — Manufactured products — other

FIGURE 16
GDP BY ECONOMIC ACTIVITY

Agriculture — other — Trade & finance

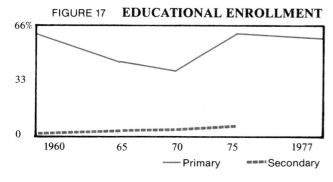

FIGURE 17 **EDUCATIONAL ENROLLMENT**

66%

33

0

1960   65   70   75   1977

—— Primary   ==== Secondary

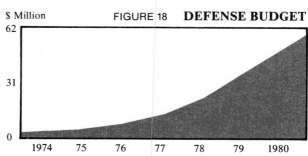

$ Million   FIGURE 18 **DEFENSE BUDGET**

62

31

0

1974   75   76   77   78   79   1980

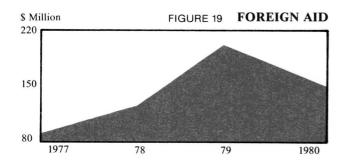

$ Million   FIGURE 19 **FOREIGN AID**

220

150

80

1977   78   79   1980

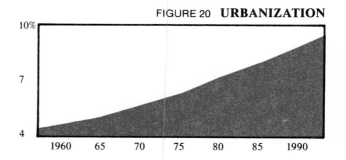

FIGURE 20 **URBANIZATION**

10%

7

4

1960   65   70   75   80   85   1990

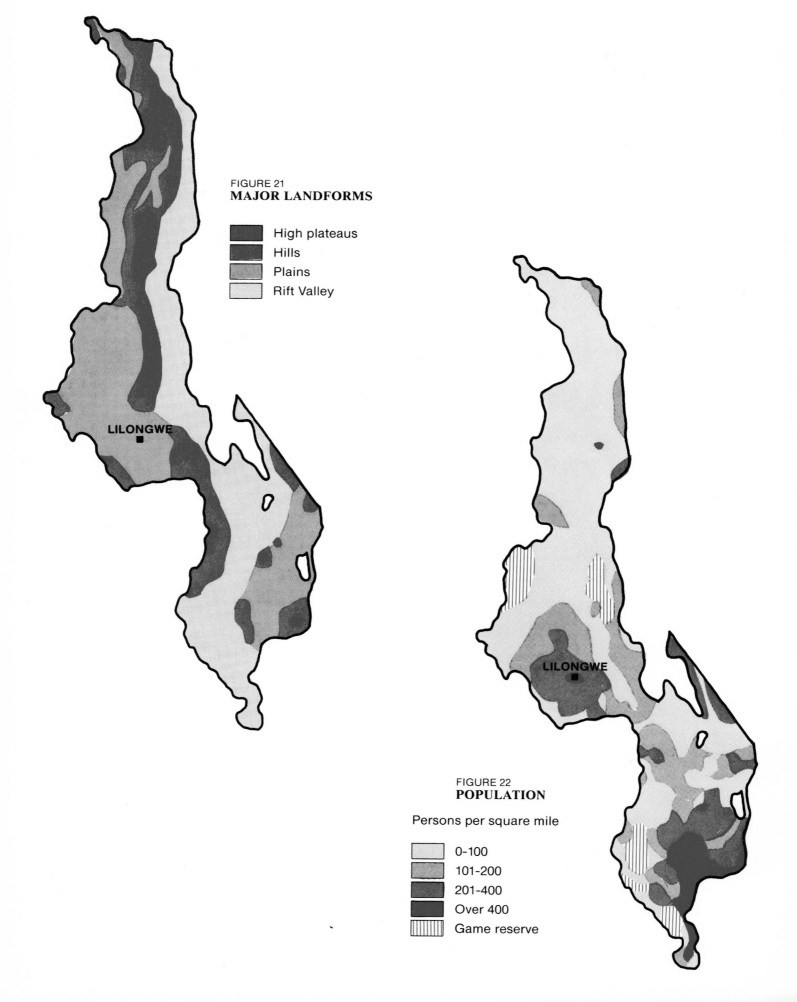

FIGURE 21
MAJOR LANDFORMS

High plateaus
Hills
Plains
Rift Valley

LILONGWE

FIGURE 22
POPULATION

Persons per square mile

0–100
101–200
201–400
Over 400
Game reserve

LILONGWE

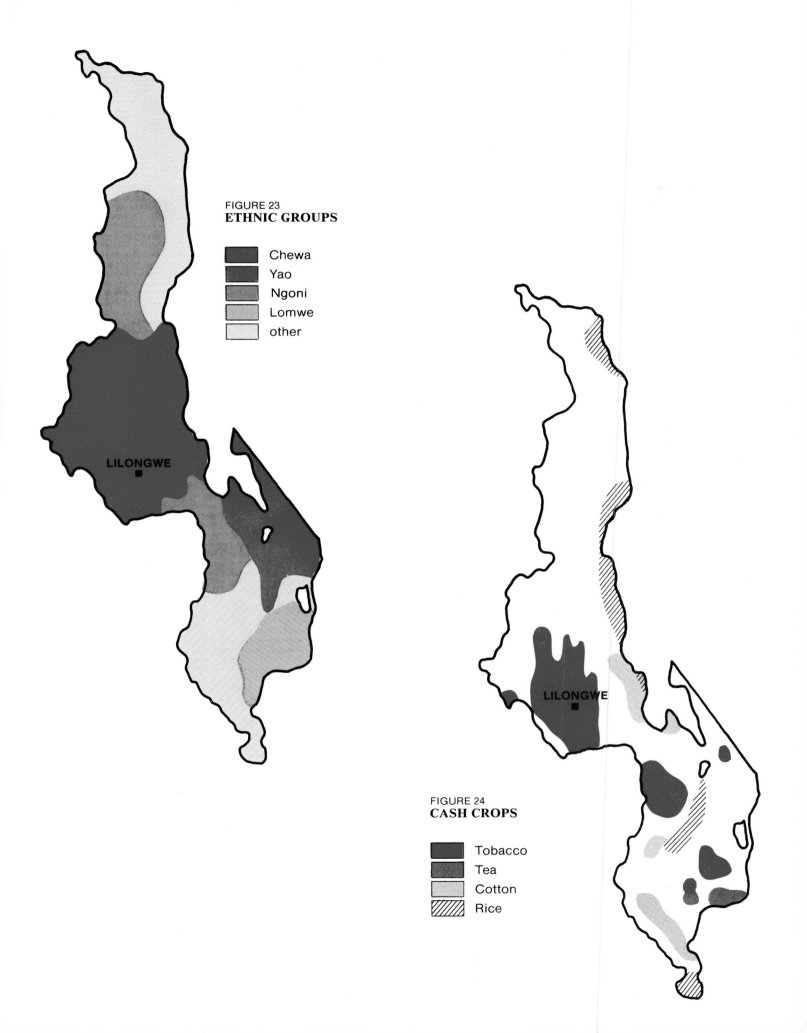

FIGURE 23
ETHNIC GROUPS

Chewa
Yao
Ngoni
Lomwe
other

LILONGWE

FIGURE 24
CASH CROPS

Tobacco
Tea
Cotton
Rice

LILONGWE

MALAYSIA

Located partly on the southern half of the Malay Peninsula and partly on the northern quarter of Borneo, Malaysia ranks 56th in land area and 50th in population. Malaysia's economy is dominated by three commodities: tin, rubber and oil; the country is among the top producers of the first two. Malaysia's rich natural resources have been by and large well managed in terms of monetary and development policy. It has had consistent trade surpluses for over a decade because the prices of its traditional exports have remained firm while at the same time these surpluses have enabled it to diversify into other commodities, such as timber. Petroleum and manufactured products have overtaken rubber as the principal foreign exchange earners since 1980. Ethnic and religious rivalries ripple through the economy periodically and the government has the task of monitoring and moderating these rivalries so that they do not tear apart the carefully balanced political and economic system.

INDONESIA

Indian Ocean

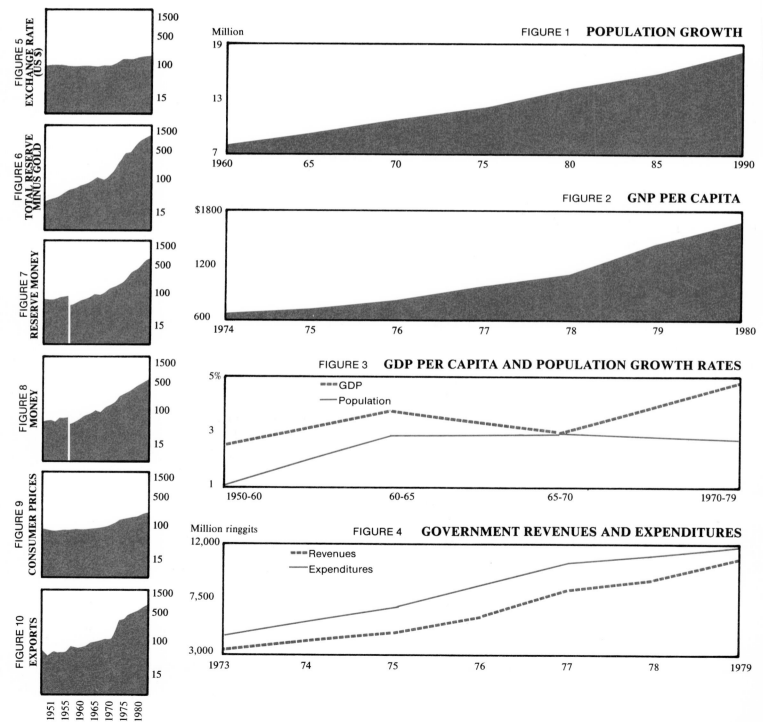

FIGURE 5 EXCHANGE RATE (US $)

FIGURE 6 TOTAL RESERVE MINUS GOLD

FIGURE 7 RESERVE MONEY

FIGURE 8 MONEY

FIGURE 9 CONSUMER PRICES

FIGURE 10 EXPORTS

FIGURE 1 **POPULATION GROWTH**

Million

FIGURE 2 **GNP PER CAPITA**

FIGURE 3 **GDP PER CAPITA AND POPULATION GROWTH RATES**

GDP
Population

FIGURE 4 **GOVERNMENT REVENUES AND EXPENDITURES**

Million ringgits

Revenues
Expenditures

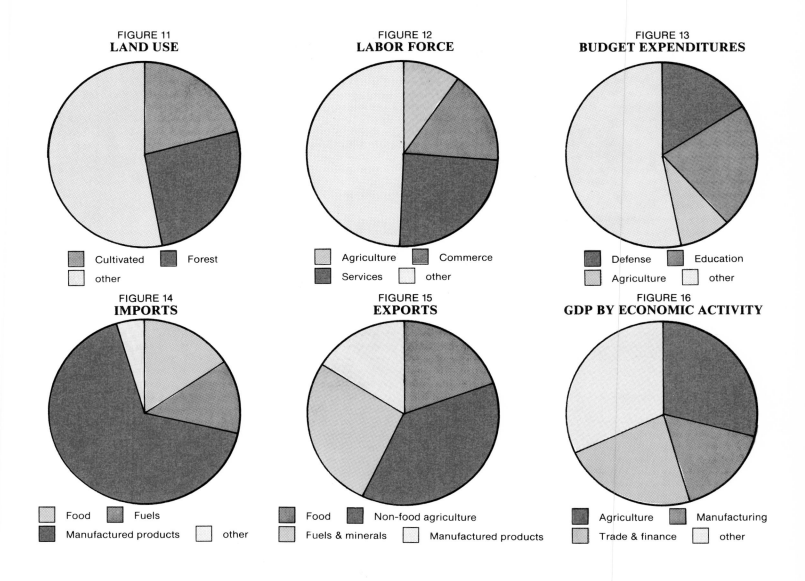

FIGURE 11
LAND USE

Cultivated Forest
other

FIGURE 12
LABOR FORCE

Agriculture Commerce
Services other

FIGURE 13
BUDGET EXPENDITURES

Defense Education
Agriculture other

FIGURE 14
IMPORTS

Food Fuels
Manufactured products other

FIGURE 15
EXPORTS

Food Non-food agriculture
Fuels & minerals Manufactured products

FIGURE 16
GDP BY ECONOMIC ACTIVITY

Agriculture Manufacturing
Trade & finance other

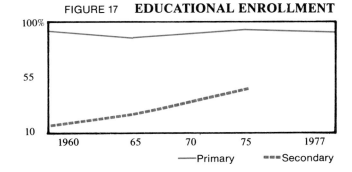

FIGURE 17   **EDUCATIONAL ENROLLMENT**

100%
55
10
1960   65   70   75   1977

——Primary   ===Secondary

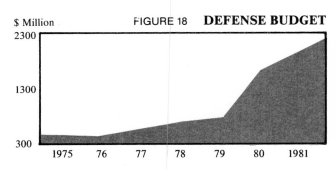

$ Million   FIGURE 18   **DEFENSE BUDGET**

2300
1300
300
1975   76   77   78   79   80   1981

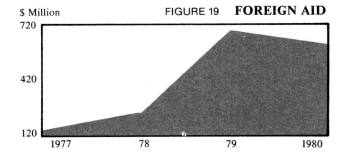

$ Million   FIGURE 19   **FOREIGN AID**

720
420
120
1977   78   79   1980

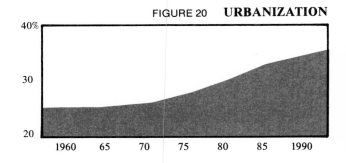

FIGURE 20   **URBANIZATION**

40%
30
20
1960   65   70   75   80   85   1990

FIGURE 21
AGRICULTURE AND LAND USE

Rubber, oil palm
Rice
Rubber, rice, coconuts
Tropical rain forest and swamp

FIGURE 22
OIL AND GAS FIELDS

□   Oil/gasfield

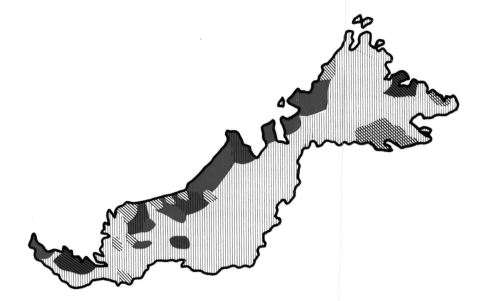

FIGURE 23
ETHNIC GROUPS

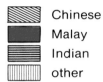 Chinese
Malay
Indian
other

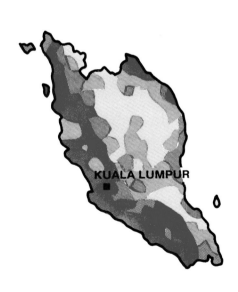

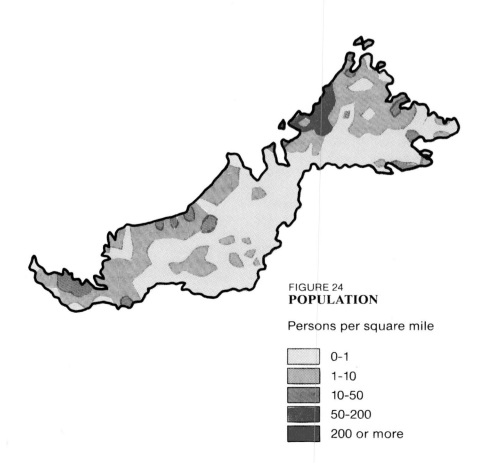

FIGURE 24
POPULATION

Persons per square mile

0–1
1–10
10–50
50–200
200 or more

MAURITANIA

A huge chunk of the Sahara Desert, Mauritania ranks 26th in land area and 128th in population, a disparity characteristic of all desert countries. About 90% of all Mauritanians live in rural areas as nomadic herdsmen, constituting the traditional subsistence sector of the Mauritanian economy. This sector, with a per capita income of only around $150, is still recovering from the great Sahelian drought of 1968-74. The modern sector accounts for about 20% of the GDP, with mining contributing two-thirds of that share. The most important natural resource is the large deposit of high-grade iron ore in the F'Derick region, exports of which account for 70% of the country's foreign exchange earnings. The cessation of hostilities with the Polisario Front has enabled the government to turn its attention once again to pressing economic problems, such as the need to control desertification and thus prevent a possible recurrence of the Sahelian drought.

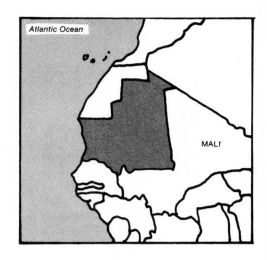

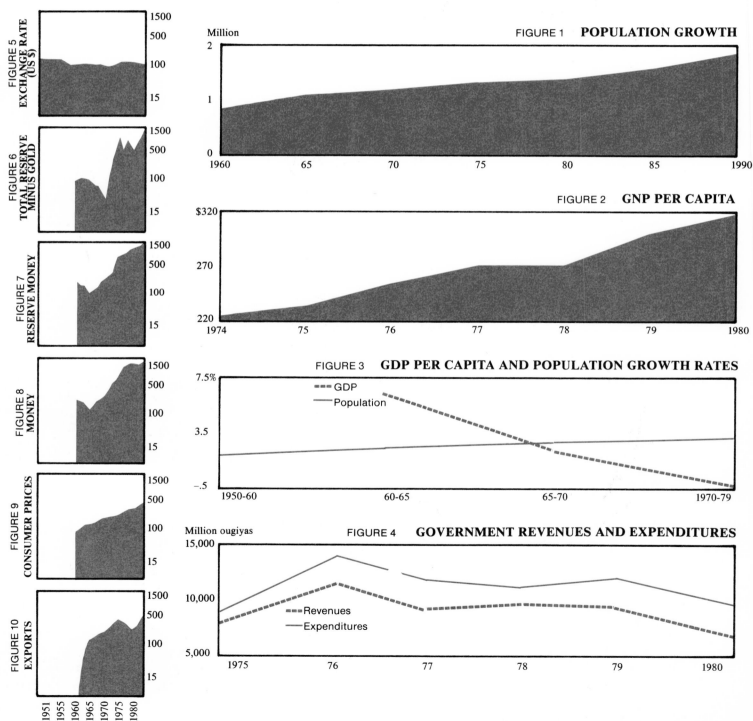

FIGURE 5 EXCHANGE RATE (US $)

FIGURE 6 TOTAL RESERVE MINUS GOLD

FIGURE 7 RESERVE MONEY

FIGURE 8 MONEY

FIGURE 9 CONSUMER PRICES

FIGURE 10 EXPORTS

FIGURE 1 **POPULATION GROWTH**

FIGURE 2 **GNP PER CAPITA**

FIGURE 3 **GDP PER CAPITA AND POPULATION GROWTH RATES**

FIGURE 4 **GOVERNMENT REVENUES AND EXPENDITURES**

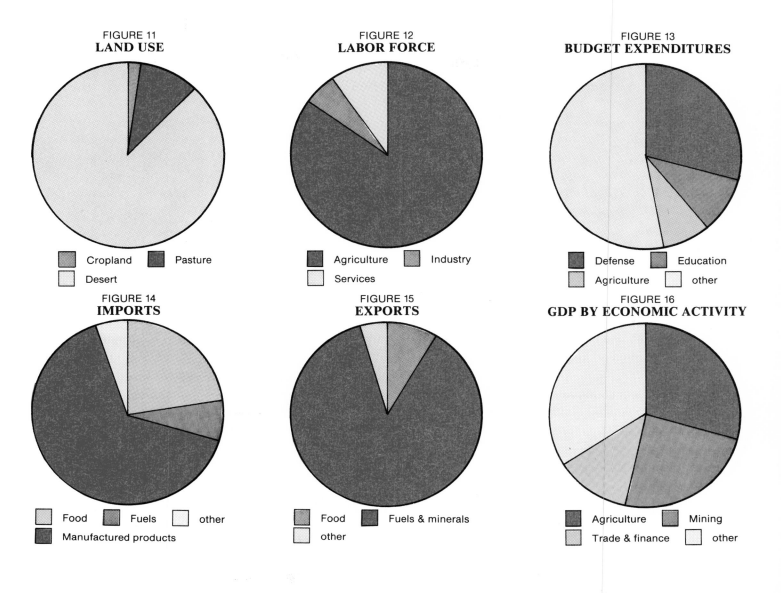

FIGURE 11
LAND USE

- Cropland
- Pasture
- Desert

FIGURE 12
LABOR FORCE

- Agriculture
- Industry
- Services

FIGURE 13
BUDGET EXPENDITURES

- Defense
- Education
- Agriculture
- other

FIGURE 14
IMPORTS

- Food
- Fuels
- other
- Manufactured products

FIGURE 15
EXPORTS

- Food
- Fuels & minerals
- other

FIGURE 16
GDP BY ECONOMIC ACTIVITY

- Agriculture
- Mining
- Trade & finance
- other

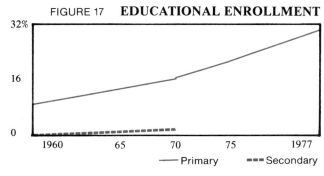

FIGURE 17 **EDUCATIONAL ENROLLMENT**

— Primary   ■■■ Secondary

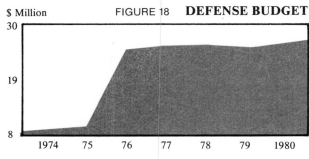

$ Million   FIGURE 18   **DEFENSE BUDGET**

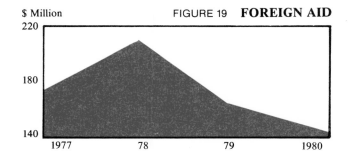

$ Million   FIGURE 19   **FOREIGN AID**

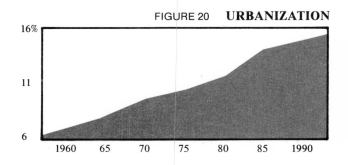

FIGURE 20   **URBANIZATION**

MAURITIUS

An island in the southwest Indian ocean, Mauritius ranks 152nd in land surface and 132nd in population. The island is one of the most overpopulated countries in the world and ranks ninth in density. The population explosion that followed the eradication of malaria during World War II has been more or less brought under control and the growth rate is now a modest 1.4% while the GNP growth rate has jumped to an encouraging 6.4%. The economy remains predominantly dependent on sugar and, like all one-product countries, suffers from boom and bust cycles induced by erratic international markets. It also shares many of the problems of mini-economies: climbing energy prices, rising government expenditures, falling foreign exchange reserves and high inflation. Apart from its economy, the most significant feature of Mauritius is that it represents a confluence of four cultures: English, French, Indian and African. Given such diverse and disparate elements, it has fused together a viable identity with few ethnic conflicts.

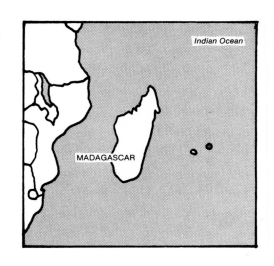

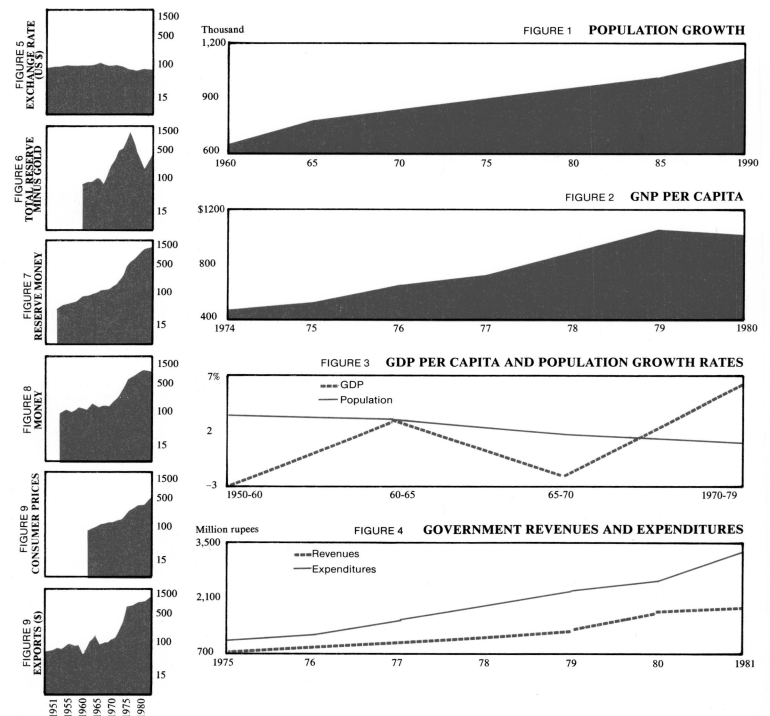

FIGURE 5 EXCHANGE RATE (US $)

FIGURE 6 TOTAL RESERVE MINUS GOLD

FIGURE 7 RESERVE MONEY

FIGURE 8 MONEY

FIGURE 9 CONSUMER PRICES

FIGURE 9 EXPORTS ($)

FIGURE 1 **POPULATION GROWTH**

FIGURE 2 **GNP PER CAPITA**

FIGURE 3 **GDP PER CAPITA AND POPULATION GROWTH RATES**

FIGURE 4 **GOVERNMENT REVENUES AND EXPENDITURES**

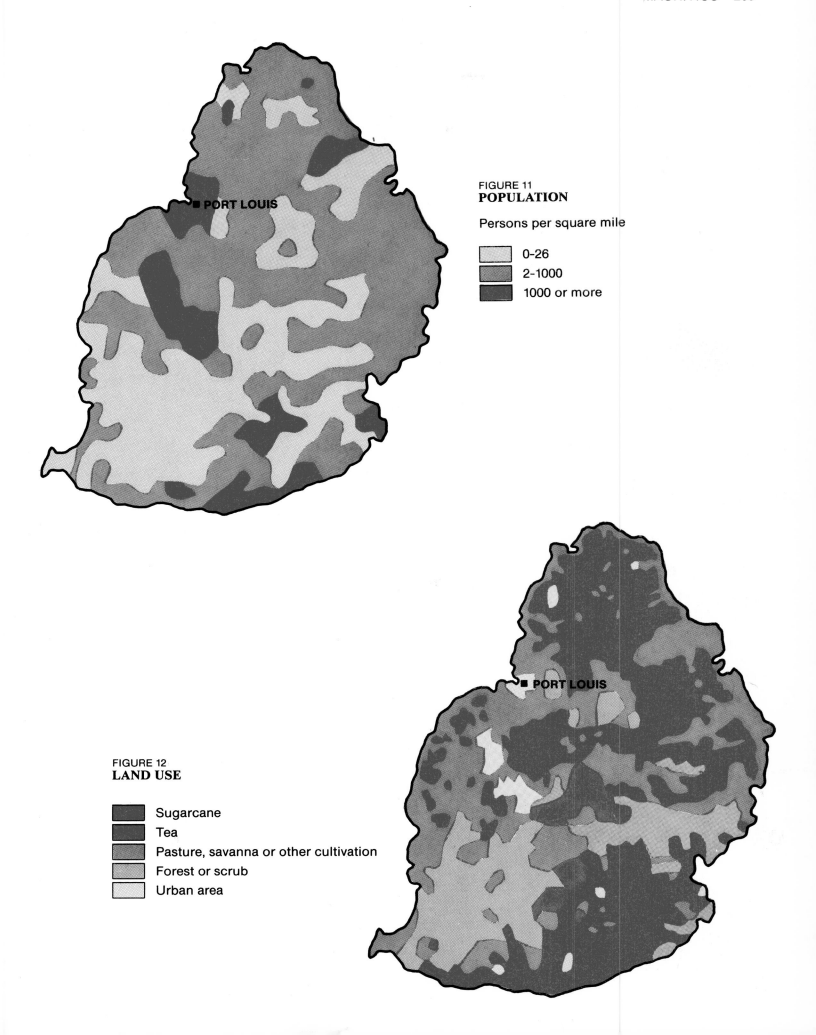

FIGURE 11
POPULATION

Persons per square mile

0-26
2-1000
1000 or more

■ PORT LOUIS

FIGURE 12
LAND USE

Sugarcane
Tea
Pasture, savanna or other cultivation
Forest or scrub
Urban area

■ PORT LOUIS

MEXICO

The third largest country in Latin America, the 12th largest in the world, the 11th most populous, and the largest Spanish-speaking country in the world, Mexico has all the attributes of a great nation but somehow misses that title because of national flaws that neither historians nor economists have been able to pinpoint. With its immense natural resources, it should appear among the top 10 in a broad array of indicators but surprisingly it does not. It has no solid strength in any particular area. Recently, the surge in oil production had led observers to call it the Saudi Arabia of the Western Hemisphere. The economic momentum these expectations generated has not been sustained; further, substantial increases in oil exports have not prevented an overall deterioration in the trade balance, largely because of imports required for escalating domestic investment. The economy became overheated because of an uncontrolled flow of petrodollars and ill-conceived development plans.

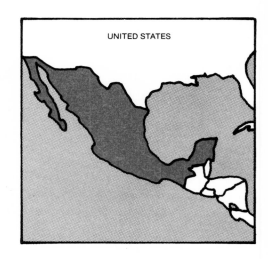

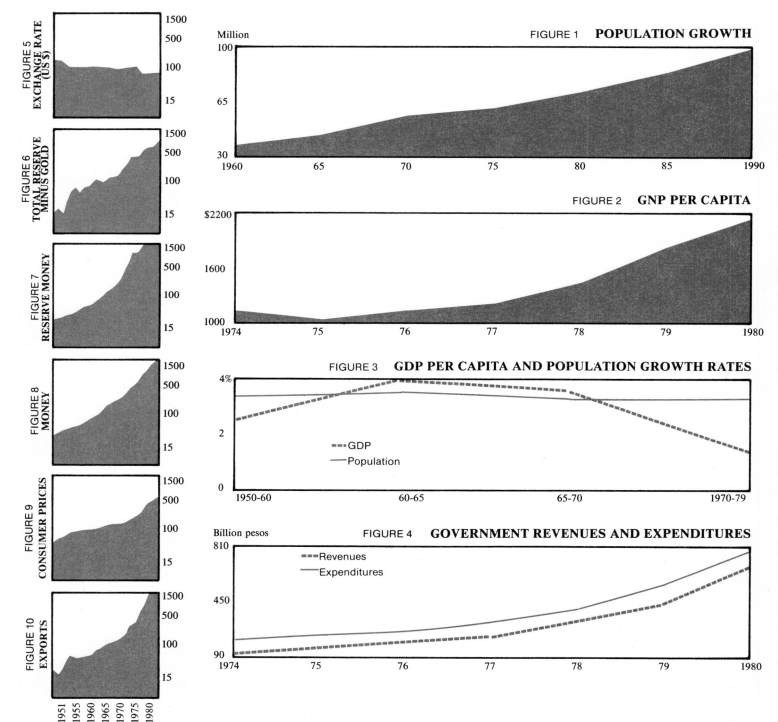

FIGURE 5 EXCHANGE RATE (US $)

FIGURE 6 TOTAL RESERVE MINUS GOLD

FIGURE 7 RESERVE MONEY

FIGURE 8 MONEY

FIGURE 9 CONSUMER PRICES

FIGURE 10 EXPORTS

FIGURE 1 **POPULATION GROWTH**

FIGURE 2 **GNP PER CAPITA**

FIGURE 3 **GDP PER CAPITA AND POPULATION GROWTH RATES**

FIGURE 4 **GOVERNMENT REVENUES AND EXPENDITURES**

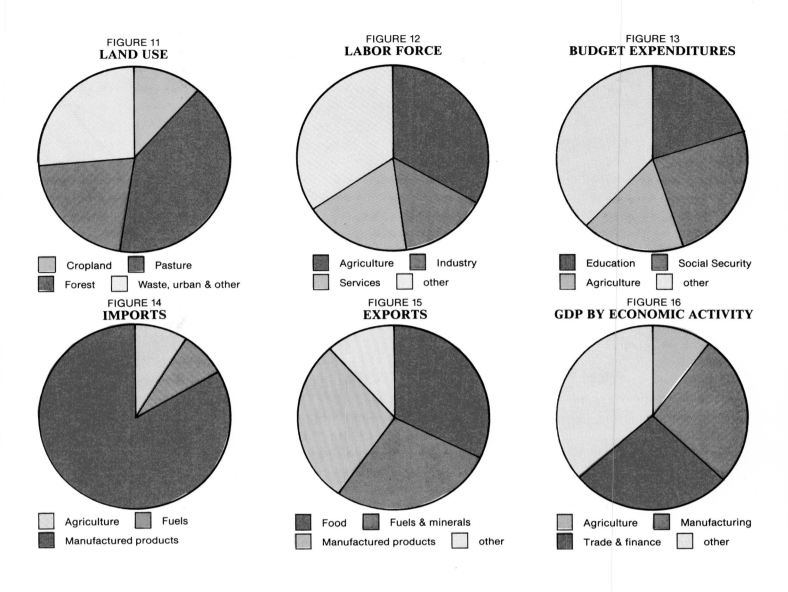

FIGURE 11
LAND USE

☐ Cropland   ■ Pasture
■ Forest   ☐ Waste, urban & other

FIGURE 12
LABOR FORCE

■ Agriculture   ■ Industry
■ Services   ☐ other

FIGURE 13
BUDGET EXPENDITURES

■ Education   ■ Social Security
■ Agriculture   ☐ other

FIGURE 14
IMPORTS

☐ Agriculture   ■ Fuels
■ Manufactured products

FIGURE 15
EXPORTS

■ Food   ■ Fuels & minerals
■ Manufactured products   ☐ other

FIGURE 16
GDP BY ECONOMIC ACTIVITY

■ Agriculture   ■ Manufacturing
■ Trade & finance   ☐ other

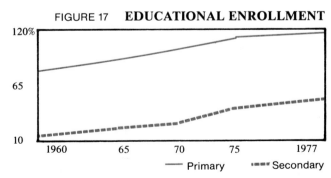

FIGURE 17   **EDUCATIONAL ENROLLMENT**

120%

65

10

1960   65   70   75   1977

—— Primary   ▬▬▬ Secondary

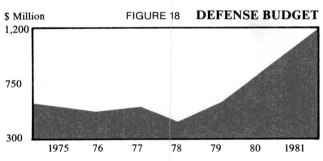

$ Million   FIGURE 18   **DEFENSE BUDGET**

1,200

750

300

1975   76   77   78   79   80   1981

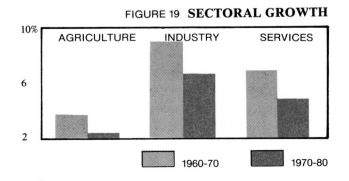

FIGURE 19   **SECTORAL GROWTH**

10%   AGRICULTURE   INDUSTRY   SERVICES

6

2

☐ 1960-70   ■ 1970-80

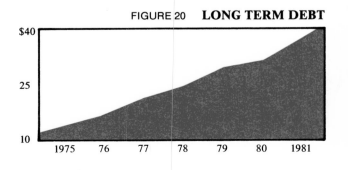

FIGURE 20   **LONG TERM DEBT**

$40

25

10

1975   76   77   78   79   80   1981

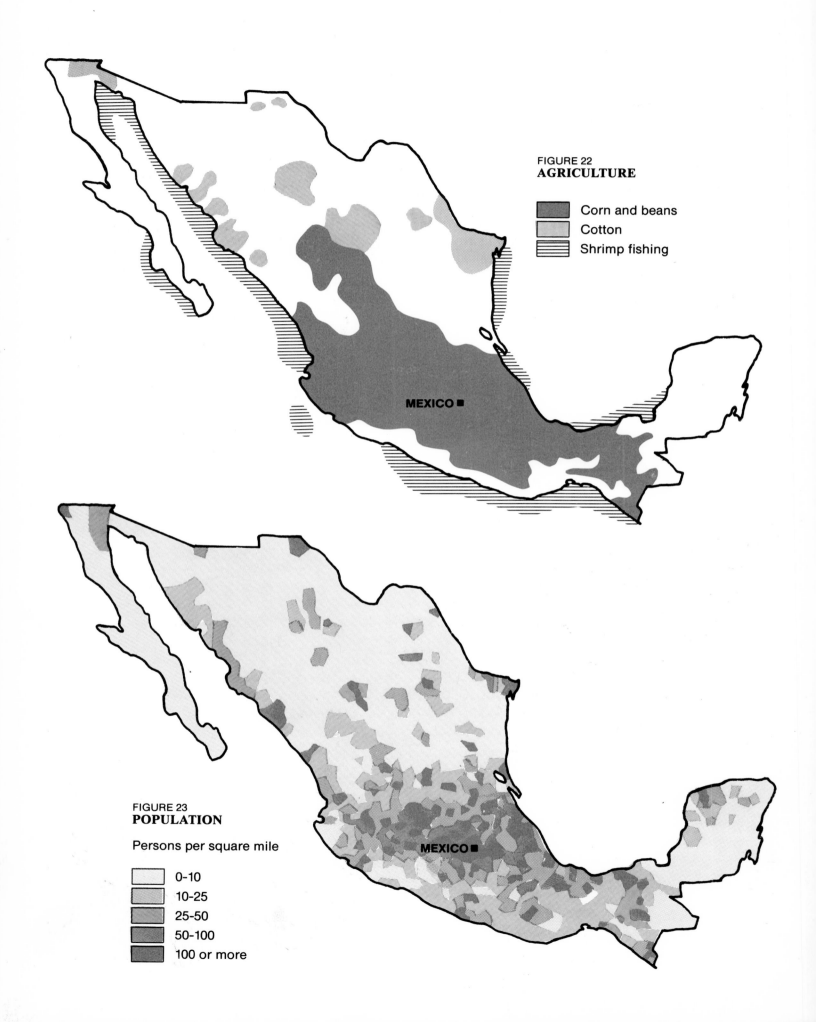

FIGURE 22
AGRICULTURE

Corn and beans
Cotton
Shrimp fishing

MEXICO ■

FIGURE 23
POPULATION

Persons per square mile

0-10
10-25
25-50
50-100
100 or more

MEXICO ■

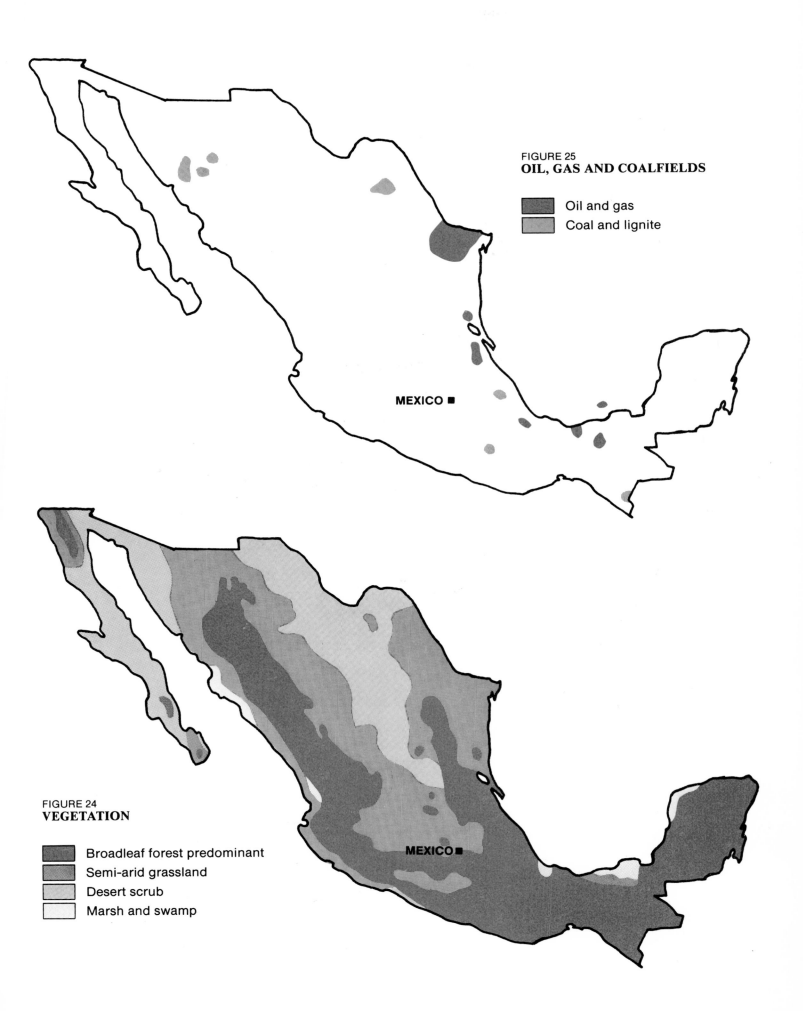

FIGURE 25
OIL, GAS AND COALFIELDS

Oil and gas

Coal and lignite

MEXICO ■

FIGURE 24
VEGETATION

Broadleaf forest predominant

Semi-arid grassland

Desert scrub

Marsh and swamp

MEXICO ■

MOROCCO

Morocco ranks 50th in land area and 36th in population. Politically stable, Morocco has not experienced the kind of violent upheavals that sister Arab nations have had to confront. The economic implications of this stability are evident: Morocco is the favorite North African destination of Western tourists as well as of French and U.S. capital. The continued fighting in Western Sahara has been a political and economic liability and has alienated Morocco from its neighbors. Outweighing these disadvantages is the fact that the issue has served to unify the nation and divert its attention from internal problems. While mining contributes only a small percentage of the GDP, it accounts for 30 to 50% of export earnings. Over 90% of mining output consists of phosphate, of which Morocco is the world's leading exporter. With the decline in phosphate prices beginning in the mid-1970s, Morocco has recorded massive trade deficits which the remittances of Moroccan workers abroad have only partially offset.

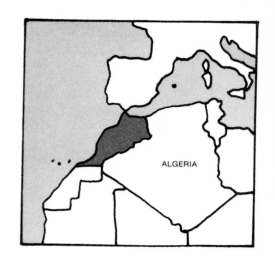

ALGERIA

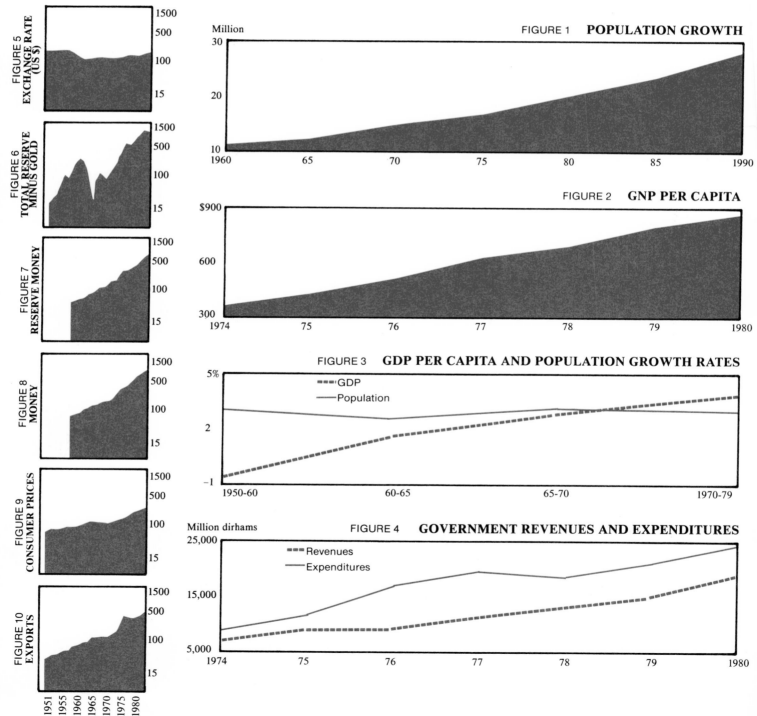

FIGURE 5 EXCHANGE RATE (US $)

FIGURE 6 TOTAL RESERVE MINUS GOLD

FIGURE 7 RESERVE MONEY

FIGURE 8 MONEY

FIGURE 9 CONSUMER PRICES

FIGURE 10 EXPORTS

FIGURE 1 **POPULATION GROWTH**

FIGURE 2 **GNP PER CAPITA**

FIGURE 3 **GDP PER CAPITA AND POPULATION GROWTH RATES**
GDP
Population

FIGURE 4 **GOVERNMENT REVENUES AND EXPENDITURES**
Million dirhams
Revenues
Expenditures

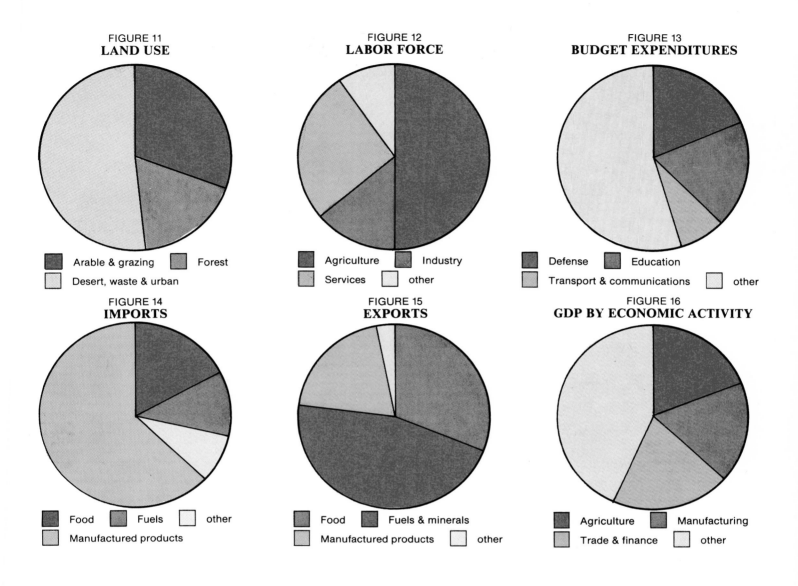

FIGURE 11
LAND USE

Arable & grazing   Forest

Desert, waste & urban

FIGURE 12
LABOR FORCE

Agriculture   Industry

Services   other

FIGURE 13
BUDGET EXPENDITURES

Defense   Education

Transport & communications   other

FIGURE 14
IMPORTS

Food   Fuels   other

Manufactured products

FIGURE 15
EXPORTS

Food   Fuels & minerals

Manufactured products   other

FIGURE 16
GDP BY ECONOMIC ACTIVITY

Agriculture   Manufacturing

Trade & finance   other

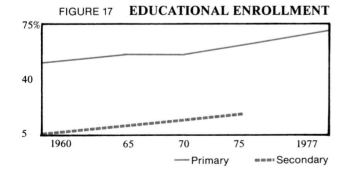

FIGURE 17   **EDUCATIONAL ENROLLMENT**

75%

40

5

1960   65   70   75   1977

——Primary   ▪▪▪▪Secondary

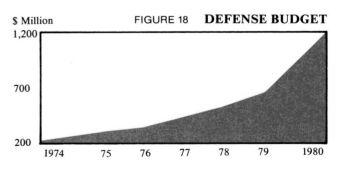

$ Million   FIGURE 18   **DEFENSE BUDGET**

1,200

700

200

1974   75   76   77   78   79   1980

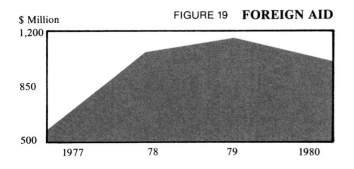

$ Million   FIGURE 19   **FOREIGN AID**

1,200

850

500

1977   78   79   1980

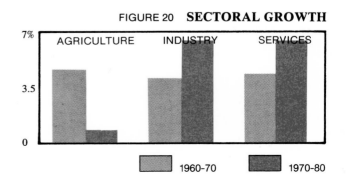

FIGURE 20   **SECTORAL GROWTH**

7%   AGRICULTURE   INDUSTRY   SERVICES

3.5

0

1960-70   1970-80

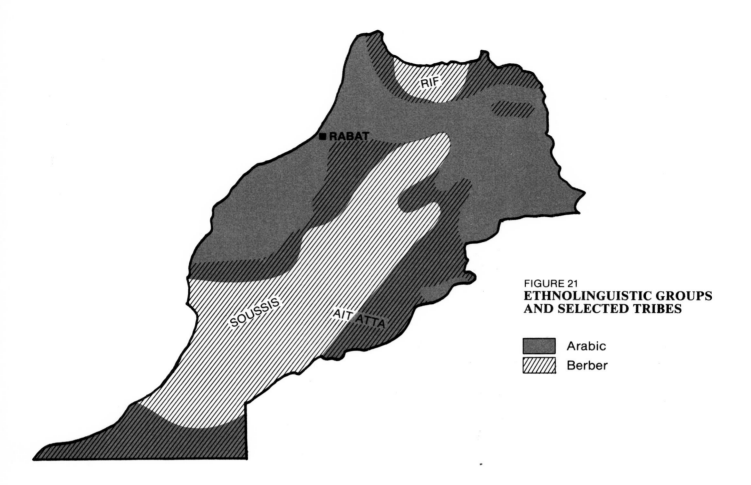

FIGURE 21
**ETHNOLINGUISTIC GROUPS
AND SELECTED TRIBES**

Arabic
Berber

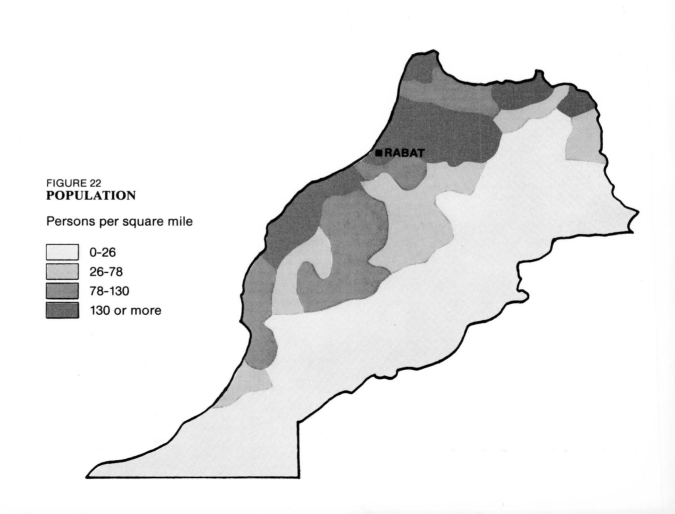

FIGURE 22
POPULATION

Persons per square mile

0-26
26-78
78-130
130 or more

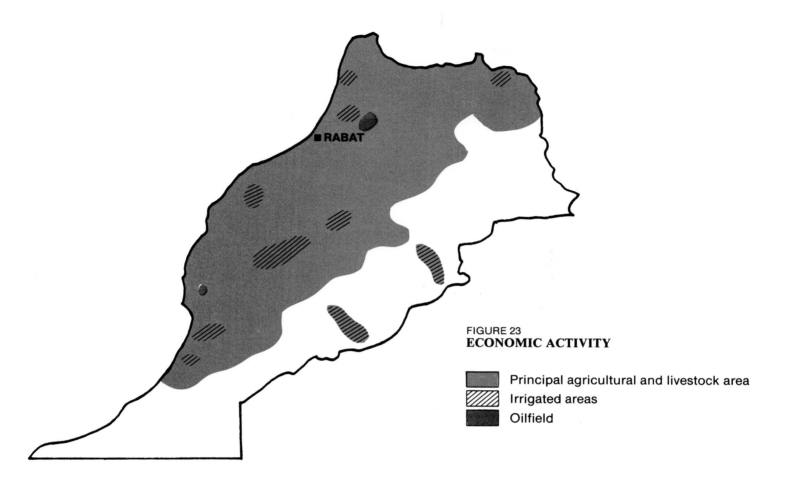

FIGURE 23
ECONOMIC ACTIVITY

Principal agricultural and livestock area
Irrigated areas
Oilfield

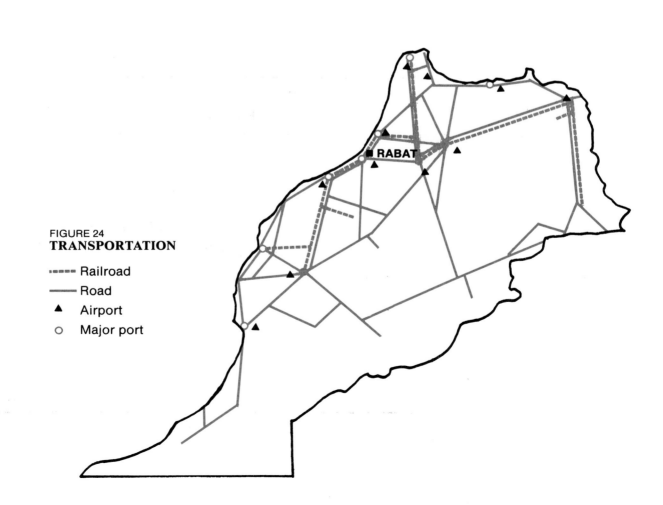

FIGURE 24
TRANSPORTATION

- - - - Railroad
—— Road
▲ Airport
○ Major port

MOZAMBIQUE

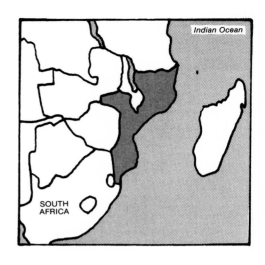

One of the youngest independent nations in Africa, Mozambique ranks 33rd in land area and 66th in population. One of the 10 poorest countries, its per capita GNP declined by 5.3% in the 1970s while the population grew by 2.5%. The country is heavily urbanized, a legacy of Portuguese rule, and ranks first in Africa in this respect. The other legacies of Portuguese rule are being gradually erased (except for the continued use of the Portuguese language). The establishment of black rule in Zimbabwe lifted one of the principal burdens on the country's economy. Agriculture remains the mainstay of the economy, but with the exodus of white and Asian farmers, output has fallen below pre-independence levels and Mozambique has had to import as much as 40% of its food requirements in recent years. The Marxist government has undertaken full control and ownership of the major sectors of the economy, but foreign capital is welcome and joint ventures with multinationals are permitted under certain conditions.

FIGURE 1 **POPULATION GROWTH**

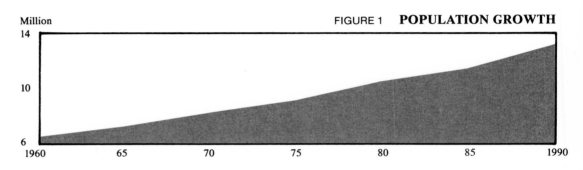

FIGURE 2 **GNP PER CAPITA**

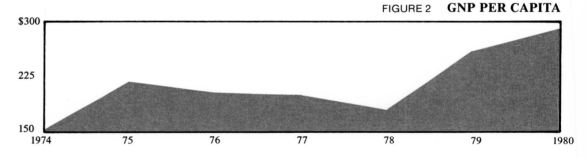

I.M.F.
DATA
UNAVAILABLE

FIGURE 3 **GDP PER CAPITA AND POPULATION GROWTH RATES**

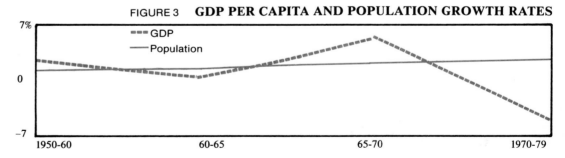

FIGURE 4 **URBANIZATION**

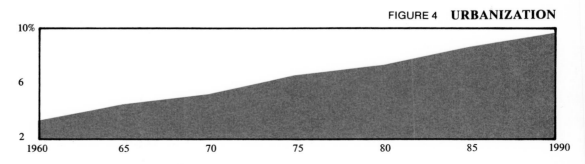

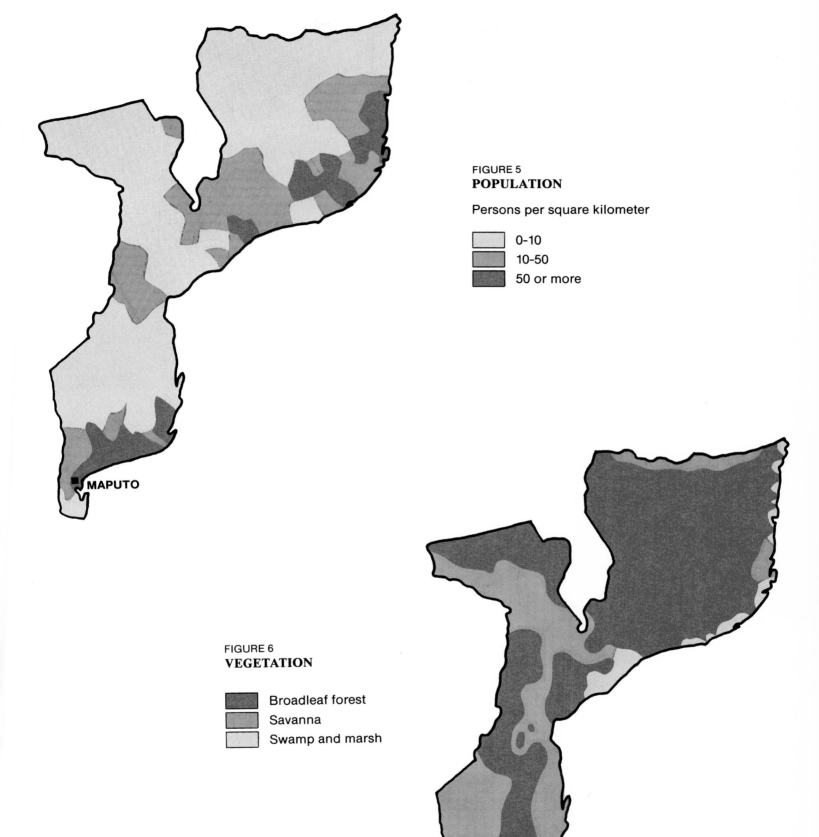

FIGURE 5
POPULATION

Persons per square kilometer

	0-10
	10-50
	50 or more

FIGURE 6
VEGETATION

	Broadleaf forest
	Savanna
	Swamp and marsh

MAPUTO

MAPUTO

NEPAL

The world's only Hindu kingdom, located on the southern slopes of the Himalayas, Nepal ranks 88th in land area and 47th in population. Sandwiched between two of the largest nations in the world, without any access to the sea, Nepal has no strategic or political leverage; further, its economic resources are meager to begin with, affording little opportunity for development. Nearly 90% of the work force is engaged in agriculture, at or below the subsistence level. Only about 30% of the land is farmed, while a third or more is forested. Two institutions—cooperatives (organized in units called *sajhas*) and a cluster of government agricultural agencies—sustain agricultural activities. While foreign trade has shown large and growing deficits, these deficits have been offset by positive balances in the services and transfers accounts, especially remittances by tourists and the famed Gurkha troops serving abroad. Over a million Indians are believed to live in Nepal and they control much of the import and export businesses.

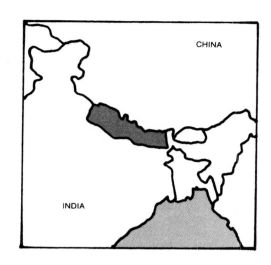

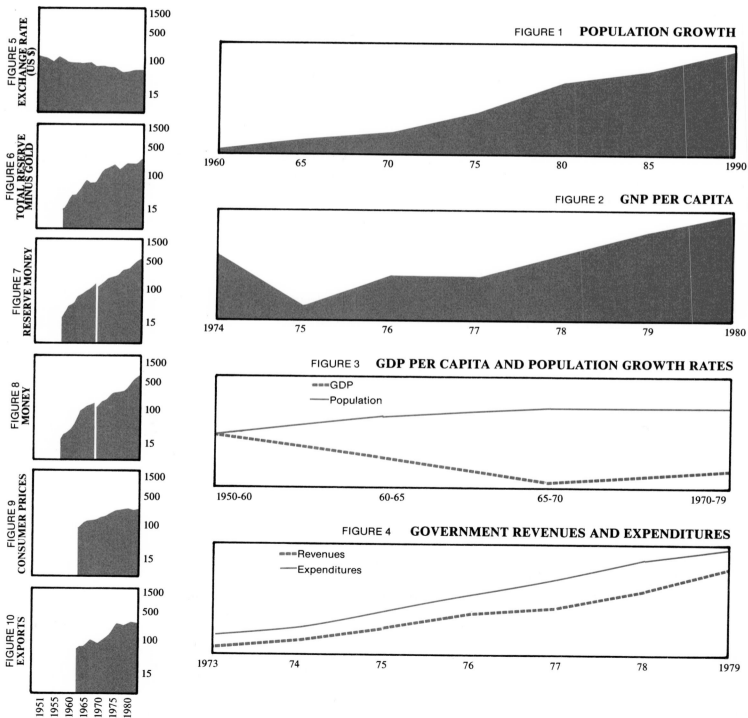

FIGURE 5 EXCHANGE RATE (US $)

FIGURE 6 TOTAL RESERVE MINUS GOLD

FIGURE 7 RESERVE MONEY

FIGURE 8 MONEY

FIGURE 9 CONSUMER PRICES

FIGURE 10 EXPORTS

FIGURE 1 **POPULATION GROWTH**

FIGURE 2 **GNP PER CAPITA**

FIGURE 3 **GDP PER CAPITA AND POPULATION GROWTH RATES**

FIGURE 4 **GOVERNMENT REVENUES AND EXPENDITURES**

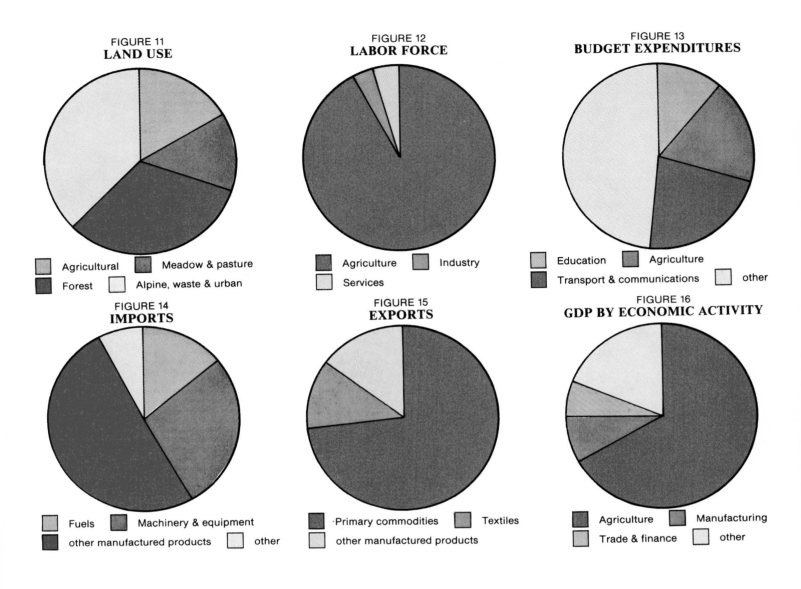

FIGURE 11
LAND USE

Agricultural　Meadow & pasture
Forest　Alpine, waste & urban

FIGURE 12
LABOR FORCE

Agriculture　Industry
Services

FIGURE 13
BUDGET EXPENDITURES

Education　Agriculture
Transport & communications　other

FIGURE 14
IMPORTS

Fuels　Machinery & equipment
other manufactured products　other

FIGURE 15
EXPORTS

·Primary commodities　Textiles
other manufactured products

FIGURE 16
GDP BY ECONOMIC ACTIVITY

Agriculture　Manufacturing
Trade & finance　other

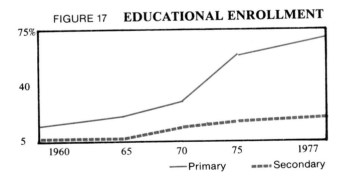

FIGURE 17　**EDUCATIONAL ENROLLMENT**

75%

40

5

1960　65　70　75　1977

——Primary　■■■■Secondary

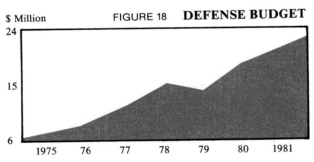

$ Million　FIGURE 18　**DEFENSE BUDGET**

24

15

6

1975　76　77　78　79　80　1981

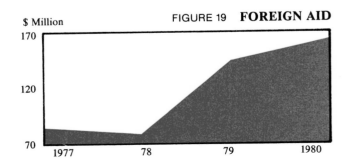

$ Million　FIGURE 19　**FOREIGN AID**

170

120

70

1977　78　79　1980

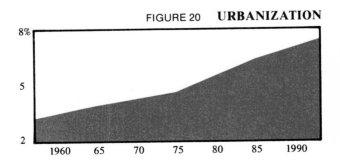

FIGURE 20　**URBANIZATION**

8%

5

2

1960　65　70　75　80　85　1990

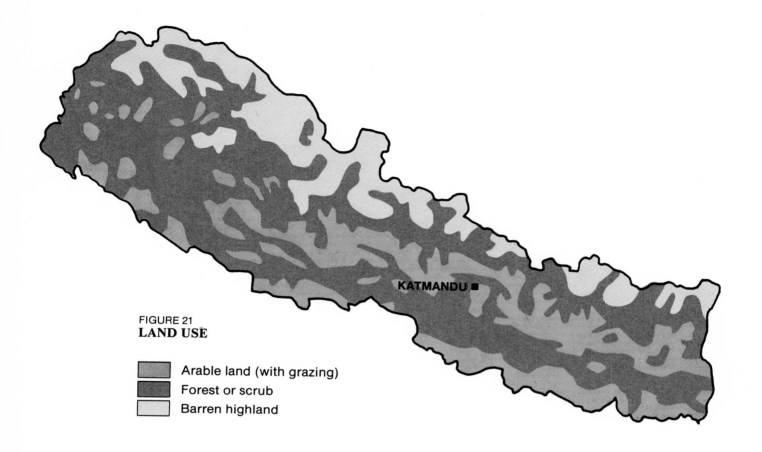

FIGURE 21
LAND USE

- Arable land (with grazing)
- Forest or scrub
- Barren highland

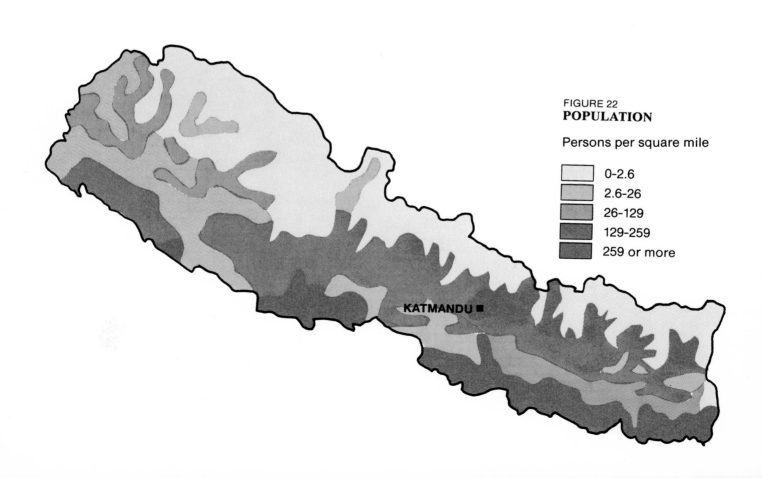

FIGURE 22
POPULATION

Persons per square mile

- 0-2.6
- 2.6-26
- 26-129
- 129-259
- 259 or more

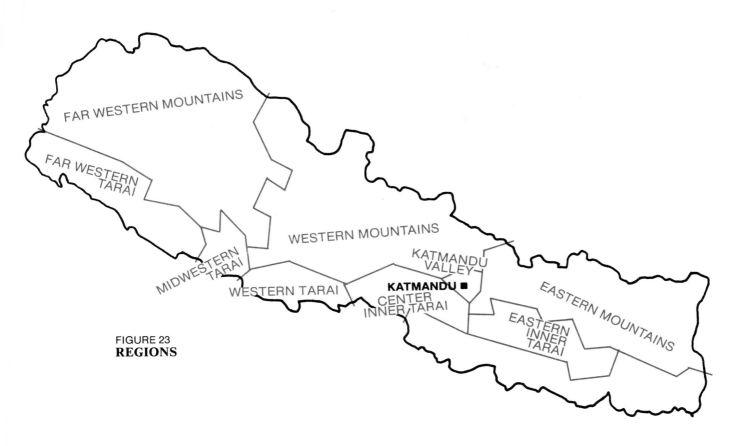

FIGURE 23
REGIONS

FAR WESTERN MOUNTAINS

FAR WESTERN TARAI

MIDWESTERN TARAI

WESTERN MOUNTAINS

WESTERN TARAI

CENTER INNER TARAI

KATMANDU VALLEY

KATMANDU ■

EASTERN INNER TARAI

EASTERN MOUNTAINS

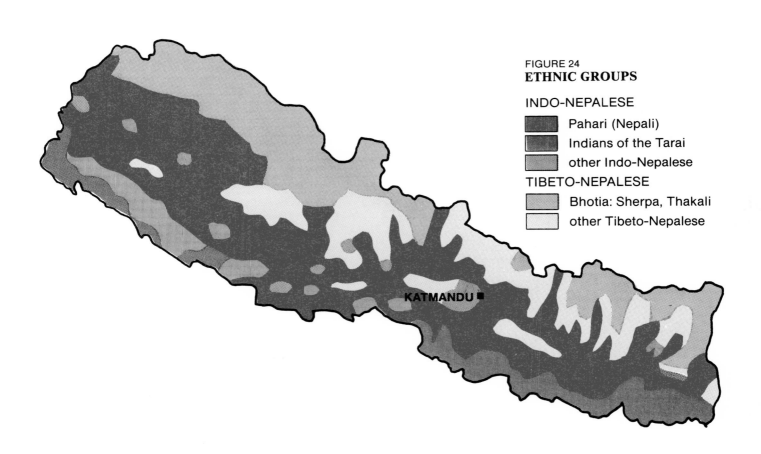

FIGURE 24
ETHNIC GROUPS

INDO-NEPALESE

Pahari (Nepali)

Indians of the Tarai

other Indo-Nepalese

TIBETO-NEPALESE

Bhotia: Sherpa, Thakali

other Tibeto-Nepalese

KATMANDU ■

NICARAGUA

The largest of the Central American republics, Nicaragua ranks 90th in land area and 116th in population. Relatively prosperous until the 1970s, the Nicaraguan economy suffered two major reverses since then: the earthquake that struck Managua in 1972 and the civil war that began in 1979 and continues even today, although the protagonists have reversed roles. In 1978 alone the GDP fell by nearly 7% and in 1979 by another 25%. One of the first acts of the Sandinistas was to nationalize the vast interest controlled by the Somoza family, as well as the *Samocistas,* the ex-president's associates, that formerly comprised one-tenth of the Nicaraguan economy. While this step proved relatively easy, further direction was lost in conflicting pressures; within the junta communist counsel prevailed and the split between moderates and extremists became sharper. As the United States began siding with the right-wing faction, it was obvious that the civil war was not over and the country could yet become another Cuba.

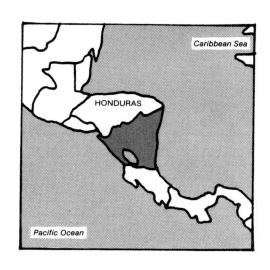

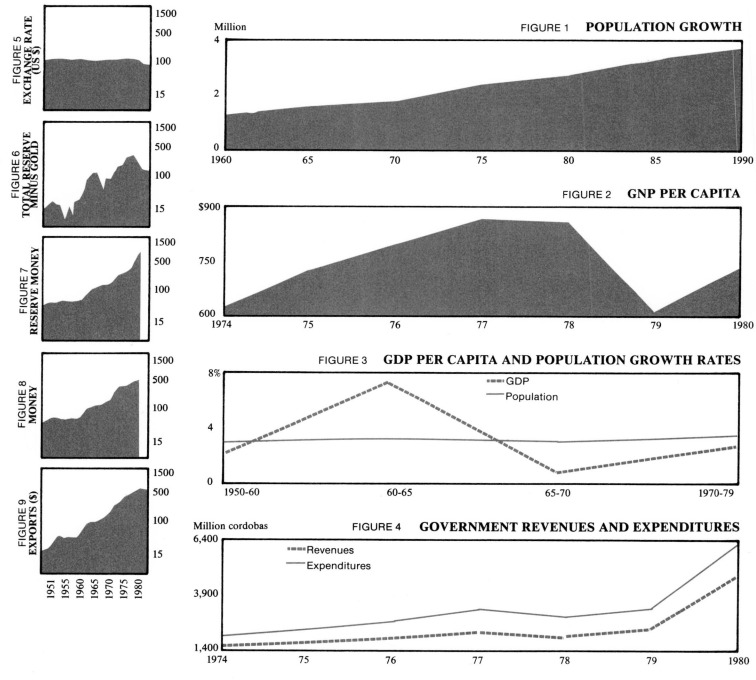

FIGURE 5 EXCHANGE RATE (US $)

FIGURE 6 TOTAL RESERVE MINUS GOLD

FIGURE 7 RESERVE MONEY

FIGURE 8 MONEY

FIGURE 9 EXPORTS ($)

FIGURE 1 **POPULATION GROWTH**

FIGURE 2 **GNP PER CAPITA**

FIGURE 3 **GDP PER CAPITA AND POPULATION GROWTH RATES**

FIGURE 4 **GOVERNMENT REVENUES AND EXPENDITURES**

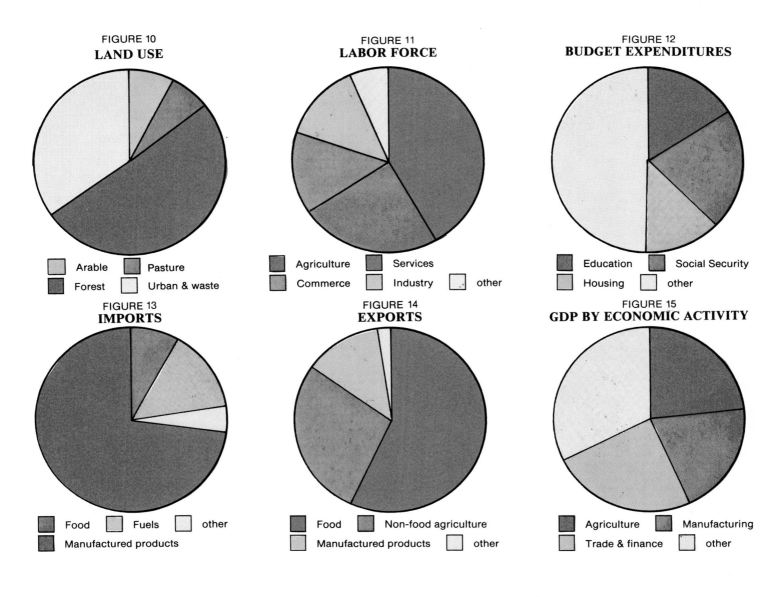

FIGURE 10
LAND USE

Arable   Pasture
Forest   Urban & waste

FIGURE 11
LABOR FORCE

Agriculture   Services
Commerce   Industry   other

FIGURE 12
BUDGET EXPENDITURES

Education   Social Security
Housing   other

FIGURE 13
IMPORTS

Food   Fuels   other
Manufactured products

FIGURE 14
EXPORTS

Food   Non-food agriculture
Manufactured products   other

FIGURE 15
GDP BY ECONOMIC ACTIVITY

Agriculture   Manufacturing
Trade & finance   other

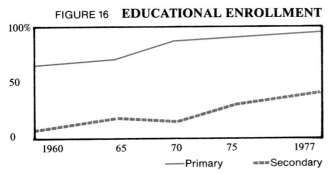

FIGURE 16   **EDUCATIONAL ENROLLMENT**

Primary   Secondary

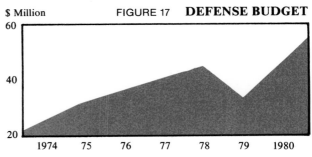

$ Million   FIGURE 17   **DEFENSE BUDGET**

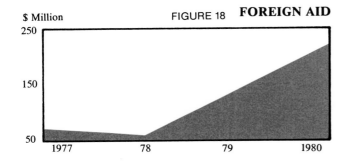

$ Million   FIGURE 18   **FOREIGN AID**

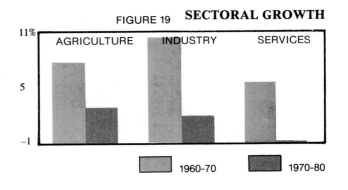

FIGURE 19   **SECTORAL GROWTH**

AGRICULTURE   INDUSTRY   SERVICES

1960-70   1970-80

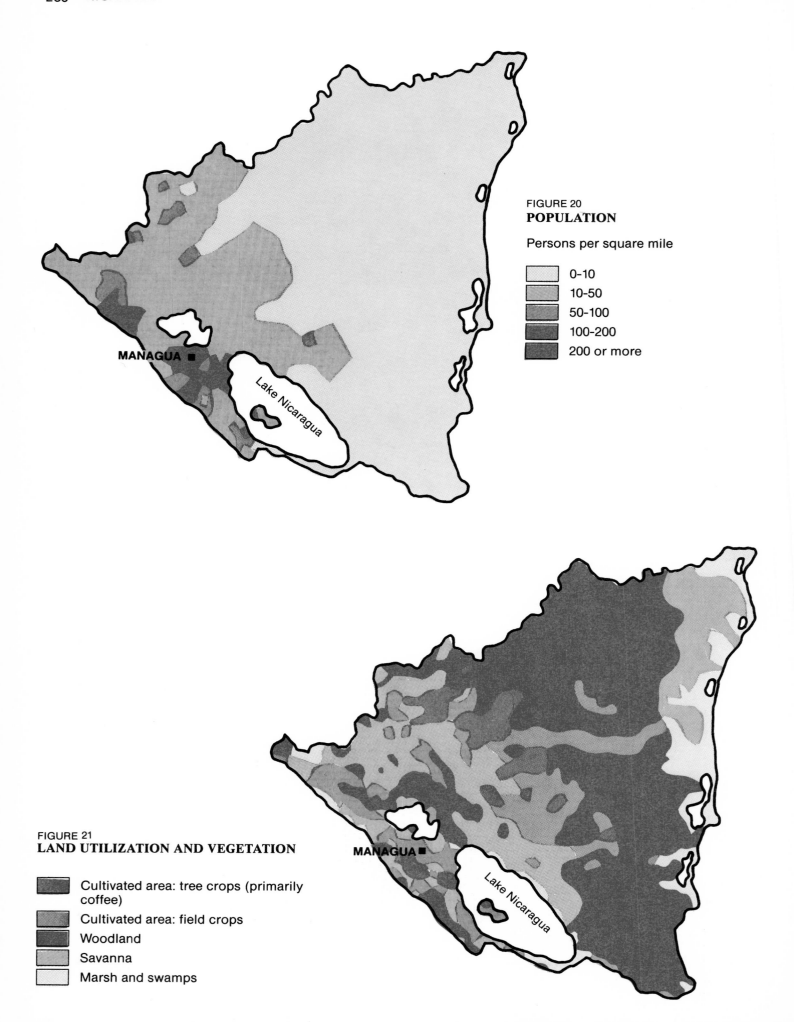

FIGURE 20
POPULATION

Persons per square mile

0–10

10–50

50–100

100–200

200 or more

MANAGUA ■

Lake Nicaragua

FIGURE 21
LAND UTILIZATION AND VEGETATION

Cultivated area: tree crops (primarily coffee)

Cultivated area: field crops

Woodland

Savanna

Marsh and swamps

MANAGUA ■

Lake Nicaragua

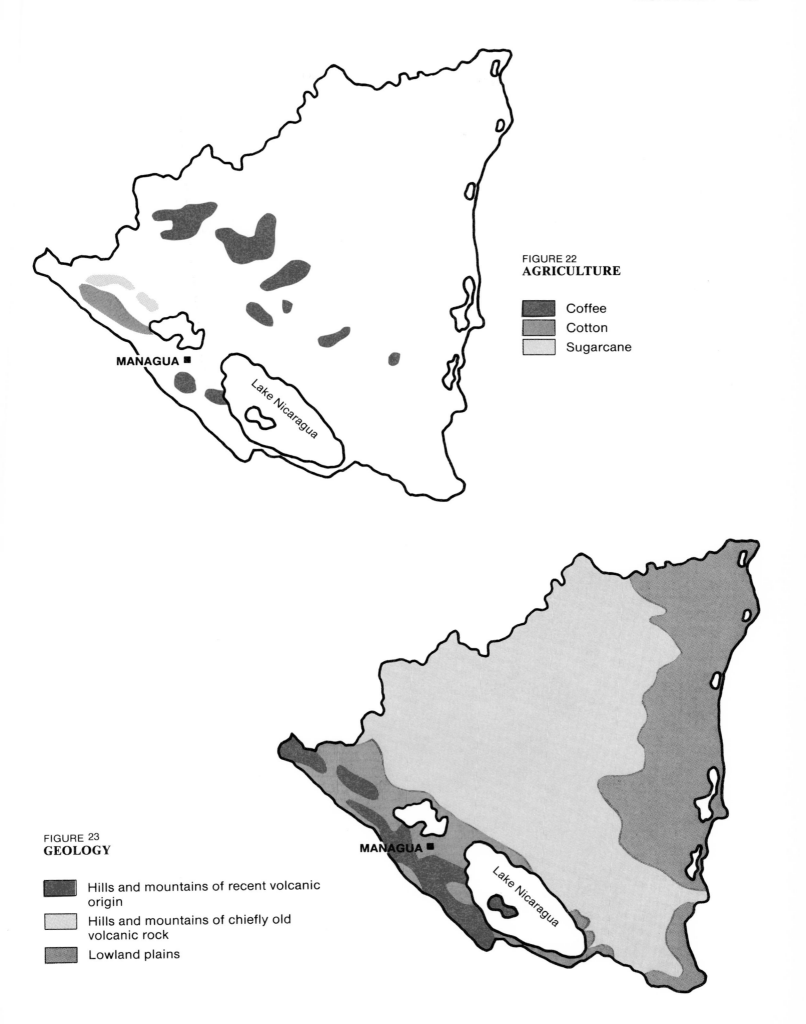

FIGURE 22
AGRICULTURE

Coffee
Cotton
Sugarcane

MANAGUA ■

Lake Nicaragua

FIGURE 23
GEOLOGY

Hills and mountains of recent volcanic origin

Hills and mountains of chiefly old volcanic rock

Lowland plains

MANAGUA ■

Lake Nicaragua

NIGER

Landlocked Niger, located on the southern fringe of the Sahara Desert, ranks 19th in land area and 84th in population. Land size is misleading because only 3% of the land is cultivable. Livestock raising, the traditional activity of the nomads, is only slowly recovering from the great Sahelian drought that resulted in the loss of two-thirds of the country's cattle stock. The country's destitution is reflected in the fact that it has the eighth highest death rate in the world. The most promising economic sector is mining; the country is rich in uranium and coal. Uranium production accounts for approximately two-thirds of the country's trade receipts, projected at over $1 billion annually by the year 1988. Known reserves total more than 100,000 tons. France, the country's major trade partner, absorbs the bulk of its uranium exports.

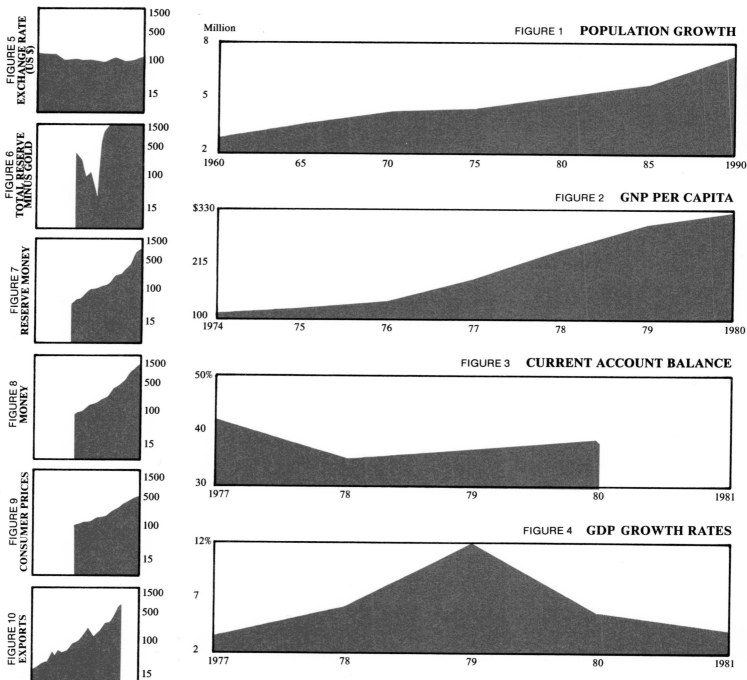

FIGURE 5 EXCHANGE RATE (US $)

FIGURE 6 TOTAL RESERVE MINUS GOLD

FIGURE 7 RESERVE MONEY

FIGURE 8 MONEY

FIGURE 9 CONSUMER PRICES

FIGURE 10 EXPORTS

FIGURE 1   **POPULATION GROWTH**

FIGURE 2   **GNP PER CAPITA**

FIGURE 3   **CURRENT ACCOUNT BALANCE**

FIGURE 4   **GDP GROWTH RATES**

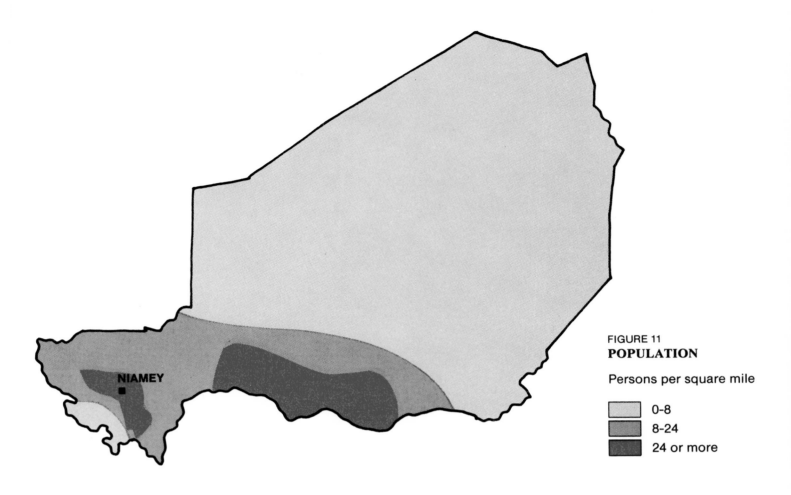

FIGURE 11
POPULATION

Persons per square mile

	0-8
	8-24
	24 or more

NIAMEY

FIGURE 12
AGRICULTURE

	Peanuts
	Grazing
	Rice
	Millet and sorghum
	Cotton

NIAMEY

NIGERIA

The most populous country in Africa, accounting for 25% of black Africa's population, Nigeria ranks 29th in land area and 84th in population. Its population density is twice as high as the African average. According to Ray Cline, it is also the most powerful nation in Africa, with the highest GNP, the largest standing army and the largest crude oil production. Despite such attributes of power, Nigeria is in effect a low-income country and its economy is not much different from those of its African neighbors. Ethnic conflicts, pervasive bureaucratic inefficiency, corruption, sectoral imbalances, all tend to distort economic growth patterns and slow development initiatives. Nevertheless, oil wealth, estimated at over $22 million per year, has brought new opportunities and an expanded national vision. The impact of oil is felt in every area, but especially in construction, industry and transportation. A number of large-scale industrial projects have been planned in collaboration with overseas firms.

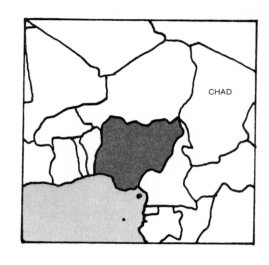

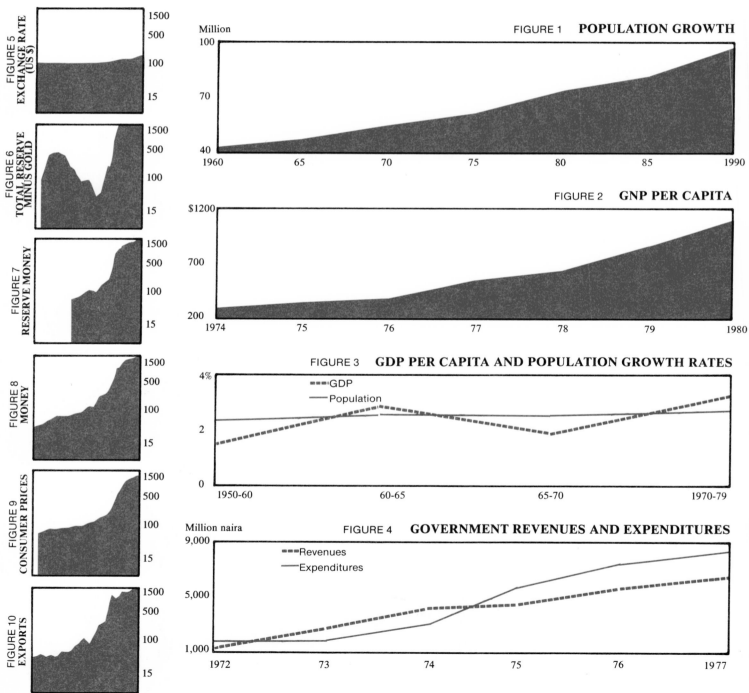

FIGURE 5 EXCHANGE RATE (US $)

FIGURE 6 TOTAL RESERVE MINUS GOLD

FIGURE 7 RESERVE MONEY

FIGURE 8 MONEY

FIGURE 9 CONSUMER PRICES

FIGURE 10 EXPORTS

FIGURE 1 **POPULATION GROWTH**

FIGURE 2 **GNP PER CAPITA**

FIGURE 3 **GDP PER CAPITA AND POPULATION GROWTH RATES**

FIGURE 4 **GOVERNMENT REVENUES AND EXPENDITURES**

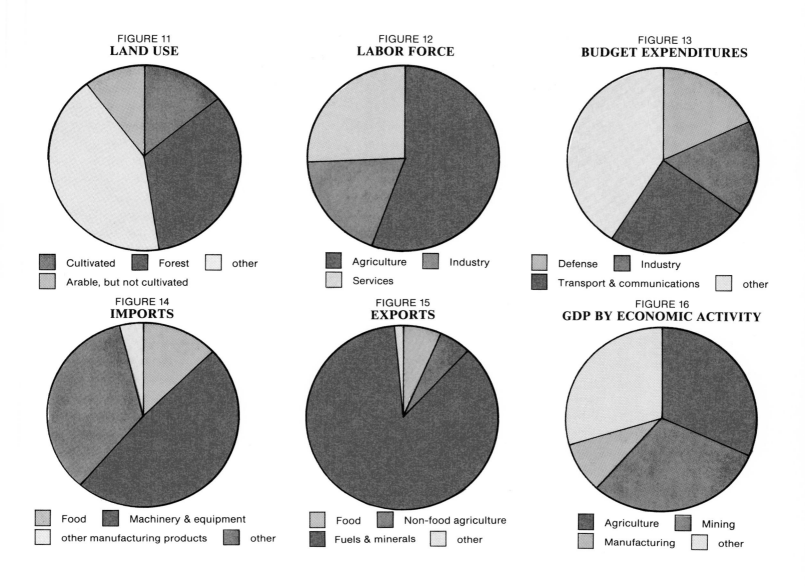

FIGURE 11
LAND USE

Cultivated ■ Forest ■ other
Arable, but not cultivated

FIGURE 12
LABOR FORCE

Agriculture ■ Industry
Services

FIGURE 13
BUDGET EXPENDITURES

Defense ■ Industry
Transport & communications ■ other

FIGURE 14
IMPORTS

Food ■ Machinery & equipment
other manufacturing products ■ other

FIGURE 15
EXPORTS

Food ■ Non-food agriculture
Fuels & minerals ■ other

FIGURE 16
GDP BY ECONOMIC ACTIVITY

Agriculture ■ Mining
Manufacturing ■ other

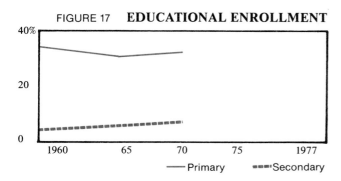

FIGURE 17 **EDUCATIONAL ENROLLMENT**

40%

20

0

1960   65   70   75   1977

—— Primary   ▪▪▪▪Secondary

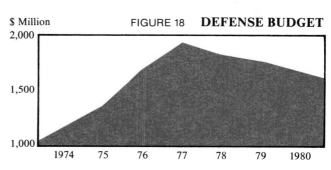

$ Million   FIGURE 18 **DEFENSE BUDGET**

2,000

1,500

1,000

1974   75   76   77   78   79   1980

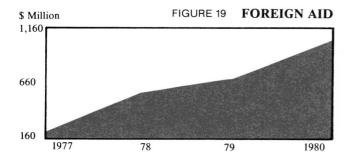

$ Million   FIGURE 19 **FOREIGN AID**

1,160

660

160

1977   78   79   1980

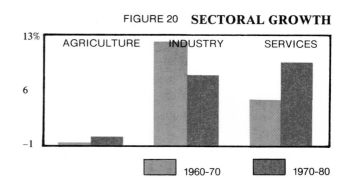

FIGURE 20 **SECTORAL GROWTH**

13%   AGRICULTURE   INDUSTRY   SERVICES

6

-1

■ 1960-70   ■ 1970-80

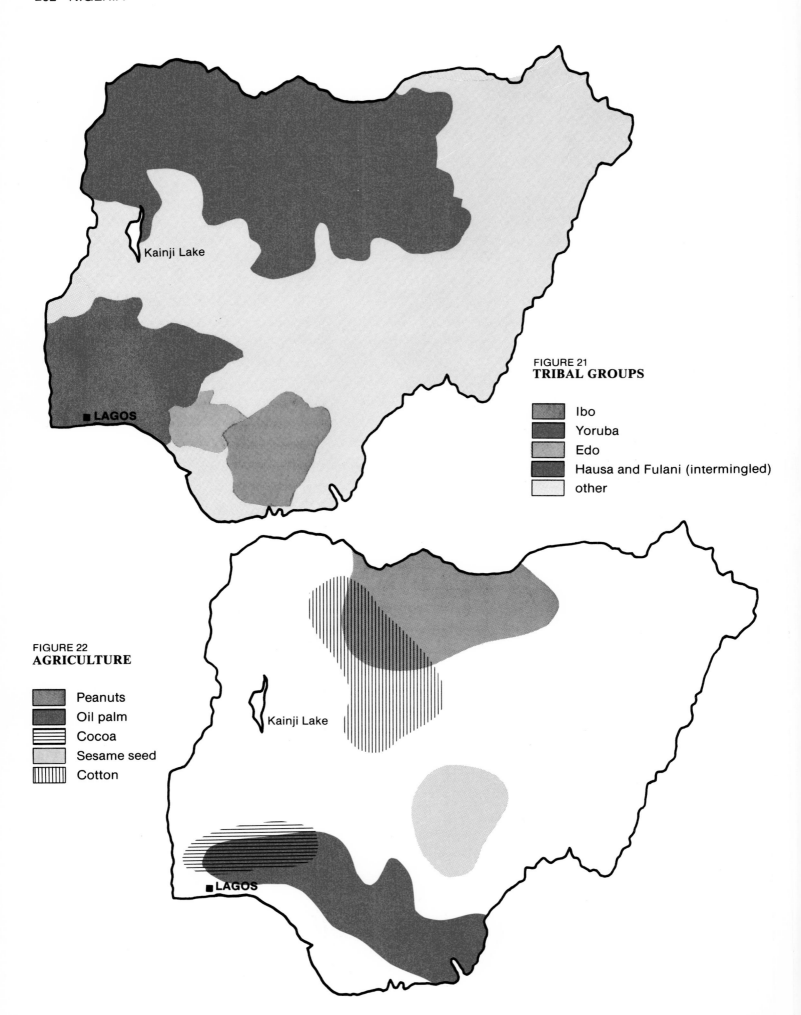

FIGURE 21
TRIBAL GROUPS

Ibo

Yoruba

Edo

Hausa and Fulani (intermingled)

other

Kainji Lake

■ LAGOS

FIGURE 22
AGRICULTURE

Peanuts

Oil palm

Cocoa

Sesame seed

Cotton

Kainji Lake

■ LAGOS

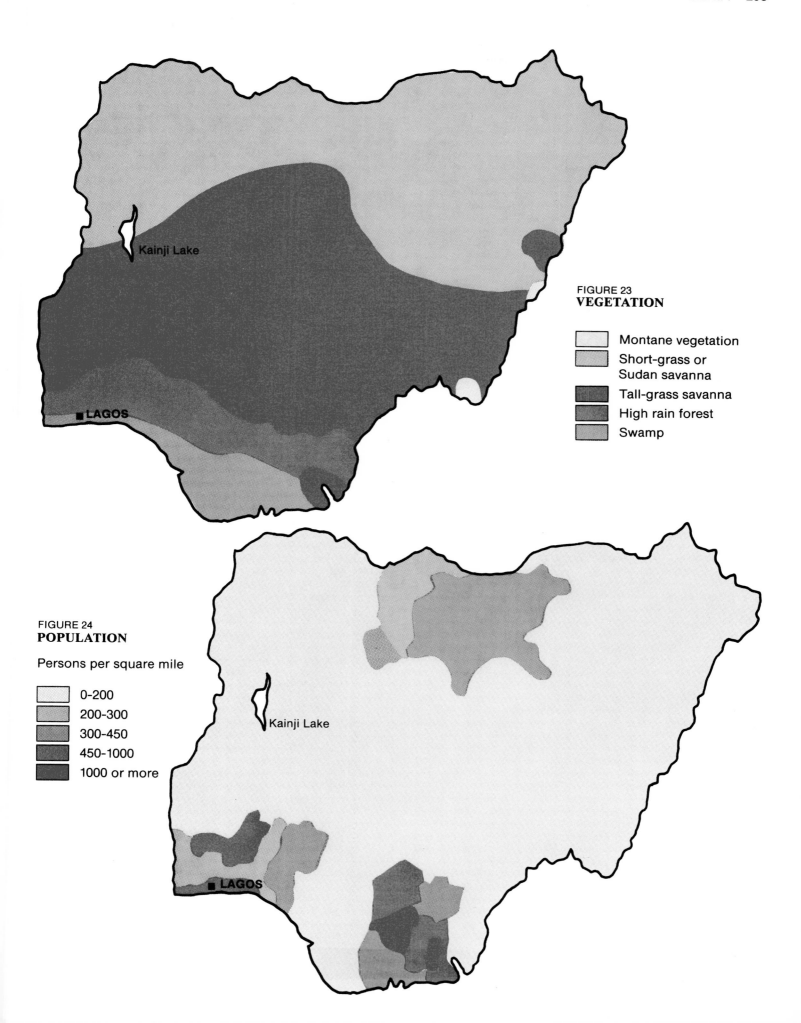

FIGURE 23
VEGETATION

Montane vegetation

Short-grass or
Sudan savanna

Tall-grass savanna

High rain forest

Swamp

Kainji Lake

LAGOS

FIGURE 24
POPULATION

Persons per square mile

0-200

200-300

300-450

450-1000

1000 or more

Kainji Lake

LAGOS

PAKISTAN

Carved out of the old Indian empire, Pakistan is the third largest country on the Indian subcontinent and ranks 32nd in land area and ninth in size of population. Unlike India, Pakistan's political history since independence has been troubled: three wars with India, border skirmishes with Afghanistan, the secession of Bangladesh, separatist movements of Pathans and Baluchis, and a succession of authoritarian regimes have twisted and scarred the national ego. The so-called Islamization, launched by President Zia, has only served to legitimize an increasingly authoritarian regime. The Pakistani economy displays all the negative characteristics of underdevelopment. The Zia government has, on the one hand, loosened central government's direct involvement in the economy by opening up to private investors a number of industries that were formerly government monopolies; on the other hand martial law has been used to interfere in routine business activities and harass both business and labor.

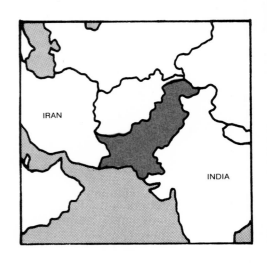

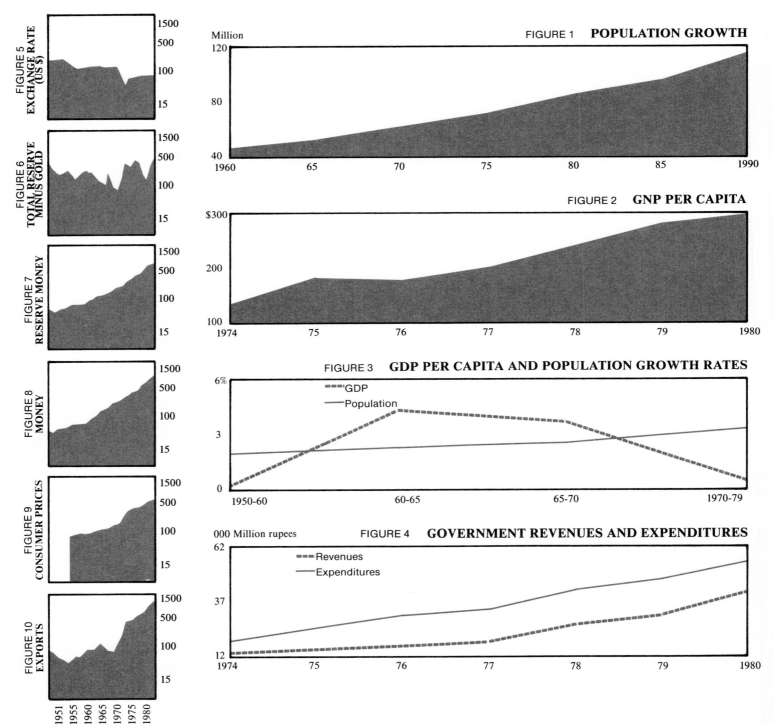

FIGURE 5 EXCHANGE RATE (US $)

FIGURE 6 TOTAL RESERVE MINUS GOLD

FIGURE 7 RESERVE MONEY

FIGURE 8 MONEY

FIGURE 9 CONSUMER PRICES

FIGURE 10 EXPORTS

FIGURE 1 **POPULATION GROWTH**

FIGURE 2 **GNP PER CAPITA**

FIGURE 3 **GDP PER CAPITA AND POPULATION GROWTH RATES**

FIGURE 4 **GOVERNMENT REVENUES AND EXPENDITURES**

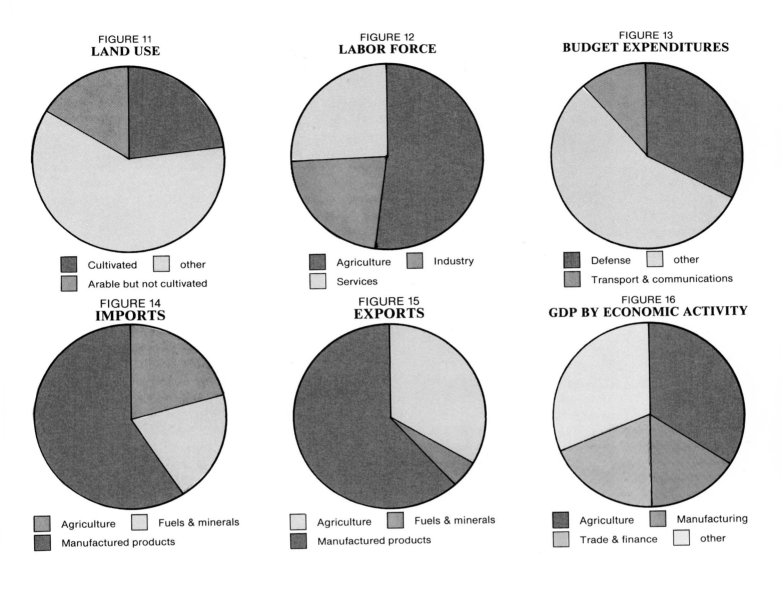

FIGURE 11
LAND USE

Cultivated
Arable but not cultivated
other

FIGURE 12
LABOR FORCE

Agriculture
Services
Industry

FIGURE 13
BUDGET EXPENDITURES

Defense
Transport & communications
other

FIGURE 14
IMPORTS

Agriculture
Manufactured products
Fuels & minerals

FIGURE 15
EXPORTS

Agriculture
Manufactured products
Fuels & minerals

FIGURE 16
GDP BY ECONOMIC ACTIVITY

Agriculture
Trade & finance
Manufacturing
other

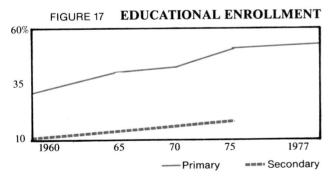

FIGURE 17   **EDUCATIONAL ENROLLMENT**

—— Primary   ▪▪▪▪ Secondary

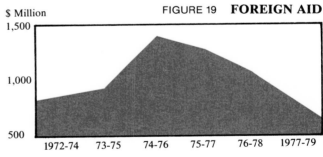

$ Million   FIGURE 19   **FOREIGN AID**

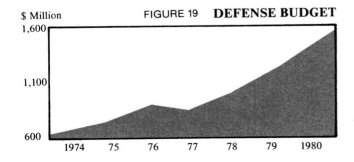

$ Million   FIGURE 19   **DEFENSE BUDGET**

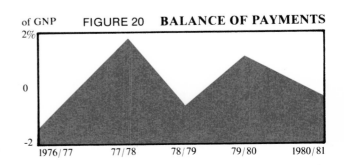

of GNP   FIGURE 20   **BALANCE OF PAYMENTS**

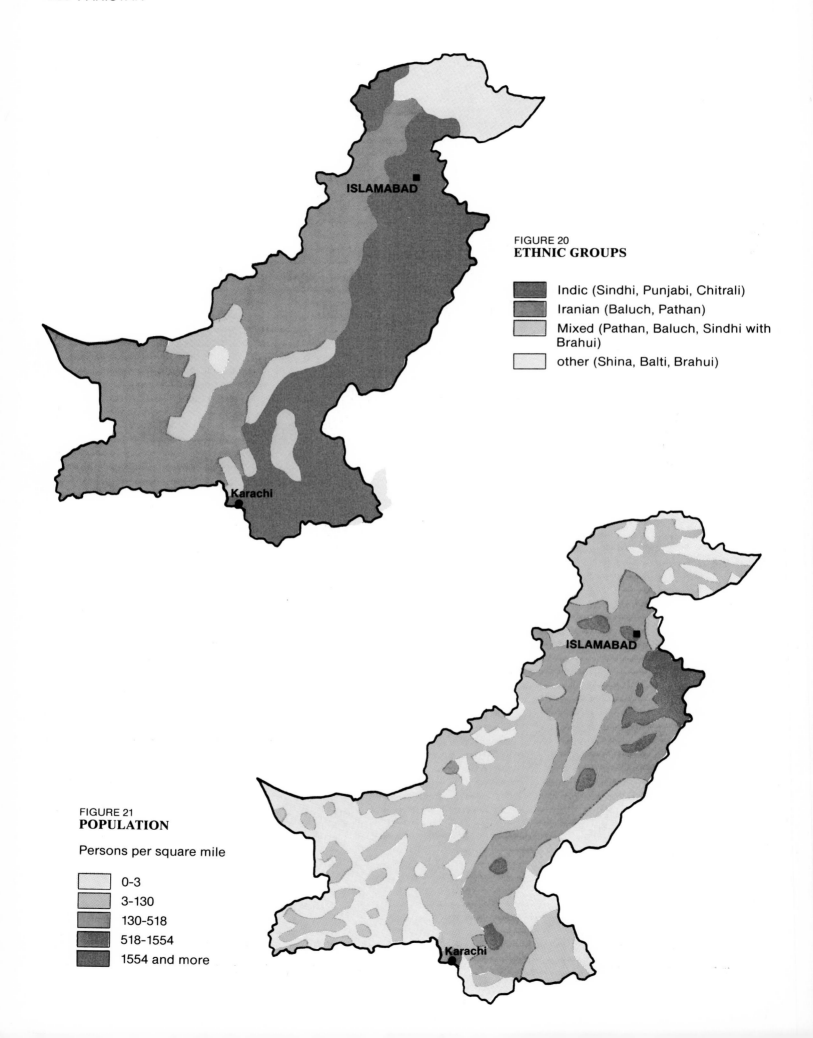

FIGURE 20
ETHNIC GROUPS

Indic (Sindhi, Punjabi, Chitrali)
Iranian (Baluch, Pathan)
Mixed (Pathan, Baluch, Sindhi with Brahui)
other (Shina, Balti, Brahui)

FIGURE 21
POPULATION

Persons per square mile

0-3
3-130
130-518
518-1554
1554 and more

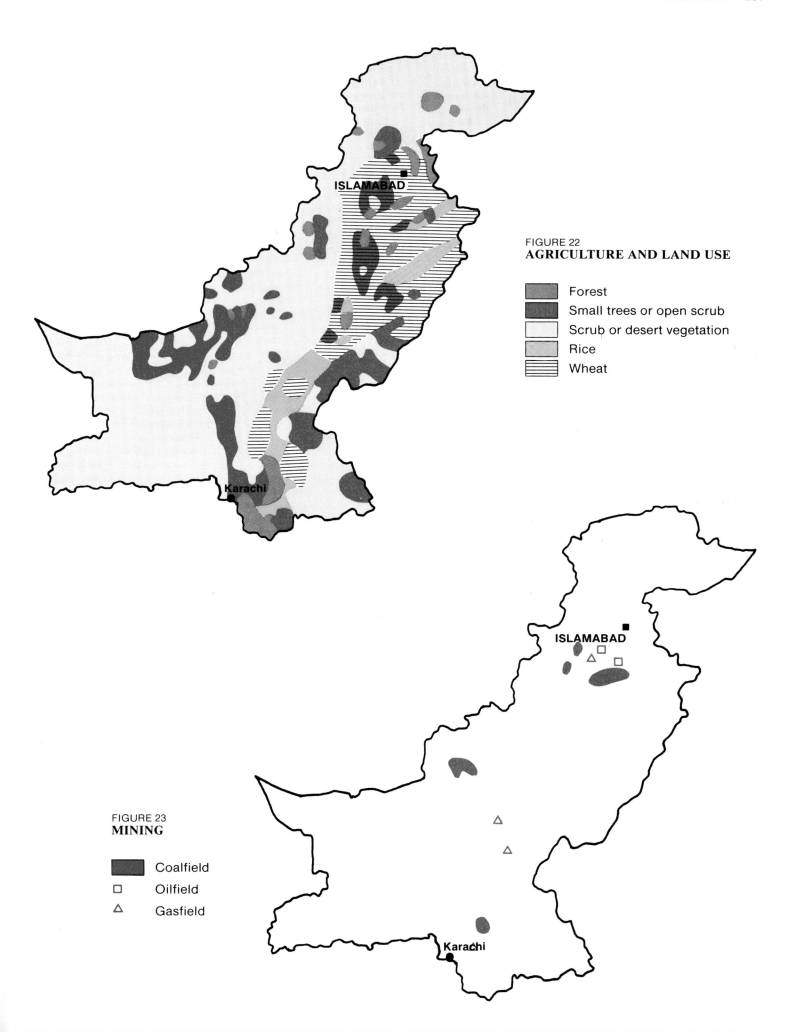

FIGURE 22
AGRICULTURE AND LAND USE

Forest
Small trees or open scrub
Scrub or desert vegetation
Rice
Wheat

ISLAMABAD

Karachi

FIGURE 23
MINING

Coalfield
Oilfield
Gasfield

ISLAMABAD

Karachi

PANAMA

Panama, the least populous mainland republic in Latin America, ranks 122nd in population and 108th in land area in the world. The Panamanian economy is based not so much on domestic resources but on three service sectors: banking, transit operations through the Panama Canal and use of its flag as a flag of convenience. Since 1968 Panama has developed into a major international banking and financial center capitalizing on its location, absence of exchange regulations, liberal banking laws and the use of the U.S. dollar as effective currency. Although second to Liberia in the gross registered tonnage flying its flag, Panama has been gaining ground, with the number of ships on the Panamanian registry growing at 14% annually. Revenues from traffic through the Panama Canal have reached record levels; nevertheless, the Canal itself is less significant for the economy than the free zone at Colon, which has become in recent years the hub of a vast commercial and industrial complex as well as a distribution point for exports to all Latin America.

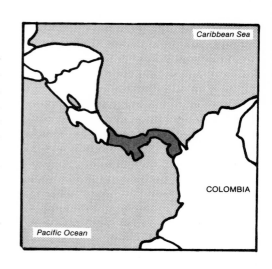

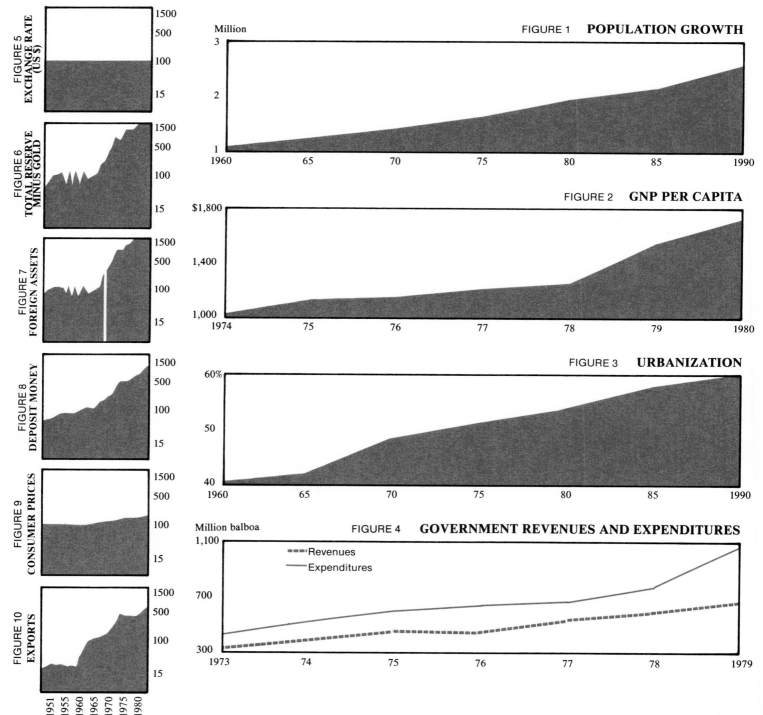

FIGURE 5 EXCHANGE RATE (US $)

FIGURE 6 TOTAL RESERVE MINUS GOLD

FIGURE 7 FOREIGN ASSETS

FIGURE 8 DEPOSIT MONEY

FIGURE 9 CONSUMER PRICES

FIGURE 10 EXPORTS

FIGURE 1 **POPULATION GROWTH**

FIGURE 2 **GNP PER CAPITA**

FIGURE 3 **URBANIZATION**

FIGURE 4 **GOVERNMENT REVENUES AND EXPENDITURES**

- - - Revenues
—— Expenditures

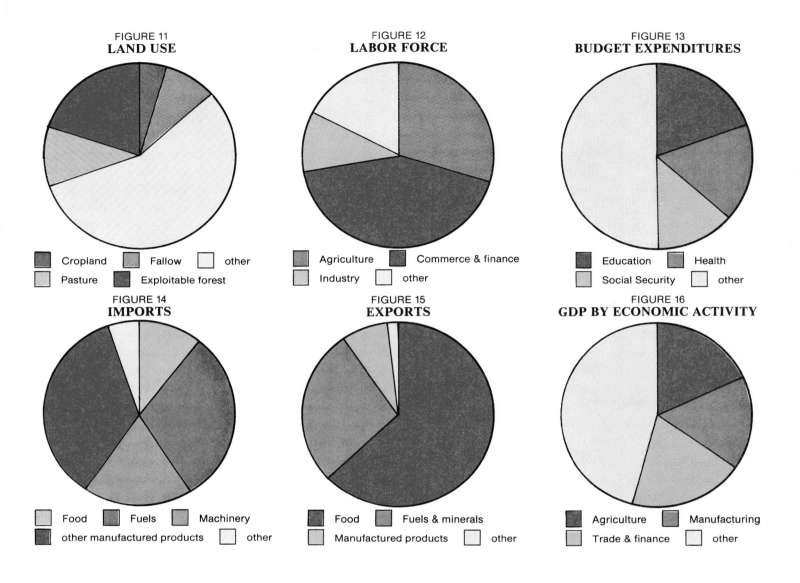

FIGURE 11
LAND USE

Cropland Fallow other
Pasture Exploitable forest

FIGURE 12
LABOR FORCE

Agriculture Commerce & finance
Industry other

FIGURE 13
BUDGET EXPENDITURES

Education Health
Social Security other

FIGURE 14
IMPORTS

Food Fuels Machinery
other manufactured products other

FIGURE 15
EXPORTS

Food Fuels & minerals
Manufactured products other

FIGURE 16
GDP BY ECONOMIC ACTIVITY

Agriculture Manufacturing
Trade & finance other

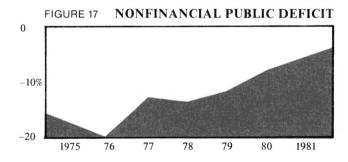

FIGURE 17 **NONFINANCIAL PUBLIC DEFICIT**

0

−10%

−20

1975 76 77 78 79 80 1981

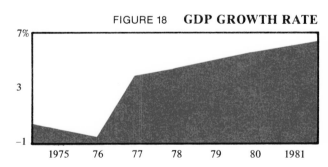

FIGURE 18 **GDP GROWTH RATE**

7%

3

−1

1975 76 77 78 79 80 1981

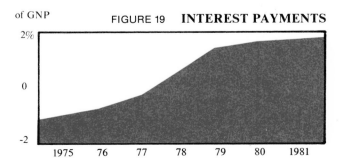

of GNP

FIGURE 19 **INTEREST PAYMENTS**

2%

0

−2

1975 76 77 78 79 80 1981

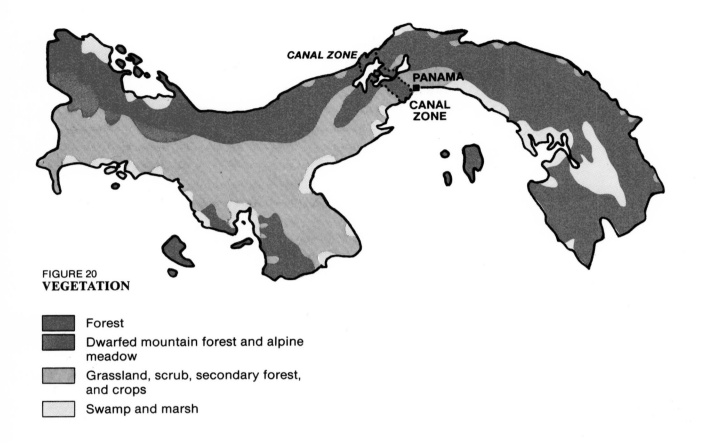

FIGURE 20
VEGETATION

Forest

Dwarfed mountain forest and alpine meadow

Grassland, scrub, secondary forest, and crops

Swamp and marsh

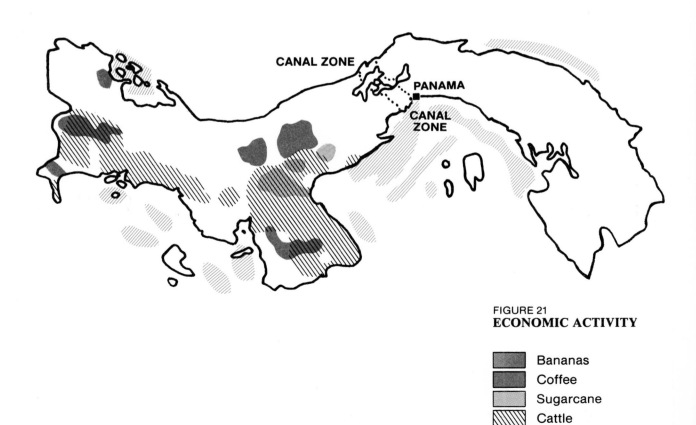

FIGURE 21
ECONOMIC ACTIVITY

Bananas

Coffee

Sugarcane

Cattle

Fishing

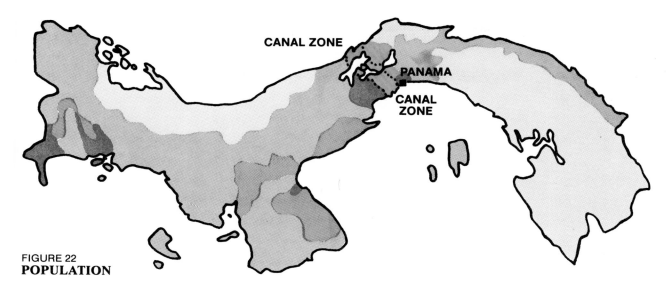

FIGURE 22
POPULATION

Persons per square mile

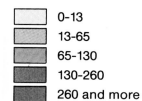

0-13
13-65
65-130
130-260
260 and more

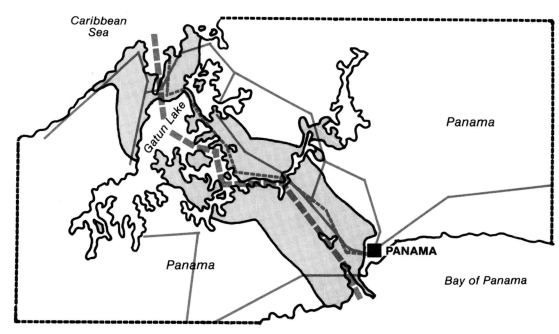

FIGURE 23
CANAL ZONE
(United States Administration)

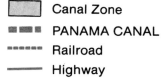

Canal Zone
PANAMA CANAL
Railroad
Highway

PERU

The third largest country in Latin America, Peru is the 17th largest in the world and the 40th most populous. Its fabled wealth in minerals and precious metals still contributes to the economy, accounting for over half the country's exports. Peru is the world's fourth ranking exporter of silver and eighth ranking exporter of copper. It was among the top six producers of molybdenum in the world and led South America in the extraction of seven other minerals, including zinc and lead. Since 1950, Peru has built up a large fishing industry and until the depletion of anchovy stocks in the mid-1970s, provided nearly half the world's supply of fishmeal. Agriculture and industry are dominated by the country's wealthy elite, contributing to manifest inequality with the poorest 20% receiving only 2% of the national income while the top 10% receive over 45%. Helped by strong oil revenues and fiscal discipline, Peru rode out a period of near-bankruptcy in the late 1970s.

BRAZIL

Pacific Ocean

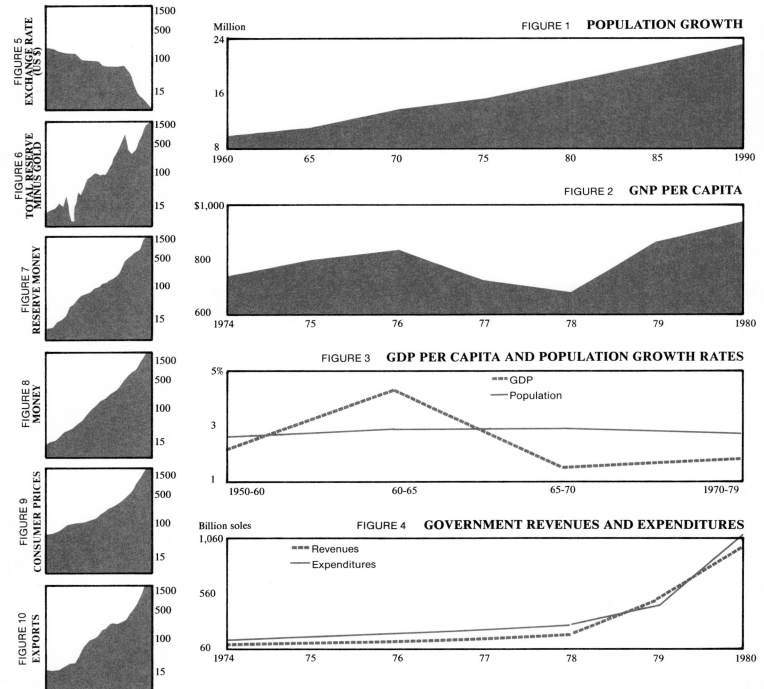

FIGURE 5 EXCHANGE RATE (US $)

FIGURE 6 TOTAL RESERVE MINUS GOLD

FIGURE 7 RESERVE MONEY

FIGURE 8 MONEY

FIGURE 9 CONSUMER PRICES

FIGURE 10 EXPORTS

FIGURE 1 **POPULATION GROWTH**

FIGURE 2 **GNP PER CAPITA**

FIGURE 3 **GDP PER CAPITA AND POPULATION GROWTH RATES**

FIGURE 4 **GOVERNMENT REVENUES AND EXPENDITURES**

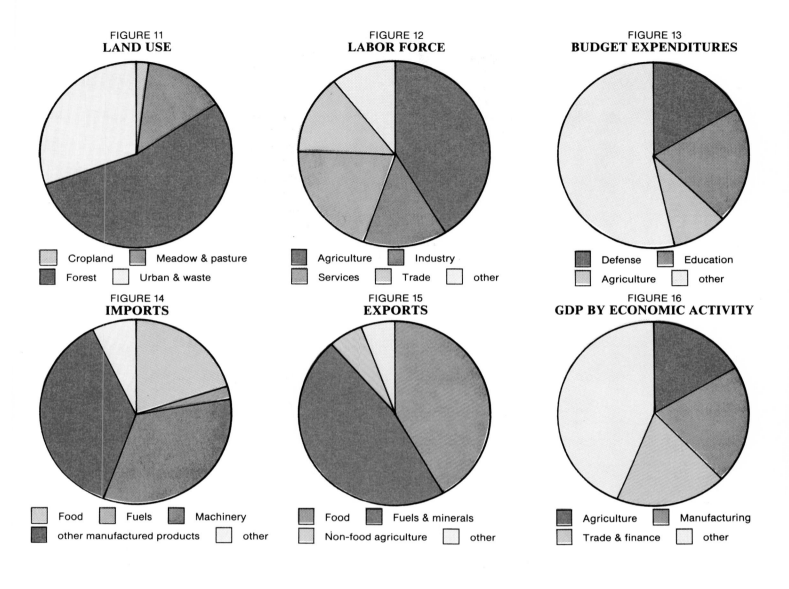

FIGURE 11
LAND USE

Cropland   Meadow & pasture
Forest   Urban & waste

FIGURE 12
LABOR FORCE

Agriculture   Industry
Services   Trade   other

FIGURE 13
BUDGET EXPENDITURES

Defense   Education
Agriculture   other

FIGURE 14
IMPORTS

Food   Fuels   Machinery
other manufactured products   other

FIGURE 15
EXPORTS

Food   Fuels & minerals
Non-food agriculture   other

FIGURE 16
GDP BY ECONOMIC ACTIVITY

Agriculture   Manufacturing
Trade & finance   other

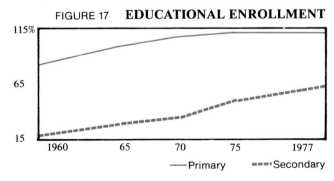

FIGURE 17   **EDUCATIONAL ENROLLMENT**

115%

65

15

1960   65   70   75   1977

——— Primary   ===== Secondary

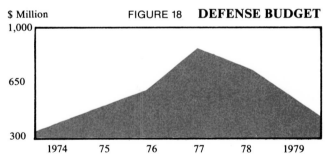

$ Million   FIGURE 18   **DEFENSE BUDGET**

1,000

650

300

1974   75   76   77   78   1979

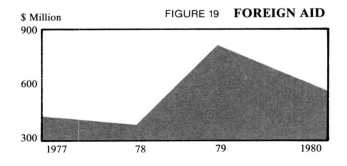

$ Million   FIGURE 19   **FOREIGN AID**

900

600

300

1977   78   79   1980

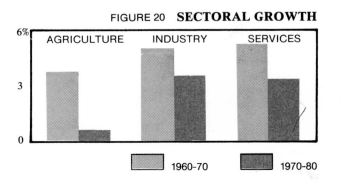

FIGURE 20   **SECTORAL GROWTH**

6%   AGRICULTURE   INDUSTRY   SERVICES

3

0

1960-70   1970-80

PHILIPPINES

An archipelago of some 7,000 islands and islets, the Philippines ranks 61st in land area and 16th in population. Despite adequate natural resources, Philippines has remained a backward country by and large and even the authoritarian rule of President Ferdinand Marcos has not helped its economy to match the spectacular growth of neighbors such as South Korea, Taiwan and Singapore. Ironically, the exodus of some half a million workers has turned into a blessing, as their remittances are helping to ease the country's balance of payments shortage. Philippines ended the 1970s on a downbeat note, with a heavy burden of foreign indebtedness, chronic balance of payments deficits and galloping inflation. As a result of IMF intervention, the government has agreed to adopt a series of measures designed to bring down the inflation rate, set limits on government and commercial borrowing, introduce new taxes and promote exports. In the absence of any political crises, the Philippine economy should do better in the eighties than it did in the seventies.

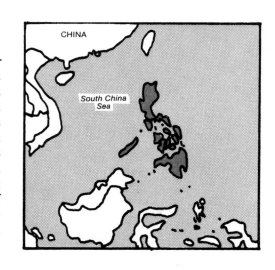

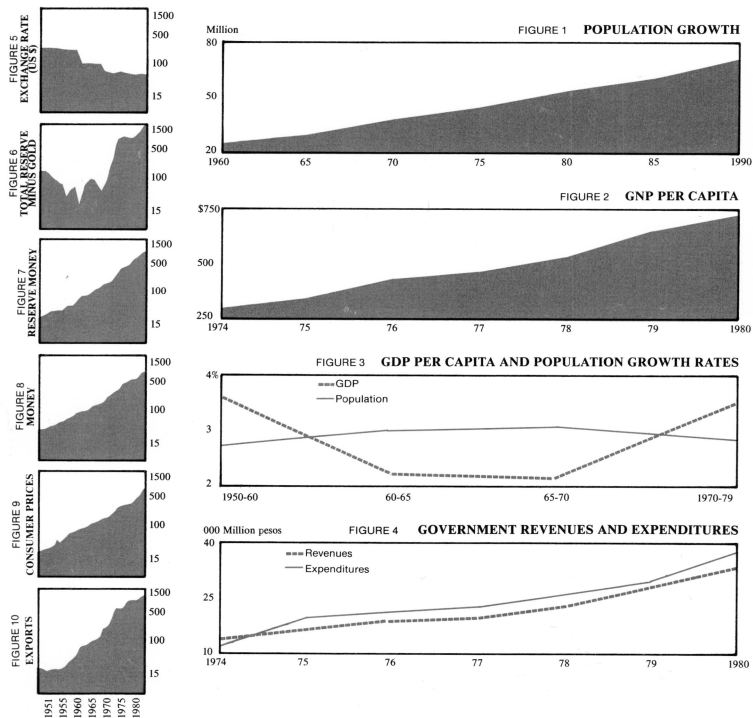

FIGURE 5 EXCHANGE RATE (US $)

FIGURE 6 TOTAL RESERVE MINUS GOLD

FIGURE 7 RESERVE MONEY

FIGURE 8 MONEY

FIGURE 9 CONSUMER PRICES

FIGURE 10 EXPORTS

FIGURE 1 **POPULATION GROWTH**

FIGURE 2 **GNP PER CAPITA**

FIGURE 3 **GDP PER CAPITA AND POPULATION GROWTH RATES**

FIGURE 4 **GOVERNMENT REVENUES AND EXPENDITURES**

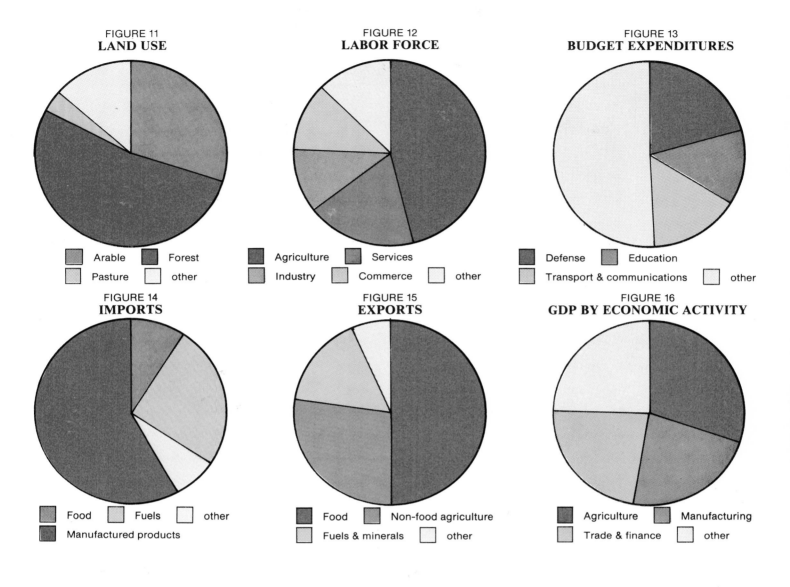

FIGURE 11
LAND USE

Arable | Forest
Pasture | other

FIGURE 12
LABOR FORCE

Agriculture | Services
Industry | Commerce | other

FIGURE 13
BUDGET EXPENDITURES

Defense | Education
Transport & communications | other

FIGURE 14
IMPORTS

Food | Fuels | other
Manufactured products

FIGURE 15
EXPORTS

Food | Non-food agriculture
Fuels & minerals | other

FIGURE 16
GDP BY ECONOMIC ACTIVITY

Agriculture | Manufacturing
Trade & finance | other

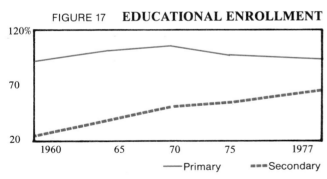

FIGURE 17 **EDUCATIONAL ENROLLMENT**

120%

70

20

1960   65   70   75   1977

——Primary   ===Secondary

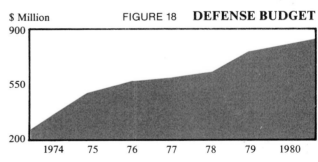

$ Million   FIGURE 18 **DEFENSE BUDGET**

900

550

200

1974   75   76   77   78   79   1980

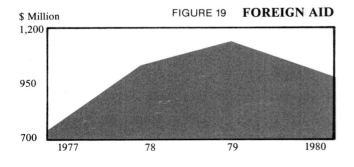

$ Million   FIGURE 19 **FOREIGN AID**

1,200

950

700

1977   78   79   1980

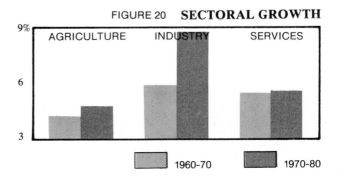

FIGURE 20 **SECTORAL GROWTH**

9%

AGRICULTURE   INDUSTRY   SERVICES

6

3

1960-70   1970-80

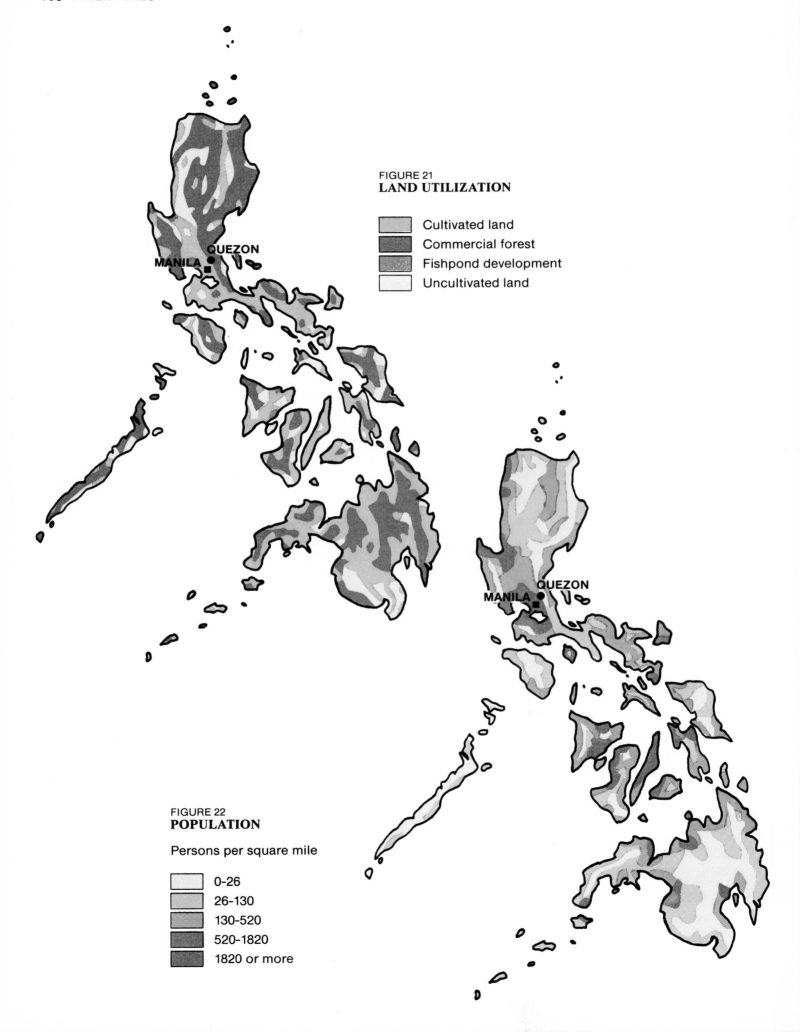

FIGURE 21
LAND UTILIZATION

Cultivated land
Commercial forest
Fishpond development
Uncultivated land

QUEZON
MANILA

FIGURE 22
POPULATION

Persons per square mile

0-26
26-130
130-520
520-1820
1820 or more

QUEZON
MANILA

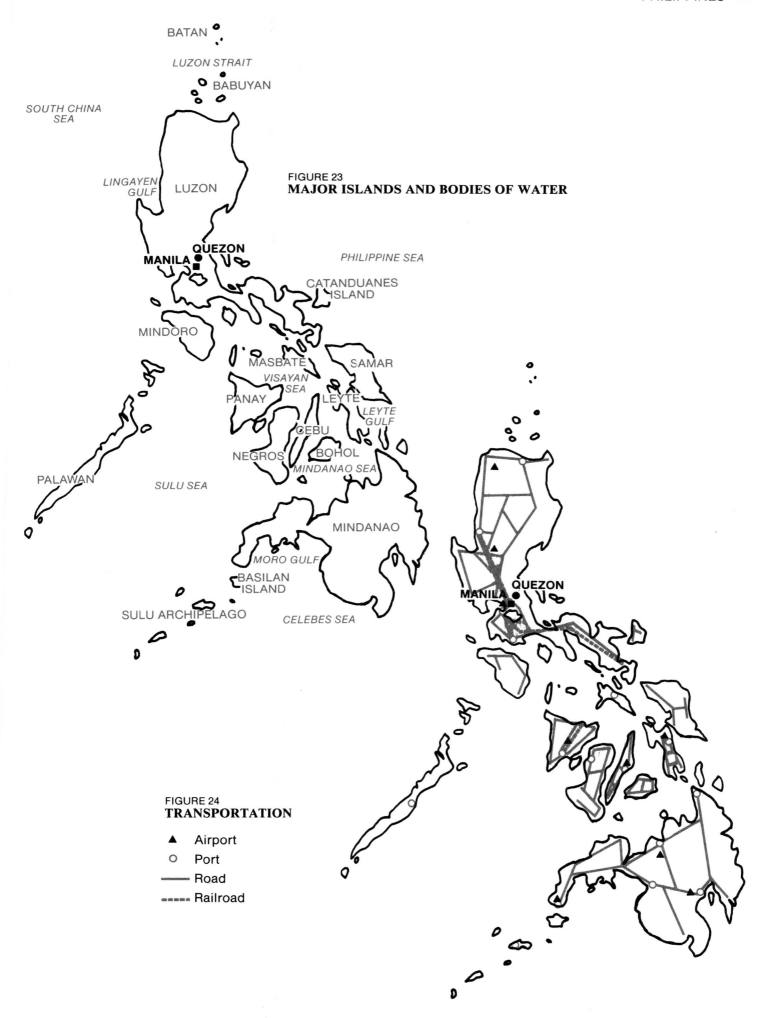

BATAN

LUZON STRAIT

BABUYAN

SOUTH CHINA
SEA

LINGAYEN
GULF LUZON

FIGURE 23
MAJOR ISLANDS AND BODIES OF WATER

PHILIPPINE SEA

QUEZON
MANILA

CATANDUANES
ISLAND

MINDORO

MASBATE SAMAR

VISAYAN
SEA

PANAY LEYTE

LEYTE
GULF

CEBU

NEGROS BOHOL

MINDANAO SEA

PALAWAN

SULU SEA

MINDANAO

MORO GULF

BASILAN
ISLAND

SULU ARCHIPELAGO CELEBES SEA

MANILA **QUEZON**

FIGURE 24
TRANSPORTATION

▲ Airport
○ Port
— Road
----- Railroad

SAUDI ARABIA

The mecca of petroleum, Saudi Arabia occupies about four-fifths of the Arabian Peninsula and ranks 75th in land area and 67th in population. However, it must be borne in mind that a true census has never been held in the country and in any official enumeration, nomads are left out and women are generally underreported. Saudi Arabia appears in the top 10 in virtually all energy-related rankings: It ranks third in energy production, second in production of crude petroleum, fifth in natural gas reserves, first in petroleum reserves and, naturally, first in balance of trade. Reversing the familiar UN category, it is the one country most favorably affected by the current adverse economic conditions. The ripple effect of oil is felt in all other sectors, especially in industrial growth rate, construction, defense expenditures, education and consumption. The country's foreign exchange reserves went over the $100 billion mark by the early 1980s.

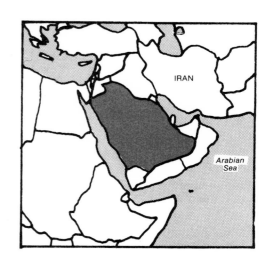

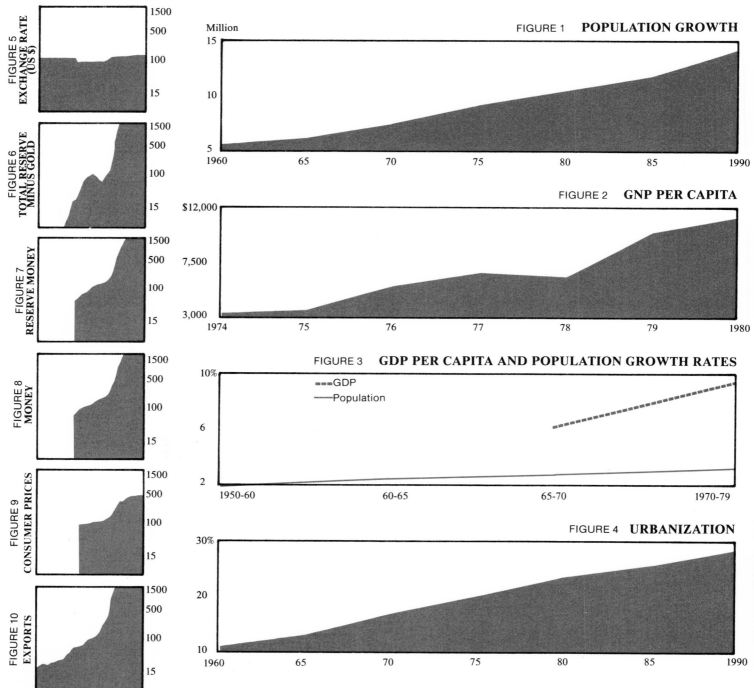

FIGURE 5 EXCHANGE RATE (US $)

FIGURE 6 TOTAL RESERVE MINUS GOLD

FIGURE 7 RESERVE MONEY

FIGURE 8 MONEY

FIGURE 9 CONSUMER PRICES

FIGURE 10 EXPORTS

FIGURE 1 **POPULATION GROWTH**

FIGURE 2 **GNP PER CAPITA**

FIGURE 3 **GDP PER CAPITA AND POPULATION GROWTH RATES**

FIGURE 4 **URBANIZATION**

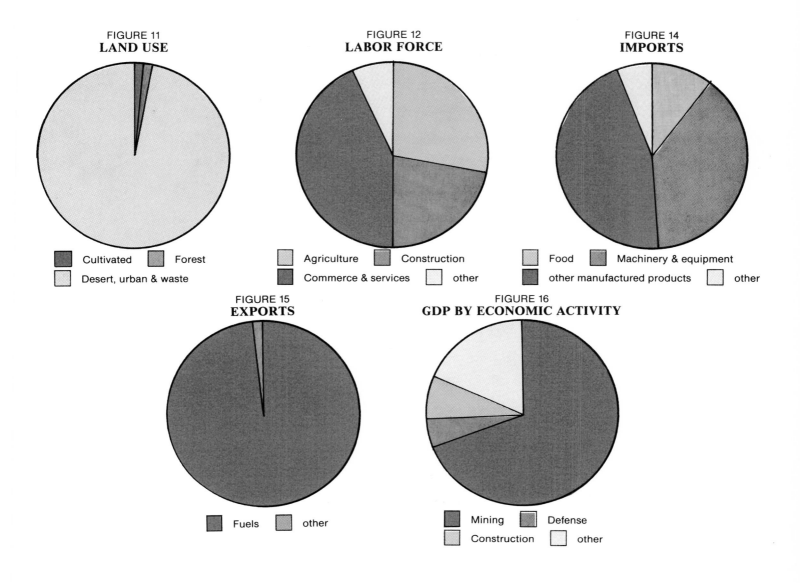

FIGURE 11
LAND USE

Cultivated
Forest
Desert, urban & waste

FIGURE 12
LABOR FORCE

Agriculture
Construction
Commerce & services
other

FIGURE 14
IMPORTS

Food
Machinery & equipment
other manufactured products
other

FIGURE 15
EXPORTS

Fuels
other

FIGURE 16
GDP BY ECONOMIC ACTIVITY

Mining
Defense
Construction
other

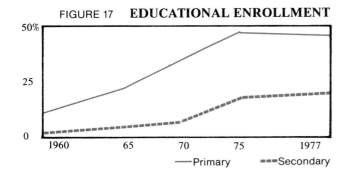

FIGURE 17 **EDUCATIONAL ENROLLMENT**

——Primary ▪▪▪Secondary

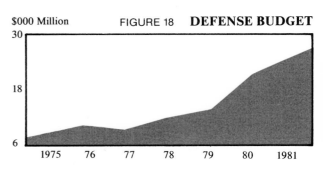

$000 Million FIGURE 18 **DEFENSE BUDGET**

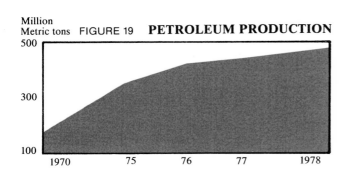

Million
Metric tons FIGURE 19 **PETROLEUM PRODUCTION**

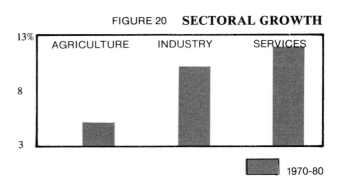

FIGURE 20 **SECTORAL GROWTH**

AGRICULTURE INDUSTRY SERVICES

1970-80

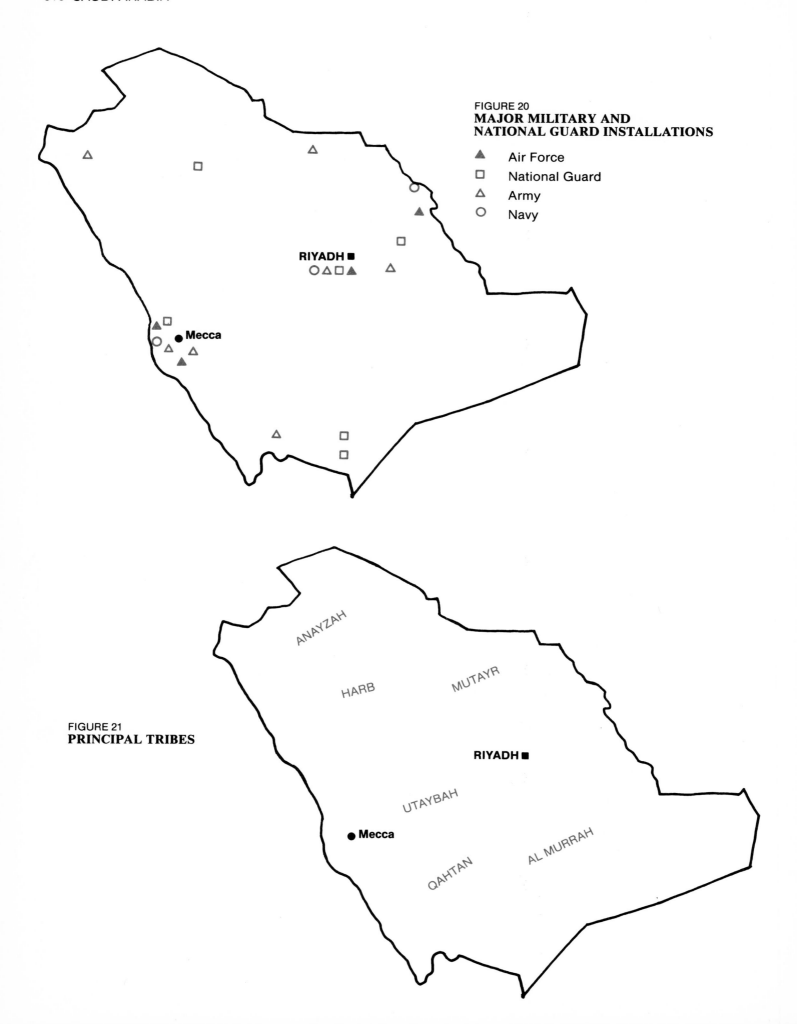

FIGURE 20
**MAJOR MILITARY AND
NATIONAL GUARD INSTALLATIONS**

▲ Air Force
☐ National Guard
△ Army
○ Navy

RIYADH ■

● Mecca

FIGURE 21
PRINCIPAL TRIBES

ANAYZAH

HARB

MUTAYR

RIYADH ■

UTAYBAH

● Mecca

QAHTAN

AL MURRAH

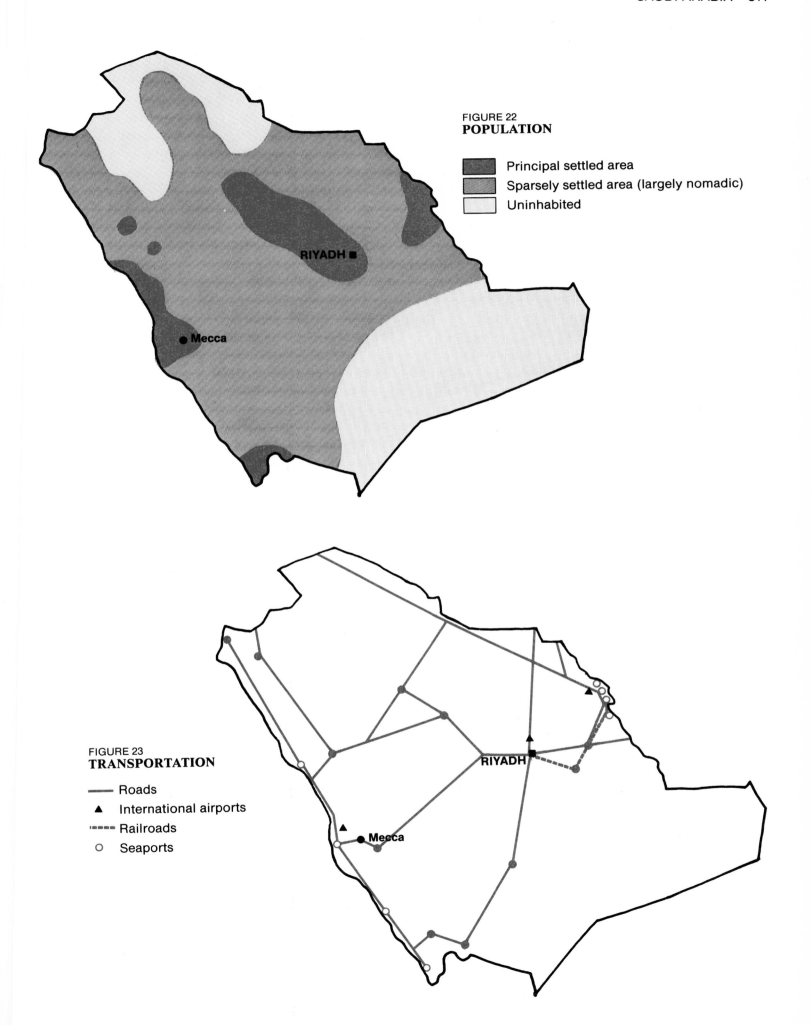

FIGURE 22
POPULATION

- Principal settled area
- Sparsely settled area (largely nomadic)
- Uninhabited

RIYADH

Mecca

FIGURE 23
TRANSPORTATION

— Roads
▲ International airports
----- Railroads
○ Seaports

RIYADH

Mecca

SENEGAL

Located about the middle of the western bulge of Africa, Senegal ranks 78th in land area and 86th in population. Senegal has been one of the showcases of francophone Africa, although it has not been spared the rough sledding that most other Sahelian nations have experienced. Since the export of peanuts (the principal crop, in the production of which Senegal ranks fourth in the world) provides about 80% of export earnings, a single bad harvest can throw the economy into a tailspin. As a hedge against such disastrous years, a $250 million development plan was launched in 1977, primarily to reduce dependence on groundnuts and, secondarily, to develop an irrigation system that will stabilize production. Former President Leopold Senghor's policy of gradualist socialism has led the state to play an increasingly active role in the economy. Although Senegal's growth potentials are limited, it can always count on generous aid from France, its principal financial patron, and from the EEC and international agencies.

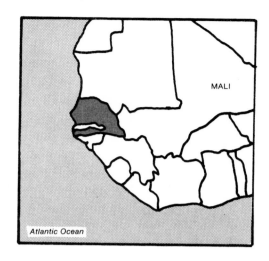

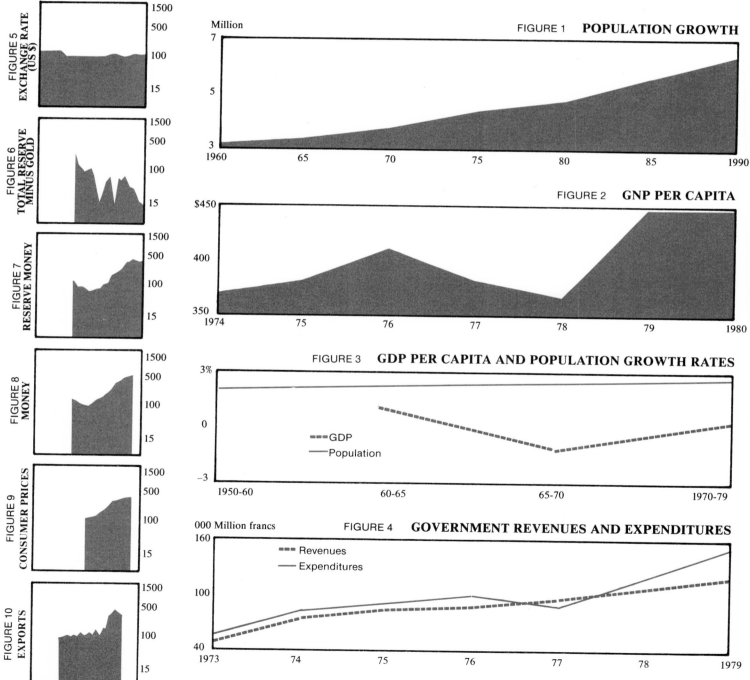

FIGURE 5 EXCHANGE RATE (US $)

FIGURE 6 TOTAL RESERVE MINUS GOLD

FIGURE 7 RESERVE MONEY

FIGURE 8 MONEY

FIGURE 9 CONSUMER PRICES

FIGURE 10 EXPORTS

FIGURE 1 **POPULATION GROWTH**

FIGURE 2 **GNP PER CAPITA**

FIGURE 3 **GDP PER CAPITA AND POPULATION GROWTH RATES**

FIGURE 4 **GOVERNMENT REVENUES AND EXPENDITURES**

FIGURE 11
LAND USE

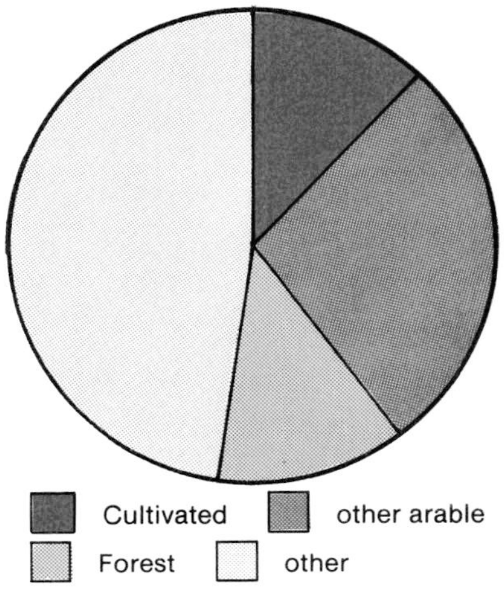

Cultivated   other arable
Forest   other

FIGURE 12
LABOR FORCE

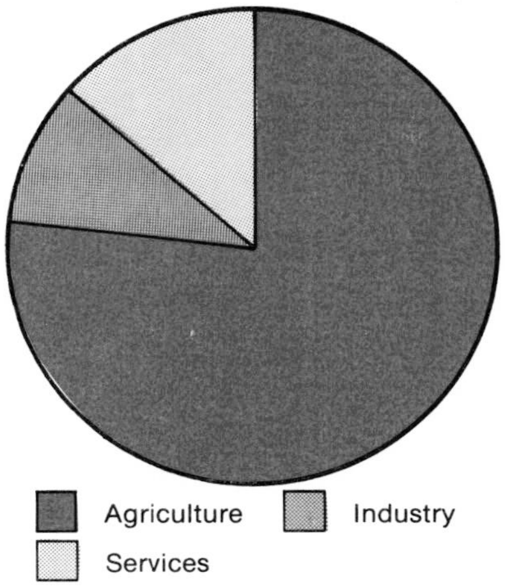

Agriculture   Industry
Services

FIGURE 13
BUDGET EXPENDITURES

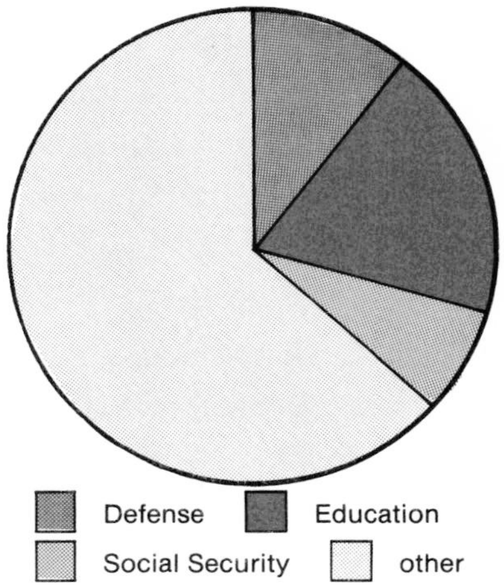

Defense   Education
Social Security   other

FIGURE 14
IMPORTS

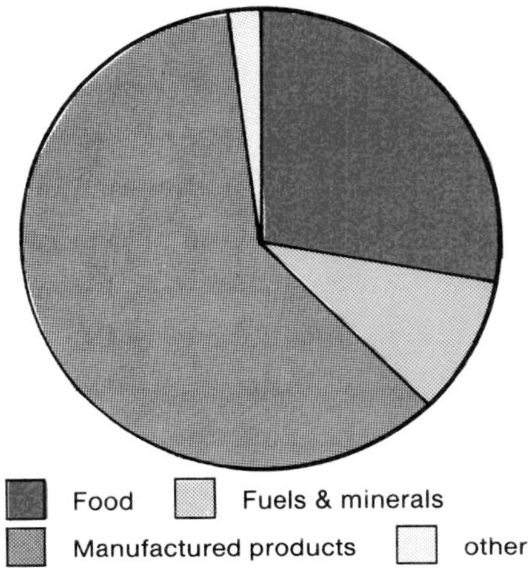

Food   Fuels & minerals
Manufactured products   other

FIGURE 15
EXPORTS

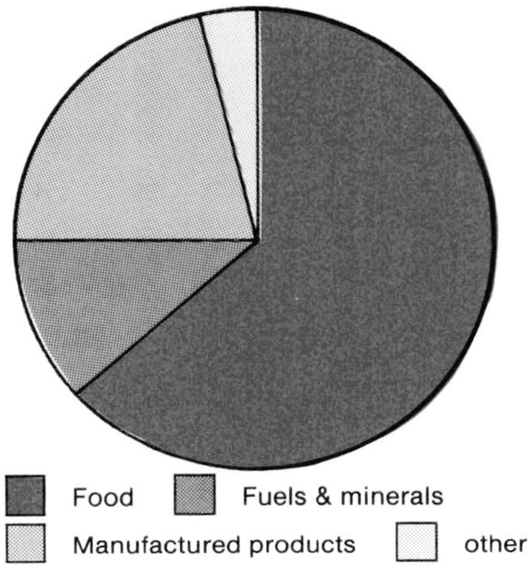

Food   Fuels & minerals
Manufactured products   other

FIGURE 16
GDP BY ECONOMIC ACTIVITY

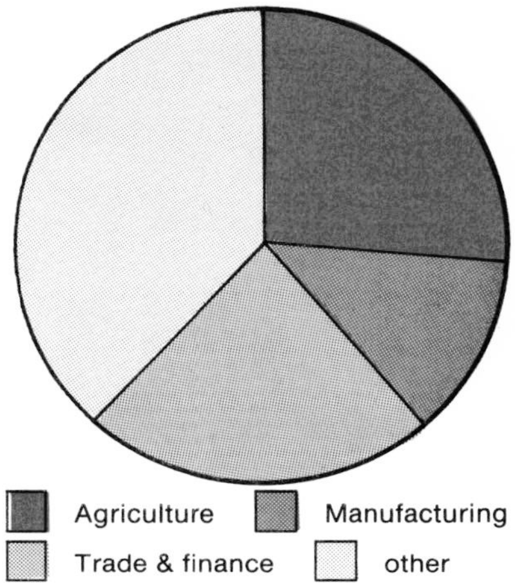

Agriculture   Manufacturing
Trade & finance   other

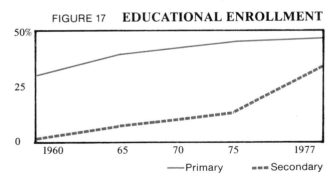

FIGURE 17 **EDUCATIONAL ENROLLMENT**

50%

25

0

1960   65   70   75   1977

——Primary   ===Secondary

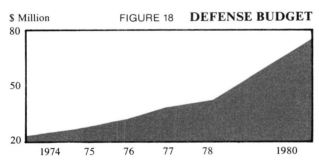

$ Million   FIGURE 18 **DEFENSE BUDGET**

80

50

20

1974   75   76   77   78   1980

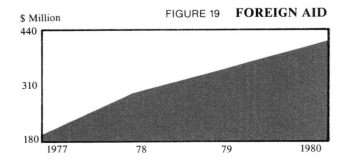

$ Million   FIGURE 19 **FOREIGN AID**

440

310

180

1977   78   79   1980

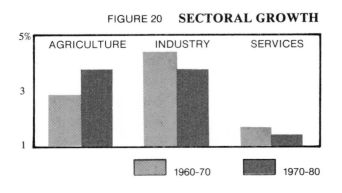

FIGURE 20 **SECTORAL GROWTH**

5%   AGRICULTURE   INDUSTRY   SERVICES

3

1

1960-70   1970-80

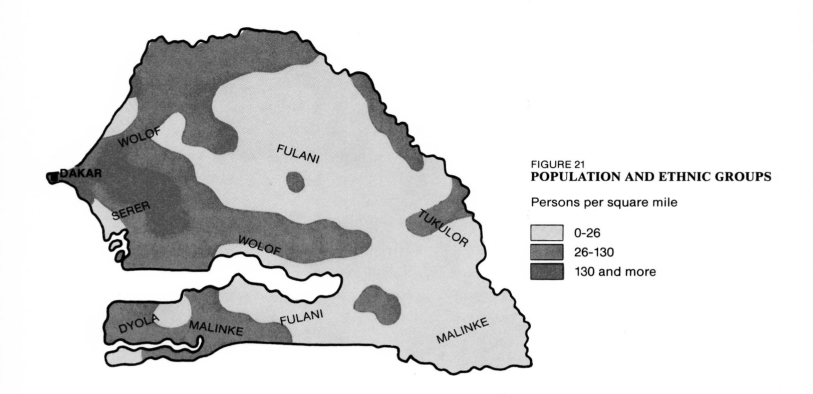

FIGURE 21
POPULATION AND ETHNIC GROUPS

Persons per square mile

- 0-26
- 26-130
- 130 and more

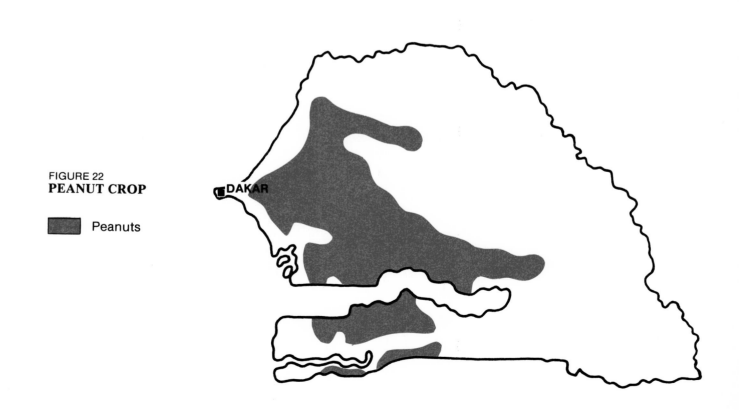

FIGURE 22
PEANUT CROP

Peanuts

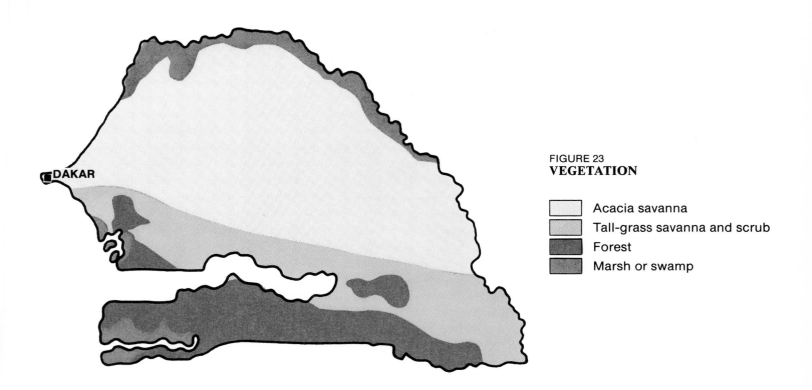

FIGURE 23
VEGETATION

Acacia savanna
Tall-grass savanna and scrub
Forest
Marsh or swamp

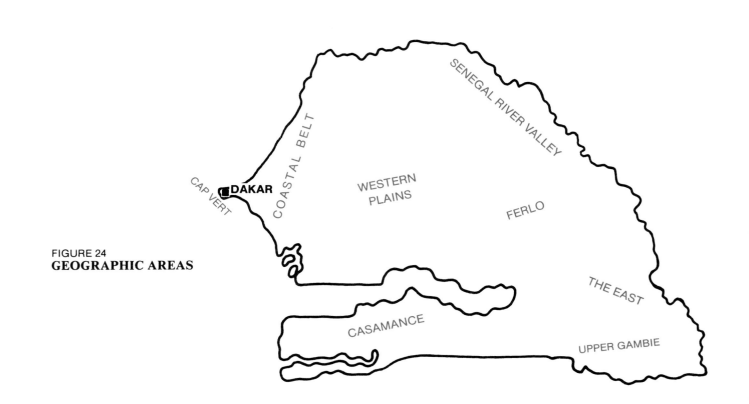

FIGURE 24
GEOGRAPHIC AREAS

SIERRA LEONE

Located in West Africa, wedged in between Liberia and Guinea, Sierra Leone ranks 109th in land area and 104th in population. Even though agriculture employs two-thirds of the economically active population, mining is the major economic activity, the principal minerals being diamonds, iron ore, bauxite, and titanium, which together account for 80% of the country's exports by value. The country also claims the third largest deposit of rutile, a form of titanium oxide. Sierra Leone closed the 1970s with its economy on a falling curve in all areas: an annual trade deficit of over $100 million, an inflation rate over 20%, chronic budget deficits, a ratio of debt servicing to exports of over 25%, and a per capita GNP that had declined every year since 1975. But these difficulties have not turned foreign creditors away primarily because the country has a substantial resource base in terms of mineral deposits and considerable potential for expansion of agriculture.

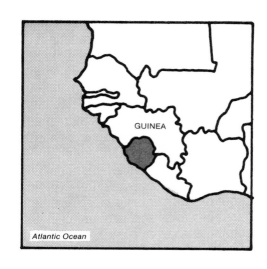

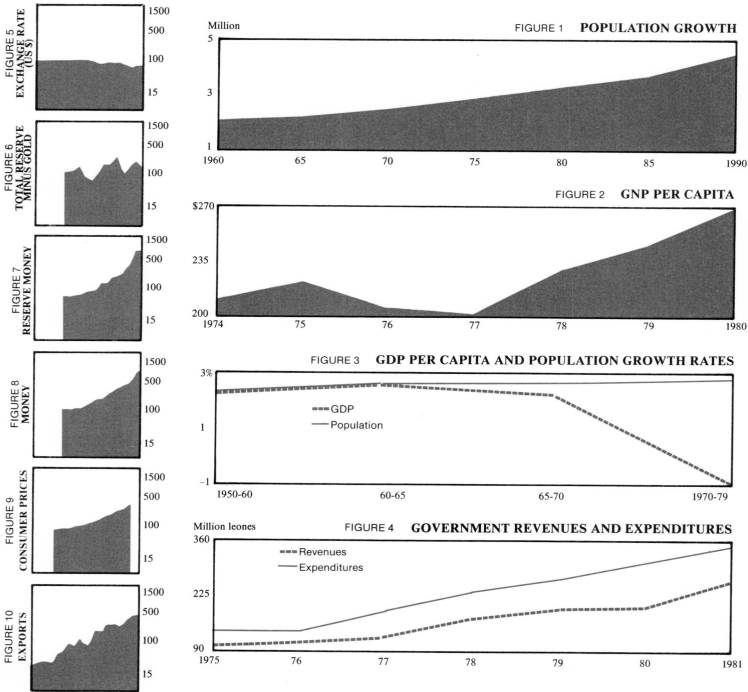

FIGURE 5 EXCHANGE RATE (US $)

FIGURE 6 TOTAL RESERVE MINUS GOLD

FIGURE 7 RESERVE MONEY

FIGURE 8 MONEY

FIGURE 9 CONSUMER PRICES

FIGURE 10 EXPORTS

FIGURE 1 **POPULATION GROWTH**

FIGURE 2 **GNP PER CAPITA**

FIGURE 3 **GDP PER CAPITA AND POPULATION GROWTH RATES**

FIGURE 4 **GOVERNMENT REVENUES AND EXPENDITURES**

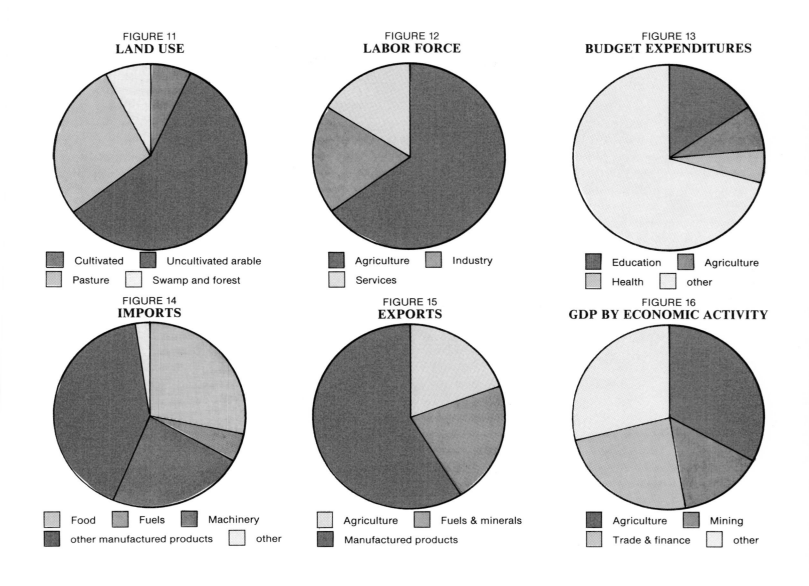

FIGURE 11
LAND USE

- Cultivated
- Uncultivated arable
- Pasture
- Swamp and forest

FIGURE 12
LABOR FORCE

- Agriculture
- Industry
- Services

FIGURE 13
BUDGET EXPENDITURES

- Education
- Agriculture
- Health
- other

FIGURE 14
IMPORTS

- Food
- Fuels
- Machinery
- other manufactured products
- other

FIGURE 15
EXPORTS

- Agriculture
- Fuels & minerals
- Manufactured products

FIGURE 16
GDP BY ECONOMIC ACTIVITY

- Agriculture
- Mining
- Trade & finance
- other

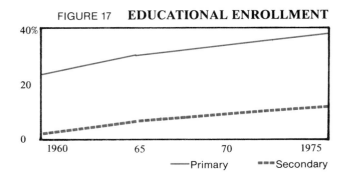

FIGURE 17 **EDUCATIONAL ENROLLMENT**

— Primary   ▪▪▪ Secondary

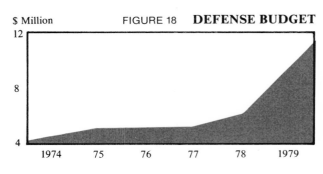

$ Million   FIGURE 18 **DEFENSE BUDGET**

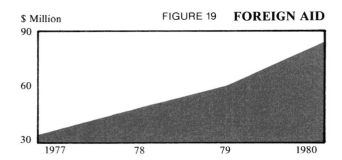

$ Million   FIGURE 19 **FOREIGN AID**

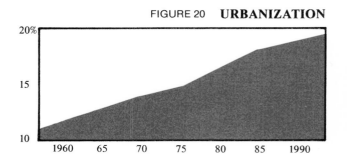

FIGURE 20 **URBANIZATION**

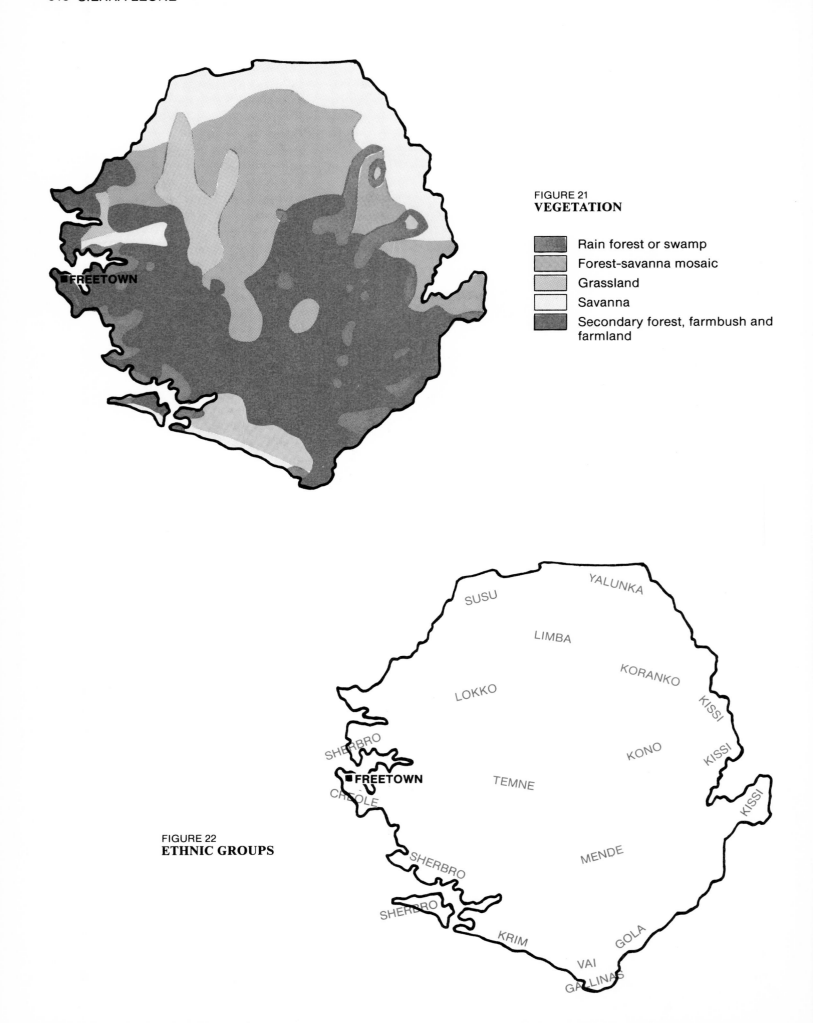

FIGURE 21
VEGETATION

Rain forest or swamp
Forest-savanna mosaic
Grassland
Savanna
Secondary forest, farmbush and farmland

FIGURE 22
ETHNIC GROUPS

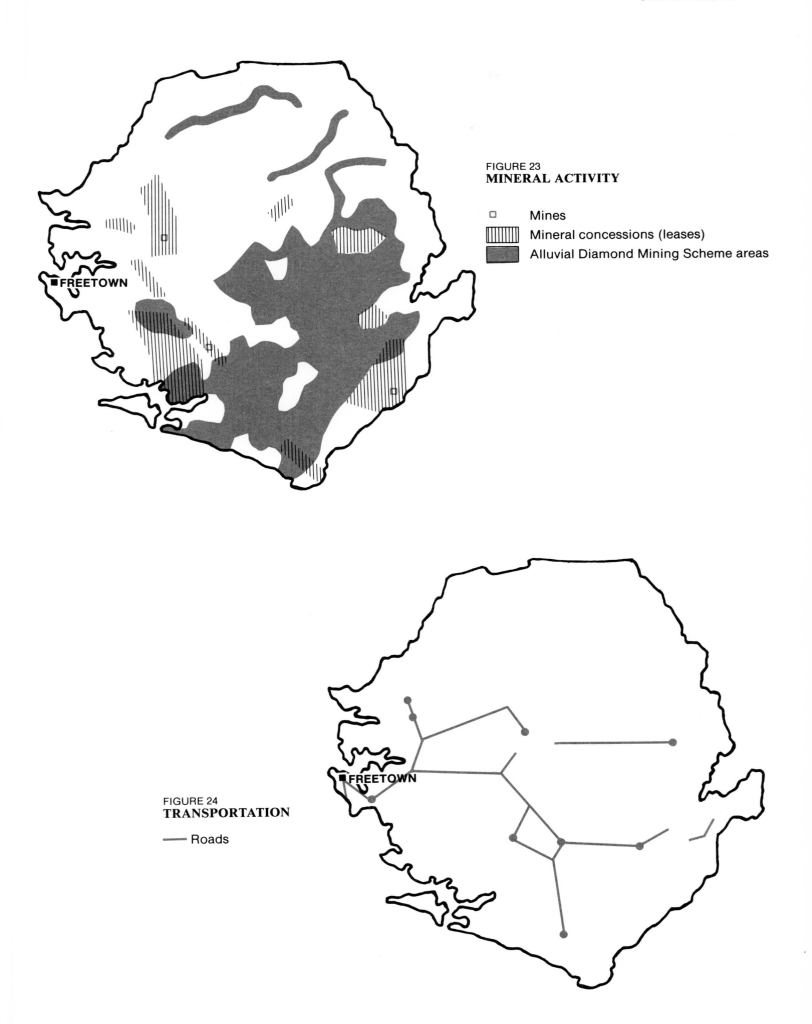

FIGURE 23
MINERAL ACTIVITY

☐   Mines

▥   Mineral concessions (leases)

▦   Alluvial Diamond Mining Scheme areas

■FREETOWN

FIGURE 24
TRANSPORTATION

—— Roads

■FREETOWN

SINGAPORE

One of the world's great commercial centers and entrepots, Singapore ranks among the bottom in land area but is the third most densely populated and urbanized country. It is also an interesting amalgam of three important Asian races: Chinese, Malay and Indian. Because of its high per capita income ($4,480 in 1980) the UN ranks it a developed country. Traditionally geared to the entrepot trade, it ranks fourth in the world in exports and imports per capita and the port of Singapore is the fourth largest in the world in cargo handled. However, in recent years the government has shifted its economic strategy to place greater emphasis on industrialization, making Singapore a regional leader in shipbuilding, electronics and oil refining. Singapore has also developed a reputation as an international financial center, competing with the Bahamas in attracting offshore U.S. dollars. Singapore's move into capital-intensive, technologically sophisticated industries is expected to pay off in the eighties, reinforcing its status as the linchpin of the Southeast Asian economy.

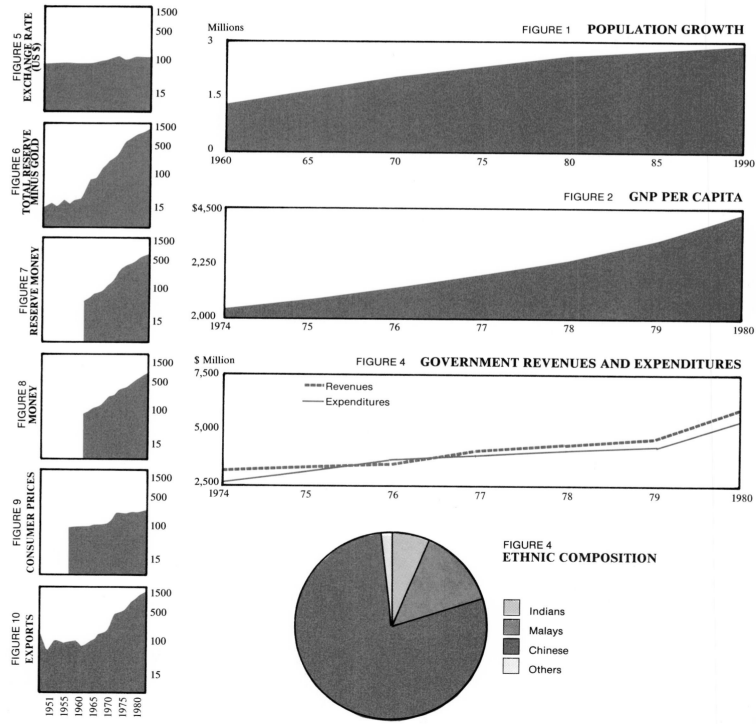

FIGURE 5 EXCHANGE RATE (US $)

FIGURE 6 TOTAL RESERVE MINUS GOLD

FIGURE 7 RESERVE MONEY

FIGURE 8 MONEY

FIGURE 9 CONSUMER PRICES

FIGURE 10 EXPORTS

FIGURE 1 **POPULATION GROWTH**

FIGURE 2 **GNP PER CAPITA**

FIGURE 4 **GOVERNMENT REVENUES AND EXPENDITURES**

Revenues
Expenditures

FIGURE 4
ETHNIC COMPOSITION

Indians
Malays
Chinese
Others

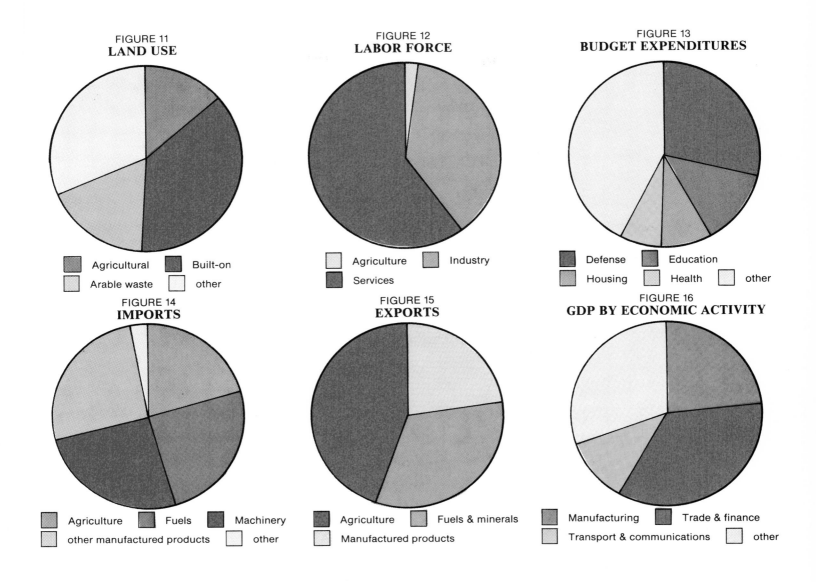

FIGURE 11
LAND USE

Agricultural
Arable waste
Built-on
other

FIGURE 12
LABOR FORCE

Agriculture
Services
Industry

FIGURE 13
BUDGET EXPENDITURES

Defense
Housing
Education
Health
other

FIGURE 14
IMPORTS

Agriculture
other manufactured products
Fuels
Machinery
other

FIGURE 15
EXPORTS

Agriculture
Manufactured products
Fuels & minerals

FIGURE 16
GDP BY ECONOMIC ACTIVITY

Manufacturing
Transport & communications
Trade & finance
other

FIGURE 17
RUBBER PRODUCTION

SINGAPORE
Rubber plantation
Jurong Industrial Estate

SOMALIA

The tip of the horn of Africa, Somalia ranks 39th in land area and 102nd in population. Already among the poorest nations of the world, Somalia is now burdened with the crushing losses it suffered in the 1977-78 war with Ethiopia; if that were not enough, it has to feed nearly a million refugees from the Ogaden region at a time when the nation has lost a fourth of its livestock and suffered severe setbacks in agricultural production as a result of drought. Despite problems of such awesome magnitude, the economy is limping along and has actually made progress in some areas. The 1979-81 three-year development plan projected an expenditure of $1.2 billion, including $221 million for the construction of a dam across the Juba at Bardera which is expected to provide irrigation for half a million acres of cropland and yield 115 million kwh of hydroelectric power annually. Most Western investment in the economy was eliminated through large-scale nationalization measures in 1975.

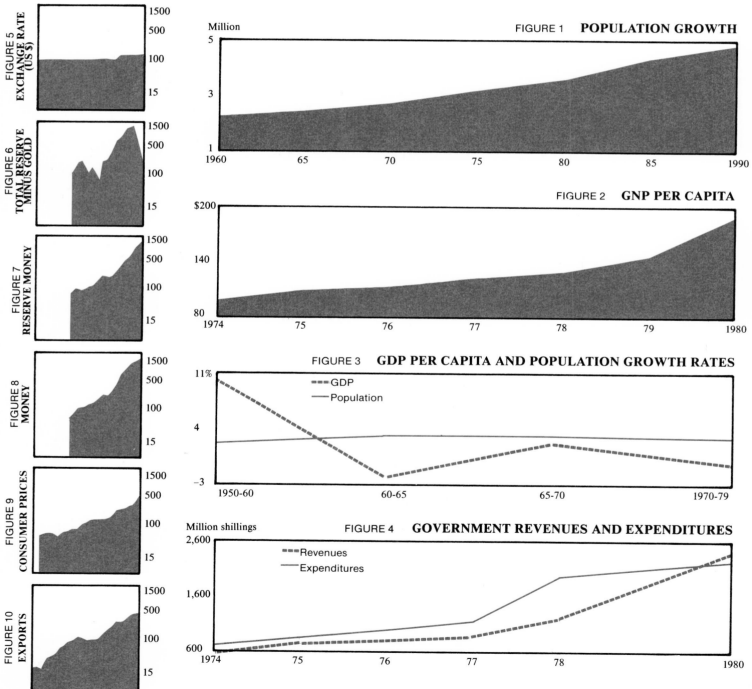

FIGURE 5 EXCHANGE RATE (US $)

FIGURE 6 TOTAL RESERVE MINUS GOLD

FIGURE 7 RESERVE MONEY

FIGURE 8 MONEY

FIGURE 9 CONSUMER PRICES

FIGURE 10 EXPORTS

FIGURE 1 **POPULATION GROWTH**

FIGURE 2 **GNP PER CAPITA**

FIGURE 3 **GDP PER CAPITA AND POPULATION GROWTH RATES**

FIGURE 4 **GOVERNMENT REVENUES AND EXPENDITURES**

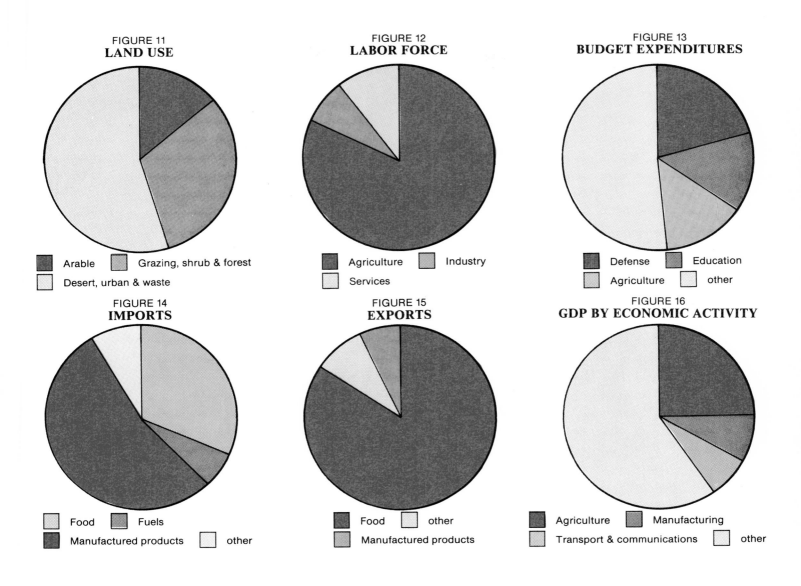

FIGURE 11
LAND USE

Arable
Grazing, shrub & forest
Desert, urban & waste

FIGURE 12
LABOR FORCE

Agriculture
Industry
Services

FIGURE 13
BUDGET EXPENDITURES

Defense
Education
Agriculture
other

FIGURE 14
IMPORTS

Food
Fuels
Manufactured products
other

FIGURE 15
EXPORTS

Food
other
Manufactured products

FIGURE 16
GDP BY ECONOMIC ACTIVITY

Agriculture
Manufacturing
Transport & communications
other

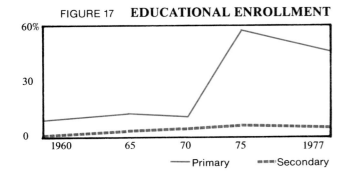

FIGURE 17   **EDUCATIONAL ENROLLMENT**

60%

30

0

1960   65   70   75   1977

—— Primary   ▪▪▪ Secondary

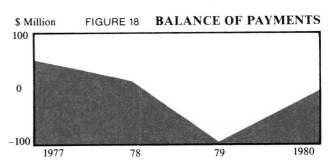

$ Million   FIGURE 18   **BALANCE OF PAYMENTS**

100

0

-100

1977   78   79   1980

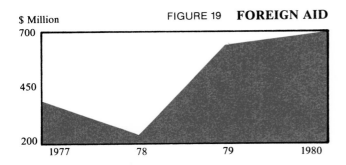

$ Million   FIGURE 19   **FOREIGN AID**

700

450

200

1977   78   79   1980

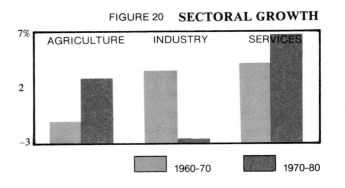

FIGURE 20   **SECTORAL GROWTH**

7%   AGRICULTURE   INDUSTRY   SERVICES

2

-3

1960-70   1970-80

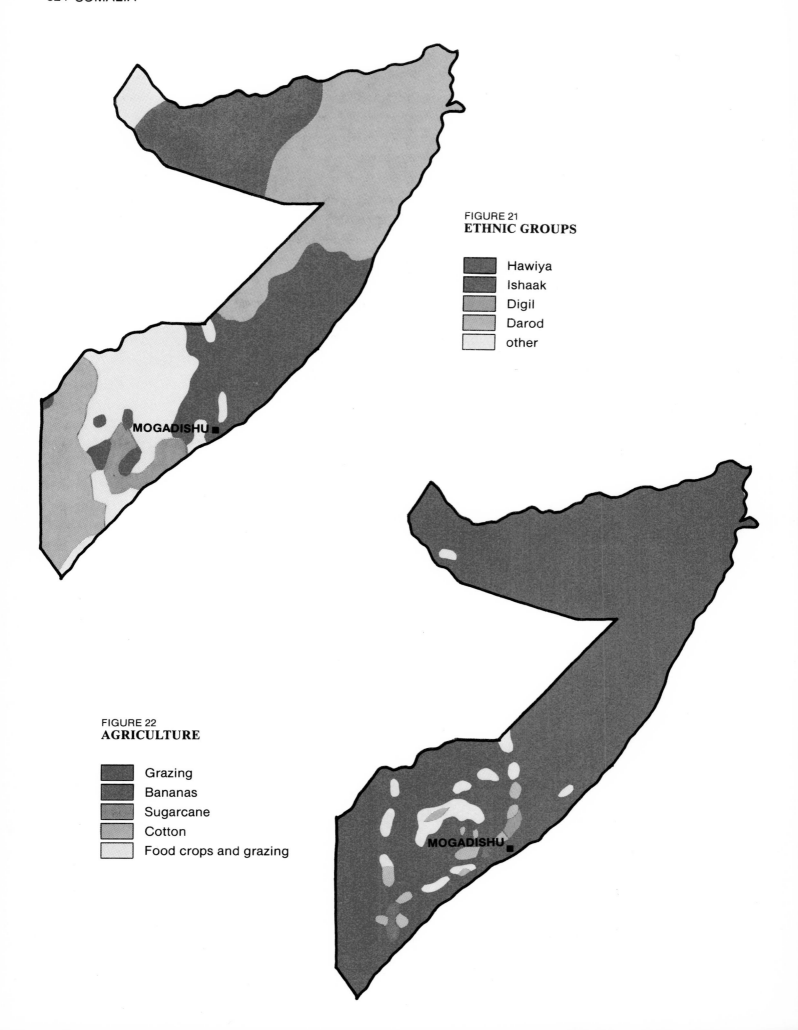

FIGURE 21
ETHNIC GROUPS

Hawiya
Ishaak
Digil
Darod
other

MOGADISHU ■

FIGURE 22
AGRICULTURE

Grazing
Bananas
Sugarcane
Cotton
Food crops and grazing

MOGADISHU ■

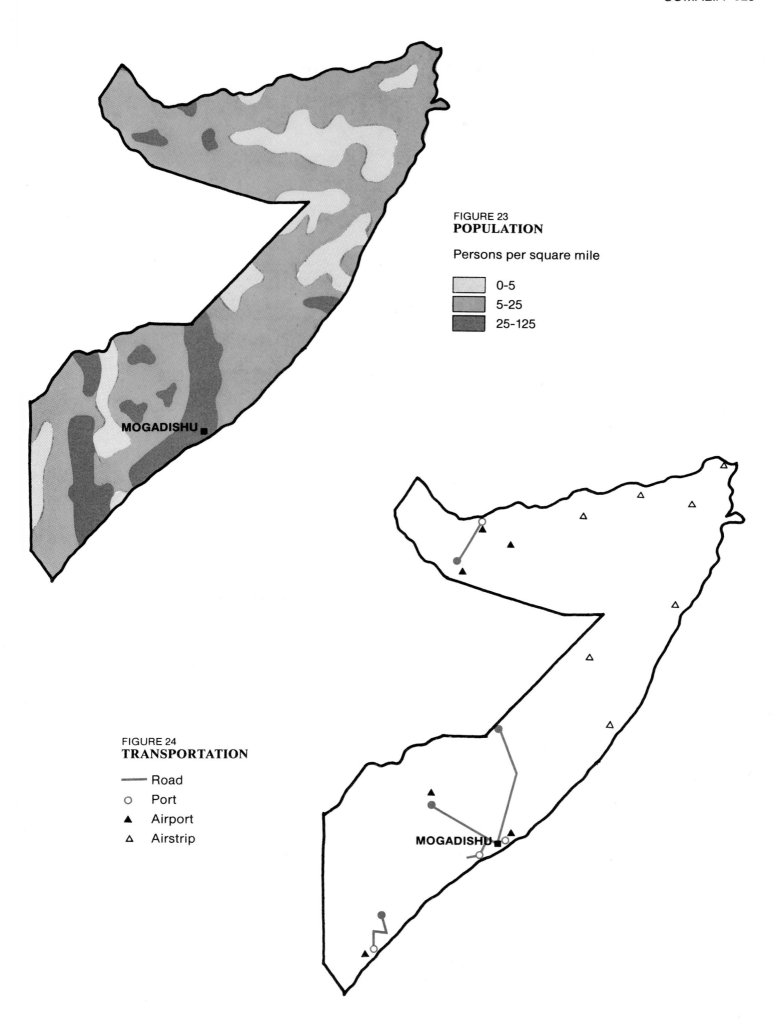

FIGURE 23
POPULATION

Persons per square mile

0-5
5-25
25-125

MOGADISHU

FIGURE 24
TRANSPORTATION

— Road
○ Port
▲ Airport
△ Airstrip

MOGADISHU

SRI LANKA

A pear-shaped island in the Indian Ocean southeast of India, Sri Lanka ranks 111th in land area and 44th in population. Along with all other countries in the Indian subcontinent, it is officially classified as a low-income country seriously affected by recent adverse economic conditions. However, it fares better than other countries in the region on the physical quality of life index. Three major plantation crops account for by far the bulk of Sri Lankan exports: tea, rubber and coconuts. Despite declining production, it remains the world's second largest exporter of tea. Official economic policies have swung from extreme leftist under the two Bandaranaikes to free-enterprise under the Senanaikes and President Jayawardene. The economy is expected to benefit as a result of the relaxation of controls both on domestic business as well as foreign investors. Nevertheless, some 60% of the economy is still in government hands and many of the socialist programs of the Bandaranaike governments remain.

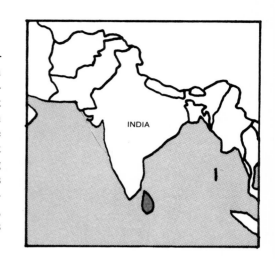

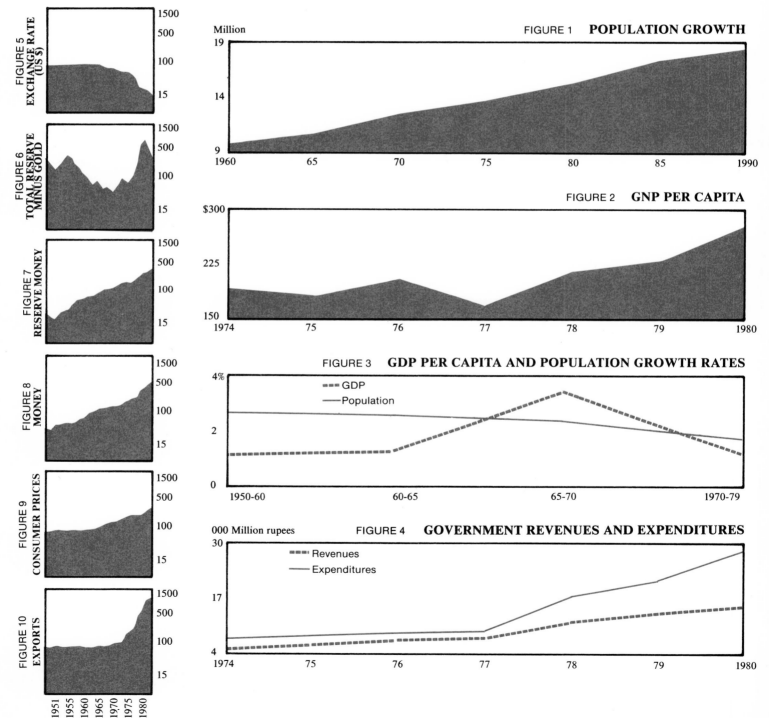

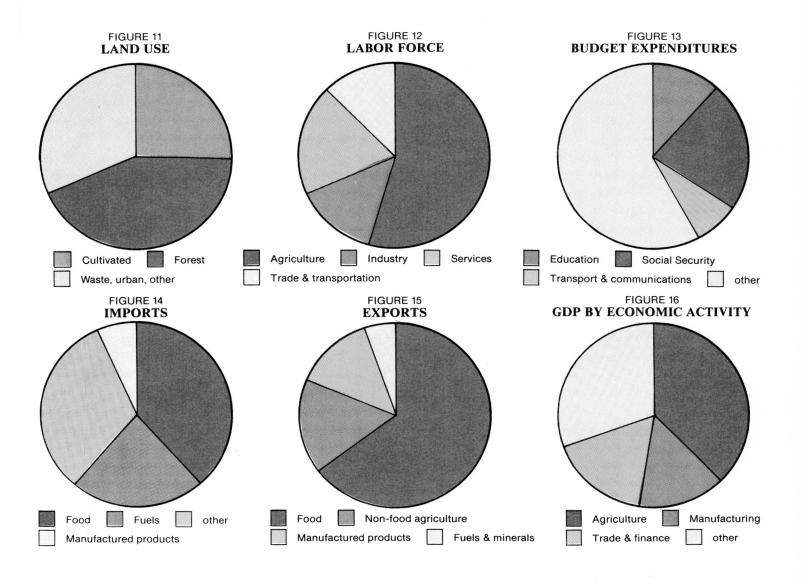

FIGURE 11
LAND USE

Cultivated   Forest
Waste, urban, other

FIGURE 12
LABOR FORCE

Agriculture   Industry   Services
Trade & transportation

FIGURE 13
BUDGET EXPENDITURES

Education   Social Security
Transport & communications   other

FIGURE 14
IMPORTS

Food   Fuels   other
Manufactured products

FIGURE 15
EXPORTS

Food   Non-food agriculture
Manufactured products   Fuels & minerals

FIGURE 16
GDP BY ECONOMIC ACTIVITY

Agriculture   Manufacturing
Trade & finance   other

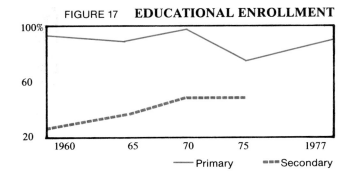

FIGURE 17   **EDUCATIONAL ENROLLMENT**

——— Primary   ▄▄▄ Secondary

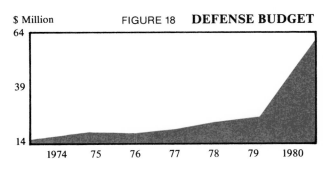

$ Million   FIGURE 18   **DEFENSE BUDGET**

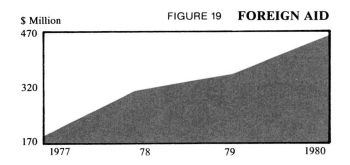

$ Million   FIGURE 19   **FOREIGN AID**

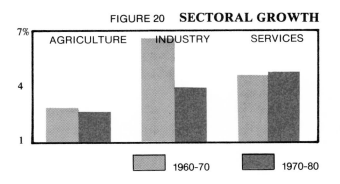

FIGURE 20   **SECTORAL GROWTH**

AGRICULTURE   INDUSTRY   SERVICES

1960-70   1970-80

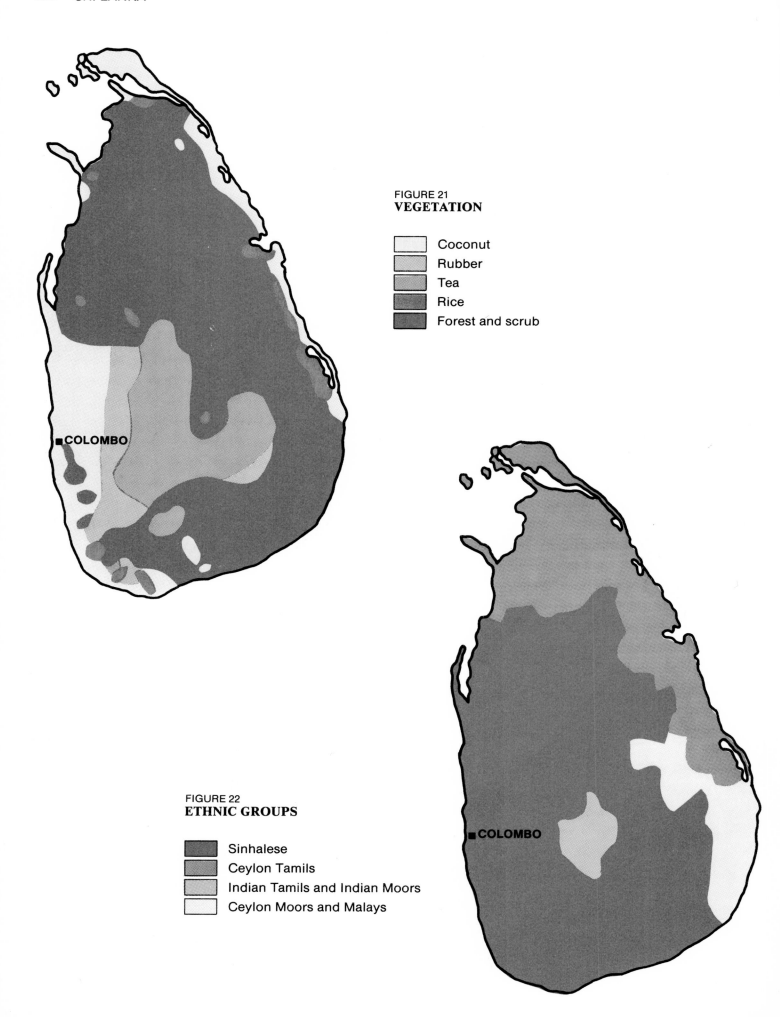

FIGURE 21
VEGETATION

Coconut
Rubber
Tea
Rice
Forest and scrub

■COLOMBO

FIGURE 22
ETHNIC GROUPS

Sinhalese
Ceylon Tamils
Indian Tamils and Indian Moors
Ceylon Moors and Malays

■COLOMBO

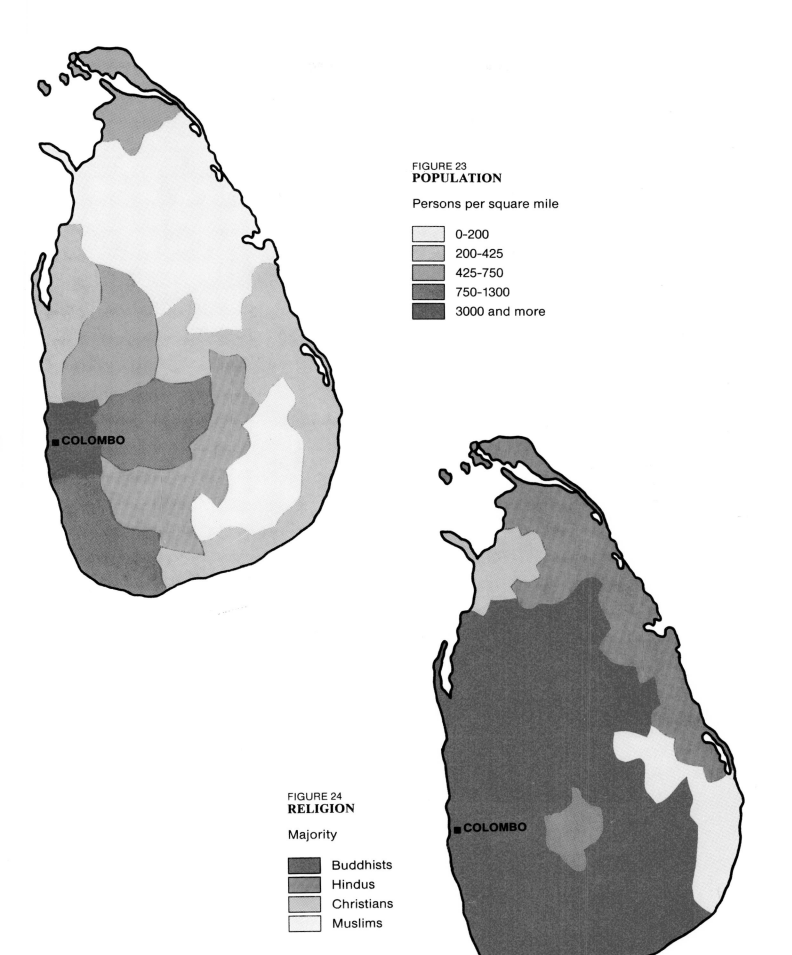

FIGURE 23
POPULATION

Persons per square mile

0-200
200-425
425-750
750-1300
3000 and more

■ COLOMBO

FIGURE 24
RELIGION

Majority

Buddhists
Hindus
Christians
Muslims

■ COLOMBO

SUDAN

The largest country in Africa, Sudan ranks ninth in land area but only 35th in population. The potentials for growth that flow from sheer physical size have only been partially realized. A number of reasons have been advanced for such underdevelopment: inadequate transportation facilities, presence of nearly half a million refugees from Eritrea, Uganda, Chad and other countries, misallocation of resources in the agricultural sector, political instability, ethnic rivalries between the predominantly Muslim north and the pagan south, and chronic trade deficits. Of the 200 million acres of cultivable land (which, if properly utilized, could turn the country into the breadbasket of Africa), only 10% is being cultivated. Historically, cotton has been the principal commodity but most people tend to associate the country with gum arabic, of which Sudan produces four-fifths of the world's supply. One encouraging sign for the future direction of the economy is Saudi Arabia's and the UAE's substantial investments in Sudanese development projects.

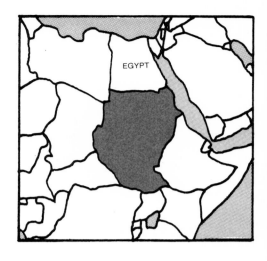

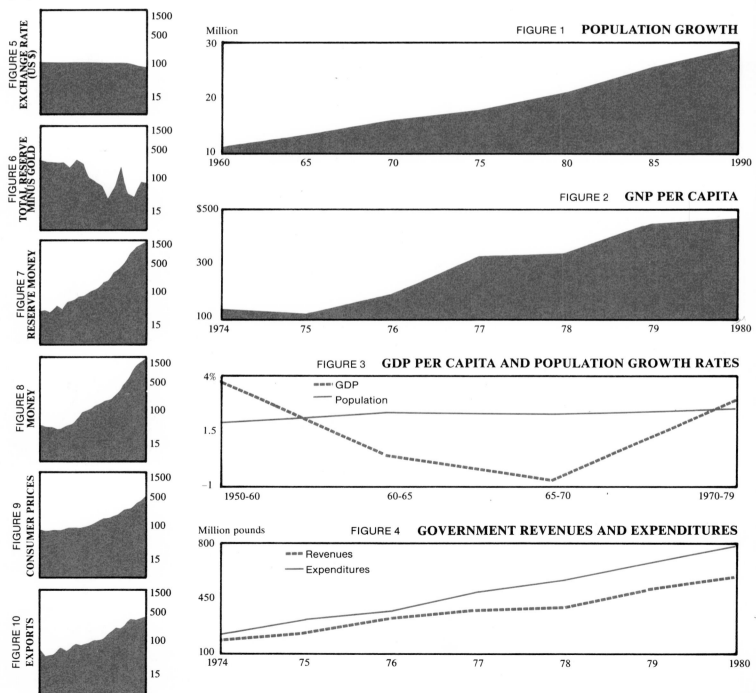

FIGURE 5 — EXCHANGE RATE (US $)

FIGURE 6 — TOTAL RESERVE MINUS GOLD

FIGURE 7 — RESERVE MONEY

FIGURE 8 — MONEY

FIGURE 9 — CONSUMER PRICES

FIGURE 10 — EXPORTS

FIGURE 1 **POPULATION GROWTH**

FIGURE 2 **GNP PER CAPITA**

FIGURE 3 **GDP PER CAPITA AND POPULATION GROWTH RATES**

FIGURE 4 **GOVERNMENT REVENUES AND EXPENDITURES**

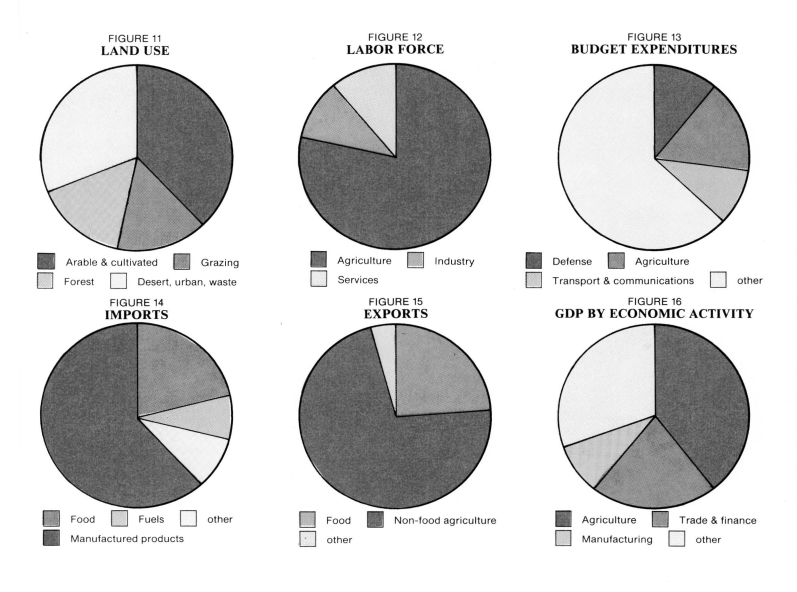

FIGURE 11
LAND USE

Arable & cultivated   Grazing
Forest   Desert, urban, waste

FIGURE 12
LABOR FORCE

Agriculture   Industry
Services

FIGURE 13
BUDGET EXPENDITURES

Defense   Agriculture
Transport & communications   other

FIGURE 14
IMPORTS

Food   Fuels   other
Manufactured products

FIGURE 15
EXPORTS

Food   Non-food agriculture
other

FIGURE 16
GDP BY ECONOMIC ACTIVITY

Agriculture   Trade & finance
Manufacturing   other

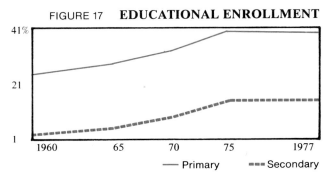

FIGURE 17   **EDUCATIONAL ENROLLMENT**

41%

21

1

1960   65   70   75   1977

—— Primary   === Secondary

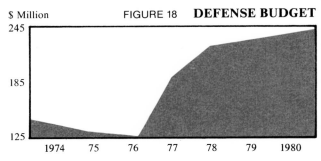

$ Million   FIGURE 18   **DEFENSE BUDGET**

245

185

125

1974   75   76   77   78   79   1980

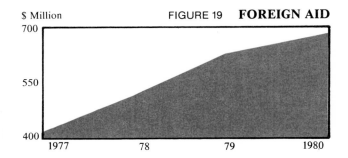

$ Million   FIGURE 19   **FOREIGN AID**

700

550

400

1977   78   79   1980

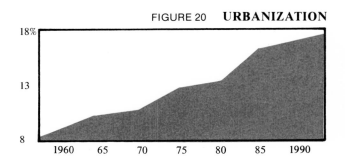

FIGURE 20   **URBANIZATION**

18%

13

8

1960   65   70   75   80   85   1990

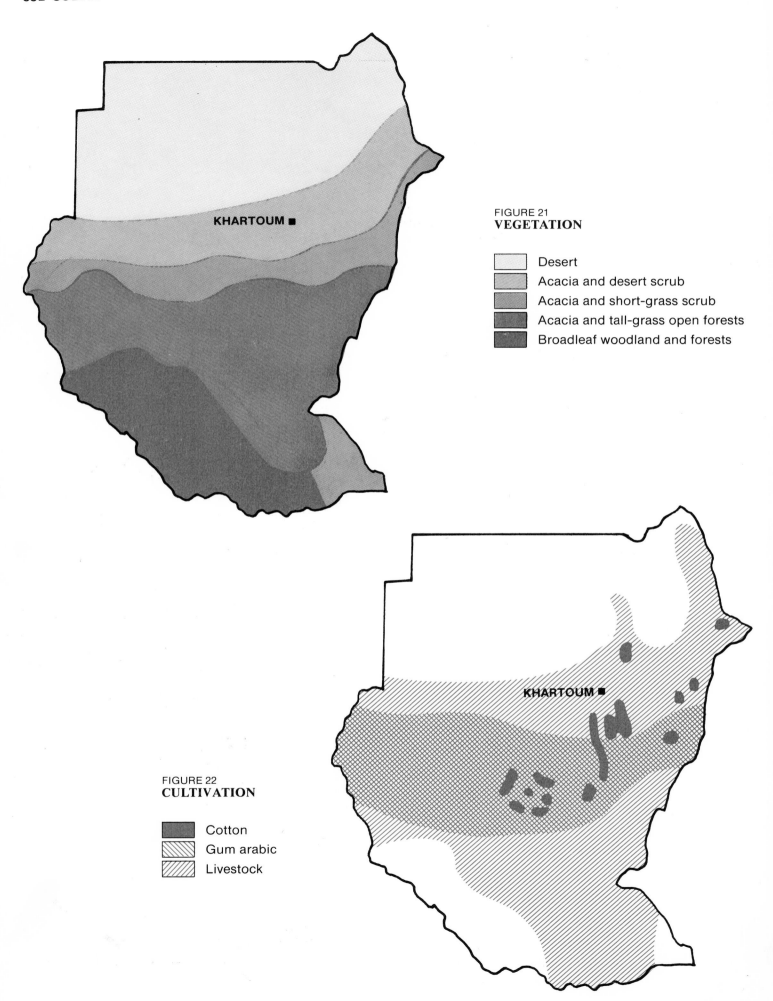

FIGURE 21
VEGETATION

KHARTOUM ■

	Desert
	Acacia and desert scrub
	Acacia and short-grass scrub
	Acacia and tall-grass open forests
	Broadleaf woodland and forests

FIGURE 22
CULTIVATION

KHARTOUM ■

	Cotton
	Gum arabic
	Livestock

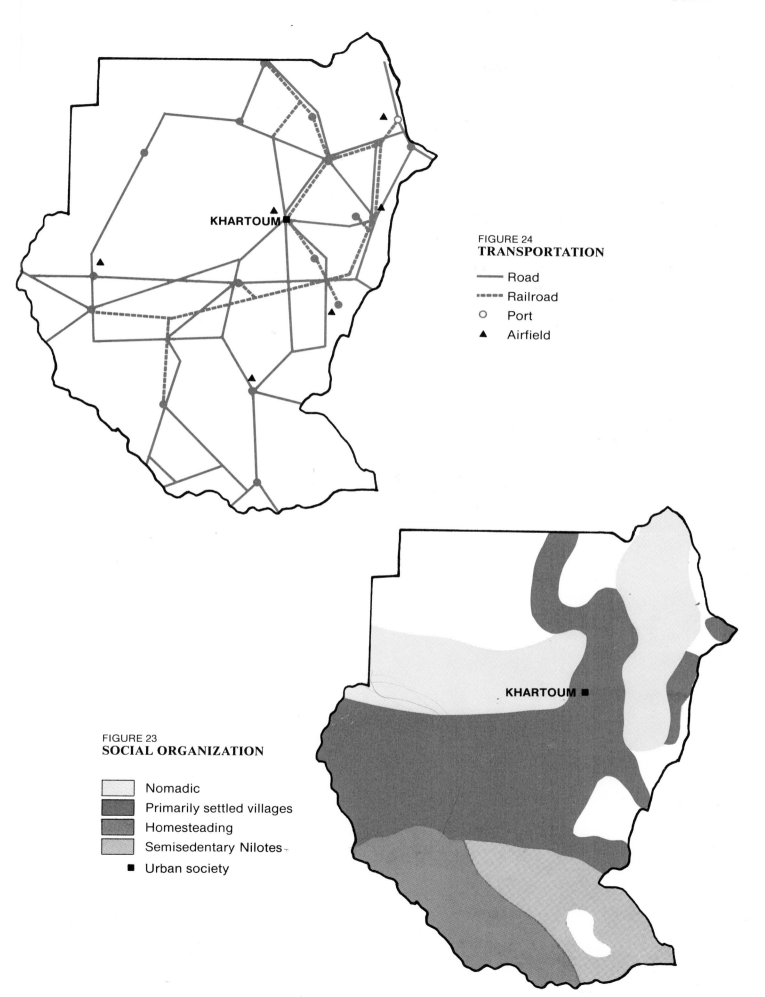

FIGURE 24
TRANSPORTATION

——— Road
- - - - Railroad
○ Port
▲ Airfield

KHARTOUM ■

FIGURE 23
SOCIAL ORGANIZATION

Nomadic
Primarily settled villages
Homesteading
Semisedentary Nilotes
■ Urban society

KHARTOUM ■

SYRIA

Ranking 80th in land area and 63rd in population, Syria, once a byword for political instability, has become, since the rise of President Assad to power in 1971, one of the most stable nations in the region, although internal dissensions continue to erupt off and on. A decade of relative peace and stability has helped to firm up the economy, producing many encouraging signs, such as first rank on the mineral production index, second rank on the construction index, fourth on the manufacturing index, first rank in the annual growth rate of energy production and eighth rank in the annual growth rate of agriculture. During 1974-75 the economy reached an annual growth rate of 13% and, despite inflationary pressures, maintained a growth rate of 4.6% for the entire decade of the seventies. Major factors contributing to such a performance were massive aid from richer Arab nations, realistic economic planning and higher prices for oil exports. Although highly centralized and state-controlled, the economy retains some private sector flavor.

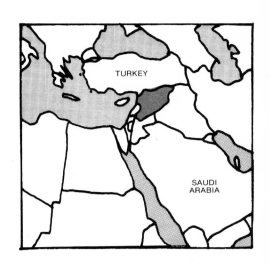

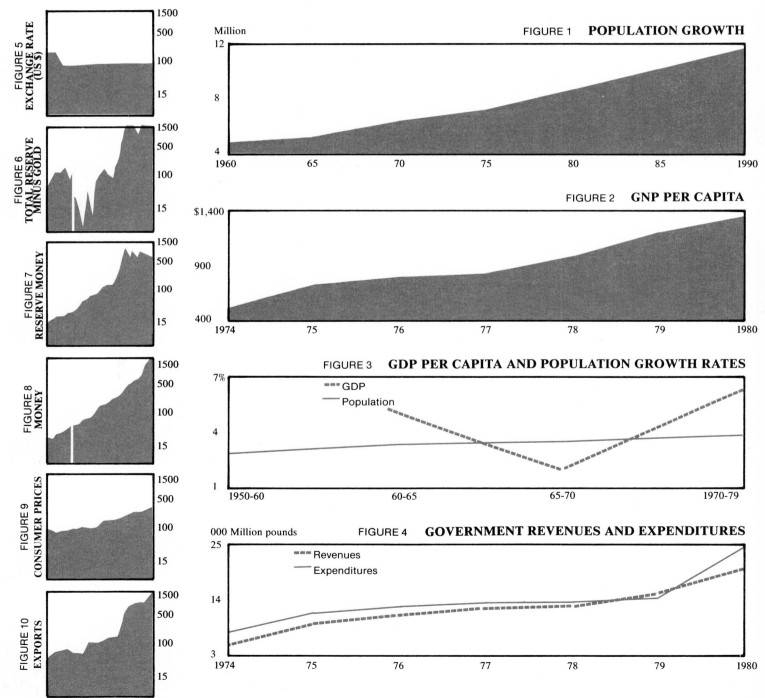

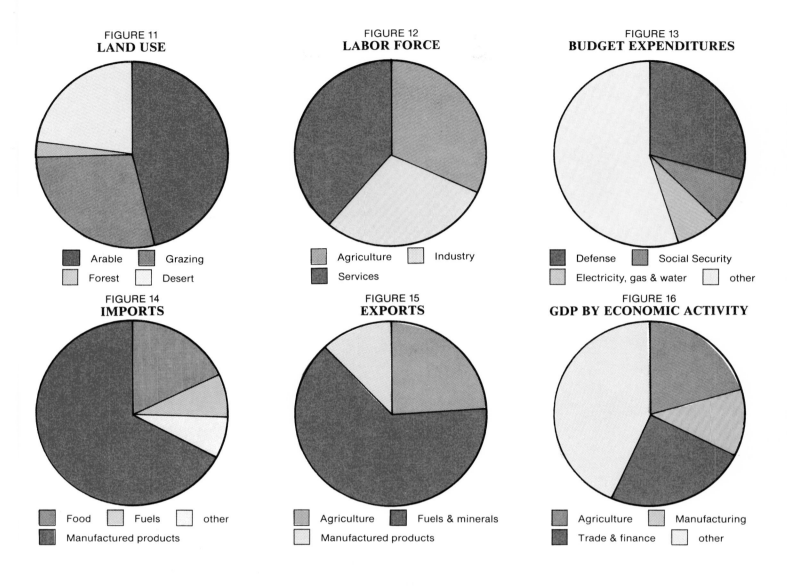

FIGURE 11
LAND USE

Arable Grazing
Forest Desert

FIGURE 12
LABOR FORCE

Agriculture Industry
Services

FIGURE 13
BUDGET EXPENDITURES

Defense Social Security
Electricity, gas & water other

FIGURE 14
IMPORTS

Food Fuels other
Manufactured products

FIGURE 15
EXPORTS

Agriculture Fuels & minerals
Manufactured products

FIGURE 16
GDP BY ECONOMIC ACTIVITY

Agriculture Manufacturing
Trade & finance other

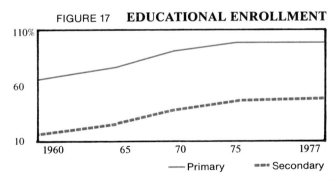

FIGURE 17 **EDUCATIONAL ENROLLMENT**

110%

60

10
1960   65   70   75   1977

—— Primary   ▪▪▪ Secondary

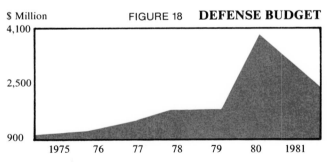

$ Million   FIGURE 18   **DEFENSE BUDGET**
4,100

2,500

900
1975   76   77   78   79   80   1981

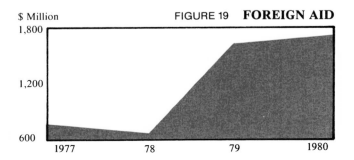

$ Million   FIGURE 19 **FOREIGN AID**
1,800

1,200

600
1977   78   79   1980

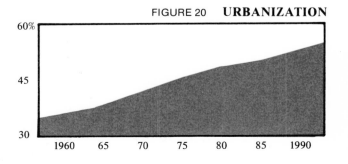

FIGURE 20 **URBANIZATION**
60%

45

30
1960   65   70   75   80   85   1990

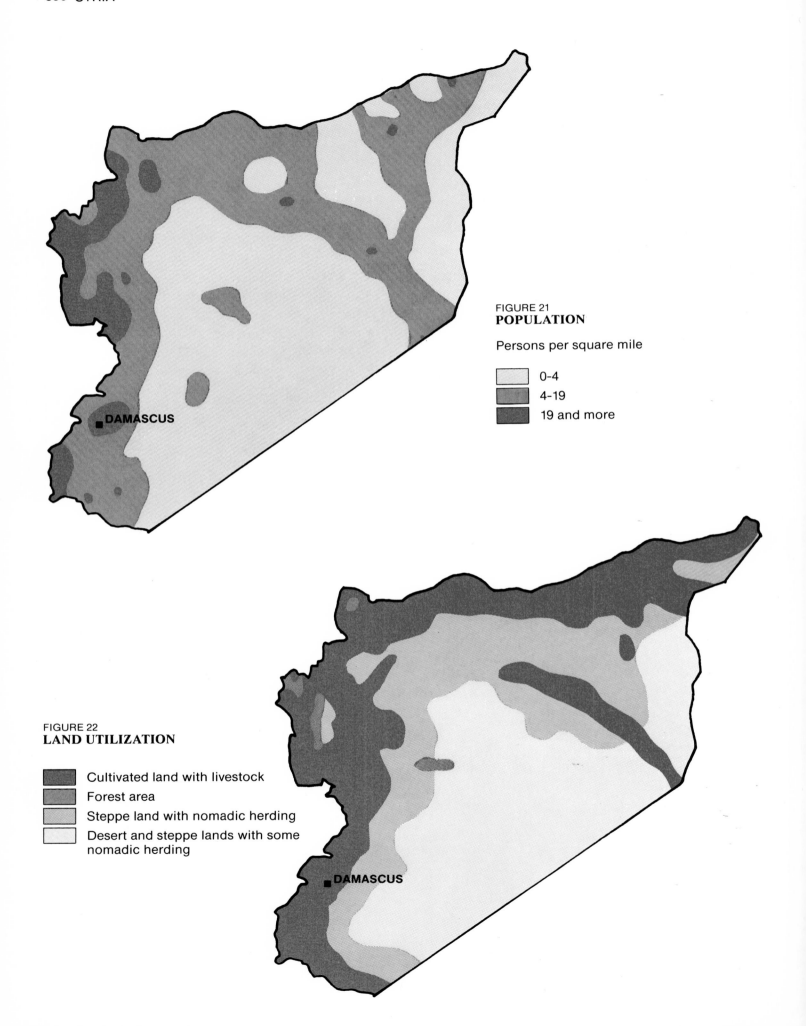

FIGURE 21
POPULATION

Persons per square mile

0-4

4-19

19 and more

■ DAMASCUS

FIGURE 22
LAND UTILIZATION

Cultivated land with livestock

Forest area

Steppe land with nomadic herding

Desert and steppe lands with some
nomadic herding

■ DAMASCUS

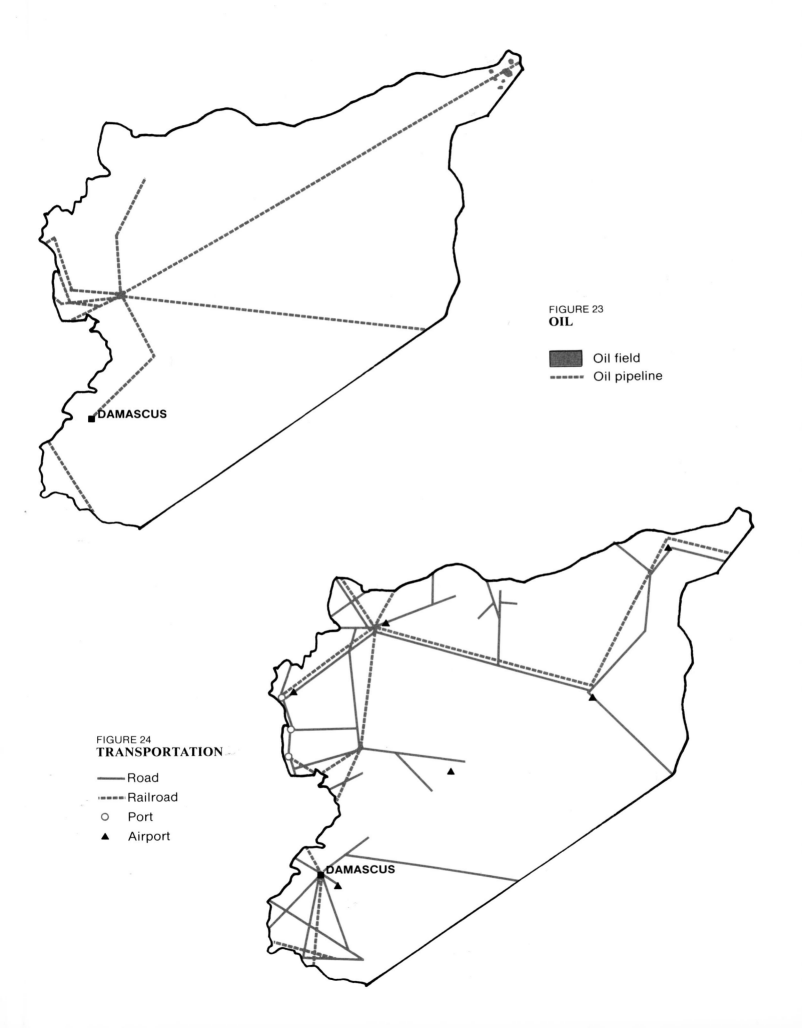

FIGURE 23
OIL

Oil field
Oil pipeline

FIGURE 24
TRANSPORTATION

Road
Railroad
○ Port
▲ Airport

DAMASCUS

DAMASCUS

TANZANIA

Located in East Africa, Tanzania ranks 28th in land area and 38th in population. It has known only one president since independence and his philosophy has guided its economic and political development. The basic principles of this ideology were set forth in the 1967 Arusha Declaration and are embodied in the concept known as *ujamaa* (Swahili for familyhood), expounded in President Nyerere's *Socialism and Rural Development*. *Ujamaa* is a practical form of rural organization in which the communal village (*ujamaa vijijini*) is the basic unit of development planning. The post-Arusha development strategy of egalitarianism, self-reliance and social transformation has borne some fruits; yet Tanzania remains one of the world's poorest countries, with nearly 30% of the GDP derived from subsistence activities. During the latter half of the 1970s, the country experienced severe economic distress—principally caused by its war against Idi Amin, estimated to have cost it $500 million—and survived only through foreign aid.

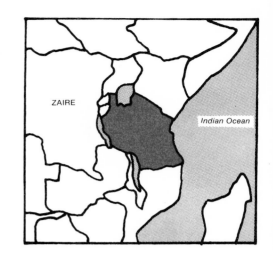

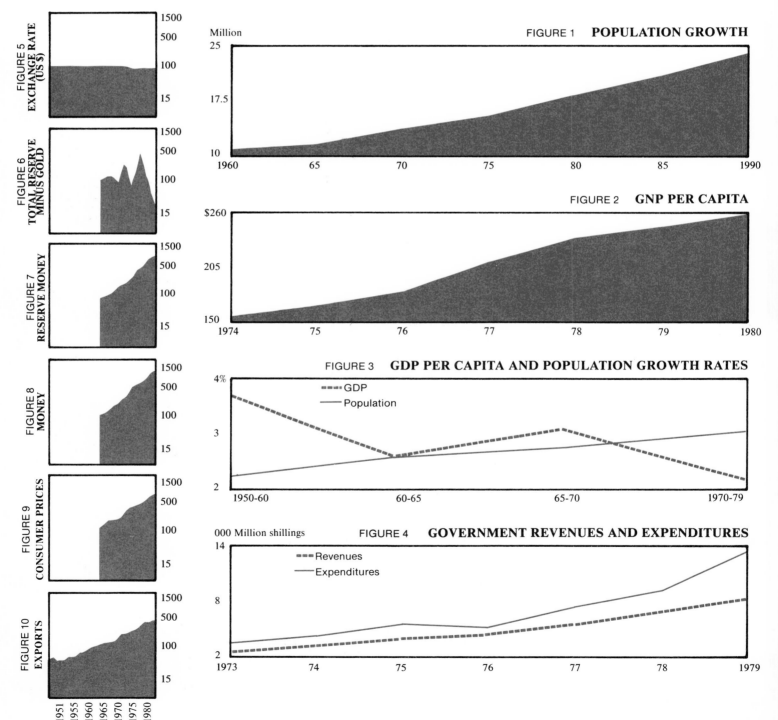

FIGURE 5 EXCHANGE RATE (US $)

FIGURE 6 TOTAL RESERVE MINUS GOLD

FIGURE 7 RESERVE MONEY

FIGURE 8 MONEY

FIGURE 9 CONSUMER PRICES

FIGURE 10 EXPORTS

FIGURE 1 **POPULATION GROWTH**

FIGURE 2 **GNP PER CAPITA**

FIGURE 3 **GDP PER CAPITA AND POPULATION GROWTH RATES**

FIGURE 4 **GOVERNMENT REVENUES AND EXPENDITURES**

FIGURE 11
LAND USE

Cultivated
Grassland
Brush & forest
Inland water

FIGURE 12
LABOR FORCE

Agriculture
Industry
Services

FIGURE 13
BUDGET EXPENDITURES

Defense
Education
Agriculture
other

FIGURE 14
IMPORTS

Food
Fuels
Machinery
other manufactured products
other

FIGURE 15
EXPORTS

Agriculture
Fuels & minerals
Manufactured products

FIGURE 16
GDP BY ECONOMIC ACTIVITY

Agriculture
Manufacturing
Trade & finance
other

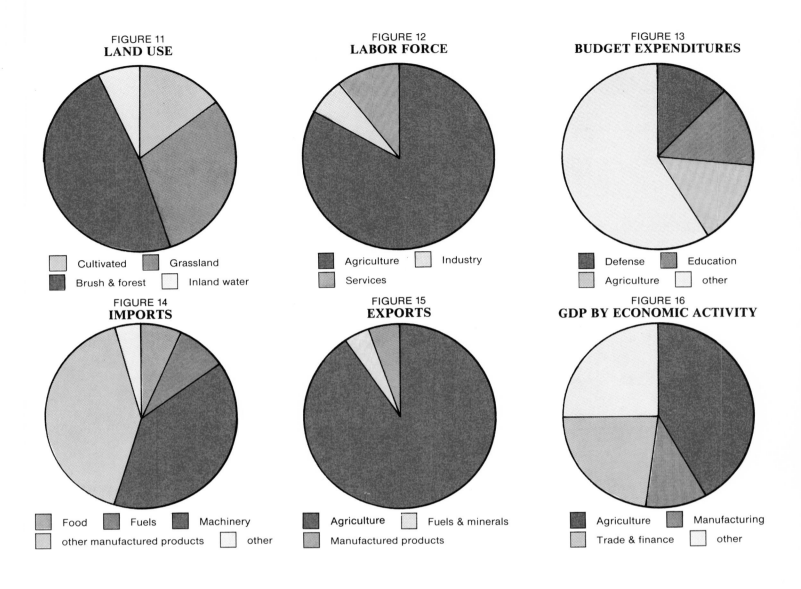

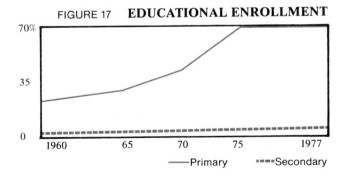

FIGURE 17 **EDUCATIONAL ENROLLMENT**

70%

35

0

1960   65   70   75   1977

——— Primary   ▪▪▪▪ Secondary

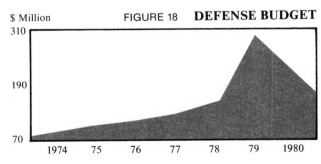

$ Million   FIGURE 18   **DEFENSE BUDGET**

310

190

70

1974   75   76   77   78   79   1980

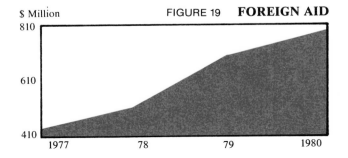

$ Million   FIGURE 19   **FOREIGN AID**

810

610

410

1977   78   79   1980

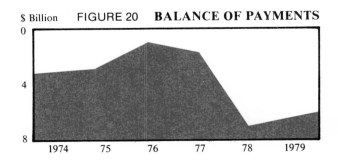

$ Billion   FIGURE 20   **BALANCE OF PAYMENTS**

0

4

8

1974   75   76   77   78   1979

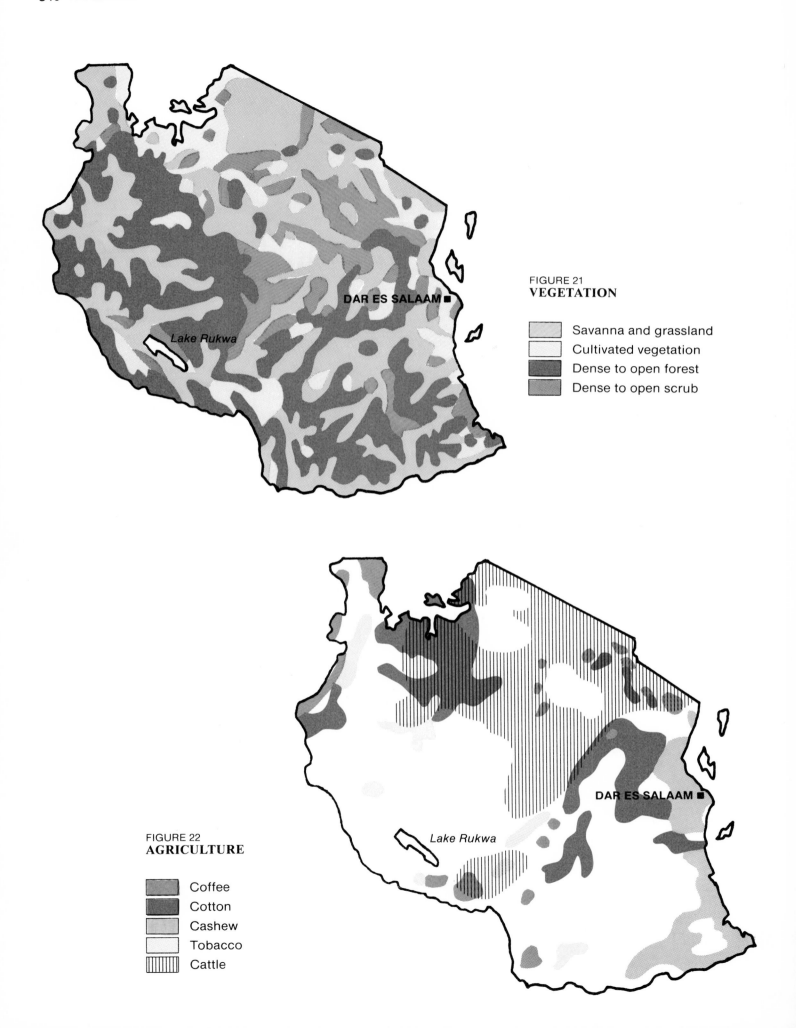

FIGURE 21
VEGETATION

Savanna and grassland
Cultivated vegetation
Dense to open forest
Dense to open scrub

DAR ES SALAAM ■

Lake Rukwa

FIGURE 22
AGRICULTURE

Coffee
Cotton
Cashew
Tobacco
Cattle

DAR ES SALAAM ■

Lake Rukwa

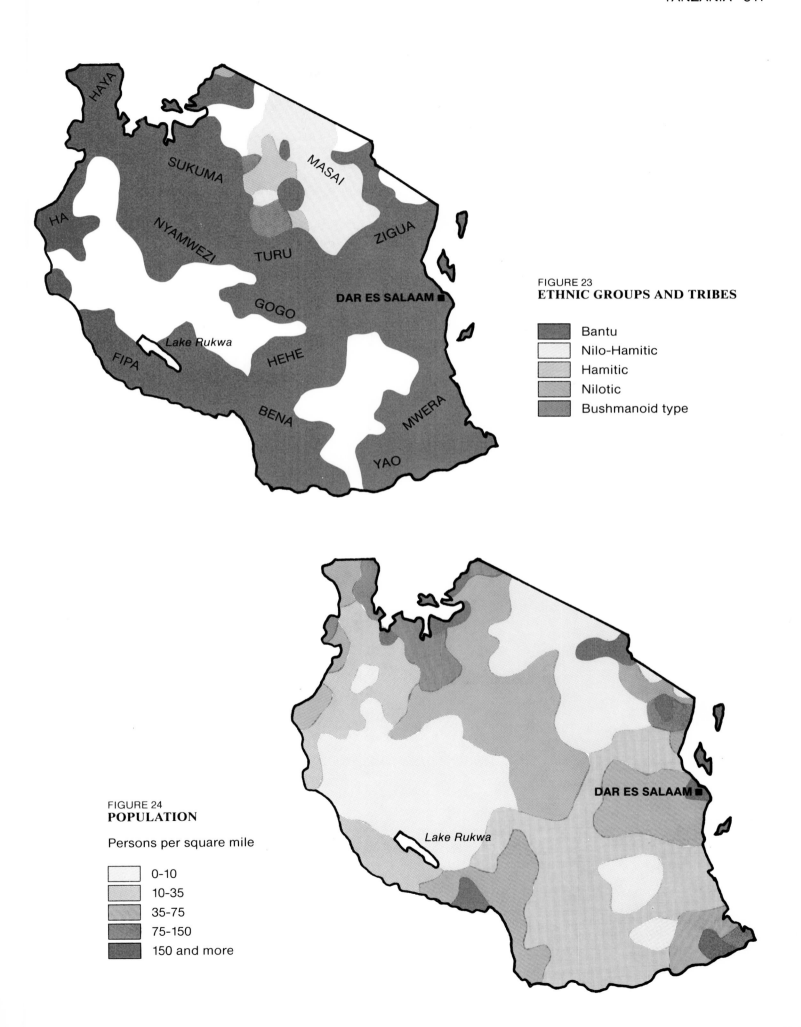

FIGURE 23
ETHNIC GROUPS AND TRIBES

- Bantu
- Nilo-Hamitic
- Hamitic
- Nilotic
- Bushmanoid type

FIGURE 24
POPULATION

Persons per square mile

- 0-10
- 10-35
- 35-75
- 75-150
- 150 and more

THAILAND

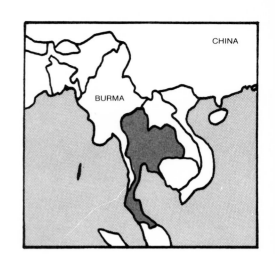

The world's largest Buddhist nation, Thailand ranks 45th in land area and 17th in population. An island of stability in a region ravaged by war and insurgency, Thailand emerged from the seventies with fewer economic scars than her neighbors. The challenges and threats were many and serious, including one of history's largest influxes of refugees and the withdrawal of U.S. military bases. Yet the character of the economy remained unchanged and economic crises never reached flash point. Agriculture employs 75% of the labor force and contributed 26% of the GDP. The country's conservative fiscal policies have helped it to earn a solid international credit rating. External debt remains a small percent of GDP and debt servicing constitutes less than 3% of the value of exported goods and services. Although the country is hospitable to foreign capital, there is considerable nationalist sentiment (expressed in periodic demonstrations) against Japanese domination of the market; over 500 Japanese firms are believed to have invested in Thailand from 1951 to 1978.

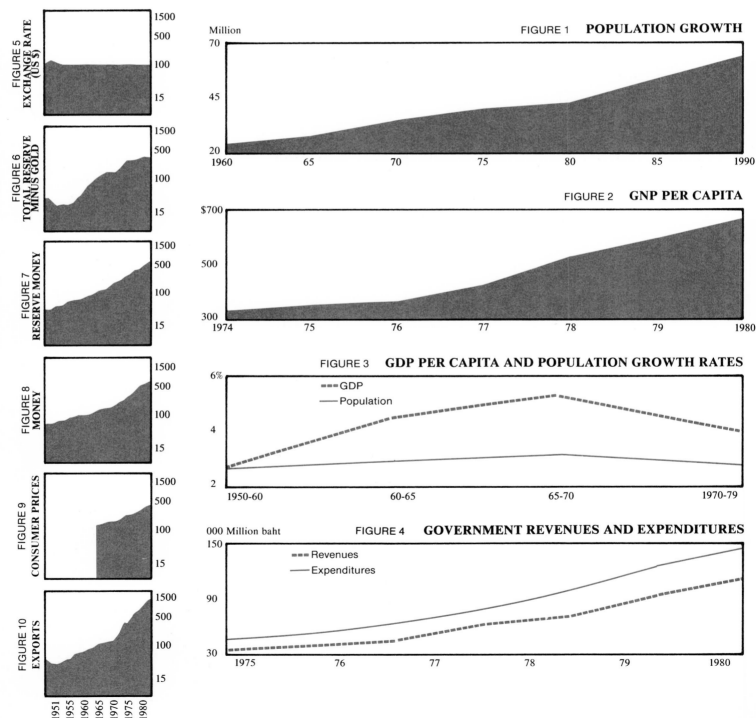

FIGURE 5 — EXCHANGE RATE (US $)

FIGURE 6 — TOTAL RESERVE MINUS GOLD

FIGURE 7 — RESERVE MONEY

FIGURE 8 — MONEY

FIGURE 9 — CONSUMER PRICES

FIGURE 10 — EXPORTS

FIGURE 1 **POPULATION GROWTH**

FIGURE 2 **GNP PER CAPITA**

FIGURE 3 **GDP PER CAPITA AND POPULATION GROWTH RATES**

FIGURE 4 **GOVERNMENT REVENUES AND EXPENDITURES**

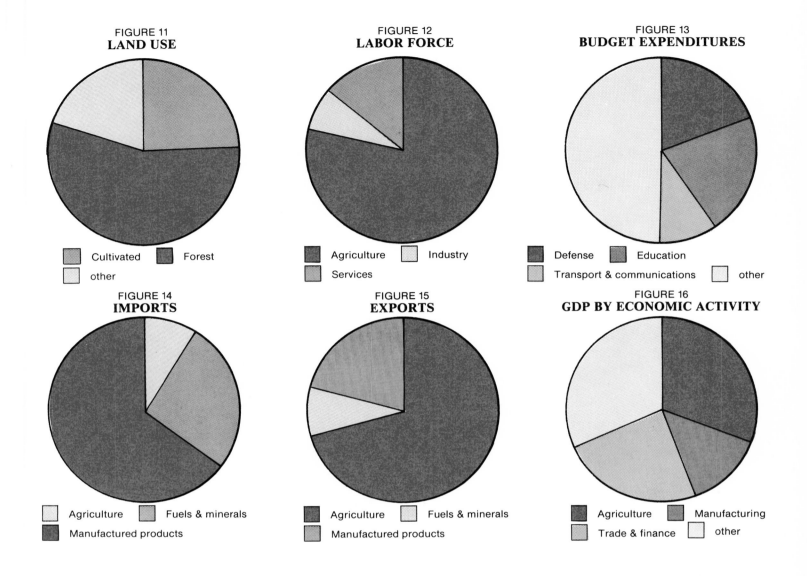

FIGURE 11
LAND USE

Cultivated Forest
other

FIGURE 12
LABOR FORCE

Agriculture Industry
Services

FIGURE 13
BUDGET EXPENDITURES

Defense Education
Transport & communications other

FIGURE 14
IMPORTS

Agriculture Fuels & minerals
Manufactured products

FIGURE 15
EXPORTS

Agriculture Fuels & minerals
Manufactured products

FIGURE 16
GDP BY ECONOMIC ACTIVITY

Agriculture Manufacturing
Trade & finance other

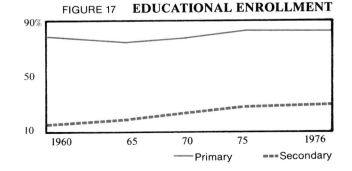

FIGURE 17 **EDUCATIONAL ENROLLMENT**

90%

50

10

1960   65   70   75   1976

——Primary ===Secondary

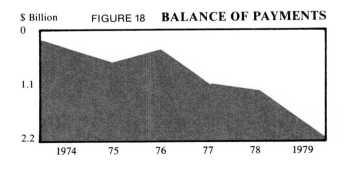

$ Billion FIGURE 18 **BALANCE OF PAYMENTS**

0

1.1

2.2

1974   75   76   77   78   1979

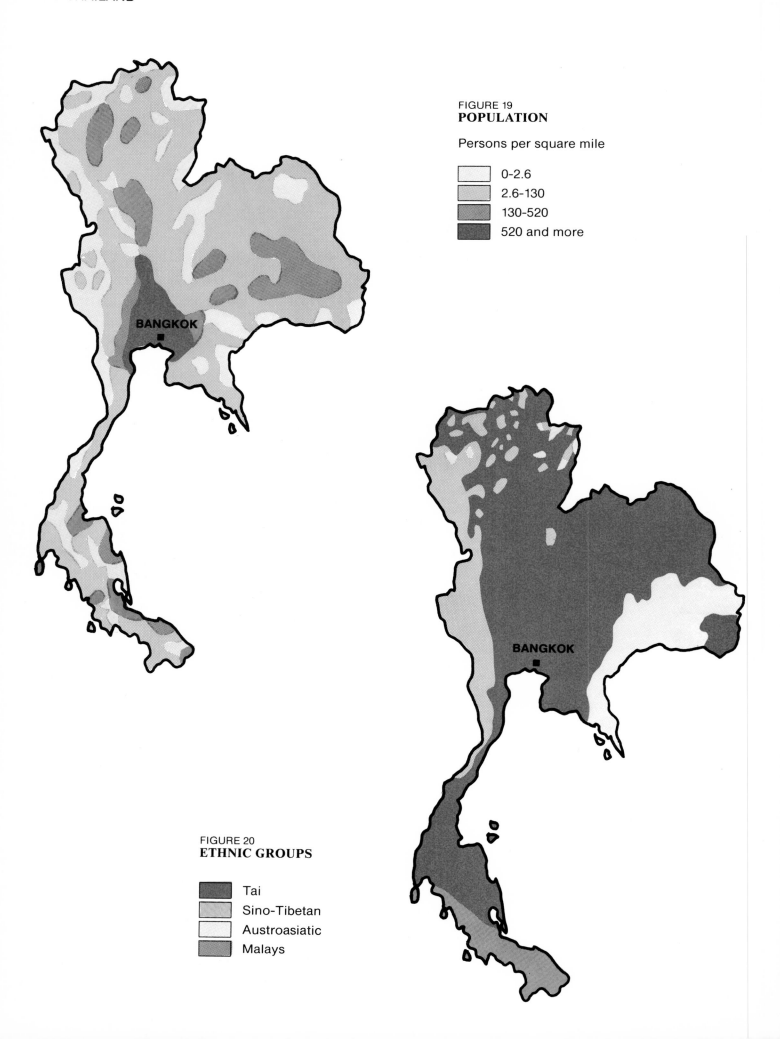

FIGURE 19
POPULATION

Persons per square mile

0-2.6
2.6-130
130-520
520 and more

FIGURE 20
ETHNIC GROUPS

Tai
Sino-Tibetan
Austroasiatic
Malays

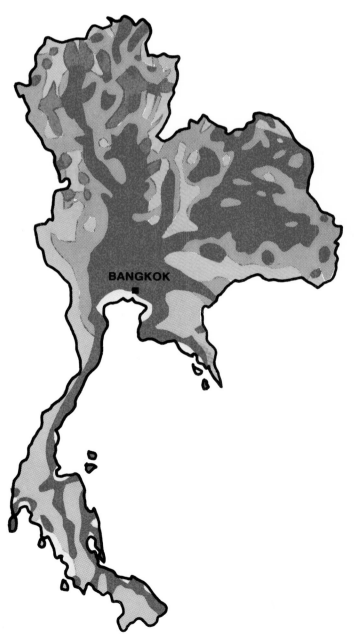

FIGURE 21
ECONOMIC ACTIVITY

Agricultural area (mainly rice)
Rubber
Teak
Fishing

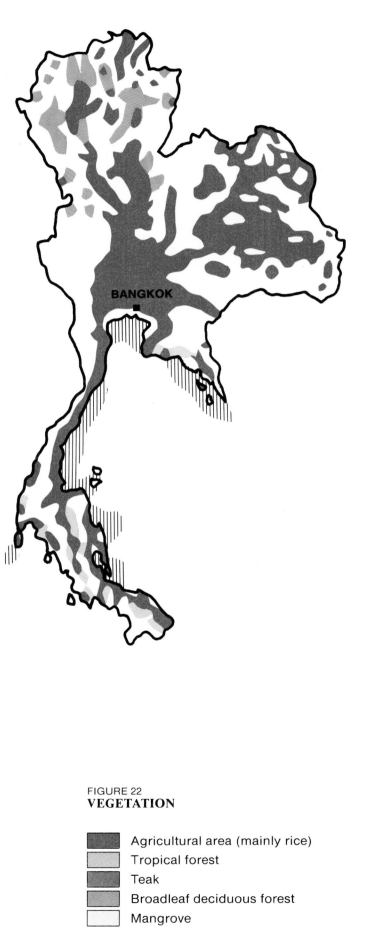

FIGURE 22
VEGETATION

Agricultural area (mainly rice)
Tropical forest
Teak
Broadleaf deciduous forest
Mangrove

TUNISIA

Located on the eastern end of the Maghrebian littoral, Tunisia ranks 85th in land area and 77th in population. Like Tanzania, Guinea and other countries, Tunisia has known only one president since independence, and his personality and that of his country are inextricably related. After a long spell of indifferent economic performance, the country began to rally in the mid 1970s and the annual growth rate of per capita GNP rose to 5.7% through the seventies. The key factor in this turnaround was the abandonment of the socialist programs of earlier years and the move toward a mixed economy with adequate incentives for private investment. Pari passu, the relative share of agriculture in the GDP fell from 24% in 1961 to 18% in 1978 while that of industry rose to 30% from 18%. The discovery of petroleum in 1964 has also helped to spur the economy and cushion it against erratic performance in other sectors. Production is dominated by foreign companies, with the state being only a limited participant.

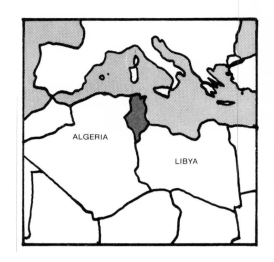

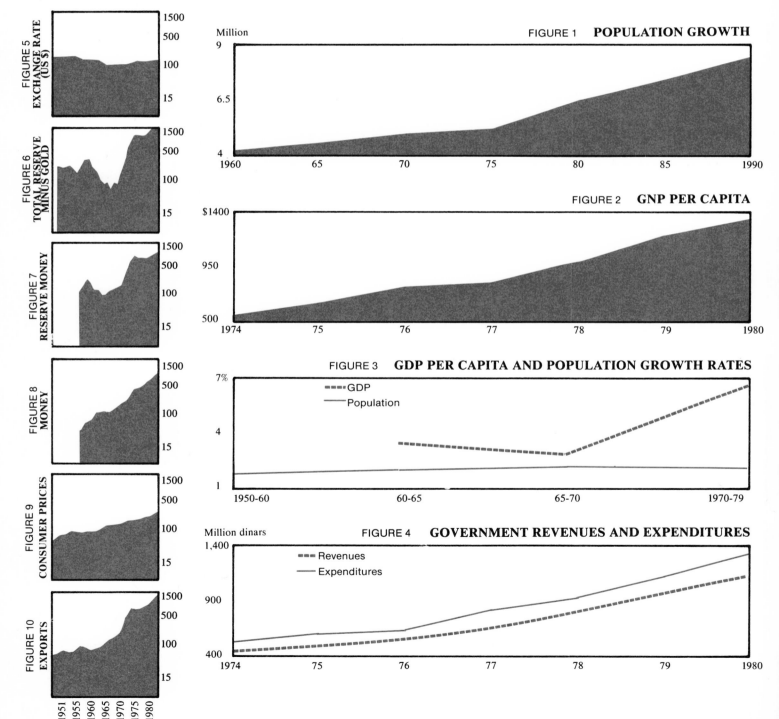

FIGURE 5 EXCHANGE RATE (US $)

FIGURE 6 TOTAL RESERVE MINUS GOLD

FIGURE 7 RESERVE MONEY

FIGURE 8 MONEY

FIGURE 9 CONSUMER PRICES

FIGURE 10 EXPORTS

FIGURE 1 **POPULATION GROWTH**

FIGURE 2 **GNP PER CAPITA**

FIGURE 3 **GDP PER CAPITA AND POPULATION GROWTH RATES**

FIGURE 4 **GOVERNMENT REVENUES AND EXPENDITURES**

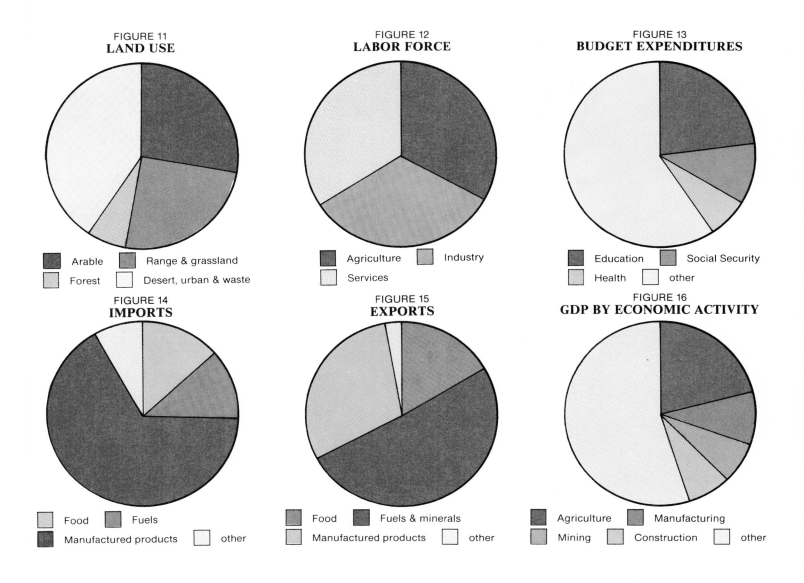

FIGURE 11
LAND USE

Arable   Range & grassland
Forest   Desert, urban & waste

FIGURE 12
LABOR FORCE

Agriculture   Industry
Services

FIGURE 13
BUDGET EXPENDITURES

Education   Social Security
Health   other

FIGURE 14
IMPORTS

Food   Fuels
Manufactured products   other

FIGURE 15
EXPORTS

Food   Fuels & minerals
Manufactured products   other

FIGURE 16
GDP BY ECONOMIC ACTIVITY

Agriculture   Manufacturing
Mining   Construction   other

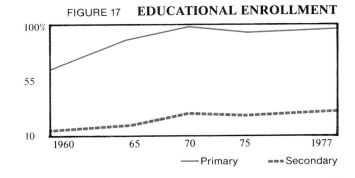

FIGURE 17   **EDUCATIONAL ENROLLMENT**

100%
55
10
1960   65   70   75   1977

——Primary   ===Secondary

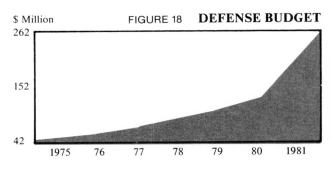

$ Million   FIGURE 18   **DEFENSE BUDGET**

262
152
42
1975   76   77   78   79   80   1981

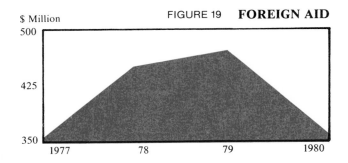

$ Million   FIGURE 19   **FOREIGN AID**

500
425
350
1977   78   79   1980

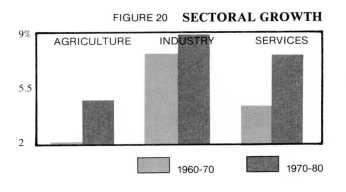

FIGURE 20   **SECTORAL GROWTH**

9%   AGRICULTURE   INDUSTRY   SERVICES
5.5
2

1960-70   1970-80

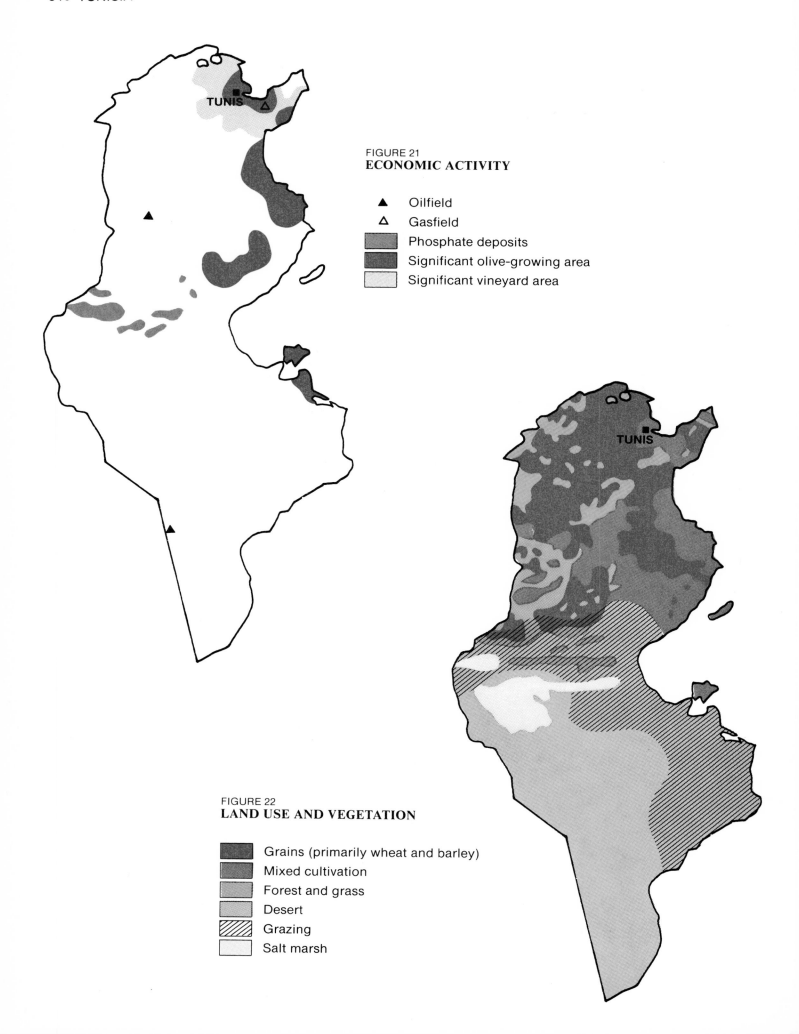

FIGURE 21
ECONOMIC ACTIVITY

▲ Oilfield
△ Gasfield
Phosphate deposits
Significant olive-growing area
Significant vineyard area

FIGURE 22
LAND USE AND VEGETATION

Grains (primarily wheat and barley)
Mixed cultivation
Forest and grass
Desert
Grazing
Salt marsh

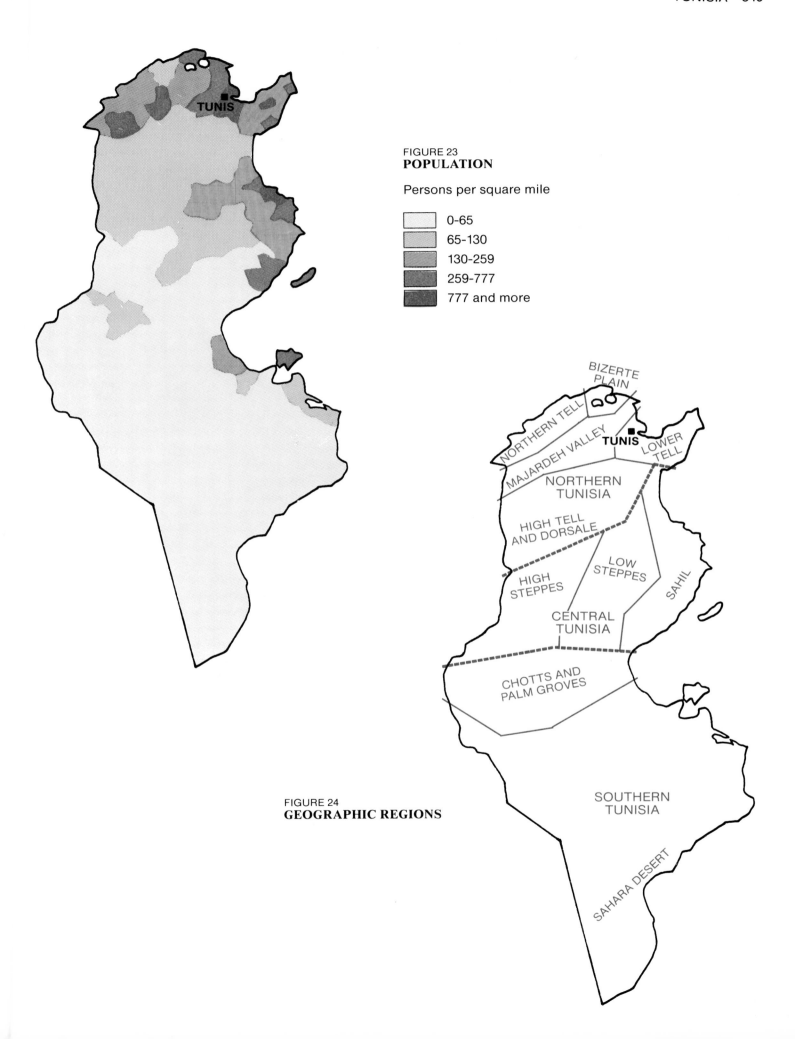

FIGURE 23
POPULATION

Persons per square mile

- 0-65
- 65-130
- 130-259
- 259-777
- 777 and more

FIGURE 24
GEOGRAPHIC REGIONS

BIZERTE PLAIN

NORTHERN TELL

MAJARDEH VALLEY

TUNIS

LOWER TELL

NORTHERN TUNISIA

HIGH TELL AND DORSALE

LOW STEPPES

SAHIL

HIGH STEPPES

CENTRAL TUNISIA

CHOTTS AND PALM GROVES

SOUTHERN TUNISIA

SAHARA DESERT

TURKEY

Straddling Europe and Asia, Turkey ranks 34th in land area and 19th in population. Still the "sick man of Europe," Turkey does not fall into neat political, social or cultural categories; it is neither European nor Asian, neither democratic nor authoritarian, neither modernized and secular nor medieval and sectarian. This anomaly extends to the economy: its population growth rate is typically Asian, 2.5% during the late 1970s, its per capita income is lower than that of any European country, and in indicators of modernization, it ranks in the middle of developing countries. Yet the government is committed to bring Turkey into the European Community and to pursue full membership, which it is likely to obtain by 1995. Political instability has made it difficult to formulate and sustain a coherent economic strategy over a sufficiently long period of time. The country continues to depend on worker remittances from Europe (generally over $1 billion every year) to meet the balance of payments deficits.

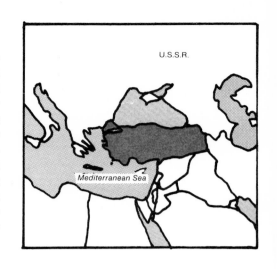

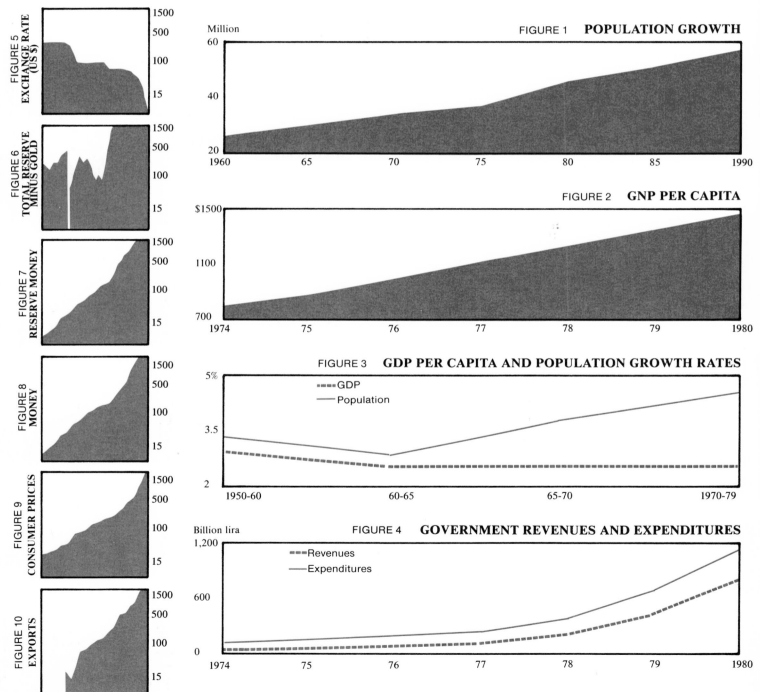

FIGURE 5 EXCHANGE RATE (US $)

FIGURE 6 TOTAL RESERVE MINUS GOLD

FIGURE 7 RESERVE MONEY

FIGURE 8 MONEY

FIGURE 9 CONSUMER PRICES

FIGURE 10 EXPORTS

FIGURE 1 **POPULATION GROWTH**

FIGURE 2 **GNP PER CAPITA**

FIGURE 3 **GDP PER CAPITA AND POPULATION GROWTH RATES**

FIGURE 4 **GOVERNMENT REVENUES AND EXPENDITURES**

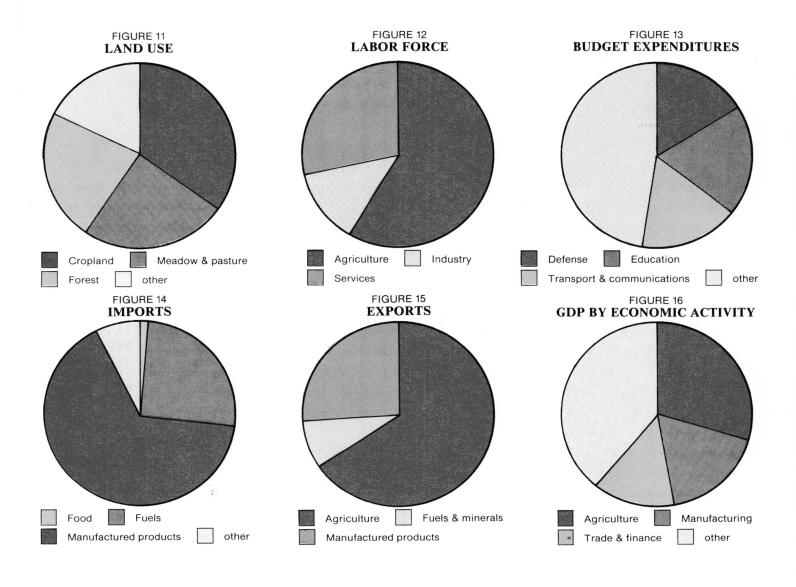

FIGURE 11
LAND USE

- Cropland
- Meadow & pasture
- Forest
- other

FIGURE 12
LABOR FORCE

- Agriculture
- Industry
- Services

FIGURE 13
BUDGET EXPENDITURES

- Defense
- Education
- Transport & communications
- other

FIGURE 14
IMPORTS

- Food
- Fuels
- Manufactured products
- other

FIGURE 15
EXPORTS

- Agriculture
- Fuels & minerals
- Manufactured products

FIGURE 16
GDP BY ECONOMIC ACTIVITY

- Agriculture
- Manufacturing
- Trade & finance
- other

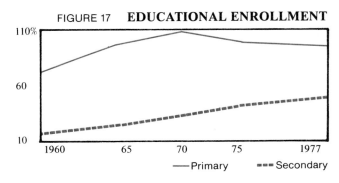

FIGURE 17 **EDUCATIONAL ENROLLMENT**

— Primary --- Secondary

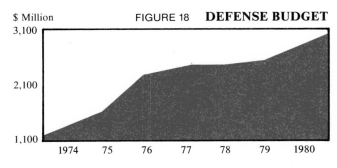

$ Million   FIGURE 18 **DEFENSE BUDGET**

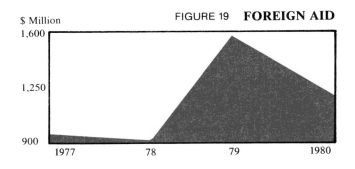

$ Million   FIGURE 19 **FOREIGN AID**

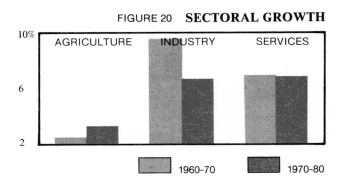

FIGURE 20 **SECTORAL GROWTH**

AGRICULTURE   INDUSTRY   SERVICES

1960-70   1970-80

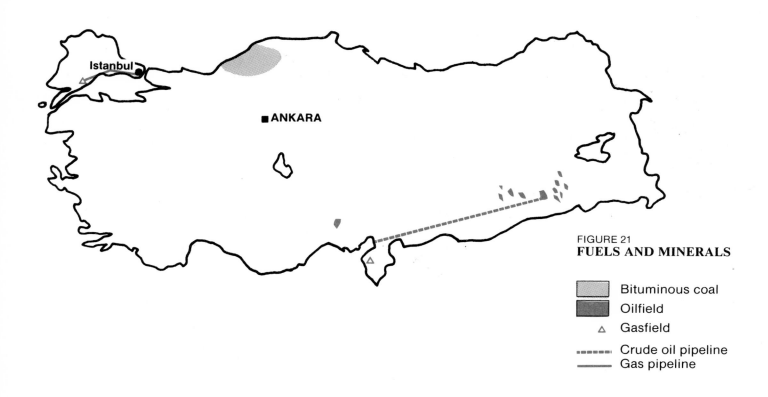

FIGURE 21
FUELS AND MINERALS

▨ Bituminous coal

▨ Oilfield

△ Gasfield

┅┅┅ Crude oil pipeline
─── Gas pipeline

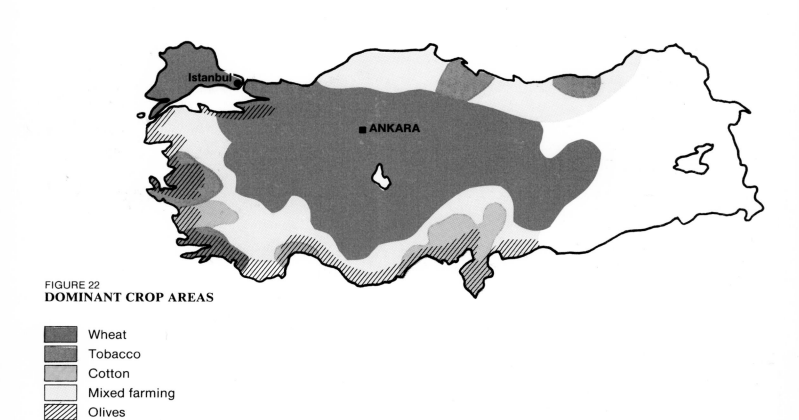

FIGURE 22
DOMINANT CROP AREAS

▨ Wheat

▨ Tobacco

▨ Cotton

▢ Mixed farming

▨ Olives

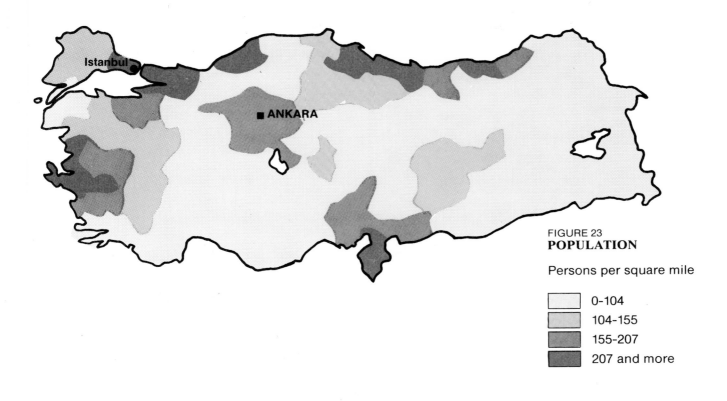

FIGURE 23
POPULATION

Persons per square mile

0-104
104-155
155-207
207 and more

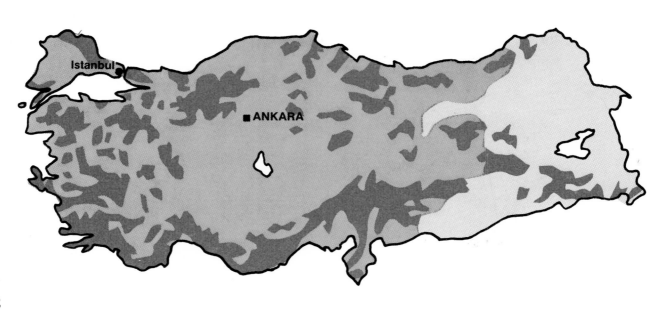

FIGURE 24
LAND USE

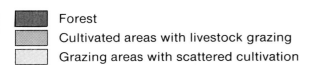

Forest
Cultivated areas with livestock grazing
Grazing areas with scattered cultivation

UGANDA

A landlocked nation in central Africa, Uganda ranks 74th in land area and 51st in population. Still recovering from the locust years of Idi Amin's rule, Uganda has found the process of rebuilding to be slow and frustrating, often one step forward and two steps back. Not merely is the cost of rebuilding, estimated at over $3 billion, beyond its reach, but political unrest and outbreaks of criminal violence continue to disrupt even existing economic activities. Although many of the foreign and Asian enterprises confiscated by Idi Amin have been restored to their former owners, there is little prospect of substantial private investment in the country. During 1979-80, Uganda regained its position as the third largest coffee grower and fifth largest cottonseed producer, although problems of transit through Kenyan territory made export of these commodities difficult.

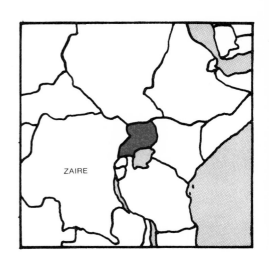

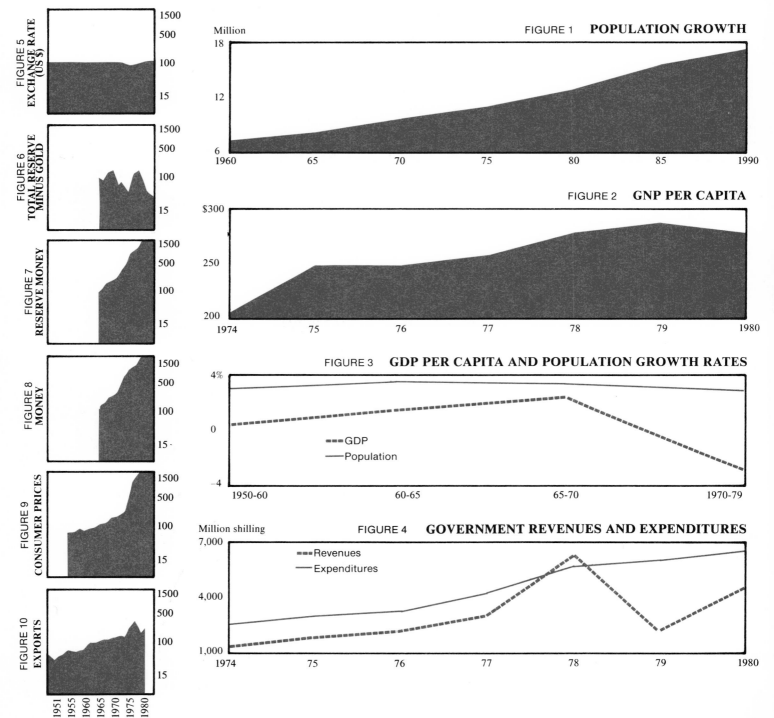

FIGURE 5 EXCHANGE RATE (US $)

FIGURE 6 TOTAL RESERVE MINUS GOLD

FIGURE 7 RESERVE MONEY

FIGURE 8 MONEY

FIGURE 9 CONSUMER PRICES

FIGURE 10 EXPORTS

FIGURE 1 **POPULATION GROWTH**

FIGURE 2 **GNP PER CAPITA**

FIGURE 3 **GDP PER CAPITA AND POPULATION GROWTH RATES**

FIGURE 4 **GOVERNMENT REVENUES AND EXPENDITURES**

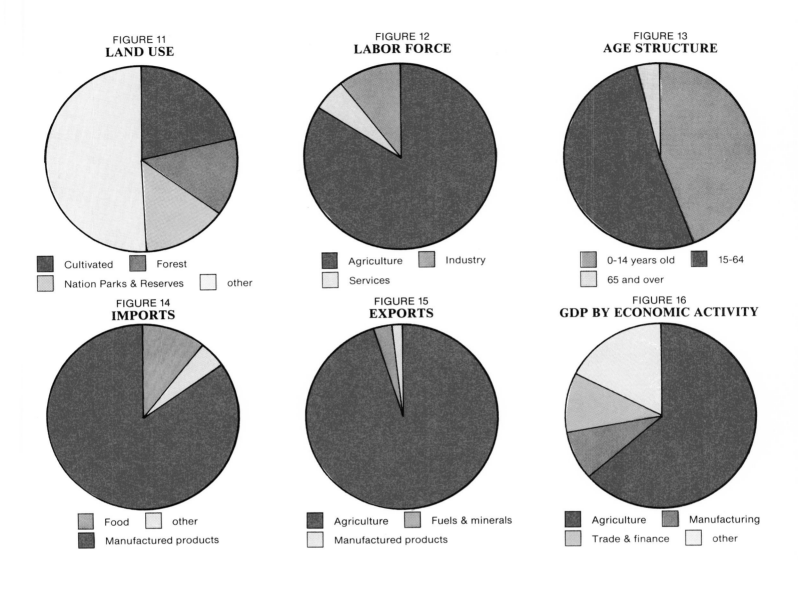

FIGURE 11
LAND USE

■ Cultivated ■ Forest
■ Nation Parks & Reserves □ other

FIGURE 12
LABOR FORCE

■ Agriculture ■ Industry
□ Services

FIGURE 13
AGE STRUCTURE

■ 0-14 years old ■ 15-64
□ 65 and over

FIGURE 14
IMPORTS

■ Food □ other
■ Manufactured products

FIGURE 15
EXPORTS

■ Agriculture ■ Fuels & minerals
□ Manufactured products

FIGURE 16
GDP BY ECONOMIC ACTIVITY

■ Agriculture ■ Manufacturing
■ Trade & finance □ other

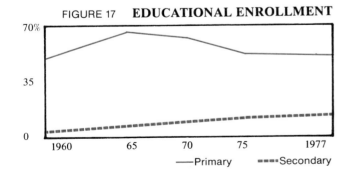

FIGURE 17 **EDUCATIONAL ENROLLMENT**

——Primary ■■■■Secondary

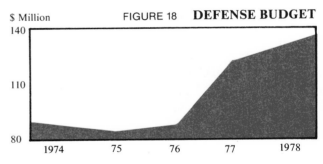

$ Million FIGURE 18 **DEFENSE BUDGET**

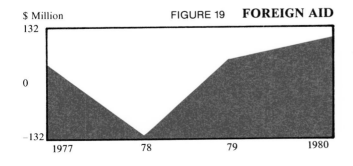

$ Million FIGURE 19 **FOREIGN AID**

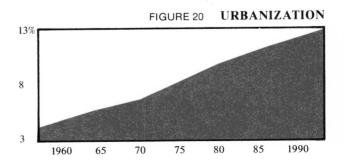

FIGURE 20 **URBANIZATION**

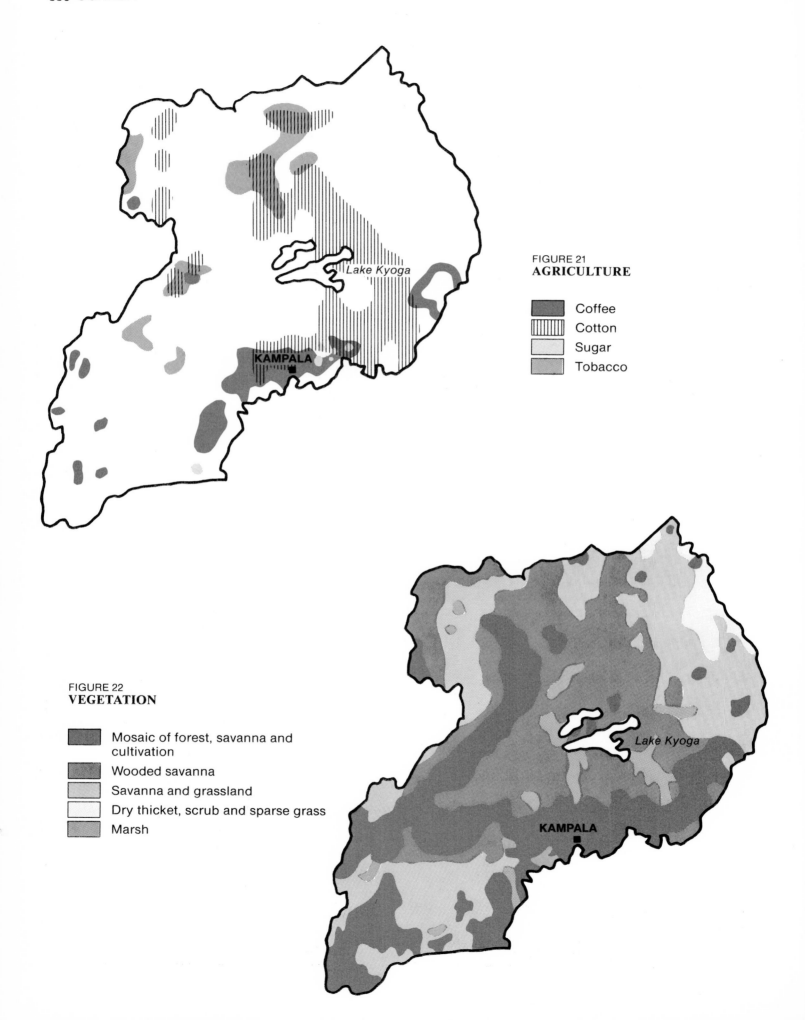

FIGURE 21
AGRICULTURE

Coffee
Cotton
Sugar
Tobacco

Lake Kyoga

KAMPALA

FIGURE 22
VEGETATION

Mosaic of forest, savanna and cultivation
Wooded savanna
Savanna and grassland
Dry thicket, scrub and sparse grass
Marsh

Lake Kyoga

KAMPALA

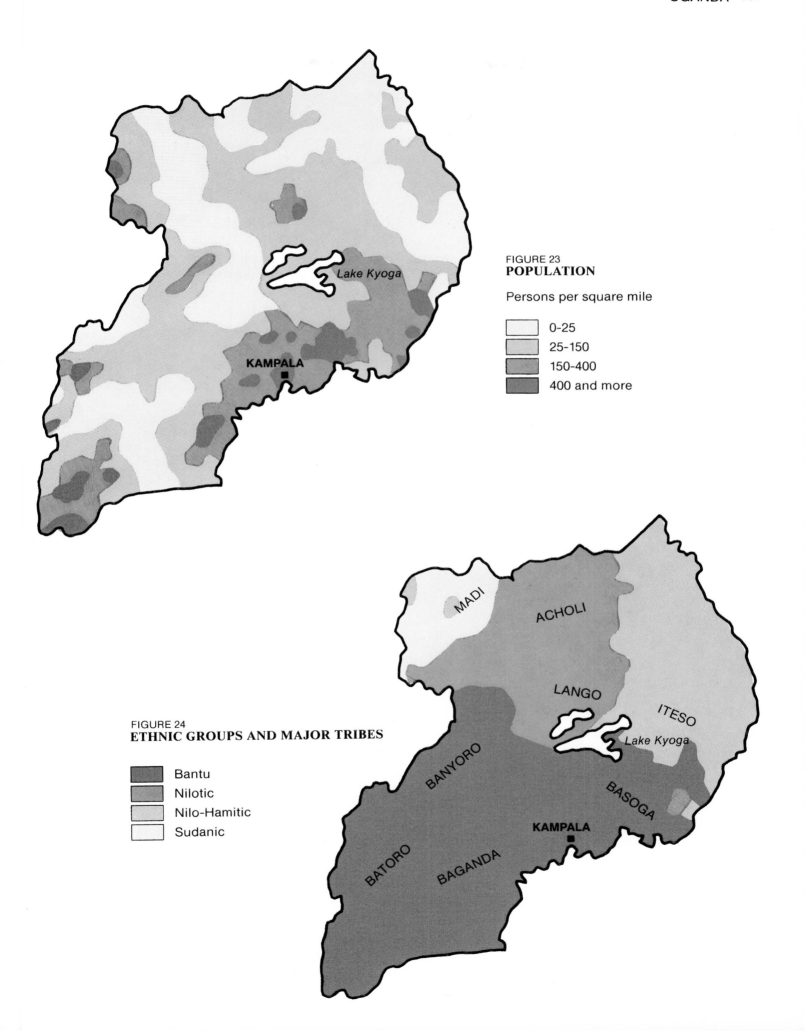

FIGURE 23
POPULATION

Persons per square mile

- 0-25
- 25-150
- 150-400
- 400 and more

Lake Kyoga

KAMPALA

FIGURE 24
ETHNIC GROUPS AND MAJOR TRIBES

- Bantu
- Nilotic
- Nilo-Hamitic
- Sudanic

MADI

ACHOLI

LANGO

ITESO

Lake Kyoga

BANYORO

BASOGA

BATORO

BAGANDA

KAMPALA

UPPER VOLTA

A landlocked country in West Africa, Upper Volta ranks 64th in land area and 75th in population. With a per capita GNP of $190, Upper Volta is classified as among the least developed of the low-income countries. Over 75% of the population subsists in absolute poverty. Agricultural production has not yet completely recovered from the 1968-74 drought that decimated the livestock and laid waste most areas of the country. Even the limited mineral resources that the country possesses, mostly gold deposits at Poura, manganese deposits at Tambao, and lesser deposits of vanadium, nickel, lead, zinc and bauxite, cannot be properly exploited for lack of transportation facilities. Manufacturing is rudimentary, and is concentrated in urban centers along the Abidjan-Niger railway. The country is a prime target for developmental aid, especially from France and the World Bank.

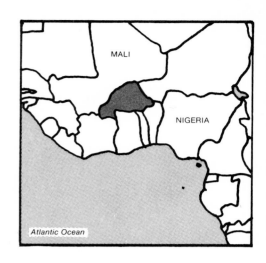

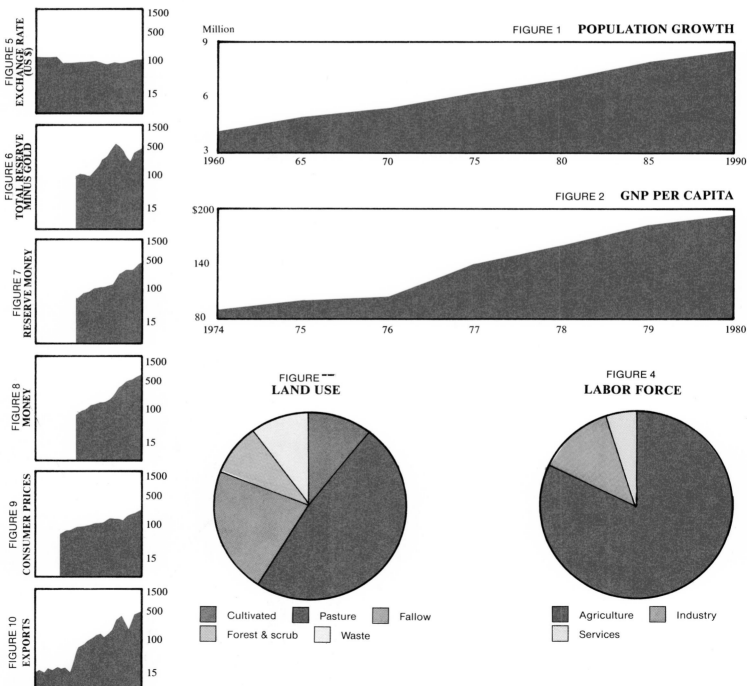

FIGURE 5 EXCHANGE RATE (US $)

FIGURE 6 TOTAL RESERVE MINUS GOLD

FIGURE 7 RESERVE MONEY

FIGURE 8 MONEY

FIGURE 9 CONSUMER PRICES

FIGURE 10 EXPORTS

FIGURE 1 **POPULATION GROWTH**

FIGURE 2 **GNP PER CAPITA**

FIGURE 3
LAND USE

Cultivated
Pasture
Fallow
Forest & scrub
Waste

FIGURE 4
LABOR FORCE

Agriculture
Industry
Services

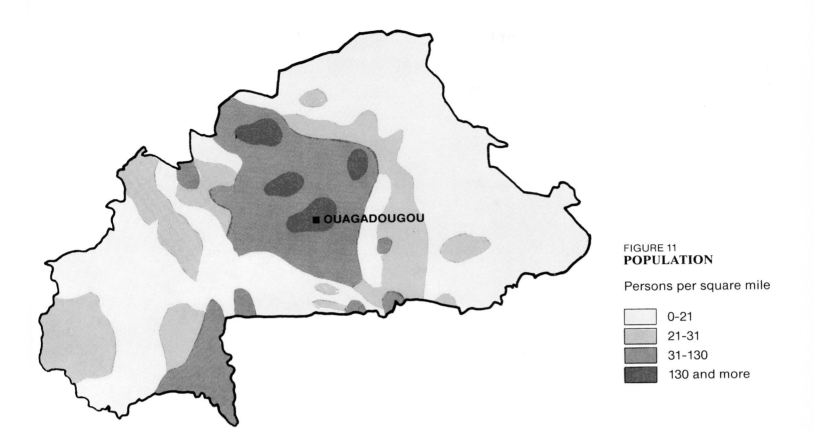

FIGURE 11
POPULATION

Persons per square mile

- 0-21
- 21-31
- 31-130
- 130 and more

■ OUAGADOUGOU

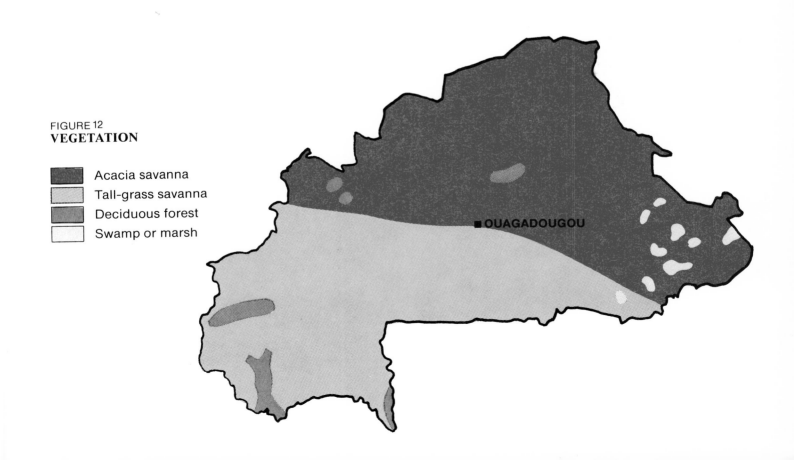

FIGURE 12
VEGETATION

- Acacia savanna
- Tall-grass savanna
- Deciduous forest
- Swamp or marsh

■ OUAGADOUGOU

URUGUAY

The second smallest independent country in South America, Uruguay ranks 82nd in land area and 107th in population. Hard hit by the fourth highest rate of inflation, its per capita GNP has been declining by 0.3% annually, and it ranks third in all three gauges of inflation: the wholesale price index, the consumer price index and the rent index. Uruguay's richest resource is its livestock, raised on 70% of its agricultural land, and it ranks high in all indicators related to livestock. The country is expected to be a net exporter of electricity by 1984 when the Salto Grande venture on the Rio Uruguay with an installed capacity of 1,980 megawatts and the Palma Power plant on the Rio Negro with an installed capacity of 300 megawatts go on stream. Meanwhile, the rising costs of the country's extensive domestic social programs and the declining market for agricultural exports have placed its economy in a double bind and might produce the kind of social unrest that led to military intervention over a decade ago.

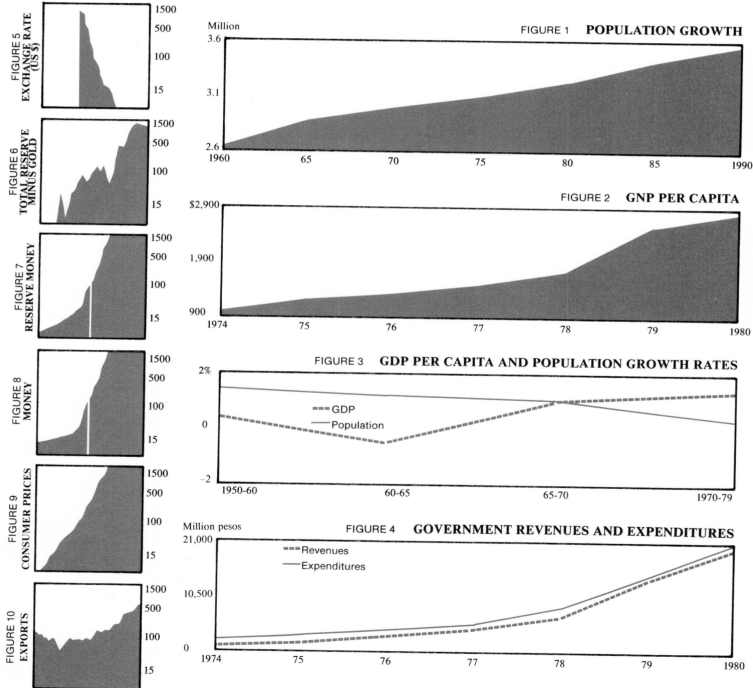

FIGURE 5 EXCHANGE RATE (US $)

FIGURE 6 TOTAL RESERVE MINUS GOLD

FIGURE 7 RESERVE MONEY

FIGURE 8 MONEY

FIGURE 9 CONSUMER PRICES

FIGURE 10 EXPORTS

FIGURE 1 **POPULATION GROWTH**

FIGURE 2 **GNP PER CAPITA**

FIGURE 3 **GDP PER CAPITA AND POPULATION GROWTH RATES**

FIGURE 4 **GOVERNMENT REVENUES AND EXPENDITURES**

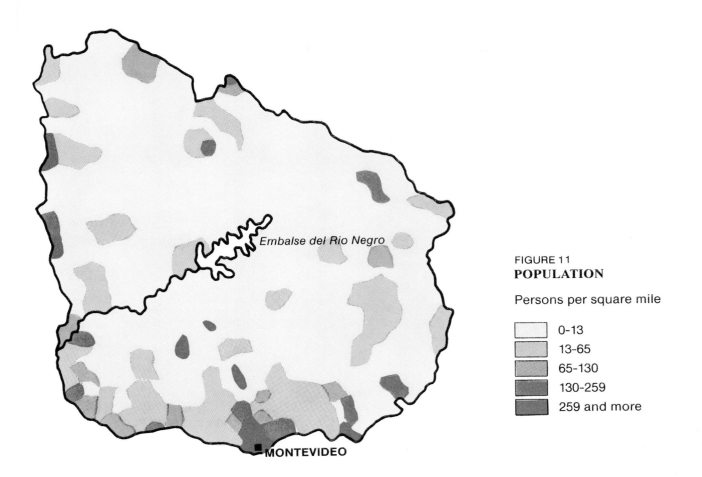

Embalse del Rio Negro

MONTEVIDEO

FIGURE 11
POPULATION

Persons per square mile

0-13
13-65
65-130
130-259
259 and more

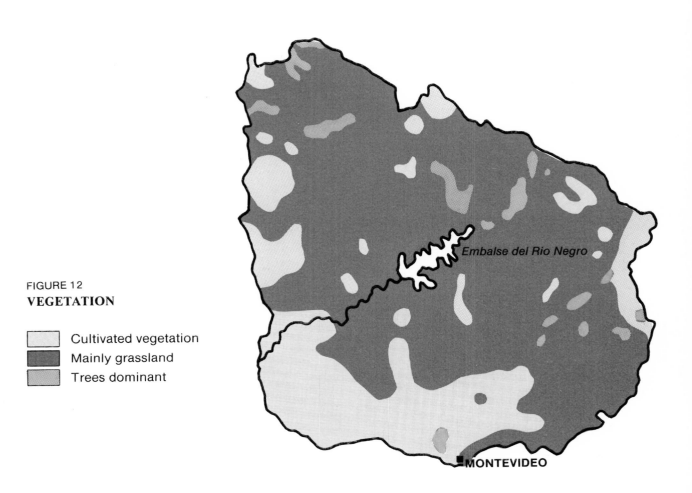

Embalse del Rio Negro

MONTEVIDEO

FIGURE 12
VEGETATION

Cultivated vegetation
Mainly grassland
Trees dominant

VENEZUELA

The country with the highest per capita GNP in Latin America, Venezuela ranks 30th in land area and 48th in population. It is one of the world's major oil-producing and oil-exporting nations, ranking sixth in production and third in exports. Petroleum accounts for nearly one-third of GDP, two-thirds of government revenues, and over 90% of export earnings. Proven reserves are currently estimated at 18 billion barrels of crude, in addition to 42 billion cubic feet of natural gas. Venezuela is also a major producer of iron ore and bauxite. Over 60% of the economy remains in private hands and this proportion is not likely to change dramatically in the future. Despite substantial oil revenues, Venezuela has above average foreign indebtedness, estimated at over $12 billion. Debt service is an unusually high 9.4% and constitutes 16% of exports. The government is gambling on exploiting the heavy oil belt complex at Orinoco, a project estimated to cost $8 billion. The future of Venezuela's economy will hinge on the success of this project.

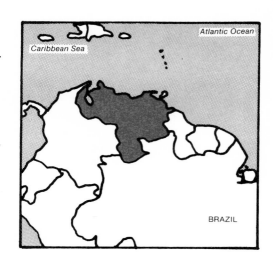

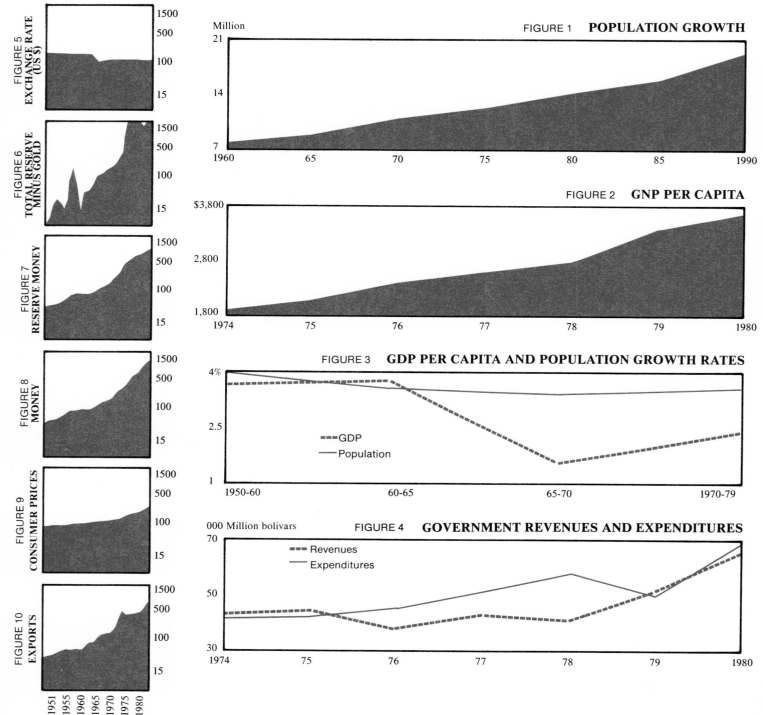

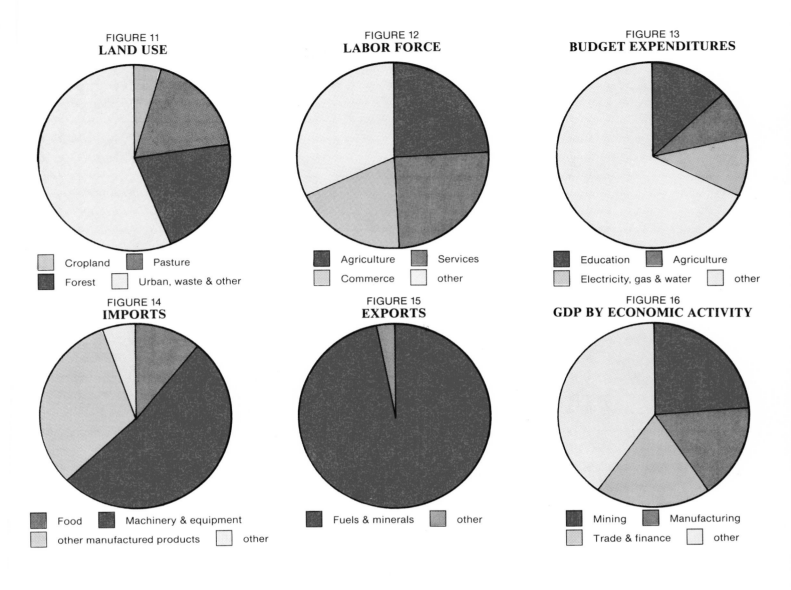

FIGURE 11
LAND USE

- Cropland
- Pasture
- Forest
- Urban, waste & other

FIGURE 12
LABOR FORCE

- Agriculture
- Services
- Commerce
- other

FIGURE 13
BUDGET EXPENDITURES

- Education
- Agriculture
- Electricity, gas & water
- other

FIGURE 14
IMPORTS

- Food
- Machinery & equipment
- other manufactured products
- other

FIGURE 15
EXPORTS

- Fuels & minerals
- other

FIGURE 16
GDP BY ECONOMIC ACTIVITY

- Mining
- Manufacturing
- Trade & finance
- other

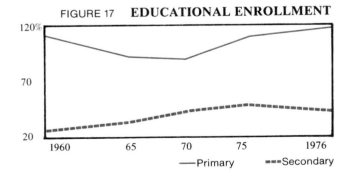

FIGURE 17 **EDUCATIONAL ENROLLMENT**

— Primary ▪▪▪Secondary

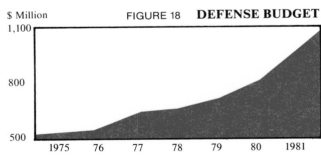

$ Million   FIGURE 18 **DEFENSE BUDGET**

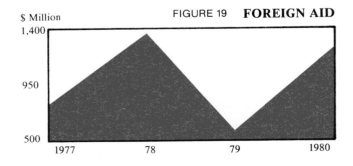

$ Million   FIGURE 19 **FOREIGN AID**

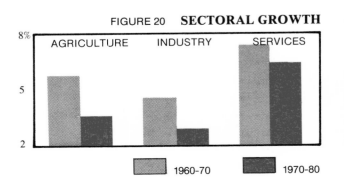

FIGURE 20 **SECTORAL GROWTH**

AGRICULTURE   INDUSTRY   SERVICES

- 1960-70
- 1970-80

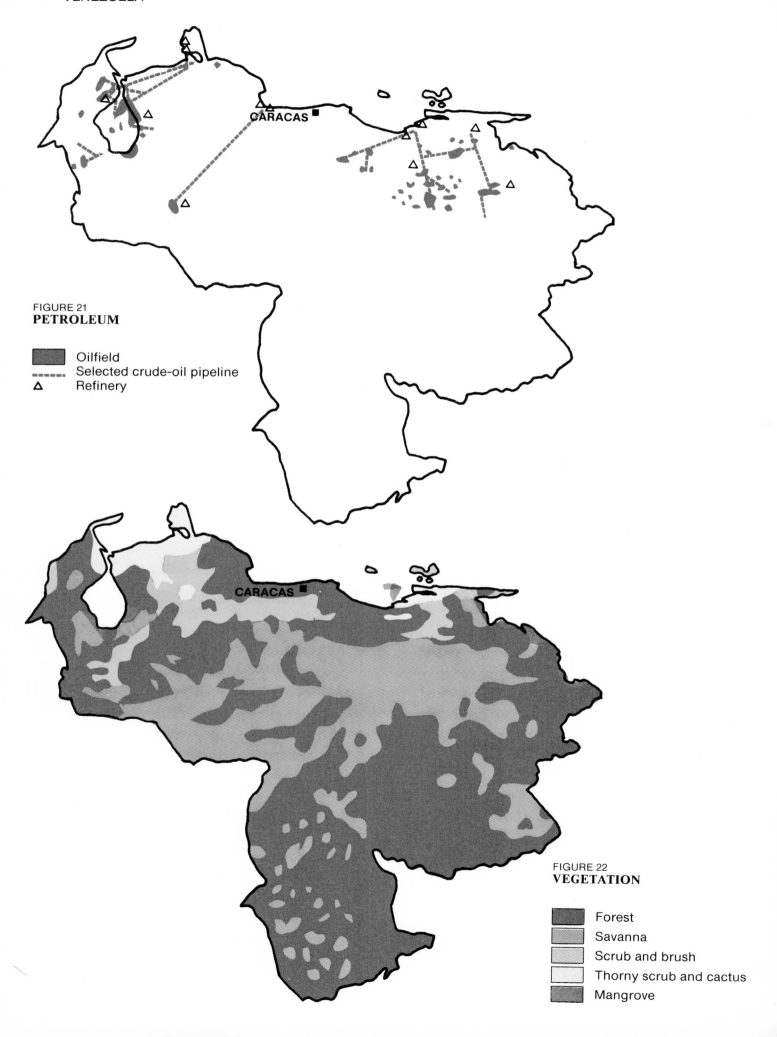

FIGURE 21
PETROLEUM

Oilfield
Selected crude-oil pipeline
△ Refinery

CARACAS ■

FIGURE 22
VEGETATION

Forest
Savanna
Scrub and brush
Thorny scrub and cactus
Mangrove

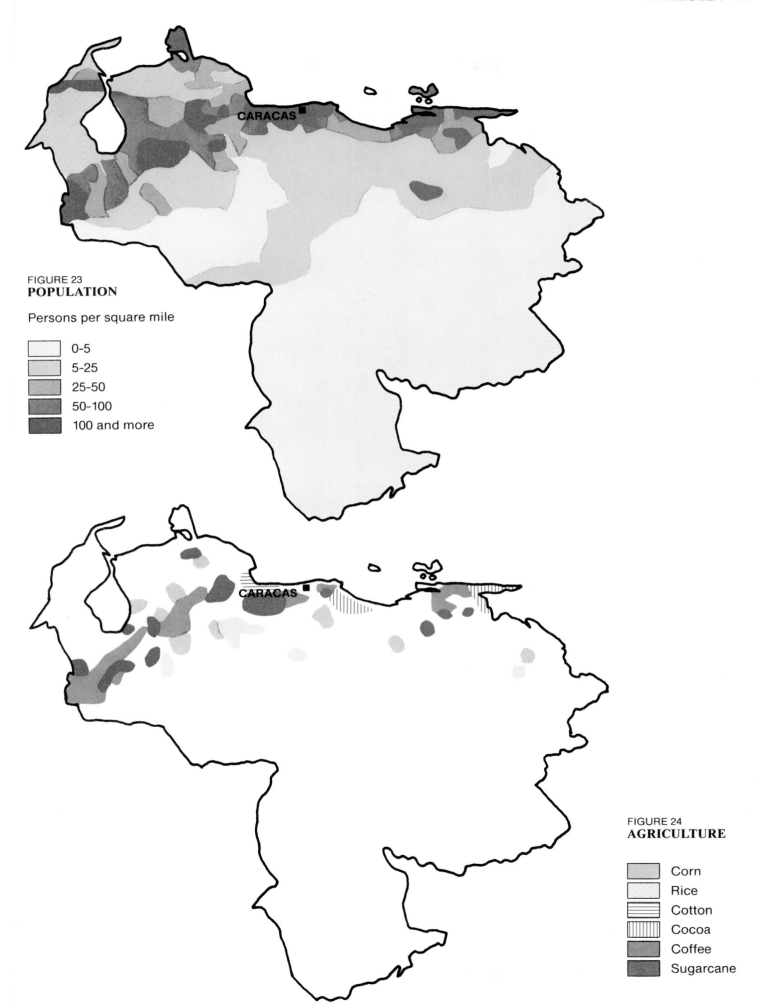

FIGURE 23
POPULATION

Persons per square mile

0-5
5-25
25-50
50-100
100 and more

CARACAS

FIGURE 24
AGRICULTURE

Corn
Rice
Cotton
Cocoa
Coffee
Sugarcane

CARACAS

YEMEN ARAB REPUBLIC

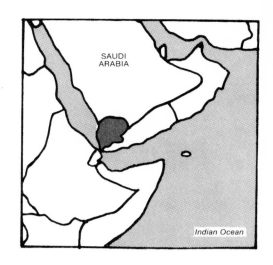

A country out of the Middle Ages, the Yemen Arab Republic ranks 79th in land area and 68th in population. What is significant about the economy is neither its agriculture (although it accounts for nearly all the country's exports, 83% of its employment and a third of its GDP) nor its manufacturing, but the fact that nearly half the GDP is generated by 1 million Yemenis—half the country's adult male work force—who are working abroad. Remittances from these workers are estimated at over $1.5 billion. In addition to these remittances, the economy has been supported by Saudi Arabian subsidies, motivated partly by the political necessity of having a buffer against the Marxist-dominated Southern Yemen. Nearly 90% of the population remains without piped water or electricity or the benefits of literacy. But for a country that, until the civil war of 1962, was a stranger to modern civilization, it has been a remarkable transformation, riding on the coattails of richer Arab neighbors, right into the 20th century.

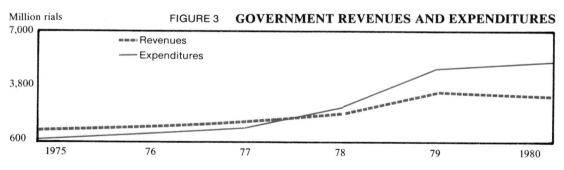

Million

FIGURE 1 **POPULATION GROWTH**

I.M.F.
DATA
UNAVAILABLE

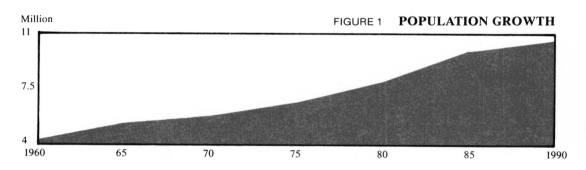

FIGURE 2 **GNP PER CAPITA**

Million rials

FIGURE 3 **GOVERNMENT REVENUES AND EXPENDITURES**

- ▪▪▪ Revenues
- —— Expenditures

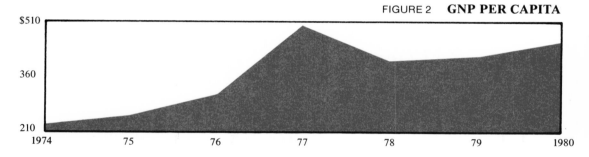

Million rials

FIGURE 4 **EXPORTS AND IMPORTS**

- ▪▪▪ Exports
- —— Imports

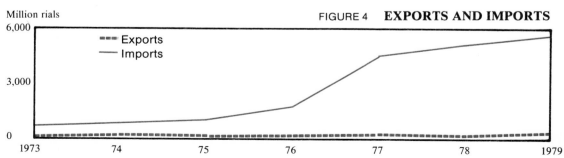

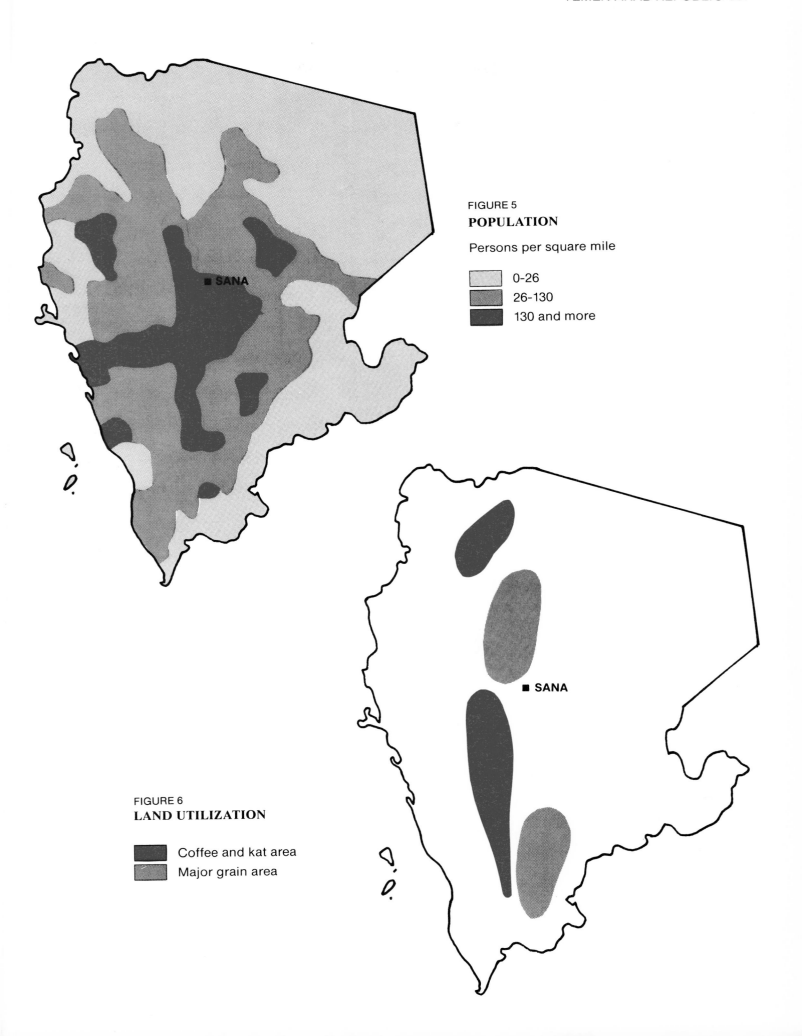

FIGURE 5
POPULATION

Persons per square mile

0-26
26-130
130 and more

■ SANA

FIGURE 6
LAND UTILIZATION

Coffee and kat area
Major grain area

■ SANA

PEOPLE'S DEMOCRATIC REPUBLIC OF YEMEN

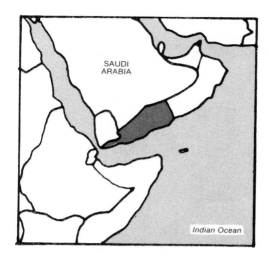

Located on the southeastern coast of the Arabian Peninsula, Southern Yemen ranks 62nd in land area and 124th in population, both behind its northern neighbor. But it shares with the other Yemen its status as one of the least developed low-income countries, a label it is likely to keep for the foreseeable future. Once a tranquil British colony noted for its port of Aden with its oil refinery, it has become since independence the Cuba of the Middle East. A clear Soviet military presence has been established with Socotra Island as a Soviet naval station. There are probabily no less than 10,000 foreign personnel, of which 4,000 are Cubans and the rest Russians. Ironically, the country receives foreign aid not only from the Soviet bloc but also from Kuwait, UAE and Iraq, and these subsidies, along with remittances from Yemeni workers abroad (estimated at over $300 million annually), have enabled PDRY to maintain a respectable balance of payments and even provide capital for investment.

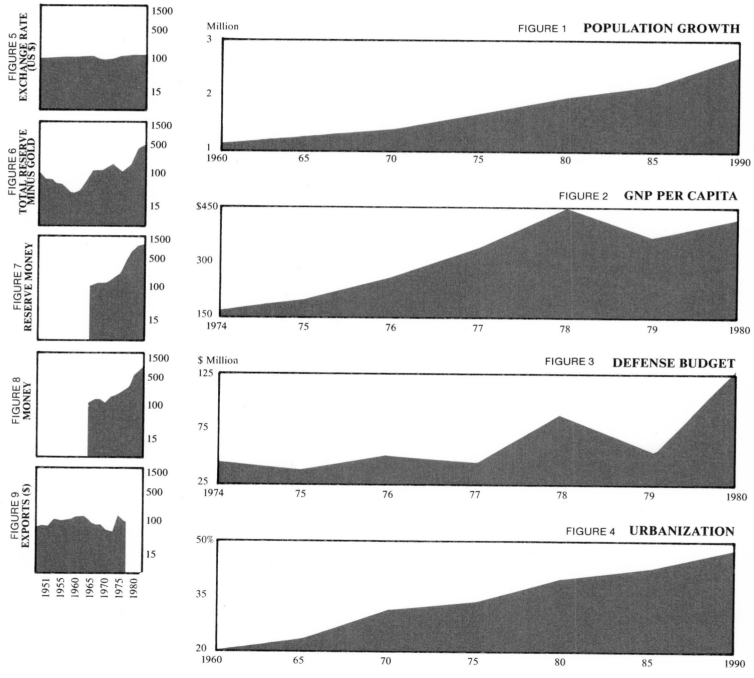

FIGURE 5 EXCHANGE RATE (US $)

FIGURE 6 TOTAL RESERVE MINUS GOLD

FIGURE 7 RESERVE MONEY

FIGURE 8 MONEY

FIGURE 9 EXPORTS ($)

FIGURE 1 **POPULATION GROWTH**

FIGURE 2 **GNP PER CAPITA**

FIGURE 3 **DEFENSE BUDGET**

FIGURE 4 **URBANIZATION**

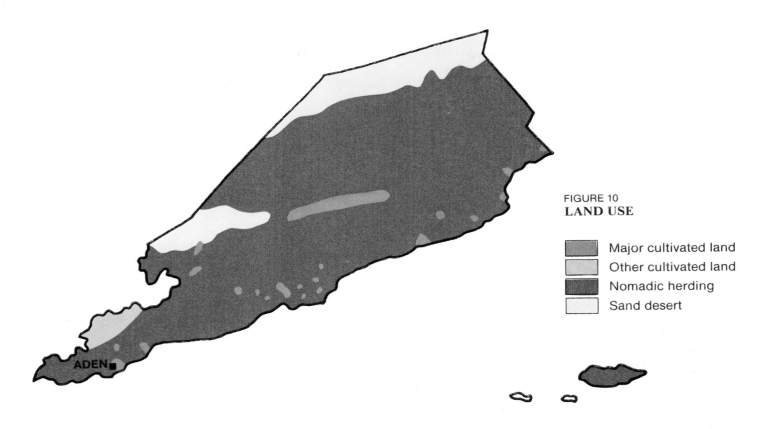

FIGURE 10
LAND USE

Major cultivated land
Other cultivated land
Nomadic herding
Sand desert

FIGURE 11
POPULATION

Persons per square mile

Uninhabited
0-1
1-10
10-50
50 and more

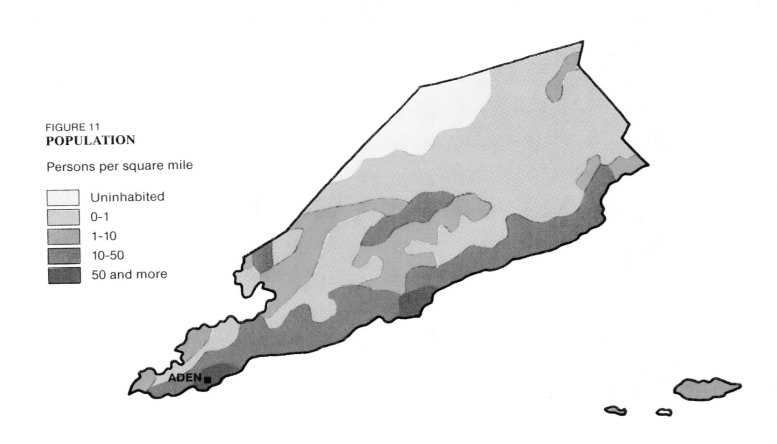

ZAIRE

Located in south central Africa, Zaire is the third largest country in Africa and ranks 11th in land area and 28th in population in the world. Drained by one of the longest rivers in Africa, Zaire ranks sixth in inland navigation and its hydroelectric potential is estimated at 13% of the world total. It is a treasurehouse of minerals, from cobalt and industrial diamonds (in both of which it leads all countries) to copper (sixth rank), tin (ninth rank) and manganese (10th rank). Yet it has been plagued throughout the first two decades of independence by political and administrative failures that have resulted in a staggering foreign debt, an inflation rate of nearly 100% and a scandalous inequality of wealth. The crisis reached flash point in the late 1970s and the economy was rescued from imminent collapse by a team of international aid agencies. Zaire entered the 1980s with mixed economic prospects; while mining appeared to be holding its own, the industrial sector had declined, its contribution to the GDP falling from 13% in 1960 to 7% in 1978.

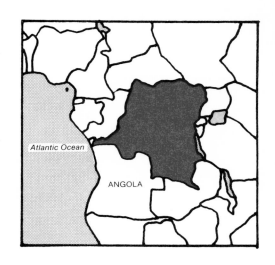

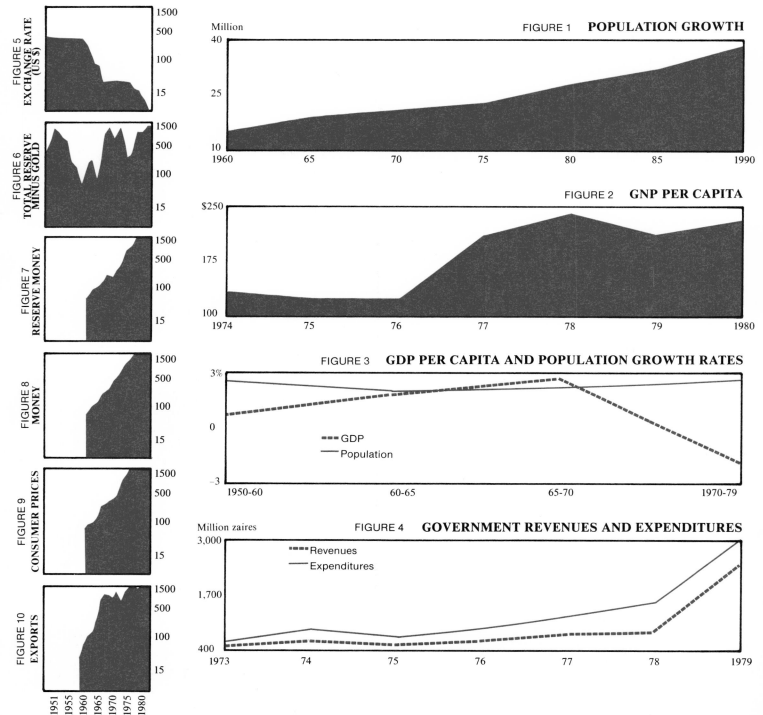

FIGURE 5 EXCHANGE RATE (US $)

FIGURE 6 TOTAL RESERVE MINUS GOLD

FIGURE 7 RESERVE MONEY

FIGURE 8 MONEY

FIGURE 9 CONSUMER PRICES

FIGURE 10 EXPORTS

FIGURE 1 **POPULATION GROWTH**

FIGURE 2 **GNP PER CAPITA**

FIGURE 3 **GDP PER CAPITA AND POPULATION GROWTH RATES**

--- GDP
— Population

FIGURE 4 **GOVERNMENT REVENUES AND EXPENDITURES**

Million zaires

--- Revenues
— Expenditures

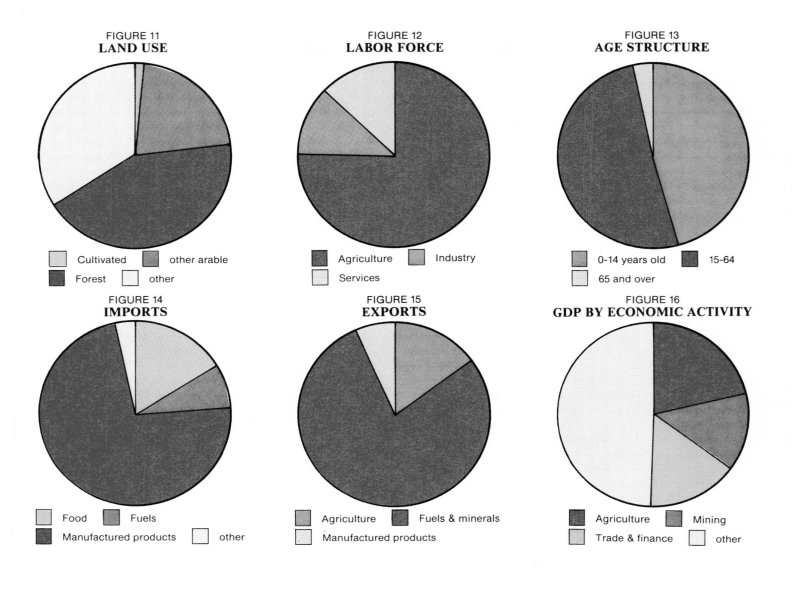

FIGURE 11
LAND USE

Cultivated | other arable
Forest | other

FIGURE 12
LABOR FORCE

Agriculture | Industry
Services

FIGURE 13
AGE STRUCTURE

0-14 years old | 15-64
65 and over

FIGURE 14
IMPORTS

Food | Fuels
Manufactured products | other

FIGURE 15
EXPORTS

Agriculture | Fuels & minerals
Manufactured products

FIGURE 16
GDP BY ECONOMIC ACTIVITY

Agriculture | Mining
Trade & finance | other

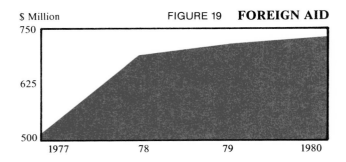

FIGURE 17 **EDUCATIONAL ENROLLMENT**

100%
50
0
1960 — 65 — 70 — 75 — 1977
—— Primary   ■■■ Secondary

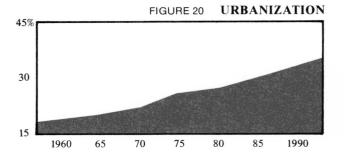

$ Million   FIGURE 18 **DEFENSE BUDGET**

210
110
10
1973 — 74 — 75 — 76 — 77 — 78 — 1979

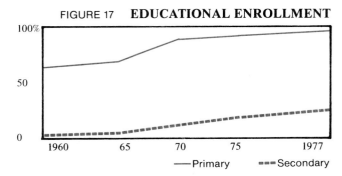

$ Million   FIGURE 19 **FOREIGN AID**

750
625
500
1977 — 78 — 79 — 1980

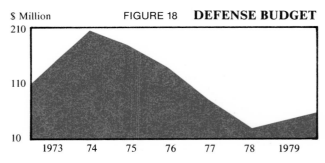

FIGURE 20 **URBANIZATION**

45%
30
15
1960 — 65 — 70 — 75 — 80 — 85 — 1990

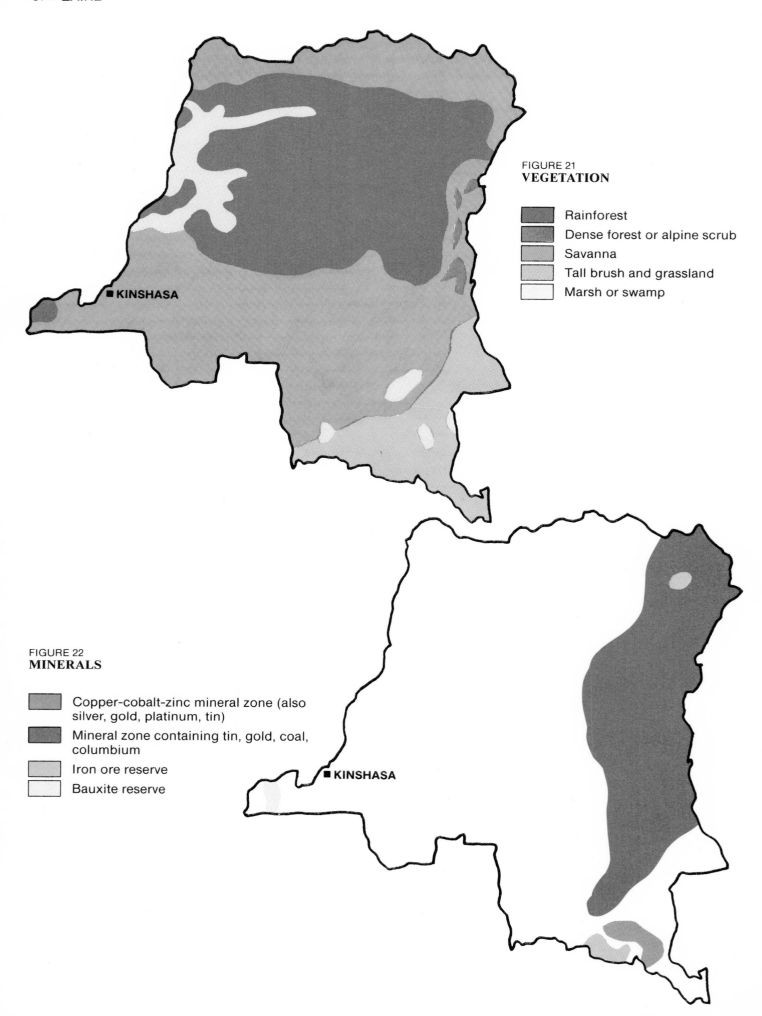

FIGURE 21
VEGETATION

■ KINSHASA

Rainforest
Dense forest or alpine scrub
Savanna
Tall brush and grassland
Marsh or swamp

FIGURE 22
MINERALS

Copper-cobalt-zinc mineral zone (also silver, gold, platinum, tin)
Mineral zone containing tin, gold, coal, columbium
Iron ore reserve
Bauxite reserve

■ KINSHASA

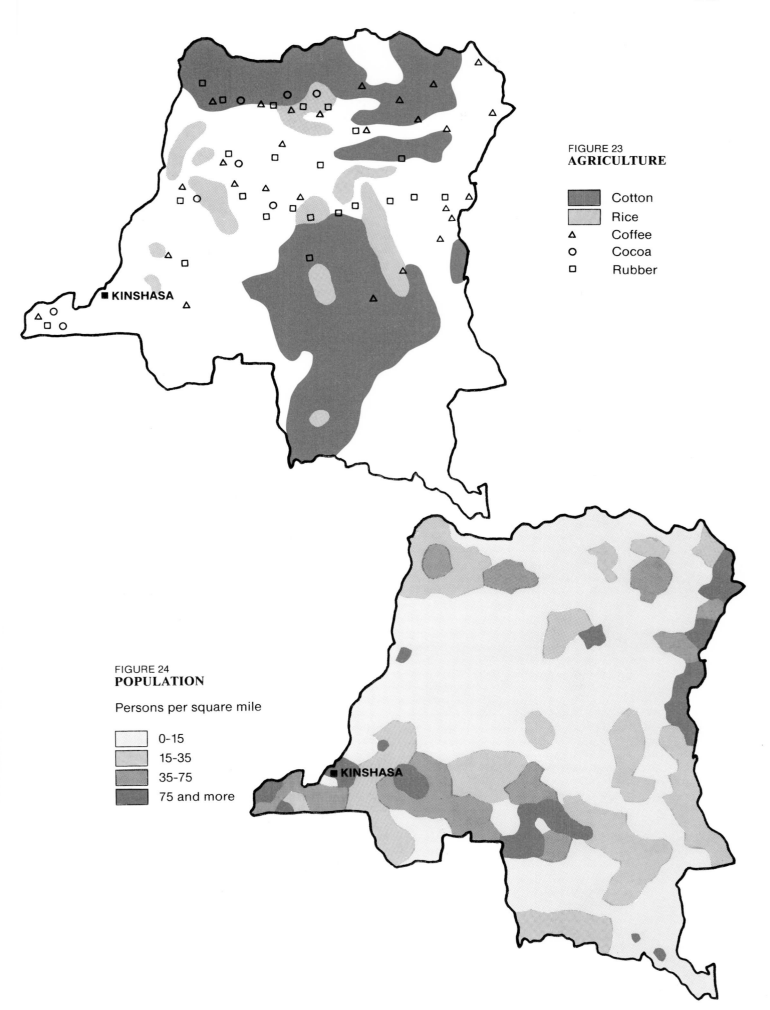

FIGURE 23
AGRICULTURE

Cotton
Rice
△ Coffee
○ Cocoa
□ Rubber

KINSHASA

FIGURE 24
POPULATION

Persons per square mile

0-15
15-35
35-75
75 and more

KINSHASA

ZAMBIA

A landlocked country in central Africa, Zambia ranks 36th in land area and 80th in population. It is considered a lower middle-income country, a relatively high status for African countries, but it owes that label solely to the fact that it is the world's fourth largest copper producer. The country's official ideology is an African variety of socialism based on traditional egalitarianism and communality. In accordance with this ideology, the Kaunda regime in 1968 assumed full control and direction of the economy and of some industries. Some of the harsher features of this program were relaxed following the economic crisis of the mid-1970s and emphasis on private sector participation was renewed. The crisis was the collapse of the world copper market, which reduced the share of copper mining in the Zambian GDP from 45% to 13%. As a result, all sectors declined, unemployment rose by 7.5% and the GDP fell by 4%. The establishment of Zimbabwe and recent surges in world market prices for copper and cobalt have restored some stability to the economy.

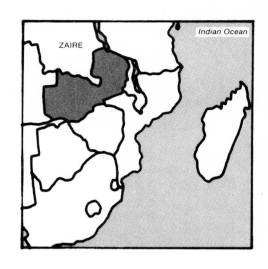

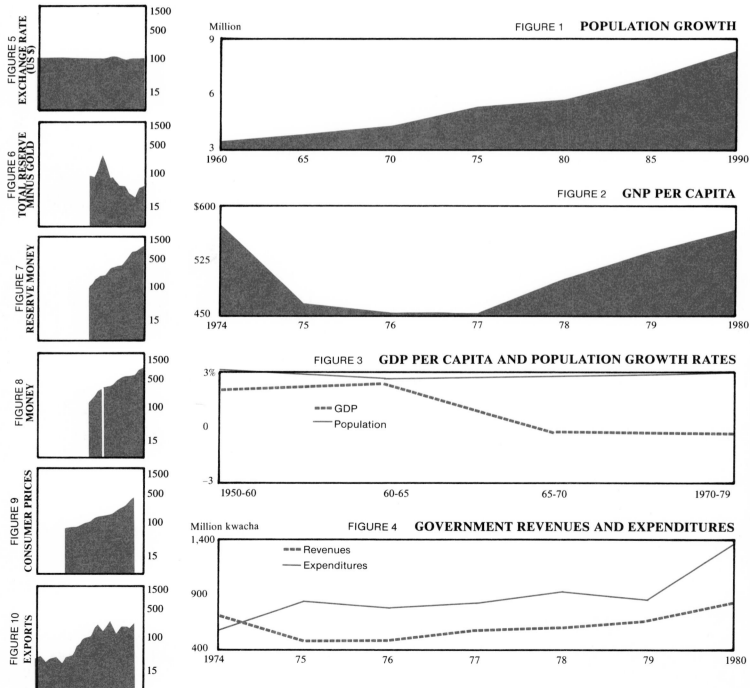

FIGURE 5 EXCHANGE RATE (US $)

FIGURE 6 TOTAL RESERVE MINUS GOLD

FIGURE 7 RESERVE MONEY

FIGURE 8 MONEY

FIGURE 9 CONSUMER PRICES

FIGURE 10 EXPORTS

FIGURE 1 **POPULATION GROWTH**

FIGURE 2 **GNP PER CAPITA**

FIGURE 3 **GDP PER CAPITA AND POPULATION GROWTH RATES**

FIGURE 4 **GOVERNMENT REVENUES AND EXPENDITURES**

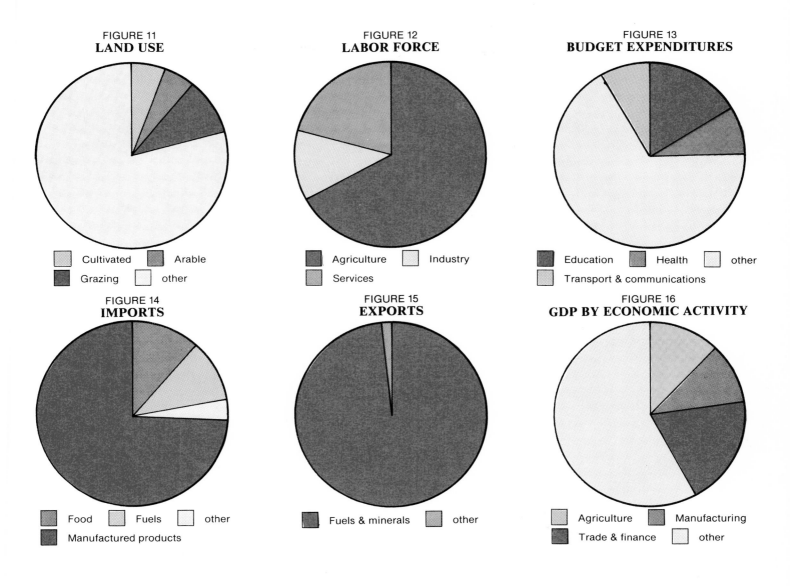

FIGURE 11
LAND USE

- Cultivated
- Arable
- Grazing
- other

FIGURE 12
LABOR FORCE

- Agriculture
- Industry
- Services

FIGURE 13
BUDGET EXPENDITURES

- Education
- Health
- other
- Transport & communications

FIGURE 14
IMPORTS

- Food
- Fuels
- other
- Manufactured products

FIGURE 15
EXPORTS

- Fuels & minerals
- other

FIGURE 16
GDP BY ECONOMIC ACTIVITY

- Agriculture
- Manufacturing
- Trade & finance
- other

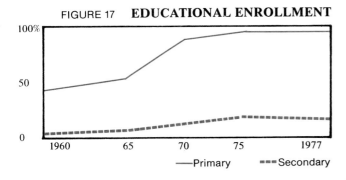

FIGURE 17 **EDUCATIONAL ENROLLMENT**

—— Primary ---- Secondary

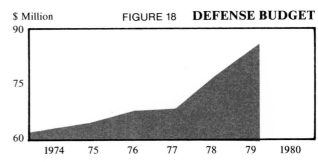

$ Million   FIGURE 18 **DEFENSE BUDGET**

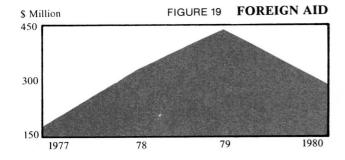

$ Million   FIGURE 19 **FOREIGN AID**

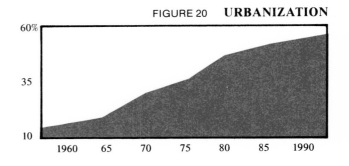

FIGURE 20 **URBANIZATION**

ZIMBABWE

The youngest independent nation in Africa, Zimbabwe ranks 55th in land area and 70th in population. Its economy, while already well established through the years of white rule, has had only three years to adjust to the responsibilities and opportunities of freedom. The Robert Mugabe government began on a moderate note—thus surprising those who had expected his performance to match his Marxist rhetoric—but was soon prodded by extremists as well as opposition from the Joshua Nkomo group into more hardline positions. The funds needed for reconstruction and social reform, including land redistribution, estimated at $2 billion, can only be forthcoming from Western nations if the government forswears its professions of socialism and nationalization. Given political moderation and stability, Zimbabwe's economic prognosis is unusually bright. By African standards, it already has a well-developed infrastructure and a strong agricultural and industrial base, painfully built up during the white rule.

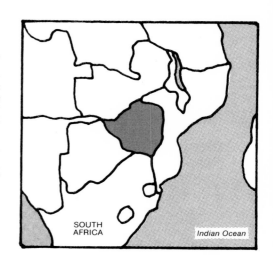

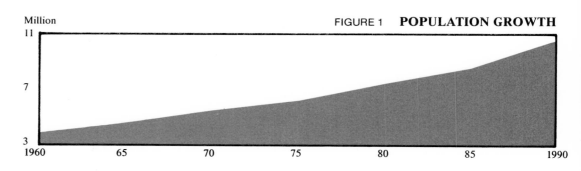

FIGURE 1 **POPULATION GROWTH**

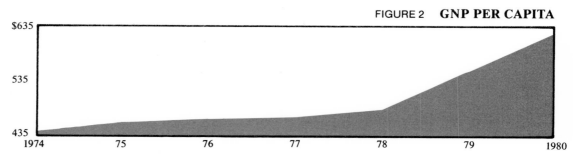

FIGURE 2 **GNP PER CAPITA**

I.M.F.
DATA
UNAVAILABLE

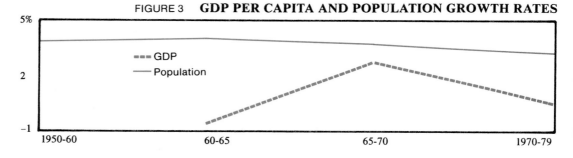

FIGURE 3 **GDP PER CAPITA AND POPULATION GROWTH RATES**

=== GDP
— Population

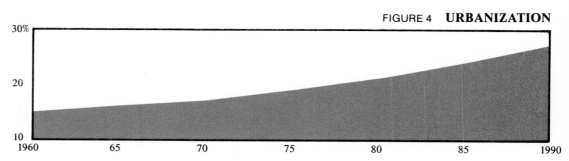

FIGURE 4 **URBANIZATION**

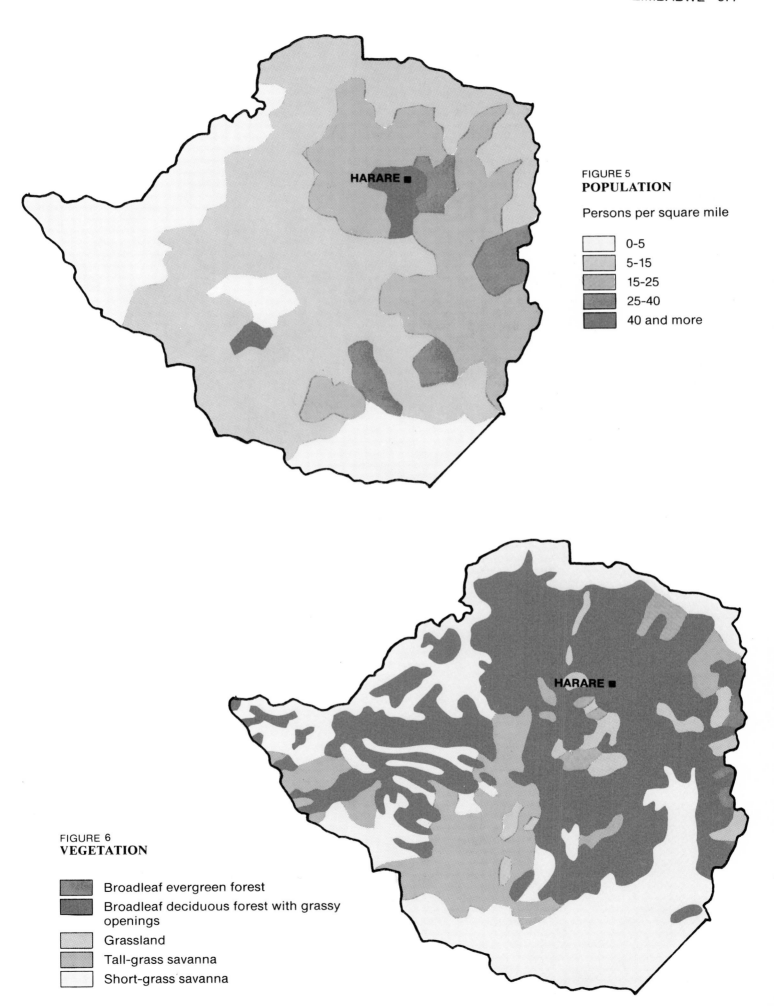

FIGURE 5
POPULATION

Persons per square mile

HARARE ■

	0-5
	5-15
	15-25
	25-40
	40 and more

FIGURE 6
VEGETATION

	Broadleaf evergreen forest
	Broadleaf deciduous forest with grassy openings
	Grassland
	Tall-grass savanna
	Short-grass savanna

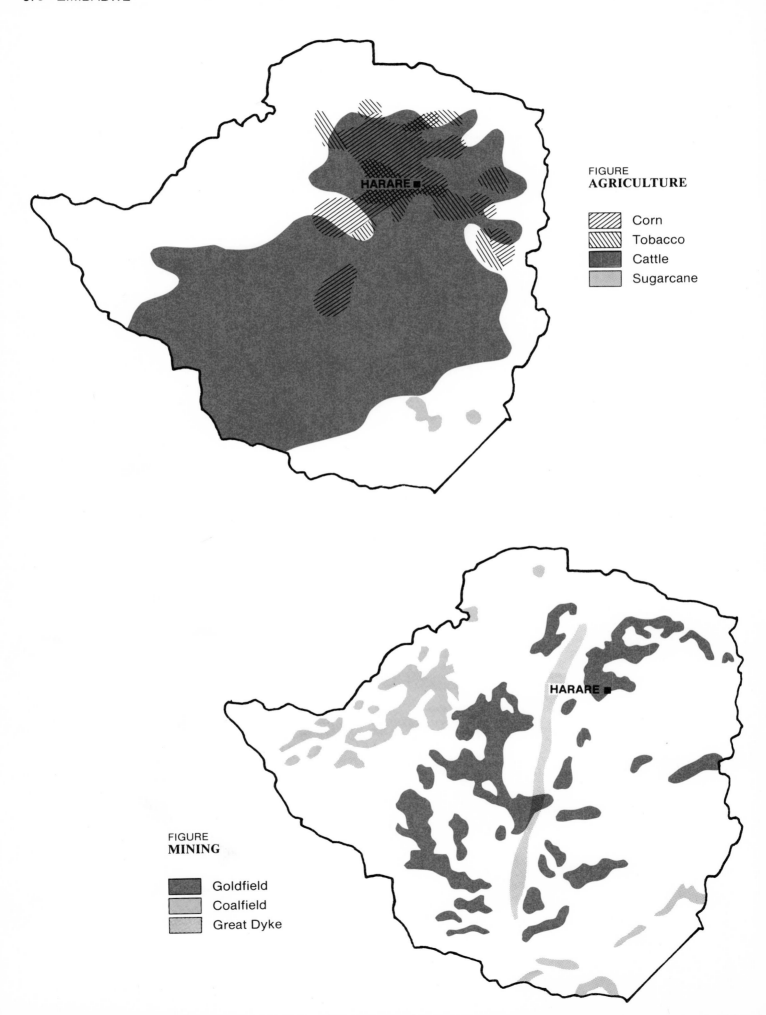

FIGURE
AGRICULTURE

Corn
Tobacco
Cattle
Sugarcane

HARARE■

FIGURE
MINING

Goldfield
Coalfield
Great Dyke

HARARE■

INDEX

Abidjan—222, 223
Abortion—18
Accra—186, 187
Addis Ababa—178, 179
Aden—369
Afghanistan—104-107
Age distribution—12, 13, 15, 189, 217, 221, 251, 355, 371
Agricultural machinery—63
Agriculture—59, 60, 61, 63, 65, 66. See also by country
Aid—40-42, 70. See also by country
Alexandria—170, 171
Algeria—108-11
Algiers—110, 111
Aluminum—138, 224
Amazon River—130, 131
Amman—230, 231
Amortization payments—26
Anchovies—302
Angola—112-13
Ankara—352, 353
Antananarivo—256, 257
Antimony—126
Argentina—114-17
Armed forces. See Defense
Arms exports and imports—45, 46, 47

Baghdad—218, 219
Balance of payments. See by country
Balance of trade—91
Bananas—153, 166, 188, 200, 226, 300, 324
Banghazi—252, 253
Bangkok—344, 345
Bangladesh—118-21
Banking—244, 298
Barley—214, 348
Bauxite—192, 194, 224, 227, 316, 358, 362, 372
Beans—272
Beirut—244, 245
Benin—122-25
Birth rates—14, 19, 79
Bismuth—126
Bogota—152, 153
Bolivia—126-27
Bombay—206, 207
Brasilia—130, 131
Brazil—128-31
Brazzaville—154
Buenos Aires—116, 117
Burma—132-35

Cairo—170, 171
Calcutta—206, 207
Calories—54, 62, 67
Cambodia—136-37
Cameroon—138-41
Caracas—364, 365
Cashews—340
Cassava—61
Cattle—62, 63, 114, 288, 300, 340,

378
Cereal grains—61, 111, 114, 145, 149, 166, 178, 214, 230, 289, 348, 367. See also Corn; Wheat
Chad—142-45
Chemicals—238
Chile—146-49
Chinese assistance—208, 236
Cholera—84
Citrus fruit—111, 226
Cloves—254
Coal—150, 214, 241, 273, 288, 297, 352, 372, 378
Cobalt—370, 372, 374
Cocoa—131, 138, 141, 150, 166, 184, 187, 220, 222, 226, 292, 365, 373
Coconuts—141, 226, 264, 326, 328
Coffee—131, 138, 141, 150, 153, 160, 166, 175, 178, 188, 190, 200, 211, 220, 222, 226, 254, 256, 287, 300, 340, 354, 356, 365, 367, 373
Colombia—150-53
Colombo—328, 329
Colon—298
Colonial powers
  England—138, 184, 194, 232, 268, 368
  France—108, 122, 138, 142, 198, 220, 254, 268, 274, 288, 312, 358
  Portugal—112, 278
  Spain—270
Columbium—372
Commodities—26, 29, 91
Communications—97-100
Communist aid—42
Conakry—193
Congo—154-55
Consumer prices—25, 26. See also by country
Contraceptive use—21
Copper—112, 149, 302, 370, 372, 374
Copra—211
Corn—117, 166, 211, 272, 365, 378
Costa Rica—156-57
Cotton—117, 124, 131, 138, 141, 142, 153, 166, 168, 175, 190, 261, 272, 287, 289, 292, 324, 330, 332, 340, 352, 354, 356, 365, 373
Cuba—112, 158-61, 368

Dakar—314, 315
Damascus—336, 337
Dar es Salaam—340, 341
Dates—214
Deaths, war—48
Debt—26, 29, 30, 31, 37
Defense—41, 43-49. See also by country
Deficits—28, 31
Dental health occupations—76
Desertification—58
Dhaka—120, 121
Diamonds—112, 187, 316, 319, 370
Diet patterns—64

Djakarta—210, 211
Dominican Republic—162-63
Drugs—150

Economic aid—40-42, 70. See also by country
Ecuador—164-67
Education—3, 69-73. Public education expenditures— 3, 69, 70. Pupil-teacher ratios —73
Egypt—168-71
Electricity—90, 322, 360, 370
Electronics—320
El Salvador—172-75
Emeralds—150
Energy—1, 86-90. See also by country
Environment—58, 68. See also Land Use; Vegetation
Ethiopia—176-79
Ethnic groups. See by country
Euphrates River—216, 218, 219
Exchange rates—26. See also by country
Excreta disposal—74
Export earnings—4, 28. See also by country
Exports—27, 29, 45, 46, 47, 92-96. See also by country

Family planning—17, 18, 21
Fat—63
Female population—15, 16
Fertilizer—59, 65
Financial institutions—32, 40, 41
Fishing—56, 124, 272, 300, 302, 345
Fishmeal—302
Food production—1, 53, 57, 62, 63, 64. See also by country
Foreign aid—40-42, 70. See also by country
Foreign exchange reserves—4, 31, 33. See also by country
Fort-Lamy—144, 145
Freetown—318, 319
Fruit—111, 149, 226, 230. See also specific fruit by name

Gabon—180-83
Ganges River—120, 121, 206, 207
Gas, natural—104, 108, 111, 170, 214, 264, 273, 297, 308, 348, 352, 362
GDP—27, 30, 39, 66. See also by country
Georgetown—196, 197
Ghana—184-87
GNP—2, 26, 30, 31, 34, 35, 36, 37, 69. See also by country
Gold—26, 358, 372, 378
Gold Coast—184
Government expenditures. See by country
Government revenues. See by country

Grapes—111, 230, 348
Gross Domestic Product. See GDP
Gross National Product. See GNP
Guatemala—188-91
Guatemala City—190, 191
Guinea—192-93
Gum arabic—330, 332
Guyana—194-97

Haiti—198-99
Harare—377, 378
Havana—160, 161
Health—3, 19, 20, 44, 74-85, 136. Public health expenditures—3, 82. See also Food production; Population
Health occupations—75, 78
Henequen—160
Honduras—200-203

Imports—31, 45, 46, 47, 92-96. See also by country
Income distribution—32
Income growth—33
Independence—6, 9
India—204-207
Indonesia—208-11
Infant mortality rate—2, 81, 83
Inflation—27
Interest payments—26, 31
International banks—32, 40, 41
Investment—30, 31, 94
Iran—212-15
Iraq—216-19
Iron—104, 112, 149, 180, 183, 222, 246, 248, 266, 316, 362, 372
Irrawaddy River—134, 135
Irrigation—59, 65
Islamabad—296, 297
Istanbul—352, 353
Ivory Coast—220-23

Jamaica—224-27
Java—208
Jordan—228-31

Kabul—106, 107
Kampala—356, 357
Karachi—296, 297
Kat—367
Katmandu—282, 283
Kenya—232-35
Khartoum—332, 333
Kingston—226, 227
Kinshasa—372, 373
Korea, North—236-37
Korea, South—238-41
Kuala Lumpur—264, 265

Labor—31, 50-52, 59. See also by country
Lagos—292, 293
Land use—55, 59, 60. See also by country
Laos—242-43
Law enforcement—101

Lead—302, 358
Leadership changes—7
Lebanon—244-45
Liberia—246-49
Libreville—182, 183
Libya—250-53
life expectancy—19, 20, 74, 80, 83,
Lilongwe—260, 261
Linguistic groups. See by country
Literacy—2, 69, 83
Livestock—145, 149, 166, 215, 219,
  253, 269, 277, 288, 289, 322, 324,
  332, 336, 348, 353, 358, 360
Loans—31, 32, 40, 41
Luanda—113
Lumber—131, 132, 138, 154, 183,
  220, 345

Madagascar—254-57
Maize—61, 64
Malaria—85
Malawi—258-61
Malaysia—262-65
Male population—15, 16
Managua—284, 286, 287
Malinese—149, 358, 370
Manila—306, 307
Manufactures—28, 92, 94, 96
Maputo—279
Mauritania—266-67
Mauritius—268-69
Meat production—62, 114
Mecca—310, 311
Media—97-100
Mekong River—243
Mexico—270-73
Mexico City—272, 273
Migration—52, 78
Military aid—41, 42
Military bases—49
Military expenditures—31, 43, 44,
  47
Military governments—8
Millet—61, 64, 145, 289
Mogadishu, 324, 325
Molybdenum—302
Money supply—38. See also by
  country
Monrovia—248, 249
Montevideo—361
Morocco—274-77
Mortality rates—2, 14, 19, 24, 81.
  Infants—2, 81, 83
Mozambique—278-79

Nairobi—234, 235
National parks—68, 234

Nepal—280-83
New Delhi—206, 207
Newspapers—97
Niamey—289
Nicaragua—284-87
Nickel—158, 358
Niger—288-89
Nigeria—290-93
Nile River—170, 171
Nitrates—149
Nomads and nomadic herding—
  110, 111, 145, 178, 266, 336, 369
Nuts—141, 312, 340. See also
  Peanuts

ODA—31, 40
Oil—2, 32, 87, 108, 111, 112, 128,
  132, 138, 149, 154, 164, 170, 180,
  181, 208, 212, 213, 214, 216, 217,
  219, 250, 251, 253, 262, 264, 270,
  273, 277, 290, 297, 302, 308, 309,
  320, 334, 337, 346, 348, 352, 362,
  364, 368
Oilseed crops—178, 292
Olives—111, 230, 348, 352
Orinoco—362
Ouagadougou—359
Overseas Development Assistance.
  See ODA

Pakistan—294-97
Palm oil—124, 141, 211, 264, 292
Panama—298-301
Panama Canal—298, 300, 301
Panama City—300, 301
Parks, national—68, 234
Peanuts—138, 145, 289, 292, 312,
  314
Peru—302-303
Petroleum. See Oil
Philippines—304-307
Phnom Penh—137
Phosphate—228, 274, 348
Physical quality of life index—83
Physician density—78
Plantain—61
Platinum—372
Point-Noire—154
Political divisions—5
Political independence—6, 9
Political instability—7
Population—2, 10-24, 79, 81.
  Female and male—15, 16. See
  also by country
Port-au-Prince—198, 199
Port Louis—269
Porto-Novo—124, 125
Potatoes—61, 64, 166
Poverty, absolute—29

Protein—60
Public education expenditures—3,
  69, 70
Public health expenditures—3, 82
Pupil-teacher ratios—73
Purchasing power—31, 93
P'Yongyang—237

Quebracho—117
Quezon—306, 307
Quito—166, 167

Rabat—276, 277
Radios—99
Rangoon—134, 135
Religions. See by country
Resource transfer—31
Rice—61, 64, 132, 134, 145, 160,
  194, 197, 208, 211, 214, 256, 261,
  264, 289, 297, 328, 345, 365, 373
Rio de Janeiro—130, 131
Riyadh—310, 311
Rubber—138, 211, 246, 248, 262,
  264, 321, 326, 328, 345, 373
Rutile—316

Salada River—116, 117
Sana—367
San Salvador—174, 175
Santiago—146, 148, 149
Sao Paulo—130, 131
Saudi Arabia—212, 228, 308-11
Sectoral growth. See by country
Security forces—101
Senegal—312-15
Seoul—240-41
Sesame seed—292
Shipping—244, 246, 320
Shrimp—272
Sierra Leone—316-19
Silver—302, 372
Singapore—320-21
Sisal—256
Somalia—322-25
Sorghum—64, 145, 289
Soviet bloc nations—104, 158, 176,
  236, 268
Sri Lanka—326-29
Staple crops—61. See also by
  country and crop
Sudan—330-33
Sugar—117, 131, 153, 158, 160, 166,
  188, 194, 197, 226, 268, 269, 287,
  300, 324, 356, 365, 378
Syria—334-37

Tanzania—338-41
Tea—138, 211, 214, 261, 269, 326,
  328

Teak—345
Tegucigalpa—202, 203
Tehran—212, 214, 215
Telephones—98
Televisions—100
Thailand—342-45
Tigris River—216, 218, 219
Tin—262, 370, 372
Titanium—316
Tobacco—138, 160, 211, 256, 261,
  340, 352, 356, 378
Tourism—200, 224, 244, 274, 280
Trade—26, 91-96
Transportation. See by country
Tripoli—252, 253
Tunis—348, 349
Tunisia—346-49
Turkey—350-53

Ubangi River—154
Uganda—354-57
Upper Volta—358-59
Uranium—180, 288
Urbanization. See by country
Uruguay—360-61
U.S. exports—93, 94, 95

Valparaiso—146
Vanadium—358
Vanilla—254, 256
Vegetables—111. See also specific
  vegetable by name.
Vegetation—55. See also by
  country
Venezuela—362-65
Vientiane—242, 243

War deaths—48
Waste disposal systems—74
Water supply—74, 77
Western allies—164, 188, 200, 228,
  274, 298, 342
Wheat—61, 64, 117, 214, 297, 348,
  352
Wool—138
Workers' remittance—31, 350

Yams—61, 64
Yaounde—140, 141
Yemen Arab Republic—366-67
Yemen, People's Democratic
  Republic of—368-69

Zaire—370-73
Zaire River—154
Zambia—374-75
Zimbabwe—376-78
Zinc—302, 358, 372